Representative Plays by American Dramatists

Edited with
Historical and Critical Introductions

By Montrose J. Moses

In Three Volumes

Volume I 1765–1819
Volume II 1815–1858
Volume III 1856–1911

ROOTS AND SOURCES OF THE AMERICAN THEATRE

SONNECK, Oscar ....Early Opera in America

CARSON, William, G.B. ......Managers In Distress:
The St. Louis Stage, 1840-1844

LUDLOW, Noah Miller ......Dramatic Life as I Found It.
With a lengthy introduction by Prof. Francis Hodge (Univ. of Texas) and new index by Prof. Napier Wilt (Univ. of Texas)

MOSES, Montrose, J. (ed.) ....Representative Plays By American Dramatists, 3 vols.
Vol. 1, 1765-1819
Vol. 2, 1815-1858
Vol. 3, 1856-1917

BROWN, Thomas Allston ....History of the New York Stage
From The First Performance In 1732 To 1901. Three Volumes.

MOSES, Montrose, J. ....The American Dramatist. Revised edition.

Representative Plays by American Dramatists

Edited, with an Introduction to Each Play

By Montrose J. Moses

1856-1911

Illustrated with Portraits, and Original Playbills

BENJAMIN BLOM, INC.

New York

First published by E. P. Dutton & Co. Inc., 1921,
Copyright renewed by Mrs. Leah H. Moses, 1948
Reissued by Benjamin Blom, Inc. 1964 by arrangement with Mrs. L. H. Moses.

Printed in U.S.A. by
NOBLE OFFSET PRINTERS, INC.
NEW YORK 3, N. Y.

To

BRANDER MATTHEWS

Friend of the American Theatre

To whom all Critics of the Theatre are beholden.

Table of Contents

INTRODUCTION

The present volume of "Representative Plays by American Dramatists" includes many hitherto unpublished manuscripts. These are for the first time made available in authoritative form to the student of the American theatre. The Editor has tried consistently to adhere to his original basis of selection: to offer only those texts not generally in circulation and not used elsewhere in other anthologies. Exactions of copyright have sometimes compelled him to depart from this rule. He has been somewhat embarrassed, editorially, by the ungenerous haste with which a few others have followed closely in his path, even to the point of reproducing plays which were known to be scheduled for this collection. For that reason there have been omitted Mr. William Gillette's "Secret Service," available to readers in so many forms, and Mr. Percy Mackaye's "The Scarecrow." No anthology of the present historical scope, however, can disregard George Henry Boker's "Francesca da Rimini" or Bronson Howard's "Shenandoah." In the instance of Mr. Langdon Mitchell's "The New York Idea," it is possible to supersede all previous issues of this refreshing comedy by offering a text which, as to stage directions, has been completely revised by the author. Mr. Mitchell wishes to have this regarded as the correct version, and has himself prepared the "copy" of same. Because of the easy accessibility of Dion Boucicault's "The Octoroon; or, Life in Louisiana," it was thought best to omit this Irish-American playwright, whose jovial prolixity enriched the American stage of the '60's and '70's. His "London Assurance" is included in the present Editor's collection of "Representative British Dramas: Victorian and Modern."

Of more historical significance than Joseph Jefferson's final version of "Rip Van Winkle," are the two texts upon which Boucicault and Jefferson based their play. It has been possible to offer the reader a comparative arrangement of the John Kerr and Charles Burke dramatizations.

In the choice of Steele Mackaye's "Paul Kauvar; or, Anarchy" a period is illustrated which might be described as transitional.

Executors of the Augustin Daly estate are not ready to allow any of Daly's original plays or adaptations to be published. The consequence is "Paul Kauvar" must stand representative of the eighteen-eighty fervour of Lester Wallack, A. M. Palmer, and Daly, who were in the Mackaye tradition.

Oliver Bunce's "Love in '76" has been selected for the same reason that one might select Clyde Fitch's Revolutionary or Civil War pieces—because of its bloodless character; because it is one of the rare parlour comedies of the period.

Of the new pieces, Fitch's "The Moth and the Flame" has remained unpublished until now. It exemplifies many of his most sprightly observational qualities. "The Truth" and "The Girl with the Green Eyes" are more mature, but are no less Fitchean than this. Mr. David Belasco's "The Return of Peter Grimm" is as effective in the reading as it was on the stage under his triumphant management. Mr. Eugene Walter's "The Easiest Way," at the last moment, was released from publication in the *Drama League Series of Plays*; it still stands as America's most cruelly realistic treatment of certain city conditions. In the choice of Mr. Augustus Thomas's "In Mizzoura"—"The Witching Hour" having so often been used in dramatic collections—the Editor believes he has represented this playwright at a time when his dramas were most racy and native.

This third volume, therefore, brings examples of the present American stagecraft to date. Had his policy of selection not been exclusive, but rather inclusive of plays easily accessible to the student, the Editor might have reached out for Mr. George C. Hazelton's and Mr. Benrimo's "The Yellow Jacket," Mr. Charles Kenyon's "Kindling," and Mr. A. E. Thomas's "Her Husband's Wife." He might likewise have included William Vaughn Moody's "The Great Divide." These are all representative plays by American dramatists for some future anthologist, when present editions become rare.

But here are offered plays that will enrich the American dramatic library because of their rarity, and for that reason others have been excluded, which are easily procurable in print.

Through the courteous co-operation of Dr. Fred W. Atkinson, Professor Brander Matthews, officials of the New York Public Library, The Library Society of Philadelphia, Mr. Robert Gould Shaw, Custodian of the Dramatic Collection of Harvard

College Library, and through the generous response of the owners of copyrights and manuscripts, the present volume is made possible. The Editor, through every phase of his work, has had the unswerving encouragement and assistance of his wife.

MONTROSE J. MOSES.

New Hartford, Conn.
August, 1920.

BIBLIOGRAPHY OF GENERAL WORKS

A large bibliography of standard works on the American Theatre was given in Volume I of the present collection. A very few of the titles have been repeated here, with the additional inclusion of books which will present the essential spirit of modern American playwriting. Some of these works mentioned contain further bibliographies, and these will enable the student to go as far in the field as desired. There are still unblazed trails for the research worker, but these trails are becoming fewer and fewer, as interest in the study of American Drama as a social and artistic force progresses.

ATKINSON, F. W. American Plays. Private Catalogue. Brooklyn, N. Y.

BAKER, GEORGE PIERCE. Dramatic Technique. Boston· Houghton. 1919.

BURTON, RICHARD. The New American Drama. New York: Crowell. 1913.

CHANDLER, FRANK W. Aspects of Modern Drama. New York: Macmillan.

CHENEY, SHELDON. The Art Theatre. New York: Knopf. 1917.

CHENEY, SHELDON. The New Movement in the Theatre. New York: Kennerley. 1914.

CHENEY, SHELDON. The Out-of-door Theatre. New York: Kennerley. 1918.

CRAWFORD, MARY C. The Romance of the American Theatre. Boston: Little, Brown. 1913.

DALY, JOSEPH FRANCIS. Life of Augustin Daly. New York: Macmillan. 1917.

DICKINSON, THOMAS H. The Case of the American Drama. Boston: Houghton. 1915.

DICKINSON, THOMAS H. Chief Contemporary Dramatists. Boston: Houghton. 1915.

HAMILTON, CLAYTON. Problems of the Playwright. New York: Holt. 1917.

HAMILTON, CLAYTON. Studies in Stagecraft. New York: Holt. 1914.

HAMILTON, CLAYTON. The Theory of the Theatre. New York: Holt. 1910.

HENDERSON, ARCHIBALD. The Changing Drama. New York: Holt. 1914.

HORNBLOW, ARTHUR. A History of the Theatre in America. 2 vols. Philadelphia: Lippincott. 1919. (The files of the *Theatre Magazine* are invaluable as a record of current stage events. Mr. Hornblow has been the editor of this magazine for many years, from its beginning.)

HUTTON, LAURENCE. Curiosities of the American Stage. New York: Harper. 1891.

IRELAND, JOSEPH N. Records of the New York Stage from 1750–1860. 2 vols. 1866.

KROWS, ARTHUR E. Play Production in America. New York: Holt. 1916.

MACKAY, CONSTANCE D. The Little Theatre in the United States. New York: Holt. 1917. (See also Thomas H. Dickinson's book on the same subject.)

MACKAYE, PERCY. The Civic Theatre. New York: Kennerley. 1912.

MACKAYE, PERCY. The Playhouse and the Play. New York: Macmillan. 1909.

MODERWELL, HIRAM K. The Theatre of To-day. New York: Lane. 1914.

MOSES, MONTROSE J. The American Dramatist. Boston: Little, Brown. 1917.

MOSES, MONTROSE J. Famous Actor-Families in America. New York: Crowell. (o.p.)

MOSES, MONTROSE J. The Drama (1860–1918). See The Cambridge History of American Literature. Volume III, Chapter XVIII. Also comprehensive bibliography.

NATHAN, GEORGE JEAN. Another Book of the Theatre. New York: Huebsch. 1915.

NATHAN, GEORGE JEAN. The Popular Theatre. New York: Knopf. 1918.

PENCE, JAMES HARRY. The Magazine and the Drama. New York: Dunlap Society. 1896.

PHELPS, WILLIAM LYON. The Twentieth Century Theatre. New York: Macmillan. 1918.

POLLOCK, CHANNING. The Footlights Fore and Aft. Boston: Badger. 1911.

QUINN, A. H. Representative American Plays. New York: Century. 1917.

REED, PERLEY I. The Realistic Presentation of American Characters in Native American Plays Prior to Eighteen Seventy. Ohio State University Bulletin. Vol. 22, No. 26, May, 1918.

RODEN, ROBERT F. Later American Plays. New York: Dunlap Society. 1900.

ROLLAND, ROMAIN. The People's Theatre. New York: Holt. 1918. (Giving the principles which are spreading and forming a democratic conception of the theatre.)

RUHL, ARTHUR. Second Nights. New York: Scribner. 1914.

SHIPMAN, LOUIS E. The True Adventures of a Play. New York: Kennerley. 1914.

INDIVIDUAL BIBLIOGRAPHIES FOR PLAYS

Rip Van Winkle

Dion Boucicault. "Dramatization of Rip Van Winkle." *Critic* (New York), No. 66, vol. 3, pp. 158-59, April 7, 1883.—Brown, T. Allston. "History of the New York Stage." 3 vols. New York: Dodd, Mead. 1903.—H. C. Bunner. On Jefferson's Rip. See Matthews and Hutton: "Actors and Actresses in Great Britain and the United States." 5 vols. 1886.—J. B. Clapp and E. F. Edgett. "Plays of the Present." New York: Dunlap Society, 1902.—George William Curtis. On Jefferson's Rip. *Harper's Magazine*, March, 1871.—L. Clarke Davis. "Among the Comedians." *Atlantic Monthly*, 19:750-61, June, 1867.—L. Clarke Davis. "At and After the Play." *Lippincott*, July, 1879.—Durang. "History of the Philadelphia Stage." Published in the Philadelphia *Dispatch*.—*The Galaxy*, February, 1868. On Hackett's Rip.—*Harper's Magazine*, 67:617. The Legend of Rip Van Winkle.—Laurence Hutton. "Curiosities of the American Stage." New York: Harper. 1891.—Laurence Hutton. "Plays and Players." New York: Hurd & Houghton. 1875.—Joseph Jefferson. "Autobiography." New York: Century. 1890.—Jefferson's version of "Rip." New York: Dodd, Mead. 1895.—Jefferson, Intimate Recollections of (by Eugénie Paul Jefferson). New York: Dodd, Mead. 1909.—Jefferson's Rip is detailed in the following magazines: *Ev. Sat.*, 10: 152, 162.—*Radical* (S. Johnson), 6: 133.—*Nation* (A. G. Sedgwick), 9:247.—*Atlantic Monthly* (L. C. Davis), 19:750.—*Appleton*, 19:146.—*Scribner*, 1:216, December, 1870.—*Harper*, 42:614, April, 1871.—*Atlantic Monthly*, 52:695.—"The Original of Rip Van Winkle." *Lon. M.*, 5:229.—N. M. Ludlow. "Dramatic Life as I Found It." St. Louis: G. I. Jones & Co. 1880.—Brander Matthews. On Jefferson's Rip. *Scribner*. July, 1879.—Brander Matthews. "These Many Years." New York: Scribner. 1917.—Henry Morley. Journal of a London Playgoer. September 23, 1886.—Montrose J. Moses. "Famous Actor-Families in America." Chapters and Bibliographies under Hackett, Jefferson, Boucicault. New York: Crowell. 1906. (o.p.)—

H. P. Phelps. "Players of a Century." Albany, 1880.—Sol. F. Smith. "Theatrical Management in the West and South for Thirty Years." New York: Harper. 1868.—J. B. Thompson, D. D. "The Genesis of the Rip Van Winkle Legend." *Old Ulster*. Kingston, N. Y. 1914. Vol. 10:13–26.—Eugene Tompkins and Quincy Kilby. "History of the Boston Theatre." Boston: Houghton Mifflin. 1908.—J. Rankin Towse. On Jefferson's Rip. *Century*, January, 1884.—J. Rankin Towse. "Sixty Years of the Theatre." New York: Funk & Wagnalls. 1916.—J. H. Wainwright. Rip Van Winkle. Libretto. Lacy Acting Edition. Vol. 39.—Walsh (T.). Dion Boucicault. The Career of. New York: Dunlap Society, 1915.—F. C. Wemyss. "Twenty-six Years of the Life of an Actor and Manager." New York: Burgess, Stringer & Co. 1847. On Hackett's Rip.—Francis Wilson. "Joseph Jefferson: Reminiscences of a Fellow Player." New York: Scribner. 1906.—William Winter. "The Life of David Belasco." 2 vols. New York: Moffat, Yard & Co. 1918.—William Winter. The Jeffersons. Boston: J. R. Osgood & Co. 1881. (See also the Macmillan Life of Jefferson, by Winter. 1894.)—William Winter. "Other Days." New York: Moffat, Yard. 1908.—William Winter. "The Wallet of Time." 2 vols. New York: Moffat, Yard. 1913. (Besides the Rip references, see also J. T. Raymond and Irving's "Wolfert's Roost.")

George Henry Boker

General references for Boker, see Allibone, Lamb's Biographical Dictionary, Appleton's Cyclopedia of American Biography, National Cyclopedia of American Biography, Warner's Library of the World's Best Literature.—Lawrence Barrett, A Professional Sketch of. By Elwyn A. Barron. Chicago: Knight & Leonard Co. 1889. (For a review of Barrett's opening in "Francesca," Philadelphia, see telegraphic report in the New York *Tribune*, September 15, 1882, p. 15.)—Alfred Bates. Drama. Vol. XX. p. 70.—Biographical Encyclopedia of Pennsylvanians of the Nineteenth Century. Philadelphia: Galaxy Publishing Co. 1874. p. 370.—Magazine references to Boker: *Atlantic Monthly*, 65:427, March, 1890. *Book Buyer*, 1900, 21:47. *Critic*, January 11, 1890; April 12, 1890; 1898, 33:240. *Harper's Monthly*, 1882, 4:633. *Harper's Weekly*, 1871, 15:1173; 1890, 34:32. *Sewanee Review* (J. W. Krutch), October, 1917, 25:457–68.—Biographie du très honorable Georges H. Boker. Ministre des Etats Unis Amérique auprès de la Sublime Porte. *L'Orient Illustré Journal Hebdomadaire*, Constantinople, 22 Aug., 1874.—Reception tendered by the Members of the Union League of Philadelphia to George H. Boker, Minister of the United States to Turkey, Friday Evening, December 22, 1871. Philadelphia: 1872.—Cambridge History of American Literature. New York: Putnam. 1917. 1:494. Bibliography.—Century Association: Bryant Festival. 1865. 19.—J. B. Clapp and E. F. Edgett. "Plays of the Present." New York: Dunlap Society. 1902.—E. L. Davenport. A Biography, by E. F. Edgett. New York: Dunlap Society. 1901. (A complete bibliography of Davenport is in Moses' "Famous Actor-Families in America.")—Duyckinck, E. A. and G. L. "Cyclopedia of American Literature." Philadelphia: William Rutter & Co. 1877. 2 vols. 2:710.—Knickerbocker Gallery. 1855. p. 59.—Charles Godfrey Leland. A Biography. By Elizabeth Robins Pennell. 2 vols. Boston: Houghton Mifflin.—Charles Godfrey Leland. Memoirs. 2 vols. London: Heinemann. 1893.—Charles Godfrey Leland. Reminiscences of George H. Boker. *The American*, 1890, March 1. 19:392–94.—Charles Godfrey Leland. *Sartain's Magazine*, 1851, 8:369–78.—George Parsons Lathrop. George H. Boker. Authors at Home. xxvii. *Critic*. n.s. vol. 9, April 14, 1888.—Morris. "Makers of Philadelphia." p. 78.—Oberholtzer. "Literary History of Philadelphia." Quinn, A. H. "The Dramas of George Henry Boker." *Pub. of Modern Language Association of America*. Vol. 32, no. 2, n.s., Vol. XXV, June, 1917, pp. 233–66.—T. Buchanan Read, A Memoir of. Philadelphia, 1889.—Augustus C. Rogers. "Sketches of Our Representatives Abroad."—Henry Simpson. "Lives of Eminent Philadelphians." Philadelphia: William Brotherhead. 1859. Charles S. Boker. By Joseph R. Chandler. (With portrait.) pp. 93–107.—Edmund Clarence Stedman. Life and Letters of. Edited by Laura Stedman and George M. Gould. New York: Moffat, Yard. 1910. 2 vols.—Edmund Clarence Stedman. "Poets of America." Boston: Houghton. 1892.—Edmund Clarence Stedman. "An American Anthology." Boston: Houghton. 1900.—E. C. Stedman and Ella M. Hutchinson. "A Library of American Literature." New York: C. L. Webster & Co. 1889. 8:111–18.—Richard Henry Stoddard. "Recollections Personal and Literary." Edited by Ripley Hitchcock. Introduction by Edmund Clarence Stedman. New York: Barnes. 1903.—

Richard Henry Stoddard. Recollections of George Henry Boker. *Lippincott*, June, 1890, 45:856–67.—Bayard Taylor, Life and Letters of. Edited by Marie Hansen-Taylor and Horace E. Scudder. 2 vols. Boston: Houghton. 1885.—W. P. Trent. "William Gilmore Simms." Boston: Houghton. 1892.—William Winter. "The Wallet of Time." 2 vols. New York: Moffat, Yard. 1913.

Oliver Bell Bunce

Appleton's Cyclopedia of American Biography.—Appleton's Annual Cyclopedia. 1890.—T. Allston Brown. "History of the New York Stage." New York: Dodd, Mead. 1903. 3 vols.—Articles about Bunce in the magazines: *Critic*, May 24, 1890; 16:262.—*Literary World* (Boston), 21:192.—Articles by Bunce: "The Players." *Appleton's Journal*, April 3, 1869.—"Some of Our Actors." *The Galaxy*. 5:165.—"Ellen Tree." See Editor's Table, *Appleton's Journal*, October, 1880.—For notices of "Love in '76" see the advertisement in the New York *Tribune*, February 28, 1857, and see also the New York *Herald*, March 2, 1857.—W. P. Eaton. "The American Stage of To-day." Boston: Small, Maynard. 1908. pp. 259–69. "Where is Our Drama of '76?"—Laurence Hutton. "Curiosities of the American Stage." New York: Harper. 1891.—Lamb. Biographical Dictionary of the United States.

Steele Mackaye

Percy Mackaye. "Steele Mackaye, Dynamic Artist of the American Theatre." *The Drama*, November, 1911, pp. 138–61; February, 1912, pp. 153–73.—(Notices of Mackaye's "Paul Kauvar" in the New York *Tribune* for December 25, 1887, and other New York papers for the same date. Mr. Percy Mackaye has in preparation a Life of his father.)—Montrose J. Moses. "The American Dramatist." Boston: Little, Brown. 1917. Chapter VIII.—William Winter. "Life of David Belasco." New York: Moffat, Yard. 1918. 2 vols. Consult indexes.

Bronson Howard

William Archer. "English Dramatists of To-day." London: Sampson Low, Marston, Searle, & Rivington. 1882. Chapter on Howard.—Johnson Briscoe. "The Pioneer American Dramatist." *Green Book*, 11:749–56. May, 1914.—J. B. Clapp and E. F. Edgett. "Plays of the Present." New York: Dunlap

Society. 1902.—Barrett H. Clark. "The British and American Drama of To-day." New York: Holt. 1915. Howard, with bibliography, pp. 219–27.—Eleanor Eustace. "Drama in War Time." *Green Book Album.* 4:776–85.—James L. Ford. "The Banker's Daughter." *Munsey,* 34:122, 199.—Daniel Frohman and I. Marcosson. Charles Frohman, A Biography. Manager and Man. New York: Harper. 1916. Chapter VI.—Daniel Frohman. "Memories of a Manager." New York: Doubleday, Page. 1911.—Articles by Bronson Howard: "The American Drama." *Sunday Magazine,* October 7, 1906, reproduced in this volume.—"The Autobiography of a Play." With an Introduction by Augustus Thomas. *Dramatic Museum of Columbia University.* New York, 1914. Papers on Play-making. 11. Series 1. (This is also reprinted in the Memorial Volume mentioned below.) "The Literary Value of Mediocrity." (In the Memorial Volume, see Howard's address: "Trash on the Stage and the Lost Dramatists of America." p. 115.)—"In Memoriam:" Addresses delivered at the Memorial Meeting, Sunday, October 18, 1908, at the Lyceum Theatre, New York. New York, 1910.—"Old Dry Ink." *Dramatic Mirror.* Christmas, 1896. 37:939.—"Our Schools for the Stage." *Century,* 61:28–37.—*Bookman,* 10:195 ("The Work of Bronson Howard").—*Century Magazine,* 3:465 ("The Plays of Bronson Howard").—Hamilton Wright Mabie. "American Plays Old and New." *Outlook.* December 28, 1912. pp. 945–55.—Brander Matthews. Bronson Howard. *North American Review.* 1908, 188:504–13. (This essay is also in "Gateways to Literature." New York: Scribner. 1912. pp. 279–96.—Brander Matthews. "These Many Years." New York: Scribner. 1917.—Clara Morris. "Life on the Stage." (See chapter on "Saratoga"), New York: McClure, Phillips. 1902.—Montrose J. Moses. "The American Dramatist." Boston: Little, Brown. 1917. Chapter V.—(A notice of "Shenandoah" is in the New York *Tribune,* September 10, 1889.)—T. Edgar Pemberton. "Sir Charles Wyndham." London, 1904. —J. Rankin Towse. Bronson Howard. *Book Buyer,* March, 1898. 16:113–17.—William Winter. "The Life of David Belasco." 2 vols. New York: Moffat, Yard. 1918. Consult Indexes for references to Howard.

Augustus Thomas

Barrett H. Clark. "The British and American Drama of To-day." New York: Holt. 1915. Thomas, with bibliography.

—Montrose J. Moses. "The American Dramatist." Boston: Little, Brown. 1917. Chapter IX.—Walter P. Eaton. "At the New Theatre and Others." Boston: Small, Maynard. 1910. "Mr. Thomas's New Birth." ("The Harvest Moon.") pp. 109–16.—Walter P. Eaton. "Plays and Players." Cincinnati: Stewart & Kidd. 1916. "As Augustus Thomas Thinks." pp. 25–33.—Walter P. Eaton. "The American Stage of To-day." Boston: Small, Maynard. 1908. "The Witching Hour."—Frederick M. Smith. "Mr. Augustus Thomas and Some of His Works." *Sewanee Review.* April, 1907. XV:192–98.—William Winter. "The Wallet of Time." 2 vols. New York: Moffat, Yard. 1913. "The Plays of Augustus Thomas." 2:529–57.—Mr. Thomas wrote the introduction to Bronson Howard's "Autobiography of a Play." See also his Introductions to the edition of his plays issued by Messrs. Samuel French. A political article, "The Claims of the Candidates," lauding W. J. Bryan, was written by Mr. Thomas, and published in the *North American Review*, June, 1908, 187:801–6.

Clyde Fitch

Archie Bell. "The Clyde Fitch I Knew." New York: Broadway Publishing Co. 1909.—Bibliography of Clyde Fitch. "Modern Drama and Opera." Vol. II. Boston: The Boston Book Co. 1915. pp. 60–65.—(Notices of "The Moth and the Flame" are in the New York *Times*, April 12, 1898 and April 17, 1898. E. A. Dithmar.)—Martin Birnbaum. Critical Appreciation. *Independent*, 67:123–31.—Barrett H. Clark. "The British and American Drama of To-day." New York: Holt. 1915. Fitch, with bibliography.—Walter P. Eaton. "At the New Theatre." Boston: Small, Maynard. 1910. "The Case of Clyde Fitch." pp. 258–83. This was also published in *Scribner's*, 46:490–97.—Norman Hapgood. "The Stage in America. 1897–1900." New York: The Macmillan Co. 1901. (References to Fitch, Howard, and Thomas.)—Montrose J. Moses. "The American Dramatist." Boston: Little, Brown. 1917. Chapter X and bibliography.—Clement Scott. "Drama of Yesterday and To-day." New York: The Macmillan Co. 1899. 2 vols.—L. C. Strang. "Plays and Players of the Last Quarter Century."—For the "Beau Brummell" dispute, both sides, see the biographies of Richard Mansfield, by Paul Wilstach and William Winter. A Memorial Edition of "The Plays of Clyde Fitch," edited by Montrose J. Moses and Virginia Gerson, 4 vols., has been issued by Little, Brown & Co. Boston. 1915.

Langdon Mitchell

William Archer. "The New York Idea." London *Tribune*, May 27, 1907.—J. B. Clapp and E. F. Edgett. "Plays of the Present." New York: Dunlap Society. 1902. (Reference to "Becky Sharp.")—Norman Hapgood. "The Stage in America. 1897–1900." New York: The Macmillan Co. 1901.—Joyce Kilmer. Langdon Mitchell, Interview with. New York *Times*, February 20, 1916.—William Winter. "The Wallet of Time." New York: Moffat, Yard. 1913. 2 vols. "The Acting of Mrs. Fiske."

Eugene Walter

Barrett H. Clark. "The British and American Drama of To-day." New York: Holt. 1915. With bibliography.—Denig, L. "Vicissitudes of a Playwright." *Theatre*, 21:235, May, 1915.—"The Easiest Way" (Excerpts). *Current Literature*, 51:73–81.—"The Easiest Way." *Dramatist*, 4:379, July, 1913.—Walter P. Eaton. "At the New Theatre and Others." Boston: Small, Maynard. 1910. pp. 93–98.—Walter P. Eaton. "The American Stage of To-day." ("Paid in Full.") Boston: Small, Maynard. 1908. pp. 45–57.—Walter P. Eaton. "Plays of Eugene Walter." *American Magazine*, November, 1910, 71:121–23.—Ada Patterson. Interview with Eugene Walter. *Theatre*, October, 1908. 8:272–76.—Peirce, Francis Lamont. "Eugene Walter: An American Dramatic Realist." *Drama*. February, 1916. Vol. 6.—Eugene Walter. Sketch of. *Green Book Album*, January, 1911, 5:186–87.—William Winter. "The Life of David Belasco." 2 vols. New York: Moffat, Yard. 1918. References in the Indexes to "The Easiest Way," "Just a Wife."—William Winter. "The Wallet of Time." 2 vols. New York: Moffat, Yard. 1913. 2:374; 479–88.—For contemporary criticism on Walter consult the Dramatic Index, and the Indexes of the New York *Tribune* and *Times*.

David Belasco

Such articles by Mr. Belasco as "The Business of Theatrical Management," Philadelphia *Saturday Evening Post*, June 7, 1919, may be found by consulting the Dramatic Index. They are more or less amplified expressions of opinion which were dwelt upon in his extended Reminiscences, written for *Hearst's Magazine*, beginning March, 1914. Constant references to Mr. Belasco are to be found in Winter's "Wallet of Time." But the monumental "Life of David Belasco," 2 vols., by Winter, will give all the biographical data necessary for the student to have. It is issued by Moffat, Yard, New York, 1918. Consult likewise Montrose J. Moses' "The American Dramatist." Chapter VII. Boston: Little, Brown. 1917. See also Walter P. Eaton's "Plays and Players." Cincinnati: Stewart & Kidd. 1916. "Warfield in the Spirit World," pp. 17–24. "Belasco and Hypnotism" (Locke's "The Case of Becky"), pp. 59–65.

RIP VAN WINKLE

A LEGEND OF THE CATSKILLS

Charles Burke

RIP VAN WINKLE

This is the history of the evolution of a play. Many hands were concerned in its growth, but its increase in scenic effect as well as in dialogue was a stage one, rather than prompted by literary fervour. No dramatization of Washington Irving's immortal story has approached the original in art of expression or in vividness of scene. But, if historical record can be believed, it is the actor, rather than the dramatist, who has vied with Irving in the vitality of characterization and in the romantic ideality of figure and speech. Some of our best comedians found attraction in the rôle, yet, though Charles Burke and James A. Herne are recalled, by those who remember back so far, for the very Dutch lifelikeness of the genial old drunkard, Joseph Jefferson overtops all memories by his classic portrayal.

As far as literary value of the versions is concerned, it would be small loss if none of them were available. They form a mechanical frame-work as devoid of beauty as the skeleton scarecrow in Percy Mackaye's play, which was based on Hawthorne's "Feathertop" in "Mosses from an Old Manse." It was only when the dry bones were clothed and breathed into by the actor's personality that the dramatizations lived. One can recall no plot that moves naturally in these versions; the transformation of the story into dialogue was mechanical, done by men to whom hack-work was the easiest thing in the world. Comparing the Kerr play with the Burke revision of it, when the text is strained for richness of phrase it might contain, only one line results, and is worth remembering; it is Burke's original contribution,—"Are we so soon forgot when we are gone?"

The frequency with which "Rip Van Winkle" was dramatized would indicate that, very early in the nineteenth century, managers of the theatre were assiduous hunters after material which might be considered native. Certainly *Rip* takes his place with *Deuteronomy Dutiful*, *Bardwell Slote*, *Solon Shingle* and *Davy Crockett* as of the soil.

Irving's "Sketch Book" was published in 1819, and, considering his vast interest in the stage, and the dramatic work done by him in conjunction with John Howard Payne, it is unfortunate that he himself did not realize the dramatic possibilities of his story. There is no available record to show that he either approved or disapproved of the early dramatizations. But there is ample record to show that, with the beginning of its stage career, nine years after publication, "Rip" caught fire on the stage both in America and in London. Mr. James K. Hackett is authority for the statement that among his father's papers is a letter from Irving congratulating him upon having made so much from such scant material.

The legendary character of Irving's sources, as traced in German folk-lore, does not come within the scope of this introduction. The first record of a play is Thomas Flynn's appearance as *Rip* in a dramatization made by an unnamed Albanian, at the South Pearl Street Theatre, Albany, N. Y., May 26, 1828. It was given for the benefit of the actor's wife, and was called "Rip Van Winkle; or, The Spirits of the Catskill Mountains." Notice of it may be found in the files of the Albany *Argus*. Winter, in his Life of Joseph Jefferson, reproduces the prologue. Part of the cast was as follows:

Derrick Van Slous—Charles B. Parsons
Knickerbocker—Moses S. Phillips
Rip Van Winkle—Thomas Flynn
Lowenna—Mrs. Flynn
Alice—Mrs. Forbes

Flynn was a great friend of the elder Booth, and Edwin bore Thomas as a middle name.

In 1829, Charles B. Parsons was playing "Rip" in Cincinnati, Ohio, but no authorship is mentioned in connection with it, so it must be inferred that it was probably one of those stock products so characteristic of the early American theatre. Ludlow, in his "Dramatic Life," records "Rip" in Louisville, Kentucky, November 21, 1831, and says that the Cincinnati performance occurred three years before, making it, therefore, in the dramatic season of 1828–29, this being Rip's "first representation West of the Alleghany Mountains, and, I believe, the first time on any stage." Ludlow proceeds to state that, while in New York, in the summer of 1828, an old stage friend of his offered to sell him a manuscript version of "Rip," which, on his recommendation, he proceeded to purchase "without reading it." And then the manager indicates how a character part is built to catch the interest of the audience, by the following bit of anecdote:

It passed off there [in Cincinnati] without appearing to create any interest more than a drama on any ordinary subject, with the exception of one speech, which was not the author's, but introduced without my previous knowledge by one of the actors in the piece. This actor was a young gentleman of education, who was performing on the stage under the name of Barry; but that was not his real name, and he was acting the part of *Nicholas Vedder* in this drama. In the scene where *Rip* returns to his native village after the twenty years of sleep that he had passed through, and finds the objects changed from what he remembered them,—among other things the sign over the door of the tavern where he used to take his drinks,—he enquires of *Vedder*, whom he had recognized, and to whom he had made himself known, who that sign was intended to represent, saying at the same time that the head of King George III used to hang there. In reply to him, instead of speaking the words of the author, Mr. Barry said, "Don't you know who that is? That's George Washington." Then *Rip* said, "Who is George Vashingdoner?" To which Barry replied, using the language of General Henry (see his "Eulogy on Washington," December 26, 1799), "He was first in war, first in peace, and first in the hearts of his countrymen!" This woke the Cincinnatians up.

Joseph Jefferson rejected this emendation later on, giving as his reason that, once an audience is caught in the flare of a patriotic emotion, it is difficult for an actor to draw them back effectively to the main currents of his story. We have Ludlow's statement to the effect that Burke's version was not unlike that produced by him as early as 1828–29, in the middle West. Could it have had any relationship to the manuscript by Kerr?

In Philadelphia, at the Walnut Street Theatre, on October 30, 1829, William Chapman appeared as *Rip*, supported by Elizabeth and J. (probably John) Jefferson. Winter suggests that the dramatization may have been Ludlow's, or it may have been the first draft of Kerr's. Though it is generally conceded that the latter play was the one used by James H. Hackett, in a letter received by the Editor from Mr. James K. Hackett, it is suggested that his father made his own version, a statement not proved, but substantiated by Winter.

The piece was given by Hackett, at the Park Theatre, New York, on August 22, 1830, and Sol Smith, in his "Theatrical

Management in the West and South," declares, "I should despair of finding a man or woman in an audience of five hundred, who could hear [his] utterance of five words in the second act, 'But she was mine vrow' without experiencing some moisture in the eyes." While the *Galaxy*, in a later year, for February, 1868, states: "His *Rip Van Winkle* is far nearer the ordinary conception of the good-for-nothing Dutchman than Mr. Jefferson's, whose performance is praised so much for its naturalness." The statement, by Oliver Bell Bunce, is followed by this stricture against Jefferson: "Jefferson, indeed, is a good example of our modern art. His naturalness, his unaffected methods, his susceptible temperament, his subtleties of humour and pathos are appreciated and applauded, yet his want of breadth and tone sometimes renders his performance feeble and flavourless." On the day before its presentment by Hackett, the New York *Evening Post* contained the following notice:

> Park Theatre, Mr. Hackett's Benefit. Thursday, 22d inst. First night of Rip Van Winkle and second night of Down East.—Mr. Hackett has the pleasure of announcing to his friends and the public that his Benefit is fixed for Thursday next, 22d inst., when will be produced for the first time the new drama of "Rip Van Winkle; or, The Legend of the Kaatskill Mountains"—(founded on Washington Irving's celebrated tale called "Rip Van Winkle")—with appropriate Dutch costumes; the River and Mountain scenery painted by Mr. Evers, all of which will be particularly described in the bills of the day.—Principal characters—*Rip Van Winkle*, Mr. Hackett; *Knickerbocker*, Mr. Placide; *Vedder*, Mr. Chapman; *Van Slous*, Mr. Blakely; *Herman*, Mr. Richings; *Dame Rip Van Winkle*, Mrs. Wheatley; *Alice*, Mrs. Hackett; *Lowenna*, Mrs. Wallack.

Durang refers to the dramatist who is reputed to have done the version for Mr. Hackett, as "Old Mr. Kerr," an actor, who appeared in Philadelphia under the management of F. C. Wemyss. However much of an actor John Kerr was, he must have gained some small reputation as a playwright. In 1818, Duncombe issued Kerr's "Ancient Legends or Simple and Romantic Tales," and at the Harvard Library, where there is a copy of this book, the catalogue gives Kerr's position in London at the time as Prompter of the Regency Theatre. He must have ventured, with a relative, into independent publishing, for there was issued, in 1826, by J. & H. Kerr, the former's freely translated melodramatic romance, "The Monster and Magician; or,

The Fate of Frankenstein," taken from the French of J. T. Merle and A. N. Béraud. He did constant translation, and it is interesting to note the similarity between his "The Wandering Boys! or, The Castle of Olival," announced as an original comedy, and M. M. Noah's play of the same name.

There is valuable material in possession of Mr. James K. Hackett for a much needed life of his father. This may throw light on his negotiations with Kerr; it may also detail more thoroughly than the records now show why it was that, when he went to England in 1832, he engaged Bayle Bernard to make a new draft of the piece, given in New York at the Park Theatre, September 4, 1833. It may have been because he saw, when he reached London, a version which Bernard had shaped for the Adelphi Theatre, 1831-32, when Yates, John Reeve, and J. B. Buckstone had played together. But I am inclined to think that, whatever the outlines of the piece as given by Hackett, it was his acting which constituted the chief creative part of the performance. Like Jefferson, he must have been largely responsible for the finished product.

Hackett's success in dialect made him eager for any picturesque material which would exploit this ability. Obviously, local character was the best vehicle. That was his chief interest in encouraging American plays. Bayle Bernard had done writing for him before "Rip." In 1831, J. K. Paulding's "The Lion of the West" had proven so successful, as to warrant Bernard's transferring the popular *Col. Nimrod Wildfire* to another play, "The Kentuckian." Then, in 1837, Hackett corresponded with Washington Irving about dramatizing the "Knickerbocker History," which plan was consummated by Bernard as "Three Dutch Governors," even though Irving was not confident of results. Hackett went out of his way for such native material. Soon after his appearance as *Rip*, the following notice appeared in the New York *Evening Post*, for April 24, 1830:

Prize Comedy.—The Subscriber, desirous of affording some pecuniary inducement for more frequent attempts at dramatizing the manners and peculiarities of our own country, and the numerous subjects and incidents connected with its history, hereby offers to the writer of the best Comedy in 3 acts, in which a principal character shall be an original of this country, the sum of Two Hundred and Fifty Dollars—the decision to be made by a committee of competent literary gentlemen, whose names shall duly be made public.

The manuscripts to be sent to the address of the subscriber through the Post Office, before *1st September, next*, each accompanied with a letter communicating the address to which the author would desire his production returned, if unsuccessful, together with his *name* in a *sealed enclosure*, which will only be opened in the event of his obtaining the Prize.

Jas. H. Hackett,
64 Reed Street, New York

Many such prize contests were the fashion of the day.

Mr. James K. Hackett, in reminiscence, writes: "My mother used to tell me that Joe Jefferson played the part like a German, whereas *Rip* was a North River Dutchman, and in those days dialects were very marked in our country. But my father soon became identified with the part of *Falstaff*, and he used to say, 'Jefferson is a younger man than I, so I'll let him have *Rip*. I don't care to play against him'."

A stage version of the Irving story was made by one John H. Hewitt, of Baltimore, and during the season of 1833–34 was played in that city by William Isherwood. It was after this that Charles Burke (1822–1854) turned his attention to the play, and, as is shown in the text here reproduced, drew heavily upon Kerr. Winter says that he depended also upon the dramatic pieces used by Flynn and Parsons. The date of the first essayal of the part in New York was January 7, 1850, at the New National Theatre. But, during the previous year, he went with the play to the Philadelphia Arch Street Theatre, where his half-brother, Joseph, appeared with him in the rôle of *Seth*. Durang, however, disagrees with this date, giving it under the heading of the "Summer Season of 1850 at the Arch Street Theatre," and the specific time as August 19. In his short career Burke won an enviable position as an actor. "He had an eye and a face," wrote Joe Jefferson, "that told their meaning before he spoke, a voice that seemed to come from the heart itself, penetrating—but melodious." He was slender, emaciated, sensitive, —and full of lively response to things. Like all of the Jeffersons, he was a born comedian, and critics concede that W. E. Burton feared his rivalry. Between Burke and his half-brother, there was a profound attraction; they had "barn stormed" together, and through Burke's consideration it was that Joe was first encouraged and furthered in Philadelphia. Contrasting Burton and Burke, Jefferson wrote in his "Autobiography:"

Burton coloured highly, and laid on the effects with a liberal brush, while Burke was subtle, incisive and refined. Burton's features were strong and heavy, and his figure was portly and ungainly. Burke was lithe and graceful. His face was plain, but wonderfully expressive. The versatility of this rare actor was remarkable, his pathos being quite as striking a feature as his comedy. . . . His dramatic effects sprung more from intuition than from study; and, as was said of Barton Booth, "the blind might have seen him in his voice, and the deaf have heard him in his visage."

But the height of Jefferson's praise was reached when he said: "Charles Burke was to acting what Mendelssohn was to music. He did not have to work for his effects, as I do; he was not analytical, as I am. Whatever he did came to him naturally, as grass grows or water runs; it was not talent that informed his art, but genius."

Such was the comedian who next undertook the rôle of *Rip*. How often his own phrase, "Are we so soon forgot," has been applied to the actor and his art! The only preservative we have of this art is either in individual expressions of opinion or else in contemporary criticism. Fortunately, John Sleeper Clarke, another estimable comedian of the Jefferson family, has left an impression of how Burke read that one famous line of his. He has said:

> No other actor has ever disturbed the impression that the profound pathos of Burke's voice, face, and gesture created; it fell upon the senses like the culmination of all mortal despair, and the actor's figure, as the low, sweet tones died away, symbolized more the ruin of the representative of the race than the sufferings of an individual: his awful loss and loneliness seemed to clothe him with a supernatural dignity and grandeur which commanded the sympathy and awe of his audience.

Never, said Clarke, who often played *Seth* to Burke's *Rip*, was he disappointed in the poignant reading of that line—so tender, pathetic and simple that even the actors of his company were affected by it.

However much these various attempts at dramatization may have served their theatrical purpose, they have all been supplanted in memory by the play as evolved by Jefferson and Boucicault, who began work upon it in 1861. The incident told by Jefferson of how he arrived by his decision to play *Rip*, as his father had done before him, is picturesque. One summer day, in 1859, he lay in the loft of an old barn, reading the "Life and Letters of Washington Irving," and his eye fell upon this passage:

September 30, 1858. Mr. Irving came in town, to remain a few days. In the evening went to Laura Keene's Theatre to see young Jefferson as *Goldfinch* in Holcroft's comedy, "The Road to Ruin." Thought Jefferson, the father, one of the best actors he had ever seen; and the son reminded him, in look, gesture, size, and "make," of the father. Had never seen the father in *Goldfinch*, but was delighted with the son.

This incident undoubtedly whetted the interest of Joseph Jefferson, and he set about preparing his version. He had played in his half-brother's, and had probably seen Hackett in Kerr's. All that was needed, therefore, was to evolve something which would be more ideal, more ample in opportunity for the exercise of his particular type of genius. So he turned to the haven at all times of theatrical need, Dion Boucicault, and talked over with him the ideas that were fulminating in his brain. Clark Davis has pointed out that in the Jefferson "Rip" the credits should thus be measured:

Act I.—Burke + Jefferson + Boucicault ending.
Act II.—Jefferson.
Act III.—Burke + Jefferson + ending suggested by Shakespeare's "King Lear."

But, however the credit is distributed, Jefferson alone made the play as it lives in the memories of those who saw it. It grew by what it fed on, by accretions of rich imagination. Often times, Jefferson was scored for his glorification of the drunkard. He and Boucicault were continually discussing how best to circumvent the disagreeable aspects of *Rip's* character. Even Winter and J. Rankin Towse are inclined to frown at the reprobate, especially by the side of Jefferson's interpretation of *Bob Acres* or of *Caleb Plummer*. There is no doubt that, in their collaboration, Boucicault and Jefferson had many arguments about "Rip." Boucicault has left a record of the encounters:

"Let us return to 1865," he wrote. "Jefferson was anxious to appear in London. All his pieces had been played there. The managers would not give him an appearance unless he could offer them a new play. He had a piece called 'Rip Van Winkle', but when submitted for their perusal, they rejected it. Still he was so desirous of playing *Rip* that I took down Washington Irving's story and read it over. It was hopelessly undramatic. 'Joe', I said, 'this old sot is not a pleasant figure. He lacks romance. I dare say you made a fine sketch of the old beast, but there is no interest in him. He may be picturesque, but he is not dramatic. I would prefer to start him in a play as a young scamp, thoughtless, gay, just such a curly-head, good-humoured fellow as all the village girls would love, and the children and dogs would run after'. Jefferson threw up his hands in despair. It was totally opposed to his artistic preconception. But I insisted, and he reluctantly conceded. Well, I wrote the play as he plays it now. It was not much of a literary production, and it was with some apology that it was handed to him. He read it, and when he met me, I said: 'It is a poor thing, Joe'. 'Well', he replied, 'it is good enough for me'. It was produced. Three or four weeks afterward he called on me, and his first words were: 'You were right about making *Rip* a young man. Now I could not conceive and play him in any other shape'."

When finished, the manuscript was read to Ben Webster, the manager of the Haymarket Theatre, London, and to Charles Reade, the collaborator, with Boucicault, in so many plays. Then the company heard it, after which Jefferson proceeded to study it, literally living and breathing the part. Many are the humourous records of the play as preserved in the Jefferson "Autobiography" and in the three books on Jefferson by Winter Frances Wilson and Euphemia Jefferson.

On the evening of September 4, 1865, at the London Adelphi, the play was given. Accounts of current impressions are extant by Pascoe and Oxenford. It was not seen in New York until September 3, 1866, when it began a run at the Olympic, and it did not reach Boston until May 3, 1869. From the very first, it was destined to be Jefferson's most popular rôle. His royalties, as time progressed, were fabulous, or rather his profits, for actor, manager, and author were all rolled into one. He deserted a large repertory of parts as the years passed and his strength declined. But to the very end he never deserted *Rip*. At his death the play passed to his son, Thomas. The Jefferson version has been published with an interpretative introduction by him.

When it was first given, the play was scored for the apparent padding of the piece in order to keep Jefferson longer on the stage. The supernatural elements could not hoodwink the critics, but, as Jefferson added humanity to the part, and created a poetic, lovable character, the play was greatly strengthened.

In fact Jefferson was the play. His was a classic embodiment, preserved in its essential details in contemporary criticism and vivid pictures.

THEATRE

FOR THE BENEFIT

OF

Mrs. SHARPE

AND HER LAST APPEARANCE, prior to her departure for the South—on which occasion

Mr. Hackett

Has kindly consented to perform.

On Wednesday Evening, Oct. 18

Will be produced, 1st time in America, the Tragedy in 5 acts, of

THE BRIDAL

As altered from a Tragedy of Beaumont & Fletcher, by Messrs MACREADY *and* SHERIDAN KNOWLES, *and now performing in London with great applause.* 1837

Arcanus,	(King of Rhodes)	Mr. Richings
Melantius		Fredericks
Amintor		Mason
Lysippus	(brother to the King)	Wells
Diphibus,	(brother of Melantius & Evadne)	Nexsen
Cleon,		Garland
Calliranex,	(Kinsman to Aspasia,)	Wheatley
Archas	(Keeper of the Prison)	Bedford
Strato,		Isherwood
Diagoras,		Johnson
Assasin		King
Dion,		Gallott

Nobles, Guards, &c.

EVADNE	(Wife of Amintor,)	**MRS. SHARPE**
Aspasia	(formerly betrothed to Amintor)	Mrs. Richardson
Antiphole,		Pritchard
Olympias		Conway
Dula		Durie
Cleanthe		Miss Bedford

Ladies, &c. &c.

—IN ACT 2—

A GREEK PAS DE DEUX,

WILL BE DANCED

By MR. & MRS. CHECKENI.

After which, the Drama of

Rip Van Winkle!

Or—A Legend of the Catskill Mountains.

Characters in Act First—or 1763.

RIP VAN WINKLE, a North River Dutchman ***Mr. HACKETT***

Derrick Van Tassel, the Burgomaster........................Mr. Clarke
Nicholas Vedder, a Farmer,..................................Isherwood
Brom Van Brunt, a Schoolmaster,..............................Fisher
Rory Van Clump, Landlord of George 3d Tavern,..............Wells
Henderick Hudson, Capt. of the Spirit Crew of the Dutch
discovery ship 'Half Moon".....................................Hayden
Richard Juet, his Mate,..
Dirk Quackenboss,....................................

Dutchmen, Spirit Crew, &c.

Dame Van Winkle, Rip's Scolding Wife,..........Mrs. Wheatley
Alice, Rip's Sister,...Chippindale

Between the first and Second Acts a period of Twenty Years is supposed to elapse.

RIP VAN WINKLE, the Sleeper, now a Stranger in his Native Village,..................MR. HACKETT

Herman Van Tassel,....Son of the late Burgomaster Contracted to Gertrude,..............Mr. Wheatley
Abram Higginbottom....late Brom Van Brunt.........Fisher
Bradford.............in love with Gertrude.........Richings
Perseverance Peashell....Landlord of Washington Hotel,...Povey
Hiram, } ....Yankee Wits................ { King
Ebenezer, } { Wells
Young Rip Van Winkle,..Bancker
District Judge..Nexsen
Gertrude Van Winkle contracted to Herman ...Miss E. Turnbull
Dame Van Winkle formerly Alice Van Winkle....Chippindale

A Double Hornpipe by Mast & Miss Wells.

To conclude with, the FIRST ACT of the Farce of the

Kentuckian

Or—A Trip to New-York.

Nimrod Wildfire, - Mr. Hackett

Mr. Freeman .... Mr. Clarke
Percival, ... Wheatley
Pompey, ... Povey
Tradesman, ... Gallott
Mrs. Luminary, ...Mrs. Wheatley
Mrs. Freeman.... .... Vernon
Mary, ... Durie
Servant, ... Conway
Caroline .... Miss Turnbull

Thursday—Third Night of the Engagement of

MISS TREE

ION,

[illegible] ....Miss Tree

And, ANIMAL MAGNETISM.

☞ Friday and Saturday Evenings MISS TREE will perform.

RIP VAN WINKLE

A LEGEND OF THE CATSKILLS

A ROMANTIC DRAMA IN TWO ACTS

ADAPTED FROM WASHINGTON IRVING'S SKETCH BOOK

By CHARLES BURKE

[It is common knowledge that "Rip Van Winkle," as a play, was a general mixture of several versions when it finally reached the hands of Joseph Jefferson. From Kerr to Burke, from Burke to Boucicault, from Boucicault to Jefferson was the progress. The changes made by Burke in the Kerr version are so interesting, and the similarities are so close, that the Editor has thought it might be useful to make an annotated comparison of the two. This has been done, with the result that the reader is given two plays in one. The title-page of the Kerr acting edition runs as follows: "Rip Van Winkle; A Legend of Sleepy Hollow. A Romantic Drama in Two Acts. Adapted from Washington Irving's Sketch-Book by John Kerr, Author of 'Therese', 'Presumptive Guilt', 'Wandering Boys', 'Michael and Christine', 'Drench'd and Dried', 'Robert Bruce', &c., &c. With Some Alterations, by Thomas Hailes Lacy. Theatrical Publisher. London." The Burke version, used here as a basis, follows the acting text, without stage positions, published by Samuel French. An opera on the subject of "Rip Van Winkle," the libretto written by Wainwright, was presented at Niblo's Garden, New York, by the Pyne and Harrison Troupe, Thursday, September 27, 1855. There was given, during the season of 1919–20, by the Chicago Opera Association, "Rip Van Winkle: A Folk Opera," with music by Reginald de Kovan and libretto by Percy Mackaye, the score to be published by G. Schirmer. New York.]

CAST OF CHARACTERS

First performed at the West London Theatre (under the management of Mr. Beverley).

RIP VAN WINKLE

A Legend of the Sleepy Hollow.

CHARACTERS

Act I. 1763

	Original	*Walnut St. Philadelphia*
Deidrich Van Slaus	Mr. Sanger	Mr. Porter
Herman (his Son)	" N. Norton	" Read
Knickerbocker (a Schoolmaster)	" S. Beverley	" J. Jefferson
Rory Van Clump (a Landlord)	" C. Osborne	" Greene
		" Chapman
Rip Van Winkle	" H. Beverley	" Hackett
Nicholas Vedder	" T. Santer	" Sefton
Peter Clausen	" Cogan	" James
Gustave	Master Kerr	Miss Anderson
Dame Van Winkle	Mrs. Porter	Mrs. B. Stickney
Alice	" W. Hall	" S. Chapman
Lowena	Miss Kerr	Miss Eberle
Imp of the Mountain	W. Oxberry, Jun.	W. Wells

The Spectre Crew of the Mountains, Farmers, &c.

A Lapse of Twenty Years occurs between the Acts.

Act II. 1783.

Herman Van Slaus	Mr. H. Norton	Mr. Read
Seth Kilderkin	———	———
Knickerbocker	" S. Beverley	" J. Jefferson
Nicholas Vedder	" T. Santer	" Sefton
Gustave	———	———
Young Rip	———	———
		" Chapman
Rip Van Winkle	" H. Beverley	" Hackett
Alice Van Knickerbocker	Mrs. W. Hall	Mrs. S. Chapman
Lowena	Miss Kerr	Miss Eberle
Jacintha	———	———

CAST OF THE CHARACTERS

	Bowery Theatre New York 1857	*Arch Street Theatre Philadelphia* 1850	*Broadway Theatre New York* 1855	*Metropolitan Theatre Buffalo* 1857
ACT I—1763				
RIP VAN WINKLE (a Dutchman)	Mr. F. S. Chanfrau	Mr. C. Burke	Mr. Hackett	Mr. F. S. Chanfrau
KNICKERBOCKER (a Schoolmaster)	" Whiting	" J. L. Baker	" Norton	" B. G. Rogers
DERRIC VAN SLAUS (the Burgomaster)	" Ferdon	" Marsh	" McDonall	" Ross
HERMAN VAN SLAUS (his son)	" Blake	" Henkins	———	" Ferrell
NICHOLAS VEDDER (friend to Rip)	" Baker	" ———	" Anderson	" Stephens
CLAUSEN	" Edson	" Bradford	———	" Leak
RORY VANCLUMP (a Landlord)	" Foster	" Worrell	" Price	" Boynton
GUSTAFFE	" F. Hodges	" Mortimore	Miss Wood	" Kent
DAME VAN WINKLE	Mrs. Axtel	Mrs. Hughs	Mrs. Bellamy	Miss Wells
ALICE	" Fitzgerald	Miss Wood	" Sylvester	Mrs. C. Henri
LORRENNA	Miss Wallis	" E. Jones	Miss Henry	La Petite Sarah
SWAGGRINO (Spirits of the Catskills)	Mr. Williams	Mr. Brown	Mr. Lamy	Mr. Henri
GAUDERKIN (Spirits of the Catskills)	" Barry	" Ray	———	" McAuley
ICKEN (Spirits of the Catskills)	" Bennett	" Ross	———	" Ferris
ACT II.—1783.—*A lapse of twenty years is supposed to occur between the First and Second Acts.*				
RIP VAN WINKLE (the dreamer)	Mr. F. S. Chanfrau	Mr. C. Burke	Mr. Hackett	Mr. F. S. Chanfrau
HERMAN VAN SLAUS	" Blake	" Henkins	" Warwick	" Ferrell
SETH SLOUGH	" Denham	" J. Jefferson	" Whiting	" Stephens
KNICKERBOCKER	" Whiting	" J. L. Baker	" Norton	" B. G. Rogers
THE JUDGE	" Pelham	" Anderson	———	" Spackman
GUSTAFFE	" F. Hodges	" Mortimore	" Levere	" Kent
RIP VAN WINKLE, JR.	" Thompson	" Stanley	" Ryder	" McAuley
FIRST VILLAGER	" Bennett	" Thomas	" Brown	" Ferris
SECOND VILLAGER	" Alkins	" Sims	" Hoffman	" Judson
ALICE KNICKERBOCKER	Mrs. Fitzgerald	Miss Wood	Mrs. Sylvester	Mrs. C. Henri
LORRENNA	" J. R. Scott	" E. Jones	" Allen	Miss Tyson

COSTUME

RIP—*First dress:*—A deerskin coat and belt, full brown breeches, deerskin gaiters, cap. *Second dress:*—Same, but much worn and ragged.

KNICKERBOCKER—*First dress:*—Brown square cut coat, vest and breeches, shoes and buckles. *Second dress:*—Black coat, breeches, hose, &c.

DERRIC VAN SLAUS—Square cut coat, full breeches, black silk hose, shoes and buckles—*powder.*

HERMAN—*First dress:*—Ibid. *Second dress:*—Black frock coat, tight pants, boots and tassels.

VEDDER, CLAUSEN, RORY—Dark square cut coats, vests, breeches, &c.

GUSTAFFE—Blue jacket, white pants, shoes.

SETH SLOUGH—Gray coat, striped vest, large gray pants.

JUDGE—Full suit of black.

YOUNG RIP—A dress similar to Rip's first dress.

DAME—Short gown and quilted petticoat, cap.

ALICE—*First dress:*—Bodice, with half skirt, figured petticoat. *Second dress:*—Brown satin bodice and skirt, &c.

LORRENNA, Act 1—A child.

LORRENNA, Act 2—White muslin dress, black ribbon belt, &c.

RIP VAN WINKLE

ACT I.

SCENE I.—*A Village.—House, with a sign of* "George III."—*Two or three tables.*—VILLAGERS *discovered, smoking.* VEDDER, KNICKERBOCKER, RORY, CLAUSEN *at table. Chorus at rise of curtain.*

CHORUS.

In our native land, where flows the Rhine,
In infancy we culled the vine;
Although we toiled with patient care,
But poor and scanty was our fare.

SOLO.

Till tempting waves, with anxious toil,
We landed on Columbia's soil;
Now plenty, all our cares repay,
So laugh and dance the hours away.

CHORUS.

Now plenty, all our cares repay,
So laugh and dance the hours away;
Ha, ha, ha! Ha, ha, ha!
So laugh, ha, ha! and dance the hours away.

VEDDER. Neighbour Clausen, on your way hither, saw you anything of our friend, Rip Van Winkle? Where there's a cup of good liquor to be shared, he's sure to be on hand—a thirsty soul.

KNICKERBOCKER. Truly, the man that turns up his nose at good liquor is a fool, as we Dutchmen have it; but cut no jokes on Rip; remember, I'm soon to be a member of his family; and any insult offered to him, I shall resent in the singular number, and satisfaction must follow, as the Frenchmen have it.

VEDDER. So, Knickerbocker, you are really determined to marry Rip's sister, the pretty Alice?

KNICKERBOCKER. Yes, determined to be a prisoner in Hymen's chains, as the lovers have it. I've got Rip's consent, I've got Alice's consent, and I've got my own consent.

CLAUSEN. But have you got the dame's consent, eh?

KNICKERBOCKER. There I'm dished and done up brown; would you believe it? she calls me a long, scraggy, outlandish animal, and that I look like two deal boards glued together!

RORY. Here comes Alice, and with her, Rip's daughter.

Enter ALICE, *with* LORRENNA. [LOWENA] [1]

ALICE. Come along, loiterer! Woe betide us when we get home, for having tarried so long! What will the dame say?

LORRENNA. Well, it's not my fault, for you have been up and down the lane a dozen times, looking for the schoolmaster, Knickerbocker.

ALICE. Hold your tongue, Miss, it's no such thing.

LORRENNA. You know you love him.

ALICE. How do you know that, Miss Pert?

LORRENNA. I can see it; and seeing is believing, they say. Oh, you're monstrous jealous of him, you know you are.

KNICKERBOCKER *advances.*

ALICE. Jealous! I, jealous of him? No, indeed, I never wish to see his ugly face again.

KNICKERBOCKER. Say not so, sweet blossom of the valley, for in that case I shall shoot myself in despair.

ALICE. Oh, don't think of such a thing, for then your ghost might haunt me.

LORRENNA. And I'm sure you would rather have him than his ghost, wouldn't you, Alice?

KNICKERBOCKER. That's a very smart child. But Alice, sweet Alice, can't I drop in this evening, when the old folks are out of the way?

ALICE. Not for the world; if the dame were to find you in the house, I don't know what would happen.

LORRENNA. Don't you know, Alice, mammy always goes out for an hour in the evening, to see her neighbour, Dame Wrigrim; now, if you [*To* KNICKERBOCKER.] come at eight o'clock, and throw some gravel at the window, there's no knowing but you might see Alice.

[1] So spelled in the Kerr version.

KNICKERBOCKER. That's an uncommon clever girl; but, Alice, I'm determined to turn over a new leaf with Dame Van Winkle; the next time I see her, I'll pluck up [my] courage and say to her—

DAME. [*Without.*] Alice! Alice! odds bodikins and pins, but I'll give it you when I catch you.

The VILLAGERS *exit.*

KNICKERBOCKER. Run, Alice, run!

[ALICE, LORENNA *and* KNICKERBOCKER *run to right.*

DAME. [*Without.*] Alice!

[ALICE, LORRENNA *and* KNICKERBOCKER *exeunt hastily.*

RORY. Egad! the dame's tongue is a perfect scarecrow!

VEDDER. The sound of her voice sets them running just as if she were one of the mountain spirits, of whom we hear so much talk. [But where the deuce can Rip be all this while? [RIP *sings without.*] But talk of the devil and his imps appear.] [1]

Enter RIP VAN WINKLE, *with gun, game-bag, &c.*

RIP. Rip, Rip, wass is dis for a business. You are a mix nootze unt dat is a fact. Now, I started for de mountains dis mornin', determined to fill my bag mit game, but I met Von Brunt, de one-eyed sergeant—[comma see hah, unt brandy-wine hapben my neiber friend];[2] well, I couldn't refuse to take a glass mit him, unt den I tooks anoder glass, unt den I took so much as a dozen, [do] [3] I drink no more as a bottle; he drink no more as I—he got so top heavy, I rolled him in de hedge to sleep a leetle, for his one eye got so crooked, he never could have seed his way straight; den I goes to de mountain, [do] [4] I see double, [d——d] [5] a bird could I shooted. But I stops now, I drinks no more; if anybody ask me to drink, I'll say to dem—[VEDDER *comes down, and offers cup to him.*]—here is your [go-to-hell],[6] and your family's [go-to-hell],[6] and may you all live long and [prosper].[7] [*Drinks.*

VEDDER. Why, neighbour Rip, where have you been all day?

[1] Assigned to CLAUSEN in the Kerr version. Preceding this bracket,
CLAUSEN. Well, she is a tartar, there's no denying that.
VEDDER. No! but if she were my wife instead of Rip's, I warrant I'd soon tame her.
CLAUSEN. Not you! But where the deuce . . .

[2] Not in the Kerr version.

[3] "but" in K.

[4] "but as" in K.

[5] "not a" in K.

[6] "Goot-hell" in K.

[7] "brosber" in K. In this speech, there is a variation in dialect as "v" for "w" in such words as "was," and "v" for "o" in such a word as "one."

We feared some of the [Elfin] [1] goblins of the Catskill had caught you.

RIP. Ha, ha! I never see no ghosts, though I've fought mit *spirits* in my time, ha, ha!

VEDDER. And they always throw you, eh? ha, ha!

RIP. Dat's a fact! Ha, ha, ha!

VEDDER. But, Rip, where have you been?

RIP. Oh, very hard at work [2]—very busy; dere is nothing slipped [fun my fingers as was come at abe.] [3]

RORY. They appear to have slipped through your game bag though, for its full of emptiness.—Ha, ha, ha!

RIP Ho, ho, ho! cut no jokes at my *bag* or I'll gib you de sack.

VEDDER. Come, Rip, sit down, take a pipe and a glass and make yourself comfortable.

RIP. [Nine, nine—ech con neiched—] [4] it behoves a man to look after his interest unt not drink all de while, I shall den be able to manage—

VEDDER. Your wife, Rip?

RIP. Manage mine [frow] [5]? Can you fly to de moon on a [paper][6] kite? Can you drink all de beer and brandy-wine at one gulp? when you can do dat, mine goot [im himmel] [7] you can manage mine [frow]. [*All laugh.* [8]

RORY.[9] Take one glass, Rip.

RIP. No, I won't touch him.

VEDDER. Come, come, lay hold.

RIP. Now I'll be [d——d fun] [10] I does.

VEDDER. Well, if you won't. [*All go to table but* RIP.

RIP. Dere is [a] [11] drinks, dere is [a][11] drinks; I have [conquered] [12] temptation at last. Bravo resolution! bravo resolution; resolution, you shall have one glass for dat.[13] [*Goes to table.*

OMNES. Ha, ha, ha!

[1] Not in K.
[2] "vork" in K.
[3] "froo my fingers as vas comeatable," in K.
[4] "Nein, nein" in K.
[5] "frau" in K.
[6] "baber" in K.
[7] "freund, den" in K.
[8] Here is given in Kerr, the following:
VEDDER. I wish she was my wife, I'd manage her.
RIP. And I wish she vas your vife too, or anybody's vife, so long as she vasn't mine vife.
[9] RORY'S speech, in K., begins with "Come."
[10] "stewed vhen" in K.
[11] "der" in K.
[12] "gonguered" in K.
[13] In K., variation only in dialect form.

RORY. Here, Rip, here's a glass at your service, and as for the contents I'll warrant it genuine and no mistake.

[*Gives* RIP *a cup.*

RIP. Rory, here is your [go-to-hell],[1] unt your family's [go-to-hell],[1] un may you all live long unt [prosper].[2]

RORY. Come, Rip, give us a stave.

VEDDER. Yes, yes, Rip, a stave, for the old dame will be after you soon and then we will all have to make a clearance.

RIP. Oh, tunner wasser! [won't][3] my old woman skin me when I get home.

VEDDER and RORY. Ha, ha, ha! come, the song, the song.

RIP. Well, here is Rip Van Winkle's warning to all single fellows.

SONG.—RIP.

List, my friends, to caution's voice,
Ere de marriage knot you tie;
It is [the devil],[4] mit shrews to splice,
Dat nobody can deny, deny,
Dat nobody can deny.

Chorus.—That nobody can deny, &c.

When a wife to rule once wishes,
Mit poor spouse 'tis all my eye,
I'm [d——d] [5] if she don't wear de breeches,
Dat nobody can deny, deny,
Dat nobody can deny.

Chorus.—That nobody can deny, &c.

Yet dere is a charm about dem,
Do dere voices are so high
We can't do mit'em, [*Pause.*
Nor we can't do mit-out 'em,
Dat nobody can deny, deny,
Dat nobody can deny.

Chorus.—That nobody can deny, &c.[6]

1 "goot-hell" in K.
2 "brosber" in K.
3 "vont" in K. The present edition does not attempt to indicate such slight variations and differences.
4 "der tyfil" in K.
5 "stewed" in K.
6 In this song, "v" takes the place of "w" in K.

DAME. [*Without.*] Rip, Rip! I'll stretch your ears when I get hold of them.

RIP. [Mine goot im himmel],[1] dere is my frow.

DAME. [*Without.*] Rip! you lazy varmint! Rip!

RIP. [*Gets under the table with bottle.*] Look out, boys! de wild cat's coming.

Music.—VEDDER, RORY *and* CLAUSEN, *at table.—Enter* DAME, *with a stick.*

DAME. Where is this wicked husband of mine! odds bodikins and pins! I heard his voice; you've hid him somewhere! you ought to be ashamed of yourselves to inveigle a husband from a tender, loving spouse; but I'm put upon by all, because they know the mildness of my temper.—[*They laugh.*]—Odds bodikins and curling irons, but some of you shall laugh the other sides of your mouths—I'll pull your pates for you.[2]

Music.—Chases them round table; they exit.—DAME *upsets table and discovers* RIP.

DAME. Oh, you Rip of all rips! what have you to say for yourself?

RIP. Here is your [go-to-hell],[3] unt your family's[3], unt may you all live long and [prosper].

DAME. [*Pulling him down the stage by the ear.*] I'm cool—that is to say not very hot: but the mildest temper in the world would be in a passion at such treatment. Get home, you drunken monster, or I sha'n't be able to keep my hands off you. Tell me, sir, what have you been about all day?

RIP. Hard at work, my dumpsy dumpsy; de first ting I see dis morning was a fine fat rabbit.

DAME. A rabbit? Oh, I do like rabbits in a stew; I like everything in a stew.

RIP. I be [d——d] [4] but dat is a fact.

DAME. Well, well, the rabbit?

RIP. I was going to tell you, well, dere was de rabbit feeding in de grass.

[1] "Der tyfil" in K.

[2] In K. there follows:
VEDDER. Oh, I wish I was your husband, Dame Winkle. [*Exit.*
DAME. You, my husband, you! [*To the others.*] Out of my sight, reprobates.

[3] "goot-hell" in K.

[4] "stewed" in K.

DAME. Well, well, Rip?

RIP. I [puts] [1] my gun to my shoulder—

DAME. Yes,—

RIP. I takes goot aim mit him.

DAME. Yes,—

RIP. I [pulls] [2] my trigger, unt—

DAME. Bang went the gun and down the rabbit fell.

RIP. Eh? snap went [de] [3] gun and off de rabbit run. Ha, ha, ha!

DAME. No!

RIP. I be [d——d fun] [4] dat is a fact.

DAME. And you shot nothing?

RIP. Not dat time; but de next time, I picks me my flint, unt I [creeps] [5] up to de little [pond] [6] by de old field, unt dere—what do you [tink] [7] I see?

DAME. Ducks?

RIP. More as fifty black ducks—ducks as big as [a goose] [8]—well, I hauls up again.

DAME. And so will I [*Raising stick.*] if you miss fire this time.

RIP. Bang!

DAME. How many down?

RIP. [One!] [9]

DAME. Not more than one duck out of fifty?

RIP. Yes, a great deal more as [one] duck.

DAME. Then you shot more than one?

RIP. Yes, more as one duck,—I shot one old bull.

DAME. What?

RIP. I'm [d——d fun] dat is a fact! dat was one down, and [my goot im himmel] [10] how he did roar and bellow, unt lash his tail, unt snort and sneeze, unt sniff! Well, de bull puts right after me, unt I puts right away fun de bull: well, de bull comes up mit me just as I was climbing de fence, unt he catch me mit his horns fun de [seat] [11] of my breeches, unt sent me flying more

1 "buts" in K.
2 "bulls" in K.
3 "der" in K.
4 "stewed but" in K.
5 "creebs" in K.
6 "bond" in K.
7 "think" in K.
8 "gooses" in K.
9 "von" in K.
10 "den" in K.
11 "back" in K.

as a mile high.—Well, by-and-bye directly, I come down aready in a big tree, unt dere I sticks fast, unt den—

DAME. You went fast asleep for the rest of the day.

RIP. Dat's a fact. How[1] you know dat? you must be a witch.

DAME. [*Catching him by the collar.*] Home, sir, home! you lazy scamp. [*Beating him.*

RIP. But, mine lublicka frow—

DAME. Home! [*Beating him.*

RIP. [Nine! nine!—][2]

DAME. Home! [*Beats him.*

RIP. [Mine goot im himmel.][3] [*Music.—*DAME *beats him off.*

SCENE II.—*A Plain Chamber.*

Enter DERRIC VAN SLAUS.[4]

[1] "do" follows "how" in K.

[2] "Nein, nein" in K.

[3] In K., Rip's speech is "Ter tyfil! but I have cotch him dis time!"

[4] "*and* HERMAN" in K. The scene, which is different, runs as follows:

HERMAN. Lecture me as much as you will, father, if at the close of your sermon you are prepared to supply me with the money that I need.

DERRIC. Money! that is eternally your cry. Your extravagances have almost ruined and soon will dishonour me. Oh! I am but justly punished for my mad indulgence of a son who was born only to be my bane and curse.

HERMAN. If you could but invent some fresh terms for my reproach! such frequent repetition becomes, I assure you, very wearisome.

DERRIC. You have caused me to plunge into debt, and I am now pursued by a host of creditors.

HERMAN. We must find a way to quiet them. And for the money I now require—

DERRIC. Not another dollar do you obtain from me. Already, to supply your cravings, I have misappropriated some of the public money, and I must replace it soon if I would avert the shame and degradation with which I now am threatened.

HERMAN. And from which I will save you.

DERRIC. You?

HERMAN. Yes, I! Rip van Winkle, your tenant—

DERRIC. What has that idle, dissipated fellow to do with the present matter?

HERMAN. Much, as I will show you, and his daughter more.

DERRIC. His daughter?

HERMAN. Now scarcely seven years old, I believe. This girl has an aunt residing in New York, who has long since, in consequence of an affront received from Van Winkle, discarded the whole family. But I have discovered that, of which they have no notion.

DERRIC. What do you mean?

HERMAN. Why, that the whole of this aunt's fortune, and she is immensely rich, must of necessity, at the old lady's death, become the inheritance of the little Lowena.

DERRIC. And in what way can that affect us?

HERMAN. You shall hear. I have already caused a contract to be prepared, and to which you must obtain Rip Van Winkle's signature.

DERRIC. What is that contract?

HERMAN. You shall read it presently. Van Winkle is an easy soul, and at present, I believe, your debtor.

DERRIC. Yes, considerably in arrears with the rent of the tenement, which he holds from me.

HERMAN. Obtain his signature to the contract I am about to give you, and 'twill be a security on which money may be raised to any amount.

DERRIC. You amaze me, I—

HERMAN. You must have cash, father, to relieve you from your unpleasant difficulties, and I, for those delights of youth without which there is no advantage in being young. [*Exeunt.*

DERRIC. Should the present application fail, I am a ruined man; all my speculations will be frustrated, and my duplicity exposed; yes, the dissipation of my son must inevitably prove his ruin as well as mine. To supply his wants, the public money has been employed; and, if unable to replace it, heaven knows what may be the consequence. But my son is now placed with an able advocate in New York, and should he pursue the right path, there may be still hopes of his reformation.

HERMAN. [*Without.*] My father, you say, is this way?

DERRIC. What voice is that; my son? What can have recalled him thus suddenly? Some new misadventure.—Oh, my forboding thoughts!

Enter HERMAN.

DERRIC. Herman, what brings you back? Are all my cautions thus lightly regarded, that they can take no hold upon your conduct?

HERMAN. You have good cause for warmth, sir, but learn the reason of my disobedience, ere you condemn. Business of importance has urged me hither—such as concerns us both most intimately.

DERRIC. Some fresh extravagance, no doubt, to drain my little left, and set a host of creditors loose upon me.

HERMAN. Not so, sir, but the reverse. List! you know our neighbour, Rip Van Winkle?

DERRIC. Know him? Aye, his idleness is proverbial; you have good cause to recollect him too, since 'twas by his courage your life was preserved, when attacked by the famished wolf.

HERMAN. He has a daughter scarcely seven years old; now, the attorney whom I serve has been employed to draw up the will and settle the affairs of this girl's aunt, who, for some slight offered by Van Winkle, has long since discarded the family. At her death, the whole of her immense wealth, in cash and land, is the inheritance of the girl, who is, at this moment, the richest presumptive heiress in the land.

DERRIC. What connection can Van Winkle's fortune have with ours?

HERMAN. Listen! Were it possible to procure his signature to a contract that his daughter, when of age, should be married to me, on this security money might be raised by us to any amount. Now, my good father, am I comprehensible?

DERRIC. Truly, this seems no visionary dream, like those in which, with fatal pertinacity, you have so oft indulged; and, on recollection, the rent of his tenement is in arrears; 'twill offer favourable opportunity for my calling and sounding him; the contract must be your care.

HERMAN. 'Tis already prepared and lacks only his signature. —[*Presenting it.*] Lawyers, who would do justice to their clients, must not pause at conscience; 'tis entirely out of the question when their own interest is concerned.

DERRIC. Herman, I like not this black-leg manner of proceeding: yet it augurs thou wilt be no pettifogger. I'll to Van Winkle straight and, though not legalized to act, yet in this case I can do work which honest lawyers would scorn. [*Exit.*

HERMAN. [*Solus.*] True; the honest lawyer lives by his reputation, and therefore pauses to undertake a cause he knows unjust: but how easily are some duped. Can my father for a moment suppose that the rank weeds of youth are so easily uprooted? No! what is to be done, good father of mine, but to serve myself? young men of the present generation cannot live without the means of entering into life's varieties and this supply will henceforth enable me to do so, to the fullest extent of my ambitious wishes. [*Exit.*

SCENE III.—RIP'S *Cottage.—Door.—Window in flat.—A closet in flat, with dishes, shelves, &c.—Clothes-basket, with clothes.——Table, chairs, arm-chair, with cloak over it.—Broom on stage.*

KNICKERBOCKER *enters cautiously.*

KNICKERBOCKER. Zooks! I'm venturing into a tiger's den in quest of a lamb. All's clear, however; and, could I but pop on little Alice, how we would bill and coo. She comes! lie still, my fluttering heart.

Enter ALICE.[1]

ALICE. [*Without observing* KNICKERBOCKER.] There, there, go to sleep. Ah! Knickerbocker, how I love you, [spite of all the strange ways that you pursue.] [2]

KNICKERBOCKER. [*Aside.*] Sensible, susceptible soul! [But merit ever meets its recompense.] [3]

[1] *"speaking off, to the child,"* in K.
[2] Not in K.
[3] Not in K.

ALICE. No wonder I am fascinated; [his figure is so elegant, and then his education! I never see him, but I am ready to jump into his loving arms. [*Turning, she is caught in the embrace of* KNICKERBOCKER.] [1]

KNICKERBOCKER. This is too much for human nature to support; [this declaration is a banquet that gods might prize.[2]] Beauteous angel! hear me, whilst I proclaim—

[*Kneeling.*

DAME. [*Without.*] Go along, you drunken brute.

KNICKERBOCKER. The devil! 'tis Dame Van Winkle! [what's to become of me?

ALICE. If you're found here I'm ruined! you must conceal yourself—but where?

KNICKERBOCKER. That's the important question; oh,][3] I'll hop into the cupboard.

ALICE. Not for the world! she is sure to want something out of it. Here, here, get into this clothes-basket, and let me cover you over with the foul linen.

KNICKERBOCKER. It's a very foul piece of business altogether but I must stomach it whether I will or no.

Music.—She puts him into the basket and covers him with linen.

DAME *enters, dragging in* RIP.

DAME. And now, sir, I've got you home, what have you to say for yourself, I should like to know?

RIP. Nothing, [my] [4] darling, de least said is soonest mended, and so you shall have all de talk to yourself.—Now ain't dat liberal?

DAME. Where's all the game you were to bring home?

RIP. On de wing still: wouldn't venture to come mitin fire; for though dey missed mine gun, dere's one ting for certain, I never miss your blowing up.

DAME. My blowing up! Odds bodikins and pins! I shall never be able to contain myself! Where's the money to pay the rent, you oaf?

RIP. I don't know.—Do you?

DAME. You'll go to prison, and that'll be the end on't.

[1] Not in K. Instead, "he is so handsome, his figure is so elegant."
[2] Not n K.
[3] Not in K.
[4] "mein" in K.

RIP. Come, no more quarrelling to-night. [We'll][1] see about de rent money to-morrow morning.

DAME. To-morrow! it's always to-morrow with you. So, Alice, you are sitting and idling as usual, just like your brother, a precious pair of soft pates.

RIP. Soft [pate][2]—pretty hard I guess, or it would have been [fructured][3] long since and dat's a fact.

DAME. And now, Alice, come with me that I may satisfy myself how you have disposed of the children, for in these matters you are just such a crawler as that vagrum there, [*Is retiring.*] that terrapin!

RIP. Terrapin! Ah, dame, I leaves you to go the whole hog, but hark'ee, my lovey, before you go, won't you return de leetle bottle which you manage to get from me [last night]?[4]

DAME. Odds bodikins, and pins! A man already drunk, and asking for more liquor! You sha'n't have a drop, you sot, that you shall not. The bottle indeed! not you, eh! faith!

[*Exit with* ALICE.

RIP. [Tunder][5] take me if I don't [think][6] but what she has [finished][7] it herself, and dat's de fact. My nose always sniffs like a terrier's; 'tis in de cupboard, her Hollands;—so, here goes to nibble.

Music.—RIP *opens the closet door cautiously, and is rummaging for a bottle, when he treads on* KNICKERBOCKER, *who roars out lustily.* RIP, *in his sudden alarm, upsets the* [*porcelain and glass*];[8] *and, falling, rolls into the middle of the chamber, quaking in every limb, and vociferating loudly.*

RIP. Help! murder! fire! thieves!

KNICKERBOCKER, [*in the interim*][9], *darts out of the closet, and,* [*beyond the consciousness of future proceeding*][10], *throws himself into the arm-chair.*—ALICE, *entering hastily, throws a cloak over him, which hides him from observation.*—DAME *enters, alarmed.*

DAME. Odds bodikins and pins! what's the matter, now?

[1] "Ve'll" in K.
[2] "bate" in K.
[3] "broken" in K. Also add "by your knocks."
[4] Not in K.
[5] "Tonner" in K.
[6] "tink" in K.
[7] "finish" in K.
[8] "crockery" in K.
[9] Not in K.
[10] Not in K.

RIP. [*Raising his head cautiously.*] Matter, indeed! [the devil's][1] in the cupboard! Oh, la! I'll be swammed.

DAME. In the cupboard!—[*Going there, sees china broken; squalling.*]—All my fine porcelain destroyed! monster! vile, rapacious monster! A devil, indeed, has been in the cupboard, and that's you. The china, presented to me by my grand relations, which I set such store on, smashed into a thousand pieces; 'tis too much for my weak nerves. I shall swoon! I shall faint! [*She sinks in the arm-chair, but immediately starts up, and, squalling, falls into* RIP'S *arms.*—KNICKERBOCKER *regains the closet, unobserved by all, save* ALICE.

DAME. Heaven have mercy on us! there was somebody in the chair! somebody in the chair!

RIP. Phoo! there's nothing in de chair, save your old cloak, [*Tossing it aside.*] dat's all.

DAME. I'm so alarmed—so agitated, that—Alice, put your hand into my pocket and you'll find a bottle. [ALICE *produces a bottle.*

RIP. [*Aside.*] A leetle bottle! Oh, dat's de [private][2] cupboard. Alice, let me hold de leetle bottle, whilst you fetch a glass for the old woman. [ALICE, *hastening off, brings a wine-glass, which* RIP *fills and gives to* DAME.

RIP. Here's your [go-to-hell],[3] and your family's and may you live long and [prosper][4]. [*Drinks from the bottle;* ALICE, *in the interim, proceeds to the closet and brings* KNICKERBOCKER *out, who is making for the door, when, hearing some one approach, he again escapes to his retreat.*

ALICE. [*At door.*] Oh, aunt! aunt! here's the burgomaster coming up the garden.

DAME. Odds bodikins and pins! the burgomaster! what's to be done now? Coming for the rent! What's to be done now, I say?

RIP. I'll go to bed and [think][5].

[*Crosses.*

DAME. You sha'n't go to bed! you must make some fresh excuse;—you're famous at them to me;—you have got into the hobble and must get out of it as well as you can; I shall go and

[1] "der tyfil's" in K.
[2] "brivate" in K.
[3] "goot-hell" in K.
[4] "brosber" in K.
[5] "tink" in K.

consult my friend, Dame Wrigrim; and Alice, should the pedlar woman come, desire her not to leave any more of her rubbish here.

As DAME *retires, she meets* DERRIC[1] *to whom she curtseys.*

DERRIC. Good evening, Dame.

DAME. Your honour's servant. [*Exit* DAME.

RIP. [*Aside.*] La! what a stew I'm in. Alice take yourself off, 'tis full time. Wish I was off too, mit all my heart and soul.

ALICE. [*Aside.*] Dear, dear! what will become of my poor Knickerbocker. [*Exit.*

DERRIC. Well, honest Rip, how wags the world with you?

RIP. Bad enough, sir, for though [labouring][2] from morn to night, I can make no advance in de world, though my industry is proverbial, and dat's a fact.

DERRIC. Why, where the bottle is concerned, few, I believe, can boast so much industry.

RIP. Dat is a fact; but I suppose you have called concerning de rent. [*Aside.*] How my heart [goes and comes!][3] [*Aloud.*] Now if your honour will be so [good][4] enough to—

DERRIC. To write the receipt: certainly.

RIP. Nine, nine! [*Aside.*] I'm stewed alive mit [perspiration.][5]

DERRIC. We'll talk of the rent at a future period! There is another affair on which I wish to consult you.

RIP. Take a chair, your honour.—[*Aside, rubbing his hands together.*]—It's all right, by de hookey.—[*Aloud.*]—Take a glass mit me. [*They take chairs.*

DERRIC. You know my only son, [whose life you preserved?][6]

RIP. Yes; and a [wild][7] harum-scarum [dog][8] he is. [*Drinks.*

DERRIC. He [is now stationed in New York, studying the law, and][8] has become a staid, sober, prudent youth; and [now][9], 'tis my wish that he should settle in this, his native place, and [that he][10] marry some honest girl, who is altogether unacquainted with the frivolities of cities; and I have been thinking that in a

[1] "entering" inserted, in K.
[2] "I vork" in K.
[3] "bit-and-bat" in K.
[4] "goot" in K.
[5] "bersbiration" in K.
[6] Not in K.
[7] "vild" and "tog" in K.
[8] Not in K.
[9] Not in K.
[10] Not in K.

few years your daughter will be grown up, and would make a suitable match for him. True, there will be some disparity in their ages, but as the years are on the side of the husband, so 'twill be all the better for the wife, in having a matured preceptor.

RIP. Beg [pardon],[1] sir; but it strikes me you are only carrying on your rigs mit me.

DERRIC. No, on my honour; and, to convince you that I'm in earnest, I have brought with me a contract, by which our offspring, when of age, are bound to intermarry, or forfeit their several fortunes. I shall settle all mine on Herman, and I shall expect you to do the same for your daughter.

RIP. Yah! yah! [ech woll][2]; I'll give her all [I got][2]; all my money; but she must be [d——d][3] smart if she can find ['em.][4] Take a drink, [Mr.][5] Burgomaster. [*Drinks.*

DERRIC. Well, here are the two contracts, both binding and legally drawn.

RIP. Yah! yah! [*Drinks.*—DERRIC *gives him the pen.*] What you want me to do mit dis?

DERRIC. Merely sign your name.

RIP. Me, [put][6] my name to dat [paper],[6] mitout my old woman knowing?—mine goot [friend],[7] she would skin me. [*Noise in closet.*] [Schat! you witch!][8]

DERRIC. But I was about to propose, on condition of your signing the contract, to let you live rent free, in future.

RIP. Rent free! I'll sign! but [stop]![9] my old woman [must][9] play [old hob][10] mit me—so put down dat I can break dat contract, if I choose, in twenty years and a day.—[*Noise.*]—[Schat! you witch!][11]

DERRIC. [*Writing.*] As you please.[12] [*Noise.*

RIP. Schat! you witch![13] [*Drinks.*

DERRIC. Is that a cat, friend Rip? [*Writing.*

[1] "bardon" in K.
[2] Not in K.
[3] "uncommon" in K.
[4] "him" in K.
[5] "Mynheer" in K.
[6] "boot" and "baber" in K.
[7] "freund" in K.
[8] In K, "S-ss cat! be quiet wid you!"
[9] "Stob" and "vould" in K.
[10] "der tyfil" in K.
[11] In K, "S-s cat! you be quiet, or I will skin you as my vife skins me."
[12] K. adds, "I will take care to get him so completely in my power that he shall not dare, however he might desire it, to avail himself of the power which that addition to the contract will give him."
[13] In K., the line reads, "S-s cat! I vill cut off your tail."

RIP.—I don't know if it is a cat—but, if it is my dog [Snider],[1] I wouldn't be in his skin when de old woman comes back.

DERRIC. There, friend Rip, I have inserted, at your request, this codicil: "Should the said Rip Van Winkle think fit to annul this contract, within twenty years and a day, he shall be at full liberty to do so."

RIP. Yah, yah! [dos][2] is recht—dat is goot. Now [Mr.][2] Burgomaster, what you want me to do?

DERRIC. Sign it!

RIP. Wass?

DERRIC. Sign!

RIP. Give me de [paper][3].—[*Takes it.*]—How my head turns round.—[*Reading.*]—"Should the said Rip Van Winkle"—yah, yah! dat is me.—"Rip Van Winkle—twenty years and a day."—Oh, dat is all recht.—[*Writing.*]—R-i-p V-a-n—[*Noise.*]—Schat! you witch! W-i-n-k-l-e—now, dere he is.

DERRIC. And there is the counterpart. [*Gives it.*

RIP. Dis is for me, eh? I'll put him in my breast [pocket][4]—yah, yah.

DERRIC. Now, Rip, I must bid you good evening.

RIP. Stop! Take some more liquor. Why, de bottle is empty. Here! Alice! Alice! get some more schnapps for de burgomaster.

DERRIC. No, not to-night. [*Rising.*] But, should you want any you will always find a bottle for you at your old friend Rory's; so, good-night.

RIP. Stop, [Mr.][5] Burgomaster! I will go and get dat bottle now.—[*Rising.*]—Alice, Alice! [comma see hah!][6]

Enter ALICE.

RIP. Alice, give me mine hat. [*Alice gives it.*] Now, take care of de house till I comes back: if de old woman comes before I gets home, tell her I am gone out mit de burgomaster on [par—par—tick—partickler][7] business.[8] [*Exit, with* DERRIC.

1 "Schneider" in K.
2 "dat ist" in K; also "Mynheer."
3 "baber" in K.
4 "bocket" in K.
5 "Mynheer" in K.
6 Not in K.
7 "bar-bar-tick-bartickler" in K.
8 K. has also:
ALICE. She wont believe it.
RIP. Tell her—I'll be stewed fun it's a fact.

ALICE *advances, and brings on* KNICKERBOCKER *from the closet.*

ALICE. So, Mr. Knickerbocker, you are still here.

KNICKERBOCKER. Yes, all that's left of me! and, now that the coast is clear, I'll give them leg bail, as the lawyers have it; and if ever they catch me here again—[*He goes towards the door, and returns in sudden alarm.*] Oh dear! oh dear! here's mother Van Winkle coming back. I shall never get out of this mess.

ALICE. It's all your own fault! Why would you come to-night!

KNICKERBOCKER. I shall never be able to come again—the cross vixen will take care of that if she catches me here.

ALICE. [There is but one method of avoiding her wrath;][1] slip on the clothes the old pedlar woman brought for sale, and I'll warrant you'll soon be tumbled out of the house.

KNICKERBOCKER. With a good thrashing to boot, I suppose. [No matter, if I can but slip out of the house, I don't care what I slip into.][2] [KNICKERBOCKER *sits in arm-chair, and is attired by* ALICE *in a woman's dress: on rising, the petticoats but reach his knees.*] Confound the lower garments! they're too short [by half.][3]

ALICE. 'Tis your legs are too long [by half!][4]; stoop down; [say as little as possible, and you'll not be discovered.][4]

[*He again sits.*

DAME *enters.*

DAME. [Well, I've got back and I see Mr. Van Slaus is gone! but][5] where's that varlet, Rip; out again? Oh, that Rip! that Rip! I'll certainly be the death of him; or he will of me, which is most likely. Alice, who have you in the chair?

ALICE. The pedlar woman, aunt, who has come for the things she left.

DAME. The pedlar woman—hark'ee gossip: bring no more of your rubbish here. Take yourself off, and let me have a clear house.

KNICKERBOCKER. [*Aside.*] 'Gad, I wish I was safely cleared out of it. [KNICKERBOCKER *rises, hobbles forward; but, forgetting the shortness of the petticoats, in curtseying, is discovered by the* DAME, *from the exposure of his legs.*

[1] Not in K.
[2] In K, only "But, never mind."
[3] Not in K.
[4] Not in K.
[5] Not in K.

DAME. Odds bodikins and pins! who have we here! an imposter! but you shall pay for it; this is a pedlar woman, indeed, with such lanky shanks. [*She rushes up to door and locks it—then, with a broom pursues him round; he flings bonnet in her face.*

KNICKERBOCKER. Needs must, when the devil drives—so here goes.

He jumps through the window [*which is dashed to pieces*] [1]*—and disappears.—*DAME *rushes up, with broom, towards window.—* ALICE *laughs.*

DAME. What! laugh at his misconduct, hussey. One's just as bad as the other. All born to plague me. Get you to bed—to bed, I say. [DAME *drives* ALICE *off, and follows.*

SCENE IV.—*Half dark.—A front wood.—The report of a gun is heard; shortly after,* RIP *enters, with his fowling piece.*

RIP. [Whip-poor-Will! egad, I think they'll whip poor Rip.][2]—[*Takes aim at bird; it flashes in the pan.*]—Another miss! Oh, curse the misses and the missusses! hang me if I can get a single shot at the sky-flyers. [Wish] [3] I had one of de German guns which Knickerbocker talks so much about—one dat fires round[4] corners; la! how I'd bring dem down! bring dem down! were I to wing as many daily as would fill a dearborn, Dame wouldn't be satisfied—not that she's avaricious—but den she must have something or somebody to snarl at, and I'm the unlucky dog at whom she always lets fly. Now, she got at me mit de broomstick so soon as I got back again; if I go home again, she will break my back. Tunner wasser! how sleepy I am—I can't go home, she will break my back— so I will sleep in de mountain to-night, and to-morrow I turn over a new leaf and drink no more liquor.[5]

VOICE. [*Outside:*] Rip Van Winkle.

*A dead pause ensues.—Suddenly a noise like the rolling of cannon-balls is heard—then a discordant shout of laughter.—*RIP *wakes and sits up astonished.*

[1] Not in K.
[2] Not in K.
[3] "I vishes" in K. No attempt is being made to indicate small differences of dialect.
[4] "der" inserted in K.
[5] In K., stage direction, "[*Lies down.*]".

RIP. What [the deuce][1] is that? [my wife][1] at mine elbow? Oh, no, nothing of the kind: I must have been dreaming; so I'll contrive to nap, since I'm far enough from her din.

[*Reclines and sleeps.*[2]

VOICE. [*Outside.*] Rip Van Winkle. [*The laugh being repeated,* RIP *again awakes.*[3]

RIP. I can't be mistaken dis time. Plague on't, I've got among the spirits of the mountains, metinks, and haven't a drop of spirits left to keep them off.

SWAGGRINO.[4] [*Without.*] Rip Van Winkle! Rip Van Winkle.

RIP. Rip Van Winkle! that's me to a certainty.

Music.—[SWAGGRINO, *the grotesque dwarf, enters*],[5] *bending beneath the weight of a large cask which he bears on his shoulder.—He pauses, examines* RIP, *then invites him to assist him in placing the cask on the ground, which* RIP *complies with.*

RIP. Hang me, if he hasn't brought my heart up into my mouth: what an outlandish being, [a sea snake,][6] by dunder!

Music.—[SWAGGRINO,][7] *pointing to the cask,* [*entreats*][7] RIP'S *assistance in bearing it up the mountains.*

RIP. Want me to help you up mit it? Why not say so at first, my old codger? What a queer old chap, to be sure; but I can't let him toil up the mountain with such a heavy load as dat, no, no, and so, old [broad][8] chops, I'll help you.

Music.—[DWARF][9] *assists in placing cask on* RIP'S *shoulder. A loud laugh is heard;* RIP *is alarmed, but* [DWARF][9] *signs him to proceed and be of good courage—leads way up rocks. Another peal of laughter, and* RIP *hastily follows him.*

SCENE V.—*Dark.—The Sleepy Hollow, in the bosom of the mountains, occupying the extreme extent of the stage—stunted trees, fragments of rock in various parts.—Moon in the horizon;*

1 "der debil" in K.; also "mein frau."
2 In K., the stage directions are: [*Lies down to sleep.*
3 In K., the speech takes this form:
VOICE. [*Without.*] Rip Van Winkle!
4 No name in K., only "VOICE."
5 In K., read, "*One of the* SPECTRE CREW *enters.*"
6 Not in K.
7 "*The* IMP" in K.; also "asks."
8 "pale" in K.
9 "IMP" in K.

the entrance to this wild recess being by an opening from the abyss in the rear of the glen.

Music.—GROTESQUE DUTCH FIGURES *with [enormous][1] masked heads and lofty tapering hats, discovered playing [at cards in various places—others at Dutch pins—battledores and shuttlecocks—the majority seated on a rock drinking and smoking.][2]*

GAUDERKIN. Since on earth this only day,
In fifty years we're given to stray,
We'll keep it as a holiday!
So brothers, let's be jolly and gay.

[ICKEN.][3] But question, where's that lazy [wight,][3]
Who, soon as sun withdrew it's light,
Was for the earth's rich beverage sent,
And has such time in absence spent.

GAUDERKIN. Perhaps [with some][1] misfortune he's been doomed to meet,
Cross'd, no doubt, on the road by mortal feet.

ICKEN. And what the punishment that you decree
On him, who on our mysteries makes free?

GAUDERKIN. Twenty years in slumber's chain,
Is the fate that we ordain:
Yet, if merry wight he prove,
Pleasing dreams his sleep shall move.

ICKEN. Our brother comes, and up the rugged steep,
A mortal, see, Swaggrino's presence keep.

OMNES. Twenty years in slumber's chain,
Is the fate that we ordain.
He comes! he comes! let silence reign!—
Let silence reign! let silence reign!

The SPIRITS *retire up and station themselves in motionless attitudes.*

Music.—[SWAGGRINO][4] *ascends by the opening in the rear followed by* RIP, *with the keg.*—RIP *advances on the left, and, with the assistance of his conductor, places the cask on the rock.*—
The SPIRITS *remain immovable.*

[1] Not in K.
[2] In K., reads, "*at Dutch pins—the majority seated on a rock drinking and smoking—thunder reverberates each time a bowl is delivered.*"
[3] "ICHEN" in K.; also "sprite."
[4] "*The* IMP" in K.

RIP. I'm a dead man, to a certainty. Into what strange company have I tumbled! crikey, what will become of me? Dear, dear! would I were home again, even though along with [Dame][1] Van Winkle.

Music.—The FIGURES *severally advance, and stare at him, then resume their game.* SWAGGRINO *taps the cask; motions the astonished* RIP *to assist him in distributing its contents into various flagons; an injunction with which he complies.*—SWAGGRINO *helps his companions.*

RIP. After all, they seem a harmless set, and there can be no argument with them, for they appear to be all dumbies.—[Lord were my wife][2] as silent. They're a deadly, lively, jolly set; but I wonder what kind of spirits dese spirits are [drinking!][3] Surely, dere can be no harm in taking a drop along mit dem.—[*Fills a flagon.*]—Here goes!—Gentlemen, here's your [go-to-hells,][4] and your [broad chopped][5] family's, and may you all live long and prosper. [*Drinks.*]

OMNES. Ha, ha, ha!

Music.—A grotesque dance ensues, during which RIP *continues to supply himself from the keg.—He at length joins in the dance, and becomes so exhausted, that he reels forward and sinks in front. The dancing ceases, the* SPIRITS *utter three "ho, ho, ho's!"—* [*Some of them sink.*] [6]

END OF ACT I.

ACT II

SCENE I.—*The last of the First Act repeated; but the distance now presents a richly cultivated country.—The bramble is grown into a lofty tree, and all that remains of* RIP'S *gun is its rusty barrel, which is at the foot of the tree.*

Bird Music.—RIP *discovered extended on the ground, asleep; his hair grey, and beard grown to an unusual length.—The hour of*

[1] "Frau" in K.
[2] In K., "If mein wife vere"
[3] "trinking" in K.
[4] "goot-hells" in K.
[5] Not in K. Instead, "Your family's goot-hells."
[6] In K., the stage directions end, "*Moon very bright. Tableau.*"

the scene is gray dawn and birds from sky and hill are chirping.[1]

RIP. [*Speaking in his sleep.*] Mother Van Winkle! [Dame][2] Van Winkle! what are you arter? Don't be always badgering; will you never allow poor Rip a moment's quiet? Curse it! don't throw de hot water about so, you'll scald one's eyes, and so you will, and no mistake; and so you have. [*He awakens in sudden emotion.*] Eh! by dunder! what's all dis,—where am I—in the name of goodness where am I? [*Gazing around.*] On the Catskill Mountains, by all that's miraculous! Egad! my rib will play the very devil with me for stopping out all night. There will be a fine peal sounded when I get home. [*Rises.*] [3] How confoundedly stiff and sore my joints do feel; surely I must have been sleeping for a pretty long time! Asleep! [no;] [4] I was awake and enjoying myself with as jolly a rum set of codgers as ever helped to toom out a keg of Hollands. I danced, and egad, drank with them, till I was pretty blue, and dat's no mistake;—but confound it, they shouldn't have caught me napping, for 'tis plain they have taken themselves off [like an unceremonious pack of—pack of—give an eye tooth to know who they were.][5] [*Looking around.*] Where is my gun? I left it on a little bush. [*On examining he finds the rusty barrel of his gun.*] Hillo! [come up, here's a grab!][6] the unmannerly set of sharpers! stolen one of the best fowling-pieces that ever made a crack: and left this [worthless,][7] rusty barrel, by way of exchange! What will Dame Van Winkle say to this!

[1] In K., the scene opens thus:
The AERIAL SPIRITS *in Tableau.—Dance of the* SPIRITS *to the gleams of the rising sun.—Tableau.*
SPIRIT OF THE MOUNTAIN. [*Speaks.*]

Wake, sleeper, wake, rouse from thy slumbers,
The rosy cheeked dawn is beginning to break,
The dream-spell no longer thy spirit encumbers,
Gone is its power, then wake, sleeper, wake.

The Spirits of Night can no longer enchain thee,
The breeze of the morn now is striving to shake
Sweet dewdrops like gems from the copsewood and forest tree,
All nature is smiling, then wake, sleeper, wake.

Tableau.—They disappear as the clouds gradually pass away and a full burst of bright sunshine illumines the scene.

[2] "Frau" in K.
[3] In K., stage direction reads, "*Rises with difficulty.*" All through this speech in K., the dialect is pronounced.
[4] "nein" in K.
[5] Not in K.
[6] In K., "donner unt blitzen."
[7] Not in K.

By the hookey! but she'll comb my hair finely! Now, I went to sleep beneath that hickory;—'twas a mere bush. Can I be dreaming still? Is there any one who will be [good] [1] enough to tell me whether it is so or not? Be blowed if I can make head or tail [o'nt.] [2] One course only now remains,—to pluck up resolution, go back to Dame Van Winkle, and by dunder! she'll soon let me know whether I'm awake or not! [3]

[*Music.—Exit.*

SCENE II.[4]—*A well-furnished apartment in the house of* KNICKERBOCKER.

[1] "goot" in K.
[2] In K., "of him."
[3] In K., speech ends, [*Moves painfully.*] "My legs do seem as if they vould not come after me."
[4] Scene II, in K., reads as follows:

SCENE SECOND.—*Chamber.*

Enter NICHOLAS VEDDER *and* DAME VEDDER (*formerly* DAME VAN WINKLE).

DAME. 'Tis very hard for the poor girl.
VEDDER. Yes; but 'tis your fault. You shouldn't have had a fool and a sot for your first husband.
DAME. [*Aside.*] And I didn't ought to have had a bear for my second.
VEDDER. What did you say?
DAME. Nothing—nothing.
VEDDER. Well, don't say it again. Because Lowena will have to be the wife of Herman Van Slaus, that's settled!
DAME. But he's a most disreputable man, and my poor child detests him.
VEDDER. Well, she won't be the first wife that has detested her husband.
DAME. No; I should think not, indeed.
VEDDER. You should think not! What do you mean by that?
DAME. Nothing!
VEDDER. Well, don't mean it again. What, do you suppose that I'll suffer my daughter-in-law to sacrifice her fortune—a fortune of which we shall have our share? —Herman has promised that.
DAME. Herman will promise anything; and you know that my poor girl is doatingly fond of young Gustaffe.
VEDDER. Well, I can't help that; but I am not going to allow her to make a beggar of herself and us too, for any nonsense about the man of her heart.
DAME. Her's will break if she is compelled to—
VEDDER. Nonsense—a woman's heart is about the toughest object in creation.
DAME. You have given me plenty of proof that you think so.
VEDDER. What do you intend to imply by that?
DAME. Nothing!
VEDDER. Well, don't imply it again—don't, because—

Enter KNICKERBOCKER *and* ALICE, *arm-in-arm—both grown stout.*

KNICKERBOCKER. Halloa! what's going on—a matrimonial tiff? My wife has just been giving me a few words, because I told her that she waddles up and down, and rolls about like one of our butter-laden luggers in a squall, as the Dutchmen have it.
ALICE. You have no occasion to talk, Mr. Knickerbocker, for, I am sure, your corporation—
KNICKERBOCKER. Yes, I belong to the town corporation, and to look respectable, am obliged to have one of my own. Master Vedder, a word with you. [*Talks aside with him.*
ALICE. [*Going to* DAME.] You wish now, that my poor brother Rip hadn't died, don't you?

LORRENNA, *now a woman, enters.*

LORRENNA. Alas, what a fate is mine! Left an orphan at an early age,—a relation's bounty made me rich, but, to-day, this fatal day—poverty again awaits me unless I bestow my hand without my heart! Oh, my poor father! little did you know the misery you have entailed upon your child.

KNICKERBOCKER *and* ALICE *enter, arm in arm. They are much more corpulent than when seen in Act I and dressed in modern attire,*—ALICE *in the extreme of former fashion.*

KNICKERBOCKER. Decided that cause in the most judgematical like manner. White wasn't black. Saw that in a twinkling; no one disputed my argument. [*Speaking as entering.*] Come along, spouse! Lauks! how you do waddle up and down, side to side, like one of our butter-laden luggers in a squall, as the Dutchmen have it. Ah, Lorrenna, you here? but you appear more depressed than customary. Those saddened looks are by no means pleasing to those who would ever wish to see you cheerful. What the dickens prevents your being otherwise when all around are so anxious for your happiness!

LORRENNA. Truly, am I beholden for your protection and ever grateful. But to place a smile on the brow whilst sorrow lingers in the bosom is a deceptive penance to the wearer—painful to those around who mark and must perceive the vizard; to say that I am happy would be inconsistent with truth. The persecutions of Herman Van Slaus—

DAME. [*Sighing.*] But I thought Nicholas Vedder would have been just as easy to manage; he was as mild as a dove before our marriage.

ALICE. You ought to have known that to be allowed to wear the inexpressibles by two husbands was more than the most deserving of our sex had any right to expect.

DAME. Oh, dear me! I never thought that I should live to be any man's slave.

ALICE. Ah, we never know what we may come to! but your fate will be a warning and example for me, if Mr. Knickerbocker should take it into his head to leave me a widow.

VEDDER. Mrs. Vedder, what are you whispering about there?

DAME. Nothing!

VEDDER. Well, don't whisper it any more.

ALICE. [*Aside,* to DAME.] Come along with me.

VEDDER. Mrs. Vedder, take yourself out of the room.

ALICE. Mr. Knickerbocker, I shall expect you to follow me immediately.

[*Exeunt* ALICE *and* DAME.

KNICKERBOCKER. And this is the last day of the term fixed on by the agreement!

VEDDER. Yes; and Herman is resolute, and so am I.

KNICKERBOCKER. I am sorry for poor Lowena.

VEDDER. She shouldn't have had a fool for a father.

KNICKERBOCKER. It was unfortunate, but I can't exactly see that it was her fault.

[*Exeunt.*

ALICE. Ah! my dear Lorrenna, many a restless night have I had on that varlet's account, as spouse knows.

KNICKERBOCKER. That's as true as there's ghosts in the Catskills, as Dutchmen have it; for be darned if a single night passes that Alice suffers me to go to sleep peaceably.

ALICE. Well, well; cheer thee, my niece; there is bounteous intelligence in store; nor think there is any idle fiction in this brain, as our divine poets picture.

KNICKERBOCKER. There, there, Alice is getting into her romance again,—plain as my fist—she has been moonified ever since she became a subscriber for books at the new library! Planet struck, by gum, as philosophers have it, and—

ALICE. And you have said so little to the purpose, that I must now interpose. My dear Lorrenna—Gustaffe—'tis your aunt who speaks—

KNICKERBOCKER. There, now, pops in her word before a magistrate.

LORRENNA. My Gustaffe! ha! say!—

KNICKERBOCKER. Would have told you in a brace of shakes, as gamblers have it, if she hadn't thrown the dice first. Yes, my pretty chicky—Gustaffe's vessel is now making up the Hudson; so, cheer thee! cheer thee, I say! your lover is not far off.

LORRENNA. Gustaffe so near? blessed intelligence! Oh, the happiest wishes of my heart are gratified! But are you certain? Do not raise my hopes without cause. Are you quite certain? speak, dear aunt; are you indeed assured, Gustaffe's vessel has arrived?

KNICKERBOCKER. Didn't think fit to break the news too suddenly, but you have it.

ALICE. "The ship with wide-expanded canvas glides along and soon"—I forget the remainder of the quotation; but 'tis in the delectable work, "Robinson Crusoe"—soon will you hear him hail. [*A knock is heard.*] My stars foretell that this is either him—

KNICKERBOCKER. Or somebody else, as I suppose.

Enter SOPHIA.

SOPHIA. Oh, sir; Squire Knickerbocker, Herman, son of the late Derric Van Slaus, is in the hall.

ALICE. That's not the him whom I expected, at all events.

KNICKERBOCKER. Son of the individual whom I succeeded as burgomaster? Talk of the devil—now, I don't know how it is, but I'm always squalmish when in company of these lawyers that's of his cast. *Qui Tam.*

SOPHIA. He wishes to be introduced. What is your pleasure?

KNICKERBOCKER. Let him be so, by all means. An honest man needn't fear the devil. [*Exit* SOPHIA.

LORRENNA. Excuse my presence, uncle. To hear him repeat his claims, would but afflict a heart already agonized: and with your leave, I will withdraw. [*Exit.*

KNICKERBOCKER. Aye, aye; let me alone to manage him, as a barrister says to his client when he cross-questions a witness. See Miss Lorrenna to her chamber, Mrs. Knickerbocker. This Herman is a d—d rogue, as the English have it; and he'll go to the dominions below, as the devil will have it, and as I have had it for the last twenty years.

ALICE. And I tell you, to your comfort, if you don't send the varlet quick off with a flea in his ear, you shall have it. Yes, Squire Knickerbocker, you shall have it, be assured. So says Mrs. Knickerbocker, you shall have it. [*Exit.*

KNICKERBOCKER. Truly, I've had plenty of it from you for the last eighteen years.

Enter HERMAN.

HERMAN. Sir, I wait upon you once more. The period is now expired when my just claim, which you have so long protracted, can be vainly disputed. A vain and idle dispute of justice.

KNICKERBOCKER. Precious fine, indeed, sir,—but, my ward has a mighty strong reluctance to part with her fortune, and much more so to make you her partner for life. You are not exactly to her liking, nor to her in the world's generally.

HERMAN. One or the other she is compelled to. You are aware, sir, that the law is on my side! the law, sir—the law, sir!

KNICKERBOCKER. Oh, yes! And, no doubt, every quibble that it offers will be twisted to the best purpose for your interest. You're a dabster at chicane, or you're preciously belied.

HERMAN. You will not, I presume, dispute the signature of the individual who formed the contract?

KNICKERBOCKER. Oh, no! not dispute Rip's signature, but his error in judgement. I happened to be a cabinet councillor at the very moment my deceased relative, who was ***non compos mentis***, at the time, clapped his pen to a writing, artfully extracted from him by your defunct father, whose memory is better forgotten than remembered. . . . .

HERMAN. Sir, I came here, not to meet insult; I came hither, persuaded you would acknowledge my right, and to prevent a publicity that may be painful to both parties. You are inclined to dispute them; before a tribunal shall they be arbitrated; and, knowing my claims, Mr. Knickerbocker, know well that Lorrenna or her fortune must be mine. . . . . [*Exit.*

KNICKERBOCKER. You go to Davy Jones, as the seamen have it. Lorrenna shall never be yours, and if ever she wants a cent whilst I have one, my name isn't Knickerbocker;—damme, as the dandies have it.

LORRENNA *enters, with* ALICE.

LORRENNA. My dear guardian, you have got rid of Herman, I perceive. . . . .

KNICKERBOCKER. I wish I had, with all my soul; but he sticks to his rascally undertaking like a crab to its shell; egad, there will be no dislodging him unless he's clapped into a cauldron of boiling water, as fishmongers have it. . . . .

ALICE. And boiled to rags. But, husband! husband, I say!

KNICKERBOCKER. Mr. Knickerbocker, my dear, if you please.

ALICE. Well, then, Mr. Knickerbocker, my dear, if you please, we have been looking out at the window to ascertain who came and went, and have discovered a fine, handsome fellow galloping towards the town, and I shouldn't at all wonder if it wasn't—

GUSTAFFE *rushes in.*

LORRENNA. [*Hurries to him.*] My dear, dear Gustaffe!

GUSTAFFE. [*Embracing her.*] My tender, charming Lorrenna!

KNICKERBOCKER. Why, Gustaffe! Bless us! why, how the spark has grown. . . . .

ALICE. Not quite so corpulent as you, spouse.

KNICKERBOCKER. Spouse! Mr. Knickerbocker, if you please. Truly, wife, we have both increased somewhat in corporal, as well as temporal substance, since Gustaffe went to sea. But you know, Alice—

ALICE. Mrs. Knickerbocker, if you please.

KNICKERBOCKER. Well, Mrs. Knickerbocker—

GUSTAFFE. Why, Knickerbocker, you have thriven well of late.

KNICKERBOCKER. I belong to the corporation, and we must support our corporation as well as it. But not a word about the pig, as the butchers have it, when you were a little boy, and Alice courting me.

ALICE. I court you, sirrah? what mean you?

KNICKERBOCKER. Sirrah! Mr. Knickerbocker, if you please. Why, then, deary—we didn't like anyone to intrude on our society; do you take the hint? as the gamblers have it. Come along, Alice—Mrs. Knickerbocker, I would say—let us leave the lovers to themselves.

ALICE. Again they meet, and sweet's the love that meets return.

Exeunt KNICKERBOCKER *and* ALICE, *singing in concert,* "Again they meet."

GUSTAFFE. My dear Lorrenna, why this dejected look?—It is your own Gustaffe enfolds you in his arms.

LORRENNA. Alas! I am no longer worthy of your love,—your friendship. A fatal bond extracted from my lamented father has severed us forever—I am devoid of fortune.

GUSTAFFE. Lorrenna, you have been the star that has guided my bark,—thee, my compass—my north pole,—and when the magnet refuses its aid to the seaman, then will he believe that you have foundered in affection, or think that I would prove faithless from the loss of earthly pittance.

LORRENNA. Shoals,—to speak in your nautical language—have long, on every side, surrounded me; but, by my kind uncle's advice, must we be guided. [*Exit.*

SCENE III.—*The Town of* RIP'S *nativity, instead of the Village as presented in first scene of the drama.—It is now a populous and flourishing settlement.—On the spot where* RORY'S *tap-house formerly stood, is a handsome hotel, and the sign of* "George III" *is altered into that of* "George Washington." *A settee in front, with table.—The harbour is filled with shipping.—Music at the opening of the scene.*

SETH [SLOUGH,][1] *the landlord, enters from the Hotel.—Loud shouts.*

[1] In K., "Kilderkin."

SETH. Well, I reckon the election's about bustin' up. If that temperance feller gets in I'm bound to sell out; for a rum-seller will stand no more chance with him than a bob-tail cow in fly time.—[*Laugh.*]—Hollo! who is this outlandish critter? he looks as if he had been dead for fifty years and was dug up to vote against the temperance ticket.—

Music.—Enter MALE *and* FEMALE VILLAGERS, *laughing.*[1] —*Enter* RIP,—*they gather round him.*

RIP. Where I was I wonder? my neiber frints, "knost you ty spricken?"[2]

VILLAGERS. Ha, ha, ha!

1ST VILLAGER. I say, old feller, you ain't seed nothing of no old butter firkin with no kiver on, no place about here?

RIP. No butter firkin mit no kiver no place, no I ain't seen him.

VILLAGERS. Ha, ha, ha!

1ST VILLAGER. Who's your barber?—[*Strokes his chin.—All laugh and exeunt.*

RIP. I can't understand dis: everything seems changed.—[*Strokes his chin.*]—Why, I'm changed too; why, my beard's as long as a goat's.

SETH. [*Coming down.*] Look here, old sucker, I guess you had better go home and get shaved.

RIP. My old woman will shave me when I gets home! Home, where is my home? I went to the place where it used to was, and it wasn't dere. Do you live in Catskill?

SETH. Well, I rather guess I dus—

RIP. Do you know where I live?

SETH. Well, to look at you, I should think you didn't live nowhere in particular, but stayed round in spots.

RIP. You live in Catskill?

SETH. Certain.

RIP. You don't know dat I belong here?

SETH. No, I'm darned if I do. I should say you belonged to Noah's ark—

RIP. Did you never hear in Catskill of one Rip Van Winkle?

SETH. What, Rip Van Winkle, the greatest rum-sucker in the country?

[1] In K., "*and pointing at* RIP, *who comes* on."
[2] In K., "Vhere I was I wonder? my kneiber freunds, sprechen sie deutsch?"

RIP. Dat is a fact—dat is him! ha! ha! now we shall see.

SETH. Oh, yes, I've heard of him; the old coon's been dead these twenty years.

RIP. Den I am dead and dat is a fact. Well, poor Rip is dead. I'm sorry for dat.—Rip was a goot fellow.

SETH. I wish there was a whole grist just like him in Catskill. Why, they say he could drink rum enough in one day to swim in.

RIP. Don't talk so much about rum; you makes me so dry as never was.

SETH. Hold on a spell then, and I'll fetch you something to wet your whistle. [*Exit into house.*

RIP. Why, here is another change! dis was Rory's house last night, [SETH *re-enters.*] mit de sign of George the Third.

[SETH. The alteration of my sign is no bad sign for the country, I reckon.][1]

RIP. [*Reading.*] "George Washington,"—who is he? [I remember a shoot of dat name, dat served under Braddock, before I went to sleep.

SETH. [*Giving him jug.*] Well, if you've been asleep I guess he ar'n't: his enemies always found him wide awake and kicking; and that shoot, as you call him, has planted the tree of liberty so everlasting tight in Yankeeland, that all the kingdoms of the earth can't root it out.][2]

RIP. Well, here is General Washington's goot health, and his family's goot health, ant may dey all live long ant prosper. So poor Rip Van Winkle is dead, eh? [Now comes de poser;][3] if Rip is dead, [what has become of his old woman?][4]

SETH. She busted a blood-vessel swearing at a Yankee pedlar, and has gone to kingdom come long ago.

RIP. De old woman dead too? den her clapper is stopped at last. [*Pause.*] So de old woman is dead; well, she led me a hard

[1] Not in K.

[2] Not in K. After "who is he," read, "I do not know him, but—" and continue with next RIP speech.

[3] "But, now, I'm going to ask a ticklish question" in K. This speech is in dialect in K.

[4] In K., "is his old voman dead too?"

SETH. No. She's alive and kicking.

RIP. Kicking—yes, she always vas dat.

SETH. And she's married agin.

RIP. She's done what agin?

SETH. She's got a second husband.

RIP. Second husband!—I pities the poor creetur. But there vas—vill you tell me, my friend—

SETH. I can't stop any longer, because—

life—she was de wife of my bosom, she was mine frow for all dat. [*Whimpering.*] I'm dead too, unt dat is a fact. Tell me my frient—

SETH. I can't stop any longer—the polls are almost closing, and I must spread the game for the boys. Hurrah, for rum drinking and cheap licence for the retailers! that's my ticket. [*Re-enter* VILLAGERS, *shouting.*][1] Here, boys, see what you can make of this old critter.—I give him up for the awfulest specimen of human nature in the States.

[*Exit into house.*

2D VILLAGER. Are you a Federal or a Democrat?

RIP. Fiddle who? damn who's cat?

2D VILLAGER. What's your politics?

RIP. Oh, I am on de safe side dere; I am a faithful subject of King George!

2D VILLAGER. He's a Tory! Kill him! Duck him!

VILLAGERS. [To the horse pond! Duck him.][2]

Music.—They seize RIP *and are about hurrying him off when* GUSTAFFE *rushes in and throws them off.*[3]

GUSTAFFE. Stand back, [cowards.][4]

[1] In K., the stage directions are, "VILLAGERS *hurry on, shouting.*"
[2] In K., read, "Duck him—duck him."
[3] In K., read, "*Music. All are rushing on* RIP.—GUSTAVE *enters.*"
[4] In K., read, are you not ashamed—a score of you to attack a single man?

RIP. [*Aside.*] Yes. I *am* a single man—now my vife is marry agin; dat is a fact! From this point, the two plays differ so that what remains in Kerr is here reproduced.

GUSTAVE. And a poor old, gray-haired man.

RIP. Yes, I am poor, dat is a fact; but I know I'm not old, and I can't be gray-haired.

GUSTAVE. Take yourselves off! What cause had you given them to attack you?

VILLAGERS *sneak off.*

RIP. I don't know—do you?

GUSTAVE. [*Smiling.*] How should I—

RIP. I say—vhere do I live?

GUSTAVE. Don't you know?

RIP. I'm stewed fun I does. But, young man, you seems to know somezing, so, perhaps you knows Rip Van Winkle?

GUSTAVE. Young Rip Van Winkle—I should think I do.

RIP. [*Aside.*] Here is von vhat knows me! dat is goot!

GUSTAVE. I only wish his father hadn't gone away and died, twenty years ago.

RIP. [*Aside.*] His fader! Ah! he means my young Rip, and I'm dead myself arter all—dat is a fact.

GUSTAVE. Poor old Rip Van Winkle—perhaps you know his daughter?

RIP. His daughter—yes, I tink I—and she is not dead, like her fader?

GUSTAVE. No, thank heaven! and she would have been my wife before this, but for—

RIP. But for what, young man?

Enter LOWENA.

LOWENA. Gustave. [*Moving to him.*

GUSTAVE. Ah! dear Lowena!

RIP. Lowena! Ah! dat is my daughter—and I have a son too, a lublicka boy; but my daughter is a girl, and I always lub my leetle girl so much, ven she vas only so big—and I must not hug her now to my poor heart, because she—she has got another fader—and I am dead—yes, dey all tell me dat is a fact! I am dead to meinself and—and I am dead to my leetle girl.

LOWENA. Oh, yes, Gustave, it is indeed a sad misfortune for us both, that my father should have entered into a contract which had for its object to coerce me into becoming the wife of Herman Van Slaus.

RIP. [*Aside.*] Yes, dat is a fact. I remember, de burgomaster come to my house last night mit a paper, and I wrote my name down on it; but I vas trunk.

GUSTAVE. And having loved you so long, is it now impossible that you can become my wife?

LOWENA. No, not impossible; but—oh, my poor dear father, if you had but survived to see this day!

RIP. [*Aside.*] I wish what I had—but I am dead, dat is a fact.

Enter HERMAN VAN SLAUS.

LOWENA. Oh, Gustave! see, protect me from that wicked man—I will be thine, and only thine!

HERMAN. No, Lowena; you will be *mine*, for you will not be suffered to resign into my hands that fortune of which I covet the possession, but which would lose half its value to me if you come not with it.

RIP. [*Aside.*] Dat is young Slaus; and he is as big a tam rascal as vas his resbectable fader.

HERMAN. Hereafter, Lowena, I will cause you to repent that you have given a rival to the man to whom, from your very childhood, you have been pledged and bound.

RIP. Herman Van Slaus, *you* are bledged to old Nick, and vill never be redeemed.

HERMAN. Who is this miserable old wretch?

GUSTAVE. I would kill you sooner than you should become the husband of my heart's adored.

Enter KNICKERBOCKER *and* ALICE.

KNICKERBOCKER. So, there you are, Master Herman, sticking to your rascally work like a crab to its shell, as fishmongers have it.

ALICE. I should like to throw him into a saucepan of boiling water till he was done to rags.

RIP. [*Aside.*] Dat is my sister Alice—and dat is Knickerbocker—how fat they both is got since last night! What great big suppers they must have eat!

Enter NICHOLAS VEDDER *and* DAME VEDDER.

DAME. Oh, do, try if you cannot save my poor girl!

RIP. [*Aside.*] Tonner unt blitzen! dat is mein frau! [*Retreating.*] No, no! I forget—she not is mine frau now! [*Chuckles.*

DAME. Let him take half the fortune and—

VEDDER. What is that you observe?

DAME. Nothing—nothing!

VEDDER. Then don't observe it any more.

DAME. I—I only—

VEDDER. [*Shouting.*] Silence!

RIP. [*Aside.*] Dat is goot! [*Laughing.*] Mine frau have caught a Tartar. De second one make her pay for de virst. Ha, ha, ha! I'm stewed fun dat is a fact!

HERMAN. Nicholas Von Vedder, say—[*Producing paper.*]—is this contract to be fulfilled?

VEDDER. Certainly. Lowena, the time for trifling is past; you have delayed until the very last hour, and must now at once consent to become Herman's wife.

LOWENA. Never! Welcome poverty, if I may be wealthy only with that man for my husband. Whatever privations I may be made to endure, I shall not repine; for he whom I love will share them with me.

RIP. [*Aside.*] Dat is mine own girl, I vill swear to dat.

GUSTAVE. I am poor, Lowena, but my love will give me courage to toil manfully, and heaven will smile upon my efforts and enable me to replace that fortune which, for my sake, you so readily sacrifice.

HERMAN. Well, be it as you will. This document gives me a claim which may not be evaded. [*Reads.*] "We, Deidrich Van Slous, Burgomaster, and Rip Van Winkle, desirous of providing for the prosperity of our offspring, do hereby mutually

OMNES. Cowards!

GUSTAFFE. Yes, cowards! who but cowards would rush in numbers one grey-haired man?

RIP. Yah, yah, dat's a fact!

GUSTAFFE. Sheer off! you won't? then damme, here's at ye. [*Drives them off.*] Tell me, old man, what cause had you given them to attack you?

RIP. I don't know: do you?

GUSTAFFE. You appear bewildered: can I assist you?

RIP. Just tell me where I live, dat's all I want to know.

GUSTAFFE. And don't you know?

RIP. I'm d—d fun I does.

GUSTAFFE. What is your name?

RIP. Why, I was Rip Van Winkle.

GUSTAFFE. Rip Van Winkle? impossible!

RIP. Well, I won't swear to it myself.

GUSTAFFE. Stay,—you have a daughter?

RIP. To be sure I has: a pretty little girl about so old—Lorrenna; and I have a son too, a lublicka boy, but my daughter is a girl.

agree that Herman Van Slous, and Lowena Van Winkle, shall be united on the demand of either. Whosoever of those contracted fails in fulfilling the agreement shall forfeit their fortune to the party complaining.—Rip Van Winkle—Deidrich Van Slous."

RIP. [*Aside.*] Yes, dat is a fact—I remember dat baber, and I've got him somevheres. [*Feels in his pockets.*

VEDDER. Lowena, I command that you consent to become Herman's wife—I will not suffer that your fortune be sacrificed to—

HERMAN. And here is the now useless codicil.

RIP. [*Advancing, paper in hand.*] Let me read it. [*All turn amazedly towards him.*] "Should the said Rip Van Winkle tink fit to annul dis contract vithin twenty years and a day, he shall be at full liberty to do so."

HERMAN. How came you by that document?

RIP. You see I've got it, and dat is a fact.

HERMAN. Who gave it to you?

RIP. Your old blackguard of a fader.

DAME. Oh, you are—you are—

RIP. Yes, I am—I am Rip Van Winkle! [*All start.*—DAME, *with a loud scream, falls into* KNICKERBOCKER'S *arms.*] Dere! for de first time in my life, I have doubled up my old woman!

KNICKERBOCKER *carries off* DAME.

LOWENA. Oh, it is my father—my dear, dear father! [*Runs into his arms.*

RIP. Yes, and you are mein taughter, my darling dat I always was love so! Oh, bless your heart, how you have grown since last night as you was a little girl.

ALICE. [*Embracing him.*] Oh, my poor dear brother.

RIP. Yes, I tink I am your broder 'cos you is my sister.

KNICKERBOCKER *returns.*

ALICE. And here is my husband.

RIP. He is a much deal uglier, dan he used to vas before.

KNICKERBOCKER. [*Embracing him.*] My blessed brother-in-law.

VEDDER. Ah! and now you have come back, I suppose you want your wife!

RIP. No, I'll be tam if I do! You've got her, and you keep her—I von't never have her no more.

GUSTAFFE. Do you remember entering into a contract, binding your daughter to marry Herman Van Slaus?

RIP. Oh! I remember, de burgomaster came to my house last night mit a paper, and I wrote my name down on it, but I was drunk.

GUSTAFFE. Last night! His brain wanders: yet it must be he; come, come with me, old man.

RIP. Where are you going to take me to?

GUSTAFFE. Your daughter.

RIP. Yes, yes, take me to my child. Stop, my gracious!—I am so changed,—suppose she should forget me too; no, no, she can't forget her poor father. Come, come!

[*Exeunt.*

SCENE IV.—KNICKERBOCKER'S *House as before.*

KNICKERBOCKER, ALICE *and* LORRENNA *enter.*

KNICKERBOCKER. Give me joy, dears; I'm elected unanimously—elected a member of the Legislature.

ALICE. Why, spouse!

KNICKERBOCKER. Mr. Knickerbocker, if you please, my dear; damme! I'm so happy I could fly to the moon, jump over a steeple, dance a new fandango on stilts. [*Dances.*] Fal, lal, la.

Enter HERMAN.

KNICKERBOCKER. Well, sir, what the devil do you want?

HERMAN. I came to claim this lady's fortune or her hand.

VEDDER. I sha'n't have her—I have done with her, and glad to be rid of her. [*Exit.*

RIP. Ha, ha! Then my poor frau is a vidder, with two husbands, an' she ain't got none at all.

HERMAN. It is Rip Van Winkle, and alive!

RIP. Yes, and to the best of my belief, I have not never been dead at all.

HERMAN. And I am left to poverty and despair. [*Exit.*

RIP. And serve you right too—I'm stewed fun dat is fact. [*Looking round.*] But I had a leetle boy, last night—vhere is my young baby boy, my leetle Rip?

ALICE. I saw him just now—oh, here he is.

Enter, young RIP VAN WINKLE, *a very tall young man.*

RIP. Is dat my leetle baby boy? How he is grown since last night. Come here, you young Rip. I am your fader. Vell, he is much like me—he is a beautiful leetle boy.

KNICKERBOCKER. But tell us, Rip, where have you hid yourself for the last twenty years?

RIP. Ech woll! ech woll! Vhen I take mine glass, I vill tell mine strange story, and drink the health of mine friends—and, ladies and gentlemen, I will drink to your good hells and your future families, and may you all—and may Rip Van Winkle too—live long and brosber.

Curtain.

ALICE. Knock him down, spouse.

KNICKERBOCKER. Mr. Knickerbocker, my dear.

ALICE. Oh, bother! I know if he comes near my niece, woman as I am, I'll scratch his eyes out.

HERMAN. Mr. Knickerbocker.

KNICKERBOCKER. The honourable member from ——— County, if you please.

HERMAN. The judge of the district will this day arrive and give judgement on my appeal; my rights are definitive, and I question the whole world to controvert them. We shall meet before the tribunal; then presume to contend longer if you dare. [*Exit.*

KNICKERBOCKER. 'Twill be difficult, no doubt, but we'll have a wrangle for the bone, as the dog's have it; there will be no curs found in our party, I'll be sworn. [*Aside.*] Hang me, but I'm really a little chop fallen and there is a strange sense of dizziness in my head which almost overcomes me.

LORRENNA. My dear uncle, what is to be done in this emergency?

KNICKERBOCKER. Done! your fortune is done for: but if you ever want a cent whilst I have one, may I be sent to the devil, that's all.

GUSTAFFE. [*Entering.*] Bravo! Nunkey Knickerbocker! you are no blind pilot. Awake to breakers and quicksand, Knickerbocker.

KNICKERBOCKER. Knickerbocker! the honourable Mr. Knickerbocker, if you please; I'm now a member of the Legislature and, curse me, if I'd change my dignified station as representative of an independent people, for that of the proudest potentate who holds supremacy by corruption or the bayonet. [*Exeunt.*

SCENE LAST.—*The Court House.—An arm-chair at the back, in front of which is a large table, covered with baize.—On each side a gallery.—On the right of table are chairs.*

Music.—The JUDGE *discovered, seated.—The galleries filled with auditors.*—HERMAN.—KNICKERBOCKER.

JUDGE. Mr. Knickerbocker, you will please to bring your client into court.

KNICKERBOCKER *goes off, and returns with* LORRENNA *and* ALICE.

JUDGE. Be pleased to let your ladies take seats.

[LORRENNA *and* ALICE *sit.*

HERMAN. And now, sir, I presume 'tis time to enter on my cause. Twenty years have elapsed since this contract, this bond was signed by the father of that lady, by which she or her fortune were made mine. Be pleased to peruse. [*Presenting the document to the* JUDGE.

JUDGE. [*Reading.*] "We, Derric Van Slaus, Burgomaster, and Rip Van Winkle, desirous of providing for the prosperity of our offspring, do hereby mutually agree that Herman Van Slaus and Lorrenna Van Winkle shall be united on the demand of either. Whosoever of those contracted, fails in fulfilling this agreement, shall forfeit their fortune to the party complaining.

"Rip Van Winkle,
"Derric Van Slaus."

But here's a codicil. "Should the said Rip Van Winkle think fit to annul this contract within twenty years and a day, he shall be at full liberty to do so. (Signed) Derric Van Slaus." The document is perfect in every form. Rip Van Winkle, 'tis stated, is defunct. Is there any one present to prove his signature?

HERMAN. Mr. Knickerbocker, if he dare be honest, will attest it.

KNICKERBOCKER. Dare be honest, sir! presume you to question my veracity? How was that bond obtained?

HERMAN. Why should you ask? The late Rip Van Winkle, anxious for the prosperity of his offspring, though too indolent to provide for their subsistence, persuaded my deceased father to form this alliance.

KNICKERBOCKER. It's a lie! Hum!—

JUDGE. Restrain this violence! a court of justice must not be swayed by such proceedings.

HERMAN. Behold! sir, a picture of their general effrontery. In a public tribunal to threaten those, who, in pleading their own rights, but advocate the cause of justice.

LORRENNA. [*Comes down stage.*] All my hopes vanish—bleak and dreary is the perspective.

HERMAN. [*Advances.*] At last I triumph! Now, lady, your hand or your inheritance.

LORRENNA. My hand! never! Welcome were every privation to an union with one so base.

JUDGE. It appears, then, that this signature is not denied by the defendant, and in that case the contract must stand in full force against her.

LORRENNA. Oh, Alice, take me home: poverty, death, anything rather than wed the man I cannot love.

[*She is led off by* ALICE.

KNICKERBOCKER. Why, damn it, Judge!

JUDGE. Mr. Knickerbocker!

KNICKERBOCKER. I beg pardon, I meant no disrespect to the court, but I had thought after—

JUDGE. I have decided, Mr. Knickerbocker.

KNICKERBOCKER. Oh! you have decided. Yes, and a damned pretty mess you've made of it. But I sha'n't abide by your decision; I'll appeal to a higher court. I am now a member of the Legislature, and if they allow such blocks as you on the bench, I'll have a tax upon timber, sir—yes, sir, a tax upon timber.

[*Exit, in a rage.*

JUDGE. Twenty years and a day is the period within which the contract could be cancelled by the negature of Rip Van Winkle, and as he has rendered no opposition during this lengthened time—

HERMAN. 'Tis not very probable, sir, that he will alter his intentions by appearing to do so within the few brief hours that will complete the day. Can the grave give up its inmates? No, no! Who dare pretend to dispute my rights? The only one who could do so has been dead these twenty years.

Enter GUSTAFFE *and* RIP.

GUSTAFFE. 'Tis false! Rip Van Winkle stands before you!

OMNES. Rip Van Winkle!

HERMAN. You, Rip Van Winkle! Van Winkle come back after such a lapse of time? Impossible!

RIP. Nothing at all impossible in anything Rip Van Winkle undertakes, and, though all of you are in the same story, dat he has been gone so long, he is nevertheless back soon enough, to your sorrow, my chap.

HERMAN. If this, indeed, be Rip Van Winkle, where has he hid himself for twenty years?

JUDGE. What answer do you make to this?

RIP. Why, dat I went up in de mountains last night, and got drunk mit some jolly dogs, and when I come back dis morning I found myself dead for twenty years.

HERMAN. You hear him, sir.

JUDGE. This is evidently an impostor; take him into custody.

GUSTAFFE. Stay! delay your judgement one moment till I bring the best of proofs—his child and sister. [*Exit.*

HERMAN. If you are Rip Van Winkle, some one here would surely recognize you.

RIP. To be sure dey will! every one knows me in Catskill. [*All gather round him and shake their heads.*] No, no, I don't know dese peoples—dey don't know me neither, and yesterday dere was not a dog in the village but would have wagged his tail at me; now dey bark. Dere's not a child but would have scrambled on my knees—now dey run from me. Are we so soon forgotten when we're gone? Already dere is no one wot knows poor Rip Van Winkle.

HERMAN. So, indeed, it seems.

RIP. And have you forgot de time I saved your life?

HERMAN. Why, I—I—I—

RIP. In course you have! a short memory is convenient for you, Herman.

HERMAN. [*Aside.*] Should this indeed be he! [*Aloud.*] I demand judgement.

JUDGE. Stay! If you be Rip Van Winkle you should have a counterpart of this agreement. Have you such a paper?

RIP. Paper! I don't know; de burgomaster gave me a paper last night. I put it in my breast, but I must have loosed him. No, no—here he is! here is de paper! [*Gives it to* JUDGE, *who reads it.*

JUDGE. 'Tis Rip Van Winkle! [*All gather round and shake hands with him.*

RIP. Oh! everybody knows me now!

HERMAN. Rip Van Winkle alive! then I am dead to fortune and to fame; the fiends have marred my brightest prospects, and nought is left but poverty and despair. [*Exit.*

GUSTAFFE. [*Without.*] Room there! who will keep a child from a long lost father's arms?

Enter GUSTAFFE, *with* LORRENNA, ALICE *and* KNICKERBOCKER.

LORRENNA. My father! [*Embraces* RIP.

RIP. Are you mine daughter? let's look at you. Oh, my child—but how you have grown since you was a little gal. But who is dis?

ALICE. Why, brother!—

RIP. Alice! give us a hug. Who is dat?

ALICE. Why, my husband—Knickerbocker.

RIP. Why Knick, [*Shakes hands.*] Alice has grown as big round as a tub; she hasn't been living on pumpkins. But where is young Rip, my baby?

KNICKERBOCKER. Oh, he was in the court-house just now. Ah! here he comes!

Enter RIP VAN WINKLE, JR.

RIP. Is dat my baby? come here, Rip, come here, you dog; I am your father. What an interesting brat it is.

KNICKERBOCKER. But tell us, Rip, where have you hid yourself for the last twenty years?

RIP. Ech woll—ech woll. I will take mine glass and tell mine strange story and drink the health of mine frients. Unt, ladies and gents, here is your goot health and your future families and may you all live long and prosper.

THE END.

FRANCESCA DA RIMINI

A TRAGEDY

Francesca, i tuoi martiri a lagrimar
mi fanno tristo e pio.—Dante.

Inferno. v. 75 *seq.*

George Henry Boker

GEORGE HENRY BOKER
(1823-1890)

The name of George Henry Boker suggests a coterie of friendships—a group of men pledged to the pursuit of letters, and worshippers at the shrine of poetry. These men, in the pages of whose published letters and impressions are embedded many pleasing aspects of Boker's temperament and character, were Bayard Taylor, Richard Henry Stoddard, and Charles Godfrey Leland, the latter known familiarly in American literature as "Hans Breitmann." These four, in different periods of their lives, might have been called "the inseparables"—so closely did they watch each other's development, so intently did they await each other's literary output, and write poetry to each other, and meet at Boker's, now and again, for golden talks on Sundays. Poetry was a passion with them, and even when two—Boker and Taylor—were sent abroad on diplomatic missions, they could never have been said to desert the Muse—their literary activity was merely arrested. One of the four—Stoddard—often felt, in the presence of Boker, a certain reticence due to lack of educational advantages; but in the face of Boker's graciousness—a quality which comes with culture in its truest sense,—he soon found himself writing Boker on matters of style, on qualities of English diction, and on the status of American letters—a stock topic of conversation those days.

Boker was a Philadelphian, born there on October 6, 1823,—the son of Charles S. Boker, a wealthy banker, whose financial expertness weathered the Girard National Bank through the panic years of 1838-40, and whose honour, impugned after his death, in 1857, was defended many years later by his son in "The Book of the Dead," reflective of Tennyson's "In Memoriam," and marked by a triteness of phrase which was always Boker's chief limitation, both as a poet and as a dramatist.

He was brought up in an atmosphere of ease and refinement, receiving his preparatory education in private schools, and entering Princeton in 1840. On the testimony of Leland, who, being related to Boker, was thrown with him in their early years, and who avows that he always showed a love for the theatre, we learn that the young college student bore that same distinction of manner which had marked him as a child, and was to cling to him as a diplomat. Together as boys, these two would read their "Percy's Reliques," "Don Quixote," Byron and Scott—and while they were both in Princeton, Boker's room possessed the only carpet in the dormitory, and his walls boasted shelves of the handsomest books in college.

"As a mere schoolboy," wrote Leland, "Boker's knowledge of poetry was remarkable. I can remember that he even at nine years of age manifested that wonderful gift that caused him many years after to be characterized by some great actor—I think it was Forrest—as the best reader in America. . . :While at college . . . Shakespeare and Byron were his favourites. He used to quiz me sometimes for my predilections for Wordsworth and Coleridge. We both loved Shelly passionately."

In fact, Leland claims that Boker was given to ridicule the "Lakers;" had he studied them instead, he would have added to his own poetry a naturalness of expression which it lacked.

He was quite the poet of Princeton in his day, quite the gentleman Bohemian. "He was," writes Leland, "quite familiar, in a refined and gentlemanly way, with all the dissipations of Philadelphia and New York." His easy circumstances made it possible for him to balance his ascetic taste for scholarship with riding horse-back. To which almost perfect attainment, he added the skilled ability to box, fence and dance. He graduated from Princeton in 1842, and the description of him left to us by Leland reveals a young man of nineteen, six feet tall, whose sculptured bust, made at this time, was not as much like him "as the ordinary busts of Lord Byron." In later years he was said to bear striking resemblance to Hawthorne. His marriage to Miss Julia Riggs, of Maryland, followed shortly after his graduation, in fact, while he was studying law, a profession which was to serve him in good stead during his diplomatic years, but which he threw over for the stronger pull of poetry, whose Muse he could court without the necessity of driving it hard for support. Yet he was concerned about literature as a paying profession for others. On April 26, 1851, he wrote to Stoddard: "Alas! alas! Dick, is it not sad that an American author cannot live by magazine writing? And this is wholly owing to the want of our international copyright law. Of course it is little to me whether magazine writers get paid or not; but it is so much to you, and to a thousand others." The time, until 1847, was spent in foreign travel, but it is interesting to note, as indication of no mean literary attainment in the interim, that Princeton, during this period, bestowed on him the degree of M.A., for merit in letters.

1848 was a red-letter year for Boker. It witnessed the publication of his first volume of verse, "The Lessons of Life, and other Poems," and it introduced him to Bayard Taylor and to R. H. Stoddard. Of the occasion, Taylor writes on October 13, to Mary Agnew:

Young Boker, author of the tragedy, "Calaynos," a most remarkable work, is here on a visit, and spent several hours to-night with me. He is another hero,—a most notable, glorious mortal! He is one of our band, and is, I think, destined to high renown as an author. He is nearly my own age, perhaps a year or two older, and he has lived through the same sensations, fought the same fight, and now stands up with the same defiant spirit.

This friendship was one of excellent spiritual sympathy and remarkable external similarities and contrasts. One authority has written of their late years:

In certain ways, he and his friend, Bayard Taylor, made an interesting contrast with each other. Here was Boker [circa 1878] who had just come back from diplomatic service abroad; and here, too, was Taylor, who was just going abroad as minister to Berlin. Both were poets; they were fellow-Pennsylvanians and friends; and they were men of large mould physically, and of impressive presence; yet they were very dissimilar types. Boker, though massive and with a trace of the phlegmatic in his manner (perhaps derived from his Holland ancestors, the Bôchers, who had come thither from France, and had then sent a branch into England, from which the American family sprang), was courtly, polished, slightly reserved. His English forefathers had belonged to the Society of Friends, as had also Taylor's family in Pennsylvania,—another point in common. But Taylor's appearance, as his friends will remember, was somewhat bluff and rugged; his manner was hearty and open.

Launched in the literary life, therefore, Boker began to write assiduously. "Calaynos," the tragedy referred to by Taylor, went into two editions during 1848, and the following year was played by Samuel Phelps at Sadler's Wells Theatre, London, May 10. From the New York *Tribune* office, on May 29, 1849, Taylor wrote:

Your welcome letter came this morning, and from the bottom of my heart was I rejoiced by it. I can well imagine your feeling of triumph at this earnest of fame. . . . I instantly hunted up the London "Times" and found "Calaynos" advertised for performance, —second night. I showed it to Griswold, who was nearly as much surprised and delighted as myself. Of course he will make good mention of it in his book. It will *sell* immensely for you, and especially just now, when you are coming out with "Anne Bullen" [sic.]. I shall not fail to have a notice of it in to-morrow morning's "Tribune."

Some authorities state that it was given by Phelps without Boker's consent. Another, who examined Boker's manuscripts, in possession of the poet's daughter-in-law, Mrs. George Boker, records that Barrett made cuts in the play, preparatory to giving it, Boker, even, revising it in part. The American première was reserved for James E. Murdoch, at the Philadelphia Walnut Street Theater, January 20, 1851, and it was revived at the same playhouse in April, 1855, by E. L. Davenport. As Stoddard says of it, one "should know something—the more the better—about the plays that Dr. Bird and Judge Conrad wrote for Forrest and his successors, about Poe's 'Politian', Sargent's 'Velasco', Longfellow's 'Spanish Student'."

His choice of subject, in this, his first drama, indicated the romantic aloofness of Boker's mind, for he was always anxious to escape what Leland describes him as saying was a "practical, soulless, Gradgrind age." In fact, Boker had not as yet found himself; he was more the book-lover than the student of men he afterwards became.

"Read Chaucer for strength," he advises Stoddard on January 7, 1850, "read Spenser for ease and sweetness, read Milton for sublimity and thought, read Shakespeare for all these things, and for something else which is his alone. Get out of your age as far as you can."

These young men were not quickly received, and they regarded the utilitarian spirit of the time as against them. To Stoddard Boker once confessed: "Were poetry forged upon the anvil, cut out with the axe, or spun in the mill, my heaven, how men would wonder at the process! What power, what toil, what ingenuity!"

Boker's correspondence with Stoddard began in a letter, dated September 5, 1849, announcing overtures made by the London Haymarket Theatre for his new tragedy, "Anne Boleyn," which he was contemplating sending them in sheets. "I have also the assurance," he announces, "that Miss Cushman will bring it out in this country, provided she thinks her powers adapted to it."

Boker's pen was energetic, and it moved at a gait which shows how fertile was his imagination. "The inseparables" cheered the way for each other in the face of official journalistic criticism. Taylor declared "Anne Boleyn" far in advance of "Calaynos," prophesying that it would last. "Go ahead, my dear poet," he admonishes, "it will soon be your turn to damn those who would willingly damn you." Together these friends were always planning to storm the citadel of public favour with poetry, but Boker seems to have been the only one to whom the theatre held out attraction. By August 12, 1850, he was sending news to Stoddard that "The Betrothal" would be staged the following month. In good spirits, he writes:

The manager is getting it up with unusual care and splendour. Spangles and red flannels flame through it from end to end. I even think of appearing before the curtain on horseback, nay, of making the whole performance equestrian, and of introducing a hippopotamus in the fifth act. What think you? Have you and your miserable lyrics ever known such glory? If the play should take *here*, you benighted New-Yorkers will be illuminated with it immediately after it has run its hundredth night in the city which is so proud of its son.

This was the second of his pieces to be given performance, "Anne Boleyn" never seeing the boards. "The Betrothal" was produced at the Philadelphia Walnut Street Theatre, on September 25, 1850, and opened in New York, on November 18 of the same year. Taylor wrote to its author, on December 4: "I saw the last night. . . . It is even better as an acting play than I had anticipated, but it was very badly acted. I have heard nothing but good of it, from all quarters." It was Elizabethan in tone, quite in the spirit of that romantic drama practised by such American authors as Willis, Sargent and others. How it was received when presented in London, during 1853, is reflected in Boker's letter to Stoddard, dated October 9, 1853:

I have read the *Times* notice of the "Betrothal." It is honey to most of the other newspaper criticisms. . . . Notwithstanding, and taking the accounts of my enemies for authority, the play was unusually successful with the audience on that most trying occasion, the first night. . . . The play stands a monument of English injustice. Mark you, it was not prejudice that caused the catastrophe; it was fear lest I should get a footing on their stage, of which "Calaynos" had given them timely warning.

"The Widow's Marriage," in manuscript, and never published, was accepted by Marshall, manager of the Walnut, and is noted by Boker, in a letter to Stoddard, October 12, 1852, the chief handicap confronting him being the inability to find someone suited to take the leading rôle. Stoddard's own comment was:

Whether [it] was ever produced I know not, but I should say not, for the part of the principal character, *Lady Goldstraw*, is one which no actress whom I remember could have filled to the satisfaction of her creator. The fault of this character (me judice) is that it is too good to be played on a modern stage. It ought to have been written for antiquity two hundred years ago.

Boker was right when he referred to himself as "prolific" at this time. He already had produced, in 1851, according to markings on the manuscript, a piece called "All the World a Mask," and he had written "The Podesta's Daughter," a dramatic sketch, issued, with "Miscellaneous Poems," in 1852. Toward the end of this year, he completed "Leonor de Guzman."

"Her history," he writes to Stoddard, on November 14, "you will find in Spanish Chronicles relating to the reigns of Alfonso XII of Castile and his son, Peter the Cruel. There are no such subjects for historical tragedy on earth as are to be found in the Spanish history of that period. I am so much in love with it that I design following up 'Leonor de Guzman' by 'Don Pedro'. The present tragedy, according to the judgment of Leland, is the very best play I have written, both for the closet and the stage. Perhaps I am too ready to agree with him, but long before he said it I had formed the same judgment."

This tragedy was performed at the Philadelphia Walnut Street Theatre, on October 3, 1853, and at the New York Broadway Theatre, on April 24, 1854. Boker wrote to his friends, showing his customary concern about an actress skilled enough for the rôle of his heroine. When, finally, for the Philadelphia première, Julia Dean was decided upon, he thus expressed his verdict to Stoddard, after the opening performance: "Miss Dean, as far as her physique would admit, played the part admirably, and with a full appreciation of all those things which you call its beauties."

During these years of correspondence with his friends, Boker was determining to himself the distinction between *poetic* and *dramatic* style,

"Seriously, Dick," he writes to Stoddard, on October 6, 1850, "there is, to my mind, no English diction for your purposes equal to Milton's in his minor poems. Of course any man would be an intensified ass who should attempt to reach the diction of the 'Paradise Lost', or aspire to the tremendous style of Shakespeare. You must not confound things, though. A Lyric diction is one thing—a Dramatic diction is another, requiring the utmost force and conciseness of expression,—and Epic diction is still another; I conceive it to be something between the Lyric and Dramatic, with all the luxuriance of the former, and all the power of the latter."

He must have written to Taylor in the same vein, for, in a letter from the latter, there is assurance that he fully understands what a slow growth dramatic style must be. But Boker was not wholly wed to theatrical demands; he still approached the stage in the spirit of the poet who was torn between loyalty to poetic indirectness, and necessity for direct dialogue. On January 12, 1853, he writes to Stoddard:

Theatricals are in a fine state in this country; every inducement is offered to me to burn my plays as fast as I write them. Yet, what can I do? If I print my plays, the actors take them up, butcher, alter and play them, without giving me so much as a hand in my own damnation. This is something beyond even heavenly rigour; and so I proceed to my own destruction, with the proud consciousness that, at all events, it is my own act. *À propos*, have you ever read the English acting copy of my "Calaynos"? A viler thing was never concocted from like materials.

Whether or not the play, "The Bankrupt," preceded or followed the writing of "Francesca da Rimini" in 1853, we have no way of determining; but it would seem that it progressed no further in its stage career than in manuscript form, it being the only play on a modern theme attempted by Boker. Then, it seems, he was hot on the trail of the Francesca love story told in Dante, and used by so many writers in drama and poetry. It is this play, conceded to be his best, which is included in the present collection, and which calls for analysis and history by itself.

Taylor's collection of "Poems at Home and Abroad," dedicated to Boker in 1855, suggests that the two must have continually talked over the possibilities of gathering their best effusions in book form. Did not Taylor write, as early as June 30, 1850, "You must come out in the Fall with a volume of poems. Stoddard will, and so, I think, will I. You can get a capital volume, with your 'Song', 'Sir John', 'Goblet', and other things. . . . The publishing showmen would of course parade our wonderful qualities, and the snarling critics in the crowd would show their teeth; but we would be as unmoved as the wax statues of Parkman and Webster, except that there might now and then be a sly wink at each other, when nobody was looking." The two friends had been separated for some time, while Taylor wandered over the face of the globe, writing from Cairo, in the shadow of the pyramids, and exclaiming, in Constantinople (July 18, 1852), "There is a touch of the East in your nature, George."

In 1856, Boker prepared his two volumes of "Plays and Poems" for the press. He had won considerable reputation as a sonneteer, and this was further increased by the tradition that Daniel Webster had quoted him at a state dinner in Washington. As yet he was merely a literary poet, and a literary dramatist whose name is usually linked with that Philadelphia group discussed in Vol. II of this collection.*

Writing of the Philadelphia of 1868, Leland says:

[It was] "the Philadelphia when 'Emily Schaumbeg' was the belle and Penington's 'store' was the haunt of the booklover, when snow fell with old fashioned violence, and Third Street was convulsed by old-fashioned panics, when everybody went mad over Offenbach, when one started for New York from the Walnut Street Ferry, when George Boker was writing his dramas and George Childs was beginning to play the public Mæcenas." Oftentimes the sturdy figure of Walt Whitman could be seen walking on Broad Street, while Horace Greely, buried in newspapers, travelled aboard a boat between New York and Philadelphia.

It was the Civil War that not only turned Boker's pen to the Union Cause, but changed him politically from a Democrat to a staunch Republican. In fact, his name is closely interwoven with the rehabilitation of the Republican party in Philadelphia. He often confessed that his conscience hurt him many times when he realized he cast his first vote for Buchanan. "After that," he is quoted as having said, "the sword was drawn; it struck me that politics had vanished entirely from the scene—that it was now merely a question of patriotism or disloyalty." His "Poems of the War," issued in 1864, contained such examples of his

*Duyckinck recalls that, in 1862, R. T. Conrad's "Devotional Poems" were published, edited by Boker.

martial and occasional ability as the "Dirge for a Soldier," "On the Death of Philip Kearney" and "The Black Regiment," besides "On Board the Cumberland" and the "Battle of Lookout Mountain."

About this time, there was founded the Union League Club, with Boker as the leading spirit; through his efforts the war earnestness of the city was concentrated here; from 1863-71 he served as its secretary; from 1879-84 as its President; and his official attitude may be measured in the various annual reports of the organization. But even in those strenuous days—at the period when the Northern spirits lagged over military reverses, and at the time when the indecision of General McClellan drew from him the satiric broadside,—"Tardy George"—privately printed in 1865—Boker's thoughts were concerned with poetry. His official laureate consciousness did not serve to improve the verse. His "Our Heroic Themes"—written for the Harvard Phi Beta Kappa—was mediocre in everything but intent, recalling what Taylor wrote to him: "My Harvard poem, [he had read it in 1850 before the same fraternity] poor as it is, was received with great applause; but, alas! I published it, and thus killed the tradition of its excellence, which, had I not done so, might still have been floating around Harvard."

In 1869, Boker issued "Königsmark, The Legend of the Hounds and other Poems," and this ended his dramatic career until his return from abroad, and until Lawrence Barrett came upon the scene with his revival of "Francesca da Rimini" and his interest in Boker's other work, to the extent of encouraging him to recast "Calaynos" and to prepare "Nydia" (1885), later enlarged from two acts to a full sized drama in "Glaucus" (1886), both drawing for inspiration on Bulwer's "The Last Days of Pompeii."

President Grant sent Boker to Constantinople, as U. S. Minister (his appointment dated November 3, 1871)—an honour undoubtedly bestowed in recognition of his national service. Here he remained four years, "and during that time secured the redress for wrongs done American subjects by the Syrians, and successfully negotiated two treaties, one having reference to the extradition of criminals, and the other to the naturalization of subjects of little power in the dominions of the other." A reception was tendered him on December 22, 1871, by members of the Union League Club, and among those present were Bayard

Taylor, Col. George Boker, of the Governor's staff, and son of Boker, and Dr. Charles S. Boker, his brother. Among those who spoke were Robeson, Secretary of the Navy, and Cameron, U. S. Senator from Pennsylvania. Congratulatory letters were received from Bryant, James T. Fields, Stoddard, Lowell, Longfellow, Aldrich, Curtis, and Stedman. On this occasion, Taylor said: "I know the ripeness and soundness of his mind, the fine balance of his intellectual qualities."

On December 24, 1871, Boker wrote to Leland:

> The scarcest thing with me just now is time. I might give you a shilling at a pinch, but a half hour is an article which I do not happen to have about me. . . . By the way, your rhapsody over the East in "M. K." ["Meister Karl"] had something to do with my acceptance of the Turkish Mission; and if you have been lying, I shall find you out, old boy.

Boker's enthusiasm for Turkish scenery was unbounded, but his difficulties as a diplomat were due to his ignorance of the tongue, and his distrust of interpreters. But by the time his Government was ready to transfer him to another post—that of Minister to Russia (January 3, 1875)—he was heartily sick of his wrangling with the Crescent, and glad, as he wrote Leland, "to shake the dust of this dismal old city from my shoes, and prepare my toes for a freezing at St. Petersburg." He echoed his distaste in later years by writing: "I hate the East so profoundly that I should not return to it if there were no other land in which I could live." This promotion to the Russian court—it was a Russian, Ignatieff, who characterized him as "of true diplomatic stuff"—was made in 1875, and he remained there two years.

> "While in Russia," we learn, "he was the only one of our Ministers at foreign courts who was able to checkmate Spain in her controversy with us about the *Virginius.* He baffled the Spanish Ambassador at St. Petersburg, and influenced Gortschakoff to send a despatch to Madrid, which caused Spain to apologize to the United States; thus averting serious complications."

Diplomatic life was not wholly distasteful to him; he possessed social distinction which made him popular at both courts, so much so, indeed, that the Czar cabled to Washington, when a change of administration brought Boker's tenure of office to a close, asking if it were not possible to have him retained. He had had his difficulties at the Porte, as Lowell had had at Madrid.

But his artistic nature responded quickly to the picturesqueness of his surroundings. "Within a mile of me," he writes Leland from Turkey,—"for I am now living at Therapia upon the Bosphorus—there is a delicious encampment of the black tents of a tribe of Gypsies." While he was in Russia he was continually supplying Leland with information about gypsies.

He went to Egypt, at the invitation of the Sultan, and—as though recalling Taylor's longing, in 1852, when he was in Cairo, to have Boker with him—took a trip up the Nile, with Leland, whom he had invited to accompany him. Under the palm trees at Misraim, he had his first meeting with Emerson. The varied foreign travel had broadened his taste, and he was quickly responsive to what he saw. Writes Leland:

I have been with him many times in the Louvre, the great galleries of London and St. Petersburg, and studied with him the stupendous and strange remains of Egyptian art in the Boulak Museum and the Nile temples, but never knew anyone, however learned he might be in such matters, who had a more sincere enjoyment of their greatest results. I remember that he manifested much more interest and deeper feeling for what he saw in Egypt than did Emerson, who was there at the same time, and with whom I conversed daily.

On January 15, 1878, Boker withdrew from diplomatic life, returning to the United States, where he resumed literary work, his chief interest in the stage being revived by his association with Barrett. His home in Philadelphia—one of the literary centres of the time,—bore traces of his Turkish stay—carpets brought from Constantinople, Arabic designs on the draperies, and rich Eastern colours in the tapestried chairs. His experience was obliged to effect his writing, if not in feeling, at least in expression. I note in his "Monody," written at the time of the death of his friend, the poet, T. Buchanan Read (1822-1872), such lines as "the hilly Bosphorus," and ". . . For the hills of Ancient Asia through my trembling tears glimmer like fabrics. . . ." As early as 1855, he had written for the *U. S. Gazette and North American*, an article on Read comparing his "New Pastoral" with the poetry of Cowper and Thompson. But Read to-day is familiar because of his "Sheridan's Ride." We are told that Boker had a work-room where he delighted in designing metal scrolls.

There was a slight revival of public interest in his poems, which necessitated the reprinting of several of his books.

"The last time when I saw him," Stoddard recalls in 1890, "was at the funeral of Taylor, at Cedarcroft, a little more than ten years ago. We rode to the grave, on a hillside, and we rode back to the house. And now he has gone to the great majority!" Boker died in Philadelphia, January 2, 1890. "He takes place with Motley on our roll of well-known authors," George Parsons Lathrop has written, "and it is even more remarkable that he should have cultivated poetry in Philadelphia, where the conditions were unfavourable, than that Motley should have taken up history in Boston, where the conditions were wholly propitious."

It is by "Francesca da Rimini" that Boker is best remembered. In a letter to Stoddard, March 3, 1853, he writes:

You will laugh at this, but the thing is so. "Francesca da Rimini" is the title. Of course you know the story,—everyone does; but you nor any one else, do not know it as I have treated it. I have great faith in the successful issue of this new attempt. I think all day, and write all night. This is one of my peculiarities, by the bye: a subject seizes me soul and body, which accounts for the rapidity of my execution. My muse resembles a whirlwind: she catches me up, hurries me along, and drops me all breathless at the end of her career.

And soon this was followed by the letter so often quoted, showing the white-heat of his enthusiasm:

Now that "Francesca da Rimini" is done,—all but the polishing, —I have time to look around and see how I have been neglecting my friends during my state of "possession." Of course you wish to know my opinion of the bantling; I shall suppose you do, at all events. Well, then, I am better satisfied with "Francesca da Rimini" than with any of my previous plays. It is impossible for me to say what you, or the world, will say of it; but if it do not please you both, I do not know what I am about. The play is more dramatic than former ones, fiercer in its display of intense passions, and, so far as mere poetry goes, not inferior, if not superior, to any of them. In this play I have dared more, risked more, than I ever had courage to do before. *Ergo*, if it be not a great triumph, it will certainly be a great failure. I doubt whether you, in a hundred guesses, could hit upon the manner in which I have treated the story. I shall not attempt to prejudice you regarding the play; I would rather have you judge for yourself, even if your decision be adverse. Am I not the devil and all for rapid composition? My speed frightens me, and makes me fearful of the merits of my work. Yet, on coolly going over my work, I find little to object to, either as to the main design or its details. I touch up, here and there, but I do little more. The reason for my rapid writing is that I never attempt putting pen to paper before my design is perfectly mature. I never start with one idea, trusting to the glow of poetical composition for the remainder. That will do in lyrical poetry, but it would be death and damnation to dramatic. But just think of it!—twenty-eight hundred lines in about three weeks! To look back upon such labour is appalling! Let me give you the whole history of my manner of composition in a few words. If it be not interesting to you, you differ from me, and I mistake the kind of matters that interest you. While I am writing I eat little, I drink nothing, I meditate my work, literally, all day. By the time night arrives I am in a highly nervous and excited state. About nine o'clock I begin writing and smoking, and I continue the two exercises, *pari passu*, until about four o'clock in the morning. Then I reel to bed, half crazy with cigar-smoke and poesy, sleep five hours, and begin the next day as the former. Ordinarily, I sleep from seven to eight hours; but when I am writing, but five,—simply because I cannot sleep any longer at such times. The consequence of this mode of life is that at the end of a long work I sink at once like a spent horse, and have not energy enough to perform the ordinary duties of life. I *feel* my health giving way under it, but really I do not care. I am ambitious to be remembered among the martyrs.

This letter is not only significant of Boker's method of workmanship; it is, as well, measure of his charm as a letter writer. For, in correspondence with his close friends, he was as natural with them, as full of force and brightness, as he was in conversation. We find Taylor thanking him at one time, when in distress over family illness and death, for his sustaining words of comfort; we find Leland basking in the warmth of his sheer animal spirits. To the latter, Boker once wrote:

Dear old Charley, you are the only man living with whom I can play the fool through a long letter and be sure that I shall be clearly understood at the end. To say that this privilege is cheerful is to say little, for it is the breath of life to a man of a certain humour.

The "Francesca" note, therefore, is typical of Boker's enthusiasm. When Stoddard read the play, we wonder whether he saw in it any similarities to Leigh Hunt's poem on the same subject? For once he had detected in Boker's verses the influence of Hunt. There are critics who claim Boker had read closely Hugo's "Le Roi s'Amuse." But there is only one real comparison to make—with Shakespeare, to the detriment of Boker. His memory beat in Elizabethan rhythm, and beat haltingly. The present Editor began noting on the margin of his copy parallelisms of thought and expression in this "Francesca" and in the plays of Shakespeare; these similarities became so many, were so apparent, that it is thought best to omit them. The text used is not based on the manuscripts left by Boker, nor has it been compared with the acting copy made, in 1855, for E. L. Davenport, as has already been done elsewhere in print. I have preferred to use the text finally prepared by Boker for his published plays, this being the one which met with his approval. In 1882, Lawrence Barrett, with the aid of William Winter, prepared an acting version of "Francesca," and it was this which Mr. Otis Skinner used, when he revived the piece in 1901.

A notice in The New York *Tribune* for 1882 suggests that when E. L. Davenport first essayed "Francesca da Rimini," in 1855, it was in one-act. I can find no corroboration of this statement. The play-bill here reproduced specifically announces a *five* act tragedy, and it is to be inferred that the form of the play, as given at the Broadway Theatre, New York, September 26, 1855,* was the only one used by him. Winter claims that as *Lanciotto*, Davenport was "unimaginative, mechanical, and melodramatic," and that the whole piece "proved tedious." This is strange, considering the heroic and romantic characteristics in Davenport's method of acting. It may be that he attempted Boker's play because of his interest in the development of American drama. He had assisted Mrs. Mowatt in her career as playwright, and, during his full life, his name was identified with Boker's "Calaynos," George H. Miles's tragedy, "De Soto, the Hero of the Mississippi," and Conrad's "Jack Cade." But the concensus of opinion is that Boker's "Francesca da Rimini," as given by Davenport, was a failure.

An examination of the cast in the Davenport program with the cast as it was when Boker issued the play, indicates that the text must have been considerably changed, and certain characters omitted, when, at the suggestion of Winter, Lawrence Barrett promised to revive it during the summer of 1882. The scholarly turn of Barrett's mind must have made him ponder it well during a trip he made abroad at the time, and Boker, meanwhile, must have been cutting the cloth to suit the actor's ideas. Barron, one of Barrett's biographers, claims that "Mr. Barrett

*We find a record of Mrs. John Drew having, as *Francesca*, [supported Davenport when the play was taken to Philadelphia.

saw great possibilities in the work, and with his practical assistance the play was suitably changed, new situations were effected, a more picturesque colouring was given the scenes and story, and all that was repellant in the too close following of Dante [!] was removed." The play was given by Barrett, at Haverly's Theatre, Chicago, on September 14, 1882, Otis Skinner playing *Paolo*, and Marie Wainwright appearing as *Francesca*. In Winter's estimate of the performance, we find the dominant characteristics being "moderation" and "balanced growth." He says of *Lanciotto:* "Alertness of the brain sustained it, at every point, in brilliant vigour, and it rose in power, and expanded in terrible beauty, accordingly as it was wrought upon by the pressure of circumstances and the conflict of passions."

The memory of this must have affected the interpretation of Mr. Skinner, when, as *Lanciotto*, in his revival of the piece at the Chicago Grand Opera House, August 22, 1901, with Aubrey Boucicault as *Paolo*, Marcia Van Dresser as *Francesca*, and William Norris as *Pepe*, he met with such success. "D'Annunzio gives us the soldier and the brute," he wrote me in 1904. "Boker's hero is an idealist—almost a dreamer." The fact is, Boker was recalling his memories of *Othello* and *Richard III*, if not of *Hamlet*, as Skinner suggests. In another respect did the Barrett performance affect the later revival. The portrayal of *Pepe*, by Norris, was based on what he called "the James tradition," Louis James having, as Winter wrote, "a laughter that is more terrible than malice."

Lawrence Barrett's interest in the American drama was never very pronounced. He sought Boker's "Francesca da Rimini," as he sought W. D. Howells' "Yorick's Love" (given at Cleveland, Ohio, October 26, 1878), because the rôles therein suited his temperament. Between him and Boker, there was some misunderstanding of short duration, about royalties, but this was bridged over, and Boker's final attempts at playwriting were made for him. The reader is referred to Vol. 32, n.s. Vol. XXV, no. 2, June, 1917, of the *Publications of the Modern Language Association of America*, for statements as to Boker's "profits" from the stage.

After Otis Skinner's revival of "Francesca da Rimini," it was played for a while by Frederick Ward and Louis James in association (1893) and by Frank C. Bangs in 1892.

Hosts of dramas have been written on "Francesca da Rimini," and every poet has essayed at one time or another to surpass Dante's incomparable lines. Music scores have glorified this passionate love story, while marble and canvas have caught the external expression of it. In its portrayal, actual history has taken on legendary character, and so "Francesca da Rimini" now ranks as a theme with the history of Lancelot and Guinevere, of Tristan and Isolde. It has become the inspiration for Maeterlinck in "Pelléas and Mélisande," who has viewed the Italian passion through a mirage of mysticism.

Into "The Divine Comedy," the account of Francesca and Paolo is dropped, keen, sensitive and delicate, as though the poet, a friend of those concerned, wished to cover the hard fact of illicit love in an ecstacy of human feeling. Dante, the supreme master of his age, the incomparable lover of Beatrice, differentiated this tragedy from countless incidents of like character which marked his age. Had the story been preserved only in the form recorded by Boccaccio, it would have been lost in its minor details of history; whereas Dante has glorified it.

By the very fact that Dante places the two lovers in the circle of the Lustful, it is clear that he realized the enormity of their sin. The theory that his friendship with Guido Novella, the nephew of Francesca, made Dante refrain from entering fully into the incident, will not hold, when it is remembered that the cantos of the Inferno were written in 1300, seventeen years before the poet reached Ravenna, and accepted the hospitality of the Polenta house. Dante's infinite compassion is, therefore, the cause for the compressed poetry of this famous passage.

Dante's Francesca lines have been infinitely translated. Longfellow is conscientious; Byron chafes to be freed of the original Italian, and his lines are irksome; Rossetti sees and feels, but he is laboured. Dante, infinitely translated, remains supreme.

The poems on this ideal love legend are of infinite variety. Tassoni describes Paolo, the warrior, consumed with ravishing love, "shrunk with misery;" he fails to reach the youthful passion, and is as mediaevally chivalric as is Chaucer in "The Knightes Tale" of Palamon and Arcite. Leigh Hunt resorts to stilted narrative and description.

Byron once thought to write a drama on this subject; had he done so, Silvio Pellico might have had a formidable rival. More or less, all the playwrights have gone to Italian history, and the more exact they became, the more gross the situation. F. Marion Crawford fell on this rock of accuracy, when he wrote his Francesca play for Mme. Sarah Bernhardt.

Silvio Pellico, who wrote the first drama on "Francesca da Rimini" known to modern playgoers, lived his early life in an intensely religious atmosphere, and suffered imprisonment later because of his patriotic tendencies; it is not surprising, therefore, to find in his play—first a national appeal that was to win it applause from all Italy, and then, more important still, a purity of tone that struggled most nobly against an inevitable, passionate end. *Paolo* is the one who, after some scruples, succumbs; *Francesca* is infinitely conscious that she is a wife; *Giovanni* is suspicious. It would seem that Pellico's play is the first that realized the theatrical possibilities of the story; research has brought to light no play manuscript previous to his.

In the handling of his details, Pellico's incongruities and artificialities are many. *Paolo* returns from knightly deeds in Asia, to find his father dead—the *Malatesta Verucchio* who died in 1312, twenty-seven years after *Giovanni* committed the murder; therefore Pellico gives to the deformed brother the power that history does not wholly accord. The dramatist would avoid the indelicacy he finds in the reading incident, recounting it only in a situation during which *Francesca* holds aloof in a wild effort to stifle her love. Throughout the play, there is this ruthless twisting, in a desire to conceal wrong and unpardonable sin.

Turning to Uhland's fragmentary ideas, which even he himself was doubtful whether he could handle, an atmosphere confronts us as mediaevally German as the "Der arme Heinrich" of Hartmann von Aue, which was the inspirational source for Longfellow's "The Golden Legend." Uhland shows heaviness in conception, and a conventionality, thoroughly at variance with the tragedy's original passion. Romantic as he is, he has robbed the story of its warm southern nature, and has thrown his Dante aside to deal with false situation. He seems willing to let fact and spirit go. *Paolo* is a knight who tilts and worships a glove. Uhland thinks, and he is not alone in his belief, that *Francesca* had been promised to *Paolo* before *Giovanni* was wedded to her; yet if *Paolo's* marriage with *Orabile*, in 1269, is to be recognized as correct, historically, logical deductions from dates would discountenance the statement. Neither have I found commentaries to support the theory that *Paolo* was older than *Giovanni*, as Uhland sets forth in his play. The servant in Boccaccio here becomes a jealous lover. It is interesting to note the variations of this counter-element in the many play versions of the story—the element that urges *Giovanni's* suspicion to quick action—the dramatic force of *Pepe* in Boker; the disappointed motherhood and embittered love of *Lucrezia* in Stephen Phillips; the inborn savagery of *Malatestino* in D'Annunzio; the innocent unconsciousness of *Concordia* in Crawford, which finds similarity in a scene in Maeterlinck's "Pelléas and Mélisande," between father and little son. Further, in Uhland, a distorted glimpse of a colourless reportorial figure of Dante, gathering material for his poem, is as meaningless as it is unnecessary for atmosphere.

Stephen Phillips, in his Francesca drama, ignores altogether Italian temperament; save for the fact that he occasionally mentions the Tyrant of Rimini, Pesaro and Florence, and that he adheres to historic names, there is more of the English hamlet romance in the piece, than Italian passion. And that cannot be said of Shakespeare's "Romeo and Juliet." Perhaps one may claim for Phillips some of the simplicity of Dante, but there is not the humanity. Undeniably, the English poet is happy in phrase and imagery, but his genius is not so dramatic as it is poetic; he has some of the great lyrical feeling of Tennyson, and he has that which distinguishes the poet from the dramatist—the power to *describe* situation. One cannot deny the appeal of his girl-Francesca, nor the beauty of many of his haunting lines; but no warm impression of the situation is gained, and the characters are peculiarly inactive at inopportune times. Mr. Phillips's talent was predominantly undramatic; he was too much the poet to allow his feeling to be guided by historical material. Yet, as acted, the play was charmingly simple.

On the other hand, D'Annunzio, in his drama, saturates himself with the history of Italy. In bulk, his play has not the slightest claim to simplicity; the main object of the dramatist seemed to have been to overweight the scenes with the licentious and rude Italy of the thirteenth century; extraneous side-issues burden the progress of the plot. Yet D'Annunzio has taken care that this does not affect his central theme. On the stage, the scenes appear cumbersome, and the action moves slowly; but, after analyzing the book, it may be claimed for this "Francesca da Rimini," that it reflects the age in which the tragedy occurred.

Much artistic construction is shown in the contrast of the Polenta and Malatesta families, and, repellent as he is at times, D'Annunzio has moments of great poetic fervour; his fire swings forth in many of *Francesca's* speeches, that alternate with the languor of her symbolic nature.

That his drama on Francesca was definitely constructed for theatrical effect, was openly avowed by Marion Crawford. At the beginning of the French version made for Mme. Bernhardt, he placed material that showed his intention of dealing with fact in the manner of a novelist, and regardless of the sweetness of Dante. To him, *Concordia* is fourteen, since he considers 1289 as the date of the tragedy, and, with his details from Boccaccio's commentary, he has coarsened *Francesca*, making her bitterness full of the spleen that could only accompany maturity. A striking point is to be noted in the strong vein of Catholicism that colours many of the speeches.

Paolo's wife, *Orabile*, moves through the D'Annunzio play with only slight mention—to show the husband's avoidance of her—to draw attention to her deep-rooted aversion to *Francesca*. Mr. Crawford also brings her on the scene, and has *Paolo* the cause of her death, wittingly distorting history, since *Orabile* died many years after the murder of her husband.

The only American drama on the subject is that by Boker; it is a peculiarly contradictory piece of work, since, from the standpoint of the stage, it is essentially and effectively dramatic, while as literature it is imitative of the Elizabethan style. Boker's poetic imagery is distinctly borrowed, and his choice of words disappointingly colloquial. Yet, over and above the mere story, he has succeeded in portraying a strong character in his *Pepe*. The historical setting of the play is slight, yet sufficient to localize the piece, and his *dramatis personæ* are faithfully distinct in outline, though at times devoid of consuming passion.

Phillips as a dramatist has the fault of being diffuse; Boker's style is prosaically plain. Were it not for over-elaboration, D'Annunzio's play might supplant all others because of its spirit. Could we take from Phillips his simplicity, from D'Annunzio his Italian intensity, and from Boker his proportion, and could we add these to Crawford's realization of situation, toned away from his melodramatic tendencies, an ideal drama on "Francesca da Rimini" might be constructed.

But the revitalizing power that was given Shakespeare, has been bequeathed to none who have followed Dante. The one beauty of the Francesca story is the simple element that permeates the dark motive. The genius required to deal with it lies in this: to make one conscious of the tragedy in a touch that recalls the beauty of spring.

It is strange that no other poet than Dante has succeeded in catching this beauty. No poet, writing directly on the theme, has the subtle feeling which may be compared with that of the Italian. Richard Le Gallienne is infinitely superior to Hunt; Lowell and Gilder beyond the lesser poets,—but all fade before the master. They treat of the vision of Hell, with its whirling wind; of the two in close embrace; there is the kiss that ends the reading of a self-same love; there is the flash of a dagger that joins them eternally in death. These are the themes for the songs. The artists have done with brush and pencil, what the poets have tried in sonnets and verse. But it is Dante who dominates them everyone.

To me, after tracing in part the development of this Italian tragedy, there remains the charm of Dante's simplicity, and were one to ask, who, among the moderns, have partially reflected his passion, I should turn to Keats' insatiable thirst for beauty in his sonnet, "A Dream, After reading Dante's Episode of Paolo and Francesca," and his account of it in a letter to George and Georgiana Keats (February 14, 1819), and to Carlyle's appreciation of tragedy and love, in "The Hero as a Poet."

Boker's "Francesca da Rimini" will stand largely because, in structure and in directness, it is strikingly effective for the stage.

BROADWAY THEATRE

LESSEE..Mr. E. A. MARSHALL
STAGE MANAGER..Mr. W. R. BLAKE

SECOND WEEK OF THE
REGULAR SEASON!

CONTINUATION OF THE ENGAGEMENT OF THE EMINENT

AMERICAN ACTOR!

MR. E. L. DAVENPORT

FIRST TIME ON ANY STAGE OF

THE TRAGEDY

By G. H. BOKER, Esq., author of "Calaynos," "Betrothal," &c., called

Francesca da Rimini

IN WHICH THE EMINENT AMERICAN ACTOR

MR. E. L. DAVENPORT

Will appear in an entirely

ORIGINAL CHARACTER!!

This production of a popular and most talented Native Author will be brought forward with the efficient aid of

ESTABLISHED PERFORMERS!

NEW AND APPROPRIATE SCENERY!!

COSTUMES, PROPERTIES, DECORATIONS!!!

APPOINTMENTS, MUSIC and PAGANTRY!!!!

WEDNESDAY EVENING, SEPT. 26, 1855,

Will be presented the Tragedy, in five acts, by G. H. BOKER, Esq., entitled

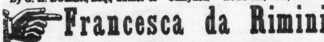

FRANCESCA

DA

RIMINI

CHARACTERS REPRESENTED.

GUELPHS.

Malatesto, (Lord of Rimini)....................................Mr. Whiting
LANCIOTTO......} his sons }..................Mr. E. L. DAVENPORT
Paolo.............}   }.....................................Mr. Lanergan
Pepe, (the Jester)..Mr. C. Fisher
Rosalvi.........} Young Nobles—companions of Paolo }.....Mr. Walters
Malvechi.......}   }....Mr. Harcourt
Civanti.........}   }......Mr. Cutter
Reue, (a Troubadour)..Mr. Vincent
Nobles, Soldiers, Pages, Troubadours, Attendants, &c., &c.

GHIBELINS.

Guido da Polinta, (Lord of Ravenna)..........................Mr. Canoll
The Cardinal Vecchino..Mr. Hodges
Fiorenzi } Nobles of Malatesto's Court }..........................Mr. Willet
Beppo .   }   }..............................Josaike
Henrico, (Captain of the Guard)...............................Mr. Fordyck
Antonio, (a leader of the Forces)..............................Mr. Wright
Nobles, Dignitaries of the Church, Soldiers, Pages, Banner Bearers, Messengers, &c.
Francesca da Rimini, (Daughter o Guido)....................Mme Ponisi
Rilta, (her attendent)......................................Miss J. Manners

---

To conclude with the popular Farce of

☞ POOR PILLICODDY

Mr. Pillicoddy..Mr. W. A. Chapman | Capt. O'Scuttle.......Mr. Seymour
Mrs. Pollicoddy.......Mrs. Warren | Mrs. O'Scuttle.......Mrs. Seymour
Sarah Blunt...Miss J. Manners

☞TO-MORROW EVENING—A NEW TRAGEDY, in which

MR. E L. DAVENPORT

Will appear.

TREASURER...Mr. P. WARREN
ASSISTANT TREASURER...Mr. NAGLE

☞Doors open at three quarters past 6 o'clock—Performances will commence an half past 7, precisely.

Howard F. Snowden, Printer, 163 Pearl Street, (Courier and Enquirer • Bee.)

FRANCESCA DA RIMINI

*A TRAGEDY IN FIVE ACTS**

By GEORGE H. BOKER

* The text that follows was compared with Lawrence Barrett's copy of the second edition, now in the library of The Players, New York. The title page reads: Plays and Poems: | by | George H. Boker | In two volumes | Vol. I | Second Edition | Boston: | Ticknor and Fields. | MDCCCLVII. | | Boker's copyright, 1856.

DRAMATIS PERSONÆ

McVicker's Theatre, Chicago, November 6, 1882

MALATESTA, *Lord of Rimini*	Mr. B. G. Rogers.
GUIDO DA POLENTA, *Lord of Ravenna*	Mr. F. C. Mosley.
LANCIOTTO, *Malatesta's son*	Mr. Lawrence Barrett.
PAOLO, *His brother*	Mr. Otis Skinner.
PEPÉ,* *Malatesta's jester*	Mr. Louis James.
CARDINAL, *Friend to Guido*	Mr. Charles Rolfe.
RENÉ,* *A troubadour*	Mr. Percy Winter.
FRANCESCA DA RIMINI, *Guido's daughter*	Miss Marie Wainwright.
RITTA, *Her maid*	Miss Rosie Batchelder.

Lords, Ladies, Knights, Priests, Soldiers, Pages, Attendants, &c.

Grand Opera House, Chicago, August 26, 1901.

MALATESTA, *Lord of Rimini*	Mr. W. J. Constantine.
GUIDO DA POLENTA, *Lord of Ravenna*	M. E. A. Eberle.
LANCIOTTO, *Malatesta's son*	Mr. Otis Skinner.
PAOLO, *His brother*	Mr. Aubrey Boucicault.
PEPÉ, *Malatesta's jester*	Mr. William Norris.
CARDINAL, *Friend to Guido*	Mr. Frederick von Rensselar.
RENÉ, *A troubadour*	Mr. Fletcher Norton.
FRANCESCA DA RIMINI, *Guido's daughter*	Miss Marcia Van Dresser.
RITTA, *Her maid*	Miss Gertrude Norman.

Lords, Ladies, Knights, Priests, Soldiers, Pages, Attendants, &c.

SCENE. *Rimini, Ravenna, and the neighbourhood.*

TIME. *About 1300 A. D.*

* In the original edition, the accents in the names of PEPÉ and RENÉ are used only in the Dramatis Personæ, and not in the body of the book.

FRANCESCA DA RIMINI

ACT I.

SCENE I. *Rimini. The Garden of the Palace.* PAOLO *and a number of noblemen are discovered, seated under an arbour, surrounded by* RENE, *and other troubadours, attendants, &c.*

PAOLO. I prithee, Rene, charm our ears again
With the same song you sang me yesterday.
Here are fresh listeners.

RENE. Really, my good lord,
My voice is out of joint. A grievous cold—

[*Coughs.*

PAOLO. A very grievous, but convenient cold,
Which always racks you when you would not sing.

RENE. O, no, my lord! Besides, I hoped to hear
My ditty warbled into fairer ears,
By your own lips; to better purpose, too.

[*The* NOBLEMEN *all laugh.*

FIRST NOBLEMAN. Rene has hit it. Music runs to waste
In ears like ours.

SECOND NOBLEMAN. Nay, nay; chaunt on, sweet Count.

PAOLO. [*Coughing.*] Alack! you hear, I've caught poor Rene's cough.

FIRST NOBLEMAN. That would not be, if we wore petticoats.

[*The others laugh.*

PAOLO. O, fie!

FIRST NOBLEMAN. So runs the scandal to our ears.

SECOND NOBLEMAN. Confirmed by all our other senses, Count.

FIRST NOBLEMAN. Witnessed by many a doleful sigh, poured out
By many a breaking heart in Rimini.

SECOND NOBLEMAN. Poor girls!

FIRST NOBLEMAN. [*Mimicking a lady.*] Sweet Count! sweet Count Paolo! O!
Plant early violets upon my grave!
Thus go a thousand voices to one tune.

[*The others laugh.*

PAOLO. 'Ods mercy! gentlemen, you do me wrong.

FIRST NOBLEMAN. And by how many hundred, more or less?

PAOLO. Ah! rogues, you'd shift your sins upon my shoulders.

SECOND NOBLEMAN. You'd bear them stoutly.

FIRST NOBLEMAN. It were vain to give
Drops to god Neptune. You're the sea of love
That swallows all things.

SECOND NOBLEMAN. We the little fish
That meanly scull about within your depths.

PAOLO. Go on, go on! Talk yourselves fairly out.
[PEPE *laughs without.*
But, hark! here comes the fool! Fit company
For this most noble company of wits!

[*Enter* PEPE, *laughing violently.*]

Why do you laugh?

PEPE. I'm laughing at the world.
It has laughed long enough at me; and so
I'll turn the tables. Ho! ho! ho! I've heard
A better joke of Uncle Malatesta's
Than any I e'er uttered. [*Laughing.*

ALL. Tell it, fool.

PEPE. Why, do you know—upon my life, the best
And most original idea on earth:
A joke to put in practice, too. By Jove!
I'll bet my wit 'gainst the stupidity
Of the best gentleman among you all,
You cannot guess it.

ALL. Tell us, tell us, fool.

PEPE. Guess it, guess it, fools.

PAOLO Come, disclose, disclose!

PEPE. He has a match afoot.—

ALL. A match!

PEPE. A marriage.

ALL. Who?—who?

PEPE. A marriage in his family.

ALL. But, who?

PEPE. Ah! there's the point.

ALL. Paolo?

PEPE. No.

FIRST NOBLEMAN. The others are well wived. Shall we turn Turks?

PEPE. Why, there's the summit of his joke, good sirs.
By all the sacred symbols of my art—
By cap and bauble, by my tinkling bell—
He means to marry Lanciotto!
[*Laughs violently.*

ALL. [*Laughing.*] Ho!—

PAOLO. Peace! peace! What tongue dare echo yon fool's laugh?
Nay, never raise your hands in wonderment:
I'll strike the dearest friend among ye all
Beneath my feet, as if he were a slave,
Who dares insult my brother with a laugh!

PEPE. By Jove! ye're sad enough. Here's mirth's quick cure!
Pretty Paolo has a heavy fist,
I warn you, sirs. Ho! ho! I trapped them all;
[*Laughing.*]
Now I'll go mar old Malatesta's message. [*Aside.*
[*Exit.*

PAOLO. Shame on ye, sirs! I have mistaken you.
I thought I harboured better friends. Poor fops,
Who've slept in down and satin all your years,
Within the circle Lanciotto charmed
Round Rimini with his most potent sword!—
Fellows whose brows would melt beneath a casque,
Whose hands would fray to grasp a brand's rough hilt,
Who ne'er launched more than braggart threats at foes!—
Girlish companions of luxurious girls!—
Danglers round troubadours and wine-cups!—Men
Whose best parts are their clothes! bundles of silk,
Scented like summer! rag-men, nothing more!—
Creatures as generous as monkeys—brave
As hunted hares—courteous as grinning apes—
Grateful as serpents—useful as lap-dogs—
[*During this, the* NOBLEMEN, *&c., steal off.*]
Ha!
I am alone at last! So let me be,
Till Lanciotto fill the vacant room
Of these mean knaves, whose friendship is but breath. [*Exit.*

SCENE II.

The Same. A Hall in the Castle. Enter MALATESTA *and* LANCIOTTO.

MALATESTA. Guido, ay, Guido of Ravenna, son—
Down on his knees, as full of abject prayers
For peace and mercy as a penitent.

LANCIOTTO. His old trick, father. While his wearied arm
Is raised in seeming prayer, it only rests.
Anon, he'll deal you such a staggering blow,
With its recovered strength, as shall convert
You, and not him, into a penitent.

MALATESTA. No, no; your last bout levelled him. He reeled
Into Ravenna, from the battle-field,
Like a stripped drunkard, and there headlong fell—
A mass of squalid misery, a thing
To draw the jeering urchins. I have this
From faithful spies. There's not a hope remains
To break the shock of his great overthrow.
I pity Guido.

LANCIOTTO. 'Sdeath! go comfort him!
I pity those who fought, and bled, and died,
Before the armies of this Ghibelin.
I pity those who halted home with wounds
Dealt by his hand. I pity widowed eyes
That he set running; maiden hearts that turn,
Sick with despair, from ranks thinned down by him;
Mothers that shriek, as the last stragglers fling
Their feverish bodies by the fountain-side,
Dumb with mere thirst, and faintly point to him,
Answering the dame's quick questions. I have seen
Unburied bones, and skulls—that seemed to ask,
From their blank eye-holes, vengeance at my hand—
Shine in the moonlight on old battle-fields;
And even these—the happy dead, my lord—
I pity more than Guido of Ravenna!

MALATESTA. What would you have?

LANCIOTTO. I'd see Ravenna burn,
Flame into heaven, and scorch the flying clouds;
I'd choke her streets with ruined palaces;
I'd hear her women scream with fear and grief,

As I have heard the maids of Rimini.
All this I'd sprinkle with old Guido's blood,
And bless the baptism.

MALATESTA. You are cruel.

LANCIOTTO. Not I;
But these things ache within my fretting brain.
The sight I first beheld was from the arms
Of my wild nurse, her husband hacked to death
By the fierce edges of these Ghibelins.
One cut across the neck—I see it now,
Ay, and have mimicked it a thousand times,
Just as I saw it, on our enemies.—
Why, that cut seemed as if it meant to bleed
On till the judgment. My distracted nurse
Stooped down, and paddled in the running gore
With her poor fingers; then a prophetess,
Pale with the inspiration of the god,
She towered aloft, and with her dripping hand
Three times she signed me with the holy cross.
'Tis all as plain as noon-day. Thus she spake,—
"May this spot stand till Guido's dearest blood
Be mingled with thy own!" The soldiers say,
In the close battle, when my wrath is up,
The dead man's blood flames on my vengeful brow
Like a red planet; and when war is o'er,
It shrinks into my brain, defiling all
My better nature with its slaughterous lusts.
Howe'er it be, it shaped my earliest thought,
And it will shape my last.

MALATESTA. You moody churl!
You dismal knot of superstitious dreams!
Do you not blush to empty such a head
Before a sober man? Why, son, the world
Has not given o'er its laughing humour yet,
That you should try it with such vagaries.—Poh!
I'll get a wife to teach you common sense.

LANCIOTTO. A wife for me! [*Laughing.*

MALATESTA. Ay, sir, a wife for you.
You shall be married, to insure your wits.

LANCIOTTO. 'Tis not your wont to mock me.

MALATESTA. How now, son!
I am not given to jesting. I have chosen
The fairest wife in Italy for you.
You won her bravely, as a soldier should:
And when you'd woo her, stretch your gauntlet out,
And crush her fingers in its steely grip.
If you will plead, I ween, she dare not say—
No, by your leave. Should she refuse, howe'er,
With that same iron hand you shall go knock
Upon Ravenna's gates, till all the town
Ring with your courtship. I have made her hand
The price and pledge of Guido's future peace.

LANCIOTTO. All this is done!

MALATESTA. Done, out of hand; and now
I wait a formal answer, nothing more.
Guido dare not decline. No, by the saints,
He'd send Ravenna's virgins here in droves,
To buy a ten days' truce.

LANCIOTTO. Sir, let me say,
You stretch paternal privilege too far,
To pledge my hand without my own consent.
Am I a portion of your household stuff,
That you should trade me off to Guido thus?
Who is the lady I am bartered for?

MALATESTA. Francesca, Guido's daughter.—Never frown;
It shall be so!

LANCIOTTO. By heaven, it shall not be!
My blood shall never mingle with his race.

MALATESTA. According to your nurse's prophecy,
Fate orders it.

LANCIOTTO. Ha!

MALATESTA. Now, then, I have struck
The chord that answers to your gloomy thoughts.
Bah! on your sibyl and her prophecy!
Put Guido's blood aside, and yet, I say,
Marry you shall.

LANCIOTTO. 'Tis most distasteful, sir.

MALATESTA. Lanciotto, look ye! You brave gentlemen,
So fond of knocking out poor people's brains,
In time must come to have your own knocked out:
What, then, if you bequeath us no new hands,

To carry on your business, and our house
Die out for lack of princes?

LANCIOTTO. Wed my brothers:
They'll rear you sons, I'll slay you enemies.
Paolo and Francesca! Note their names;
They chime together like sweet marriage-bells.
A proper match. 'Tis said she's beautiful;
And he is the delight of Rimini,—
The pride and conscious centre of all eyes,
The theme of poets, the ideal of art,
The earthly treasury of Heaven's best gifts!
I am a soldier; from my very birth,
Heaven cut me out for terror, not for love.
I had such fancies once, but now—

MALATESTA. Pshaw! son,
My faith is bound to Guido; and if you
Do not throw off your duty, and defy,
Through sickly scruples, my express commands,
You'll yield at once. No more: I'll have it so! [*Exit.*

LANCIOTTO. Curses upon my destiny! What, I—
Ho! I have found my use at last—What, I,
I, the great twisted monster of the wars,
The brawny cripple, the herculean dwarf,
The spur of panic, and the butt of scorn—
I be a bridegroom! Heaven, was I not cursed
More than enough, when thou didst fashion me
To be a type of ugliness,—a thing
By whose comparison all Rimini
Holds itself beautiful? Lo! here I stand,
A gnarléd, blighted trunk! There's not a knave
So spindle-shanked, so wry-faced, so infirm,
Who looks at me, and smiles not on himself.
And I have friends to pity me—great Heaven!
One has a favourite leg that he bewails,—
Another sees my hip with doleful plaints,—
A third is sorry o'er my huge swart arms,—
A fourth aspires to mount my very hump,
And thence harangue his weeping brotherhood!
Pah! it is nauseous! Must I further bear
The sidelong shuddering glances of a wife?
The degradation of a showy love,

That over-acts, and proves the mummer's craft
Untouched by nature? And a fair wife, too!—
Francesca, whom the minstrels sing about!
Though, by my side, what woman were not fair?
Circe looked well among her swine, no doubt;
Next me, she'd pass for Venus. Ho! ho! ho! [*Laughing.*]
Would there were something merry in my laugh!
Now, in the battle, if a Ghibelin
Cry, "Wry-hip! hunchback!" I can trample him
Under my stallion's hoofs; or haggle him
Into a monstrous likeness of myself:
But to be pitied,—to endure a sting
Thrust in by kindness, with a sort of smile!—
'Sdeath! it is miserable!

Enter PEPE.

PEPE. My lord—
LANCIOTTO. My fool!
PEPE. We'll change our titles when your bride's bells ring—
Ha, cousin?
LANCIOTTO. Even this poor fool has eyes,
To see the wretched plight in which I stand.
[*Aside.*]
How, gossip, how?
PEPE. I, being the court-fool,
Am lord of fools by my prerogative.
LANCIOTTO. Who told you of my marriage?
PEPE. Rimini!
A frightful liar; but true for once, I fear.
The messenger from Guido has returned,
And the whole town is wailing over him.
Some pity you, and some the bride; but I,
Being more catholic, I pity both.
LANCIOTTO. Still, pity, pity! [*Aside. Bells toll.*] Ha! whose knell is that?
PEPE. Lord Malatesta sent me to the tower,
To have the bells rung for your marriage-news.
How, he said not; so I, as I thought fit,
Told the deaf sexton to ring out a knell.
[*Bells toll.*]
How do you like it?

LANCIOTTO. Varlet, have you bones,
To risk their breaking? I have half a mind
To thresh you from your motley coat!
[*Seizes him.*

PEPE. Pardee!
Respect my coxcomb, cousin. Hark! ha, ha! [*Laughing.*]

[*Bells ring a joyful peal.*]

Some one has changed my music. Heaven defend!
How the bells jangle. Yonder graybeard, now,
Rings a peal vilely. He's more used to knells,
And sounds them grandly. Only give him time,
And, I'll be sworn, he'll ring your knell out yet.

LANCIOTTO. Pepe, you are but half a fool.

PEPE. My lord,
I can return the compliment in full.

LANCIOTTO. So, you are ready.

PEPE. Truth is always so.

LANCIOTTO. I shook you rudely; here's a florin.
[*Offers money.*

PEPE. No:
My wit is merchandise, but not my honour.

LANCIOTTO. Your honour, sirrah!

PEPE. Why not? You great lords
Have something you call lordly honour; pray,
May not a fool have foolish honour, too?
Cousin, you laid your hand upon my coat—
'T was the first sacrilege it ever knew—
And you shall pay it. Mark! I promise you.

LANCIOTTO. [*Laughing.*] Ha, ha! you bluster well. Upon my life,
You have the tilt-yard jargon to a breath.
Pepe, if I should smite you on the cheek—
Thus, gossip, thus—[*Strikes him.*] what would you then demand?

PEPE. Your life!

LANCIOTTO. [*Laughing.*] Ha, ha! there is the camp-style, too,
A very cut-throat air! How this shrewd fool
Makes the punctilio of honour show!
Change helmets into coxcombs, swords to baubles,
And what a figure is poor chivalry!
Thanks for your lesson, Pepe. [*Exit.*

PEPE. Ere I'm done,
You'll curse as heartily, you limping beast!
Ha! so we go—Lord Lanciotto, look!
[*Walks about, mimicking him.*]
Here is a leg and camel-back, forsooth,
To match your honour and nobility!
You miscreated scarecrow, dare you shake,
Or strike in jest, a natural man like me?—
You curséd lump, you chaos of a man,
To buffet one whom Heaven pronounces good!
[*Bells ring.*]
There go the bells rejoicing over you:
I'll change them back to the old knell again.
You marry, faugh! Beget a race of elves;
Wed a she-crocodile, and keep within
The limits of your nature! Here we go,
Tripping along to meet our promised bride,
Like a rheumatic elephant!—ha, ha! [*Laughing.*
[*Exit, mimicking* LANCIOTTO.

SCENE III.

The Same. A Room in the Same. Enter LANCIOTTO, *hastily.*

LANCIOTTO. Why do these prodigies environ me?
In ancient Rome, the words a fool might drop,
From the confusion of his vagrant thoughts,
Were held as omens, prophecies; and men
Who made earth tremble with majestic deeds,
Trembled themselves at fortune's lightest threat.
I like it not. My father named this match
While I boiled over with vindictive wrath
Towards Guido and Ravenna. Straight my heart
Sank down like lead; a weakness seized on me,
A dismal gloom that I could not resist;
I lacked the power to take my stand, and say—
Bluntly, I will not! Am I in the toils?
Has fate so weakened me, to work its end?
There seems a fascination in it, too,—
A morbid craving to pursue a thing
Whose issue may be fatal. Would that I
Were in the wars again! These mental weeds

Grow on the surface of inactive peace.
I'm haunted by myself. Thought preys on thought.
My mind seems crowded in the hideous mould
That shaped my body. What a fool am I
To bear the burden of my wretched life,
To sweat and toil under the world's broad eye,
Climb into fame, and find myself—O, what?—
A most conspicuous monster! Crown my head,
Pile Cæsar's purple on me—and what then?
My hump shall shorten the imperial robe,
My leg peep out beneath the scanty hem,
My broken hip shall twist the gown awry;
And pomp, instead of dignifying me,
Shall be by me made quite ridiculous.
The faintest coward would not bear all this:
Prodigious courage must be mine, to live;
To die asks nothing but weak will, and I
Feel like a craven. Let me skulk away
Ere life o'ertask me. [*Offers to stab himself.*

Enter PAOLO.

PAOLO. [*Seizing his hand.*] Brother! what is this?
Lanciotto, are you mad? Kind Heaven! look here—
Straight in my eyes. Now answer, do you know
How near you were to murder? Dare you bend
Your wicked hand against a heart I love?
Were it for you to mourn your wilful death,
With such a bitterness as would be ours,
The wish would ne'er have crossed you. While we're bound
Life into life, a chain of loving hearts,
Were it not base in you, the middle link,
To snap, and scatter all? Shame, brother, shame!
I thought you better metal.

LANCIOTTO. Spare your words.
I know the seasons of our human grief,
And can predict them without almanac.
A few sobs o'er the body, and a few
Over the coffin; then a sigh or two,
Whose windy passage dries the hanging tear;
Perchance, some wandering memories, some regrets;
Then a vast influx of consoling thoughts—

Based on the trials of the sadder days
Which the dead missed; and then a smiling face
Turned on to-morrow. Such is mortal grief.
It writes its histories within a span,
And never lives to read them.

PAOLO. Lanciotto,
I heard the bells of Rimini, just now,
Exulting o'er your coming marriage-day,
While you conspired to teach them gloomier sounds.
Why are you sad?

LANCIOTTO. Paolo, I am wretched;
Sad's a faint word. But of my marriage-bells—
Heard you the knell that Pepe rang?

PAOLO. 'Twas strange:
A sullen antic of his crabbed wit.

LANCIOTTO. It was portentous. All dumb things find tongues
Against this marriage. As I passed the hall,
My armour glittered on the wall, and I
Paused by the harness, as before a friend
Whose well-known features slack our hurried gait;
Francesca's name was fresh upon my mind,
So I half-uttered it. Instant, my sword
Leaped from its scabbard, as with sudden life,
Plunged down and pierced into the oaken floor,
Shivering with fear! Lo! while I gazed upon it—
Doubting the nature of the accident—
Around the point appeared a spot of blood,
Oozing upon the floor, that spread and spread—
As I stood gasping by in speechless horror—
Ring beyond ring, until the odious tide
Crawled to my feet, and lapped them, like the tongues
Of angry serpents! O, my God! I fled
At the first touch of the infernal stain!
Go—you may see—go to the hall!

PAOLO. Fie! man,
You have been ever played on in this sort
By your wild fancies. When your heart is high,
You make them playthings; but in lower moods,
They seem to sap the essence of your soul,
And drain your manhood to its poorest dregs.

LANCIOTTO. Go look, go look!

PAOLO. [*Goes to the door, and returns.*] There sticks the sword, indeed,
Just as your tread detached it from its sheath;
Looking more like a blessed cross, I think,
Than a bad omen. As for blood—Ha, ha!
[*Laughing.*]
It sets mine dancing. Pshaw! away with this!
Deck up your face with smiles. Go trim yourself
For the young bride. New velvet, gold, and gems,
Do wonders for us. Brother, come; I'll be
Your tiring-man, for once.

LANCIOTTO. Array this lump—
Paolo, hark! There are some human thoughts
Best left imprisoned in the aching heart,
Lest the freed malefactors should dispread
Infamous ruin with their liberty.
There's not a man—the fairest of ye all—
Who is not fouler than he seems. This life
Is one unending struggle to conceal
Our baseness from our fellows. Here stands one
In vestal whiteness with a lecher's lust;—
There sits a judge, holding law's scales in hands
That itch to take the bribe he dare not touch;—
Here goes a priest with heavenward eyes, whose soul
Is Satan's council-chamber;—there a doctor,
With nature's secrets wrinkled round a brow
Guilty with conscious ignorance;—and here
A soldier rivals Hector's bloody deeds—
Out-does the devil in audacity—
With craven longings fluttering in a heart
That dares do aught but fly! Thus are we all
Mere slaves and alms-men to a scornful world,
That takes us at our seeming.

PAOLO. Say 't is true;
What do you drive at?

LANCIOTTO. At myself, full tilt.
I, like the others, am not what I seem.
Men call me gentle, courteous, brave.—They lie!
I'm harsh, rude, and a coward. Had I nerve
To cast my devils out upon the earth,
I'd show this laughing planet what a hell

Of envy, malice, cruelty, and scorn,
It has forced back to canker in the heart
Of one poor cripple!

PAOLO. Ha!

LANCIOTTO. Ay, now 'tis out!
A word I never breathed to man before.
Can you, who are a miracle of grace,
Feel what it is to be a wreck like me?
Paolo, look at me. Is there a line,
In my whole bulk of wretched contraries,
That nature in a nightmare ever used
Upon her shapes till now? Find me the man,
Or beast, or tree, or rock, or nameless thing,
So out of harmony with all things else,
And I'll go raving with bare happiness,—
Ay, and I'll marry Helena of Greece,
And swear I do her honour!

PAOLO. Lanciotto,
I, who have known you from a stripling up,
Never observed, or, if I did, ne'er weighed
Your special difference from the rest of men.
You're not Apollo—

LANCIOTTO. No!

PAOLO. Nor yet are you
A second Pluto. Could I change with you—
My graces for your nobler qualities—
Your strength, your courage, your renown—by heaven,
We'd e'en change persons, to the finest hair.

LANCIOTTO. You should be flatterer to an emperor.

PAOLO. I am but just. Let me beseech you, brother,
To look with greater favour on yourself;
Nor suffer misty phantoms of your brain
To take the place of sound realities.
Go to Ravenna, wed your bride, and lull
Your cruel delusions in domestic peace.
Ghosts fly a fireside; 't is their wont to stalk
Through empty houses, and through empty hearts.
I know Francesca will be proud of you.
Women admire you heroes. Rusty sages,
Pale poets, and scarred warriors, have been
Their idols ever; while we fair plump fools

Are elbowed to the wall, or only used
For vacant pastime.

LANCIOTTO. To Ravenna?—no!
In Rimini they know me; at Ravenna
I'd be a new-come monster, and exposed
To curious wonder. There will be parade
Of all the usual follies of the state;
Fellows with trumpets, tinselled coats, and wands,
Would strut before me, like vain mountebanks
Before their monkeys. Then, I should be stared
Out of my modesty; and when they look,
How can I tell if 't is the bridegroom's face
Or hump that draws their eyes? I will not go.
To please you all, I'll marry; but to please
The wonder-mongers of Ravenna—Ha!
Paolo, now I have it. You shall go,
To bring Francesca; and you'll speak of me,
Not as I ought to be, but as I am.
If she draw backward, give her rein; and say
That neither Guido nor herself shall feel
The weight of my displeasure. You may say,
I pity her—

PAOLO. For what?

LANCIOTTO. For wedding me.
In sooth, she'll need it. Say—

PAOLO. Nay, Lanciotto,
I'll be a better orator in your behalf,
Without your promptings.

LANCIOTTO. She is fair, 't is said;
And, dear Paolo, if she please your eye,
And move your heart to anything like love,
Wed her yourself. The peace would stand as firm
By such a match.

PAOLO. [*Laughing.*] Ha! that is right: be gay!
Ply me with jokes! I'd rather see you smile
Than see the sun shine.

LANCIOTTO. I am serious.
I'll find another wife, less beautiful,
More on my level, and—

PAOLO. An empress, brother,
Were honoured by your hand. You are by much

Too humble in your reckoning of yourself.
I can count virtues in you, to supply
Half Italy, if they were parcelled out.
Look up!

LANCIOTTO. I cannot: Heaven has bent me down.
To you, Paolo, I could look, however,
Were my hump made a mountain. Bless him, God!
Pour everlasting bounties on his head!
Make Crœsus jealous of his treasury,
Achilles of his arms, Endymion
Of his fresh beauties,—though the coy one lay,
Blushing beneath Diana's earliest kiss,
On grassy Latmos; and may every good,
Beyond man's sight, though in the ken of heaven,
Round his fair fortune to a perfect end!
O, you have dried the sorrow of my eyes;
My heart is beating with a lighter pulse;
The air is musical; the total earth
Puts on new beauty, and within the arms
Of girding ocean dreams her time away,
And visions bright to-morrows!

Enter MALATESTA *and* PEPE.

MALATESTA. Mount, to horse!

PEPE. [*Aside.*] Good Lord! he's smiling! What's the matter now?
Has anybody broken a leg or back?
Has a more monstrous monster come to life?
Is hell burst open?—heaven burnt up? What, what
Can make yon eyesore grin?—I say, my lord,
What cow has calved?

PAOLO. Your mother, by the bleat.

PEPE. Right fairly answered—for a gentleman!
When did you take my trade up?

PAOLO. When your wit
Went begging, sirrah.

PEPE. Well again! My lord,
I think he'll do.

MALATESTA. For what?

PEPE. To take my place.
Once fools were rare, and then my office sped;

But now the world is overrun with them:
One gets one's fool in one's own family,
Without much searching.

MALATESTA. Pepe, gently now.
Lanciotto, you are waited for. The train
Has passed the gate, and halted there for you.

LANCIOTTO. I go not to Ravenna.

MALATESTA. Hey! why not?

PAOLO. For weighty reasons, father. Will you trust
Your greatest captain, hope of all the Guelfs,
With crafty Guido? Should the Ghibelins
Break faith, and shut Lanciotto in their walls—
Sure the temptation would be great enough—
What would you do?

MALATESTA. I'd eat Ravenna up!

PEPE. Lord! what an appetite!

PAOLO. But Lanciotto
Would be a precious hostage.

MALATESTA. True; you're wise;
Guido's a fox. Well, have it your own way.
What is your plan?

PAOLO. I go there in his place.

MALATESTA. Good! I will send a letter with the news.

LANCIOTTO. I thank you, brother. [*Apart to* PAOLO.

PEPE. Ha! ha! ha!—O! O! [*Laughing.*

MALATESTA. Pepe, what now?

PEPE. O! lord, O!—ho! ho! ho! [*Laughing.*

PAOLO. Well, giggler?

PEPE. Hear my fable, uncle.

MALATESTA. Ay.

PEPE. Once on a time, Vulcan sent Mercury
To fetch dame Venus from a romp in heaven.
Well, they were long in coming, as he thought;
And so the god of spits and gridirons
Railed like himself—the devil. But—now mark—
Here comes the moral. In a little while,
Vulcan grew proud, because he saw plain signs
That he should be a father; and so he
Strutted through hell, and pushed the devils by,
Like a magnifico of Venice. Ere long,
His heir was born; but then—ho! ho!—the brat

Had wings upon his heels, and thievish ways,
And a vile squint, like errant Mercury's,
Which honest Vulcan could not understand;—
Can you?

PAOLO. 'Sdeath! fool, I'll have you in the stocks.
Father, your fool exceeds his privilege.

PEPE. [*Apart to* PAOLO.] Keep your own bounds, Paolo. In the stocks
I'd tell more fables than you'd wish to hear.
And so ride forth. But, cousin, don't forget
To take Lanciotto's picture to the bride.
Ask her to choose between it and yourself.
I'll count the moments, while she hesitates,
And not grow gray at it.

PAOLO. Peace, varlet, peace!

PEPE. [*Apart to him.*] Ah, now I have it. There's an elephant
Upon the scutcheon; show her that, and say—
Here's Lanciotto in our heraldry!

PAOLO. Here's for your counsel!

[*Strikes* PEPE, *who runs behind* MALATESTA.

MALATESTA. Son, son, have a care!
We who keep pets must bear their pecks sometimes.
Poor knave! Ha! ha! thou'rt growing villainous!

[*Laughs and pats* PEPE.

PEPE. Another blow! another life for that! [*Aside.*

PAOLO. Farewell, Lanciotto. You are dull again.

LANCIOTTO. Nature will rule.

MALATESTA. Come, come!

LANCIOTTO. God speed you, brother!
I am too sad; my smiles all turn to sighs.

PAOLO. More cause to haste me on my happy work.

[*Exit with* MALATESTA.

PEPE. I'm going, cousin.

LANCIOTTO. Go.

PEPE. Pray, ask me where.

LANCIOTTO. Where, then?

PEPE. To have my jewel carried home:
And, as I'm wise, the carrier shall be
A thief, a thief, by Jove! The fashion's new.

[*Exit.*

LANCIOTTO. In truth, I am too gloomy and irrational.
Paolo must be right. I always had
These moody hours and dark presentiments,
Without mischances following after them.
The camp is my abode. A neighing steed,
A fiery onset, and a stubborn fight,
Rouse my dull blood, and tire my body down
To quiet slumbers when the day is o'er,
And night above me spreads her spangled tent,
Lit by the dying cresset of the moon.
Ay, that is it; I'm homesick for the camp.

[*Exit.*

ACT II.

SCENE I. *Ravenna. A Room in* GUIDO'S *Palace. Enter* GUIDO *and a* CARDINAL.

CARDINAL. I warn thee, Count.
GUIDO. I'll take the warning, father,
On one condition: show me but a way
For safe escape.
CARDINAL. I cannot.
GUIDO. There's the point.
We Ghibelins are fettered hand and foot.
There's not a florin in my treasury;
Not a lame soldier, I can lead to war;
Not one to man the walls. A present siege,
Pushed with the wonted heat of Lanciotto,
Would deal Ravenna such a mortal blow
As ages could not mend. Give me but time
To fill the drainéd arteries of the land.
The Guelfs are masters, we their slaves; and we
Were wiser to confess it, ere the lash
Teach it too sternly. It is well for you
To say you love Francesca. So do I;
But neither you nor I have any voice
For or against this marriage.
CARDINAL. 'T is too true.
GUIDO. Say we refuse: Why, then, before a week,
We'll hear Lanciotto rapping at our door,
With twenty hundred ruffians at his back.

What's to say then? My lord, we waste our breath.
Let us look fortune in the face, and draw
Such comfort from the wanton as we may.

CARDINAL. And yet I fear—

GUIDO. You fear! and so do I.
I fear Lanciotto as a soldier, though,
More than a son-in-law.

CARDINAL. But have you seen him?

GUIDO. Ay, ay, and felt him, too. I've seen him ride
The best battalions of my horse and foot
Down like mere stubble: I have seen his sword
Hollow a square of pikemen, with the ease
You'd scoop a melon out.

CARDINAL. Report declares him
A prodigy of strength and ugliness.

GUIDO. Were he the devil—But why talk of this?—
Here comes Francesca.

CARDINAL. Ah! unhappy child!

GUIDO. Look you, my lord! you'll make the best of it;
You will not whimper. Add your voice to mine,
Or woe to poor Ravenna!

Enter FRANCESCA *and* RITTA.

FRANCESCA. Ha! my lord—
And you, my father!—But do I intrude
Upon your counsels? How severe you look!
Shall I retire?

GUIDO. No, no.

FRANCESCA. You moody men
Seem leagued against me. As I passed the hall,
I met your solemn Dante, with huge strides
Pacing in measure to his stately verse.
The sweeping sleeves of his broad scarlet robe
Blew out behind, like wide-expanded wings,
And seemed to buoy him in his level flight.
Thinking to pass, without disturbing him,
I stole on tip-toe; but the poet paused,
Subsiding into man, and steadily
Bent on my face the lustre of his eyes.
Then, taking both my trembling hands in his—
You know how his God-troubled forehead awes—

He looked into my eyes, and shook his head,
As if he dared not speak of what he saw;
Then muttered, sighed, and slowly turned away
The weight of his intolerable brow.
When I glanced back, I saw him, as before,
Sailing adown the hall on out-spread wings.
Indeed, my lord, he should not do these things:
They strain the weakness of mortality
A jot too far. As for poor Ritta, she
Fled like a doe, the truant.

RITTA. Yes, forsooth:
There's something terrible about the man.
Ugh! if he touched me, I should turn to ice.
I wonder if Count Lanciotto looks—

GUIDO. Ritta, come here. [*Takes her apart.*

RITTA. My lord.

GUIDO. 'Twas my command,
You should say nothing of Count Lanciotto.

RITTA. Nothing, my lord.

GUIDO. You have said nothing, then?

RITTA. Indeed, my lord.

GUIDO. 'Tis well. Some years ago,
My daughter had a very silly maid,
Who told her sillier stories. So, one day,
This maiden whispered something I forbade—
In strictest confidence, for she was sly:
What happened, think you?

RITTA. I know not, my lord.

GUIDO. I boiled her in a pot.

RITTA. Good heaven! my lord.

GUIDO. She did not like it. I shall keep that pot
Ready for the next boiling.
[*Walks back to the others.*

RITTA. Saints above!
I wonder if he ate her! Boil me—me!
I'll roast or stew with pleasure; but to boil
Implies a want of tenderness,—or rather
A downright toughness—in the matter boiled,
That's slanderous to a maiden. What, boil me—
Boil me! O! mercy, how ridiculous!
[*Retires, laughing.*

Enter a MESSENGER.

MESSENGER. Letters, my lord, from great Prince Malatesta.
[*Presents them, and exit.*

GUIDO. [*Aside.*] Hear him, ye gods!—"from great Prince Malatesta!"
Greeting, no doubt, his little cousin Guido.
Well, well, just so we see-saw up and down.
[*Reads.*]
"*Fearing our treachery*,"—by heaven, that's blunt,
And Malatesta-like!—"*he will not send*
His son, Lanciotto, to Ravenna, but"—
But what?—a groom, a porter? or will he
Have his prey sent him in an iron cage?
By Jove, he shall not have her! O! no, no;
"*He sends his younger son, the Count Paolo,*
To fetch Francesca back to Rimini."
That's well, if he had left his reasons out.
And, in a postscript—by the saints, 't is droll!—
"'*T would not be worth your lordship's while to shut*
Paolo in a prison; for, my lord,
I'll only pay his ransom in plain steel:
Besides, he's not worth having." Is there one,
Save this ignoble offshoot of the Goths,
Who'd write such garbage to a gentleman?
Take that, and read it. [*Gives letter to* CARDINAL.

CARDINAL. I have done the most.
She seems suspicious.

GUIDO. Ritta's work.

CARDINAL. Farewell!

FRANCESCA. Father, you seem distempered.

GUIDO. No, my child,
I am but vexed. Your husband's on the road,
Close to Ravenna. What's the time of day?

FRANCESCA. Past noon, my lord.

GUIDO. We must be stirring, then.

FRANCESCA. I do not like this marriage.

GUIDO. But I do.

FRANCESCA. But I do not. Poh! to be given away,
Like a fine horse or falcon, to a man
Whose face I never saw!

RITTA. That's it, my lady.

GUIDO. Ritta, run down, and see if my great pot
Boils to your liking.
RITTA. [*Aside.*] O! that pot again!
My lord, my heart betrays me; but you know
How true 'tis to my lady. [*Exit.*
FRANCESCA. What ails Ritta?
GUIDO. The ailing of your sex, a running tongue.
Francesca, 'tis too late to beat retreat:
Old Malatesta has me—you, too, child—
Safe in his clutch. If you are not content,
I must unclose Ravenna, and allow
His son to take you. Poh, poh! have a soul
Equal with your estate. A prince's child
Cannot choose husbands. Her desires must aim,
Not at herself, but at the public good.
Both as your prince and father, I command;
As subject and good daughter, you'll obey.
FRANCESCA. I knew that it must be my destiny,
Some day, to give my hand without my heart;
But—
GUIDO. But, and I will but you back again!
When Guido da Polenta says to you,
Daughter, you must be married,—what were best?
FRANCESCA. 'Twere best Francesca, of the self-same name,
Made herself bridal garments. [*Laughing.*
GUIDO. Right!
FRANCESCA. My lord,
Is Lanciotto handsome—ugly—fair—
Black—sallow—crabbed—kind—or what is he?
GUIDO. You'll know ere long. I could not alter him,
To please your taste.
FRANCESCA. You always put me off;
You never have a whisper in his praise.
GUIDO. The world reports it.—Count my soldiers' scars,
And you may sum Lanciotto's glories up.
FRANCESCA. I shall be dutiful, to please you, father.
If aught befall me through my blind submission,
Though I may suffer, you must bear the sin.
Beware, my lord, for your own peace of mind!
My part has been obedience; and now
I play it over to complete my task;

And it shall be with smiles upon my lips,—
Heaven only knows with what a sinking heart!

[*Exeunt.*

SCENE II.

The Same. Before the Gates of the City. The walls hung with banners, flowers, &c., and crowded with citizens. At the side of the scene is a canopied dais, with chairs of state upon it. Music, bells, shouts, and other sounds of rejoicing, are occasionally heard. Enter GUIDO, *the* CARDINAL, NOBLEMEN, KNIGHTS, GUARDS, *&c., with banners, arms, &c.*

GUIDO. My lord, I'll have it so. You talk in vain.
Paolo is a marvel in his way:
I've seen him often. If Francesca take
A fancy to his beauty, all the better;
For she may think that he and Lanciotto
Are like as blossoms of one parent branch.
In truth, they are, so far as features go—
Heaven help the rest! Get her to Rimini,
By any means, and I shall be content.
The fraud cannot last long; but long enough
To win her favour to the family.

CARDINAL. 'Tis a dull trick. Thou hast not dealt with her
Wisely nor kindly, and I dread the end.
If, when this marriage was enjoined on thee,
Thou hadst informed Francesca of the truth,
And said, Now daughter, choose between
Thy peace and all Ravenna's; who that knows
The constant nature of her noble heart
Could doubt the issue? There'd have been some tears,
Some frightful fancies of her husband's looks;
And then she'd calmly walk up to her fate,
And bear it bravely. Afterwards, perchance,
Lanciotto might prove better than her fears,—
No one denies him many an excellence,—
And all go happily. But, as thou wouldst plot,
She'll be prepared to see a paragon,
And find a satyr. It is dangerous.
Treachery with enemies is bad enough,
With friends 'tis fatal.

GUIDO. Has your lordship done?

CARDINAL. Never, Count Guido, with so good a text.
Do not stand looking sideways at the truth;
Craft has become thy nature. Go to her.
GUIDO. I have not heart.
CARDINAL. I have. [*Going.*
GUIDO. Hold, Cardinal!
My plan is better. Get her off my hands,
And I care not.
CARDINAL. What will she say of thee,
In Rimini, when she detects the cheat?
GUIDO. I'll stop my ears up.
CARDINAL. Guido, thou art weak,
And lack the common fortitude of man.
GUIDO. And you abuse the license of your garb,
To lesson me. My lord, I do not dare
To move a finger in these marriage-rites.
Francesca is a sacrifice, I know,—
A limb delivered to the surgeon's knife,
To save our general health. A truce to this.
Paolo has the business in his hands:
Let him arrange it as he will; for I
Will give Count Malatesta no pretext
To recommence the war.
CARDINAL. Farewell, my lord.
I'll neither help nor countenance a fraud.
You crafty men take comfort to yourselves,
Saying, deceit dies with discovery.
'Tis false; each wicked action spawns a brood,
And lives in its succession. You, who shake
Man's moral nature into storm, should know
That the last wave which passes from your sight
Rolls in and breaks upon eternity! [*Exit.*
GUIDO. Why, that's a very grand and solemn thought:
I'll mention it to Dante. Gentlemen,
What see they from the wall?
NOBLEMAN. The train, my lord.
GUIDO. Inform my daughter.
NOBLEMAN. She is here, my lord.

Enter FRANCESCA, RITTA, LADIES, ATTENDANTS, *&c.*

FRANCESCA. See, father, what a merry face I have,
And how my ladies glisten! I will try

To do my utmost, in my love for you
And the good people of Ravenna. Now,
As the first shock is over, I expect
To feel quite happy. I will wed the Count,
Be he whate'er he may. I do not speak
In giddy recklessness. I've weighed it all,—
'Twixt hope and fear, knowledge and ignorance,—
And reasoned out my duty to your wish.
I have no yearnings towards another love:
So, if I show my husband a desire
To fill the place with which he honours me,
According to its duties, even he—
Were he less noble than Count Lanciotto—
Must smile upon my efforts, and reward
Good will with willing grace. One pang remains.
Parting from home and kindred is a thing
None but the heartless, or the miserable,
Can do without a tear. This home of mine
Has filled my heart with two-fold happiness,
Taking and giving love abundantly.
Farewell, Ravenna! If I bless thee not,
'Tis that thou seem'st too blessed; and 'twere strange
In me to offer what thou 'st always given.

GUIDO. [*Aside.*] This is too much! If she would rail a while
At me and fortune, it could be endured. [*Shouts, music, &c., within.*

FRANCESCA. Ha! there's the van just breaking through the wood!
Music! that's well; a welcome forerunner.
Now, Ritta—here—come talk to me. Alas!
How my heart trembles! What a world to me
Lies 'neath the glitter of yon cavalcade!
Is that the Count?

RITTA. Upon the dapple-gray?

FRANCESCA. Yes, yes.

RITTA. No; that's his—

GUIDO. [*Apart to her.*] Ritta!

RITTA. Ay; that's—that's—

GUIDO. Ritta, the pot! [*Apart to her.*

RITTA. O! but this lying chokes! [*Aside.*]
Ay, that's Count Somebody, from Rimini.

FRANCESCA. I knew it was. Is that not glorious?

RITTA. My lady, what?
FRANCESCA. To see a cavalier
Sit on his steed with such familiar grace.
RITTA. To see a man astraddle on a horse!
It don't seem much to me.
FRANCESCA. Fie! stupid girl!
But mark the minstrels thronging round the Count!
Ah! that is more than gallant horsemanship.
The soul that feeds itself on poesy,
Is of a quality more fine and rare
Than Heaven allows the ruder multitude.
I tell you, Ritta, when you see a man
Beloved by poets, made the theme of song,
And chaunted down to ages, as a gift
Fit for the rich embalmment of their verse,
There's more about him than the patron's gold.
If that's the gentleman my father chose,
He must have picked him out from all the world.
The Count alights. Why, what a noble grace
Runs through his slightest action! Are you sad?
You, too, my father? Have I given you cause?
I am content. If Lanciotto's mind
Bear any impress of his fair outside,
We shall not quarrel ere our marriage-day.
Can I say more? My blushes speak for me:
Interpret them as modesty's excuse
For the short-comings of a maiden's speech.
RITTA. Alas! dear lady! [*Aside.*
GUIDO. [*Aside.*] 'Sdeath! my plot has failed,
By overworking its design. Come, come;
Get to your places. See, the Count draws nigh.

GUIDO *and* FRANCESCA *seat themselves upon the dais, surrounded by* RITTA, LADIES, ATTENDANTS, GUARDS, *&c. . Music, shouts, ringing of bells, &c. Enter* MEN-AT-ARMS, *with banners, &c.;* PAGES *bearing costly presents on cushions; then* PAOLO, *surrounded by* NOBLEMEN, KNIGHTS, MINSTRELS, *&c., and followed by other* MEN-AT-ARMS. *They range themselves opposite the dais.*

GUIDO. Ravenna welcomes you, my lord, and I
Add my best greeting to the general voice.

This peaceful show of arms from Rimini
Is a new pleasure, stranger to our sense
Than if the East blew zephyrs, or the balm
Of Summer loaded rough December's gales,
And turned his snows to roses.

PAOLO. Noble sir,
We looked for welcome from your courtesy,
Not from your love; but this unhoped for sight
Of smiling faces, and the gentle tone
In which you greet us, leave us naught to win
Within your hearts. I need not ask, my lord,
Where bides the precious object of my search;
For I was sent to find the fairest maid
Ravenna boasts, among her many fair.
I might extend my travel many a league,
And yet return, to take her from your side.
I blush to bear so rich a treasure home,
As pledge and hostage of a sluggish peace;
For beauty such as hers was meant by Heaven
To spur our race to gallant enterprise,
And draw contending deities around
The dubious battles of a second Troy.

GUIDO. Sir Count, you please to lavish on my child
The high-strained courtesy of chivalry;
Yet she has homely virtues that, I hope,
May take a deeper hold in Rimini,
After the fleeting beauty of her face
Is spoiled by time, or faded to the eye
By its familiar usage.

PAOLO. As a man
Who ever sees Heaven's purpose in its works,
I must suppose so rare a tabernacle
Was framed for rarest virtues. Pardon me
My public admiration. If my praise
Clash with propriety, and bare my words
To cooler judgment, 'tis not that I wish
To win a flatterer's grudged recompense,
And gain by falsehood what I'd win through love.
When I have brushed my travel from my garb,
I'll pay my court in more befitting style.

Music. Exit with his train.

GUIDO. [*Advancing.*] Now, by the saints, Lanciotto's deputy
Stands in this business with a proper grace,
Stretching his lord's instructions till they crack.
A zealous envoy! Not a word said he
Of Lanciotto—not a single word;
But stood there, staring in Francesca's face
With his devouring eyes.—By Jupiter,
I but half like it!

FRANCESCA. [*Advancing.*] Father?

GUIDO. Well, my child.

FRANCESCA. How do you like—

GUIDO. The coxcomb! I've done well!

FRANCESCA. No, no; Count Lanciotto?

GUIDO. Well enough.
But hang this fellow—hang your deputies!
I'll never woo by proxy.

FRANCESCA. Deputies!
And woo by proxy!

GUIDO. Come to me anon.
I'll strip this cuckoo of his gallantry!

[*Exit with* GUARDS, *&c.*

FRANCESCA. Ritta, my father has strange ways of late.

RITTA. I wonder not.

FRANCESCA. You wonder not?

RITTA. No, lady:
He is so used to playing double games,
That even you must come in for your share.
Plague on his boiling! I will out with it. [*Aside.*]
Lady, the gentleman who passed the gates—

FRANCESCA. Count Lanciotto? As I hope for grace,
A gallant gentleman! How well he spoke!
With what sincere and earnest courtesy
The rounded phrases glided from his lips!
He spoke in compliments that seemed like truth.
Methinks I'd listen through a summer's day,
To hear him woo.—And he must woo to me—
I'll have our privilege—he must woo a space,
Ere I'll be won, I promise.

RITTA. But, my lady,
He'll woo you for another.
FRANCESCA. He?—ha! ha! [*Laughing.*]
I should not think it from the prologue, Ritta.
RITTA. Nor I.
FRANCESCA. Nor any one.
RITTA. 'Tis not the Count—
'Tis not Count Lanciotto.
FRANCESCA. Gracious saints!
Have you gone crazy? Ritta, speak again,
Before I chide you.
RITTA. 'Tis the solemn truth.
That gentleman is Count Paolo, lady,
Brother to Lanciotto, and no more
Like him than—than—
FRANCESCA. Than what?
RITTA. Count Guido's pot,
For boiling waiting-maids, is like the bath
Of Venus on the arras.
FRANCESCA. Are you mad,—
Quite mad, poor Ritta?
RITTA. Yes; perhaps I am.
Perhaps Lanciotto is a proper man—
Perhaps I lie—perhaps I speak the truth—
Perhaps I gabble like a fool. O! heavens,
That dreadful pot!
FRANCESCA. Dear Ritta!—
RITTA. By the mass,
They shall not cozen you, my gentle mistress!
If my lord Guido boiled me, do you think
I should be served up to the garrison,
By way of pottage? Surely they would not waste me.
FRANCESCA. You are an idle talker. Pranks like these
Fit your companions. You forget yourself.
RITTA. Not you, though, lady. Boldly I repeat,
That he who looked so fair, and talked so sweet,
Who rode from Rimini upon a horse
Of dapple-gray, and walked through yonder gate,
Is not Count Lanciotto.
FRANCESCA. This you mean?
RITTA. I do, indeed!

FRANCESCA. Then I am more abused—
More tricked, more trifled with, more played upon—
By him, my father, and by all of you,
Than anything, suspected of a heart,
Was ever yet!
RITTA. In Count Paolo, lady,
Perchance there was no meditated fraud.
FRANCESCA. How, dare you plead for him?
RITTA. I but suppose:
Though in your father—O! I dare not say.
FRANCESCA. I dare. It was ill usage, gross abuse,
Treason to duty, meanness, craft—dishonour!
What if I'd thrown my heart before the feet
Of this sham husband! cast my love away
Upon a counterfeit! I was prepared
To force affection upon any man
Called Lanciotto. Anything of silk,
Tinsel, and gewgaws, if he bore that name,
Might have received me for the asking. Yes,
I was inclined to venture more than half
In this base business—shame upon my thoughts!—
All for my father's peace and poor Ravenna's.
And this Paolo, with his cavalcade,
His minstrels, music, and his pretty airs,
His showy person, and his fulsome talk,
Almost made me contented with my lot.
O! what a fool—in faith, I merit it—
Trapped by mere glitter! What an easy fool!
Ha! ha! I'm glad it went no further, girl;
[*Laughing.*]
I'm glad I kept my heart safe, after all.
There was my cunning. I have paid them back,
I warrant you! I'll marry Lanciotto;
I'll seem to shuffle by this treachery. No!
I'll seek my father, put him face to face
With his own falsehood; and I'll stand between,
Awful as justice, meting out to him
Heaven's dreadful canons 'gainst his conscious guilt.
I'll marry Lanciotto. On my faith,
I would not live another wicked day
Here, in Ravenna, only for the fear

That I should take to lying, with the rest.
Ha! ha! it makes me merry, when I think
How safe I kept this little heart of mine! [*Laughing.*

[*Exit, with* ATTENDANTS, *&c.*

RITTA. So, 'tis all ended—all except my boiling,
And that will make a holiday for some.
Perhaps I'm selfish. Fagot, axe, and gallows,
They have their uses, after all. They give
The lookers-on a deal of harmless sport.
Though one may suffer, twenty hundred laugh;
And that's a point gained. I have seen a man—
Poor Dora's uncle—shake himself with glee,
At the bare thought of the ridiculous style
In which some villain died. "Dancing," quoth he,
"To the poor music of a single string!
Biting," quoth he, "after his head was off!
What use of that?" Or, "Shivering," quoth he,
"As from an ague, with his beard afire!"
And then he'd roar until his ugly mouth
Split at the corners. But to see me boil—
O! that will be the queerest thing of all!
I wonder if they'll put me in a bag,
Like a great suet-ball? I'll go, and tell
Count Guido, on the instant. How he'll laugh
To think his pot has got an occupant!
I wonder if he really takes delight
In such amusements? Nay, I have kept faith;
I only said the man was not Lanciotto;
No word of Lanciotto's ugliness.
I may escape the pot, for all. Pardee!
I wonder if they'll put me in a bag!

[*Exit, laughing.*

SCENE III.

The Same. A Room in GUIDO'S *Palace. Enter* GUIDO *and* RITTA.

RITTA. There now, my lord, that is the whole of it:
I love my mistress more than I fear you.
If I could save her finger from the axe,
I'd give my head to do it. So, my lord,
I am prepared to stew.

GUIDO. Boil, Ritta, boil.

RITTA. No; I prefer to stew.
GUIDO. And I to boil.
RITTA. 'Tis very hard, my lord, I cannot choose
My way of cooking. I shall laugh, I vow,
In the grim headsman's face, when I remember
That I am dying for my lady's love.
I leave no one to shed a tear for me;
Father nor mother, kith nor kin, have I,
To say, "Poor Ritta!" o'er my lifeless clay.
They all have gone before me, and 'twere well
If I could hurry after them.
GUIDO. Poor child. [*Aside.*]
But, baggage, said you aught of Lanciotto?
RITTA. No, not a word; and he's so ugly, too!
GUIDO. Is he so ugly?
RITTA. Ugly! he is worse
Than Pilate on the hangings.
GUIDO. Hold your tongue
Here, and at Rimini, about the Count,
And you shall prosper.
RITTA. Am I not to boil?
GUIDO. No, child. But be discreet at Rimini.
Old Malatesta is a dreadful man—
Far worse than I—he bakes his people, Ritta;
Lards them, like geese, and bakes them in an oven.
RITTA. Fire is my fate, I see that.
GUIDO. Have a care
It do not follow you beyond this world.
Where is your mistress?
RITTA. In her room, my lord.
After I told her of the Count Paolo,
She flew to have an interview with you;
But on the way—I know not why it was—
She darted to her chamber, and there stays
Weeping in silence. It would do you good—
More than a hundred sermons—just to see
A single tear, indeed it would, my lord.
GUIDO. Ha! you are saucy. I have honoured you
Past prudence, malpert! Get you to your room!
[*Exit* RITTA.]
More of my blood runs in yon damsel's veins

Than the world knows. Her mother to a shade;
The same high spirit, and strange martyr-wish
To sacrifice herself, body and soul,
For some loved end. All that she did for me;
And yet I loved her not. O! memory!
The darkest future has a ray of hope,
But thou art blacker than the sepulchre!
Thy horrid shapes lie round, like scattered bones,
Hopeless forever! I am sick at heart.
The past crowds on the present: as I sowed,
So am I reaping. Shadows from myself
Fall on the picture, as I trace anew
These rising spectres of my early life,
And add their gloom to what was dark before.
O! memory, memory! How my temples throb! [*Sits.*

Enter FRANCESCA, *hastily.*

FRANCESCA. My lord, this outrage—
[*He looks up.*]
Father, are you ill?
You seem unhappy. Have I troubled you?
You heard how passionate and bad I was,
When Ritta told me of the Count Paolo.
Dear father, calm yourself; and let me ask
A child's forgiveness. 'Twas undutiful
To doubt your wisdom. It is over now.
I only thought you might have trusted me
With any counsel.

GUIDO. [*Aside.*] Would I had!

FRANCESCA. Ah! well,
I understand it all, and you were right.
Only the danger of it. Think, my lord,
If I had loved this man at the first sight:
We all have heard of such things. Think, again,
If I had loved him—as I then supposed
You wished me to—'twould have been very sad.
But no, dear sir, I kept my heart secure,
Nor will I loose it till you give the word.
I'm wiser than you thought me, you perceive.
But when we saw him, face to face, together,
Surely you might have told me then.

GUIDO. Francesca,
My eyes are old—I did not clearly see—
Faith, it escaped my thoughts. Some other things
Came in my head. I was as ignorant
Of Count Paolo's coming as yourself.
The brothers are so like.

FRANCESCA. Indeed?

GUIDO. Yes, yes.
One is the other's counterpart, in fact;
And even now it may not be—O! shame!
I lie by habit. [*Aside.*

FRANCESCA. Then there is a hope?
He may be Lanciotto, after all?
O! joy—

Enter a SERVANT.

SERVANT. The Count Paolo. [*Exit.*

FRANCESCA. Misery!
That name was not Lanciotto!

GUIDO. Farewell, child.
I'll leave you with the Count: he'll make it plain.
It seems 't was Count Paolo. [*Going.*

FRANCESCA. Father!

GUIDO. Well.

FRANCESCA. You knew it from the first! [*Exit* GUIDO.]
Let me begone:
I could not look him in the face again
With the old faith. Besides, 'twould anger him
To have a living witness of his fraud
Ever before him; and I could not trust—
Strive as I might—my happiness to him,
As once I did. I could not lay my hand
Upon his shoulder, and look up to him,
Saying, Dear father, pilot me along
Past this dread rock, through yonder narrow strait.
Saints, no! The gold that gave my life away
Might, even then, be rattling in his purse,
Warm from the buyer's hand. Look on me, Heaven!
Him thou didst sanctify before my eyes,
Him thou didst charge, as thy great deputy,
With guardianship of a weak orphan girl,

Has fallen from grace, has paltered with his trust;
I have no mother to receive thy charge,—
O! take it on thyself; and when I err,
Through mortal blindness, Heaven, be thou my guide!
Worse cannot fall me. Though my husband lack
A parent's tenderness, he yet may have
Faith, truth, and honour—the immortal bonds
That knit together honest hearts as one.
Let me away to Rimini. Alas!
It wrings my heart to have outlived the day
That I can leave my home with no regret! [*Weeps.*

Enter PAOLO.

PAOLO. Pray, pardon me. [*Going.*
FRANCESCA. You are quite welcome, Count.
A foolish tear, a weakness, nothing more:
But present weeping clears our future sight.
They tell me you are love's commissioner,
A kind of broker in the trade of hearts:
Is it your usual business? or may I
Flatter myself, by claiming this essay
As your first effort?
PAOLO. Lady, I believed
My post, at starting, one of weight and trust;
When I beheld you, I concluded it
A charge of honour and high dignity.
I did not think to hear you underrate
Your own importance, by dishonouring me.
FRANCESCA. You are severe, my lord.
PAOLO. No, not severe;
Say candid, rather. I am somewhat hurt
By my reception. If I feel the wound,
'Tis not because I suffer from the jest,
But that your lips should deal it.
FRANCESCA. Compliments
Appear to be the staple of your speech.
You ravish one with courtesy, you pour
Fine words upon one, till the listening head
Is bowed with sweetness. Sir, your talk is drugged;
There's secret poppy in your sugared phrase:
I'll taste before I take it.

PAOLO. Gentle lady—
FRANCESCA. I am not gentle, or I missed my aim.
I am no hawk to fly at every lure.
You courtly gentlemen draw one broad rule—
All girls are fools. It may be so, in truth,
Yet so I'll not be treated.
PAOLO. Have you been?
If I implied such slander by my words,
They wrong my purpose. If I compliment,
'Tis not from habit, but because I thought
Your face deserved my homage as its due.
When I have clearer insight, and you spread
Your inner nature o'er your lineaments,
Even that face may darken in the shades
Of my opinion. For mere loveliness
Needs inward light to keep it always bright.
All things look badly to unfriendly eyes.
I spoke my first impression; cooler thought
May work strange changes.
FRANCESCA. Ah, Sir Count, at length
There's matter in your words.
PAOLO. Unpleasant stuff,
To judge by your dark brows. I have essayed
Kindness and coldness, yet you are not pleased.
FRANCESCA. How can I be?
PAOLO. How, lady?
FRANCESCA. Ay, sir, how?
Your brother—my good lord that is to be—
Stings me with his neglect; and in the place
He should have filled, he sends a go-between,
A common carrier of others' love;
How can the sender, or the person sent,
Please overmuch? Now, were I such as you,
I'd be too proud to travel round the land
With other people's feelings in my heart;
Even to fill the void which you confess
By such employment.
PAOLO. Lady, 'tis your wish
To nettle me, to break my breeding down,
And see what natural passions I have hidden
Behind the outworks of my etiquette.

I neither own nor feel the want of heart
With which you charge me. You are more than cruel;
You rouse my nerves until they ache with life,
And then pour fire upon them. For myself
I would not speak, unless you had compelled.
My task is odious to me. Since I came,
Heaven bear me witness how my traitor heart
Has fought against my duty; and how oft
I wished myself in Lanciotto's place.
Or him in mine.

FRANCESCA. You riddle.

PAOLO. Do I? Well,
Let it remain unguessed.

FRANCESCA. You wished yourself
At Rimini, or Lanciotto here?
You may have reasons.

PAOLO. Well interpreted!
The Sphinx were simple in your skilful hands!

FRANCESCA. It has become your turn to sneer.

PAOLO. But I
Have gall to feed my bitterness, while you
Jest in the wanton ease of happiness.
Stop! there is peril in our talk.

FRANCESCA. As how?

PAOLO. 'Tis dangerous to talk about one's self;
It panders selfishness. My duty waits.

FRANCESCA. My future lord's affairs? I quite forgot
Count Lanciotto.

PAOLO. I, too, shame upon me. [*Aside.*

FRANCESCA. Does he resemble you?

PAOLO. Pray drop me, lady.

FRANCESCA. Nay, answer me.

PAOLO. Somewhat—in feature.

FRANCESCA. Ha!
Is he so fair?

PAOLO. No, darker. He was tanned
In long campaigns, and battles hotly fought,
While I lounged idly with the troubadours,
Under the shadow of his watchful sword.

FRANCESCA. In person?

PAOLO. He is shorter, I believe,
But broader, stronger, more compactly knit.
FRANCESCA. What of his mind?
PAOLO. Ah, now you strike the key!
A mind just fitted to his history,
An equal balance 'twixt desert and fame.
No future chronicler shall say of him,
His fame outran his merit; or his merit
Halted behind some adverse circumstance,
And never won the glory it deserved.
My love might weary you, if I rehearsed
The simple beauty of his character;
His grandeur and his gentleness of heart,
His warlike fire and peaceful love, his faith,
His courtesy, his truth. I'll not deny
Some human weakness, to attract our love,
Harbours in him, as in the rest of us.
Sometimes against our city's enemies
He thunders in the distance, and devotes
Their homes to ruin. When the brand has fallen,
He ever follows with a healing rain,
And in his pity shoulders by revenge.
A thorough soldier, lady. He grasps crowns,
While I pick at the laurel.
FRANCESCA. Stay, my lord!
I asked your brother's value, with no wish
To hear you underrate yourself. Your worth
May rise in passing through another's lips.
Lanciotto is perfection, then?
PAOLO. To me:
Others may think my brother over-nice
Upon the point of honour; over-keen
To take offence where no offence is meant;
A thought too prodigal of human life,
Holding it naught when weighed against a wrong;
Suspicious of the motives of his friends;
Distrustful of his own high excellence;
And with a certain gloom of temperament,
When thus disturbed, that makes him terrible
And rash in action. I have heard of this;
I never felt it. I distress you, lady?

Perhaps I throw these points too much in shade,
By catching at an enemy's report.
But, then, Lanciotto said, "You'll speak of me,
Not as I ought to be, but as I am."
He loathes deceit.

FRANCESCA. That's noble! Have you done?
I have observed a strange reserve, at times,
An over-carefulness in choosing words,
Both in my father and his nearest friends,
When speaking of your brother; as if they
Picked their way slowly over rocky ground,
Fearing to stumble. Ritta, too, my maid,
When her tongue rattles on in full career,
Stops at your brother's name, and with a sigh
Settles herself to dismal silence. Count,
These things have troubled me. From you I look
For perfect frankness. Is there naught withheld?

PAOLO. [*Aside.*] O base temptation! What if I betray
His crippled person—imitate his limp—
Laugh at his hip, his back, his sullen moods
Of childish superstition?—tread his heart
Under my feet, to climb into his place?—
Use his own warrant 'gainst himself; and say,
Because I loved her, and misjudged your jest,
Therefore I stole her? Why, a common thief
Would hang for just such thinking! Ha! ha! ha!
[*Laughing.*]
I reckon on her love, as if I held
The counsels of her bosom. No, I swear,
Francesca would despise so mean a deed.
Have I no honour either? Are my thoughts
All bound by her opinions?

FRANCESCA. This is strange!
Is Lanciotto's name a spell to all?
I ask a simple question, and straight you
Start to one side, and mutter to yourself,
And laugh, and groan, and play the lunatic,
In such a style that you astound me more
Than all the others. It appears to me

I have been singled as a common dupe
By every one. What mystery is this
Surrounds Count Lanciotto? If there be
A single creature in the universe
Who has a right to know him as he is,
I am that one.

PAOLO. I grant it. You shall see,
And shape your judgment by your own remark.
All that my honour calls for I have said.

FRANCESCA. I am content. Unless I greatly err,
Heaven made your breast the seat of honest thoughts.
You know, my lord, that, once at Rimini,
There can be no retreat for me. By you,
Here at Ravenna, in your brother's name,
I shall be solemnly betrothed. And now
I thus extend my maiden hand to you;
If you are conscious of no secret guilt,
Take it.

PAOLO. I do. [*Takes her hand.*

FRANCESCA. You tremble!

PAOLO. With the hand,
Not with the obligation.

FRANCESCA. Farewell, Count!
'Twere cruel to tax your stock of compliments,
That waste their sweets upon a trammelled heart;
Go fly your fancies at some freer game. [*Exit.*

PAOLO. O, Heaven, if I have faltered and am weak,
'Tis from my nature! Fancies, more accursed
Than haunt a murderer's bedside, throng my brain—
Temptations, such as mortal never bore
Since Satan whispered in the ear of Eve,
Sing in my ear—and all, all are accursed!
At heart I have betrayed my brother's trust,
Francesca's openly. Turn where I will,
As if enclosed within a mirrored hall,
I see a traitor. Now to stand erect,
Firm on my base of manly constancy;
Or, if I stagger, let me never quit
The homely path of duty, for the ways
That bloom and glitter with seductive sin! [*Exit.*

ACT III

SCENE I. *Rimini. A Room in the Castle.* LANCIOTTO *discovered reading.*

LANCIOTTO. O! fie, philosophy! This Seneca
Revels in wealth, and whines about the poor!
Talks of starvation while his banquet waits,
And fancies that a two hours' appetite
Throws light on famine! Doubtless he can tell,
As he skips nimbly through his dancing-girls,
How sad it is to limp about the world
A sightless cripple! Let him feel the crutch
Wearing against his heart, and then I'd hear
This sage talk glibly; or provide a pad,
Stuffed with his soft philosophy, to ease
His aching shoulder. Pshaw! he never felt,
Or pain would choke his frothy utterance.
'Tis easy for the doctor to compound
His nauseous simples for a sick man's health;
But let him swallow them, for his disease,
Without wry faces. Ah! the tug is there.
Show me philosophy in rags, in want,
Sick of a fever, with a back like mine,
Creeping to wisdom on these legs, and I
Will drink its comforts. Out! away with you!
There's no such thing as real philosophy!

[*Throws down the book.*]

[*Enter* PEPE.]

Here is a sage who'll teach a courtier
The laws of etiquette, a statesman rule,
A soldier discipline, a poet verse,
And each mechanic his distinctive trade;
Yet bring him to his motley, and how wide
He shoots from reason! We can understand
All business but our own, and thrust advice
In every gaping cranny of the world;
While habit shapes us to our own dull work,
And reason nods above his proper task.
Just so philosophy would rectify
All things abroad, and be a jade at home.

Pepe, what think you of the Emperor's aim
Towards Hungary?
PEPE. A most unwise design;
For mark, my lord—
LANCIOTTO. Why, there! the fact cries out.
Here's motley thinking for a diadem!—
Ay, and more wisely in his own regard.
PEPE. You flout me, cousin.
LANCIOTTO. Have you aught that's new?—
Some witty trifle, some absurd conceit?
PEPE. Troth, no.
LANCIOTTO. Why not give up the Emperor,
And bend your wisdom on your duties, Pepe?
PEPE. Because the Emperor has more need of wisdom
Than the most barren fool of wit.
LANCIOTTO. Well said!
Mere habit brings the fool back to his art.
This jester is a rare philosopher.
Teach me philosophy, good fool.
PEPE. No need.
You'll get a teacher when you take a wife.
If she do not instruct you in more arts
Than Aristotle ever thought upon,
The good old race of woman has declined
Into a sort of male stupidity.
I had a sweetheart once, she lectured grandly;
No matter on what subject she might hit,
'T was all the same, she could talk and she would.
She had no silly modesty; she dashed
Straight in the teeth of any argument,
And talked you deaf, dumb, blind. Whatever struck
Upon her ear, by some machinery,
Set her tongue wagging. Thank the Lord, she died!—
Dropped in the middle of a fierce harangue,
Like a spent horse. It was an even thing,
Whether she talked herself or me to death.
The latest sign of life was in her tongue;
It wagged till sundown, like a serpent's tail,
Long after all the rest of her was cold.
Alas! poor Zippa!

LANCIOTTO. Were you married, fool?
PEPE. Married! Have I the scars upon me?
No;
I fell in love; and that was bad enough,
And far enough for a mere fool to go.
Married! why, marriage is love's purgatory,
Without a heaven beyond.
LANCIOTTO. Fie, atheist!
Would you abolish marriage?
PEPE. Yes.
LANCIOTTO. What?
PEPE. Yes.
LANCIOTTO. Depopulate the world?
PEPE. No fear of that.
I'd have no families, no Malatesti,
Strutting about the land, with pedigrees
And claims bequeathed them by their ancestors;
No fellows vapouring of their royal blood;
No one to seize a whole inheritance,
And rob the other children of the earth.
By Jove! you should not know your fathers, even!
I'd have you spring, like toadstools, from the soil—
Mere sons of women—nothing more nor less—
All base-born, and all equal. There, my lord,
There is a simple commonwealth for you!
In which aspiring merit takes the lead,
And birth goes begging.
LANCIOTTO. It is so, in truth;
And by the simplest means I ever heard.
PEPE. Think of it, cousin. Tell it to your friends,
The statesmen, soldiers, and philosophers;
Noise it about the earth, and let it stir
The sluggish spirits of the multitudes.
Pursue the thought, scan it, from end to end,
Through all its latent possibilities.
It is a great seed dropped, I promise you,
And it must sprout. Thought never wholly dies;
It only wants a name—a hard Greek name—
Some few apostles, who may live on it—
A crowd of listeners, with the average dulness
That man possesses—and we organize;

Spread our new doctrine, like a general plague;
Talk of man's progress and development,
Wrongs of society, the march of mind,
The Devil, Doctor Faustus, and what not;
And, lo! this pretty world turns upside down,
All with a fool's idea!

LANCIOTTO. By Jupiter,
You hit our modern teachers to a hair!
I knew this fool was a philosopher.
Pepe is right. Mechanic means advance;
Nature bows down to Science' haughty tread,
And turns the wheel of smutty artifice:
New governments arise, dilate, decay,
And foster creeds and churches to their tastes:
At each advance, we cry, "Behold, the end!"
Till some fresh wonder breaks upon the age.
But man, the moral creature, midst it all
Stands still unchanged; nor moves towards virtue more,
Nor comprehends the mysteries in himself,
More than when Plato taught academies,
Or Zeno thundered from his Attic porch.

PEPE. I know not that; I only want my scheme
Tried for a while. I am a politician,
A wrongs-of-man man. Hang philosophy!
Let metaphysics swallow, at a gulp,
Its last two syllables, and purge itself
Clean of its filthy humours! I am one
Ready for martyrdom, for stake and fire,
If I can make my great idea take root!
Zounds! cousin, if I had an audience,
I'd make you shudder at my eloquence!
I have an itching to reform the world.

LANCIOTTO. Begin at home, then.

PEPE. Home is not my sphere;
Heaven picked me out to teach my fellow-men.
I am a very firebrand of truth—
A self-consuming, doomed, devoted brand—
That burns to ashes while I light the world!
I feel it in me. I am moved, inspired,
Stirred into utterance, by some mystic power
Of which I am the humble instrument.

LANCIOTTO. A bad digestion, sage, a bilious turn,
A gnawing stomach, or a pinching shoe.

PEPE. O! hear, but spare the scoffer! Spare the wretch
Who sneers at the anointed man of truth!
When we reached that, I and my followers
Would rend you limb from limb. There!—ha! ha! ha!
[*Laughing.*]
Have I not caught the slang these fellows preach;
A grand, original idea, to back it;
And all the stock in trade of a reformer?

LANCIOTTO. You have indeed; nor do I wonder, Pepe.
Fool as you are, I promise you success
In your new calling, if you'll set it up.
The thing is far too simple.

Trumpet sounds within.

PEPE. Hist! my lord.

LANCIOTTO. That calls me to myself.

PEPE. At that alarm,
All Rimini leaped up upon its feet.
Cousin, your bridal-train. You groan! 'Ods wounds!
Here is the bridegroom sorely malcontent—
The sole sad face in Rimini. Since morn,
A quiet man could hardly walk the streets,
For flowers and streamers. All the town is gay.
Perhaps 'tis merry o'er your misery.

LANCIOTTO. Perhaps; but that it knows not.

PEPE. Yes, it does:
It knows that when a man's about to wed,
He's ripe to laugh at. Cousin, tell me, now,
Why is Paolo on the way so long?
Ravenna's but eight leagues from Rimini—

LANCIOTTO. That's just the measure of your tongue, good fool.
You trouble me. I've had enough of you—
Begone!

PEPE. I'm going; but you see I limp.
Have pity on a cripple, gentle Count. [*Limps.*

LANCIOTTO. Pepe!

PEPE. A miracle, a miracle!
See, see, my lord, at Pepe's saintly name
The lame jog on.

MALATESTA. [*Without.*] Come, Lanciotto!
LANCIOTTO. Hark!
My father calls.
PEPE. If he were mine, I'd go—
That's a good boy! [*Pats* LANCIOTTO'S *back.*
LANCIOTTO. [*Starting.*] Hands off! you'll rue it else! [*Exit.*
PEPE. [*Laughing.*] Ha! ha! I laid my hand upon his hump!
Heavens, how he squirmed! And what a wish I had
To cry, Ho! camel! leap upon his back,
And ride him to the devil! So, we've had
A pleasant flitting round philosophy!
The Count and Fool bumped heads, and struck ideas
Out by the contact! Quite a pleasant talk—
A friendly conversation, nothing more—
'Twixt nobleman and jester. Ho! my bird,
I can toss lures as high as any man.
So, I amuse you with my harmless wit?
Pepe's your friend now—you can trust in him—
An honest, simple fool! Just try it once,
You ugly, misbegotten clod of dirt!
Ay, but the hump—the touch upon the hump—
The start and wriggle—that was rare! Ha! ha!
[*Exit, laughing.*

SCENE II.

The Same. The Grand Square before the Castle. SOLDIERS *on guard, with banners, &c.* CITIZENS, *in holiday dresses, cross the scene. The houses are hung with trophies, banners, garlands, &c. Enter* MALATESTA, *with* GUARDS, ATTENDANTS, *&c.*

MALATESTA. Captain, take care the streets be not choked up
By the rude rabble. Send to Cæsar's bridge
A strong detachment of your men, and clear
The way before them. See that nothing check
The bride's first entrance into Rimini.
Station your veterans in the front. Count Guido
Comes with his daughter, and his eyes are sharp.
Keep up a show of strength before him, sir;
And set some labourers to work upon
The broken bastion. Make all things look bright;
As if we stood in eager readiness,
And high condition, to begin a war.

CAPTAIN. I will, my lord.

MALATESTA. Keep Guido in your eye;
And if you see him looking over-long
On any weakness of our walls, just file
Your bulkiest fellows round him; or get up
A scuffle with the people; anything—
Even if you break a head or two—to draw
His vision off. But where our strength is great,
Take heed to make him see it. You conceive?

CAPTAIN. Trust me, my lord. [*Exit with* GUARDS.

Enter PEPE.

PEPE. Room, room! A hall; a hall!
I pray you, good man, has the funeral passed?

MALATESTA. Who is it asks?

PEPE. Pepe of Padua,
A learned doctor of uncivil law.

MALATESTA. But how a funeral?

PEPE. You are weak of wit.
Francesca of Ravenna's borne to church,
And never issues thence.

MALATESTA. How, doctor, pray?

PEPE. Now, for a citizen of Rimini,
You're sadly dull. Does she not issue thence
Fanny of Rimini? A glorious change,—
A kind of resurrection in the flesh!

MALATESTA. [*Laughing.*] Ha! ha! thou cunning villain! I was caught.
I own it, doctor.

PEPE. [*Aside.*] This old fool would laugh
To see me break a straw, because the bits
Were of unequal lengths. My character
Carries more dulness, in the guise of wit,
Than would suffice to break an ass's back.

[*Distant shouts, music, &c.*]

Hark! here comes Jeptha's daughter, jogging on
With timbrels and with dances.

MALATESTA. Jeptha's daughter!
How so?

PEPE. Her father's sacrifice.

MALATESTA. [*Laughing.*] Ho! ho!
You'll burst my belt! O! you outrageous wretch,
To jest at Scripture!
PEPE. You outlandish heathen,
Tis not in Scripture!
MALATESTA. Is it not?
PEPE. No more
Than you are in heaven. Mere Hebrew history.
She went up to the mountains, to bewail
The too-long keeping of her honesty.
There's woman for you! there's a character!
What man would ever think of such a thing?
Ah! we of Rimini have little cause
For such a sorrow. Would she'd been my wife!
I'll marry any woman in her case.
MALATESTA. Why, Pepe?
PEPE. Why? because, in two months' time,
Along comes father Jeptha with his knife,
And there's an end. Where is your sacrifice?
Where's Isaac, Abraham? Build your altar up:
One pile will do for both.
MALATESTA. That's Scripture, sure.
PEPE. Then I'm a ram, and you may slaughter me
In Isaac's stead.
MALATESTA. Here comes the vanguard. Where,
Where is that laggard?
PEPE. At the mirror, uncle,
Making himself look beautiful. He comes,
[*Looking out.*]
Fresh as a bridegroom! Mark his doublet's fit
Across the shoulders, and his hose!—
By Jove, he nearly looks like any other man!
MALATESTA. You'd best not let him hear you. Sirrah, knave,
I have a mind to swinge you! [*Seizes his ear.*
PEPE. Loose my ear!
You've got the wrong sow, swineherd! You're unjust.
Being his father, I was fool sufficient
To think you fashioned him to suit yourself,
By way of a variety. The thought
Was good enough, the practice damnable.
MALATESTA. Hush! or I'll clap you in the pillory.

Enter LANCIOTTO.

PEPE. [*Sings.*] Ho, ho, ho, ho!—old Time has wings—
We're born, we mourn, we wed, we bed,
We have a devilish aching head;
So down we lie,
And die, and fry;
And there's a merry end of things!

[*Music, &c., within.*]

Here come Ravenna's eagles for a roost
In Rimini! The air is black with them.
When go they hence? Wherever yon bird builds,
The nest remains for ages. Have an eye,
Or Malatesta's elephant may feel
The eagle's talons.

LANCIOTTO. You're a raven, croaker.

PEPE. And you no white crow, to insure us luck.

MALATESTA. There's matter in his croak.

PEPE. There always is;
But men lack ears.

MALATESTA. Then eyes must do our work.
Old Guido shall be looked to. If his force
Appear too great, I'll camp him out of town.

LANCIOTTO. Father, you are a sorry host.

MALATESTA. Well, well,
I'm a good landlord, though. I do not like
This flight of eagles more than Pepe. 'Sdeath!
Guido was ever treacherous.

LANCIOTTO. My lord,
You mar my holiday by such a thought.
My holiday! Dear saints! it seems to me
That all of you are mocking me.

PEPE. So—so—
Guido was ever treacherous?—so—so!

MALATESTA. So—so! How so?

PEPE. What if this treachery
Run in the blood? We'll tap a vein then—so!

MALATESTA. Sew up your mouth, and mind your fooling fool!

PEPE. Am I not fooling? Why, my lord, I thought
The fooling exquisite.

LANCIOTTO. [*Aside.*] This thoughtless knave
Hits near us sometimes with his random shafts.
Marriage for me! I cannot comprehend,
I cannot take it to my heart; the thing
Seems gross, absurd, ridiculous. Ah! well,
My father bears the folly of it all;
I'm but an actor in his comedy.
My part is bad, but I must through with it.
[*Retires.*

Shouts, music, &c., within.

PEPE. Look! here's the whole parade! Mark yonder knave—
The head one with the standard. Nature, nature!
Hadst thou a hand in such a botch-work? Why,
A forest of his legs would scarcely make
A bunch of fagots. Mark old Guido, too!
He looks like Judas with his silver. Ho!
Here's news from sweet Ravenna!

MALATESTA. [*Laughing.*] Ha! ha! ha!

PEPE. Ah! now the bride!—that's something—she is tooth-some.
Look you, my lord—now, while the progress halts—
Cousin Paolo, has he got the dumps?
Mercy! to see him, one might almost think
'T was his own marriage. What a doleful face!
The boy is ill. He caught a fever, uncle,
Travelling across the marshes. Physic! physic!
If he be really dying, get a doctor,
And cut the matter short. 'Twere merciful.

MALATESTA. For heaven's sake, cease your clamour! I shall have
No face to meet them else. 'Tis strange, for all:
What ails Paolo?

PEPE. Dying, by this hand!

MALATESTA. Then I will hang you.

PEPE. Don't take up my craft.
Wit's such a stranger in your brain that I
Scarce knew my lodger venturing from your mouth.
Now they come on again.

MALATESTA. Stand back!

PEPE. [*Looking round.*] The bridegroom?
He flies betimes, before the bride shows fight.
[*Walks back, looking for* LANCIOTTO.

Music, shouts, ringing of bells, &c. Enter MEN-AT-ARMS, *with banners, &c.*, GUIDO, CARDINAL, KNIGHTS, ATTENDANTS, *&c.; then* PAOLO, *conducting* FRANCESCA, *followed by* RITTA, LADIES, PAGES, *&c., and other* MEN-AT-ARMS. *They file around the stage, and halt.*

MALATESTA. Welcome, to Rimini, Count Guido! Welcome,
And fair impressions of our poor abode,
To you, my daughter! You are well returned,
My son, Paolo! Let me bless you, son.

[PAOLO *approaches.*]

How many spears are in old Guido's train?

[*Apart to* PAOLO.

PAOLO. Some ten-score.

MALATESTA. Footmen?

PAOLO. Double that.

MALATESTA. 'Tis well.
Again I bid you welcome! Make no show
Of useless ceremony with us. Friends
Have closer titles than the empty name.
We have provided entertainment, Count,
For all your followers, in the midst of us.
We trust the veterans of Rimini
May prove your soldiers that our courtesy
Does not lag far behind their warlike zeal.
Let us drop Guelf and Ghibelin henceforth,
Coupling the names of Rimini and Ravenna
As bridegroom's to his bride's.

GUIDO. Count Malatesta,
I am no rhetorician, or my words
Might keep more even with the love I feel:
Simply, I thank you. With an honest hand
I take the hand which you extend to me,
And hope our grasp may never lose its warmth.—
You marked the bastion by the water-side?
Weak as a bulrush. [*Apart to a* KNIGHT.

KNIGHT. Tottering weak, my lord.

GUIDO. Remember it; and when you're private, sir,
Draw me a plan.

KNIGHT. I will, my lord.

GUIDO. How's this?
I do not see my future son-in-law.

MALATESTA. Lanciotto!
LANCIOTTO. [*Advancing.*] I am here, my lord.
FRANCESCA. [*Starting.*] O! heaven!
Is that my husband, Count Paolo? You,
You then, among the rest, have played me false!
He is—[*Apart to* PAOLO.
PAOLO My brother.
LANCIOTTO [*Aside.*] Ha! she turns from me.
PEPE. [*Approaching* LANCIOTTO, *sings.*]
Around, around the lady turned,
She turned not to her lord;
She turned around to a gallant, gallant knight,
Who ate at his father's board.

A pretty ballad! all on one string though.

LANCIOTTO. Pepe, go hence! [PEPE *retires.*]
[*Aside.*] I saw her start and pale,
Turn off with horror; as if she had seen—
What?—simply me. For, am I not enough,
And something over, to make ladies quail,
Start, hide their faces, whisper to their friends,
Point at me—dare she?—and perform such tricks
As women will when monsters blast their sight?
O! saints above me, have I come so low?
Yon damsel of Ravenna shall bewail
That start and shudder. I am mad, mad, mad!
I must be patient. They have trifled with her:
Lied to her, lied! There's half the misery
Of this broad earth, all crowded in one word.
Lied, lied!—Who has not suffered from a lie?
They're all aghast—all looking at me too.
Francesca's whiter than the brow of fear:
Paolo talks.—Brother, is that well meant?
What if I draw my sword, and fight my way
Out of this cursed town? 'Twould be relief.
Has shame no hiding-place? I've touched the depth
Of human infamy, and there I rest.
By heaven, I'll brave this business out! Shall they
Say at Ravenna that Count Lanciotto,
Who's driven their shivering squadrons to their homes,
Haggard with terror, turned before their eyes

And slunk away? They'll look me from the field,
When we encounter next. Why should not I
Strut with my shapeless body, as old Guido
Struts with his shapeless heart? I'll do it! [*Offers, but shrinks back.*] 'Sdeath!
Am I so false as to forswear myself?
Lady Francesca! [*Approaches* FRANCESCA.

FRANCESCA. Sir—my lord—

LANCIOTTO. Dear lady,
I have a share in your embarrassment,
And know the feelings that possess you now.

FRANCESCA. O! you do not.

PAOLO. [*Advancing.*] My lady—

LANCIOTTO. Gentle brother,
Leave this to me. [PAOLO *retires.*

FRANCESCA. Pray do not send him off.

LANCIOTTO. 'Tis fitter so.

FRANCESCA. He comforts me.

LANCIOTTO. Indeed?
Do you need comfort?

FRANCESCA. No, no—pardon me!
But then—he is—you are—

LANCIOTTO. Take breath, and speak.

FRANCESCA. I am confused, 'tis true. But, then, my lord,
You are a stranger to me; and Paolo
I've known so long!

LANCIOTTO. Since yesterday.

FRANCESCA. Ah! well:
But the relationship between us two
Is of so close a nature, while the knowledge,
That each may have of each, so slender is
That the two jar. Besides, Paolo is
Nothing to me, while you are everything.
Can I not act? [*Aside.*

LANCIOTTO. I scarcely understand.
You say your knowledge of me, till to-day,
Was incomplete. Has naught been said of me
By Count Paolo or your father?

FRANCESCA. Yes;
But nothing definite.

LANCIOTTO. Perchance, no hint
As to my ways, my feelings, manners, or—
Or—or—as I was saying—ha! ha!—or—
[*Laughing.*]
As to my person?

FRANCESCA. Nothing, as to that.

LANCIOTTO. To what?

FRANCESCA. Your—person.

LANCIOTTO. That's the least of all. [*Turns aside.*]
Now, had I Guido of Ravenna's head
Under this heel, I'd grind it into dust!
False villain, to betray his simple child!
And thou, Paolo—not a whit behind—
Helping his craft with inconsiderate love!—
Lady Francesca, when my brother left,
I charged him, as he loved me, to conceal
Nothing from you that bore on me: and now
That you have seen me, and conversed with me,
If you object to anything in me,—
Go, I release you.

FRANCESCA. But Ravenna's peace?

LANCIOTTO. Shall not be perilled.

GUIDO. [*Coming behind, whispers her.*] Trust him not, my child;
I know his ways; he'd rather fight than wed.
'Tis but a wish to have the war afoot.
Stand firm for poor Ravenna!

LANCIOTTO. Well, my lady,
Shall we conclude a lasting peace between us
By truce or marriage rites?

GUIDO. [*Whispers her.*] The devil tempts thee:
Think of Ravenna, think of me!

LANCIOTTO. My lord,
I see my father waits you. [GUIDO *retires.*

FRANCESCA. Gentle sir,
You do me little honour in the choice.

LANCIOTTO. My aim is justice.

FRANCESCA. Would you cast me off?

LANCIOTTO. Not for the world, if honestly obtained;
Not for the world would I obtain you falsely.

FRANCESCA. The rites were half concluded ere we met.

LANCIOTTO. Meeting, would you withdraw?
FRANCESCA. No. Bitter word! [*Aside.*
LANCIOTTO. No! Are you dealing fairly?
FRANCESCA. I have said.
LANCIOTTO. O! rapture, rapture! Can it be that I—
Now I'll speak plainly; for a choice like thine
Implies such love as woman never felt.
Love me! Then monsters beget miracles,
And Heaven provides where human means fall short.
Lady, I'll worship thee! I'll line thy path
With suppliant kings! Thy waiting-maids shall be
Unransomed princesses! Mankind shall bow
One neck to thee, as Persia's multitudes
Before the rising sun! From this small town,
This centre of my conquests, I will spread
An empire touching the extremes of earth!
I'll raise once more the name of ancient Rome;
And what she swayed she shall reclaim again!
If I grow mad because you smile on me,
Think of the glory of thy love; and know
How hard it is, for such a one as I,
To gaze unshaken on divinity!
There's no such love as mine alive in man.
From every corner of the frowning earth,
It has been crowded back into my heart.
Now, take it all! If that be not enough,
Ask, and thy wish shall be omnipotent!
Your hand. [*Takes her hand.*] It wavers.
FRANCESCA. So does not my heart.
LANCIOTTO. Bravo! Thou art every way a soldier's wife;
Thou shouldst have been a Cæsar's! Father, hark!
I blamed your judgment, only to perceive
The weakness of my own.
MALATESTA. What means all this?
LANCIOTTO. It means that this fair lady—though I gave
Release to her, and to Ravenna—placed
The liberal hand, which I restored to her,
Back in my own, of her own free good-will.
Is it not wonderful?
MALATESTA. How so?

LANCIOTTO. How so!

PAOLO. Alas! 'tis as I feared! [*Aside.*

MALATESTA. You're humble?—How?

LANCIOTTO. Now shall I cry aloud to all the world,
Make my deformity my pride, and say,
Because she loves me, I may boast of it? [*Aside.*]
No matter, father, I am happy; you,
As the blessed cause, shall share my happiness.
Let us be moving. Revels, dashed with wine,
Shall multiply the joys of this sweet day!
There's not a blessing in the cup of life
I have not tasted of within an hour!

FRANCESCA. [*Aside.*] Thus I begin the practice of deceit,
Taught by deceivers, at a fearful cost.
The bankrupt gambler has become the cheat,
And lives by arts that erewhile ruined me.
Where it will end, Heaven knows; but I—
I have betrayed the noblest heart of all!

LANCIOTTO. Draw down thy dusky vapours, sullen night—
Refuse, ye stars, to shine upon the world—
Let everlasting blackness wrap the sun,
And whisper terror to the universe!
We need ye not! we'll blind ye, if ye dare
Peer with lack-lustre on our revelry!
I have at heart a passion, that would make
All nature blaze with recreated light! [*Exeunt.*

ACT IV

SCENE I. *The Same. An Apartment in the Castle. Enter* LANCIOTTO.

LANCIOTTO. It cannot be that I have duped myself,
That my desire has played into the hand
Of my belief; yet such a thing might be.
We palm more frauds upon our simple selves
Than knavery puts upon us. Could I trust
The open candour of an angel's brow,
I must believe Francesca's. But the tongue

Should consummate the proof upon the brow,
And give the truth its word. The fault lies there.
I've tried her. Press her as I may to it,
She will not utter those three little words—
"I love thee." She will say, "I'll marry you;—
I'll be your duteous wife;—I'll cheer your days;—
I'll do whate'er I can." But at the point
Of present love, she ever shifts the ground,
Winds round the word, laughs, calls me "Infidel!—
How can I doubt?" So, on and on. But yet,
For all her dainty ways, she never says,
Frankly, I love thee. I am jealous—true!
Suspicious—true! distrustful of myself;—
She knows all that. Ay, and she likewise knows,
A single waking of her morning breath
Would blow these vapours off. I would not take
The barren offer of a heartless hand,
If all the Indies cowered under it.
Perhaps she loves another? No; she said,
"I love you, Count, as well as any man;"
And laughed, as if she thought that precious wit.
I turn her nonsense into argument,
And think I reason. Shall I give her up?
Rail at her heartlessness, and bid her go
Back to Ravenna? But she clings to me,
At the least hint of parting. Ah! 'tis sweet,
Sweeter than slumber to the lids of pain,
To fancy that a shadow of true love
May fall on this God-stricken mould of woe,
From so serene a nature. Beautiful
Is the first vision of a desert brook,
Shining beneath its palmy garniture,
To one who travels on his easy way;
What is it to the blood-shot, aching eye
Of some poor wight who crawls with gory feet,
In famished madness, to its very brink;
And throws his sun-scorched limbs upon the cool
And humid margin of its shady strand,
To suck up life at every eager gasp?
Such seems Francesca to my thirsting soul;
Shall I turn off and die?

Enter PEPE

PEPE. Good-morning, cousin!

LANCIOTTO. Good-morning to your foolish majesty!

PEPE. The same to your majestic foolery!

LANCIOTTO. You compliment!

PEPE. I am a troubadour,
A ballad-monger of fine mongrel ballads,
And therefore running o'er with elegance.
Wilt hear my verse?

LANCIOTTO. With patience?

PEPE. No, with rapture.
You must go mad—weep, rend your clothes, and roll
Over and over, like the ancient Greeks,
When listening to Iliad.

LANCIOTTO. Sing, then, sing!
And if you equal Homer in your song,
Why, roll I must, by sheer compulsion.

PEPE. Nay,
You lack the temper of the fine-eared Greek.
You will not roll; but that shall not disgrace
My gallant ballad, fallen on evil times. [*Sings.*]

My father had a blue-black head,
My uncle's head was reddish—maybe,
My mother's hair was noways red,
Sing high ho! the pretty baby!

Mark the simplicity of that! 'Tis called
"The Babe's Confession," spoken just before
His father strangled him.

LANCIOTTO. Most marvellous!
You struggle with a legend worth your art.

PEPE. Now to the second stanza. Note the hint
I drop about the baby's parentage:
So delicately too! A maid might sing,
And never blush at it. Girls love these songs
Of sugared wickedness. They'll go miles about,
To say a foul thing in a cleanly way.
A decent immorality, my lord,
Is art's specific. Get the passions up,
But never wring the stomach.

LANCIOTTO. Triumphant art!

PEPE. [*Sings.*]

My father combed his blue-black head,
  My uncle combed his red head—maybe,
My mother combed my head, and said,
  Sing high ho! my red-haired baby.

LANCIOTTO. Fie, fie! go comb your hair in private.
PEPE. What!
Will you not hear? Now comes the tragedy. [*Sings.*]

My father tore my red, red head,
  My uncle tore my father's—maybe,
My mother tore both till they bled—
  Sing high ho! your brother's baby!

LANCIOTTO. Why, what a hair-rending!
PEPE. Thence wigs arose;
A striking epoch in man's history.
But did you notice the concluding line,
Sung by the victim's mother? There's a hit!

"Sing high ho! your brother's baby!"

Which brother's, pray you? That's the mystery,
The adumbration of poetic art,
And there I leave it to perplex mankind.
It has a moral, fathers should regard,—
A black-haired dog breeds not a red-haired cur.
Treasure this knowledge: you're about to wive;
And no one knows what accident—
LANCIOTTO. Peace, fool!
So all this cunning thing was wound about,
To cast a jibe at my deformity? [*Tears off* PEPE'S *cap.*]
There lies your cap, the emblem that protects
Your head from chastisement. Now, Pepe, hark!
Of late you've taken to reviling me;
Under your motley, you have dared to jest
At God's inflictions. Let me tell you, fool,
No man e'er lived, to make a second jest
At me, before your time!
PEPE. Boo! bloody-bones!
If you're a coward—which I hardly think—
You'll have me flogged, or put into a cell,

Or fed to wolves. If you are bold of heart,
You'll let me run. Do not; I'll work you harm!
I, Beppo Pepe, standing as a man,
Without my motley, tell you, in plain terms,
I'll work you harm—I'll do you mischief, man!

LANCIOTTO. I, Lanciotto, Count of Rimini,
Will hang you, then. Put on your jingling cap;
You please my father. But remember, fool,
No jests at me!

PEPE. I will try earnest next.

LANCIOTTO. And I the gallows.

PEPE. Well, cry quits, cry quits!
I'll stretch your heart, and you my neck—quits, quits!

LANCIOTTO. Go, fool! Your weakness bounds your malice.

PEPE. Yes:
So you all think, you savage gentlemen,
Until you feel my sting. Hang, hang away!
It is an airy, wholesome sort of death,
Much to my liking. When I hang, my friend,
You'll be chief mourner, I can promise you.
Hang me! I've quite a notion to be hung:
I'll do my utmost to deserve it. Hang! [*Exit.*

LANCIOTTO. I am bemocked on all sides. My sad state
Has given the licensed and unlicensed fool
Charter to challenge me at every turn.
The jester's laughing bauble blunts my sword,
His gibes cut deeper than its fearful edge;
And I, a man, a soldier, and a prince,
Before this motley patchwork of a man,
Stand all appalled, as if he were a glass
Wherein I saw my own deformity.
O Heaven! a tear—one little tear—to wash
This aching dryness of the heart away!

Enter PAOLO.

PAOLO. What ails the fool? He passed me, muttering
The strangest garbage in the fiercest tone.
"Ha! ha!" cried he, "they made a fool of me—
A motley man, a slave; as if I felt
No stir in me of manly dignity!

Ha! ha! a fool—a painted plaything, toy—
For men to kick about this dirty world!—
My world as well as theirs.—God's world, I trow!
I will get even with them yet—ha! ha!
In the democracy of death we'll square.
I'll crawl and lie beside a king's own son;
Kiss a young princess, dead lip to dead lip;
Pull the Pope's nose; and kick down Charlemagne,
Throne, crown, and all, where the old idiot sprawls,
Safe as he thinks, rotting in royal state!"
And then he laughed and gibbered, as if drunk
With some infernal ecstasy.

LANCIOTTO. Poor fool!
That is the groundwork of his malice, then,—
His conscious difference from the rest of men?
I, of all men, should pity him the most.
Poor Pepe! I'll be kinder. I have wronged
A feeling heart. Poor Pepe!

PAOLO. Sad again!
Where has the rapture gone of yesterday?

LANCIOTTO. Where are the leaves of Summer? Where the snows
Of last year's Winter? Where the joys and griefs
That shut our eyes to yesternight's repose,
And woke not on the morrow? Joys and griefs,
Huntsmen and hounds, ye follow us as game,
Poor panting outcasts of your forest-law!
Each cheers the others,—one with wild halloos,
And one with whines and howls.—A dreadful chase,
That only closes when horns sound *à mort!*

PAOLO. Thus ever up and down! Arouse yourself,
Balance your mind more evenly, and hunt
For honey in the wormwood.

LANCIOTTO. Or find gall
Hid in the hanging chalice of the rose:
Which think you better? If my mood offend,
We'll turn to business,—to the empty cares
That make such pother in our feverish life.
When at Ravenna, did you ever hear
Of any romance in Francesca's life?

A love-tilt, gallantry, or anything
That might have touched her heart?
PAOLO. Not lightly even.
I think her heart as virgin as her hand.
LANCIOTTO. Then there is hope.
PAOLO. Of what?
LANCIOTTO. Of winning her.
PAOLO. Grammercy! Lanciotto, are you sane?
You boasted yesterday—
LANCIOTTO. And changed to-day.
Is that so strange? I always mend the fault
Of yesterday with wisdom of to-day.
She does not love me.
PAOLO. Pshaw! she marries you:
'Twere proof enough for me.
LANCIOTTO. Perhaps, she loves you.
PAOLO. Me, Lanciotto, me! For mercy's sake,
Blot out such thoughts—they madden me! What, love—
She love—yet marry you!
LANCIOTTO. It moves you much.
'Twas but a fleeting fancy, nothing more.
PAOLO. You have such wild conjectures!
LANCIOTTO. Well, to me
They seem quite tame; they are my bed-fellows.
Think, to a modest woman, what must be
The loathsome kisses of an unloved man—
A gross, coarse ruffian!
PAOLO. O! good heavens, forbear!
LANCIOTTO. What shocks you so?
PAOLO. The picture which you draw,
Wronging yourself by horrid images.
LANCIOTTO. Until she love me, till I know, beyond
The cavil of a doubt, that she is mine—
Wholly, past question—do you think that I
Could so afflict the woman whom I love?
PAOLO. You love her, Lanciotto!
LANCIOTTO. Next to you,
Dearer than anything in nature's scope.
PAOLO. [*Aside.*] O! Heaven, that I must bear this! Yes, and more,—
More torture than I dare to think upon,

Spreads out before me with the coming years,
And holds a record blotted with my tears,
As that which I must suffer!

LANCIOTTO. Come, Paolo,
Come help me woo. I need your guiding eye,
To signal me, if I should sail astray.

PAOLO. O! torture, torture! [*Aside.*

LANCIOTTO. You and I, perchance,
Joining our forces, may prevail at last.
They call love like a battle. As for me,
I'm not a soldier equal to such wars,
Despite my arduous schooling. Tutor me
In the best arts of amorous strategy.
I am quite raw, Paolo. Glances, sighs,
Sweets of the lip, and arrows of the eye,
Shrugs, cringes, compliments, are new to me;
And I shall handle them with little art.
Will you instruct me?

PAOLO. Conquer for yourself.
Two captains share one honour: keep it all.
What if I ask to share the spoils?

LANCIOTTO. [*Laughing.*] Ha! ha!
I'll trust you, brother. Let us go to her:
Francesca is neglected while we jest.
I know not how it is, but your fair face,
And noble figure, always cheer me up,
More than your words; there's healing in them, too,
For my worst griefs. Dear brother, let us in. [*Exeunt.*

SCENE II.

The Same. A Chamber in the Same. FRANCESCA *and* RITTA *discovered at the bridal toilet.*

RITTA. [*Sings.*]

Ring high, ring high! to earth and sky;
A lady goes a-wedding;
The people shout, the show draws out,
And smiles the bride is shedding.

No bell for you, ye ragged few;
 A beggar goes a-wedding;
The people sneer, the thing's so queer,
 And tears the bride is shedding.

Ring low, ring low! dull bell of woe,
 One tone will do for either;
The lady glad, and beggar sad,
 Have both lain down together.

FRANCESCA. A mournful ballad!
RITTA. I scarce knew I sang.
I'm weary of this wreath. These orange-flowers
Will never be adjusted to my taste:
Strive as I will, they ever look awry.
My fingers ache!
FRANCESCA. Not more than my poor head.
There, leave them so.
RITTA. That's better, yet not well.
FRANCESCA. They are but fading things, not worth your pains:
They'll scarce outlive the marriage merriment.
Ritta, these flowers are hypocrites; they show
An outside gayety, yet die within,
Minute by minute. You shall see them fall,
Black with decay, before the rites are o'er.
RITTA. How beautiful you are!
FRANCESCA. Fie, flatterer!
White silk and laces, pearls and orange-flowers,
Would do as much for any one.
RITTA. No, no!
You give them grace, they nothing give to you.
Why, after all, you make the wreath look well;
But somewhat dingy, where it lies against
Your pulsing temple, sullen with disgrace.
Ah! well, your Count should be the proudest man
That ever led a lady into church,
Were he a modern Alexander. Poh!
What are his trophies to a face like that?
FRANCESCA. I seem to please you, Ritta.
RITTA. Please yourself,
And you will please me better. You are sad:
I marked it ever since you saw the Count.

I fear the splendour of his victories,
And his sweet grace of manner—for, in faith,
His is the gentlest, grandest character,
Despite his—

FRANCESCA. Well?

RITTA. Despite his—

FRANCESCA. Ritta, what?

RITTA. Despite his difference from Count Paolo.—

[FRANCESCA *staggers.*]

What is the matter? [*Supporting her.*

FRANCESCA. Nothing; mere fatigue.
Hand me my kerchief. I am better now.
What were you saying?

RITTA. That I fear the Count
Has won your love.

FRANCESCA. Would that be cause for fear?

[*Laughing.*

RITTA. O! yes, indeed! Once—long ago—I was
Just fool enough to tangle up my heart
With one of these same men. 'Twas terrible!
Morning or evening, waking or asleep,
I had no peace. Sighs, groans, and standing tears,
Counted my moments through the blessed day.
And then to this there was a dull, strange ache
Forever sleeping in my breast,—a numbing pain,
That would not for an instant be forgot.
O! but I loved him so, that very feeling
Became intolerable. And I believed
This false Giuseppe, too, for all the sneers,
The shrugs and glances, of my intimates.
They slandered me and him, yet I believed.
He was a noble, and his love to me
Was a reproach, a shame, yet I believed.
He wearied of me, tried to shake me off,
Grew cold and formal, yet I would not doubt.
O! lady, I was true! Nor till I saw
Giuseppe walk through the cathedral door
With Dora, the rich usurer's niece, upon
The very arm to which I clung so oft,
Did I so much as doubt him. Even then—
More is my shame—I made excuses for him.

"Just this or that had forced him to the course:
Perhaps, he loved me yet—a little yet.
His fortune, or his family, had driven
My poor Giuseppe thus against his heart.
The low are sorry judges for the great.
Yes, yes, Giuseppe loved me!" But at last
I did awake. It might have been with less:
There was no need of crushing me, to break
My silly dream up. In the street, it chanced,
Dora and he went by me, and he laughed—
A bold, bad laugh—right in my poor pale face,
And turned and whispered Dora, and she laughed.
Ah! then I saw it all. I've been awake,
Ever since then, I warrant you. And now
I only pray for him sometimes, when friends
Tell his base actions towards his hapless wife.—
O! I am lying—I pray every night! [*Weeps.*

FRANCESCA. Poor Ritta. [*Weeping.*

RITTA. No! blest Ritta! Thank kind heaven,
That kept me spotless when he tempted me,
And my weak heart was pleading with his tongue.
Pray, do not weep. You spoil your eyes for me.
But never love; O! it is terrible!

FRANCESCA. I'll strive against it.

RITTA. Do: because, my lady,
Even a husband may be false, you know;
Ay, even to so sweet a wife as you.
Men have odd tastes. They'll surfeit on the charms
Of Cleopatra, and then turn aside
To woo her blackamoor. 'Tis so, in faith;
Or Dora's uncle's gold had ne'er outbid
The boundless measure of a love like mine.
Think of it, lady, to weigh love with gold!
What could be meaner?

FRANCESCA. Nothing, nothing, Ritta.
Though gold's the standard measure of the world,
And seems to lighten everything beside.
Yet heap the other passions in the scale,
And balance them 'gainst that which gold outweighs—
Against this love—and you shall see how light
The most supreme of them are in the poise!

I speak by book and history; for love
Slights my high fortunes. Under cloth of state
The urchin cowers from pompous etiquette,
Waiving his function at the scowl of power,
And seeks the rustic cot to stretch his limbs
In homely freedom. I fulfil a doom.
We who are topmost on this heap of life
Are nearer to heaven's hand than you below;
And so are used, as ready instruments,
To work its purposes. Let envy hide
Her witless forehead at a prince's name,
And fix her hopes upon a clown's content.
You, happy lowly, know not what it is
To groan beneath the crownéd yoke of state,
And bear the goadings of the sceptre. Ah!
Fate drives us onward in a narrow way,
Despite our boasted freedom.

[*Enter* PAOLO, *with* PAGES *bearing torches.*]

Gracious saints!
What brought you here?

PAOLO. The bridegroom waits.

FRANCESCA. He does?
Let him wait on forever! I'll not go!
O! dear Paolo—

PAOLO. Sister!

FRANCESCA. It is well.
I have been troubled with a sleepless night.
My brain is wild. I know not what I say.
Pray, do not call me sister: it is cold.
I never had a brother, and the name
Sounds harshly to me. When you speak to me,
Call me Francesca.

PAOLO. You shall be obeyed.

FRANCESCA. I would not be obeyed. I'd have you do it
Because—because you love me—as a sister—
And of your own good-will, not my command,
Would please me.—Do you understand?

PAOLO. Too well! [*Aside.*]
'Tis a nice difference.

FRANCESCA. Yet you understand?
Say that you do.

PAOLO. I do.

FRANCESCA. That pleases me.
'Tis flattering if our—friends appreciate
Our nicer feelings.

PAOLO. I await you, lady.

FRANCESCA. Ritta, my gloves.—Ah! yes, I have them on;
Though I'm not quite prepared. Arrange my veil;
It folds too closely. That will do; retire. [RITTA *retires.*]
So, Count Paolo, you have come, hot haste,
To lead me to the church,—to have your share
In my undoing? And you came, in sooth,
Because they sent you? You are very tame!
And if they sent, was it for you to come?

PAOLO. Lady, I do not understand this scorn.
I came, as is my duty, to escort
My brother's bride to him. When next you're called,
I'll send a lackey.

FRANCESCA. I have angered you.

PAOLO. With reason: I would not appear to you
Low or contemptible.

FRANCESCA. Why not to me?

PAOLO. Lady, I'll not be catechized.

FRANCESCA. Ha! Count!

PAOLO. No! if you press me further, I will say
A word to madden you.—Stand still! You stray
Around the margin of a precipice.
I know what pleasure 'tis to pluck the flowers
That hang above destruction, and to gaze
Into the dread abyss, to see such things
As may be safely seen. 'Tis perilous:
The eye grows dizzy as we gaze below,
And a wild wish possesses us to spring
Into the vacant air. Beware, beware!
Lest this unholy fascination grow
Too strong to conquer!

FRANCESCA. You talk wildly, Count;
There's not a gleam of sense in what you say;
I cannot hit your meaning.

PAOLO. Lady, come!

FRANCESCA. Count, you are cruel! [*Weeps.*

PAOLO. O! no; I would be kind.

But now, while reason over-rides my heart,
And seeming anger plays its braggart part—
In heaven's name, come!

FRANCESCA. One word—one question more:
Is it your wish this marriage should proceed?

PAOLO. It is.

FRANCESCA. Come on! You shall not take my hand:
I'll walk alone—now, and forever!

PAOLO. [*Taking her hand.*] Sister!

[*Exeunt* PAOLO *and* FRANCESCA, *with* PAGES.

RITTA. O! misery, misery!—it is plain as day—
She loves Paolo! Why will those I love
Forever get themselves ensnared, and heaven
Forever call on me to succor them?
Here was the mystery, then—the sighs and tears,
The troubled slumbers, and the waking dreams!
And now she's walking through the chapel-door,
Her bridal robe above an aching heart,
Dressed up for sacrifice. 'Tis terrible!
And yet she'll smile and do it. Smile, for years,
Until her heart breaks; and the nurses ask
The doctor of the cause. He'll answer, too,
In hard thick Latin, and believe himself.
O! my dear mistress! Heaven, pray torture me!
Send back Giuseppe, let him ruin me,
And scorn me after; but, sweet heaven, spare her!
I'll follow her. O! what a world is this! [*Exit.*

SCENE III.

The Same. Interior of the Cathedral. LANCIOTTO, FRANCESCA, PAOLO, MALATESTA, GUIDO, RITTA, PEPE, LORDS, KNIGHTS, PRIESTS, PAGES, *a bridal-train of* LADIES, SOLDIERS, CITIZENS, ATTENDANTS, *&c., discovered before the High Altar. Organ music. The rites being over, they advance.*

MALATESTA. By heaven—

PEPE. O! uncle, uncle, you're in church!

MALATESTA. I'll break your head, knave!

PEPE. I claim sanctuary.

MALATESTA. Why, bridegroom, will you never kiss the bride?
We all are mad to follow you.

PEPE. Yes, yes;
Here was Paolo wetting his red lips
For the last minute. Kiss, and give him room.

MALATESTA. You heaven-forsaken imp, be quiet now!

PEPE. Then there'd be naught worth hearing.

MALATESTA. Bridegroom, come!

PEPE. Lord! he don't like it! Hey!—I told you so—
He backs at the first step. Does he not know
His trouble's just begun?

LANCIOTTO. Gentle Francesca,
Custom imposes somewhat on thy lips:
I'll make my levy. [*Kisses her. The others follow.*]
[*Aside.*] Ha! she shrank! I felt
Her body tremble, and her quivering lips
Seemed dying under mine! I heard a sigh,
Such as breaks hearts—O! no, a very groan;
And then she turned a sickly, miserable look
On pale Paolo, and he shivered too!
There is a mystery hangs around her,—ay,
Paolo knows it, too.—By all the saints,
I'll make him tell it, at the dagger's point!
Paolo!—here! I do adjure you, brother,
By the great love I bear you, to reveal
The secret of Francesca's grief.

PAOLO. I cannot.

LANCIOTTO. She told you nothing?

PAOLO. Nothing.

LANCIOTTO. Not a word?

PAOLO. Not one.

LANCIOTTO. What heard you at Ravenna, then?

PAOLO. Nothing.

LANCIOTTO. Here?

PAOLO. Nothing.

LANCIOTTO. Not the slightest hint?—
Don't stammer, man! Speak quick! I am in haste.

PAOLO. Never.

LANCIOTTO. What know you?

PAOLO. Nothing that concerns

Your happiness, Lanciotto. If I did,
Would I not tell unquestioned?

LANCIOTTO. Would you not?
You ask a question for me: answer it.

PAOLO. I have.

LANCIOTTO. You juggle, you turn deadly pale,
Fumble your dagger, stand with head half round,
Tapping your feet.—You dare not look at me!
By Satan! Count Paolo, let me say,
You look much like a full-convicted thief!

PAOLO. Brother!—

LANCIOTTO. Pshaw! brother! You deceive me, sir:
You and that lady have a devil's league,
To keep a devil's secret. Is it thus
You deal with me? Now, by the light above
I'd give a dukedom for some fair pretext
To fly you all! She does not love me? Well,
I could bear that, and live away from her.
Love would be sweet, but want of it becomes
An early habit to such men as I.
But you—ah! there's the sorrow—whom I loved
An infant in your cradle; you who grew
Up in my heart, with every inch you gained;
You whom I loved for every quality,
Good, bad, and common, in your natural stock;
Ay, for your very beauty! It is strange, you'll say,
For such a crippled horror to do that,
Against the custom of his kind! O! yes,
I love, and you betray me!

PAOLO. Lanciotto,
This is sheer frenzy. Join your bride.

LANCIOTTO. I'll not!
What, go to her, to feel her very flesh
Crawl from my touch?—to hear her sigh and moan,
As if God plagued her? Must I come to that?
Must I endure your hellish mystery
With my own wife, and roll my eyes away
In sentimental bliss? No, no! until
I go to her, with confident belief
In her integrity and candid love,
I'll shun her as a leper. [*Alarm-bells toll.*

MALATESTA. What is that?

Enter, hastily, a MESSENGER *in disorder.*

MESSENGER. My lord, the Ghibelins are up—

LANCIOTTO. And I
Will put them down again! I thank thee, Heaven,
For this unlooked-for aid! [*Aside.*

MALATESTA. What force have they?

LANCIOTTO. It matters not,—nor yet the time, place, cause,
Of their rebellion. I would throttle it,
Were it a riot, or a drunken brawl!

MALATESTA. Nay, son, your bride—

LANCIOTTO. My bride will pardon me;
Bless me, perhaps, as I am going forth;—
Thank me, perhaps, if I should ne'er return. [*Aside.*]
A soldier's duty has no bridals in it.

PAOLO. Lanciotto, this is folly. Let me take
Your usual place of honour.

LANCIOTTO. [*Laughing.*] Ha! ha! ha!
What! thou, a tilt-yard soldier, lead my troops!
My wife will ask it shortly. Not a word
Of opposition from the new-made bride?
Nay, she looks happier. O! accursed day,
That I was mated to an empty heart! [*Aside.*

MALATESTA. But, son—

LANCIOTTO. Well, father?

PEPE. Uncle, let him go.
He'll find it cooler on a battle-field
Than in his—

LANCIOTTO. Hark! the fool speaks oracles.
You, soldiers, who are used to follow me,
And front our charges, emulous to bear
The shock of battle on your forward arms,—
Why stand ye in amazement? Do your swords
Stick to their scabbards with inglorious rust?
Or has repose so weakened your big hearts,
That you can dream with trumpets at your ears?
Out with your steel! It shames me to behold
Such tardy welcome to my war-worn blade! [*Draws.*]

[*The* KNIGHTS *and* SOLDIERS *draw.*]

Ho! draw our forces out! Strike camp, sound drums,

And set us on our marches! As I live,
I pity the next foeman who relies
On me for mercy! Farewell! to you all—
To all alike—a soldier's short farewell! [*Going.*]

[PAOLO *stands before him.*]

Out of my way, thou juggler! [*Exit.*

PAOLO. He is gone!

ACT V.

SCENE I. *The Same. The Garden of the Castle.* *Enter* **PEPE,** *singing.*

PEPE. 'Tis jolly to walk in the shady greenwood
With a damsel by your side;
'Tis jolly to walk from the chapel-door,
With the hand of your pretty bride;
'Tis jolly to rest your weary head,
When life runs low and hope is fled,
On the heart where you confide:
'Tis jolly, jolly, jolly, they say,
They say—but I never tried.

Nor shall I ever till they dress their girls
In motley suits, and pair us, to increase
The race of fools. 'Twould be a noble thing,
A motley woman, had she wit enough
To bear the bell. But there's the misery:
You may make princes out of any stuff;
Fools come by nature. She'll make fifty kings—
Good, hearty tyrants, sound, cruel governors—
For one fine fool. There is Paolo, now,
A sweet-faced fellow with a wicked heart—
Talk of a flea, and you begin to scratch.
Lo! here he comes. And there's fierce crook-back's bride
Walking beside him—O, how gingerly!
Take care, my love! that is the very pace
We trip to hell with. Hunchback is away—
That was a fair escape for you; but, then,
The devil's ever with us, and that's worse.
See, the Ravenna giglet, Mistress Ritta,

And melancholy as a cow.—How's this?
I'll step aside, and watch you, pretty folks.
[*Hides behind the bushes.*

Enter PAOLO *and* FRANCESCA, *followed by* RITTA. *He seats himself in an arbour, and reads.* RITTA *and* FRANCESCA *advance.*

FRANCESCA. Ritta.
RITTA. My lady.
FRANCESCA. You look tired.
RITTA. I'm not.
FRANCESCA. Go to your chamber.
RITTA. I would rather stay.
If it may please you. I require a walk
And the fresh atmosphere of breathing flowers,
To stir my blood. I am not very well.
FRANCESCA. I knew it, child. Go to your chamber, dear.
Paolo has a book to read to me.
RITTA. What, the romance? I should so love to hear!
I dote on poetry; and Count Paolo
Sweetens the Tuscan with his mellow voice.
I'm weary now, quite weary, and would rest.
FRANCESCA. Just now you wished to walk.
RITTA. Ah! did I so?
Walking or resting, I would stay with you.
FRANCESCA. The Count objects. He told me, yesterday,
That you were restless while he read to me;
And stirred your feet amid the grass, and sighed,
And yawned, until he almost paused
RITTA. Indeed
I will be quiet.
FRANCESCA. But he will not read.
RITTA. Let me go ask him. [*Runs toward* PAOLO.
FRANCESCA. Stop! Come hither, Ritta.
[*She returns.*]
I saw your new embroidery in the hall,—
The needle in the midst of Argus' eyes;
It should be finished.
RITTA. I will bring it here.—
O no! my finger's sore; I cannot work.
FRANCESCA. Go to your room.
RITTA. Let me remain, I pray.

'Tis better, lady; you may wish for me:
I know you will be sorry if I go.

FRANCESCA. I shall not, girl. Do as I order you.
Will you be headstrong?

RITTA. Do you wish it, then?

FRANCESCA. Yes, Ritta.

RITTA. Yet you made pretexts enough,
Before you ordered.

FRANCESCA. You are insolent.
Will you remain against my will?

RITTA. Yes, lady;
Rather than not remain.

FRANCESCA. Ha! impudent!

RITTA. You wrong me, gentle mistress. Love like mine
Does not ask questions of propriety,
Nor stand on manners. I would do you good,
Even while you smote me; I would push you back,
With my last effort, from the crumbling edge
Of some high rock o'er which you toppled me.

FRANCESCA. What do you mean?

RITTA. I know.

FRANCESCA. Know what?

RITTA. Too much.
Pray, do not ask me.

FRANCESCA. Speak!

RITTA. I know—dear lady,
Be not offended—

FRANCESCA. Tell me, simpleton!

RITTA. You know I worship you; you know I'd walk
Straight into ruin for a whim of yours;
You know—

FRANCESCA. I know you act the fool. Talk sense!

RITTA. I know Paolo loves you.

FRANCESCA. Should he not?
He is my brother.

RITTA. More than brother should.

FRANCESCA. Ha! are you certain?

RITTA. Yes, of more than that.

FRANCESCA. Of more?

RITTA. Yes, lady; for you love him, too.
I've said it! Fling me to the carrion crows,

Kill me by inches, boil me in the pot
Count Guido promised me,—but, O, beware!
Back, while you may. Make me the sufferer,
But save yourself!

FRANCESCA. Now, are you not ashamed,
To look me in the face with that bold brow?
I am amazed!

RITTA. I am a woman, lady;
I too have been in love; I know its ways,
Its arts, and its deceits. Your frowning face,
And seeming indignation, do not cheat.
Your heart is in my hand.

PAOLO. [*Calls.*] Francesca!

FRANCESCA. Hence,
Thou wanton-hearted minion! hence, I say!—
And never look me in the face again!—
Hence, thou insulting slave!

RITTA. [*Clinging to her.*] O lady, lady—

FRANCESCA. Begone! [*Throws her off.*

RITTA. I have no friends—no one to love—
O, spare me!

FRANCESCA. Hence!

RITTA. Was it for this I loved—
Cared for you more than my own happiness—
Ever at heart your slave—without a wish
For greater recompense than your stray smiles?

PAOLO. [*Calls.*] Francesca!

FRANCESCA. Hurry!

RITTA. I am gone. Alas!
God bless you, lady! God take care of you,
When I am far away! Alas, alas! [*Exit weeping.*

FRANCESCA. Poor girl!—but were she all the world to me,
And held my future in her tender grasp,
I'd cast her off, without a second thought,
To savage death, for dear Paolo's sake!
Paolo, hither! Now he comes to me;
I feel his presence, though I see him not,
Stealing upon me like the fervid glow
Of morning sunshine. Now he comes too near—
He touches me—O heaven!

PAOLO. Our poem waits.
I have been reading while you talked with Ritta.
How did you get her off?

FRANCESCA. By some device.
She will not come again.

PAOLO. I hate the girl:
She seems to stand between me and the light.
And now for the romance. Where left we off?

FRANCESCA. Where Lancelot and Queen Guenevra strayed
Along the forest, in the youth of May.
You marked the figure of the birds that sang
Their melancholy farewell to the sun—
Rich in his loss, their sorrow glorified—
Like gentle mourners o'er a great man's grave.
Was it not there? No, no; 'twas where they sat
Down on the bank, by one impulsive wish
That neither uttered.

PAOLO. [*Turning over the book.*] Here it is. [*Reads.*]
"So sat
Guenevra and Sir Lancelot"—'Twere well
To follow them in that. [*They sit upon a bank.*

FRANCESCA. I listen: read.
Nay, do not; I can wait, if you desire.

PAOLO. My dagger frets me; let me take it off. [*Rises.*]
In thoughts of love, we'll lay our weapons by.
[*Lays aside his dagger, and sits again.*]
Draw closer: I am weak in voice to-day. [*Reads*]
"So sat Guenevra and Sir Lancelot,
Under the blaze of the descending sun,
But all his cloudy splendours were forgot.
Each bore a thought, the only secret one,
Which each had hidden from the other's heart,
Both with sweet mystery well-nigh overrun.
Anon, Sir Lancelot, with gentle start,
Put by the ripples of her golden hair,
Gazing upon her with his lips apart.
He marvelled human thing could be so fair;
Essayed to speak; but in the very deed,
His words expired of self-betrayed despair.
Little she helped him, at his direst need,
Roving her eyes o'er hill, and wood, and sky,

Peering intently at the meanest weed;
  Ay, doing aught but look in Lancelot's eye.
Then, with the small pique of her velvet shoe,
  Uprooted she each herb that blossomed nigh;
Or strange wild figures in the dust she drew;
  Until she felt Sir Lancelot's arm around
Her waist, upon her cheek his breath like dew.
  While through his fingers timidly he wound
Her shining locks; and, haply, when he brushed
  Her ivory skin, Guenevra nearly swound:
For where he touched, the quivering surface blushed,
  Firing her blood with most contagious heat,
Till brow, cheek, neck, and bosom, all were flushed.
  Each heart was listening to the other beat.
As twin-born lilies on one golden stalk,
  Drooping with Summer, in warm languor meet,
So met their faces. Down the forest walk
  Sir Lancelot looked—he looked, east, west, north, south—
No soul was nigh, his dearest wish to balk:
  She smiled; he kissed her full upon the mouth."

[*Kisses* FRANCESCA.]

I'll read no more! [*Starts up, dashing down the book.*

FRANCESCA. Paolo!

PAOLO. I am mad!
The torture of unnumbered hours is o'er,
The straining cord has broken, and my heart
Riots in free delirium! O, Heaven!
I struggled with it, but it mastered me!
I fought against it, but it beat me down!
I prayed, I wept, but Heaven was deaf to me;
And every tear rolled backward on my heart,
To blight and poison!

FRANCESCA. And dost thou regret?

PAOLO. The love? No, no! I'd dare it all again,
Its direst agonies and meanest fears,
For that one kiss. Away with fond remorse!
Here, on the brink of ruin, we two stand;
Lock hands with me, and brave the fearful plunge!
Thou canst not name a terror so profound
That I will look or falter from. Be bold!
I know thy love—I knew it long ago—

Trembled and fled from it. But now I clasp
The peril to my breast, and ask of thee
A kindred desperation.

FRANCESCA. [*Throwing herself into his arms.*] Take me all,
Body and soul! The women of our clime
Do never give away but half a heart:
I have not part to give, part to withhold,
In selfish safety. When I saw thee first,
Riding alone amid a thousand men,
Sole in the lustre of thy majesty,
And Guido da Polenta said to me,
"Daughter, behold thy husband!" with a bound
My heart went forth to meet thee. He deceived,
He lied to me—ah! that's the aptest word—
And I believed. Shall I not turn again,
And meet him, craft with craft? Paolo, love,
Thou'rt dull—thou'rt dying like a feeble fire
Before the sunshine. Was it but a blaze,
A flash of glory, and a long, long night?

PAOLO. No, darling, no! You could not bend me back;
My course is onward; but my heart is sick
With coming fears.

FRANCESCA. Away with them! Must I
Teach thee to love? and reinform the ear
Of thy spent passion with some sorcery
To raise the chilly dead?

PAOLO. Thy lips have not
A sorcery to rouse me as this spell. [*Kisses her*

FRANCESCA. I give thy kisses back to thee again:
And, like a spendthrift, only ask of thee
To take while I can give.

PAOLO. Give, give forever!
Have we not touched the height of human bliss?
And if the sharp rebound may hurl us back
Among the prostrate, did we not soar once?—
Taste heavenly nectar, banquet with the gods
On high Olympus? If they cast us, now,
Amid the furies, shall we not go down
With rich ambrosia clinging to our lips,
And richer memories settled in our hearts?
Francesca.

FRANCESCA. Love?
PAOLO. The sun is sinking low
Upon the ashes of his fading pyre,
And gray possesses the eternal blue;
The evening star is stealing after him,
Fixed, like a beacon, on the prow of night;
The world is shutting up its heavy eye
Upon the stir and bustle of to-day;—
On what shall it awake?
FRANCESCA. On love that gives
Joy at all seasons, changes night to day,
Makes sorrow smile, plucks out the barbéd dart
Of moaning anguish, pours celestial balm
In all the gaping wounds of earth, and lulls
The nervous fancies of unsheltered fear
Into a slumber sweet as infancy's!
On love that laughs at the impending sword,
And puts aside the shield of caution: cries,
To all its enemies, "Come, strike me now!—
Now, while I hold my kingdom, while my crown
Of amaranth and myrtle is yet green,
Undimmed, unwithered; for I cannot tell
That I shall e'er be happier!" Dear Paolo,
Would you lapse down from misery to death,
Tottering through sorrow and infirmity?
Or would you perish at a single blow,
Cut off amid your wildest revelry,
Falling among the wine-cups and the flowers,
And tasting Bacchus when your drowsy sense
First gazed around eternity? Come, love!
The present whispers joy to us; we'll hear
The voiceless future when its turn arrives.
PAOLO. Thou art a siren. Sing, forever sing;
Hearing thy voice, I cannot tell what fate
Thou hast provided when the song is o'er;—
But I will venture it.
FRANCESCA. In, in, my love! [*Exeunt.*

PEPE *steals from behind the bushes.*

PEPE. O, brother Lanciotto!—O, my stars!—
If this thing lasts, I simply shall go mad!
[*Laughs, and rolls on the ground.*]

O Lord! to think my pretty lady puss
Had tricks like this, and we ne'er know of it!
I tell you, Lanciotto, you and I
Must have a patent for our foolery!
"She smiled; he kissed her full upon the mouth!"—
There's the beginning; where's the end of it?
O poesy! debauch thee only once,
And thou'rt the greatest wanton in the world!
O cousin Lanciotto—ho, ho, ho! [*Laughing.*]
Can a man die of laughter? Here we sat;
Mistress Francesca so demure and calm;
Paolo grand, poetical, sublime!—
Eh! what is this? Paolo's dagger? Good!
Here is more proof, sweet cousin Broken-back.
"In thoughts of love, we'll lay our weapons by!"
[*Mimicking* PAOLO.]
That's very pretty! Here's its counterpart:
In thoughts of hate, we'll pick them up again!
[*Takes the dagger.*]
Now for my soldier, now for crook-backed Mars!
Ere long all Rimini will be ablaze.
He'll kill me? Yes: what then? That's nothing new,
Except to me; I'll bear for custom's sake.
More blood will follow; like the royal sun,
I shall go down in purple. Fools for luck;
The proverb holds like iron. I must run,
Ere laughter smother me.—O, ho, ho, ho! [*Exit, laughing.*

SCENE II.

A Camp among the Hills. Before LANCIOTTO'S *tent. Enter, from the tent,* LANCIOTTO.

LANCIOTTO. The camp is strangely quiet. Not a sound
Breaks nature's high solemnity. The sun
Repeats again his every-day decline;
Yet all the world looks sadly after him,
As if the customary sight were new.
Yon moody sentinel goes slowly by,
Through the thick mists of evening, with his spear
Trailed at a funeral hold. Long shadows creep,

From things beyond the furthest range of sight,
Up to my very feet. These mystic shades
Are of the earth; the light that causes them,
And teaches us the quick comparison,
Is all from heaven. Ah! restless man might crawl
With patience through his shadowy destiny,
If he were senseless to the higher light
Towards which his soul aspires. How grand and vast
Is yonder show of heavenly pageantry!
How mean and narrow is the earthly stand
From which we gaze on it! Magnificent,
O God, art thou amid the sunsets! Ah!
What heart in Rimini is softened now,
Towards my defects, by this grand spectacle?
Perchance, Paolo now forgives the wrong
Of my hot spleen. Perchance, Francesca now
Wishes me back, and turns a tenderer eye
On my poor person and ill-mannered ways;
Fashions excuses for me, schools her heart
Through duty into love, and ponders o'er
The sacred meaning in the name of wife.
Dreams, dreams! Poor fools, we squander love away
On thankless borrowers; when bankrupt quite,
We sit and wonder of their honesty.
Love, take a lesson from the usurer,
And never lend but on security.
Captain!

Enter a CAPTAIN.

CAPTAIN. My lord.
LANCIOTTO. They worsted us to-day.
CAPTAIN. Not much, my lord.
LANCIOTTO. With little loss, indeed.
Their strength is in position. Mark you, sir.
[*Draws on the ground with his sword.*]
Here is the pass; it opens towards the plain,
With gradual widening, like a lady's fan.
The hills protect their flank on either hand;
And, as you see, we cannot show more front
Than their advance may give us. Then, the rocks
Are sorry footing for our horse. Just here,
Close in against the left-hand hills, I marked

A strip of wood, extending down the gorge:
Behind that wood dispose your force ere dawn.
I shall begin the onset, then give ground,
And draw them out; while you, behind the wood,
Must steal along, until their flank and rear
Oppose your column. Then set up a shout,
Burst from the wood, and drive them on our spears.
They have no outpost in the wood, I know;
'Tis too far from their centre. On the morrow,
When they are flushed with seeming victory,
And think my whole division in full rout,
They will not pause to scrutinize the wood;
So you may enter boldly. We will use
The heart to-day's repulse has given to them,
For our advantage. Do you understand?

CAPTAIN. Clearly, my lord.

LANCIOTTO. If they discover you,
Before you gain your point, wheel, and retreat
Upon my rear. If your attack should fail
To strike them with a panic, and they turn
In too great numbers on your small command,
Scatter your soldiers through the wood:
Let each seek safety for himself.

CAPTAIN. I see.

LANCIOTTO. Have Pluto shod; he cast a shoe to-day:
Let it be done at once. My helmet, too,
Is worn about the lacing; look to that.
Where is my armourer?

CAPTAIN. At his forge.

LANCIOTTO. Your charge
Must be at sunrise—just at sunrise, sir—
Neither before nor after. You must march
At moonset, then, to gain the point ere dawn.
That is enough.

CAPTAIN. Good-even! [*Going.*

LANCIOTTO. Stay, stay, stay!
My sword-hilt feels uneasy in my grasp; [*Gives his sword.*]
Have it repaired; and grind the point. Strike hard!
I'll teach these Ghibelins a lesson. [*Loud laughter within.*]
Ha!
What is that clamour?

Enter hastily PEPE, *tattered and travel-stained.*

PEPE. News from Rimini! [*Falls exhausted.*

LANCIOTTO. Is that you, Pepe? Captain, a good-night!
[*Exit* CAPTAIN.]
I never saw you in such straits before.
Wit without words!

PEPE. That's better than—O!—O!— [*Panting.*]
Words without wit.

LANCIOTTO. [*Laughing.*] You'll die a jester, Pepe.

PEPE. If so, I'll leave the needy all my wit.
You, you shall have it, cousin.—O! O! O! [*Panting.*]
Those devils in the hills, the Ghibelins,
Ran me almost to death. My lord—ha! ha! [*Laughing.*]
It all comes back to me—O! Lord 'a mercy!—
The garden, and the lady, and the Count!
Not to forget the poetry—ho! ho! [*Laughing.*]
O! cousin Lanciotto, such a wife,
And such a brother! Hear me, ere I burst!

LANCIOTTO. You're pleasant, Pepe!

PEPE. Am I?—Ho! ho! ho! [*Laughing.*]
You ought to be; your wife's a——

LANCIOTTO. What?

PEPE. A lady—
A lady, I suppose, like all the rest.
I am not in their secrets. Such a fellow
As Count Paolo is your man for that.
I'll tell you something, if you'll swear a bit.

LANCIOTTO. Swear what?

PEPE. First, swear to listen till the end.—
O! you may rave, curse, howl, and tear your hair;
But you must listen.

LANCIOTTO. For your jest's sake? Well.

PEPE. You swear?

LANCIOTTO. I do.

PEPE. Next, swear to know the truth.

LANCIOTTO. The truth of a fool's story!

PEPE. You mistake.
Now, look you, cousin! You have often marked—
I know, for I have seen—strange glances pass
Between Paolo and your lady wife.—

LANCIOTTO. Ha! Pepe!

PEPE. Now I touch you to the quick.
I know the reason of those glances.

LANCIOTTO. Ha!
Speak! or I'll throttle you! [*Seizes him.*

PEPE. Your way is odd.
Let go my gullet, and I'll talk you deaf.
Swear my last oath: only to know the truth.

LANCIOTTO. But that may trouble me.

PEPE. Your honour lies—
Your precious honour, cousin Chivalry—
Lies bleeding with a terrible great gash,
Without its knowledge. Swear!

LANCIOTTO. My honour? Speak!

PEPE. You swear?

LANCIOTTO. I swear. Your news is ill, perchance?

PEPE. Ill! would I bring it else? Am I inclined
To run ten leagues with happy news for you?
O, Lord, that's jolly!

LANCIOTTO. You infernal imp,
Out with your story, ere I strangle you!

PEPE. Then take a fast hold on your two great oaths,
To steady tottering manhood, and attend.
Last eve, about this hour, I took a stroll
Into the garden.—Are you listening, cousin?

LANCIOTTO. I am all ears.

PEPE. Why, so an ass might say.

LANCIOTTO. Will you be serious?

PEPE. Wait a while, and we
Will both be graver than a church-yard. Well,
Down the long walk, towards me, came your wife,
With Count Paolo walking at her side.
It was a pretty sight, and so I stepped
Into the bushes. Ritta came with them;
And Lady Fanny had a grievous time
To get her off. That made me curious.
Anon, the pair sat down upon a bank,
To read a poem;—the tenderest romance,
All about Lancelot and Queen Guenevra.
The Count read well—I'll say that much for him—
Only he stuck too closely to the text,

Got too much wrapped up in the poesy,
And played Sir Lancelot's actions, out and out,
On Queen Francesca. Nor in royal parts
Was she so backward. When he struck the line—
"She smiled; he kissed her full upon the mouth;"
Your lady smiled, and, by the saints above,
Paolo carried out the sentiment!
Can I not move you?

LANCIOTTO. With such trash as this?
And so you ran ten leagues to tell a lie?—
Run home again.

PEPE. I am not ready yet.
After the kiss, up springs our amorous Count,
Flings Queen Guenevra and Sir Lancelot
Straight to the devil; growls and snaps his teeth,
Laughs, weeps, howls, dances; talks about his love,
His madness, suffering, and the Lord knows what,
Bullying the lady like a thief. But she,
All this hot time, looked cool and mischievous;
Gave him his halter to the very end;
And when he calmed a little, up she steps
And takes him by the hand. You should have seen
How tame the furious fellow was at once!
How he came down, snivelled, and cowed to her,
And fell to kissing her again! It was
A perfect female triumph! Such a scene
A man might pass through life and never see.
More sentiment then followed—buckets full
Of washy words, not worth my memory.
But all the while she wound his Countship up,
Closer and closer; till at last—tu!—wit!—
She scoops him up, and off she carries him,
Fish for her table! Follow, if you can;
My fancy fails me. All this time you smile!

LANCIOTTO. You should have been a poet, not a fool.

PEPE. I might be both.

LANCIOTTO. You made no record, then?
Must this fine story die for want of ink?
Left you no trace in writing?

PEPE. None.

LANCIOTTO. Alas!
Then you have told it? 'Tis but stale, my boy;
I'm second hearer.

PEPE. You are first, in faith.

LANCIOTTO. In truth?

PEPE. In sadness. You have got it fresh?
I had no time; I itched to reach your ear.
Now go to Rimini, and see yourself.
You'll find them in the garden. Lovers are
Like walking ghosts, they always haunt the spot
Of their misdeeds.

LANCIOTTO. But have I heard you out?
You told me all?

PEPE. All; I have nothing left.

LANCIOTTO. Why, you brain-stricken idiot, to trust
Your story and your body in my grasp! [*Seizes him.*

PEPE. Unhand me, cousin!

LANCIOTTO. When I drop you, Pepe,
You'll be at rest.

PEPE. I will betray you—O!

LANCIOTTO. Not till the judgment day. [*They struggle.*

PEPE. [*Drawing* PAOLO's *dagger.*] Take that!

LANCIOTTO. [*Wresting the dagger from him.*] Well meant,
But poorly done! Here's my return. [*Stabs him.*

PEPE. O! beast! [*Falls.*]
This I expected; it is naught—Ha! ha! [*Laughing.*]
I'll go to sleep; but you—what will you bear!
Hunchback, come here!

LANCIOTTO. Fie! say your prayers.

PEPE. Hark, hark!
Paolo hired me, swine, to murder you.

LANCIOTTO. That is a lie; you never cared for gold.

PEPE. He did, I say! I'll swear to it, by heaven!
Do you believe me?

LANCIOTTO. No!

PEPE. You lie! you lie!
Look at the dagger, cousin—Ugh!—good-night! [*Dies.*

LANCIOTTO. O! horrible! It was a gift of mine—
He never laid it by. Speak, speak, fool, speak!
[*Shakes the body.*]
How didst thou get it?—speak! Thou'rt warm—not dead—

Thou hast a tongue—O! speak! Come, come, a jest—
Another jest from those thin mocking lips!
Call me a cripple—hunchback—what thou wilt;
But speak to me! He cannot. Now, by heaven,
I'll stir this business till I find the truth!
Am I a fool? It is a silly lie,
Coined by yon villain with his last base breath.
What ho! without there!

Enter CAPTAIN *and Soldiers.*

CAPTAIN. Did you call, my lord?
LANCIOTTO. Did Heaven thunder? Are you deaf, you louts?
Saddle my horse! What are you staring at?
Is it your first look at a dead man? Well,
Then look your fill. Saddle my horse, I say!
Black Pluto—stir! Bear that assassin hence.
Chop him to pieces, if he move. My horse!
CAPTAIN. My lord, he's shoeing.
LANCIOTTO. Did I ask for shoes?
I want my horse. Run, fellow, run! Unbarbed—
My lightest harness on his back. Fly, fly! [*Exit a* SOLDIER.]
[*The others pick up the body.*]
Ask him, I pray you, if he did not lie!
CAPTAIN. The man is dead, my lord.
LANCIOTTO. [*Laughing.*] Then do not ask him!
[*Exeunt* SOLDIERS *with the body.*]
By Jupiter, I shall go mad, I think! [*Walks about.*
CAPTAIN. Something disturbs him. Do you mark the spot
Of purple on his brow? [*Apart to a* SOLDIER.
SOLDIER. Then blood must flow.
LANCIOTTO. Boy, boy! [*Enter a* PAGE.] My cloak and riding staff. Quick, quick!
How you all lag! [*Exit* PAGE.] I ride to Rimini.
Skirmish to-morrow. Wait till my return—
I shall be back at sundown. You shall see
What slaughter is then!
CAPTAIN. Ho! turn out a guard!—
LANCIOTTO. I wish no guard; I ride alone.
[*Re-enter* PAGE, *with a cloak and staff.*]
[*Taking them.*] Well done!
Thou art a pretty boy.—And now my horse!

Enter a SOLDIER.

SOLDIER. Pluto is saddled—
LANCIOTTO. 'Tis a damned black lie!
SOLDIER. Indeed, my lord—
LANCIOTTO. O! comrade, pardon me:
I talk at random. What, Paolo too,—
A boy whom I have trotted on my knee!
Poh! I abuse myself by such a thought.
Francesca may not love me, may love him—
Indeed she ought; but when an angel comes
To play the wanton on this filthy earth,
Then I'll believe her guilty. Look you, sir!
Am I quite calm?
CAPTAIN. Quite calm, my lord.
LANCIOTTO. You see
No trace of passion on my face?—No sign
Of ugly humours, doubts, or fears, or aught
That may disfigure God's intelligence?
I have a grievous charge against you, sir,
That may involve your life; and if you doubt
The candour of my judgment, choose your time:
Shall I arraign you now?
CAPTAIN. Now, if you please.
I'll trust my cause to you and innocence
At any time. I am not conscious—
LANCIOTTO. Pshaw!
I try myself, not you. And I am calm—
That is your verdict—and dispassionate?
CAPTAIN. So far as I can judge.
LANCIOTTO. 'Tis well, 'tis well!
Then I will ride to Rimini. Good-night! [*Exit.*

The others look after him amazedly, and exeunt.

SCENE III.

Rimini. The Garden of the Castle. Enter PAOLO *and* FRANCESCA.

FRANCESCA. Thou hast resolved?
PAOLO. I've sworn it.
FRANCESCA. Ah, you men
Can talk of love and duty in a breath;
Love while you like, forget when you are tired,

And salve your falsehood with some wholesome saw;
But we, poor women, when we give our hearts,
Give all, lose all, and never ask it back.

PAOLO. What couldst thou ask for that I have not given?
With love I gave thee manly probity,
Innocence, honour, self-respect, and peace.
Lanciotto will return, and how shall I—
O! shame, to think of it!—how shall I look
My brother in the face? take his frank hand?
Return his tender glances? I should blaze
With guilty blushes.

FRANCESCA. Thou canst forsake me, then,
To spare thyself a little bashful pain?
Paolo, dost thou know what 'tis for me,
A woman—nay, a dame of highest rank—
To lose my purity? to walk a path
Whose slightest slip may fill my ear with sounds
That hiss me out to infamy and death?
Have I no secret pangs, no self-respect,
No husband's look to bear? O! worse than these,
I must endure his loathsome touch; be kind
When he would dally with his wife, and smile
To see him play thy part. Pah! sickening thought!
From that thou art exempt. Thou shalt not go!
Thou dost not love me!

PAOLO. Love thee! Standing here,
With countless miseries upon my head,
I say, my love for thee grows day by day.
It palters with my conscience, blurs my thoughts
Of duty, and confuses my ideas
Of right and wrong. Ere long, it will persuade
My shaking manhood that all this is just.

FRANCESCA. Let it! I'll blazon it to all the world,
Ere I will lose thee. Nay, if I had choice,
Between our love and my lost innocence,
I tell thee calmly, I would dare again
The deed which we have done. O! thou art cruel
To fly me, like a coward, for thy ease.
When thou art gone, thou'lt flatter thy weak heart
With hopes and speculations; and thou'lt swear

I suffer naught, because thou dost not see.
I will not live to bear it!
PAOLO. Die,—'twere best;
'Tis the last desperate comfort of our sin.
FRANCESCA. I'll kill myself!
PAOLO. And so would I, with joy;
But crime has made a craven of me. O!
For some good cause to perish in! Something
A man might die for, looking in God's face;
Not slinking out of life with guilt like mine
Piled on the shoulders of a suicide!
FRANCESCA. Where wilt thou go?
PAOLO. I care not; anywhere
Out of this Rimini. The very things
That made the pleasures of my innocence
Have turned against me. There is not a tree,
Nor house, nor church, nor monument, whose face
Took hold upon my thoughts, that does not frown
Balefully on me. From their marble tombs
My ancestors scowl at me; and the night
Thickens to hear their hisses. I would pray,
But heaven jeers at it. Turn where'er I will,
A curse pursues me.
FRANCESCA. Heavens! O, say not so!
I never cursed thee, love; I never moved
My little finger, ere I looked to thee
For my instruction.
PAOLO. But my gentleness
Seems to reproach me; and, instead of joy,
It whispers horror!
FRANCESCA. Cease! cease!
PAOLO. I must go.
FRANCESCA. And I must follow. All that I call life
Is bound in thee. I could endure for thee
More agonies than thou canst catalogue—
For thy sake, love—bearing the ill for thee!
With thee, the devils could not so contrive
That I would blench or falter from my love!
Without thee, heaven were torture!
PAOLO. I must go. [*Going.*
FRANCESCA. O! no—Paolo—dearest!— [*Clinging to him.*

PAOLO. Loose thy hold!
'Tis for thy sake, and Lanciotto's; I
Am as a cipher in the reckoning.
I have resolved. Thou canst but stretch the time.
Keep me to-day, and I will fly to-morrow—
Steal from thee like a thief. [*Struggles with her.*

FRANCESCA. Paolo—love—
Indeed, you hurt me!—Do not use me thus!
Kill me, but do not leave me. I will laugh—
A long, gay, ringing laugh—if thou wilt draw
Thy pitying sword, and stab me to the heart!

[*Enter* LANCIOTTO *behind.*]

Nay, then, one kiss!

LANCIOTTO. [*Advancing between them.*] Take it: 'twill be the last.

PAOLO. Lo! Heaven is just!

FRANCESCA. The last! so be it. [*Kisses* PAOLO.

LANCIOTTO. Ha!
Dare you these tricks before my very face?

FRANCESCA. Why not? I've kissed him in the sight of heaven;
Are you above it?

PAOLO. Peace, Francesca, peace!

LANCIOTTO. Paolo—why, thou sad and downcast man,
Look up! I have some words to speak with thee.
Thou art not guilty?

PAOLO. Yes, I am. But she
Has been betrayed; so she is innocent.
Her father tampered with her. I—

FRANCESCA. 'Tis false!
The guilt is mine. Paolo was entrapped
By love and cunning. I am shrewder far
Than you suspect.

PAOLO. Lanciotto, shut thy ears;
She would deceive thee.

LANCIOTTO. Silence, both of you!
Is guilt so talkative in its defense?
Then, let me make you judge and advocate
In your own cause. You are not guilty?

PAOLO. Yes.

LANCIOTTO. Deny it—but a word—say no. Lie, lie!
And I'll believe.

PAOLO. I dare not.

LANCIOTTO. Lady, you?

FRANCESCA. If I might speak for him—

LANCIOTTO. It cannot be:
Speak for yourself. Do you deny your guilt?

FRANCESCA. No! I assert it; but—

LANCIOTTO. In heaven's name, hold!
Will neither of you answer no to me?
A nod, a hint, a sign, for your escape.
Bethink you, life is centred in this thing.
Speak! I will credit either. No reply?
What does your crime deserve?

PAOLO. Death.

FRANCESCA. Death to both.

LANCIOTTO. Well said! You speak the law of Italy;
And by the dagger you designed for me,
In Pepe's hand,—your bravo?

PAOLO. It is false!
If you received my dagger from his hand,
He stole it.

LANCIOTTO. There, sweet heaven, I knew! And now
You will deny the rest? You see, my friends,
How easy of belief I have become!—
How easy 'twere to cheat me!

PAOLO. No; enough!
I will not load my groaning spirit more;
A lie would crush it.

LANCIOTTO. Brother, once you gave
Life to this wretched piece of workmanship,
When my own hand resolved its overthrow.
Revoke the gift. [*Offers to stab himself.*

PAOLO. [*Preventing him.*] Hold, homicide!

LANCIOTTO. But think,
You and Francesca may live happily,
After my death, as only lovers can.

PAOLO. Live happily, after a deed like this!

LANCIOTTO. Now, look ye! there is not one hour of life
Among us three. Paolo, you are armed—

You have a sword, I but a dagger: see!
I mean to kill you.

FRANCESCA. [*Whispers to* PAOLO.] Give thy sword to me.

PAOLO. Away! thou'rt frantic. I will never lift
This wicked hand against thee.

LANCIOTTO. Coward, slave!
Art thou so faint? Does Malatesta's blood
Run in thy puny veins? Take that! [*Strikes him.*

PAOLO. And more:
Thou canst not offer more than I will bear.

LANCIOTTO. Paolo, what a craven has thy guilt
Transformed thee to! Why, I have seen the time
When thou'dst have struck at heaven for such a thing!
Art thou afraid?

PAOLO. I am.

LANCIOTTO. O! infamy!
Can man sink lower? I will wake thee, though:—
Thou shalt not die a coward. See! look here!
[*Stabs* FRANCESCA.

FRANCESCA. O!—O!— [*Falls.*

PAOLO. Remorseless man, dare you do this,
And hope to live? Die, murderer!
[*Draws, rushes at him, but pauses.*

LANCIOTTO. Strike, strike!
Ere thy heart fail.

PAOLO. I cannot. [*Throws away his sword.*

LANCIOTTO. Dost thou see
Yon bloated spider—hideous as myself—
Climbing aloft, to reach that wavering twig?
When he has touched it, one of us must die.
Here is the dagger.—Look at me, I say!
Keep your eyes from that woman! Look, think, choose!—
Turn here to me: thou shalt not look at her!

PAOLO. O, heaven!

LANCIOTTO. 'Tis done!

PAOLO. [*Struggling with him.*] O! Lanciotto, hold!
Hold, for thy sake! Thou wilt repent this deed.

LANCIOTTO. I know it.

FRANCESCA. [*Rising.*] Help!—O! murder!—help, help, help!
[*She totters towards them, and falls.*

LANCIOTTO. Our honour, boy. [*Stabs* PAOLO; *he falls.*

FRANCESCA. Paolo!

PAOLO. Hark! she calls.
I pray thee, brother, help me to her side.

[LANCIOTTO *helps him to* FRANCESCA.

LANCIOTTO. Why, there!

PAOLO. God bless thee!

LANCIOTTO. Have I not done well?
What were the honour of the Malatesti,
With such a living slander fixed to it?
Cripple! that's something—cuckold! that is damned!
You blame me?

PAOLO. No.

LANCIOTTO. You, lady?

FRANCESCA. No, my lord.

LANCIOTTO. May God forgive you! We are even now:
Your blood has cleared my honour, and our name
Shines to the world as ever.

PAOLO O!—O!—

FRANCESCA. Love,
Art suffering?

PAOLO. But for thee.

FRANCESCA. Here, rest thy head
Upon my bosom. Fie upon my blood!
It stains thy ringlets. Ha! he dies! Kind saints,
I was first struck, why cannot I die first?
Paolo, wake!—God's mercy! wilt thou go
Alone—without me? Prithee, strike again!
Nay, I am better—love—now—O! [*Dies.*

LANCIOTTO. [*Sinks upon his knees.*] Great heaven!

MALATESTA. [*Without.*] This way, I heard the cries.

Enter with GUIDO, ATTENDANTS, *&c.*

GUIDO. O! horrible!

MALATESTA. O! bloody spectacle! Where is thy brother?

LANCIOTTO. So Cain was asked. Come here, old men! You shrink
From two dead bodies and a pool of blood—
You soldiers, too! Come here!

[*Drags* MALATESTA *and* GUIDO *forward.*

MALATESTA. O!—O!—

LANCIOTTO. You groan!
What must I do, then? Father, here it is,—
The blood of Guido mingled with our own,
As my old nurse predicted. And the spot
Of her infernal baptism burns my brain
Till reason shudders! Down, upon your knees!
Ay, shake them harder, and perchance they'll wake.
Keep still! Kneel, kneel! You fear them? I shall prowl
About these bodies till the day of doom.

MALATESTA. What hast thou done?

GUIDO. Francesca!—O! my child!

LANCIOTTO. Can howling make this sight more terrible?
Peace! You disturb the angels up in heaven,
While they are hiding from this ugly earth.
Be satisfied with what you see. You two
Began this tragedy, I finished it.
Here, by these bodies, let us reckon up
Our crimes together. Why, how still they lie!
A moment since, they walked, and talked, and kissed!
Defied me to my face, dishonoured me!
They had the power to do it then; but now,
Poor souls, who'll shield them in eternity?
Father, the honour of our house is safe:
I have the secret. I will to the wars,
And do more murders, to eclipse this one.
Back to the battles; there I breathe in peace;
And I will take a soldier's honour back.—
Honour! what's that to me now? Ha! ha! ha! [*Laughing.*]
A great thing, father! I am very ill.
I killed thy son for honour: thou mayst chide.
O God! I cannot cheat myself with words!
I loved him more than honour—more than life—
This man, Paolo—this stark, bleeding corpse!
Here let me rest, till God awake us all!

[*Falls on* PAOLO'S *body.*

LOVE IN '76

AN INCIDENT OF THE REVOLUTION

Oliver Bell Bunce

OLIVER BELL BUNCE

(1828–1890)

The name of Oliver Bell Bunce is not prominently connected with the American Theatre. Authorities have taken little or no trouble to unearth his association with the plays and players of his time—the mid-period of the nineteenth century. Yet they all agree that, as illustration of "parlour comedy," his "Love in '76" is a satisfactory example of sprightliness and fresh inventiveness. For this reason, the small comedietta is included in the present collection. It challenges comparison with Royall Tyler's "The Contrast" for manner, and its volatile spirit involved in the acting the good services of such estimable players as Laura Keene, Stoddart, and Ringgold. In the cast also was J. G. Burnett, author of "Blanche of Brandywine," a dramatization of a novel by George Lippard, also produced by Laura Keene.

"Love in '76" was given its première at Laura Keene's Theatre, New York, on February 28, 1857, for the benefit of the Shirt Sewers' Union; and was the second offering of a double bill beginning with "Faust and Marguerite." Though the critiques of the time recognized in it a "nice little play," they balked at what was considered to be a foolish nomenclature, "Comedietta." What was liked about it, particularly, was the absence of patriotic fustian, for the national drama of the time seems to have been loaded down with long flights of fancy on the subject of liberty. Others hailed it as smart in the social sense. As late as March 31, 1892, the little play was revived by amateurs for the benefit of a monument to be erected over the neglected grave of Washington's mother.

This was not the first time Bunce had appeared as a playwright. There had been seen, on June 10, 1850, at the New York Bowery Theatre, a tragedy entitled "Marco Bozzaris; or, The Grecian Hero," and in the cast were J. Wallack, Jr., and his wife, together with John Gilbert. It was not based on the poem by Fitz-Greene Halleck, but, for its colour and plot, Bunce went direct to history. For Wallack he also wrote a tragedy, entitled "Fate; or, The Prophecy," and, according to Hutton, during the summer of 1848, the Denin Sisters produced his "Morning of Life," at the New York Chatham Theatre.

Such was the extent of Bunce's drama writing. His life was not cast in the dramatic field, but rather in the publishing world. The plays were done in his early manhood. But he was pledged in interest to the theatre, and there are many significant criticisms and descriptions in print which convey an excellent impression of his attitude toward plays, players, and acting.

Bunce was a self-made man, with an excellent grasp of literature, which served him well in his various literary ventures. His mind was cast in channels of originality, and the history of book publishing in New York must needs consider the numerous suggestions, which, as literary adviser at different times for the houses of Harper and Appleton, he saw to successful fruition. In 1872, he became Editor of *Appleton's Journal*, and it is to the files of this magazine we must turn to extract his frank reaction to the theatre of his day. He wrote novels, stories, essays, editorials, everything to win him the name of journalist; once he had a publishing house of his own, doing business under the firm name of Bunce & Co. He was always cordial toward every move to further the literary interest of the country, and was among the first to welcome the founding of the Authors Club. It may be that his "Love in '76" was a by-product of a book written by him, in 1852, and called "Romance of the Revolution."

Bunce wrote well on theatrical matters; he is much more vivid and human than many a better-known critic. Here, for instance, is an impression of the old Park Theatre, New York, in 1846.

"That was the time," he writes in "The Editor's Table" of *Appleton's Journal* for October, 1880, "when the theatre had a pit, where critics and wiseacres were wont to assemble and utter oracular things about the plays and the performers. The actors were in those days afraid of the Pit, especially at the Park, of the fourth bench from the orchestra, where the magnates of the pen sat watchful, and where old Nestors of the drama delivered their verdicts in terms that no one dared to gainsay. The Pit was entered by cellar steps, and through a half-lighted, subterranean passage. Decorative art, as we see it now in the full bloom of the Madison Square auditorium and Mr. Daly's lobby, had not even given a hint of its coming."

In *The Galaxy* for February, 1868, Bunce ventures to survey "Some of Our Actors" from the standpoint of deploring the pre-Raphaelite realism of the modern school. He scored the attempted "truth" and "fidelity" of Matilda Heron, and, in considering Maggie Mitchell's *Fanchon*, he bespoke the cause of ideality, as necessary in *Fanchon* as in *Juliet*. "Modern comedy acting," he declares, "is usually a bright, brisk touch-and-go affair, suited to modern plays; but to the mellow and artistic style of a former generation, it is as the light claret wines, now so much in use, to crusty old port."

Except in the instances of our comedians, like Murdoch, with his "lightness of manner, that grace, which I have described elsewhere as snuffing a candle in a way to make you feel that snuffing candles is the poetry of life;" Harry Placide, with whose retirement went the retirement of *Sir Peter Teazle* and *Sir Harcourt Courtley*, ("When Placide and Gilbert are gone," he writes, "Sheridan will have to be shelved"); Holland, with his intense fun in eccentric bits; Brougham, without whom "The Rivals" is difficult to endure—apart from these the stage of the time, to Bunce, was not all it should be. He valued at their worth the romantic extravagances of the Wallack family; he applauded the sound judgment, and deplored the hard manner of Davenport; he viewed calmly what he regarded to be an overestimation of Edwin Booth—one of the first criticisms of an avowedly negative character I have seen aimed directly at this actor. In other words, Bunce fought hard against the encroachment of the new times upon the acting of his early theatre days. The epitome of his old-time attitude is to be found in *Appleton's Journal* for April 3, 1869. His better mood was to be met with in his discussion of the players of Ellen Tree's type. Here are his words of censure against the new order:

"If we old files are to be believed, the art of acting is dying out, and the very tradition of the stage disappearing. . . . Very likely the spirit, which in painting we call pre-Raphaelism, is obtaining its influence on the stage, and that some of the actors are turning out of doors the traditions and formal mannerisms of the schools, and going back to nature and truth for their inspiration. . . There were very artificial methods, no doubt, among the old actors. but there was also a very consummate knowledge of the art, a great deal of breadth, force and skill, and a finished training, which the new schools do not exhibit. In aiming to be natural, some of our actors seem to have concluded that their profession is not an art. They grow heedless in the delivery of language, weakening or obscuring its meaning, and missing its significance; and in some way lose that rich and mellow colouring that characterized the bygone performers. So marked is this, that some of the old dramatic characters are abandoned altogether, because in the hands of the Realists they fade away into ineffective and colourless forms. The *Sir Peter Teazles* and *Sir Anthony Absolutes* of the old comedy require indispensably the resources of the old art, and no thin, water-gruel realism, so-called, can personate them. In avoiding the declamatory Kembletonianism of the old school, our actors are right enough; but they cannot safely disregard the skill which sharpens and chisels, as it were, the sentences; nor forego the care, study, precision and stern adherence to rules of art, that marked the old stage."

Steeped in such belief, it is small wonder that two of Bunce's plays had characteristics in them to suit a member of the Wallack family. And being such a lover of old English Comedy accounts for some of the spirit of "Love in '76."

His plea, sound in its fundamental championing of the best that has been on our stage, might well be heeded at this time (1920). It is a strong valuation of tradition—the jade who is looked at askance by the amateur players of the "little theatres," and too exacting for the average player on the professional stage.

Bunce was a New Yorker, born in that city, February 8, 1828, and dying there on May 15, 1890.

LAURA KEENE'S
NEW THEATRE,

624 BROADWAY, NEAR HOUSTON STREET.

MISS LAURA KEENE..SOLE LESSEE AND DIRECTRESS
MR. THOMAS BAKER..MUSICAL DIRECTOR

Change of Time. Doors open at half past Six. The performance will commence with the Overture at a quarter past Seven.

BENEFIT
OF THE
SHIRT-SEWERS' UNION

Sixth time of the Dramatic Poem, in three acts, entitled

FAUST AND MARGUERITE

This Drama having been misapprehended by one or two critics, it is respectfully stated that the translation has not been made by a resident dramatist, as inferred, but by the celebrated European scholar and linguist, Jonathan Birch, whose translation has been recognized by Frederick William, of Prussia, as the best rendition of the original of Goethe's Faust ever given in English to the public.

The play has been taken bodily from this translation, published by Black & Armstrong, London, and F. A. Brockhaus, Leipsig, without any alteration other than is necessary to bring it within the bounds of an evening's performance. To produce the poem as written by Goethe, would require at least three nights in performance. By reference to the edition mentioned, it will be seen that there has been no deviation from the original, except as above specified.

The fall of Marguerite, in the poem, is much more sudden than in the play, and, indeed, the exceptions taken generally to the drama concern the original author, Goethe, rather than the translation. Great care has been taken to produce the play with strict fidelity to the author, following in the architecture, costumes and groupings the celebrated *chefs d'œuvres* of REIZSCH, who devoted the best years of his life to illustrate this great work; and it should be added, also, that every note of the music in this piece is from SPOHR.

———ooo———

Music..................by..................**Spohr, arranged by Mr. Thomas Baker**
New Scenery.........by..................**Messrs. Hawthorne and Almy**
New Wardrobe.....by..................**Mr. Bullock and Assistants**
Machinery............by..................**Mr. Smart and Assistants**
Properties and Appointments............by............**Mr. W. Duverna**

Under the personal supervision of

MISS LAURA KEENE.

First time of a New American Comedietta, in two acts, by a Citizen of New York, entitled

LOVE IN '76

SATURDAY EVENING, FEB. 28th, 1857

Will be presented the great Dramatic Poem, by Goethe, translated by Jonathan Birch, Esq., and produced for the SIXTH TIME, as now adopted and arranged for this establishment under the title of

FAUST

AND

MARGUERITE

DISTRIBUTION OF CHARACTERS:

Faust, an aged scholar..Mr. C. Wheatleigh
Mephistophiles ....Mr. George Jordan
Wagner, a student, friend to Faust..Mr. Stoddart
Valentine, a soldier, brother to Marguerite..Mr. Lingham
Brander, a soldier, friend to Valentine..Mr. Alleyne
Frosh..Mr. Hayes
Siebel..Mr. Reeve
Fritz..Mr. Harcourt
Students........................Messrs. Carpenter, Jackson, Carter, Kellog
Altmayer..Mr. McDonall
Beggar..Mr. Benson
Marguerite, a young peasant girl..Miss Laura Keene
Martha, her confidante..Mrs. H. P. Grattan
Lizzie,........................ } Companions of Marguerite { ....Miss Alleyne
Barbara,........................ } Companions of Marguerite { ....Miss Howell
Witch, a creature of Mephistophiles..Mrs. Attwood
Spirits of Good........Miss Howell, Miss Wall, Miss Berkowitz, and Miss Rosa Berkowitz

Peasantry, Chorus of Demons, etc., etc.

SCENERY IN THE DRAMA:

ACT I.

Scene 1st—Faust's Laboratory..By Almy
Scene 2d—Street in Wittenburg..By Hawthorne

ACT II.

. avillion and Garden of Marguerite..By Hawthorne

ACT III.

Sce... t—Street and Cathedral in Wittenburg..By Hawthorne
Scene 2nd—Rocky Glen..By Hawthorne
Scene 3rd—Prison..By Almy
Scene 4th—Street and Cathedral—Apotheosis of Marguerite........................By Hawthorne

---

To conclude for the FIRST TIME, with a New American Comedietta, in TWO ACTS, by a Gentleman of this city, called

LOVE IN '76

Mr. Elsworth..Mr. Stoddart
Lieutenant Harry Elsworth..Mr. Ringgold
Captain Walter Armstrong..Mr. Lingham
Major Cleveland..Mr. Burnett
Captain Arbald..Mr. Benson
Lieutenant Marvin..Mr. Hayes
Apollo Metcalf..Mr. Johnston
John..Mr. Harcourt
Corporal..Mr. Leslie
Soldiers..Messrs Jackson and Kellog
Rose Elsworth..Miss Laura Keene
Kate Elsworth..Miss Alleyne
Bridget..Miss Howell

A Grand Scenic Drama, called THE SONS OF NIGHT, has been in rehearsal, and will be produced immediately.

ADMISSION.

Dress Circle and Parquette..50 Cents
Balcony Seats..........75 Cents | **Orchestra Stalls**..........One Dollar
Family Circle..........25 Cents | **Private Boxes**. Six and Eight Dollars

Box Office open from 8 in the morning throughout the day.

Children in Arms not admitted. This regulation will be rigidly enforced.

Treasurer......Mr. W. W. Gray | **Box Bookkeeper**...Mr. F. N. Cartland

HERALD PRINT.

LOVE IN '76

AN INCIDENT OF THE REVOLUTION

A COMEDIETTA IN TWO ACTS

By OLIVER BUNCE

AS PERFORMED AT LAURA KEENE'S THEATRE
NEW YORK, FEB. 28, 1857

[The acting edition of this play, with the relative positions of the performers on the stage, is published by Samuel French.]

COSTUMES.

Mr. Elsworth.—*Shad-cut brown coat, brown or black breeches, shoe-buckles.*

Lieutenant Harry Elsworth.—*Red, turned up with blue, buff breeches, high boots.*

Captain Armstrong.—*Blue, turned up with buff, white top boots.*

Major Cleveland.—*Red, turned up with white, breeches, high boots.*

Captain Arbald.—*The Same.*

Lieutenant Marvin.—*The Same.*

Apollo Metcalf.—*Gray shad, square-cut suit.*

The Ladies.—*The costumes of the period of '76.*

LOVE IN '76.

ACT I.

SCENE. *The drawing-room in the residence of* MR. EDWARD ELSWORTH. *Garden seen through doors.* ROSE ELSWORTH *occupied at a small table, stitching.* KATE ELSWORTH *stretched languidly upon a sofa, with a book in hand.* MR. EDWARD ELSWORTH *in an easy chair, with newspaper in his lap. Writing materials on table.*

KATE. Oh, dullness! dullness! I do wish Harry was at home, or Sir William would march some of his troops this way! What's the use of an army in the country, if one can't have a dance once in a while?

ROSE. What, indeed! All I desire is, sister, that they should be [*Enter* SERVANT *with letters for* MR. ELSWORTH.] left to the dance! That much they do very well.

KATE. I'm sure, Rose, I can't see what you find in these rebels to admire. As far as my observation has gone, they are only so many boors. There was Captain Arthur. Was there ever such a dunce? He had no manner whatever. He attempted once to walk a minuet with me, and I really thought he was a bear accidentally stumbled into coat and slippers.

ROSE. You're quite right! he never should have got his appointment until he had served a campaign in the drawing-room. If I were the Congress, I'd appoint none who could not bring diplomas from their dancing-masters.

ELSWORTH. Ha? 'pon my word! Very extraordinary news.

[*All coming forward.*

ROSE. What is it, papa?

ELSWORTH. There has been a battle.

ROSE. Is it possible? Oh, where, sir?

ELSWORTH. On Long Island. [*Reading.*] Washington has been defeated—has evacuated the city—is retiring northward. [*Speaking.*] I feel, my daughters, that our situation is becoming here unsafe. We shall be continually exposed to the assaults of marauders. It would be wiser, in the present aspect of affairs, for us to seek a securer residence in New York, now so fortunately in possession of Sir William Howe.

ROSE. I should prefer remaining here.

ELSWORTH. Would it be safe, Rose?

ROSE. Yes, for we neutralize each other. Your loyalty will secure you with the Tories, and my Whiggism will protect us with the other faction.

ELSWORTH. Your Whiggism, Rose? You shock me by such an avowal; and your brother, too, an officer of the King.

KATE. I don't think there is much danger, if Mr. Armstrong is near to protect us.

ELSWORTH. Mr. Armstrong?

KATE. Oh, yes, papa! He's got to be a captain.

ELSWORTH. Not a rebel, I trust.

ROSE. Not a traitor, I thank heaven.

ELSWORTH. You confound terms strangely. A traitor is one false to his king.

ROSE. False to his country, sir. A king is a creature of to-day —your country a thing of immortality.

ELSWORTH. Your King is your sovereign, by divine right and true succession.

ROSE. Then, sir, serve the Stuarts. How came the house of Hanover upon the throne? You see, sir, that if you zealous loyalists could shift off James, we, with less belief in the divine right of kings, can shift off George.

Enter MR. APOLLO METCALF.

METCALF. Good day, Mr. Elsworth. Good day, young ladies. "Good day" all, I may say.

ELSWORTH. Have you any news of the war, Mr. Metcalf?

METCALF. News—plenty of it, and mad. The country is depopulated. There isn't a youth with the first hope of a beard upon his chin, who hasn't gone with young Armstrong, to join the army.

ELSWORTH. Young Armstrong?

METCALF. To be sure, sir. He's turned out a fiery rebel, after all—and a captain, to boot.

ELSWORTH. Heaven bless me, but this is very sad. A promising youth to be led astray! Dear me, dear me! Rose, I am very sorry to say that this is certainly your fault. You have filled him with your wild, radical, and absurd heroic rhapsodies. You have made him disloyal to his King. You have put a dagger in his hand, to stab at the heart of his country. Alas! I see what the end will be—disgrace and death, ignominy and the gallows.

[ROSE *walks back to the window.*

KATE. Mr. Metcalf, how are your little charges? How flourishes the birch?

METCALF. They've all caught the spirit of the rebellion, marm, and are as untractable as bulls. Bless you, there isn't a lad over fourteen who hasn't abandoned his horn-book and gone off with Armstrong. And as for the girls, they're greater rebels than the boys. What do you think, marm? The other day they came marching in procession, and demanded to know on which side I was. I said "God save the King;" whereupon they fell upon me like a swarm of bees, armed with a thousand pins, and so pinched, and pricked, and pulled me, that there wasn't a square inch of my skin that wasn't as full of holes as a ten-year old pin-cushion. And I do believe they never would have stopped if I hadn't cried, "Huzza for Washington!"

ELSWORTH. I hope, sir, that you will not be compelled to follow the example of your scholars, and turn soldier.

METCALF. Never, sir. I content myself with teaching the young idea how to shoot, without indulging in such dangerous practices myself.

ROSE. [*From the window.*] Why, there's Harry—father, Kate—Harry is dismounting at the door.

ELSWORTH. Bless me! Is it possible?

[*All gather around the window.*

KATE. It is, I declare—and how splendid he looks. Harry! Harry!

[*All salute him, and shake their handkerchiefs.*

METCALF. [*Aside to* ROSE.] Hist! Miss Elsworth!

ROSE. Eh!

METCALF. Walter is near—a note—

ROSE. [*Seizing it, and reading hurriedly.*] Will be with you to-day—

KATE. [*Looking towards right, at the window.*] Doesn't he look fine? There's his step in the hall.

[*They all go towards door.* ROSE *conceals* WALTER'S *note.*

HARRY. [*Within.*] Rose, Kate, father!

Enter LIEUTENANT HARRY ELSWORTH. *All gather around him with exclamations of welcome.*

METCALF. [*Aside.*] I'll take occasion to steal down-stairs, and plague Bridget into a kiss or two. Delicious Bridget!

[*Exit* METCALF.

ELSWORTH. Harry! My brave lad!

ROSE. Dear brother!

HARRY. Dear sister! Father!

ELSWORTH. Stand aside, girls. Let me have a look at him. Harry! Harry! You are a splendid-looking fellow, you are. Ha, ha, ha! Your hand, my boy. You look like a soldier, sir.

HARRY. I have good news for you. I have just rode on before to acquaint you that Major Cleveland will honour your roof to-day.

ELSWORTH. He shall be welcome—open doors and open hands.

HARRY. He will remain until to-morrow. Now, girls, some of us young fellows are dying for a dance—can't we extemporize a ball?

ROSE. Good gracious, Harry! You will have to pit coat against coat—where are your ladies?

HARRY. Oh, we'd drum them up. There are a dozen families within as many miles.

ROSE. A mad idea.

HARRY. A wild one, I confess.

ELSWORTH. It would be a suitable festivity in honour of our Long Island victory. Come girls, you have my consent.

Enter SERVANT, *announcing* CAPTAIN ARMSTRONG.

Enter CAPTAIN WALTER ARMSTRONG.

ALL [*but* ROSE]. Captain Armstrong!

ARMSTRONG. Captain Armstrong!

ALL [*but* ROSE]. In the Continental service?

ARMSTRONG. In the Continental service!

ELSWORTH. I am somewhat surprised, sir, at this visit. When you were a loyal gentleman my doors were always open to you—now, in that dress, I cannot consent to receive your visits. In happier moments you were a companion of my daughters—a friend of my son—you have selected a course which must terminate that connection with my family.

ARMSTRONG. You will pardon me, sir, I trust, for this intrusion. I have reached this place with some danger, for these parts abound with a set of fellows who have a fancy for wishing everybody else's skin the colour of their own coats. Mr. Elsworth, my sense of duty has compelled me to pursue a path which has estranged me from your friendship. Let me ask frankly, sir, if it must separate me from one who has honoured me with her consideration and affection?

ELSWORTH. You allude to my daughter—to Rose—

ARMSTRONG. I do, sir.

ELSWORTH. *Mister* Armstrong—for I acknowledge no title bestowed by an unlawful authority—I would rather wed my daughter to a Turk than to one who had so forgotten his duty to his country.

[*Goes up.*—ARMSTRONG *bows.*

HARRY. Walter, we were friends once, but, as His Majesty's servant, I can offer no compromise to a rebel. *Now* you must not think of a union with our family. [*Goes up.*

ROSE. This is nothing but blind prejudice. It has neither sense nor justice. Hear me. That for which you discard him places him higher in my esteem—shows me how worthy he is of the respect and honour of every true woman. My greatest pride is that he to whom I have pledged my hand wears those colours.

ARMSTRONG. Generous girl!

ELSWORTH. Rose, you pain me inexpressibly!

ROSE. I am not a giddy girl, sir. I'm a woman—old enough to know my own heart, and to decide between right and wrong. Walter, go, and carry with you assurances of my unwavering fidelity.

Enter BRIDGET, *hurriedly.*

BRIDGET. Oh, my good gracious! dear me, good gracious! gracious, goodness, me! Such a lot of soldiers—all coming down the road.

ARMSTRONG. Eh? Red or blue?

BRIDGET. Bless me, goodness gracious, you here, Mr. Armstrong? You'd better look out, sir, for they are red coats, and there's a big number of them, too.

ARMSTRONG. I must vanish. [*Running to the window.*] Why, we're surrounded on every side. By Jove, I'm in a trap!

ROSE. What will you do?

ARMSTRONG. To the north of the house. Perhaps I can reach the forest—

BRIDGET. They're all around that way, sir.

HARRY. I wish that you could escape, Walter, without my knowledge. This is the regiment to which I belong. You were foolhardy to venture here.

ARMSTRONG. I believe I'm caged, that's certain. And I've no desire to be caught either, for they bear especial malice against me. If they should know me for the fellow who played a certain trick upon them, an hour's time would suffice for them to make me an ornament to one of your old oaks on the lawn—a style of decoration that might suit their taste, but which wouldn't accord with my fancy.

ROSE. Do they know your person?

ARMSTRONG. From description, probably.

ROSE. We must conceal you, then.

ARMSTRONG. If you've a rat hole into which you can crowd me.

HARRY. I must be ignorant of your movements. I will go and receive them. [*Exit.*

ARMSTRONG. Whose command is it?

ROSE. Major Cleveland's.

ARMSTRONG. Eh? The man of men who itches to get hold of my insignificant person. He has offered £50 for it.

KATE. [*At the window.*] Away! They are dismounting at the door.

ROSE. You, Bridget—I can trust you—quick, to the loft with him.

KATE. [*Still at the window.*] Quick! quick!

ARMSTRONG. Stow me away among your rubbish.

[ROSE *urges them off.* WALTER *snatches a kiss from* ROSE'S *hand as he exits with* BRIDGET.

KATE. I do declare Captain Arbald is below, and I am sadly deranged.

ROSE. Oh, fearfully! Run to your glass, by all means. Set your springes, for these red birds are rare game.

KATE. Sister! But I'll be revenged. [*Exit* KATE.

Enter MAJOR CLEVELAND, *ushered in by* LIEUTENANT ELSWORTH, *who withdraws.*

ELSWORTH. My dear Major Cleveland, let me welcome you zealously to this abode.

CLEVELAND. A great many thanks, my dear Elsworth. I'm delighted to meet so true-hearted a loyalist. We pushed our march to partake of your hospitality. Ah, Miss Elsworth! How shall I express my delight in finding that Time, who deals so inexorably with us, has been induced to favour you. It gives me infinite pleasure, Miss Elsworth, to meet you once again, for the recollection of the occasions we have met previously are bright spots in my memory.

ROSE. Oh, sir, I thank you.

ELSWORTH. And how, sir, comes on the royal cause? Will it be long ere these rebels are taught their duty to their King?

CLEVELAND. Have no apprehensions, my dear Elsworth. Another campaign will scatter them to the mountains, and a live rebel be so great a curiosity, that to cage one and exhibit him would make a showman's fortune.

ROSE. [*Aside.*] If he knew there were a caged one here now!

ELSWORTH. But come, Major Cleveland, where are your companions? I must see why they have not followed you.

CLEVELAND. They are delayed for a moment with the troop. By the way, Miss Elsworth, I believe that there are a couple of gentlemen without, who are old admirers of yours—Captain Arbald and Lieutenant Marvin.

ROSE. Old, Major! You flatter my taste.

CLEVELAND. Why, with beauty I thought the conquest of the morning stale matter by night.

ROSE. Oh, sir, if staleness went to make their age, they would be proverbed instead of Methuselah.

CLEVELAND. They took very much to you.

ROSE. So did the measles, sir.

CLEVELAND. They are desperately enamoured of you—would do any difficult thing—even die for you.

ROSE. So they once told me, but I courtesied, and replied that I should prefer a live rebel to even two dead loyalists.

CLEVELAND. And then—

ROSE. They vowed to live for me. I begged of them to put themselves to no such inconvenience; that I wouldn't trouble them to do anything of the kind; that if they didn't think it worth while to live for themselves, I shouldn't intrude upon any suicidal intention they might entertain.

CLEVELAND. And so they lived—

ROSE. But I had no hand in it; I am innocent; my skirts are clear of the melancholy fact.

CLEVELAND. They are noble gentlemen, Miss Elsworth. You must bear with me if I defend them. They are good soldiers, and fine-looking fellows.

ROSE. For which I thank their tailors.

CLEVELAND. Gay, dashing; brave of heart, and witty of tongue.

ROSE. Then they have been studying the almanac. When I saw them last, they hadn't a grain of wit—not even by scratching.

CLEVELAND. Really, Mr. Elsworth, your daughter has a sharp tongue.

ELSWORTH. It is her humour, sir. Her passes are but play.

CLEVELAND. I'll be sworn her heart is as true as her wit. She is—

ROSE. Rebel, sir, from top to toe!

[*Enter* ARBALD, MARVIN, *and* HARRY.]

Ah, gentlemen, my best welcome. My father will be proud to greet you—

ELSWORTH. And most happy to know you, gentlemen.

[*Enter* SERVANT, *with wine.*]

Major Cleveland, will you do me the honour—

CLEVELAND. Sir, I esteem it an honour. Gentlemen, I hope you will all fill in honour of our host. [*They gather around, fill, and drink to* MR. ELSWORTH.] Fill again, gentlemen, and honour the toast I am going to propose. The ladies! speedy priests and rings.

ROSE. A doubtfül compliment, Major Cleveland.

CLEVELAND. Can you think so?

ROSE. Ay, sir; for marriages, though called matches, are mostly sad patch-work.

CLEVELAND. And the unmarried—

ROSE. Oh, they are even worse. Old maids and old bachelors are the tossed about odds and ends of humanity.

CLEVELAND. [*Going over to her.*] The happiest wit, madam, I ever heard.

ROSE. Captain Arbald, will you grant me your arm? I'm sure you would like a turn in the garden. I shouldn't wonder if my sister were upon the grounds. Lieutenant Marvin, will you go with us? Kate is dying for the sight of a red-coat. [*Exit.*

CLEVELAND. A merry-hearted woman, Mr. Elsworth. There is a touch of sly deviltry in her composition.

ELSWORTH. I fear lest her indiscreet tongue—

CLEVELAND. Not at all, my dear friend! Lieutenant, I have been informed within an hour, that one Captain Armstrong has been seen this day within five miles of this place. On account of his connection with a certain affair, I wouldn't let him escape me at any sacrifice. I have already dispatched dragoons in his pursuit. At earliest dawn I shall expect you to head a detachment in his search. Meanwhile, sir, I should be grateful for an opportunity to repair my toilet.

HARRY. This way, sir; I myself will conduct you to a chamber. [*Exeunt* CLEVELAND *and* HARRY.

ELSWORTH. This is a situation, indeed, for a royalist gentleman! My house filled with the King's officers, and a proscribed rebel concealed above. If discovered, I tremble to think of the consequences. [*Exit.*

Enter ROSE.

ROSE. Thank heaven; I am rid of them. Now to Walter, and learn his full danger.

[*Enter* ARMSTRONG.]

Are you mad? What are you here for? Back to your hiding place at once.

WALTER. No, Rose; I shall not go.

ROSE. Why—what—

WALTER. Hear me, Rose. Ask yourself if it is an honourable course for me, a proscribed and hunted rebel, to suffer myself to be concealed in your father's house when my discovery would involve him in terrible consequences. I cannot consent to expose him to those consequences. I would rather openly deliver myself into the hands of Major Cleveland.

ROSE. Foolish man! You are ruining all. Walter, for my sake go back again. This is a ridiculous and false sense of honour.

WALTER. No, Rose, I am resolved—

ROSE. Walter, I implore you—

[*Enter* MAJOR CLEVELAND.]

[*Aside.*] Ha! Lost! [*Aloud.*] Oh, Major Cleveland, how opportune. Pray let me make you acquainted with Captain Fuller. A friend of my father's, sir—a neighbour. Captain Fuller, Major Cleveland. Allow me to commend you, gentlemen, to each other's better acquaintance.

CLEVELAND. A rebel officer. This is very extraordinary.

ROSE. Let me see you shake hands, gentlemen, for here, you know, you must be friends. If you like to cut each other's throats elsewhere, so be it; but, of course, you sheathe your swords, and swear peace in the presence of a lady.

CLEVELAND. Miss Elsworth well rebukes us. Captain Fuller, for the time being, the red and the blue rejoice under a common auspices—Miss Elsworth smiles.

[*They shake hands ceremoniously.*

ROSE. Now, gentlemen, sit down. You, Major, shall have a seat upon the sofa by my side. Captain Fuller, please, take the chair near you. [*The gentlemen seat themselves.*] Now, you see, I am between you, and shall prevent warfare. I here proclaim a truce. The Captain, Major, wants to join our ball to-night. I have promised him my hand the next after yours.

CLEVELAND. [*Scrutinizing* WALTER *closely.*] I'm quite ready, Miss Elsworth, to laugh at a joke, but really I cannot understand—

ROSE. Why two gentlemen cannot meet under my father's roof, as his guests, and not fall to tearing each other to pieces? Is it the modern way to make war in parlours, instead of the field?

CLEVELAND. Strange, very strange. Your pardon, Captain Fuller, but I cannot help remarking that you closely resemble a description I have received of one Captain Armstrong.

ROSE. Dear me, and who is Captain Armstrong, pray?

CLEVELAND. A rebel, madam.

ROSE. I like him for that.

CLEVELAND. A spy.

ROSE. But what has all this to do with Captain Fuller? I have known the Captain, Major, for some years, and I think you can take my word for it, he is no spy.

CLEVELAND. Do Captain Fuller and Captain Armstrong wear the same colours?

WALTER. All Continental officers wear the same colours.

CLEVELAND. Are they all of the same complexion, height, and [*Rising and going over to him.*] do they all wear the same love tokens? Does Captain Fuller wear Captain Armstrong's sash, worked with Captain Armstrong's name!

WALTER. [*Aside.*] The sash Rose worked and gave me. Fool! fool!

CLEVELAND. Miss Elsworth, I'm under the necessity of a disagreeable duty. I am compelled to consider our truce at an end. Young sir, you are my prisoner.

WALTER. [*Drawing and rushing between the* MAJOR *and the door.*] If you speak aloud or attempt to call aid, I will strike you dead. I shall not yield without resistance. If you molest me, blood will be shed.

CLEVELAND. [*Drawing a pistol.*] I am better armed than you supposed, sir. It would be awkward for any collision to occur in the presence of a lady, and yet I shall not hesitate to do my duty. If you are really Captain Fuller, I shall be very glad to shake hands and drink a glass of wine with you; if Captain Armstrong, you *must* become my prisoner.

ROSE. [*Standing by her chair, trembling.*] Gentlemen! Gentlemen!

WALTER. I have but one reply to make: if you attempt to arrest me, I shall defend myself—and will escape if I can.

[*Several shots fired within.*

Enter MR. METCALF *suddenly, pursued by* TWO SOLDIERS.

CLEVELAND. Ha!

METCALF. [*Not seeing* CLEVELAND, *and rushing up to* WALTER.] Bless me, Captain Armstrong.

CLEVELAND. Oh, then he is Captain Armstrong.

ROSE. [*With great suddenness.*] Captain Fuller, Mr. Metcalf—don't play your jests here—Captain Fuller, sir.

METCALF. Eh! Eh! [*Looking confused from one to another.*] A jest, Captain Fuller—capital—ha, ha, ha—[*Aside to* ROSE.] What mischief have I tumbled into now, and who is that fellow in a very red coat and a very white wig?

ROSE. [*Aside to him.*] Major Cleveland.

METCALF. Major Cleveland! We are all hanged and quartered—though for the matter of that, in my capacity of expounder of the alphabet, I've been quartered—on the neighbourhood, these ten years past. Your obedient servant, sir, your very obedient—

CLEVELAND. That will do, fellow. What was the cause of those shots just now? [*To* SOLDIERS.

METCALF. 'Pon my word, sir, it was the guns.

CLEVELAND. Pshaw!

SOLDIER. This fellow attempted to pass without the countersign.

METCALF. You see, sir, I was just about to enter to call on my friend, Mr. Elsworth, to sip an afternoon glass with him, when a big-booted fellow cried out, halt. Now, sir, the idea of asking a man well in both legs to halt, is preposterous. So I said, and walked on as straight as I could, when bang, bum, whiz, came one, two, three bullets scattering after my hide—

CLEVELAND. Have done, sir. [*To* WALTER.] I am desirous of giving you, sir, every opportunity to disprove your identity with Captain Armstrong. I chance to know that gentleman's handwriting. There is a desk with pen and ink. Will you stand that test?

WALTER. [*Aside to* ROSE.] That would never do. There isn't one of my pot-hooks that wouldn't hang me.

ROSE. [*Quickly.*] Really, Major Cleveland, you might require a more reasonable test. Don't you see the Captain has a rheumatic hand?

CLEVELAND. For a rheumatic hand, Miss Elsworth, he handled his sword somewhat skilfully, just now. You see, sir, resistance is useless. You will resign your sword, I trust.

[*The two* SOLDIERS, *at a sign from* CLEVELAND, *have come up behind* WALTER. *He is seized.*

WALTER. Ha! I am your prisoner, sir.

Enter MR. ELSWORTH *and* HARRY.

ELSWORTH. What's this?

CLEVELAND. I regret to say, my dear Elsworth, that this gentleman must, for a few hours, remain my prisoner. A mere form, sir. He will, doubtless, be free in a few days. I shall have to make use of one of your barns, sir. It is really a pity that the Captain must be deprived of the dance to-night, but I will take care that his confinement shall not be severe.

ROSE. This, sir, is a shameful breach of hospitality. Captain Armstrong is my father's guest, no less than yourself. Every consideration of delicacy and honour requires you to consider him so.

CLEVELAND. Miss Elsworth, I could wish you not to consider me wrong or cruel in this.

ROSE. I judge, sir, by what I see.

CLEVELAND. You are severe.

ROSE. I am glad you find me so.

CLEVELAND. Will you not say peace?

ROSE. War, Major Cleveland, to the last.

ELSWORTH. Daughter, more courtesy.

ROSE. Oh! father, they may chain and bind our poor country, but they cannot find a way to chain a free woman's free tongue.

CLEVELAND. Lieutenant Elsworth, I place the Captain in your charge. Conduct him to a safe place.

HARRY. This is the hard necessity of duty.

ELSWORTH. And this will really be nothing serious?

CLEVELAND. A bagatelle, I do assure you, sir.

WALTER. [*Aside.*] I thank him for calming the fears of the family—but I know how hard it will go with me.

HARRY. Walter—

WALTER. I go, Harry. Rose!

ROSE. [*Aside, with a sudden thought.*] Go! Say nothing.

WALTER. Come, sir. [*To* HARRY.

ROSE *assumes an air of cool indifference, and flings herself carelessly in a chair.* MAJOR CLEVELAND *appears astonished.* MR. ELSWORTH *and the others look surprised and incredulous.*

PICTURE TO CLOSE OF ACT.

ACT II.

SCENE.—*A Garden.—House in the background, illuminated.*

Enter ROSE *and* MAJOR CLEVELAND *from house,* ROSE *hanging on the* MAJOR'S *arm.*

ROSE. It was really absurd—was it not?—to think me the champion of that country clown. Poor fellow! I couldn't bear his discomfited looks, Major, and so, out of old companionship, what could I do less than stand up for him? There won't be anything positively serious, will there, eh? I should be sorry to have it so, inasmuch as he fell into the trap under my father's roof. But don't you think I made a good champion? It was really presumptuous for the fellow to come here, though. These rustic clowns thrust themselves everywhere.

CLEVELAND. What, Miss Elsworth, Captain Armstrong, then, is nothing—

ROSE. Nothing in the world, I assure you, but a harmless country lad! Do tell me, Major, am I not a good actor?

CLEVELAND. Excellent. I really could have supposed that this American stood high in your esteem.

ROSE. Oh, I like him well enough. He is among the best the country affords, but that is very bad, you know.

CLEVELAND. Then you bear me no malice?

ROSE. Not enough to kill a gnat.

CLEVELAND. Ah, Miss Elsworth, this assurance gives me the greatest pleasure.

ROSE. Don't hurt the poor fellow though, Major, I beg of you. I should be quite sorry if anything happened to him. He is a good-natured, useful neighbour enough—an unpolished jewel, papa calls him. Ah, Major, our social wants in this community are lamentable enough, when we are obliged to content ourselves with such a poor substitute as you have seen, for all the polish and manner of London circles.

CLEVELAND. Lamentable, indeed, Miss Elsworth!

ROSE. The war brings one boon, at least,—the society of gentlemen.

CLEVELAND. Very true, indeed.

ROSE. [*Aside.*] Hem! Major Cleveland, I'll so wheedle you this night you shall cry enough to a woman, even if it so happen that you have never done it to a man. So look to it, my valiant Major! Look to it!

CLEVELAND. Do you know, dear Miss Elsworth, that I could wish to see you in these troubled times united to some one who could afford you the protection which only a husband can extend?

ROSE. [*Behind her fan.*] Oh, Major!

CLEVELAND. [*Taking her hand.*] I cannot be mistaken in the surmise that you love already.

ROSE. [*With a sigh.*] Oh, sir!

CLEVELAND. Miss Elsworth! Rose! Confide in me! I am your friend.

ROSE. [*With affected confusion.*] I believe you, Major Cleveland. I—I—really, sir—I implore you to believe me—I have nothing to confide.

CLEVELAND. Do not be offended, Miss Elsworth. I have your interest at heart. Pardon me—but Captain Arbald—[ROSE *starts and appears agitated.*] believes, or at least hopes, that he is acceptable to you. I am very deeply his friend—very deeply yours.

ROSE. It is very pleasant to hear you say so, Major Cleveland.

CLEVELAND. Then you do look upon him with favour?

ROSE. Alas, Major Cleveland, these wars, these wars!

CLEVELAND. They separate us from those who are dearest to us—they come between us and our hearts' affections.

ROSE. Do they not daily threaten us with a heart widowhood?

CLEVELAND. Ah, Miss Elsworth—Rose, let me call you—I see you are thinking of the young Captain. You love him!

ROSE. [*Aside.*] Walter, I must save you by whatever means! [*Aloud.*] Oh, Major, let me beg of you one thing—let me hear you promise what I will ask you. You assure me you are my friend. Then grant me a pledge. Promise me to—to protect—

CLEVELAND. The Captain—

ROSE. Who is to be my husband.

CLEVELAND. You delight me. Are you then pledged?

ROSE. We are.

CLEVELAND. The young rascal. He never told me so. And jealous enough, I'll be sworn he is, to see me monopoliz your society, as I do.

ROSE. His life is almost in your hands. Often you can save him from danger.

CLEVELAND. You will marry him?

ROSE. [*Abashed.*] Yes.

CLEVELAND. I give you the pledge, then, you ask. Make him your husband, and for your sake I will defend and protect him to the extent of my power.

ROSE. Oh, sir, you make me happy. I am, Major, a foolish girl. I place, perhaps, absurdly, so much confidence in your ability to rescue him from many dangers—that I should like—should like, sir, to wear this ring [*Slipping one from his finger.*] as a friendly pledge that you will be his guardian, his watchful protector.

CLEVELAND. Let me kiss the ring upon your finger as a formal seal to my pledge.

ROSE. It becomes an oath now.

CLEVELAND. It does—sworn upon this hand.

ROSE. That you are his friend—ever to be my husband's friend.

CLEVELAND. That is the oath. I take it again!

ROSE. [*Aside.*] Now, Major Cleveland, I have you!

CLEVELAND. [*Aside.*] She shall be his—then—why then to make her mine.

ROSE. [*Aside.*] There is some libertine scheme behind all this, I feel assured. He is playing the villain. Well, well! Shall we go in?

Enter ARBALD.

CLEVELAND. Ah, Arbald. We have been looking for you.

ROSE. I believe, Captain, that I am pledged to you for the next dance.

ARBALD. It is my happiness to recollect it. But one dance is missed.

ROSE. Let me make amends.

Enter MARVIN, *hurriedly.*

MARVIN. Sir, the rebel has escaped.

CLEVELAND. Ha! What do you mean? How?

MARVIN. It is uncertain how.

CLEVELAND. He must be about the grounds somewhere. Put your fellows upon his track. Hunt him out! I wouldn't lose my hold upon him for the value of a dozen ordinary rebels.

[*Crosses.*

During this speech ARMSTRONG *glides in behind, among the shrubbery, and touches* ROSE. ROSE *starts, and slightly screams. All turn quickly toward her. She, hastily and unseen, unclasps a bracelet from her arm, and flings it behind her.*

ROSE. Gentlemen! gentlemen! gentlemen! I've lost my bracelet—a valued bracelet. Five minutes ago I had it on my arm. Major Cleveland—Captain Arbald—I beseech you to search for it. What could have become of it?

CLEVELAND. Your bracelet?

ROSE. Gentlemen, I implore you to search for it. Major, it may have been dropped in the bower. Go look for it, sir. Captain Arbald and Lieutenant Marvin, why do you stand idly there? Do you refuse to search for my jewel? I've lost a bracelet, I tell you, sirs. Is this the way you attend upon the wishes of a lady?

CLEVELAND. Really, Miss Elsworth, duty—

ROSE. Don't talk to me of duty, sir. I would not lose my bracelet for the wealth of the world. A valued token from a dear friend; I swore never to part with it. Oh, indeed, you are gallant gentlemen! You let me lose a precious jewel, and you stand staring by. I tell you, I value that bracelet with my very life.

CLEVELAND. But the escaped prisoner?

ROSE [*Passionately.*] What is the prisoner to me? What is he to my bracelet? Must I lose my bracelet for the sake of a runaway rebel—a miserable clown, who may either hang or run, I care not? Some one will tread upon my bracelet, [*Walking up and down impetuously.*] one of the common soldiers will find and keep it. I would not lose it for worlds.

ARBALD. Indeed, Miss Rose, I assure you—

ROSE. Oh, no assurances, sir. Where is your devotion to me? Where your willingness to sacrifice everything for me, as I have heard you swear more than once? If you ever expect to come into my presence again, you must first clasp that bracelet on my arm. I will hear nothing, listen to no excuse; and if you refuse to obey me, never let me see you again.

CLEVELAND. [*Aside.*] I must not lose my hold upon her, by offending her. [*Aloud.*] Gentlemen, do you remain with Miss Elsworth, and search for the lost jewel. I will myself give the necessary order for the search for the missing prisoner.

[*Exit* CLEVELAND.

ROSE. You, Captain, search yonder bower.

ARBALD. Were you there?

ROSE. Or I should not send you. [*Exit* ARBALD.] Marvin, go hunt the rooms—I cannot say what moment I dropped it.

MARVIN. I obey Miss Elsworth. [*Exit* MARVIN.

ROSE. Where can he be—if my *ruse* has only given him time.

[*Enter* WALTER, *hurriedly.*]

Good heavens! Not off! Here yet!

WALTER. Every outlet is guarded: could I reach the house—

ROSE. This way—we may steal in—

WALTER. I found your jewel, Rose!

[*As they are hurrying off, enter* MAJOR CLEVELAND.]

Caught, as I'm alive!

ROSE. Quick! away—

WALTER. It shall be so— [*Rushes off in an opposite direction.*

CLEVELAND. Ha! ho! Guard! Corporal!

[*Enter* CORPORAL *and* GUARD *rapidly, with torches.*]

That way is your prisoner. Find him, I charge you.

[*Exeunt* CORPORAL *and* GUARD.]

What am I to think, Miss Elsworth?

ROSE. [*Vehemently.*] Think! That I would give the world for Captain Armstrong to escape.

CLEVELAND. Humph! The gift would be useless. Look for yourself.

ROSE. [*Looking off; then suddenly burying her face in her hands.*] Good heavens!

CLEVELAND. [*In her ear.*] How's this, Miss Elsworth? [*She starts up, proudly.*]

[*Enter* SOLDIERS, *guarding* WALTER.]

I rejoice, sir, that we meet again.

SOLDIER. A jewel, sir, found upon the prisoner.

CLEVELAND. Ha! what's this? [*Reading the inscription by a torch.*] "To Rose, from Walter!" Madam, I understand you now. I was deceived. Permit me to be the means of restoring this valued token from a dear friend. Would it not be a strange vicissitude if the finding of the trinket should be the means of losing the friend? Conduct your prisoner hence.

[*Exeunt all but* ROSE *and* CLEVELAND.

ROSE. Major Cleveland, Captain Armstrong must be allowed to go free. I have your promise. I hold you to it.

CLEVELAND. My promise—

ROSE. Look! [*Pointing to the signet received from the* MAJOR.

CLEVELAND. Aha! Then it was Captain Armstrong, and not Captain Arbald, to whom you alluded in our interview. I was beginning to suspect the trick.

ROSE. Your shrewdness would have done you more credit if you had detected it before. As it is, I have your signet and your promise to save Captain Armstrong.

CLEVELAND. But the promise referred only to your husband.

ROSE. Captain Armstrong is my betrothed husband.

CLEVELAND. Ay, but at present is a prisoner. You see, madam, I hold the cards.

ROSE. Your pardon, sir, but I have the game.

CLEVELAND. Eh! Is not the Captain in my hands?

ROSE. Before to-morrow morning he shall be in mine.

CLEVELAND. Confound it, madam, I'll keep so strict a guard upon him, a fly sha'n't light upon him without my knowing it.

ROSE. Do so, and if you were argus-eyed into the bargain, I'd marry him before to-morrow morning.

CLEVELAND. Ha! is it come to that? I'll march this hour.

ROSE. It would be too late.

CLEVELAND. This moment, then.

ROSE. I would anticipate you.

CLEVELAND. Zounds, madam, you talk idly.

ROSE. Zounds, sir, you talk without reason.

CLEVELAND. I'll go to him at once—put a pistol to his head—blow his brains out, and—

ROSE. Make me his widow.

CLEVELAND. Deuce take it, you're mad.

ROSE. Mad if you will, Major Cleveland. It is a struggle between us. Look to it, sir. You may be bold, valourous, cunning—vastly so; but you have a woman's wit against you—so look to it!

CLEVELAND. Confound it.

ROSE. Bravo! bravo! Your passion, sir, well becomes you—

CLEVELAND. Deaths and devils! [*Exit.*

ROSE. Ha, ha, ha!

[*Enter* METCALF.]

Here! Here, Mr. Metcalf—follow Major Cleveland; watch every step; don't lose sight of him for a moment.

METCALF. Trust me; I'll be his shadow from this time forth. [*Exeunt separately.*

Enter CAPTAIN ARBALD *and* KATE.

ARBALD. Really, Miss Kate, you do me injustice—but if I could only induce you to intercede—

KATE. Plead your cause for you. [*Aside.*] Blind and stupid! Can't he see that I am dying for that my sister laughs at.

ARBALD. If I could but find that lost bracelet—

KATE. Hush! Who comes here? [*They withdraw.*

Enter MAJOR CLEVELAND, MR. ELSWORTH, LIEUTENANT ELSWORTH, *and* METCALF *behind.*

ELSWORTH. Declared to you that she would marry Captain Armstrong—

CLEVELAND. Yes, my dear sir, and I felt it my duty to acquaint you.

HARRY. I will go to the Captain and demand a satisfactory—

CLEVELAND. Your pardon, young gentleman. Captain Armstrong is now my prisoner; and I shall hold him safe for my own purposes.

ELSWORTH. In face of my commands this day pronounced. It is monstrous. I must seek out Rose, and have an explanation. [*Exit.*

KATE. [*Aside to* ARBALD.] You see, sir, how little the bracelet would plead in your cause.

ARBALD. I do, indeed. [*They saunter off.*

HARRY. I do not, sir, often ask favours of you. This day my father forbade Armstrong from entertaining any intentions relative to my sister. He has insulted me, my father, and Rose. I wish to chastise him, sir.

CLEVELAND. Tut, tut! I will not give his cunning a chance to plan another escape. The best thing you can do is to help me to prevent the possibility of the marriage.

HARRY. You are my superior. I have no choice but to obey. But I long to inflict the punishment due to his treachery. [*Exit.*

CLEVELAND. Pest on't, I love the wench. I thought, if married to Arbald, and frequently near me, my suit might flourish. But the cunning vixen caught me in my own trap. If I could only trip her now; let me see—let me see.

Enter ARBALD.

CLEVELAND. Ah, Arbald, come hither. How flourishes your suit with Miss Elsworth?

ARBALD. Badly, I must confess.

CLEVELAND. Unless we prevent it she will be married to this Armstrong before morning.

ARBALD. Is it possible?

CLEVELAND. I have my own reasons for desiring to break up the match between them—to prevent their marriage. Nothing occurs to me at all feasible to that end, but some plan to get introduced into Armstrong's presence a woman disguised as Rose.

ARBALD. And marry them?

CLEVELAND. Ay. Armstrong is on the alert for some scheme to rescue him—would fall into such a net as fishes do—and think it was his mistress' cunning to serve him.

ARBALD. But where is the woman?

CLEVELAND. Rose has a girl in attendance upon her who is near her size and figure—a mischievous wench, or I am no judge of physiognomies.

METCALF. [*Who has been listening, aside.*] Oho! [*Exits hurriedly and secretly.*

ARBALD. Bridget, they call her.

CLEVELAND. Send her to me. Fifty pounds will be more than her fidelity can stand. Luckily we have the Chaplain with us. Have him ready.

ARBALD. I'll hunt Bridget up at once. [*Exit* ARBALD.

CLEVELAND. The plan is a good one. Now, Lady Wit, those who win may laugh. But I was a blind fool ever to allow her to obtain that promise from me.

Enter METCALF.

METCALF. Hist! Major Cleveland.

CLEVELAND. Well, good fellow.

METCALF. [*Aside.*] Fellow! It is remarkable now that I, who daily make a score of urchins tremble in their shoes at the frown of my portentous brow, can't in the least make these people afraid of me. Let me see what effect one of my frightfully severe looks would have. [*Walks up to him.*

CLEVELAND. Well, sir, have you any business with me?

METCALF. No, no, sir. [*Aside.*] I suppose my urchins feel as I do now. [*Aloud.*] I've got an idea, sir, about the Captain.

CLEVELAND. Well, what idea?

METCALF. [*Aside.*] Here comes Rose—the very image of Bridget—all I wanted was to give her time. [*Aloud.*] An idea — [*Aside.*] to trap you with sword, coat, and all—

CLEVELAND. There she is—begone, fellow—you intrude upon me.

Enter ROSE, *disguised as* BRIDGET.

ROSE. [*Curtseying.*] Your Honour sent for me.

METCALF. Ha! ha! ha! Trap to catch foxes—ho! ho! ho! [*Exit.*

CLEVELAND. You look a lively, quick-witted lass.

ROSE. [*Aside.*] Now for the airs of your true lady's lady.

CLEVELAND. Do you know how to keep a silent tongue?

ROSE. Bless us! Haven't I always been in practice? Ain't I mum to what all the fine gentlemen say about the bouquets, the presents, the love notes—

CLEVELAND. How would you like to make twenty pounds?

ROSE. Oh, sir, I am quite invincible.

CLEVELAND. But twenty pounds?

ROSE. Say twenty-five.

CLEVELAND. To be paid when the contract is performed. How would you like to marry?

ROSE. Oh! good gracious!

CLEVELAND. Hush! Why the deuce do you raise that clatter?

ROSE. Lor, sir, we always do.

CLEVELAND. Be silent, or the twenty pounds—

ROSE. Twenty-five—

CLEVELAND. Twenty-five then. Marriage in jest.

ROSE. Oh!

CLEVELAND. Only in jest—to decide a wager. You must disguise yourself as your mistress, when you will be admitted into the presence of Captain Armstrong.

ROSE. Captain Armstrong.—Goodness gracious!

CLEVELAND. Hear me out. A pretended chaplain will be by, and a sham form of marriage will be gone through with—

ROSE. Only in jest? Why, what a funny joke!

CLEVELAND. Capital! capital! Ha! ha! ha!

ROSE. Ha! ha! ha! A splendid joke, sir. But I don't quite understand it.

CLEVELAND. Oh, you understand enough. You must not speak above the lowest whisper, nor let the Captain see your features. A few words and the—the—ha, ha, ha—the joke is through with—

ROSE. I see—I see.

CLEVELAND. And then to-morrow when he comes to know it—don't you see—we will have a run on the Captain—'twill be the rarest sport when found out.

ROSE. But suppose now it should turn out to be a real no-mistake marriage.

CLEVELAND. But it can't. The priest is a sham—that's the point of the joke.

ROSE. That's the point of the joke, eh?

CLEVELAND. Come, will you do it?

ROSE. Well—I am doubtful.

CLEVELAND. Only carry it out well, and you shall have fifty pounds.

ROSE. I am convinced, as old intrigues are dull, I want pastime, and would like to earn fifty pounds, and if my chances in other quarters are uninjured, why—

CLEVELAND. You will do it?

ROSE. Will the Captain think it a jest?

CLEVELAND. He thinks there is a plan on foot to introduce your mistress to him for a similar purpose.

ROSE. And when he finds that he has married plain Bridget instead of Miss Rose—what a rage he will be in! Oh, what a delightful jest—

CLEVELAND. The funniest you ever heard of. Such laughing as there will be!

ROSE. Fifty pounds—all in gold—is more than I can stand.

CLEVELAND. Then meet me in five minutes, by yonder tree.

ROSE. I'll slip on one of my mistress's dresses, and in five minutes be ready—but remember—*fifty pounds!* [*Exit* ROSE.

CLEVELAND. [*Rubbing his hands.*] The best of tricks. Ha! ha! ha! [*Exit.*

Enter METCALF *and* ELSWORTH.

ELSWORTH. Ha, ha, ha! Bravo, Metcalf! a good jest, sir.—Bridget disguised as Rose—ha! ha! ha!

METCALF. It's exquisitely funny, sir—only I think you don't quite understand it—

ELSWORTH. It's you, Metcalf, that don't understand it. It's nothing but a piece of military deviltry. Why, my innocent sir, Armstrong's confinement is only a sham—it doesn't mean anything—Cleveland told me so himself—he will be free to-night. I shouldn't wonder if they were drinking and carousing together now. Bless you, Metcalf, it's only one of Cleveland's practical jokes. But I must go and find Rose, and tell her all about it—it will give her such a laugh. How the Captain will stare when he finds it out, to be sure! [*Exit.*

METCALF. Well, wise one, if you insist upon having it in that way, why, do so—I suppose Miss Rose can fight her battles without your help. It was devilish lucky, though, I overheard that plan of theirs, or the Captain would have been victimized—damnably—ay, damnably—if it be swearing—and a capital crime at Fidlington School. I wonder where Bridget is—Bridget *bona fide*—I mean—a delicious girl,—I love her—I will conjugate her. Nobody in the walks—the marriage not over yet—bless me! I do believe that I am trembling like a refractory scholar with a prospective birching. If it should fail—but it won't, it can't—Rose is a girl to carry anything through.

Re-enter MR. ELSWORTH.

ELSWORTH. Where can Rose be, I wonder! I can't find her anywhere. Everybody inquiring for her—everybody laughing too about the jest upon Armstrong. Ah, these military fellows are such practical jokers—so full of deviltry, to be sure! Who could have thought of such a trick?

METCALF. No civilian, you may be sure, sir. [*Aside, looking off.*] Eh? There they are. The deed is done. It's all right, ha! ha! ha! I'll cut. That Major has a sanguinary way of contemplating me that has blood in it—blood! [*Aloud.*] I think I saw Rose in this direction, sir, with the Major; I dare say we can find her, if we go along.

ELSWORTH. Come, sir, then. [*Exeunt.*

Enter MAJOR CLEVELAND.

CLEVELAND. It's done, and they are fast married. Aha, my lady, who now has the game? Armstrong looked astounded, but, expecting some plan to aid him, he fell into the trap without asking a question. Now, now, my course is clear!

Enter ELSWORTH.

ELSWORTH. Where can Rose be, to be sure? The guests are leaving, and I must find her to give them a good-night. Ah, Major! Have you seen my daughter?

Enter LIEUTENANT ELSWORTH.

LIEUTENANT ELSWORTH. Sir, sir, do you not know that Rose has clandestinely been introduced into the presence of Armstrong—

ELSWORTH. No! has she, though? You d-o-n-t say so! Let me whisper a word, Master Harry—a beautiful joke—it was Bridget—

LIEUTENANT ELSWORTH. No, sir, it was Rose herself.

CLEVELAND. The young man is right.

ELSWORTH. How! What do you say?

CLEVELAND. Simply, sir, by the richest scheme in the world, this rebel's union with your daughter is rendered impossible. I told you the marriage was a jest—a sham. It was not—quite the contrary.

ELSWORTH. Do I understand you to say, sir, that you have really tricked Captain Armstrong into a marriage with—

CLEVELAND. To be sure, sir. It will be the sport of the whole army. The disgrace you feared cannot now occur. Miss Elsworth can never be that rustic's wife—thanks, sir, to my splendid idea. Aha, it was a glorious thought, glorious!

ELSWORTH. Now, damn all respect for the red-coats.

CLEVELAND. Ha!

ELSWORTH. Sir, you have been guilty of a vile scheme. You have put my house to a dishonourable use. You have betrayed one of my guests infamously. Oh! that one of His Majesty's officers could lend himself to a scheme like this.

CLEVELAND. Why, sir, I thought—

Enter ROSE *and* WALTER, *back.*

ELSWORTH. That I would sanction such a plot. Major Cleveland, your conduct has made me half a rebel. It was devilish—diabolical, sir!

CLEVELAND. But—

Enter METCALF, *dancing.*

METCALF. Armstrong has escaped.

CLEVELAND. Escaped! Again! Impossible!

METCALF. He has, or may I be birched.

Enter LIEUTENANT MARVIN.

MARVIN. Sir, the prisoner has escaped—and the woman—

CLEVELAND. By heaven! it shall not be—a hundred pounds reward for him!

ROSE. [*Approaching with* WALTER.] I claim the reward, Major Cleveland.

CLEVELAND. You! The prisoner here! How came he free?

ROSE. By your signet. The sentry knew and acknowledged it.

CLEVELAND. Miss Elsworth?

ROSE. Mrs. Armstrong, by your kind assistance.

CLEVELAND. Ha! What do you mean?

ROSE. Permit me to present you to my husband.

CLEVELAND. Your husband! What does this mean?

ROSE. I *did have* the trump card, sir, and have taken the trick.

CLEVELAND. I am bewildered—I cannot understand—

ROSE. Can't you see? [*Imitating him.*] "How would you like to make twenty pounds? Ha, ha, ha! only as jest! a splendid jest! we'll have such a run on the Captain! As I want pastime, and my prospects—"

CLEVELAND. The wench has betrayed me.

ROSE. You never spoke a word to Bridget. I was the only person you saw.

CLEVELAND. You!

ROSE. Even I. Did I act it to the life?

CLEVELAND. Caught! Tricked! Fool! By—! Madam, this is a farce.

ROSE. Sir, I know it, but it has been played out, and you unwittingly have acted the clown.

ELSWORTH. I am confounded.

CLEVELAND. The end is not yet. I refuse to be governed by a forced construction to a promise which I meant to apply differently. The rebel is still my prisoner. He is surrounded.

ROSE. If your promise is not observed to the letter, I'll proclaim you through the army. I'll degrade you in the eyes of every English officer and gentleman in the land. You disgrace your sword, sir, by this very hesitation. Your bitter, unsoldierly, and dishonourable hatred and persecution of an honourable prisoner, drove me to an extremity which nothing but a question of life or death could have persuaded me to undertake. My womanly modesty I was forced to outrage. You compelled me to stoop to things which I abhorred. But I have a brother who is an English officer; a husband who is an American one. Be careful, sir, in what way you use my name in connection with this night's work, for, be assured, they will not fail to punish a ribald, a slanderous, or a libertine tongue. Consent to Captain Armstrong's release, and your discomfiture remains a secret; refuse, and with one word, I'll have all our guests upon the spot and a public confession.

CLEVELAND. It's absurd to suppose that I'm to be bound by such figments as you have woven. The thing is too ridiculous!

ROSE. You acknowledged the binding nature of your promise, when you attempted, with such heartless cruelty, to entrap the Captain into a marriage with a servant. How would that story sound, think you? And what would be said of the sagacity and discernment of an officer who could allow such a deceit to be practised upon him as I practised upon you? Dear me! I think, Major, that you are in a quandary.

METCALF. [*Aside.*] In a ditch!

ROSE. We await your decision. Shall the Captain be free and this little jest go no further?

CLEVELAND. Miss Elsworth—

ROSE. Excuse me if I assist your memory—Mrs. Armstrong.

CLEVELAND. Madam, I yield to a woman. You fight with weapons I do not understand—

ROSE. With wit, eh?

CLEVELAND. [*Aside.*] There is no hope for me. She has me at every point. I may as well yield with what grace I can. [*Aloud.*] Miss Elsworth, I am at your mercy. May not this night's work be forgotten? Captain Armstrong, I swore if ever I caught you, that you should pay dearly for that daring trick of yours—that bold capture of a fellow-officer, sleeping by my very side—but this lady has checkmated me.

WALTER. Checkmated you, sir, and mated me.

CLEVELAND. Both were done by the same move.

ELSWORTH. And you are married, Rose?

ROSE. I will bear Walter's name when we are publicly married, sir—which now, I trust, will be with your sanction.

ELSWORTH. You have it. You have won a husband, if ever woman did.

LIEUTENANT ELSWORTH. Walter, if you were only more true to the right—

WALTER. Oh, Harry! We will discuss that question yet. I shall make you [*In his ear.*] a convert; be sure of it.

Enter CAPTAIN ARBALD *and* KATE.

KATE. Why, the company is breaking up. We missed you all, sadly. Here come the guests.

CLEVELAND. Ah, Arbald, I'm afraid you will have to forego Miss Rose, here—

ARBALD. To pluck a flower no less sweet.

ROSE. What? Why, Kate—

ARBALD. I have your sister's consent, Miss Elsworth, conditioned only that you all accord with her decision.

ROSE. And so you have been making love under the *rose* all this while. Do not doubt our good wishes.

METCALF. I wonder where Bridget is. I'll pop the question before morning.

ELSWORTH. Rose, you have neglected your friends. Let us go in.

ROSE. Our first duty is to the friends before us—

WALTER. To which faction do they adhere—red or blue?

ROSE. True blue and rebel, I'll be sworn—but I will ask them! [*Comes forward. To* ARMSTRONG.] You see, sir, they respond already. [*To the Audience.*] Do you approve the Whiggish maid, and sanction her schemes so boldly played? The heart of love is heroic in every age; and after all

What difference can we affix,
'Twixt love to-day, and Love in '76?

CURTAIN.

The End.

PAUL KAUVAR;

OR,

ANARCHY

Steele Mackaye

STEELE MACKAYE

(1844–1894)

When one realizes the sociological purpose behind Steele Mackaye's "Paul Kauvar; or, Anarchy," it is interesting to note how inefficient the old form of drama was to carry anything more than the formal romantic fervour. Compared with John Galsworthy's treatment in "Strife" and "Justice," it makes one glad that realism came and washed away all the obscuring clap-trap of that period. Daly, Boucicault, and their generation were held firmly in its grip; they could not get away from it, and they were justified in their loyalty to it by the insistent claim "The Two Orphans" and "The Lady of Lyons" had upon the public. All the more credit, therefore, that Bronson Howard, David Belasco, and James A. Herne escaped it; had the latter completely freed himself of melodrama, his plays would be better known to-day, better capable of revival, because of the true greatness of their simple realistic patches.

But where Mackaye vitalized the old style was in the vigour of his treatment. He loved the large scene, the mob movement; and he worked with a big brush. As Nym Crinkle, the popular New York *World* dramatic critic of the day, wrote: "Whatever else he may be, [he] is not a 'lisping hawthorne bud'! He doesn't embroider such napkins as the 'Abbé Constantin', and he can't arrange such waxworks as 'Elaine'. He can't stereoscope an emotion, but he can incarnate it if you give him people enough."

Mackaye's mind was large, resourceful, daring—both in the opinions it upheld, and the practical theatrical innovations it introduced into the theatre, like the double stage for the little Madison Square playhouse, in New York, which was the precursor of such modern paraphernalia as came later with the foreign revolving stages. He always stood on the threshold of modernism, advocating those principles which were to fructify in the decades to follow him. Such pioneer spirit was evident in his ardent advocacy of Delsarte methods of acting; his own work as an actor was coloured and influenced by the master whose pupil he became in the early years of his career. When one recalls the methods of Wallack, and his shy approach toward anything which was "natural," it seems very advanced to hear Mackaye echoing the Delsarte philosophy. This advocacy was nowhere better demonstrated than when, at a breakfast given him at the New York Lotos Club, he talked on the rationale of art for two hours, and held spell-bound the attention of Longfellow, Bryant, Louis Agassiz, James J. Fields, E. P. Whipple, Edwin Booth and others. He once said:

A man to be a true actor must not only possess the power to portray vividly the emotions which in any given situation would be natural to himself, but he must study the character of the man whom he impersonates, and then act as that man would act in a like situation.

Mackaye's devotion to Delsarte was manifest in the many practical ways he aided his teacher; he was rewarded by being left most of his master's manuscripts. This passionate interest in the technique of acting not only enriched his own work, but, in 1872, prompted him to open a Delsarte house (the St. James Theatre), and later interested him in a school of acting. Mackaye studied at the École des Beaux Arts and the Conservatoire, in Paris, having as an instructor at the latter institution M. Regnier. On his way back to America, Tom Taylor persuaded him to attempt *Hamlet* in London, at the Crystal Palace. This essayal met with success. It also opened the way for collaboration with Tom Taylor in the writing of "Arkwright's Wife" and "Clancarty," and with Charles Reade of "Jealousy." At this time also he commenced a dramatization of George Eliot's "Silas Marner."

There were no half-way measures about Mackaye; things of the theatre and principles of the theatre caught and held his interest. At the very last of his life, while he was at work on his "Spectatorus," which foreran the American idea of a Hippodrome, and which might have, in years to come, happily housed his son Percy's "Caliban," he was at the same time attempting to combine with it an educational aspect which would lift it above the mere spectacular. The symbolical notes which he handed his son—who was then a mere boy—for the writing of a Chorus, show the profound approach he took to all his work. Such seriousness is one of the consuming traits of Percy, whose sense of humour is probably better developed than that of his father, and whose sway of literary expression is fuller.

For none of Steele Mackaye's dramas were written with any idea of being read. They were all constructed by one fully alive to the theatre and its demands. In view of this, it is surprising how well "Paul Kauvar" flows in type. The minor editorial changes made for this edition by Mr. Percy Mackaye are based on several manuscripts, and the result is the first authentic text of the play. Steele Mackaye was always gripped in fascination by mob psychology, always eager to write of the Reign of Terror. The version here used is the mature one, given its première at Buffalo, New York, May 30, 1887. But Mr. Percy Mackaye is authority for the statement that while his father was studying with Delsarte, in Paris, he became enamoured of the Revolution, and there are two manuscripts extant, "The Denouncer" and "The Terror," which indicate that he was chipping away at his theme very early in life. He recast these sketches in the summer of 1875, while at Brattleborough, Vt., where he had a cottage on the Bliss Farm, familiar now to Rudyard Kipling lovers because of the fact that here, too, Kipling wrote, at a later day.

The years 1875 and 1887 are the mileposts between which stretched a long period of successful play-writing by Steele Mackaye. By '75, he had already written "Marriage" (1872), "Arkwright's Wife" (1873) and "Clancarty" (1874). There followed quickly "Rose Michel" (1875, in collaboration), "Queen and Woman" (1876, an adaptation from Hugo), "Won at Last" (1877), "Through the Dark" (1878), "An Iron Will" (1879, later to be called "Hazel Kirke," 1880), "A Fool's Errand" (1881, an adaptation), "Dakolar" (1884), "In Spite of All" (1885), and "Rienzi" (1886). Then came the present play, followed by "A Noble Rogue" (1888) and "Money Mad," modelled after Hugo.

In correspondence with Mr. Percy Mackaye, it is significant to hear him insisting on his father's change in sociological bearing having taken place while writing "Paul Kauvar." Timeliness was given to its initial presentment through the fact that at the moment some Chicago anarchists had been on trial, and were condemned to death. Writing of the incident, William Dean Howells recalls that:

At the house of Judge Pryor, in 1887, several of us came together in sympathy with your father, who was trying—or had vainly tried—to get the United States Supreme Court to grant the Chicago anarchists a new trial. With your father I believed that the men had been convicted on an unjust ruling, and condemned for their opinions, not for a proven crime. I remember your father's wrathful fervour, and the instances he alledged of police brutality. [Letter to Mr. Percy Mackaye.]

In a published interview, Mackaye expressed his concern for the case; but he likewise was reticent about making theatre capital out of it. He is reported to have said:

The play was first called "Paul Kauvar; or, Anarchy." Then I thought "Anarchy" would be the best title, and under that I produced it in Buffalo. After its production, the Chicago anarchists were hanged, and, to avoid a possible charge of trading on that event, I went back to my first title. Later, however, the subtitle, "Anarchy," was gradually reduced to smaller lettering and finally dropped.

The success of the play on its first night was a double triumph, for twelve hundred leading citizens had signed an invitation to have it given in Mackaye's native city, and the evening was a kind of public testimony to his position. This was one of the rare instances of an American dramatist receiving such recognition. Mackaye assumed the title-rôle, and, supporting him were Frederick de Belleville, Eben Plympton, Sidney Drew, Julian Mitchell, May Irwin, and Genevieve Lytton. Commenting on the occasion, the Buffalo *Courier* said:

It was not as a playwright alone that his friends honour Mr. Mackaye. It may be said of him with strict justice that he is one of the few men of our day who have brought to the much-abused theatre the intelligence, the skill, the learning and the genius that it so much needs in an era of speculators and buffoons. He has always been able and willing to take the pen or the rostrum, whether at Harvard or at Steinway Hall, to expound the principles upon which he has so assiduously worked for the past fifteen years.

Mackaye had chosen his theme in the same spirit that Judge Conrad had selected "Jack Cade." He wished to measure the danger of liberty, but he did so indirectly, for the play does not abound in long philosophical flights of definition and warning. He himself confessed that the subject was defined only once, in these words, spoken by the hero to the woman he loves, when she is pleading with him to flee from France. He silences her by saying:

"I must stay to war with beasts who bring disgrace upon our noble cause. The torch of liberty, which should light mankind to progress, when left in madmen's hands, kindles that blaze of anarchy whose only end is ashes."

This indicates very distinctly that Mackaye's stand for the Chicago anarchists was not due to sympathy with their political monomania, but rather championed justice which, only when rightly used, will stem the tide of overwrought minds. With the execution of these men, he believed the cause of anarchy would be strengthened by the general impression gained of their martyrdom. His attitude was widely discussed, and "Paul Kauvar" became a visible demonstration of anarchy gone mad.

Of the component elements in his play, Mackaye left a full record. It is worth preserving as indication of his motive. In an interview he said:

For many years I have devoted myself to the mechanical, as well as the artistic side of the theatre, in the hope that by improving stage mechanism I might help to develop the artistic ensemble essential to high art results in the theatre. To this end I have made numerous inventions, and designed and built several theatres. [The Madison Square and the Lyceum Theatres.]

In this work I have been almost daily in contact with labourers and mechanics of every kind, and this contact stirred in me a very deep and sincere sympathy with these classes of men. I was led to realize the greatness of obligation under which the whole world is placed by the industry, ability and devotion to duty which characterizes by far the larger portion of the working classes.

At the same time, through relations intimate and confidential, I became conscious that certain foreign ideas—the natural outgrowth of excessive poverty and despotism in the Old World—were insinuating themselves into the hearts and minds of American labourers to an extent perilous to their own prosperity and to the very life of the republic.

In this country political corruption and the grasping spirit of corporations are constantly affording the demagogue or the dreamer opportunity to preach the destruction of civil order with great plausibility, giving scope to reckless theorists who have so often, in the world's history, baffled the endeavours of the rational and patient liberalists of their day.

This excited in me an ardent desire to do what little I could as a dramatist to counteract what seemed to me the poisonous influences of these hidden forces: to write a play which might throw some light on the goal of destruction to which these influences inevitably lead, whenever the agitation between capital and labour accepts the leadership of anarchism.

The time chosen by me was that of the Terror in France, 1793–94, during which the noble fruits of the French Revolution came near to annihilation, thanks to the supremacy, for a time, of a small band of anarchical men who, in the name of liberty, invoked the tyranny of terror.

The hero of my play, *Paul Kauvar*, has for his prototype Camille Desmoulins, one of the most conspicuous and sincere sons of liberty of his day, who—in spite of his magnificent devotion to freedom—when he dared oppose the Jacobins, was beheaded at the guillotine—a martyr to national, as distinct from personal, liberty.

The typical anarchist in my play is portrayed in *Carrac*, whose prototype was Thomas Carier, sent into La Vendée as a representative of the Jacobin convention. It was this man who, without process of law, guillotined or destroyed most horribly over one hundred thousand innocent men, women, and children—in the name of liberty. He it was who invented the "republican marriage"—the drowned bodies of whose naked victims dammed the river Loire, and rendered its water pestilential.

"The *Duc de Beaumont* portrays a type of the true noblesse of France—proud, fearless, often unjust, never ignoble.

Gouroc depicts the intriguing type of noblesse whose egotism and cruelty engendered the tyranny of the monarchy, and justified its destruction.

The prototype of General Delaroche was the brave and generous *Henri de la Rochejacquelin*, young leader of the royalists in La Vendée.

By the interplay of these types, I have sought to emphasize what is truly heroic in the struggle which must ensue in all times between men and classes possessed of differing ideas. Especially it is the purpose of my play to remind the American masses, by the history of the past, not to assist foreign influences to repeat that history on this continent in the future.

A sound attitude, and one supported now (1920) daily in the conservative press, whenever I. W. W. and Bolshevist demonstrations shake the country! But "Paul Kauvar" is, to-day, not the kind of drama to drive home the lesson; fashions have changed.

On December 24, 1887, "Paul Kauvar" opened at the New York Standard Theatre, with Joseph Haworth and Annie Robe, and thereafter started on a stage career whose history is long and varied. It reached London, May 12, 1890, under the management of Augustus Harris, at the Drury Lane, with William Terriss and Jessie Millward heading the cast.

Nym Crinkle liked "Paul Kauvar" because of its vigourous masculinity. To him there was in it the "scintillant iron," "the strong arm, ruddy at times with the tongues of promethean fire."

It is a big canvas, avowedly romantic. "It is," he wrote, after the play had been running in New York some months, "a work of great propulsive power, of genuine creative ingenuity, of massive dramatic effectiveness." On that account it is well worth the preserving and the reading.

NEW NATIONAL THEATRE.

WASHINGTON, D. C.

W. H. RAPLEY, MANAGER.

SATURDAY EVENING, ... MAY 5th, 1888,

Grand Production for the Benefit of

The Statue of Washington,

TO BE PRESENTED BY

The United States to the Republic of France,

OF THE LATEST AND GREATEST NEW YORK SUCCESS,

PAUL KAUVAR,

BY

STEELE MACKAYE.

THIS PERFORMANCE IS GIVEN UNDER THE AUSPICES OF

The President and Mrs. Cleveland,

THE FOLLOWING DISTINGUISHED COMMITTEE OF LADIES:

MRS. NATHAN APPLETON,
MISS FLORENCE BAYARD,
MRS. SECRETARY FAIRCHILD,
MRS. DON M. DICKINSON,
MRS. SENATOR SHERMAN,
MRS. SENATOR HEARST,
MRS. SENATOR MANDERSON,
MRS. F. M. D. SWEAT,
MRS. SENATOR J. P. JONES,
MRS. SENATOR PALMER,
MRS. SECRETARY ENDICOTT,
MRS. JUSTICE FIELD,
MRS. SENATOR STANFORD,
MRS. SENATOR STOCKBRIDGE,
MRS. SENATOR WALTHALL,
MRS. S. V. WHITE,

AND MRS. WASHINGTON McLEAN;

And the Following Executive Committee of Ladies and Gentlemen:

MRS. SENATOR JOHN P. JONES,
MRS. SENATOR THOMAS W. PALMER,
MISS FLORENCE BAYARD,
SENATOR W. B. ALLISON,
SENATOR J. D. CAMERON,
SENATOR JOHN T. MORGAN,
REPRESENTATIVE J. J. HEMPHILL,
REPRESENTATIVE H. H. BINGHAM,
MR. M. P. HANDY,
MR. F. A. RICHARDSON,
MR. W. STILSON HUTCHINS,
MR. D. R. McKEE,
MR. JAMES R. YOUNG,
MR. W. F. O'BRIEN,

AND COL. THOMAS P. OCHILTREE.

THIS PRODUCTION IS A TRIBUTE TO THE CAUSE FREELY OFFERED BY

MR. HENRY C. MINER, - - - - - - - - - - - - - STEELE MACKAYE,

And the Following Volunteer Cast:

GENTLEMEN:

PAUL KAUVAR .... STEELE MACKAYE
HONORÉ ALBERT MAXIME, Duc de Beaumont .... FREDERIC DE BELLEVILLE
MARQUIS DE VAUX, alias GOUROC, one of the public accusers of the Revolutionary Tribunal .... WILTON LACKAYE
GENERAL DELAROCHE, Commander of the Royalist Forces in La Vendée ...... NESTOR LENNON
GENERAL KLETERRE, Commander of the Republican Forces in La Vendée ...... M. B. SNYDER
COL. LA HOGUE, on the staff of General Delaroche .... LESLIE ALLEN
DODOLPHE POTIN, an usher of the Revolutionary Tribunal; afterwards sergeant in the Battalion of the Bonnets Rouges .... SIDNEY DREW
CARRAC, a typical Anarchist and a Republican Representative in La Vendée ... GEO. FAWCETT

BOURDOTTE, a "Sans Culottes" .... EDWARD COLEMAN
GOUJON, a Corporal in the Battalion of the Bonnets Rouges .... E. M. HURD
TABOOSE, an officer of Gens d'Armes .... J. F. WENTWORTH
FIRST ORDERLY .... E. R. SPENCER
SECOND ORDERLY .... A. S. PALMER
FIRST SANS CULOTTES .... RUFUS WILLIAM
SECOND SANS CULOTTES .... R. S. MCBRIDE

LADIES:

DIANE DE BEAUMONT, daughter of the Duke .... MISS CARRIE TURNER
NANETTE POTIN .... MISS HELEN MAR
SCARLOTTE .... MISS LIZZIE RECHELLE

AND THE FOLLOWING TRAINED AUXILIARIES:

LADIES.

Miss Bunes.	Miss Moore.	Miss Becks.	Miss Marshall.
Miss Pierson.	Miss Maguire.	Miss Forster.	Miss Gianetti.
Miss Frozar.	Miss Hughes.	Miss Weltars.	Mrs. Hughes.
Miss Weeks.	Miss Naylor.	Miss Lavard.	Miss Hearn.
Miss Smith.	Mrs. Bowars.	Miss Arnold.	Mrs. Lack.

GENTLEMEN.

Mart Townsend.	Wm. Sharkey.	Chas. Belmont.	T. Mitchell.
Henry Schaffer.	Wm. Brown.	H. Marks.	B. Fisher.
W. W. Waters.	Geo. Masten.	C. M. Mackay.	Chas. Nuger.
Geo. Turner.	Frank Comstock.	T. Jarvis.	H. Frees.
F. Daley.	Wm. Chambers.	S. Sullivan.	J. Smith.
F. King.	F. Reynolds.	E. Russell.	Daniel Charles.
R. Ryan.	S. B. Caruth.	J. Godfrey.	S. Rosenthal.
J. Sheehan.	J. Sawyer.	G. B. Merton.	A. Goldsmith.
R. Mansfield.	G. Shaffer.	P. Bergar.	Jas. O'Brien.
Rufus Williams.	C. Bird.	J. J. Blake.	Wm. Mack.
Benj. Binns.	H. Hamill.	Chas. Marshall.	C. Brady.
John Kenny.	W. Sullivan.	H. Gordon.	G. Harvey.
Ben. Sharwood.	F. Medina.	M. Brickner.	C. King.
Al. Young.	Ed. Ryerson.	L. T. McDermott.	J. Macarthy.
Chas. Norman.	E. Morrison.	F. Allen.	
Geo. Hopper.	F Blake.	J. Harris.	

Charles Haslam .... Business Manager of "Paul Kauvar" Company
Jere. Stevens .... Stage Manager
Ralph Welles .... Assistant Stage Manager
John Ginsinger .... Master Mechanic of Miner's Newark Theatre
Charles W. Heinert .... Assistant Master Mechanic of Miner's Newark Theatre
Joseph Logan .... Master Mechanic "Paul Kauvar" Company
Harry Cashion .... Chief Flyman of H. C. Miner's Newark Theatre
Charles Dunlap .... Master of Properties of Miner's Newark Theatre
Ed. Lawrence .... Master of Properties of "Paul Kauvar" Company
A. C. E. Sturgis .... Chief Electrician of Miner's Newark Theatre
William Maston .... Assistant Electrician of Miner's Newark Theatre
Charles L'Orange .... Musical Director of Miner's Newark Theater

The Tableau of the "Dream" in the First Act represents

"THE TYRANNY OF TERROR."

SCENE—FRANCE. TIME, 1794.

ACT I.—THE TERROR. Scene—The interior of the study of Paul Kauvar.

ACT II.—THE INHUMANITY OF MAN.—Scene—Prison of the Conciergerie adjoining the Revolutionary Tribunal in Paris.

ACT III.—THE CONFESSION. Scene—The Grand Hall of the Chateau of Delaroche in La Vendee.

ACT IV.—ON PAROLE. Scene—Same as Act III.

Three minutes will elapse between Acts IV. and V.

ACT V.—"TWIXT LOVE AND HONOR." Scene—Same as Act IV.

The Tableau which concludes this performance, and rivals in power and beauty the famous dream scene of the first act, represents allegorically

"THE CONQUEST OF EVIL."

It is a poetic picture, full of deep thought and careful study. The central figure is that of the Angel of Conquest, with one foot upon the prostrate fiend Anarchy, holding high that irresistible weapon of progress, the Sword of Light. The fiend carries in his hands the Torch and Flag of Anarchy, and with these is about to sink into the Abyss of Darkness.

PAUL KAUVAR;

OR,

ANARCHY

A PLAY IN FIVE ACTS

By STEELE MACKAYE

[The Editor wishes to thank Mrs. Steele Mackaye and Mr. Percy Mackaye for their permission to include "Paul Kauvar" in the present Collection.

DRAMATIS PERSONAE

MEN.

PAUL KAUVAR,	*Age 30.—President of the Revolutionary Section of Fraternity. Afterwards Captain on* GENERAL KLEBER'S *staff.*
HENRI DE LA ROCHEJACQUELEIN,	*Age 22. Commander of the Royalist forces in la Vendée.*
GENERAL KLEBER,	*In command of the Republican forces in la Vendée.*
HONORÉ ALBERT MAXIME, DUC DE BEAUMONT,	*Age 65. Cousin of* LA ROCHEJACQUELEIN.
GOUROC, *alias* MARQUIS DE VAUX,	*Of the Jacobin Club, and one of the Public Accusers of the Revolutionary Tribunal.*
COLONEL LA HOGUE,	*On the staff of* LA ROCHEJACQUELEIN.
MARDOCHE, *alias the* ABBÉ DE ST. SIMON.	
JEAN LITAIS,	*A peasant of Brittany—formerly a servant of the* DUC DE BEAUMONT. *Then for a time turnkey in the prison of the Republic.*
ARISTIDES, *alias* DODOLPHE POTIN,	*An usher of the Revolutionary Tribunal, afterward Sergeant in the Battalion of the Bonnet Rouge.*
CARRAC,	*Republican Representative in Vendée.*

GOUJON,	*Private in the Battalion of the Bonnet Rouge.*
BOURDOTTE,	*Sans Culotte.*
TABOOZE	*An officer of the gens d'armes.*
ORDERLIES,	*On the Staff of* LA ROCHEJACQUELEIN.

WOMEN.

DIANE DE BEAUMONT,	*Daughter of the Duke.*
NANETTE POTIN,	*Wife of* ARISTIDES.
DENISE DUBOIS,	*Foster-sister of* LA ROCHEJACQUELEIN *and fiancée of* JEAN LITAIS.

Soldiers, Peasants, "Sans Culottes", Turnkeys, &c.

SCENE. *France.*

TIME. *1794.*

Under the title of "ANARCHY," the play was first performed at Buffalo, New York, May 30, 1887, at the Academy of Music. The following was the cast:

PAUL KAUVAR	Steele MacKaye.
GENERAL LA ROCHEJACQUELEIN	Eben Plympton.
DUC DE BEAUMONT	Frederick de Belleville.
MARQUIS DE VAUX, *alias* GOUROC	Henry Lee.
ABBÉ DE ST. SIMON	John A. Lane.
COLONEL LA HOGUE	H. B. Bradley.
CARRAC	M. B. Snyder.
ARISTIDES POTIN	Sidney Drew.
JEAN LITAIS	B. T. Ringgold.
GENERAL KLEBER	Jerome Stevens.
BOURDOTTE	Julian Mitchell.
GOUJON	Edward M. Hurd.
DIANE DE BEAUMONT	Genevieve Lytton.
NANETTE POTIN	May Irwin.
DENISE	Marie Hartley.
SCARLOTTE	Maud Hosford.
ALINE	Alice Hamilton.

Cast of the first New York performance, December 24, 1887, the Standard Theatre. The name was changed to "Paul Kauvar".

PAUL KAUVAR	Mr. Joseph Haworth.
HONORÉ ALBERT MAXIME	Mr. Edwin Varrey.
MARQUIS DE VAUX, *alias* GOUROC	Mr. Wilton Lackaye.
GENERAL DELAROCHE	Mr. Nestor Lennon.
THE ABBÉ DE ST. SIMON	Mr. B. F. Horning.
GENERAL KLETERRE	Mr. Jerome Stevens.
COLONEL LA HOGUE	Mr. Leslie Allen.
DODOLPHE POTIN, *alias* ARISTIDES	Mr. Sidney Drew.
CARRAC	Mr. George D. Fawcett.
BOURDOTTE	Mr. Edward Coleman.
GOUJON	Mr. Edward M. Hurd.
TABOOZE	Mr. Charles Mitchell.
FIRST ORDERLY	Mr. E. R. Spencer.
SECOND ORDERLY	Mr. A. E. Lohman.
FIRST SANS CULOTTE	Mr. Fred Clifton.
SECOND SANS CULOTTE	Mr. C. H. Wentworth.
DIANE DE BEAUMONT	Miss Annie Robe.
NANETTE POTIN	Miss Louise Rial.
SCARLOTTE	Miss Lillie Eldridge.

PAUL KAUVAR

ACT I.

TIME. *The Terror. 1794.*

SCENE. *Paris. Study of* PAUL KAUVAR'S *apartment.*

The decorating is in the classic style of the painter David. Old-fashioned escritoire with chair. Folding doors across corner up stage. Window, with table beneath it. Fireplace, with picture of PAUL KAUVAR *over it, and fire on andirons. Doors at the right and left of stage.*

At the Rise of Curtain, NANETTE *crosses to fireplace and shovels ashes into a pail.* POTIN *is heard outside, singing, in loud and discordant tones, "La Marseillaise."*

NANETTE.

[*Starting up angrily.*]
There's that lazy man of mine, singing, while I work.
[*Crosses to folding doors, flings them open and shouts roughly.*]
Dodolphe!—Dodolphe Potin!

POTIN.

[*Meekly, outside.*]
Aye, aye!

NANETTE.

I want you!

POTIN.

[*Outside.*]
Aye, aye!

NANETTE.

Hurry up!—Do you hear?

POTIN.

[*Appearing.*]
I could hear your sweet voice if I were deaf as Justice.

NANETTE.

Fool! Justice is blind, not deaf.

POTIN.

True! That's why you always get the better of me, dear. Justice listens too much and looks too little.

NANETTE.

Bah!

[*Pointing to pail.*]

Take that rubbish to the cellar.

POTIN.

[*Crosses, lifts pail, and looks into it.*]

Ashes!—Heigho! Every fire has its ashes.

NANETTE.

Aye—and the fire that warms a man's home may burn his house down!—Mark you that, Citizen.

POTIN.

Oh, I see! You mean a wife, who should be a comfort, often proves a curse.

NANETTE.

I mean, Citizen Potin, that in days of revolution, husbands are easily suppressed.

POTIN.

[*Starting.*]

Take care! A word against the Revolution is treason and sure death.

NANETTE.

Bah! Better death, than a life of terror like that in France to-day.

POTIN.

[*Terrified.*]

Good heavens, Nanette! Fewer words than these have guillotined our betters! Can you never hold your tongue?

NANETTE.

Never!—while I have a truth to tell.

POTIN.

Tell the truth! Good Lord, that's fatal.

NANETTE.

Aye, for in these noble days of liberty we are only free to lie.

POTIN.

[*Turning away in disgust.*]
Damn it! I must run or be ruined.
[*Starts to go, but, in passing window, recoils with a cry of dismay.*]
Sacristie!—See!—See there!
[*Points out of window.*

NANETTE.

[*Contemptuously looking out of window.*]
What now?

POTIN.

There goes the Phantom!

NANETTE.

[*Starting.*]
The dumb girl of the guillotine!

POTIN.

Who glides like a phantom through the streets, without home, friend, or occupation.

NANETTE.

[*With horror.*]
Except to stand by the scaffold, and count the heads that fall from the guillotine.

POTIN.

They say that calamity overtakes everyone she follows: that it's disaster to stand in her way, and sure death to notice her.

NANETTE.

Aye, even those who think themselves too great to believe in God, have faith in the fatal power of this pale child. My God! look there!

POTIN.

Good Lord!—It's Mademoiselle Diane! She's crossing the street in front of the Phantom.

NANETTE.

Aye!—Go.—Hurry Mademoiselle here, before she has a chance to heed this messenger of misery.

POTIN.

[*Going hurriedly.*]

Goddess of Reason, save us all!

[*Exit.*

NANETTE.

Goddess of Reason!—A fine deity for days as mad as these!

[*Crossing to mantel and looking at* KAUVAR'S *picture.*]

Ah, Citizen Kauvar!—Patriot!—Revolutionist!—Bold son of Liberty, as you are!—You'd love this age of terror less if it brought death to Mademoiselle Diane.—Yes, I've watched ye, sturdy citizen, and in spite of your stern devotion to the Republic, I suspect you carry another idol in your heart.

DIANE

[*Outside, laughing.*]

All right, Citizen,—I'll not forget; though the poor crazed girl is not half as harmful as her saner neighbours.

NANETTE.

Ah! Here she comes—Diane Leblanc,—a ray of sunlight in this prison men call Paris.

DIANE.

[*Entering with flowers.*]

Ah, Nanette! Quick! Water and a vase. See!

NANETTE.

What—flowers?

[*Brings vase.*

DIANE.

Yes, they bloom even in this reign of terror.

[*Putting flowers in vase.*]

But you see these fragile beauties are sinless, and therefore know no fear.—Is my father in his room?

NANETTE.

No. He went away an hour ago.

DIANE.

Gone an hour, and not returned? That makes me anxious!—Is Citizen Kauvar at home?

NANETTE.

Not yet! He's been away all night.

DIANE.

Good heavens!—Nanette—can anything have happened?

NANETTE.

Yes, what happens every day. Innocence is slaughtered!

DIANE.

But he—Citizen Kauvar—?

NANETTE.

Has doubtless fought all night to stop the useless flow of noble blood.

DIANE.

Yes, he is brave, merciful.

NANETTE.

Ah! He was one of the fiercest champions of Freedom when the people first arose; but now I think he'd give his life to still the tempest he did so much to rouse.

DIANE.

He will return sad and worn; we must do our best to cheer him when he comes.

NANETTE.

One look—one smile of yours will banish every thought of sorrow from his tired brain.

DIANE.

Hush, Nanette;—you must not talk like that.

A VOICE.

[*Outside.*]
Nanette!—Diane!

NANETTE.

[*Startled.*]
What's that?

DIANE.

[*Frightened.*]
My father!

DUKE.

[*Entering wildly.*]
My child! Diane!—Where is she?

DIANE.

[*Rushing to him.*]
Here!—Safe in your dear arms!

DUKE.

[*Embracing her.*]
Thank God!
[*Turning to* NANETTE.]
My good Nanette, leave us alone awhile.

NANETTE.

[*Going.*]
All right, Citizen.

DUKE.

And warn us when anyone is coming.

NANETTE.

[*At the door.*]
Don't fear! I'll stand good guard.
[*Exit.*

DIANE.

Father, why are you so moved?

DUKE.

But now, the mob seized some poor young girl they found without protection in the street. I heard of this and fearing for your life, I hurried here in awful agony of mind. Ah! Diane, this dread of peril to you is worse than the worst of deaths to me.

DIANE.

Take heart, dear father! Does not Paul Kauvar, strong and true, stand between us and danger!

DUKE.

Yes; but 'tis hard that I, a peer of France, should owe my daughter's life to a peasant's son—a workman!

DIANE.

A workman with a brush so potent that the noblest born do honour to his art. What would have been our fate but for his devotion?

DUKE.

He's a plebeian—a Republican! The sense of my obligation to him—the enemy of my race—is almost unendurable. Ah, but for you I should long since have braved the scaffold and buried humiliation in the grave.

NANETTE.

[*Hurrying in.*]

Take care!—A committee from the Section is on its way up-stairs.

DIANE.

[*In fear.*]

A committee coming here? How strange!

NANETTE.

No, not strange! Treachery is at every door. They are coming. Quick!—To your work!

[*The* DUKE *sits at the desk and pretends to write.* DIANE *sits at table and takes up sewing.* NANETTE *dusts. Knock is heard outside.* NANETTE *answers roughly.*]

Come in!

Enter GOUROC, POTIN, GOUJON *and two* SANS CULOTTES.

GOUROC.

Health and fraternity, Citizens! We come for Paul Kauvar, President of our Section.

NANETTE.

[*Gruffly.*]

He's not at home.

GOUROC.

Ah, indeed!

[*Sitting.*]

Then we will await him here.

[*All sit in silence.*

NANETTE.

[*Aside, in irritation.*]

Oh, the impudence of these men! How my nails ache to get at their ugly faces! [*Crossing.*]

How often have I told you that this apartment is not a public office?

POTIN.

But, my precious angel—

NANETTE.

Bah! Religion is abolished, and angels are suppressed! I wish friends were too!

POTIN.

[*Laughing.*]

Talk of the rack! What is it to a woman's tongue?

NANETTE.

What know you of a woman's tongue?

POTIN.

Enough to damn me, if knowledge were a crime.

NANETTE.

[*To* GOUROC.]

Come, Citizen, there's no use waiting. President Kauvar don't do business at home; you've no rights here.

GOUROC.

[*Rising sternly.*]

The patriot has unlimited rights, woman. He may dare all—violate all, in his zeal for the Republic.

NANETTE.

Well, then, dare my dusting.

[*Strikes brush into her hand and sends dust all over* GOUROC.

GOUROC.

[*Moving off, sputtering.*]

Who is this, Citizen Potin?

POTIN.

[*Proudly.*]
My wife, Citizen Gouroc.

GOUROC.

Who taught her manners?

POTIN.

The Goddess of Liberty, a rough and ready teacher.

GOUROC.

Who teaches with sharp tools.

NANETTE.

Aye—tools so sharp they often cut the fools that use them. Mark that.

GOUROC.

[*Crossing to* DIANE.]
You are the wife of President Kauvar, I suppose?
[DIANE *starts up and stares. The* DUKE *rises and advances with stern hauteur. At sight of* GOUROC, *he starts, and surveys him with amazement.*]
Well, old man, are you mad, or do you know me?

DUKE.

[*Significantly.*]
I think we have met before.

GOUROC.

Yes, and may meet again. Permit me to introduce myself. I am Citizen Gouroc, of the Jacobin Club, and one of the Public Accusers of the Revolutionary Tribunal.
[DIANE *draws close to* NANETTE.]
Now, who are you?

DUKE.

I am George Leblanc, private secretary to Paul Kauvar.

GOUROC.

Ah, indeed!—His private secretary? Then I can do my business with you. It is said that two aristocrats in disguise are lurking about this house.
[*All start.*]

I must communicate with you in secret, Citizen.
[*Turning to* DIANE.]
Are you the daughter of this old man?

DIANE.

I am his daughter, Diane Leblanc.

GOUROC.

You remain.
[*To* SANS CULOTTES.]
You, Comrades, wait across the street;
[*Exeunt* SANS CULOTTES.]
and you, Citizen Potin, take your wife, leave the room, and wait within call. You understand?

POTIN.

I do, Citizen. When the Republic commands, I obey.
[*Exit, with* NANETTE.

GOUROC.

[*Bowing with great politeness.*]
Monsieur le Duc de Beaumont.
[DIANE *starts.*

DUKE.

[*Turning with contempt.*]
Monsieur le Marquis de Vaux.

DIANE

[*Amazed.*]
This—the Marquis de Vaux?

GOUROC.

You are surprised to see me in this garb. I am equally surprised to find you the guests of Citizen Kauvar, President of the Republican Section of Fraternity.

DUKE.

Not quite as strange as discovering the dainty Marquis de Vaux a Public Accuser and the servile slave of the guillotine.

GOUROC.

Reserve your contempt till you understand the meaning of my presence here. I come to warn you against your host.

DIANE.

[*Haughtily.*]
How, sir! You suspect the loyalty of Monsieur Kauvar?

GOUROC.

What if he has trapped you here only to betray you?

DIANE.

That's impossible, sir! Monsieur Kauvar is the soul of honour and devotion.

DUKE.

Besides, his head is surety for ours. The discovery that he had sheltered us would entail his own death.

GOUROC.

Precisely! And what if the sense of that danger had prompted a denunciation, while there still was some merit in it?
[*The* DUKE *starts.* DIANE *turns aside with scorn.*]
One thing is certain: an anonymous denunciation of you, describing your disguise and your retreat, has been made to our club.

DIANE.

[*Clasping her father.*]
What!—Discovered and denounced?

GOUROC.

As Public Accuser, the denunciation fell first into my hands. I have risked my life by withholding it from the Tribunal until your safety is assured.

DUKE.

[*Giving* GOUROC *his hand.*]
Pardon, Marquis, that I did not realize before the motives of your course.

GOUROC.

Grant me, then, the privilege of saving you.

DUKE.

We will. You belong to our own race; we may trust you.

GOUROC.

Then prepare for sudden and secret flight.

DIANE.

[*Starting.*]

Flight! Where can we be safer than under our present host's protection?

GOUROC.

Under mine, Mademoiselle. Kauvar is a man of the people. To him such words as loyalty, truth and honour are but empty puffs of air.

DIANE.

[*Proudly and passionately.*]

On whose lips is there meaning purer, or prouder, than on Paul Kauvar's?

DUKE.

[*With haughty surprise.*]

Mademoiselle! When you speak so warmly, you forget the distance that separates you from one of his rank.

[*Cries in the distance of* "To the Guillotine!" *with the roll of muffled drums.*

DIANE.

[*In solemn voice.*]

Nay, father, listen!—Do we need more to remind us of the nearness of the protected to the protector?

[*The* DUKE *listens with bowed head.* GOUROC *goes to window.*

DUKE.

[*To* GOUROC, *as drums draw near.*]

Is it the patrol?

GOUROC.

[*Solemnly.*]

No. 'Tis the guard of the death-cart, with to-day's load for the guillotine.

DIANE.

[*Hiding her face.*]

This constant agitation is torture.

GOUROC.

You can easily escape it, Mademoiselle. Accept the refuge I offer you.

DUKE.

We will, Marquis, at once. Come to my room, and we will complete our plans.

[*To* DIANE.]

My child, prepare to leave this house to-night, in haste and in secret.

[*Exit with* GOUROC.

DIANE.

Fly from this house to-night?—No! I will not go! And yet I must, or tell my father the secret I have kept from him so long.

PAUL.

[*Outside.*]

I am not at home to anyone. I will not brook intrusion here.

NANETTE.

[*Outside.*]

I'll keep out all I can.

DIANE.

Paul is coming!—How can I tell him we must part?

[PAUL *enters.* DIANE *turns quickly toward him.*

PAUL.

[*Absorbed in documents he is carrying. Crossing slowly to desk, he lays the papers down and, turning, sees* DIANE.]

Diane! Thank heaven you're alone!

[DIANE *checks him by a warning gesture; crosses quickly to the door, listens a moment, then slowly approaches* PAUL, *looking back anxiously.*]

Have you no word of welcome for a very weary friend?

DIANE.

[*Throwing herself with nervous impetuosity into his arms.*]

Ah, Paul! God bless and keep you!

PAUL.

God blessed me beyond measure, when he made your heart my own.

DIANE.

[*Leading him with nervous intensity to a chair.*]

Sit here—sit here!

[*She sits beside him.*]

Let me look at your face, and listen to your voice, while I can—while I can!

PAUL.

How strangely you say this!

DIANE.

Do you remember the old days—before this reign of terror darkened all our lives—the sunny room in my father's chateau, where you taught me to paint the flowers we had gathered—oh! so gaily!—from the quaintest corners of the garden?

PAUL.

Ah, those were ideal days.—You, almost a child—a girl just blooming into womanhood, like those rosebuds in your hair.

DIANE.

Oh, how happy I was!—So happy, earth seemed heaven! So happy, sorrow seemed almost a myth!—I little dreamed that I would ever drink the bitterest dregs of that black cup.—The Revolution rushed upon us—and then, oh then!—

[*Hides her face on* PAUL'S *breast.*

PAUL.

Then we parted, I thought forever.

DIANE.

You came no longer. The sunshine lost its smile—the flowers faded.

PAUL.

And yet, amidst the fearful tumult of these distracted times, we met once more.

DIANE.

[*Starting up.*]

Oh, my God! That meeting! I see the frightful scene again! My father there before me—old—helpless, dragged from his own house by a horde of brutal beasts.—I, shrieking, fighting vainly at his side—amidst their mocking laughs and jeers. Ah! I can hear them now—yes, and high above their hideous jests, rings out a clarion voice—'tis yours—silencing this crowd of curs!—With what sublime audacity you claim my father as your cousin, saving him and me, by the coolness of your courage!—Paul, from that hour you were more than man to me; you were a God, a hero, my father's Saviour!

PAUL.

[*Rising.*]

Better than all that now—your lover—guardian—husband.

[*Embraces her, then staggers.*

DIANE.

Paul—what is it?

PAUL.

Nothing,—fatigue from last night's bitter work.

[DIANE *brings wine and offers it. He puts it away.*]

No—one kiss from you will give me more strength than all the wine in France.

[*She kisses him.*

DIANE.

Heaven knows you need more than human strength.

PAUL.

Aye, Titan strength, to stem the tide of madness that overflows the mind of France! Ah, Diane! if it were not for your dear love, I fear my mind would falter at the task before me.

DIANE.

Oh, Paul! Why undertake this task?—Why not fly to peace in other lands?

PAUL.

Fly!—Desert France in the hour of her agony?—In the awful travail which gives birth to a new and nobler era for mankind?—No, no! I love you more than life, but my Country—ah, that is mother, sister, wife, and child!

DIANE.

But Paul—

PAUL.

Hush, sweetheart, you must not make the struggle harder! The infant age is threatened with miscarriage!—The torch of

Liberty, which should light mankind to progress, if left in madmen's hands, kindles that blaze of Anarchy whose only end is ashes.

DIANE.

[*Suddenly starting.*]
Hush! Listen! What is that?

PAUL.

[*After listening.*]
Nothing, foolish child.
[*He is about to embrace her.*

DIANE.

[*Turning sadly away.*]
Nay, we are too rash! We forget the dangers that environ us.

PAUL.

Would we could forget the weak concealment that makes cowards of us both!—Oh, that something would happen to make us end this living lie!

DIANE.

[*Solemnly.*]
Perhaps that something has happened, Paul. We have been warned that we're no longer safe beneath this roof.

PAUL.

[*Amazed.*]
Warned!—By whom?

DIANE.

What matter by whom?—Enough that we've been told the Civil Guard may search the house this very day.

PAUL.

[*With sudden resolution.*]
I am glad of it. Thank fate that something forces us to tell your father you are mine.

DIANE.

Nay, Paul—I cannot, dare not tell him that!

PAUL.

Then leave the task to me.

DIANE.

'Twould be but to win his curse. You little dream the deathless pride that's rooted in his heart! To wrench out that pride would break the heart that holds it.

PAUL.

[*Bitterly.*]

Then let it break! I, too, am proud, Diane, proud as all are proud to be who owe their manhood to their God and not to the favour of a king!—If your father scorns the sacred work of heaven's hand, then he is only fit for scorn himself.

DIANE.

Oh, Paul! Be charitable!

PAUL.

Charitable! To what?—Your father's pride in the race from which he springs—the race whose iron rule for centuries stamped shame on honest labour—crowned infamy with honour—made gods of profligates and dogs of workingmen—ruining their wives—insulting their mothers—debasing their daughters, and sewing the seeds of madness in their veins?—Ah, Diane! when I face your father, 'tis not your husband who should blush for his race.

DIANE.

My father's race is mine.—I forgot its glories, and atoned its wrongs in marrying you!—But I love, revere, my father still, and have hoped each day that he would come to love you for your saving care of me—and grow content to take you as a son.

PAUL.

Who knows—perhaps he will.

DIANE.

[*Sadly.*]

Ah, no! The more you do for me, the more his pride revolts, till now I dare not tell him of our marriage.

PAUL.

Diane—listen. The time has come when you must choose between us. I staked my life in saving yours, and his! He loves but little if he hesitates to keep the precious life I saved unmarred by sorrow.

DIANE.

Well, then, so be it! Have your will! But oh, seek first his blessing for our love, before you tell him of our secret marriage.

PAUL.

My love for you will teach me tenderness for him. Go now and send him here.

[*Kissing her.*]

Courage! All may yet be well.

[*Exit* DIANE. PAUL *sits at desk wearily.*]

Hateful humiliation!—to stoop in pleading for that already mine! But patience, Paul Kauvar; he is the father of the woman you adore.

DUKE.

[*Entering and advancing to* PAUL.]

One word before we part, good friend. I thought to leave this house without farewell, but I cannot be so cruel. I have learned that this is no longer a safe retreat. I am forced to seek one safer.

PAUL.

And where will you find one, Monsieur?

DUKE.

I shall best serve you by keeping that a secret.

PAUL.

And does your daughter go with you?

DUKE.

Could you think that I would leave her here?

PAUL.

Certainly, Monsieur. If to stay seemed less perilous than to go. Why not let me replace you for awhile?

DUKE.

You guard my daughter here alone?

PAUL.

In my character of cousin to Diane Leblanc, gossip has already united us by even a closer tie.

DUKE.

To my infinite annoyance, sir.

PAUL.

Monsieur le Duc, in times like these, Madame Kauvar would be far safer than Mademoiselle de Beaumont.

DUKE.

[*With quiet hauteur.*]

There are some means of safety forbidden to my rank, sir.—Pardon me if I must say that what you suggest is one of them.

PAUL.

What if I dared to love your daughter, to hope that you would grant me the right to guard her as my wife?

DUKE.

Seriously?

PAUL.

Seriously!

DUKE.

[*Shrugging his shoulders.*]

This is another of the many insanities of the times.

PAUL.

[*Haughtily.*]

Suppose I had reason to believe that your daughter would consent?

DUKE.

[*Sternly.*]

One moment, Monsieur! Your first proposition involves but madness,—your last implies dishonour.

PAUL.

[*Indignantly.*]

Dishonour!

[*Checking himself.*]

Monsieur, honesty is honoured now, even though it be not allied to an empty title. 'Tis not a crest, but character, that measures manhood in this modern age. Therefore I do not fear to tell you—

[DUKE *turns quickly.* PAUL *hesitates.*]

that I love your daughter.

DUKE.

[*With terrible contempt.*]

And you take this time to declare it! When you have burdened me with obligations that leave me powerless at your feet? —when I must see in the demand for the daughter's hand, a possible bargain for the father's life.

[PAUL *turns fiercely. The* DUKE *checks him.*]

No more, sir! Happily I have two securities against dishonour: my child's sense of what is due to herself—my own scorn of life purchased at such a price.

PAUL.

Perhaps your daughter may not deem the protection of my name so great a degradation as yourself.—Dare you put her to the test?

DUKE.

What test can you propose?

PAUL.

[*Seating himself at desk and writing.*]

Here is a pass procured at the risk of my life.—I fill it out for George Leblanc.—It will convey you, alone, safely beyond our borders. Here is another. I make this out for George Leblanc and Diane his daughter. This will enable both of you to escape. —These passes have the signatures of the chief of police; I countersign them, thus—a double surety for you, a double risk for me.—Now, Monsieur, either one of these passes is yours, as your daughter may decide, if you will offer her the choice of remaining under my protection, or of leaving France with you.

DUKE.

[*Striking a bell.*]

The choice is at her will.

[*Enter* NANETTE.]

Send my daughter here at once.

[*Exit* NANETTE.

PAUL.

One word, Monsieur. These passes are at stake, and my life as well. I promise to be bound by the decision of your daughter. —If she decides to remain, you promise to go and leave her here with me?

DUKE.

I promise this on one condition. I pledge my honour to put the alternative fairly before her. You must pledge yours to use no word to influence her choice.

PAUL.

I pledge myself to silence.

DIANE.

[*Entering pale and anxious.*]
You sent for me, Father?

DUKE.

I did. Listen, child. I am about to leave France. By my side there is peril—here is safety. Answer frankly: will you follow me, or remain here under the protection of Monsieur Kauvar?

DIANE.

[*Aside.*]
What can this mean? He could not ask this if he knew the truth.
[*Aloud.*]
Father, I do not understand.—What shall I say?

DUKE.

What your heart prompts, child.
[*Turning away.*]
Nay, do not hesitate; I will not influence your choice even with a look.

DIANE.

If I shrink from danger, if I stay here, what becomes of you?

DUKE.

I go alone.

DIANE.

Alone to meet your peril?—Then, by the bond of a daughter's duty, my place is at my father's side.
[PAUL *staggers. The* DUKE *retires quietly to desk.* DIANE *speaks aside to* PAUL.]
Remember he is old, with none but me to comfort his last days.

PAUL.

[*With stern self-control.*]

Monsieur, the double pass for George Leblanc and Diane his daughter has been fairly won.

[*Hands the pass to the* DUKE, *bows coldly, and leaves the room without a look at* DIANE, *who falls into a chair and hides her face.*

DUKE.

[*Looking suspiciously at* DIANE.]

Could there be warrant for his strange presumption? If so, this separation is none too soon.

[*Enter* GOUROC.]

Ah, Marquis, congratulate us. We are now released from all need of burdening even you.—See! Here is a pass which opens the doors of our prison. We fly to-night to Vendée, where we hope you may soon rejoin us, and our cousin Rochejacquelein.

GOUROC.

[*Aside.*]

The devil!—

[*Aloud.*]

You are fortunate, Duke. Alas that I cannot go with you!

DUKE.

Well, come, Diane; time flies. We must prepare for our escape.

[*Going with* DIANE.]

Au revoir, Marquis.

GOUROC.

Au revoir, Monsieur le Duc, and bon voyage, Mademoiselle de Beaumont.

[*Exeunt the* DUKE *and* DIANE. GOUROC *changes to a fierce and hurried manner.*]

Ah!—Not so fast, dear Duke! You're not out of France yet. This sudden flight destroys all my plans. Again this girl, the heiress of ten millions, will get beyond my reach.—No!—death, dishonour—nothing shall snatch her from me now!—Aye, but how to prevent it?

[*Reflecting.*]

The Duke has not many years to live, and in these ticklish times old men's days are easily shortened. He dead, his daughter's at my mercy.

[*With sudden triumph.*]

I have it!—I see the way to place her wholly in my grip!—A brilliant move and easy to execute!—Kauvar knows nothing of my rank!

[*Rings bell, goes to desk and begins to look at papers.*]

Yes, these are what I need to guarantee my triumph!

[*Enter* POTIN.]

Have you any blank warrants?

POTIN.

I have!—I keep them always handy, especially for the petticoat sex.

[*Giving them.*]

I say, Comrade, I hope it's a she-man this time, for there's nothing like this—[*Making sign across throat.*] to stop the wag of a woman's tongue.

GOUROC.

Go.—Remain in the ante-room.—I may want you to summon a guard.

POTIN.

[*Going.*]

All right, Citizen! I'm always ready at the call of the Republic.

[*Exit.*

GOUROC.

Good!—Now to secure my victory!—But where can I find Kauvar?

[*Starts for door.* KAUVAR *enters, absorbed in thought, without seeing* GOUROC, *who watches him.*]

He's just in time! Fate conspires with me for success.

[PAUL *seats himself at desk and buries his face in his arms.*—GOUROC *goes over quietly and touches him on the shoulder.*

PAUL.

[*Starting up in dismay.*]

You here, Gouroc!

GOUROC.

I am, old friend,—though you seem scarce glad to see me.

PAUL.

Pardon, Comrade; you find me at a moment when my mind's absorbed with many cares.

GOUROC.

I understand;—in times like these perplexity pursues the patriot. I would not now intrude, dear friend, if duty did not force me.

PAUL.

[*With sudden suspicion.*]

Duty! And what duty can bring you here?

GOUROC.

I have important warrants for your signature.

PAUL.

[*Sitting again, with a sigh of relief.*]

Another time.—I cannot sign them now.

GOUROC.

[*Firmly.*]

Friend, the business of the Republic is sacred; it cannot be postponed.

PAUL.

[*Wearily.*]

Well, well!—What are these warrants?

[*Takes up pen carelessly.*

GOUROC.

[*Calling off papers, as he gives them to* PAUL *to sign.*]

Warrants for the arrest of Catherine Cler—

[PAUL *signs.*]

Maxime Berton—

[PAUL *signs.*]

Marie Legrand—

[PAUL *signs.*]

And this blank warrant for a suspected party, whose name that fool Potin has registered so badly that I must get him to decipher it before I can fill it in.

[PAUL *signs mechanically.*]

[*Aside.*]

'Tis done!—And she is mine!

[*Aloud.*]

Shall you be at the club to-night, friend?

PAUL.

[*Shortly.*]

No!

[*Night comes on.*

GOUROC.

What excuse shall I offer the fraternity?

PAUL.

Say I am busy—busy—[*Striking his breast.*] breaking the heart of a traitor to France!

GOUROC.

[*Going.*]

A welcome message.—I sha'n't forget it.

[*Exit.*

PAUL.

Wife gone!—Home desolated!—Naught left but the haunting memory of joy forever lost!—Ah, I am weary, heart-broken—helpless!

[*He sinks into the chair at desk, and buries his face in his arms. Slowly the light dims to darkness.*

At back, the stage is transformed into a TABLEAU OF KAUVAR'S DREAM OF ANARCHY.

Mysterious music accompanies the Dream, which consists of a tableau of the guillotine in the Place de la Revolution, in Paris, by moonlight.

Here is seen the scaffold, with its ghastly paraphernalia, surrounded by ferocious SANS CULOTTES, *and* GENS D'ARMES. *Amidst them is an old hag.*

The death-cart, with its load of victims, is seen in the foreground—the entrance to the garden with the palace of the Tuilleries in the background.

The HEADSMAN *stands ready, near the knife of the guillotine*

From the death-cart DIANE *glides on and slowly goes up the scaffold steps.*

As she reaches the top, she is seized roughly by the HEADSMAN.

At this moment PAUL *starts with a cry of agony from his chair—and at his shriek, the whole Tableau of the Dream instantly disappears.*

PAUL.

[*Starting up wildly.*]

No, no!—My life for hers!—My life for hers!

[*Waking, as the Dream disappears, he looks about dazed and bewildered; then bursts into hysterical laughter.*]

A dream!—Thank God, a dream!—Only a horrible dream!

[*Suddenly stops short in horror.*]

How dark and still the house is. My God!—Something has happened!—What is it?

[*Shrieks with terror.*]

Diane!—Diane!

NANETTE.

[*Entering with lamp.*]

What's the matter?

PAUL.

Diane—Mademoiselle Diane, where is she?

DIANE.

[*Appearing, dressed to go away.*]

Here!

PAUL.

[*Makes a spontaneous movement toward her, then checks himself and turns to* NANETTE.]

Leave us!

[NANETTE *goes silently away.* PAUL *speaks to* DIANE *hoarsely.*]

Where are you going?

DIANE.

I am going to do my duty—follow the father who would die without my care.

PAUL.

[*After a pause.*]

Yes, I remember now.—You are right.—You will be safer out of France.—The dream! The dream!

DIANE.

What dream?

PAUL.

No matter! I am resigned now! Yes, resigned—resigned—resigned!

[*Sinks sobbing into chair.*

DIANE.

No, no, Paul!—I cannot endure this!—I will stay! I will stay!

PAUL.

[*Starting up.*]

No! You must not! I dare not keep you here.—I fear the worst!

DIANE.

What do you mean?

PAUL.

Don't ask me. I do not know myself. But you—when you are gone—you will not forget me?

DIANE.

Not while memory lasts!

PAUL.

And I—perhaps I—some day—shall be free to seek you.

DIANE.

God grant that day is near!

PAUL.

And we—when we meet again, will you find courage to acknowledge who I am?

DIANE.

Nay—if you desire it—I'll prove my deathless love before I go.—I'll tell my father all.

PAUL.

No, never!—Never till I've won a name that even your proud father is forced to honour. Meantime, I ask but this—your love and trust, while I have life to strive.

DIANE.

You shall have it!—Yes, through sunshine and shadow, I will love and trust you to the end.

[*They embrace.*

DUKE.

[*Outside.*]

Nanette, the coach is ready: be quick, bear our baggage to the door.

[PAUL *and* DIANE *separate quickly. Entering, the* DUKE *glances suspiciously at the two, then advances to* PAUL.]

Paul Kauvar, let us not part in bitterness. I owe you much; I grieve to see you suffer. Courage! Believe me, I never honoured you as I do now.

[*Extends his hand.* PAUL *turns away.*]

Will you not take my hand?

PAUL.

No, Monsieur. Not until you think it worthy to guide and guard your daughter, as my wife.

DUKE.

[*Starts haughtily, then turns to* DIANE.]

Come, child! 'Tis time that we were gone.

DIANE.

[*Crossing and extending her hand to* PAUL.]

Farewell!

PAUL.

[*Taking her hand, speaks aside to her.*]

Remember, love and trust.

DIANE.

Forever!

[PAUL *kisses her hand. She comes slowly to her father, keeping her eyes in anguish on* PAUL.

[*The* DUKE *leads her toward the folding doors which are suddenly thrown open, disclosing a platoon of* GUARDS. DIANE *shrieks, the* DUKE *starts back,* PAUL *turns in horror.* TABOOZE *advances into the room.*

TABOOZE.

In the name of the Republic, I arrest Honoré Albert Maxime, heretofore Duc de Beaumont.

DIANE.

[*Clasping the* DUKE.]
Father!

PAUL.

[*Sternly.*]
What does this mean?—Whose name is on that warrant?

TABOOZE.

[*With surprise.*]
Why, your own, Citizen.
[PAUL *recoils, stunned.*

DUKE.

What! Betrayed by you?

DIANE.

No, no! It is not true!
[*Snatching the paper, looking, then with a cry.*]
Great heaven!—It is!—His name and hand!
[*She sinks down in despair.*

PAUL.

[*Passionately, to the* DUKE.]
I betray you!—I, Paul Kauvar.—'Tis false!
[*To* DIANE.]
You at least will not believe this lie.

DUKE.

[*Interposing.*]
Silence! Better death to her than the pollution of another word from you!

PAUL.

But my God!—You do not know.—She is—

DIANE.

[*Starting up wildly.*]

Stop!—I forbid you to say more!

CURTAIN.

ACT II.

SCENE. *Interior of the Prison of the Republic. A room with cells.—Entrance to outer corridor. Table with chairs near it.—As curtain rises, howls of a Mob are heard outside.*

POTIN.

[*Entering in the midst of the howls, then clapping his hands to his ears.*]

Oh, that I were deaf! Then I'd escape the shriek of my wife, and the roar of this cursed tribunal condemning poor devils to death.

[*Renewed howls.*]

Aye, that's right! Howl on, hyenas! I could howl, too, yesterday, as well as the worst of ye. But I can't now; no, not since the arrest of the poor old Duke. There he lies, in yonder cell, and here am I quartered as a witness against him—and that villain Gouroc has done all this!

[*Enter* GOUROC *quietly in the background.*]

Curse him! He rules me with a rod of red-hot iron! I wish I had him here now! By the gods! I'd take courage for once; I'd tackle him with my tongue—like my wife. I'd say—

GOUROC.

[*Advancing coolly.*]

Well, Citizen,—you'd say—?

POTIN.

[*Aside, startled.*]

The devil take you!

GOUROC.

What would you say?

POTIN.

Nothing!—anything!—everything!

GOUROC.

That's lucky!—I have much for you to say before the day is done. The trial of the Duke will soon begin. When asked who gave you the order for the Duke's arrest, you must swear that it was Paul Kauvar who did so.

POTIN.

Why, Lord help me! 'Twas you who gave me the order, and forced me to carry it, too.

GOUROC.

Possibly; but, in spite of that, my name must not be mentioned in the affair, to any one, do you hear?

POTIN.

Alas, I do!

GOUROC.

And will swear as I command?

POTIN.

[*With sudden resolution.*]
Never!

GOUROC.

Do you care to save your head?

POTIN.

Of course! What could I do without it?

GOUROC.

If you refuse to attest as I have dictated, I will declare you guilty of treason in trying to conceal the presence of the Duke in Paris. Such a declaration from me is sure perdition to you. How say you now: will you swear?

POTIN.

[*Wilting.*]
I will swear.

GOUROC.

You are wise.
[*Going.*]
Within an hour, the trial comes on. Be at hand, or—

[*Making a sign across his throat.*]
There's nothing like this to quiet a traitor's tongue.
[*Exit.*

POTIN.

[*Looking after him.*]
To lie living, and be a coward—or to lie dead, and be a corpse; that's the riddle.—No! I'll be neither a coward nor a corpse. I'll run away!—run like a brave man, enlist in the army of Vendée, and so escape damnation, and my wife.
[*Starts off.*]
Liberty, lend thy wings that I may fly—
[NANETTE *appears.*]
Ye gods!—Fate is false again!

NANETTE.

Ha! It's you, is it?

POTIN.

No, it was me; but now you're here, I'm nobody.

NANETTE.

Where's the Duke?

POTIN

[*Pointing.*]
In that cell.

NANETTE.

And I believe 'twas you betrayed him!

POTIN.

[*Indignantly.*]
That's a lie!

NANETTE.

Well said! Short and sharp, like the truth.
[*She pats* POTIN *on the back. He turns away.*]
Bravo!—But one moment! Do you know who did betray him?
[POTIN *shakes his head mournfully.*]
You do know! I can see by the wag of your head you know, and I mean to make you tell me!—But I can't stop now; I'm here to see Mam'selle Diane; where is she?

POTIN.

[*Pointing to cell.*]
There—with her father.

NANETTE.

I'll be back soon, and then I'll give you a piece of my mind.

POTIN.

Give me peace if you like, dear, but keep the mind for yourself; you've none to spare.

NANETTE.

Woe to you when next we meet!
[*She flounces out.*

POTIN.

Yes, it's woe to me whene'er we meet!—But now to fly; I've no time to lose; between my wife and Gouroc, I shall go cracked. So here's for liberty, and Vendée!
[*Exit into his room.*

Enter GOUROC, *followed by* GUARDS *escorting* MARDOCHE.

GOUROC.

[*To* GUARDS.]
You may leave the prisoner with me.
[*Exit* GUARDS.]
And so, Mardoche, you have been tried and condemned.

MARDOCHE.

Yes. Accused by beasts, tried by fools, and condemned by assassins.

GOUROC.

And of what were you accused?

MARDOCHE.

I was a quiet cobbler; I made shoes for Jacobins that pinched their toes, so I was accused of sympathy with aristocrats.

GOUROC.

Is this all the cry they raised against you?

MARDOCHE.

No. I was never heard to swear, so I was watched—and was

seen upon my knees. As piety is poison to the Republic, I was accused of being a priest! I was searched, and these were found upon me.

[*Showing a crucifix and rosary.*]

This was enough. I was immediately condemned to die.

GOUROC.

A fine fool you were, to be caught with such baubles in your bosom. Had you forgotten old mother Dupaix?

MARDOCHE.

The old woman who never gossiped, wore clean linen, and kept four cats?

GOUROC.

The same—who was therefore accused of being a Duchess in disguise, and sent to the guillotine.

MARDOCHE.

Moral:—In this age of reason, death to him who prays!

GOUROC.

Or keeps four cats! But cheer up, Citizen; I have a crumb of comfort for you yet. In your cell someone is waiting impatiently to see you.

MARDOCHE.

Who?

GOUROC.

Your sister.

MARDOCHE.

Great heavens! Of what do they accuse her?

GOUROC.

Nothing. She is here by my care to bid you farewell.—Listen and understand.—You are going to die, and leave your sister in poverty amidst the perils of the Republic.—What would you be willing to do to provide her with an independence?

MARDOCHE.

I would do anything. I can do nothing.

GOUROC.

You are mistaken. If you choose, before you die, you can place in her hands 10,000 francs.

MARDOCHE.

How?

GOUROC.

By helping me to save another man's life.

MARDOCHE.

I do not understand.

GOUROC.

The Duc de Beaumont has been discovered, and is about to be condemned. For reasons of my own, I wish to save his life. There is but one way. You, who are destined to die soon, must be disguised as the Duke, answer to his name, and go to the scaffold in his stead. Consent to do this—and you shall place in your sister's hands 10,000 francs in gold.

MARDOCHE.

What! That Jacobin of Jacobins, Gouroc, asks a cobbler to save a Duke—?

GOUROC.

Why not? The Republic is poor, the Duke is rich. He has been condemned for our glory. But if his secret escape will bring us gold, why not crown the Republic with riches as well as fame? Is not this Patriotism?

MARDOCHE.

Yes, Patriotism to-day! Yesterday and to-morrow—Jesuitism.

GOUROC.

Well, your answer. Will you save the Duke?

MARDOCHE.

[*After a pause.*]
I will.

GOUROC.

Good! In your cell you'll find everything for your disguise.

MARDOCHE.

[*As howls are heard outside.*]

Listen.—That is the voice of fraternity shrieking for fratricide!

GOUROC.

By heaven! No cobbler talks as you do!—Who are you? What are you?

MARDOCHE.

A victim—to present madness! An atonement—for past wrongs! A pledge for future progress!—The Abbé de St. Simon.

GOUROC.

Ha! As I suspected.

[SOLDIERS *are heard approaching.*]

Take care!—Hurry to your cell; they are coming for the Duke.

MARDOCHE.

And my sister—?

GOUROC.

You shall have the money at your parting.

MARDOCHE.

Thus my death will bring her more than all the years I might have lived to love her. [*Exit.*

OFFICER.

[*Entering, followed by* GUARDS, *and presenting paper to* GOUROC.]

An order for the person of Duc de Beaumont.

GOUROC.

[*Looking at order.*]

Correct.—There is his cell.

OFFICER.

[*Reading from paper at the door of* DUKE'S *cell.*]

Honoré Albert Maxime, heretofore Duc de Beaumont, you are called for trial for your life. In the name of the law, stand forth!

The DUKE *appears with* DIANE *clinging to him, followed by* NANETTE.

DUKE.

I am ready.

[*The* GUARDS *surround him.*

OFFICER.

[*To* DIANE.]

Young woman, free your father; he must follow me alone.

DIANE.

If he is guilty, then I am guilty. I have shared his prison; I claim the right to share his scaffold.

OFFICER.

You are not called, and cannot go with him.

DUKE.

Courage, child! Remember who you are, and scorn to show these miscreants what you feel.

[*Putting her gently from his breast.*]

We shall meet again.—

[*Turning to* OFFICER.]

Lead on, sir.

[*The* GUARDS *go off with the* DUKE.—DIANE *falls into a chair near table, overcome.* NANETTE *approaches her;* GOUROC *waves her back.*

GOUROC.

[*Pointing to cell.*]

Wait there, till you're wanted.

[NANETTE *goes out sullenly.* GOUROC *draws near to* DIANE.]

At last I'm free to crave your pardon for the part I'm forced to play in these dark days of tragedy.—Say you forgive me.

DIANE.

I have nothing to forgive, sir.—You did not betray my father, and if you dare to feel for such as we, then it is for the Republic to pardon your secret treachery.

GOUROC.

Always cruel, Madamoiselle. If you knew the truth, you could not wound me with your scorn.

DIANE.

[*Going.*]
If my face offends you, I will go.

GOUROC.

Stay, and be just.—I am the slave of a great purpose. I am fast securing the ruin of the Republic. My affected zeal but masks the well-aimed blows I strike at the enemies of our order.—Before many weeks have past, Robespierre will go to the scaffold, the Jacobins be ruined, and the Republic crushed.—To this great end I am content to suffer anything, even your contempt, if need be.

DIANE.

Yes, I despise all blows dealt in darkness.

GOUROC.

Even though those very blows could save your father's life?

DIANE.

[*Turning and staring at him.*]
Save my father's life?

GOUROC.

Yes; I hold it in my power to set your father free, and escape with both of you to Vendée.—Say but the word and it is done.

DIANE.

Tell me the word that I may speak it quickly.

GOUROC.

You know the past.—My one wild dream was to win you as my wife. Revolution came; I lost you in the chaos of the times; and when at last I found you, a traitor had nearly caused your death.

DIANE.

[*In anguish.*]
No more, sir! No more!

GOUROC.

But I can save you yet.

DIANE.

Save my father! That is all I ask.

GOUROC.

To save his life I must imperil my own. I am willing to do this, but—

DIANE.

[*Scornfully.*]

You must have your price!

GOUROC.

Yes—that price, the right to save and guard you as my wife. One word of hope, and I am your slave forever.

DIANE.

Such a word would be cruelty to you, and crime in me.

[*She starts to go.*

GOUROC.

[*Seizing* DIANE'S *hand.*]

Hear me, I beg—beseech—

[*A bell tolls.*]

Nay—I command!—Listen!

A VOICE.

[*Calls slowly in the distance.*]

Hubert, Marquis de Ferrand,—Comte de Vigny,—Duc de Beaumont——

[DIANE *turns in horror.*

GOUROC.

Your father is called for trial! That means certain death.

DIANE.

[*Kneeling.*]

Save him!—I will pay the price with everything I have.

GOUROC

I may hope?

DIANE.

Yes! Take hope from my despair.

GOUROC.

Then you will be my wife?

DIANE.

When he and I are free.

GOUROC.

Your father shall be saved!—I go to perfect all my plans.
[*Kissing her hand.*]
From this moment I am yours—body, mind and soul!
[*Exit hurriedly.*

DIANE.

When he has saved my father—death shall deliver me.
[*Exit.*

POTIN *enters cautiously, with various things hidden under his clothes, giving him a grotesque appearance.*

POTIN.

Now, O Fate, is your chance to protect a patriot! If I can only get away,—I shall escape perjury in Court, and tongue-lashing from my wife!—Now to run!—To run for Vendée! Better the awful thunder of masculine war than the piercing tenderness of a woman's tongue!
[*Starting to run off, he begins to sing—to the tune of the Marseillaise chorus:*]
To leave—to leave my wife!—

NANETTE.

[*Rushing in and stopping him.*]
Hold, Citizen Potin!

POTIN.

[*Wilting.*]
Oh, Republic, I am lost!

NANETTE.

Dodolphe—you're up to mischief! Speak out—what's up?

POTIN.

Patience, gentle lamb!

NANETTE.

Don't lamb me, sir!
[*Twisting him round.*]
What's this mean?
[*Tapping him.*]
Porpoise!

[*Pulling breeches from under his coat.*]
Culottes!
[*Pulling cap from his breast.*]
Ye gods, what's this?
[*Pulling hose from his pockets.*]
By heaven! A woman's hose!
[*Shaking hose in his face.*]
What does this mean?

POTIN.

Nothing, precious love! This is my uniform;—I have recruited for Vendée.

NANETTE.

You—a soldier?

POTIN.

[*Posing.*]
Yes: The safety of France demands it. I go to preserve the Republic! France beckons—while Victory extends her arms, panting to embrace my noble form!

NANETTE.

Embrace ye?
[*Putting his head under her arm.*]
Let Victory try it if she dare!

TURNKEY.

[*Entering with* GUARD.]
Citizen Potin, you are wanted as a witness.

POTIN.

Caught!—From the frying-pan into the fire!

NANETTE.

We shall meet again, my dear.

POTIN.

Don't remind me now; I'm sick enough already.
[*Enter* PAUL KAUVAR. POTIN *starts at sight of him, and speaks to the* GUARD.]
I'm ready; show the way.

PAUL.

[*To* POTIN.]

Stop!—Thank heaven I have found you! Tell me, who ordered the Duke's arrest?

POTIN.

[*Sullenly.*]

What I know of, that I'll tell only to the Court.

[*Exit.*

PAUL.

[*Turning to* NANETTE, *who is going.*]

Nanette, one word.

NANETTE.

What word can an honest woman speak that you would care to hear?

PAUL.

Justice!—I want that word, and all it signifies.

[*Mob howls outside.*

NANETTE.

Listen! Go to them—they'll give you justice, aye, and glory, for you betrayed the innocent—to glut their appetite for blood.

PAUL.

That's a lie—a vile, infamous, monstrous lie!

NANETTE.

Is it a lie that you signed the warrant for the Duke's arrest?

PAUL.

My name was forged.

NANETTE.

I know your hand too well to be deceived. I've seen the warrant; it bears your name, and written by yourself.

PAUL.

Then it was obtained by some strange trick! I've tried to learn the truth, but no one will tell me who took the warrant to the office of the Guard.

NANETTE.

I wish I could believe you.

PAUL.

[*Forcing her to face him.*]
And so you shall!—Do I look like the vilest of mankind?

NANETTE.

No; in looks you're lucky!

PAUL.

Would any man conspire to kill the wife he adores?

NANETTE.

Why ask that?

PAUL.

Because Diane de Beaumont is my wife.

NANETTE.

Your wife?

PAUL.

Yes! For me to betray her father would be to break her heart! Pain to her is the anguish of the damned to me! Can you not see that I am—I must be innocent?

NANETTE.

In these days the fairest faces mask the foulest souls! Looks and words prove nothing! Evidence alone will clear you of this crime.

PAUL.

That—I have not been able to obtain.

NANETTE.

Then get it quickly before it is too late.

PAUL.

Where is Diane—my wife?

NANETTE.

[*Pointing.*]
There!—Praying for the father she believes you betrayed.

PAUL.

No, she cannot! By the light of her own love she sees the innocence of mine.

NANETTE.

Then love is lunacy!

PAUL.

Send her here to me!

NANETTE.

She will not come.

PAUL.

I'll stake my life she will!

NANETTE.

You shall see.

[*Exit.*

JEAN LITAIS *enters, watching* PAUL *intently.*

PAUL.

Two things at any cost I must accomplish! First, prove my innocence of treachery, and save her father from the guillotine.

JEAN.

[*Advancing.*]

For that I came to help you.

PAUL.

Who are you?

JEAN.

Look well and you will see.

PAUL.

I've seen your face before, but have forgotten where we met.

JEAN.

I am Jean Litais. Six months ago, I was accused, and about to be condemned. You saw—took pity—spoke in my behalf—and by your eloquence saved my life! So now the life you saved, and all its service, is yours to use, or forfeit as you please! A lion freed a mouse—the mouse now comes to serve the lion.

PAUL.

I do not understand.

JEAN.

I am turnkey here, though once a servant of the Duke's. You love his daughter; I can help her father to escape.

PAUL.

How?

JEAN.

[*Crossing to the door.*]

This opens on a staircase leading to the river. Here's the key. I have a boat below. To-night I'll creep up the stairs and knock three times. Open, then, this door—and you'll find deliverance for those you love.

PAUL.

[*Taking the key.*]

How can I repay this deed?

JEAN.

Trust me—that is all.

PAUL.

[*Extending his hand.*]

I will—I do!

JEAN.

[*Kissing* PAUL'S *hand.*]

I'm yours in life or death.

[*Goes to door.*]

Till to-night!

[*Exit.*

PAUL.

[*Alone.*]

Saved!—Thank God!—Their freedom in my hand!—

[*Pausing.*]

And yet she does not come.—Can it be that she believes me guilty—esteems me lower than the foulest worm?

[*Enter* DIANE.]

No, no,—I was right!

[*Going toward her.*]

I knew you'd come.

DIANE.

[*Checking him.*]
Stop!—Let me look at you and say farewell.

PAUL.

Then you really think me guilty?

DIANE.

If an angel had accused you, I would say it was a lie.

PAUL.

Diane! Diane!—My loyal wife!
[*He embraces her.*

DIANE.

[*Shrinking from him.*]
No, no! I am not worthy of your love! I must save my father's life, no matter what it costs me.

PAUL.

Courage, dear heart! I hold here salvation for you both.

DIANE.

You?

PAUL.

Yes! This very night your father shall fly with us to England.

DIANE.

Ah! Then I am free! I need owe him nothing!

PAUL.

Owe whom nothing?
[*The tramp of* SOLDIERS *is heard outside.*

DIANE.

Hark!—The Guard!—Take care!

Enter the DUKE, *with* GUARD *and* POTIN.

DUKE.

[*Contemptuously to* PAUL.]
You here, traitor?

DIANE.

[*Aside to the* DUKE.]

You must not call him that. He did not betray. The proof is this—that he has come to save you.

DUKE.

And so make my debt to him a means of reaching you;—but I would not accept my life from hands unclean with treachery.

PAUL.

There's not a drop of traitor's blood within my veins!

DUKE.

Yet you signed the warrant for my arrest.

PAUL.

Then another hand than mine—unknown to me—filled in your name.

DUKE.

Plausible trickster!—We have here double proof that you are guilty.

[*Enter* GOUROC *in background.*]

The evidence of the man to whom you gave the warrant, commanding him to take it to the Guard.

PAUL.

There's no such man alive—or dead!

DUKE.

Potin, advance.

[POTIN *comes forward sullenly.*]

Repeat what you swore in court.—From whom did you receive the warrant for my arrest?

POTIN.

[*After a struggle.*]

I received it from—

[*Hesitates.*

GOUROC.

[*Aside to* POTIN.]

Take care!—If I denounce—you die!

DUKE.

Well, sir, we are waiting.

POTIN.

[*Desperately.*]

I received it—[*Pointing at* PAUL.] from him.

[PAUL *recoils with horror.* DIANE, *with cry of agony, hides her face upon her father's breast.*

PAUL.

[*Crossing to* POTIN.]

Potin, look at me.—On your word hangs the honour of your old and steadfast friend! Look in my eyes, and, in the name of your own salvation, speak nothing but the truth.

DUKE.

[*Sternly.*]

'Tis useless to intimidate the witness. He will not prove himself a perjurer, and condemn himself to death, even to please so dear a friend as you.

PAUL.

My God!—There is some wicked plot!

DUKE.

Yes—and you're the plotter.

[PAUL *falls prostrate into chair near table. Supporting* DIANE *to the door of his cell, the* DUKE *pauses and speaks.*]

Paul Kauvar, we shall never meet again.—Remember my last words.—Beggars, thieves, assassins may escape perdition; but neither here, nor hereafter, is there any hope for Judas.

[*Exit, supporting* DIANE.

[NANETTE *follows the* DUKE *off.* POTIN *goes into the opposite cell.* GOUROC *crosses to* PAUL.

GOUROC.

How's this, old Comrade? I thought you were antique in the mastery of your emotions.—A man of iron—firm as flint!

PAUL.

Agony is fire that melts the mettle of the hardest man.

GOUROC.

But why should you—a Jacobin—care for this old Duke?

PAUL.

I loved his daughter—she became my wife.

GOUROC.

[*Starting.*]

What! Diane de Beaumont is your wife?

PAUL.

Yes—has been my wife in secret—for six months.

GOUROC.

[*Aside.*]

So I have a double task! To save her—and kill her husband.

[*Aloud.*]

The same old story, Comrade, and as usual a woman mars the plot! You were a patriot, till love enmeshed you in his magic web; then you became the weakest of mankind—a husband. I am sorry, very sorry; but Paul—my friend— if I can serve you now, I beg of you command me.

PAUL.

Yes, you can serve me. You have been my friend—be more!

GOUROC.

Your sorrow seems so deep, I swear I think I'd serve it—even at the cost of conscience! Speak then, without fear.

PAUL.

Help me to save the father of my wife!—See! This key opens yonder door; to-night, at any moment, you may hear three knocks.—That signal will be given by a man who will conduct you safely out of France.

GOUROC.

A man that you can trust?

PAUL.

To the death.—I saved his life.

GOUROC.

But suppose the Duke is called before the signal comes!—I must go and find some man to take his place.

GOUROC *starts to go.* PAUL'S *face lights with a sudden resolution.*

PAUL.

Stop! The man is found.

GOUROC.

Who is he?

PAUL.

The man they call a traitor—Paul Kauvar.

GOUROC.

[*Suppressing a smile of surprise.*]
You?

PAUL.

Yes. When safely out of France, tell them of my fate. My death may convince them I loved too deeply to betray.
[*A bell begins to toll.*

A VOICE.

[*In the distance.*]
Hubert, Marquis de Ferrand,—Mardoche, alias the Abbé de St. Simon—

GOUROC.

They're calling the condemned; there's not an instant to be lost.
[*Crossing to cell.*]
In this cell there hangs an old man's coat and wig, kept here to disguise the spies connected with the prison. Luckily they'll serve your purpose well.
[*Opening cell door.*]
Quick!—Get ready to answer when the Duke is called.

PAUL.

Tell my wife I died for love of her, and honour.
[*Exit.*

GOUROC.

[*In exultation.*]
Thank luck!—This man's death clears my path, and saves the money I meant to pay the Abbé.

Enter DIANE *and* NANETTE.

DIANE.

Where is he? I must see him once again!—Paul! Paul!

[*Starting at sight of* GOUROC.]

Who's there?

GOUROC.

'Tis I! Here to save your father.

THE VOICE.

[*Outside.*]

Comte de Vigny,—André de la Roche—

GOUROC.

That's the last call of the condemned.—Your father's name stands next upon the roll.

DIANE.

Save him!—Save him!

GOUROC.

Obey me instantly, or all is lost; hide quickly in this cell! Trust to me and wait.

DIANE.

[*Going with* NANETTE *into a cell.*]

God deal with you as you now deal with me!

[*Exit.*

Tramp of GUARDS *outside.*

GOUROC.

[*Crossing to cell and calling.*]

Kauvar!—Be quick!—stand ready. By heaven!—A close shave!

OFFICER *and* GUARDS *enter.*

OFFICER.

[*Advancing.*]

Honoré Albert Maxime, Duc de Beaumont, you are called to the guillotine.

[PAUL *comes forth in silence.*]

Fall in.—Forward, march!

[*As the* GUARDS *start with* PAUL, DIANE *rushes in with a cry of agony.*

DIANE.

Father!—Father!—We have been deceived!

[DIANE *rushes into* PAUL'S *arms; he embraces her passionately.* GUARDS *force them apart and go out with* PAUL.]

[*Held back by* GOUROC *and* NANETTE, DIANE *shrieks.*]

Father—father!

DUKE.

[*Entering.*]

Diane!—What is it?

DIANE.

[*Turning in amazement and joy.*]

What!—You are there?

GOUROC.

Yes, saved by me.

DIANE.

And he—? Who was he they dragged away?

GOUROC.

A man condemned to die—whom I disguised—to take your father's place.

DIANE.

[*Falling on her knees.*]

O God! Spare this man all pain in death—and give him life eternal!

CURTAIN.

ACT III.

SCENE. *Headquarters of Royalists in Vendée. Interior of hall in old chateau. Fireplace; large doorways with staircase leading to terrace, overlooking Granville; Faubourg de Calvaire in middle ground. Doors from hall. Bay window with large table covered with papers, maps, etc. Charts near table and fireplace.*

DISCOVERED: SENTINEL *on terrace;* LA HOGUE *seated at the table busy with papers.*

At rise of curtain—drums and fifes heard in distance.

DENISE *enters, goes to terrace, gazes anxiously, then turns and crosses quickly to* LA HOGUE.

DENISE.

[*Shouting loudly.*]
Monsieur La Hogue!

LA HOGUE.

[*Gruffly.*]
Well?

DENISE.

Do you hear?

LA HOGUE.

[*Impatiently.*]
Hear what?

DENISE.

The drums and piccolos yonder.

LA HOGUE.

[*Listening.*]
I can hear nothing.
[*Drums, etc., sound more loud.*

DENISE.

But listen now, it grows louder—up from Ville d'Avranches.

LA HOGUE.

[*Starting up.*]
D'Avranches?—Ha! Re-inforcements for the Kings' army! None too soon!
[*Drums, etc., cease.*]
[*Enter an* ORDERLY, *who presents papers.* LA HOGUE *takes papers, reads, and exclaims.*]
The Count de Parame with recruits!
[*To the* ORDERLY.]
Tell your Colonel to report here instantly! General de la Rochejacquelein [*Enter* LA ROCHEJACQUELEIN.] is indignant at his delay, and—

LA ROCHEJACQUELEIN.

[*To* LA HOGUE.]
Gently, old friend! La Rochejacquelein will speak for himself.

[*To* ORDERLY.]

Ask the Count to honour me with his presence here as speedily as possible.

[*Exit* ORDERLY.]

Now these re-inforcements have arrived, we'll give these rebels battle.

LA HOGUE.

At last, thank God! And we're ready for the fight.

[*Pointing.*]

In the Faubourg de Calvaire there's hardly a house but harbours a detachment of our men.

LA ROCHE.

With that village in our hands we'll bring Granville town to terms. To-night we will assault the place at every point.

LA HOGUE.

[*Reverently.*]

And God in mercy aid King Louis' men!

LA ROCHE *and* DENISE.

[*Together.*]

Amen!

LA ROCHE.

[*To* LA HOGUE.]

Await the Count upon the terrace, and take him to my private room. But no roughness to the Colonel—try to be charming for a change.

LA HOGUE.

Bah! Leave charmers to women,—only fighters win at war! [*Exit.*

LA ROCHE.

[*To* DENISE.]

How long since you have heard from Jean Litais?

DENISE.

Not since he, my lover, went to Paris to aid the Duc de Beaumont to escape.

LA ROCHE.

This fiendish reign of terror has prevented me from hearing of the Duke till now.

DENISE.

And you have heard—?

LA ROCHE.

The worst of news! Among some papers captured in a skirmish, I found this journal, [*Producing paper.*] printed at Paris some three months ago. It contains a list of those beheaded the preceding day.—See this name I've underlined.

DENISE.

[*Reading.*]
"The Duc de Beaumont."

Enter a MAN *from panel in wall up stage.*

LA ROCHE.

Guillotined at night, upon the tenth of last October.

DENISE.

My God! If Jean has failed to save the Duke, he must be dead himself!

THE MAN.

[*Advancing.*]
Not yet!

LA ROCHE.

[*Turning quickly.*]
Who's this?

DENISE.

It's Jean!—
[*Rushing into his arms.*]
My Jean returned!

LA ROCHE.

Litais!—Is it really you?

JEAN.

Every bit of me, my lord.

DENISE.

Thank heaven!

LA ROCHE.

How did you pass the guard?

JEAN.

Faith, I know every corner of the old chateau. No guard could bar my way while I'd such news to bring! The Duke and his daughter are here—in the park.

LA ROCHE.

Alive and safe—?

JEAN.

As you are!—Grant me a guard to bring them through our lines.

LA ROCHE.

[*Strikes a bell.*]

[*Enter* ORDERLY, *who salutes.*]

See that Monsieur and his friends have safe passage through our lines.

ORDERLY *crosses stage and stands at door.*

JEAN.

In an instant we'll return.—Come, Denise; you shall see your old master once again.

DENISE.

And never let you leave my side while I have life to love you.

[*Exeunt* DENISE, JEAN *and* ORDERLY, *who salutes* GUARD *before departing. Tumult in distance.*]

LA HOGUE.

[*Entering.*]

The Count is here and anxious for the fight.

[LA ROCHEJACQUELEIN, *listening, pays no attention.* LA HOGUE *speaks impatiently.*]

Do you hear?

LA ROCHE.

Yes, I hear a tumult yonder! Can it be mutiny—revolt?

[*Enter* SECOND ORDERLY. *He presents paper to* LA ROCHEJACQUELEIN, *who reads it aloud.*]

"Have captured Jacobin soldiers. The peasants demand their lives. Shall I surrender them or hold them at your pleasure?

La Val—Captain of King's Guards."

[*To* LA HOGUE *eagerly.*]

We may obtain information from these fellows. See La Val at once, command him to guard his prisoners with his life, and send them here to me.

LA HOGUE.

But the Count is awaiting orders for to-night's attack.

LA ROCHE.

[*Going.*]
While you see La Val, I'll see the Count.
[*Exit.*

LA HOGUE.

[*To* ORDERLY.]
To Captain La Val!
[*Exit quickly with* ORDERLY.

SENTINEL.

[*Outside.*]
Who goes there?

JEAN.

[*Outside.*]
A friend!

SENTINEL.

[*Outside.*]
Advance with countersign.

ORDERLY *advances, salutes the* SENTINEL, *whispers in his ear, then steps back against balustrade of terrace as characters enter.—When characters are on,* ORDERLY *salutes* SENTINEL, *who returns salute.* ORDERLY *goes out.* SENTINEL *about faces and disappears.*

Enter JEAN, DENISE, GOUROC, NANETTE, DUKE, AND DIANE.

JEAN.

[*To the* DUKE.]
You're safe at last, Monsieur, among your friends.

DIANE.

[*Grasping* JEAN'S *hand.*]
Thanks to your devotion.

DENISE.

[*To the* DUKE.]
I will announce your coming to the General.
[*Exit.*

NANETTE.

[*To* DIANE.]
Here, child, be seated, and taste comfort once again.
[DIANE *sits near the fire; the* DUKE *and* GOUROC *at table.*]
Now try to smile a bit.

DIANE.

I have forgotten how.
[*Calling.*]
Jean!

JEAN.

[*Crossing to* DIANE.]
Yes, Madame?

DIANE.

Hush! Do not let my father hear you call me Madame.
[*Converses aside with* JEAN.

GOUROC.

[*Taking a newspaper from table.*]
Strange!—a Paris journal, dated the day after our escape.

DUKE.

[*Taking the paper.*]
There may be some notice of our flight.
[*Reads.*

JEAN.

[*To* DIANE.]
Will you never confess your marriage to Kauvar?

DIANE.

Never!—Unless he finds us with evidence of innocence none can question.

JEAN.

He will! We can trust the wit of his deep love for that.

DIANE.

So you believe him innocent?

JEAN.

As innocent as my own sweetheart, dear Denise.

[DIANE *weeps.*]

What—tears, Madame?

DIANE.

Tears of triumph—that your heart echoes mine! Ah, Jean, we two, alone, of all the world, believe he's not a traitor.

DUKE.

Here's a list of martyrs slaughtered the day that we escaped.

GOUROC.

[*Taking the paper.*]

And here's a name underlined with ink.

[*Starting up with great joy.*]

By heaven, your own!—See!—In the list of fallen heads—the Duc de Beaumont!

[*The* DUKE *takes paper.*

DIANE.

[*Coming toward* GOUROC.]

You speak of the man who took my father's place, as though you exulted in his death!—Was he an enemy of yours?

GOUROC.

I rejoice that the man's disguise was not discovered—for the report of your father's death prevented our pursuit.

DUKE.

[*Joyfully to* GOUROC.]

You remember the Abbé de St. Simon?

GOUROC.

Yes. He was condemned to die with you.

DUKE.

This journal says that he escaped from the death-cart as it rumbled to the scaffold through the crowd.

GOUROC.

[*Starting, and with great emphasis.*]

Impossible!

DUKE.

[*Holding out the paper.*]
See for yourself!
[GOUROC *takes paper eagerly.*

LA ROCHE.

[*Entering, with a cry of joy.*]
Duke!

DUKE.

[*Holding out his arms.*]
Henri!

LA ROCHE.

[*Embracing the* DUKE.]
In days of misery, a moment such as this is sweet indeed. But how did you escape? I saw your name among the guillotined.

DUKE.

[*Turning to* GOUROC.]
This gentleman wrought a way for our deliverance!—Monsieur le Marquis de Vaux.

LA ROCHE.

[*Grasping* GOUROC'S *hand.*]
Monsieur—the King's friends are all your debtors.

GOUROC.

Nay, sir, the debt is mine. 'Tis a privilege to save such precious lives.

DUKE.

[*Presenting* DIANE.]
Here's a lass you played with, years ago.

LA ROCHE.

What!—My little cousin—grown so stately and so sad! Mademoiselle, I claim a kinsman's right to kiss away these shadows.

DIANE.

And I yield the right with pleasure, cousin Henri.

LA ROCHE.

[*Kisses her.*]
Good cheer, sweet cousin! You are now protected by the

soldiers of the King, who—God willing—will punish those who brought this shadow to your face.

GOUROC.

That may not prove an easy task! Granville is overrun with rebels, who are urged to most atrocious crimes by Carrac.

LA ROCHE.

Yes—Thomas Carrac—a brutal monster, reeking with loyal blood; a loathsome anarchist, who glories in the vilest deeds.

GOUROC.

Ravishing without remorse the daughters of our race.

LA ROCHE.

If we could capture wretches such as he, it might end our civil war.

DIANE.

Is he so hard to take?

LA ROCHE.

Yes. Reptiles are worse to overcome than lions. They bite unseen, and escape by crawling. This Carrac is brave in words, but too craven to face fighting in the field. Our soldiers rarely reach these civil sinners.

DUKE.

Let us forget them here. For now we will task your hospitality for a time.

LA ROCHE.

I swear I have not felt the poverty that war entails till now. My old chateau has been dismantled—this hall alone is habitable. I feel ashamed to offer you such shabby quarters.

DUKE.

Nay, cousin, a bed of stones with friends is better than a bed of down with those we do not love.

DENISE.

[*Entering, speaks to* LA ROCHEJACQUELEIN.]
A couch and fire are ready in the room that was your mother's.

LA ROCHE.

[*To* DIANE.]
Where doubtless you'll be glad to take some rest.

DIANE.

I confess the need, Monsieur.

LA ROCHE.

Denise, show the way.
[DENISE *crosses to the door.*

DIANE.

[*At the door.*]
Till to-night, kind friends.

LA ROCHE.

Till then, good rest.
[DIANE *courtesies and goes out with* NANETTE.]
Gentlemen, I pray you, make yourselves at home; important business claims my time.—I'll rejoin you within an hour.

DUKE.

We're here to help, not mar the cause; command us in all ways.

LA ROCHE.

Presently!—Till then the poor old house is yours.
[*Exit.*
[*Exit* JEAN.

DUKE.

[*Sitting near the fire.*]
At last, praise God! We're out of reach of traitors!

GOUROC.

Not yet!—The rebel hosts have gathered here at Granville in great force. They may rout the royal army, and capture all of us.

DUKE.

No, not all, for I shall die first, fighting in the ranks.

GOUROC.

But Diane, your daughter—?

DUKE.

Must take the chances of a soldier's child.

GOUROC.

You forget her peril from this scoundrel, Carrac.—Why not put her safely out of the reach of such a brute?

DUKE.

How?

GOUROC.

There are vessels here by which we can escape to England.

DUKE.

I fly no further. I owe the King and country service here.

GOUROC.

Then let Diane go with me to friends in London. When I've found for her safe asylum, I'll return to do my duty at your side.

DUKE.

The daughter of a peer of France could hardly go so far without protection worthy of her rank.

GOUROC.

That she can secure as a Marquise, and my wife.

[*The* DUKE *turns quickly in surprise.*]

I know, dear Duke, that you are richer, nobler than myself, but then the love I bear your daughter, together with the dangers that surround her life and honour here—

DUKE.

Say no more!—There's nothing that would ease my mind so much as to see Diane your wife.

GOUROC.

Then plead my cause with her.

DUKE.

I'll more than plead.—Her perils urge me to command this marriage.

GOUROC.

Then do not lose a moment; the attack begins to-night. Before our army strikes, she and I, as man and wife, should sail for England.

NANETTE.

[*Entering.*]

Monsieur, your daughter desires a word with you—[*Glancing at* GOUROC.] alone.

DUKE.

Say I'll see her here at once.

[*Exit* NANETTE.]

I'll broach this marriage to my child without delay.

GOUROC.

[*Going.*]

I'll be at hand in case you call me.

[*Exit.*

DUKE.

[*Alone.*]

This alliance secures Diane from peril. The Marquis is young, noble,—has saved her life, and has a claim on it. She must marry while there's time to get away.

[*Enter* DIANE.]

Now, dear child, what is it?

DIANE.

Father, I loathe this useless life of mine! I long for action—danger—anything that stirs the blood, and brings oblivion.

DUKE.

Oblivion!—Nay, Diane, I have something happier to suggest than that. Time and circumstance commend to you a marriage. We owe our lives to the wisdom of a man who seeks your hand to-day.

DIANE.

The Marquis?—[*After a pause.*] I cannot marry, for I do not love him.

DUKE.

Then 'tis time you did.

DIANE.

No more, I beg of you.—It is impossible!

DUKE.

Impossible! When prompted by the wisdom of a father's love? When your escape from peril and my peace of mind demand it?

DIANE.

I cannot argue.

DUKE.

Then at least explain.

DIANE.

Alas, I dare not.

DUKE.

You fear mere frankness with your truest friend?

[DIANE *sinks into a chair and hides her face. The* DUKE *looks at her with suspicion.*]

By heaven! You hide your face as though to speak implied dishonour.

DIANE.

No, no! It is not that!

DUKE.

Then why torture me with this concealment? Have I been cruel, or faithless as a father?

DIANE.

Never!

DUKE.

Then I claim a father's sacred right to confidence. Give me one good reason why you refuse the man to whom we owe our lives?

DIANE.

I love another.

DUKE.

[*Starting.*]

Another!

[*After a pause.*]

His name—?

DIANE.

What matter, since we shall never meet again?

DUKE.

I understand at last!—'Tis Paul Kauvar!

[DIANE *bows her head.*]

So! The saviour of your father's life is scorned for his betrayer! No wonder that you blush to own it! This makes my course more clear. The safest cure for this disgraceful love will be your marriage.

DIANE.

That cannot be!

DUKE.

[*Going.*]

I say it shall!

DIANE.

[*Startled.*]

Where are you going?

DUKE.

To seek the priest! Delay is dangerous! You wed to-day and sail to-night for England.

DIANE.

No, no! Have pity! I have no right to marry.

DUKE.

[*In horror.*]

No right?

DIANE.

[*Falling at his feet.*]

I am a wife already.

DUKE.

His wife?—You, my flesh and blood, a traitor's wife!—Oh God! What have I done to merit such a blow as this?

DIANE.

Father,—forgive! Hear me!

DUKE.

[*Flinging her off, rushes to the door.*]

Henri, Marquis—here! All of you!

[*Enter* LA HOGUE, LA ROCHEJACQUELEIN, GOUROC, JEAN *and* DENISE.]

[*To* LA ROCHE.]

Call your guards! Drag this woman away! Fling her to these rebel dogs—for she is one of them!

GOUROC.

What has she done?

DUKE.

Deceived a father's love! Become the mate of my betrayer.

[*Turning on* DIANE.]

Degraded remnant of my race!—Go! Back to your own, wife of a Sans Culotte!

GOUROC.

[*Stepping between them.*]

Stay! There must be some mistake!

DUKE.

No! She has confessed that she's the wife of Paul Kauvar.

GOUROC.

That cannot be, for Paul Kauvar is dead.

DUKE.

Dead? How do you know that?

GOUROC.

Because he, disguised, took your place on the guillotine.

DIANE.

[*Rising.*]

My God!

DUKE.

What! I owe my life to him?

GOUROC.

He died to atone his treachery to you.

DIANE.

Traitors do not die to save their victims! His life was noble! His death sublime!

[*To the* DUKE.]

You have foully wronged the man who bravely met a martyr's death for you!—have scorned and spurned me from your side, because I was his wife. You have disowned me—I now disown *you!*

[*Turning, she goes swiftly up the steps to the terrace.*

LA ROCHE.

Where are you going?

DIANE.

Back to the Sans Culottes!

DUKE.

Diane!—Daughter!

DIANE.

No! Not your daughter—but his wife! No longer Diane de Beaumont—but, thank God,—Diane Kauvar!

CURTAIN.

ACT IV.

SCENE. *Same as Act III.*—DUKE *discovered seated in attitude of despair.*—GOUROC *standing near mantel.*—LA ROCHEJACQUELEIN *enters sadly.*

DUKE.

[*Rising anxiously.*]
What news?

LA ROCHE.

None.
[*The* DUKE *sinks back into chair.*

GOUROC.

Then she has positively escaped?

LA ROCHE.

While we stood dazed with horror at her words—she vanished. Our soldiers have searched, but can find no trace of her.

DUKE.

[*Starting up.*]
I will find her!

LA ROCHE.

[*Barring his way.*]
This is madness.

DUKE.

Let me pass!

LA ROCHE.

Hear me!

DUKE.

While I listen, she is lost!—An army shall not stop me.
[*Breaks from him towards door.*

DENISE.

[*Entering joyfully.*]
She is found!

ALL.

Found?

DENISE.

Yes. Jean tracked her,—they are bringing her here.

JEAN.

[*Entering.*]
General, I have not failed.

LA ROCHE.

[*Grasping his hand.*]
You never do.

LA HOGUE *enters first, followed by two* GUARDS, *whom he directs to the entrance at top of steps.*—DIANE *enters, followed by two* GUARDS.

DIANE.

[*To* LA ROCHEJACQUELEIN.]
By what authority, Monsieur, am I arrested?

DUKE.

By mine. I am your father.

DIANE.

My marriage has set me free of parental rule. I claim the

right to fly from those who have defamed my noble husband. General, command your soldiers to release me!

GOUROC.

No!—You shall not go.

DIANE.

What will prevent me?

GOUROC.

The force of your own honour.

DIANE.

Honour commands me to return to my husband's friends.

GOUROC.

Honour commands you to keep your word with me.

[DIANE *starts and turns away.*]

You promised, if I saved your father, and you were free, you'd be my wife.—I have done my part, you must do yours.

DIANE.

[*Passionately, to* GOUROC.]

Now I understand your joy when you read of the beheadal of the man who took my father's place!—You knew he was my husband.

GOUROC.

I did.

DIANE.

You planned his death to free and force me to this marriage.

GOUROC.

I did not learn that you were his wife till he was going to the guillotine.—Then he told me all, confiding you to my care. I promised him I'd shield you from all peril.—I but keep my word with him, in asking you to keep your word with me.

DIANE.

So you would wed the widow of a Sans Culotte?

GOUROC.

Your husband was my friend; I knew and honoured him.

DIANE.

Ah, you believe, then, that Potin lied when he declared he got the warrant for the Duke's arrest from Paul Kauvar?

GOUROC.

I now believe that your husband was the victim of a trick.

DIANE.

Then swear—before those who have heard the dead defamed—swear that you believe my husband was innocent of infamy.

GOUROC.

[*With deep sincerity.*]

As I hope for mercy from my God, I believe that Paul Kauvar was guiltless of dishonour.

DIANE.

[*Impressed with his sincerity.*]

Then his widow swears to keep her word with you.

[*She extends her hand to* GOUROC.

LA HOGUE *crosses, up steps, to* GUARDS, *and directs them silently to exit.—They about-face, and go out.*

GOUROC.

[*Aside, triumphantly kissing* DIANE'S *hand.*]

At last!

[*Howls of execration outside.*]

What is that?

LA ROCHE.

The mob howling at some captured rebels.

[*Enter* ORDERLY, *who presents paper.*]

[*Reading paper,* LA ROCHEJACQUELEIN *speaks to* ORDERLY.]

Conduct the prisoner here.

[*Exit* ORDERLY.]

[*Turning to* DIANE.]

Cousin, I must ask you to retire. We have secret business to transact.

DUKE.

[*Giving* DIANE *his arm.*]

We will await you in my daughter's room.

[*To* GOUROC.]

Marquis, we can complete the plans for your marriage and escape to England.

[*Exeunt* DIANE, DUKE, JEAN, DENISE *and* GOUROC.

GOUROC.

[*Aside, as he goes out.*]

Now I know that I shall triumph!

LA ROCHE.

[*To* LA HOGUE.]

When and where were these prisoners secured?

LA HOGUE.

At dawn this morning, in the centre of the Faubourg. They fought like fiends! Their leader is a veritable lion.—Though overcome by numbers, he don't seem conquered in the least!—Hang my hide! I cannot help but like him!

[*Howls renewed outside.*

ORDERLY.

[*Entering.*]

The prisoner is here, General.

LA ROCHE.

Bring him in.

[ORDERLY *beckons.—Yells outside.* GUARDS *enter and form on terrace behind entrance.—Enter* PRISONER, *who strides haughtily in.*]

[*To* ORDERLY.]

Retire and guard the doors.

[ORDERLY *right-faces.*—GUARD *goes off with* ORDERLY.]

[*Politely to* PRISONER.]

I see, sir, you're an officer.

PRISONER.

Yes.—Captain of Volunteers in the ranks of the Republic.

LA ROCHE.

To what corps do you belong?

PRISONER.

Kleber's—who waits upon the banks of the river to cut off your retreat.

LA ROCHE.

[*Smiling.*]
We do not propose to retreat, but to advance.

PRISONER.

Before another day you will be driven, routed, into the heart of Vendée.

LA ROCHE.

If boasting wins, your side will doubtless better ours.

PRISONER.

If blows win—your side is sure to fail. You've not a regiment that's trained better than a pack of boys!

LA HOGUE.

I wish he were a liar, but he isn't.

LA ROCHE.

Our boys struck hard enough, it seems, to capture you.

PRISONER.

We were ten, surprised by a battalion, and yet it cost you nearly fifty of your friends to take but ten of us.

LA HOGUE.

There he goes again riddling us with facts.

LA ROCHE.

Sir,—you know there is no quarter given to traitors found in arms against the King.

PRISONER.

France has no sovereign but the people.—It is you who are the traitors.

LA ROCHE.

Answer civilly and I may show you mercy.

PRISONER.

I neither ask, nor accept mercy. I have done my best to deal a crushing blow to you.—So call your guards, and shoot me without more waste of words.

LA ROCHE.

I see that you are brave.

PRISONER.

Brave? Because I'm not afraid to die?

[*Laughs bitterly.*]

Bah! It takes more courage sometimes to consent to live.

LA ROCHE.

You are young, a Frenchman, and—though misled—a credit to your country. If you'll give me some excuse, I swear I'd rather spare your life.

PRISONER.

[*Laughing.*]

Thank you, General; but frankly, I'd rather give you some excuse to take it.

Tremendous explosion heard in the distance. Then a second explosion. The Faubourg in middle ground is blown up and is seen to burn into a blaze.

LA ROCHE.

My God!—See!—The Faubourg!

PRISONER.

[*Triumphantly.*]

Blown up and burning!—In an hour the houses that were to shelter your attack on our defenses will be gone, and you will have to fight our forces in the open field.—That means defeat for you.

LA HOGUE.

Sacristi! Gag this rogue, or we'll be whipped before we fight.

LA ROCHEJACQUELEIN *writes hastily, and strikes a bell. Enter* GOUROC, *who starts and goes out again with a gesture of menace towards the* PRISONER. *Enter* ORDERLY.

LA ROCHE.

[*To* ORDERLY.]

Despatch these orders instantly, and send a guard with loaded muskets here at once.

[*Exit* ORDERLY.]

[*Turning despondently to* LA HOGUE.]

I fear this is a death-blow to our plans to-night.

PRISONER.

A death-blow dealt by me!—You'd better kill me quickly before I do more damage.

LA ROCHE.

You are right, sir; I should be faithless to my King if I showed you mercy now.

PRISONER.

Bravo! Mercy to enemies is as base as cruelty to friends.

LA HOGUE.

Damn me! There's no fun in killing such a fool—he seems to like it!

[*Enter* ORDERLY *with* GUARDS.

LA ROCHE.

[*To* ORDERLY.]

Take the prisoner outside and shoot him there at once.

[GUARD *crosses to* PRISONER.]

Have you any last request?

PRISONER.

But one.—You have shown me the kindness of an honest-hearted man. War has made us enemies, but, in the presence of the peace of death, I would like to feel that as Frenchmen we are friends, and ask one parting grasp from you.

LA ROCHE.

[*Grasps his hand.*]

With all my heart!—May we meet like this above.

LA HOGUE.

[*With emotion.*]

Curse these youngsters, they make me snivel like a fool.

[*He blows his nose furiously.*

The PRISONER *bows, takes his place in the platoon of* GUARDS, *who begin to march off. When they are on the terrace,* LA HOGUE *suddenly cries out.*

LA HOGUE.

Halt!—

[ORDERLY *about-faces and waits for orders.*]

You have not given us your name.

PRISONER.

I prefer to let it die with me.

LA HOGUE.

Hang it, sir! Courage is glorious even in a rebel rascal like yourself.

LA ROCHE.

Some friend may be glad to know how fearlessly you met your fate.

PRISONER.

The only ears I'd care to reach would rather never hear my name again.

LA HOGUE.

But curse your stubbornness! I want to know your name myself. Can't you be civil as well as brave?

PRISONER.

[*Laughing.*]

Well, then, to please your gentle highness, I must give it. I am Captain on the Staff of General Kleber—Captain Kauvar.

LA ROCHE *and* LA HOGUE.

[*Starting.*]

Kauvar?

PAUL.

Yes—Captain Paul Kauvar.

LA ROCHE.

[*Turning amazed to* LA HOGUE.]

What do you think of this?

LA HOGUE.

That if I had a regiment of Paul Kauvar's, I'd conquer Europe.

LA ROCHE.

My cousin's husband was guillotined. There's some mistake.

[*To* GUARD.]

Leave the prisoner, and wait outside for orders.

PAUL.

[*Stopping the* GUARD.]

Stay!—

[ORDERLY *waits for further orders.*]
[*To* LA ROCHEJACQUELEIN.]

General, I beg of you to spare me further waiting.—Make an end of this.

LA ROCHE.

When I have questioned you again.

PAUL.

I shall refuse to answer further questions.

LA ROCHE.

I may find a way to break your silence.

PAUL.

I swear you cannot do it.

LA ROCHE.

[*Motions* GUARDS *to go.*]
[ORDERLY *about-faces, goes on to terrace.* GUARDS *then march off.*]

We shall see! You've given a name that's not your own.

[PAUL *starts, but remains silent.*]

Paul Kauvar was guillotined the night of the ninth of May.

[PAUL *turns, amazed but silent.*]

He died to save my kinsman, the Duc de Beaumont.

[PAUL, *about to speak*, *checks himself.*]

He was the husband of my cousin.

PAUL.

[*Exploding.*]

Diane—your cousin?

LA ROCHE.

Ha! I thought I'd make you speak.

PAUL.

[*Eagerly.*]

You know her?—She has escaped?—Is safe?—alive?—happy?

LA ROCHE.

Oh, ho!—So you would turn the tables—question me?

PAUL.

Is she alive and well?—I ask to know but this.

LA ROCHE.

I'll tell you more, if you will answer first my questions.

PAUL.

All!—that do not force me to betray my cause.

LA ROCHE.

Explain!—You escaped the guillotine?

PAUL.

The story is too long.

LA ROCHE.

Make it brief, but answer.

PAUL.

In the death-cart I found a priest confessing those about him. He questioned me, soon saw that I was not the Duke. "My child," he said, "I die to-day, but as a priest shall be the last to mount the scaffold.—Let me take your place, assume the same disguise, while you slip from the cart and live." At first I refused, as I no longer cared for life! But when he said Diane might not escape unless I lived to aid her, I yielded.—The night was cloudy. When the moon was hidden, the priest put on my coat and wig, and as the death-cart neared the scaffold, I slipped through its slatted floor, and in the darkness mingled with the crowd.

LA ROCHE.

Who was the holy man who set you free?

PAUL.

The Abbé de St. Simon.

LA ROCHE.

Strange! We heard the Abbé had escaped.

PAUL.

He answered when the Duke was called and so was guillotined; but when the Abbé's turn had come, they could not find him, and so gave out that he'd escaped.

LA ROCHE.

Yes, I understand it now.—Proceed!

PAUL.

I found Diane had gone, believing I was guilty of a most ignoble crime. Too sick at heart to follow her, I enlisted and, seeking death, obtained promotion to my present grade.

LA ROCHE.

What if your willingness to die to save her father had convinced Diane that you were innocent, and had taught her a deeper love for you?

PAUL.

Ah! Then life would be worth living once again!—Can you have heard from her—seen her?

LA ROCHE.

You can see her for yourself—save your own life—and bring boundless joy to hers.

PAUL.

How?

LA ROCHE.

Espouse our cause!

PAUL.

What!—Betray my country?

LA ROCHE.

No.—Redeem your country!—Desert the side of those who bring disgrace upon your native land—of fiends, who drown her soil in blood!—blood bred from the noblest heroes of her history.

PAUL.

Heroes who debauched our women, and enslaved our men!—Libertines who let harlots reign in France! Despots whose arrogant descendants are crushed to-day beneath their fathers' sins!

LA ROCHE.

What, sir! You, a soldier, justify these Jacobins—anarchists like Carrac, who slaughter hundreds of defenceless women every day, and even outrage little children?

PAUL.

Anarchists are monsters your race bred when it brutalized their mothers.

LA ROCHE.

Enough, sir! I see that I must leave you to your fate.

PAUL.

But Diane, my wife! Give me one word of her.

LA ROCHE.

Yes. You shall know that she believes you innocent, is sick with grief and desolation in thinking you are dead.

PAUL.

You have seen her, then?

LA ROCHE.

Yes—here, within an hour.

PAUL.

She is here now, within call—?

[LA ROCHEJACQUELEIN *makes sign of assent.* PAUL *kneels at his feet.*]

My God! In pity's name, let me see her once again.

LA ROCHE.

And so re-open the old wounds?—re-awaken hope, but to deepen her despair?

PAUL.

[*Rising slowly.*]

No, no! You're right. I will not purchase joy at the cost of pain to her!—Call your guards. I die happy, knowing she'll remember me with love.

LA ROCHE.

For her sake renounce rebellion, and I unite you both forever.

PAUL.

Better I should never see her face again than be unworthy of her love.

LA HOGUE.

Great Cæsar! Here's an eagle facing death in loyalty to carrion crows!—The noble bird is mad! We must not kill, but cure him.

LA ROCHE.

What do you propose?

LA HOGUE.

Put him on parole. Let him give his word that he'll not fight until he's exchanged.

LA ROCHE.

True! Captain Kauvar, you are a prisoner of war, a man of proven honour.—Give me your word that you will not lift your sword against the King, till you're exchanged, and you're paroled and free.

PAUL.

Free with honour, to see my wife once more?

LA ROCHE.

Yes!

PAUL.

Oh, generous foe! Next to my country, my life belongs to you.

LA ROCHE.

I have your word?

PAUL.

[*Raising his hand.*]
You have.

LA ROCHE.

Captain Kauvar, you are paroled.

PAUL.

And my wife?

LA ROCHE.

[*Going.*]
Shall come to you at once.
[*Exit.*

PAUL.

Great heavens!—I'm going mad with joy!
[*Turning to* LA HOGUE.]
Colonel, I must explode or die!
[*He embraces* LA HOGUE.

LA HOGUE.

[*Submitting with gusto.*]
Damme! Embraced by a Sans Culotte! I like it, too!

Artillery is heard in the distance.

PAUL.

[*Looking off.*]
By heavens!—The Republicans are sweeping down from Granville!
[*To* LA HOGUE.]
Colonel, see! My comrades have attacked you under cover of the town I burned.
[*Crash of artillery again.*

LA HOGUE.

Damnation!

Enter LA ROCHEJACQUELEIN.

ORDERLY.

[*Rushing in.*]
General, the enemy are upon us!

LA ROCHE.

[*Excitedly to* LA HOGUE.]
Quick!—To arms!—We must rouse and lead our men!

PAUL.

But Diane—my wife?

LA ROCHE.

Gone!—to England.
[*Handing a paper.*]
Read, and remember, whatever be my fate, you are on parole.
[*He rushes off with* LA HOGUE.

The crash of firearms increases.

PAUL.

[*Reading.*]
"Dear Henri:—The town is burning, my daughter in peril. I see Diane embarked for England, and join you on the field. —Duc de Beaumont."—Gone!—No! I will find her, and fly with her myself.

[*Noise of battle outside.*—PAUL *is about to go, but stops.*]

No, no! My God!—She's lost to me again! I cannot go to seek her, for I'm a prisoner on parole!

[*He falls prostrate on the stairs.*

CURTAIN.

ACT V.

SCENE. *Same as Act IV—one hour later. Noise of battle in distance.*—PAUL *discovered looking on and listening in excitement.* —*Noise increases and sounds nearer.*

PAUL.

[*Triumphantly.*]

Ah!—The enemy weakens!—gives way!—falls back!—The Royalists fly!—The Republic wins!—Progress triumphs!

[*The noise of battle grows louder, but the cries of triumph from Republicans decrease, then die away.*—PAUL *checks his joy and speaks in changed tones.*]

And I—I have no part in this glorious play—because I'm on parole.

[*Walking up and down excitedly.*]

What torture!—to be here; with heart aflame, and limbs all free; to see the fight, and yet be bound to idleness by an oath, as much a prisoner as though in fetters at the bottom of a cell!

[*Changing his whole manner.*]

And Diane—where is she? But now within my reach—almost in my arms—naught between us but a promise, a mere breath—that breath as strong as adamantine walls to part us!

JEAN.

[*Entering, sees* PAUL *and cries out.*]

Kauvar!

PAUL.

[*Turning, starts.*]

Jean Litais!

JEAN.

You, alive?

PAUL.

My wife!—Where is she?

JEAN.

Don't ask me!

PAUL.

You promised to save her.

JEAN.

I did.—But for the burning of the Faubourg, and the attack of the rebels, she would be alive and safe.

PAUL.

And now—?

JEAN.

She's lost!—She, with her father and the Marquis, fell into an ambush—were fired on from every side—

PAUL.

Killed! And I am her assassin!

JEAN.

You?

PAUL.

Yes! I planned the burning of the Faubourg, placed the mines that blew it up, and opened a way for our attack.—In serving my country, I have killed my wife!

JEAN.

You are a soldier, then,—one of the blues?

PAUL.

Yes—and captured there at dawn.
[*Points at the Faubourg.*

JEAN.

And not shot?

PAUL.

No—paroled!—paroled!—paroled!

JEAN.

Impossible! The watchword on both sides is "No mercy."

PAUL.

La Rochejacquelein spared my life, that I might once more see my wife.—Useless generosity, for she had gone to meet her death!

JEAN.

But he—the General—was merciful, magnanimous to you?

PAUL.

He was. I owe him an eternal debt.

JEAN.

Are you willing to pay your debt?

PAUL.

With my life!

JEAN.

His army is routed. He will be captured—shot like a dog, unless he's saved.

PAUL.

He must be saved.

JEAN.

There's a secret passage from this castle to the glen. If I could put his pursuers off his track, he would escape.

PAUL.

Bring the General here and leave the rest to me.

JEAN.

You will aid him?

PAUL.

I will.—Be quick; we're wasting time.

[JEAN *crosses to door and beckons; enter* LA HOGUE, LA ROCHEJACQUELEIN *and* DENISE.

PAUL.

[*Pulling off his coat and crossing.*]
General, off with your coat!

LA ROCHE.

What does this mean?

PAUL.

You were merciful to me—'tis my turn now! We exchange uniforms; I am captured in your place, mislead your pursuers while you escape.

LA ROCHE.

For you to assist me is treason to your cause.

PAUL.

Ingratitude is treason to my God!—I owe you more than life; let men call this what they will; I have a divine right to pay my debt.

LA ROCHE.

I refuse to let you do a deed that may bring dishonour on your head.

PAUL.

Then I refuse to owe my life to you.—Accept my assistance, or [*Drawing pistol from the belt of* LA ROCHEJACQUELEIN.] with my own hand I'll shoot the prisoner you paroled.

LA HOGUE.

[*Grasping* PAUL'S *arm.*]
Stop! This can be arranged.

PAUL.

How?

LA HOGUE.

You are a prisoner on parole.—The General is as good as captured now.—Let him release you from your word, then his escape will only be an exchange of prisoners.

PAUL.

Will you consent to this?

LA ROCHE.

No, I cannot. The exchange would not be fair to the side you serve. I am a General; you, but a Captain.

LA HOGUE.

But we have the other prisoners, the comrades of the Captain; we can shoot them all at once, or exchange them if we choose for you.

PAUL.

Free them—and I but make a fair exchange in helping you to get away.

[*Shouts outside.*

[*Cheers.*

JEAN.

My God! The crowd rush on this way.

DENISE.

[*Kneeling to* LA ROCHEJACQUELEIN.]

In Mercy's name—!

LA HOGUE.

The King's cause dies with you!—You are bound to live for him!

LA ROCHE.

[*Stripping off his coat.*]

Enough—I consent.

DENISE.

Thank God!

PAUL *and* LA ROCHEJACQUELEIN *exchange uniforms.*

LA ROCHE.

By heavens! I never thought to wear this colour on my back! I do it for King Louis' sake.

PAUL.

And I wear this in honour of the King of Kings, who is our common Father.

LA ROCHE.

My saviour!

PAUL.

Nay, your brother!

PAUL *and* LA ROCHEJACQUELEIN *look in each other's eyes a moment, then part in silence.* JEAN *and* DENISE *cross to panel in wall.* LA ROCHEJACQUELEIN *crosses and turns.*

LA ROCHE.

[*Saluting* PAUL.]

Long live the King!

PAUL.

[*Saluting* LA ROCHEJACQUELEIN.]
Long live the Republic!

LA HOGUE.

[*As* LA ROCHEJACQUELEIN *goes out.*]
Your comrades are there.
[*Pointing.*]
This key will set them free.

PAUL.

[*Taking* LA HOGUE'S *hand.*]
Our lives are yours!—Farewell!

LA HOGUE.

Damme! I never thought I'd live to love a Sans Culotte!
[*As* LA HOGUE *goes out,* JEAN *crosses to* PAUL.

JEAN.

When you are recognized, our pursuit will recommence.

PAUL.

How much time is needed to make sure your escape?

JEAN.

At least one hour.—If your disguise is discovered in less time, you will have risked your life in vain.

PAUL.

Don't fear!

JEAN.

I have your word, and no matter what happens, you will play your part for one whole hour?

PAUL.

You have my word, however tragic this comedy may become.

JEAN.

When the General is free, I shall return.
[*A bell tolls the hour of Two.*]
Listen! Remember, you have pledged your honour to endure all things for an hour. Till then—God help you!
[*Exit.*

Shouts and yells outside from Republican soldiers; PAUL *sits near the fire and pays no attention. Firing outside, followed by cries and cheers.*

POTIN.

[*Outside.*]

This way!—This way!—That's his nest!—We'll find the bird in there!

[*Rushes on, followed by* SOLDIERS.]

[*Looking around.*]

Deserted! The rogue of a royal General is hiding like a mouse! We'll unearth him!—Come on!

[*He is going toward door, followed by his* MEN, *when he sees* PAUL, *and starts back.*]

Halt!

[*Points at* PAUL.]

See!—There is La Rochejacquelein!

[*To the* MEN.]

Make ready—Aim!

[SOLDIERS *aim at* PAUL, *who does not move.*]

[*To* PAUL.]

General La Rochejacquelein, we recognize your uniform. Surrender!

[PAUL *does not move.*]

General, your sword, or we fire!

PAUL.

[*Rising coolly.*]

Fire!

POTIN.

We do not want to kill you.

[*Advancing with extended hand.*]

We'd rather have your sword.

PAUL.

[*Recognizing* POTIN, *speaks aside.*]

Potin!—The wretch!—He may recognize me before the hour is up!

[*He draws his sword and extends it backward.*

POTIN.

[*Taking the sword.*]

General, you are our prisoner.

[*To* SOLDIERS.]

Comrades, to us—a squad of the battalion of the Bonnet Rouge—is due the glory of taking the leader of these Royalist Brigands!—Hurrah for our Battalion!

[*All cheer.*

VOICES.

[*Outside.*]

Long live the Republic!

POTIN.

[*Looking off.*]

Bah! Here come the rabble—a crowd of anarchists!

GOUJON.

Who never share the fighting.

POTIN.

But claim all the glory fighting brings.

GOUJON.

Curse these civil shouters!

SOLDIERS *all groan. Cries of* "Carrac! Carrac!" *with cheers heard outside.*

POTIN.

Here they come, led on by Scarlotte—

GOUJON.

Scarlotte! A woman in form—a fury in nature!

POTIN.

Like my wife.

[*Cheers outside.*]

Good heavens! Worse and worse! Yonder comes Carrac—the king of curs!—Damme! The devil himself is a saint compared with him.

GOUJON.

The beast!

POTIN.

The bloodiest beast of all—a tiger!

[*To* SOLDIERS.]

Quick, form on this side [*Pointing to the left.*] and protect the General.—This hog will want to eat him, before we can deliver him to Kleber and get the credit of his capture.

[SOLDIERS *form in front of* PAUL.

SCARLOTTE.

[*Outside.*]

This way, you fools!—Death to Rochejacquelein. Come on!

MOB.

[*Outside.*]

Death to Rochejacquelein!

SCARLOTTE.

[*Entering, followed by* MOB.]

Rochejacquelein!—Rochejacquelein!—Where is Rochejacquelein?

MOB.

Down with Rochejacquelein! Down with Rochejacquelein!

BOURDOTTE.

[*Appearing.*]

Silence! Here comes Carrac, the great Carrac—representative of the Republic—who never spares an enemy!

[*Comes down stage.*

POTIN.

And never makes a friend.

MOB.

Carrac!—Carrac!—Long live Carrac!

CARRAC *appears, followed by a second* MOB, *and makes a gesture commanding silence.*

CARRAC.

So—this is the ancestral hall of that cursed kin of kings, La Rochejacquelein!—Ha! He's doubtless sneaking like a coward in some safe corner of his den. Is the place surrounded?

BOURDOTTE.

On every side.

SCARLOTTE.

Good!—Tear his house about his ears!

CARRAC.

Aye—strip the old hawk's nest.

MOB.

Aye!—Aye!

[*The* MOB *dismantle the house, with yells of exultation.*

SCARLOTTE.

[*Urging them on.*]

Heroes of Liberty!—demolish every trace of beauty in the place!

Amid a scene of anarchic rage and turmoil, the room is stript stark.

CARRAC.

Well done—noble levellers of the age!—Pull the boasted culture of the nobility to the gutter.—Bravo!—We've demolished the old nest; now to hunt the young hawk down!

MOB.

Aye!—Aye!

POTIN.

[*Waving the* MOB *back.*]

Stop!—La Rochejacquelein is found!

SCARLOTTE.

Where is he?

POTIN.

There—our prisoner.

SCARLOTTE.

Drag him to the river!

MOB.

Aye—to the river!

POTIN.

Stand back!—He belongs to our battalion.

CARRAC.

What insolence is this? We demand his surrender here—to us.

POTIN.

We surrender him to none but our own Colonel.

CARRAC.

We are the people and supreme!—We represent the civil power of the State, that rules the soldier.

MOB.

Aye!—Aye!

POTIN.

[*To the* SOLDIERS.]

Make ready!—Aim!

[SOLDIERS *aim;—the* MOB *fall back.*]

You're ten to one.—Come on, you civil rulers, and take him if you can.

CARRAC.

This is treason!

SCARLOTTE.

Aye—treason!—Treason!

[*The* MOB *groan.*

POTIN.

Soldiers have no rulers but their officers!

CARRAC.

Someone go for General Kleber. Bid him come at once—to quell this mutiny.

SCARLOTTE.

I will bring him.

[*Crosses.*]

Death to all who dare to balk the people's will!

[*Exit.*

BOURDOTTE.

Meantime, Citizen Carrac, we have some prisoners here at hand that we can dispatch at once.

CARRAC.

How many?

BOURDOTTE.

Five.—Two men, and three women—perfect beauties!

CARRAC.

Bravo! Their beauty and their lives are ours!

[*Cheers from* MOB.]

Bring them in!

[*Exeunt eight* SANS CULOTTES.]

Citizens, we've won to-day a glorious victory.

POTIN.

There he goes boasting, when he never struck a blow.

CARRAC.

Let's complete our triumph—prove our power—

MOB.

Bravo!—Bravo!

CARRAC.

You are the people!—You are France!—Let the Nation voice her will through you.—What shall we do with our prisoners?

BOURDOTTE.

Kill them.

MOB.

Aye—kill them—kill them!

BOURDOTTE.

Drown the men like puppies, and put the women to public shame!

MOB.

Aye! Aye!

CARRAC.

The voice of the people is the voice of God.—Have your will—it is God's command!

Enter CITIZENS, *dragging the* DUKE, GOUROC, DIANE, NANETTE, *and* ALINE, *a young girl.*

The MOB *groan and laugh mockingly.*

The young girl is dragged forward—two SANS CULOTTES *contending for her.*

FIRST SANS CULOTTE.

She's mine!

SECOND SANS CULOTTE.

You lie!—I caught her first!

ALINE.

Mercy!—Kill me if you will,—but spare me this!

CARRAC.

[*Laughing.*]
Citizens,—behold your victims!
[MOB *rush forward with ferocious yells.*

DUKE.

[*Interposing.*]
No, no!—Let my grey hairs suffice!
[*The* MOB *pause.*

PAUL.

[*Starting up, speaks aside.*]
My God!—That voice!
[*During what follows,* PAUL—*screened from the* MOB'S *view by his soldier* GUARDS—*expresses in pantomime his conflicting emotions.*

CARRAC.

[*To the* DUKE.]
Who are you?

GOUROC.

[*Speaking quickly.*]
We are Citizens of the Republic!—He [*Pointing at the* DUKE.] is George Leblanc—and I, Citizen Gouroc of the Committee of Public Safety.
[CARRAC *and* MOB *draw back with astonishment.*

PAUL.

[*Aside.*]
And Diane!—Is she there?—I must see!
[*Starts, stops.*]
No, no!—They would know me; the hour is not up!

CARRAC.

You, Citizen Gouroc?—I don't believe it.

GOUROC.

[*Holding out papers.*]
Here are our credentials.

CARRAC.

They may be forgeries.

MOB.

Aye—forgeries! forgeries!

CARRAC.

[*To the* MOB.]

Silence! While we proceed in our examination.

[*The* MOB *utter low murmurs.* CARRAC *turns to* NANETTE.]

Who are you?

NANETTE.

[*Advancing defiantly.*]

I am Citizeness Nanette Potin.

POTIN.

[*Aside.*]

My wife!—

[*Sneaks behind comrades.*

CARRAC.

Ha, wait!

[*Seeing* DIANE, *he drags her forth.*]

By the gods!—here's a feast for Jupiter himself.—Speak out, delicious wench, and tell us who you are.

DIANE.

I am Diane—

GOUROC.

[*Interrupting quickly.*]

She is Diane Gouroc.—

[*Pointing at the* DUKE.]

His daughter and my wife.

PAUL.

[*Exploding.*]

Liar!

[*All start and turn toward* PAUL, *who speaks aside.*]

God help me!—I forget; the hour is not ended.

CARRAC.

Who is it calls this citizen a liar?

GOUJON.

The prisoner.

CARRAC.

Ah, ha! It seems he knows these citizens.—In the name of the law and the Republic, I summon instantly as a witness Henri de la Rochejacquelein.

DIANE.

My cousin captured?

[*All turn toward her, amazed.*

GOUROC.

[*Starting.*]

My God!—We're lost!

CARRAC.

So—the prisoner is the beauty's cousin.

[*To* GOUROC.]

Traitor! You have lied!—This convicts you all.

MOB.

To the guillotine!—To the guillotine!

BOURDOTTE.

No! A marriage! A Republican marriage!

MOB.

Aye! A marriage! marriage!

[BOURDOTTE *drags forth* NANETTE.

NANETTE.

What are you going to do?

BOURDOTTE.

Tie you to this man and throw you in the river.—That's the way we marry Royalists!

[*The* MOB *laugh mockingly.*

NANETTE.

[*Shrieking.*]

Help!

POTIN.

[*Exploding.*]

Damnation!—Tongue or no tongue, I must save her.

[*Bounds forward and frees his wife.*]

Nanette!

NANETTE.

[*Joyfully embracing* POTIN.]

Dodolphe!

CARRAC.

What does this mean?

POTIN.

This is my wife; the wife of a soldier of the Republic, and so, sacred to her country.

SOLDIERS.

Aye! Aye!

POTIN.

[*Pointing to* GOUROC.]

Do what you like with him—for such cattle as he deserve to die!

[GOUROC *turns and glowers.*]

Glare! Who cares? I'm a soldier. 'Tis my turn now!—You shall pay dearly for making me a perjurer!

[*To* MOB.]

Citizens, this devil here forced me to swear falsely against a patriot.

BOURDOTTE.

When was this?

POTIN.

Three months ago in Paris.—I was secretary to my Section.—This man had a blank warrant signed by our president, Paul Kauvar.—He made me fill it in with the name of the Duc de Beaumont—and, after, falsely swear that Kauvar had ordered the arrest.

[*Cries of execration from the* MOB.

DIANE.

Father! You hear? It is to him that we owe our agony!—One of your own race.

POTIN.

Kauvar was his friend—this dog betrayed him!

NANETTE.

Yes, while he himself was all the time a Marquis in disguise.

PAUL.

He, my friend—a traitor!

CARRAC.

Death to the brigand!

MOB.

Death to him! To the river! Drown him!
[*They seize* GOUROC.

GOUROC.

[*Breaking away from them.*]
Fiends—I defy you, and escape you!
[*Draws pistol, fires, and falls dead.*

BOURDOTTE.

[*Feeling* GOUROC'S *breast.*]
Dead.—Dead as potted pork.

CARRAC.

And the people cheated of their just revenge!

CITIZENS *bear* GOUROC'S *body off.*

BOURDOTTE.

Ah, look, we have still the old Aristo and his daughter!

MOB.

Aye!—Aye! Away with them! Away with them!
[*They rush on the* DUKE *and* DIANE.

PAUL.

My God! Will this hour never end?

CARRAC.

[*To the* MOB.]
Here! Strip her! Drive her to her death!
[*The* MOB *howls.*—DIANE *breaks from* CARRAC.—*Bell tolls.*

PAUL.

[*With a cry of joy.*]
The hour strikes!—I'm free!

[CARRAC *seizes* DIANE *again and drags her to the centre of the stage.*

Rushing from his concealed position, PAUL *tears* DIANE, *fainting, from the arms of* CARRAC, *whom he flings to the ground—warning back the* MOB, *who pause for a moment, staring in amazement.*

BOURDOTTE.

Ha—the brigand—kill him!—

MOB.

[*Advancing.*]
Kill him!—Kill him!

POTIN.

[*Aiming, with* SOLDIERS.]
Halt!—He is our prisoner.
[*The* MOB *recoil.*

PAUL.

[*Flinging off his coat and hat.*]
No! Not your prisoner! Your officer!—Captain on Kleber's staff: Captain Paul Kauvar.

DIANE.

[*With a cry—quivering, incredulous.*]
Paul!—Alive!

PAUL.

Heaven is merciful at last!
[*He takes her in his arms.*

POTIN.

By the gods, it is!—The Citizen Kauvar!

GOUJON.

Then La Rochejacquelein has got away?

CARRAC.

[*Rising, to* PAUL.]
If you are a soldier of the Republic, how is it we find you in the coat of a brigand?

PAUL.

That's my affair, not yours.

CARRAC.

What! You refuse to answer? [*Coming close to* PAUL.] Do you know who I am?

PAUL.

[*With quiet, increasing intensity, before which* CARRAC *is utterly cowed.*]

Yes,—Carrac—an anarchist—a fiend—in the name of liberty invoking the tyranny of terror! An assassin—shouting fraternity and committing fratricide! A libertine—claiming equality with the good, while ravishing the pure! A monster—part vulture, part toad—who, in the holy name of progress, makes our Country and our Cause revolting to the world!

BOURDOTTE.

Ha! See! Carrac recoils! He's found his match at last!—

[*The* MOB *laugh and jeer.*

SCARLOTTE.

[*Appearing.*]

Room there!—Room for General Kleber.

MOB.

[*Falling back on both sides.*]

Kleber!—Kleber!—Long live Kleber!

KLEBER.

[*Entering with three* OFFICERS.]

I am told there is mutiny—treason here. Who and where are the accused?

CARRAC.

[*Pointing at* PAUL.]

There stands the worst of them!

KLEBER.

[*Astounded.*]

Captain Kauvar!—Of what is he accused?

CARRAC.

Treachery to France! He has worn the colours of the Royal Cause.

GOUJON.

We arrested him as Rochejacquelein.

CARRAC.

Whom he has aided to escape.

KLEBER.

A terrible charge! The punishment is instant death.—Captain Kauvar, what have you to say?

PAUL.

But little.—I led last night the band of men who mined the Faubourg and cleared the road for our army to advance.

KLEBER.

A desperate undertaking, crowned with great success!—We gave you all up as dead.

PAUL.

We should have been, but for the clemency of Rochejacquelein. He spared my men, and put me on parole. He could have shot us all, but by letting him escape I saved the band of patriots to whom our army owes its victory to-day.

[*All cheer.*

KLEBER.

Captain Kauvar, you did right!

[*The* MOB *cheer.*

CARRAC.

Citizens, the watchword sent from Robespierre to Vendée was this: "Death without mercy to the Aristocrats."

[*Pointing at the* DUKE.]

Here is one, at least; I claim him for the guillotine.

MOB.

Aye—to the guillotine! To the guillotine!

KLEBER.

[*As the* MOB *rush on the* DUKE.]

Halt!

[*The* MOB *fall back.*]

Citizens, I bring you glorious news! These despatches have just reached me on the field. They come from the National Convention at the Capitol of France. Listen!

[*Reads.*]

"The tyrant Robespierre has been guillotined. The reign of

terror is at an end. Proclaim amnesty, mercy, and fraternity to all Frenchmen in Vendée."

[*All cheer.*

CARRAC.

Robespierre dead! What will the people do without the guillotine?

PAUL.

Drive anarchists and Carracs out of France!

BOURDOTTE.

Aye! Away with him! Away with him!

[*Rushing on* CARRAC, *the* MOB *nearly tear him to pieces as they bear him away.*

SCARLOTTE.

[*Fighting the* MOB.]
Ingrates—traitors—dogs—ye shall not harm him—back! back! back!

[*Exit, facing the* MOB, *and trying to save* CARRAC.

JEAN.

[*Bounding in from panel, speaks to* PAUL.]
You see I have returned!

DUKE.

And the General?

JEAN.

Has escaped to England, [*Pointing to* PAUL.] thanks to him.

KLEBER.

[*Taking a cross from his own breast, and advancing to* PAUL.]
Captain Kauvar, you risked almost certain death to purchase victory for France. In the name of the Republic, I decorate you for heroic courage on the field!

[*He places the cross on* PAUL'S *breast. All cheer.*

DUKE.

[*Extending his hand to* PAUL.]
My son!—

[PAUL *clasps it.*

DIANE.

At last, thank God, dear France is free of tyrants.

PAUL.

Liberty is wed to Justice, and Anarchy is ended!

CURTAIN.

End of the Play.

SHENANDOAH

A MILITARY COMEDY

Bronson Howard

BRONSON HOWARD

(1842–1908)

The present Editor has just read through some of the vivacious correspondence of Bronson Howard—a sheaf of letters sent by him to Brander Matthews during a long intercourse. The time thus spent brings sharply to mind the salient qualities of the man—his nobility of character, his soundness of mind, his graciousness of manner, and his thorough understanding of the dramatic tools of his day and generation. To know Bronson Howard was to be treated to just that human quality which he put into even his hastily penned notes—and, as in conversation with him, so in his letters there are repeated flashes of sage comment and of good native wit. Not too often can we make the plea for the gathering and preserving of such material. Autobiography, after all, is what biography ought to be—it is the live portrait by the side of which a mere appreciative sketch fades. I have looked through the "Memorial" volume to Bronson Howard, issued by the American Dramatists Club (1910), and read the well-tempered estimates, the random reminiscences. But these do not recall the Bronson Howard known to me, as to so many others—who gleams so charmingly in this correspondence. Bronson Howard's plays may not last—"Fantine," "Saratoga," "Diamonds," "Moorcraft," "Lillian's Last Love"—these are mere names in theatre history, and they are very out of date on the printed page. "The Banker's Daughter," "Old Love Letters" and "Hurricanes" would scarcely revive, so changed our comedy treatment, so differently psychologized our emotion. Not many years ago the managerial expedient was resorted to of re-vamping "The Henrietta"—but its spirit would not behave in new-fangled style, and the magic of Robson and Crane was broken. In the American drama's groping for "society" comedy, one might put "Saratoga," and even "Aristocracy," in advance of Mrs. Mowatt's "Fashion" and Mrs. Bateman's "Self;" in the evolution of domestic problems, "Young Mrs. Winthrop" is interesting as an early breaker of American soil. But one can hardly say that, either for the theatre or for the library, Bronson Howard is a permanent factor. Yet his influence on the theatre is permanent; his moral force is something that should be perpetuated. Whatever he said on subjects pertaining to his craft—his comments on play-making most especially,—was illuminating and judicious. I have been privileged to read the comments sent by him to Professor Matthews during the period of their collaboration together over "Peter Stuyvesant;" they are practical suggestions, revealing the peculiar way in which a dramatist's mind shapes material for a three hours' traffic of the stage—the willingness to sacrifice situation, expression—any detail, in fact, that clogs the action. Through the years of their acquaintance, Howard and Matthews were continually wrangling good-naturedly about the relation of drama to literature. Apropos of an article by Matthews in *The Forum*, Howard once wrote:

I note that you regard the 'divorce' of the drama from literature as unfortunate. I think the divorce should be made absolute and final; that the Drama should no more be wedded to literature, on one hand, than it is to the art of painting on the other, or to music or mechanical science. Rather, perhaps, I should say, we should recognize poligamy for the Drama; and all the arts, with literature, its Harem. Literature may be Chief Sultana—but not too jealous. She is always claiming too large a share of her master's attention, and turning up her nose at the rest. I have felt this so strongly, at times, as to warmly deny that I was a 'literary man', insisting on being a 'dramatist'.

Then, in the same note, he adds in pencil: "Saw 'Ghosts' last night. Great work of art! Ibsen a brute, personally, for writing it."

In one of the "Stuyvesant" communications, Howard is calculating on the cumulative value of interest; and he analyzes it in this mathematical way:

So far as the important act is concerned, I have felt that this part of it was the hardest part of the problem before us. We were certain of a good beginning of the act and a good, rapid, dramatic end; but the middle and body of it I felt needed much attention to make the act substantial and satisfactory. To tell the truth, I was quietly worrying a bit over this part of the play, while you were expressing your anxiety about the 2nd act—which never bothered me. There *must* be 2nd acts and there *must* be last acts—audiences resign themselves to them; but 3rd acts—in 4 and 5 act plays—they *insist* on, and *will* have them good. The only exception is where you astonish them with a good 2nd act—then they'll take their siesta in the 3rd—and wake up for the 4th.

This psychological time-table shows how calculating the dramatist has to be, how precise in his framework, how sparing of his number of words. In another note, Howard says:

This would leave the acts squeezed "dry", about as follows:—Act 1, 35 minutes; Act 2, 30; Act 3, 45; Act 4, 20—total, 130—2 hrs., 10 min., curtain up: entr'acts, 25 min. Total—2 hrs., 35 min.—8:20 to 10:55.

There are a thousand extraneous considerations bothering a play that never enter into the evolution of any other form of art. After seeing W. H. Crane, who played "Peter Stuyvesant" when it was given, Howard writes Matthews of the wisdom shown by the actor in his criticism of "points" to be changed and strengthened in the manuscript.

"A good actor," he declares, "whom I always regard as an original creator in art—beginning at the point where the dramatist's pen stops—approaches a subject from such a radically different direction that we writers cannot study his impressions too carefully in revising our work." Sometimes, conventions seized the humourous side of Howard. From England, around 1883, he wrote, "Methinks there is danger in the feeling expressed about 'local colouring.' English managers would put the Garden of Eden in Devonshire, if you adapted Paradise Lost for them—and insist on giving Adam an eye-glass and a title."

Howard was above all an American; he was always emphasizing his nationality; and this largely because the English managers changed "Saratoga" to "Brighton," and "The Banker's Daughter" to "The Old Love and the New." I doubt whether he relished William Archer's inclusion of him in a volume of "English Dramatists of To-day," even though that critic's excuse was that he "may be said to occupy a place among English dramatists somewhat similar to that occupied by Mr. Henry James among English novelists." Howard was quick to assert his Americanism, and to his home town he wrote a letter from London, in 1884, disclaiming the accusation that he was hiding his local inheritance behind a French technique and a protracted stay abroad on business. He married an English woman—the sister of the late Sir Charles Wyndham—and it was due to the latter that several of his plays were transplanted and that Howard planned collaboration with Sir Charles Young.

But Howard was part of American life—born of the middle West, and shouldering a gun during the Civil War to guard the Canadian border near Detroit against a possible sympathetic uprising for the Confederacy. Besides which—a fact which makes the title of "Dean of the American Drama" a legitimate insignia,—when, in 1870, he stood firm against the prejudices of A. M. Palmer and Lester Wallack, shown toward "home industry," he was maintaining the right of the American dramatist. He was always preaching the American spirit, always analyzing American character, always watching and encouraging American thought.

Howard was a scholar, with a sense of the fitness of things, as a dramatist should have. Evidently, during the collaboration with Professor Matthews on "Stuyvesant," discussion must have arisen as to the form of English "New Amsterdamers," under Knickerbocker rule, would use. For it called forth one of Howard's breezy but exact comments, as follows:

A few more words about the "English" question: As I said, it seems to me, academical correctness, among the higher characters, will give a prim, old-fashioned tone: and *you* can look after this, as all my own work has been in the opposite direction in art. I have given it no thought in writing this piece, so far.

I would suggest the following special points to be on the alert for, even in the *best* present-day use of English:—some words are absolutely correct, now, yet based on events or movements in history since 1660. An evident illustration is the word "boulevard" for a wide street or road; so "avenue," in same sense, is New Yorkese and London imitation—even imitated from us, I imagine, in Paris: this would give a nineteenth century tone; while an "avenue lined with trees in a bowery" would not. Don't understand that I am telling you things. I'm only illustrating—to let you know what especial things in language I hope you will keep your eye on. Of course *Anneke* couldn't be "electrified"—but you may find many less evident blunders than that would be. She might be shocked, but couldn't "receive a shock." We need free colloquial slang and common expressions; but while "get out" seems all right from *Stuyvesant* to *Bogardus*, for *Barry* to say "Skedadle" would put him in the 87th New York Vols., 1861–64. Yet I doubt whether we have any more classic and revered slang than that word.

The evident ease, yet thoroughness, with which Mr. Howard prepared for his many tasks, is seen in his extended reading among Civil War records, before writing "Shenandoah." The same "knowledge" sense must have been a constant incentive to Professor Matthews, in the preparation of "Peter Stuyvesant."

"The manual of arms," Howard declares, "is simply *great.* I think we can get the muskets pointed at *Barket* in about 4 or 5 orders, however; taking the more picturesque ones, so far as may be possible. I went over the [State] librarian's letter with a nephew with the most modern of military training: and as I was at a militaryschool in 1860—just two centuries after our period—we had fun together. Even with an old muzzle loader—Scott's Tactics— it was "Load and fire in ten motions," *now* antiquated with the breech-loaders of to-day. The same operation, in 1662, required 28 motions, as we counted. By the bye, did I tell you that I found the flint-lock invented (in Spain) in 1625—and it "soon" spread over Europe? I felt, however, that the intervening 37 years would hardly have carried it to New Amsterdam; especially as the colony was neglected in such matters.

From these excerpts it is apparent that Howard had no delusions regarding the "work" side of the theatre; he was continually insisting that dramatic art was dependent upon the *artisan* aspects which underlay it. This he maintained, especially in contradiction to fictional theories upheld by the adherents of W. D. Howells.

One often asks why a man, thus so serious and thorough in his approach toward life, should have been so transitorily mannered in his plays, and the reason may be in the very *artisan* character of his work. Mr. Howard delivered a lecture before the Shakespeare Society of Harvard University, at Sanders Theatre, in 1886 (later given, 1889, before the Nineteenth Century Club, in New York), and he called it "The Autobiography of a Play." In the course of it, he illustrated how, in his own play, called "Lillian's Last Love," in 1873, which one year later became "The Banker's Daughter," he had to obey certain unfailing laws of dramatic construction during the alterations and re-writing. He never stated a requirement he was not himself willing to abide by. When he instructed the Harvard students, he was merely elucidating his own theatre education. "Submit yourselves truly and unconditionally," he admonished, "to the laws of dramatic truth, so far as you can discover them by honest mental exertion and observation. Do not mistake any mere defiance of these laws for originality. You might as well show your originality by defying the law of gravitation." Mr. Howard was not one to pose as the oracle of a new technique;

in this essay he merely stated sincerely his experience in a craft, as a clinical lecturer demonstrates certain established methods of treatment.

In his plays, vivacity and quick humour are the distinguishing characteristics. Like his contemporary workers, he was alive to topics of the hour, but, unlike them, he looked ahead, and so, as I have stated in my "The American Dramatist," one can find profit in contrasting his "Baron Rudolph" with Charles Klein's "Daughters of Men," his "The Henrietta" with Klein's "The Lion and Mouse," and his "The Young Mrs. Winthrop" with Alfred Sutro's "The Walls of Jericho." He was an ardent reader of plays, as his library—bequeathed to the American Dramatists Club, which he founded—bears witness. The fact is, he studied Restoration drama as closely as he did the modern French stage. How often he had to defend himself in the press from the accusation of plagiarism, merely because he was complying with the stage conventions of the moment!

It is unfortunate that his note-books are not available. But luckily he wrote an article at one time which shows his method of thrashing out the moral matrix of a scenario himself. It is called "Old Dry Ink." Howard's irony slayed the vulgar, but, because in some quarters his irony was not liked, he was criticized for his vulgarities. Archer, for example, early laid this defect to the influence of the Wyndham policy, in London, of courting blatant immorality in plays for the stage.

Howard's femininity, in comparison with Fitch's, was equally as observant; it was not as literarily brilliant in its "small talk." But though the effervescent chatter, handled with increasing dexterity by him, is now old-fashioned, "Old Dry Ink" shows that the scenes in his plays were not merely cleverly arrived at, but were philosophically digested. How different the dialogue from the notes!

This article was written in 1906; it conveys many impressions of early feminine struggles for political independence. The fact is, Mr. Howard often expressed his disappointment over the showing women made in the creative arts, and that he was not willing to let the bars down in his own profession is indicated by the fact that, during his life-time, women dramatists were not admitted as members into the club he founded.

The reader is referred to two other articles by Mr. Howard—one, "Trash on the Stage," included in the "Memorial" volume;

the other, on "The American Drama," which is reproduced here, because, written in 1906, and published in a now obsolete newspaper magazine, it is difficult of procuring, and stands, possibly, for Mr. Howard's final perspective of a native drama he did so much to make known as native.

The most national of Howard's plays is "Shenandoah;" it is chosen for the present volume as representative of the military drama, of which there are not many examples, considering the Civil War possibilities for stage effect. Clyde Fitch's "Barbara Frietchie," James A. Herne's "Griffith Davenport," Fyles and Belasco's "The Girl I Left Behind Me," Gillette's "Secret Service," and William DeMille's "The Warrens of Virginia"—a mere sheaf beside the Revolutionary list which might be compiled.

According to one authority, "Shenandoah" was built upon the foundations of a play by Howard, produced at Macauley's Theatre, Louisville, Kentucky. As stated by Professor Matthews, the facts are that Howard took a piece, "Drum Taps," to Lester Wallack; who, true to his English tradition, said that if it was changed in time from the Civil War to the Crimean, he might consider it. It is certain, however, that if the cast of characters, as first given under the management of Montgomery Field, at the old Boston Museum, November 19, 1888, be compared with the program of the New York Star Theatre, September 13, 1889, it will be found that the manuscript must have been considerably altered and shifted, before it reached the shape now offered here as the authentic text. The fact of the matter is, it was not considered a "go" in Boston; we are informed that such managers as Palmer and Henry E. Abbey prophesied dire end for the piece. But Charles Frohman hastened to Boston, on the advice of his brother, Daniel, and, giving half-interest in the piece to Al Hayman, he arranged with Field for rights, procured "time" at the Star Theatre with Burnham, and, as is told in "C. F.'s" biography, hastened to Stamford, Connecticut, to talk with Howard. According to this source, he said to the playwright:

"You are a very great dramatist, Mr. Howard, and I am only a theatrical manager, but I think I can see where a possible improvement might be made in the play. For one thing, I think two acts should be merged into one, and I don't think you have made enough out of Sheridan's ride."

The opening night, with General Sherman in the audience, was a memorable occasion. It was the beginning of "C. F.'s" rapid rise to managerial importance, it ushered in the era of numberless road companies playing the same piece, it met with long "runs," and the royalty statements mounted steadily in bulk for Howard. It was the success of the hour.

But "Shenandoah" is undoubtedly conventional; its melodramatic effects are dependent on stage presentment rather than on the printed page. In fact, so much an artisan of the theatre was Mr. Howard that he was always somewhat skeptical of the modern drama in print. When he was persuaded to issue his last piece, "Kate," in book form, he consented to the publisher's masking it as a novel in dialogue, hoping thus, as his prefatory note states, "to carry the imagination directly to scenes of real life and not to the stage." To the last there was a distinction in his mind between literature and the drama. It is since this was written that the play form, nervous and quick, even in its printed shape, has become widely accepted.

"Shenandoah" is a play of pictorial effects and swiftly changing sentiment. Were there a national repertory, this would be included among the plays, not because of its literary quality, but because of the spirit to be drawn from its situations, framed expressly for the stage, and because of its pictures, dependent wholly upon stage accessory. It is an actable play, and most of our prominent actors, coming out of the period of the late 80's, had training in it.

THE AMERICAN DRAMA

by

BRONSON HOWARD

In considering the present standing of the American drama, compared with the time when there was little or nothing worthy of the name, the one significant fact has been the gradual growth of a body of men engaged in writing plays. Up to the time I started in 1870, American plays had been written only sporadically here and there by men and women who never met each other, who had no personal acquaintance of any kind, no sympathies, no exchange of views; in fact, no means of building up such a body of thought in connection with their art as is necessary to form what is called a school.

In what we now style Broadway productions the late Augustin Daly stood absolutely alone, seeing no other future for his own dramatic works except by his own presentation of them. Except for Daly, I was practically alone; but he offered me the same opportunity and promise for the future that he had given to himself. From him developed a school of managers willing and eager to produce American plays on American subjects. Other writers began to drop into the profession; but still they seldom met, and it was not until about 1890 that they suddenly discovered themselves as a body of dramatists. This was at a private supper given at the Lotos Club to the veteran playwright Charles Gaylor, who far antedated Daly himself. To the astonishment of those making the list of guests for that supper, upward of fifty men writing in America who produced plays were professionally entitled to invitations, and thirty-five were actually present at the supper. A toast to seven women writers not present was also honoured.

This was the origin of the American Dramatists Club. The moment these men began to know each other personally, the process of intellectual attrition began, which will probably result eventually in a strong school. That supper took place only sixteen years ago; so we are yet only in the beginning of the great movement. Incidentally, it is also necessarily the beginning of a school of dramatic criticism of that art. It is difficult to suppose that a body of critics, merely learned in the dramatic art of Europe, can be regarded as forming a school of America.

To go to Paris to finish your education in dramatic art, and return to New York and make comments on what you see in the theatre, is not to be an American dramatic critic, nor does it tend in any way to found a school of American dramatic criticism. The same is true of the man who remains in New York and gets his knowledge of the drama from reading foreign newspapers and books.

I stated in a former article in this magazine, "First Nights in London and New York," that is was only within the last twenty-five or thirty years that a comparison between the cities and the conditions had become possible, for the reason that prior to that time there was really no American drama. There were a few American plays, and their first productions did not assume the least importance as social events. As far as any comparison is possible between the early American dramatists (I mean the first of the dramatists who were the starting point in the later '60's and early '70's) and those of the present day, I think of only two important points. There was one advantage in each case. The earlier dramatists had their choice of many great typical American characters, such as represented in *Solon Shingle*, *Colonel Sellers*, *Joshua Whitcomb*, *Bardwell Slote*, *Mose*, *Davy Crockett*, *Pudd'nhead Wilson*, and many others.

This advantage was similar in a small way to the tremendous advantage that the earliest Greek dramatists had in treating the elemental emotions; on the other hand, we earlier writers in America were liable to many errors, some of them actually childish, which the young dramatist of to-day, in constant association with his fellow playwrights, and placing his work almost in daily comparison with theirs, could not commit. To do so a man would have to be a much greater fool than were any of us; and the general improvement in the technical work of plays by young dramatists now, even plays that are essentially weak and which fail, is decided encouragement and satisfaction to one of my age who can look back over the whole movement.

The American dramatist of to-day, without those great and specially prominent American characters who stood, as it were, ready tc go on the stage, has come to make a closer study of American society than his predecessors did. They are keen also in seizing strikingly marked new types in American life as they developed before the public from decade to decade.

A notable instance is the exploitation by Charles Klein of the present-day captain of industry in "The Lion and the Mouse." The leading character in the play is differentiated on the stage, as in life, from the Wall Street giant of about 1890, as illustrated in one of my own plays, "The Henrietta." Mr. Klein's character of the financial magnate has developed in this country since my active days of playwriting, and the younger dramatist was lying in wait, ready for him, and ready to seize his peculiarities for stage purposes.

Another thing is the fact that our dramatists are doing what our literary men have done, namely, availing themselves of the striking local peculiarities in various parts of the country. A marked illustration of this now before the public is Edward Milton Royle's "Squawman," recently at Wallack's Theatre. The dramatist has caught his picture just in the nick of time, just before the facts of life in the Indian Territory are passing away. He has preserved the picture for us as George W. Cable, the novelist, preserved pictures of Creole life of old New Orleans, made at the last possible moment.

I could go on mentioning many other plays illustrating phases of life and society in America, and there could be no better or more positive proof that a school of American dramatists already exists. This school will undoubtedly continue to improve in the technical quality of its work, exactly as it has done in the past, and probably with more rapidity.

The question has been discussed as to whether we are ever likely to produce an Ibsen or a Shaw, and under what conditions he would be received. As far as concerns what may happen in the future in the way of producing absolutely great dramatists and great plays, using the word 'great' in the international and historical sense, the opinion of anyone on that subject is mere guesswork and absolutely valueless.

The greatest drama in history was produced by Greece about four or five centuries before Christ, and for a few generations afterward. Since Æschylus, Sophocles, and Euripides, Greece has scarcely given us anything. Aristophanes and Menander are of course remembered, but the writers who endeavoured to follow in the footsteps of the masters were of far inferior merit. The Roman Empire existed for nearly two thousand years without producing any drama of its own worthy of the name. The Romans were not a dramatic people. The works of the so-called Latin dramatists, such as those of Plautus and Terence, were mere imitations of the Greek.

France and England had sudden bursts of greatness followed by general mediocrity, with occasional great writers whose advent could not possibly have been predicted by anything in art preceding them. Even the exception to this in France, in the middle of the nineteenth century, was apparently a flash of light that disappeared almost as suddenly as it came. What is the use of posing as a prophet with such a record of the past? Anyone else is at liberty to do so. I would as soon act as harlequin. Was there any wise man in England who, twenty-four hours before that momentous event in April, 1564, could predict that a baby named William Shakespeare would be born the next day? To say that an American dramatist is to appear this year or in a thousand years who will make an epoch is simply ridiculous.

That Ibsen exercised and will exercise great influence on American dramatists there can be little doubt. His skill was no mere accident. He was the most finished development of the French school of the nineteenth century, as well as the most highly artificial individual dramatist of that school. I call it the strictly logical school of dramatic construction. I use the word 'artificial' in its more artistic sense, as opposed to the so-called natural school. His subjects of course were national, and not French. Whether his pessimism was national or personal, I have not been able to discover. It seemed to me that he was a pessimistic man dealing with a nation inclined to pessimism, but that had nothing to do with the technical qualities of the man any more than the national peculiarities of Denmark had to do with Thorvaldsen as a follower of Greek sculpture.

As to the policy of our theatre managers, I confess that they do follow each other; but it is simply because they think the leader they happen to be following has discovered a current of temporary popular taste. The authors have the same interest as the managers, and you will always find them watching the public taste in the same manner.

Occasionally an individual dramatist, and not always the best from a technical point of view, will develop such a strong personal bias as to write on subjects suggested by his own tastes, without any regard to the current of popular wishes. If he is a strong enough man he will become a leader of the public in his dramatic tastes. Sometimes in rare instances he will influence the public so decidedly that he compels the contemporary school of writers to follow him. This has been the case in all periods. I need not mention Shakespeare, as everything said about him is a matter of course.

Take the vile dramatic era of Charles II. Wycherley led the brutes, but Congreve came up and combatted with his brilliant comedies the vileness of the Restoration school, and Hallam says of him that he introduced decency to the stage that afterward drove his own comedies off it. A little after Congreve, the school, so to speak, for we have nothing but the school, was so stupid that it brought forth no great writers, and produced weak, sentimental plays. Then came Goldsmith, who wrote "She Stoops to Conquer" actually as a protest against the feeble sentimentality I have referred to. Richard Brinsley Sheridan was made possible by Goldsmith. We went on after that with a school of old comedies. When we speak of the "old comedies," I am not talking about Beaumont and Fletcher, nor Wycherley, nor Vanbrugh, nor even Congreve, but of the comedy of Goldsmith in the third quarter of the eighteenth century down to Bulwer Lytton's "Money" and Boucicault's "London Assurance," bringing us to about 1840. Then there swung a school of what we call the palmy days of old comedy, and in the '40's it dwindled to nothing, and England and America waited until the early '60's. Then came Tom Robertson with his so-called "tea-cup and saucer" school, which consisted of sententious dialogue, simple situations, conventional characterizations, and threads of plots, until Pinero and Jones put a stop to the Robertson fad.

This proves in my judgment that the school always starts by being shown what the popular taste is, and follows that, until some individual discovery that the popular taste is changed. The tendency of the school is always to become academic and fixed in its ideas—it is the individual who points to the necessary changes. Schools and these special individuals are interdependent.

As to the present comedies in America: in the first place, it is impossible as a rule to decide fully what are the tendencies of a school when one is living in the midst of its activities. There is no marked tendency now; and as far as I can see it is only the occasional man who discovers the tendency of the times. Pinero undoubtedly saw that the public was tired of the "tea-cup and saucer." Probably had he not thought so, he would have gone on in that school.

Undoubtedly more plays are written to order than are written on the mere impulse of authors, independently of popular demand. The "order" play simply represents the popular demand as understood by managers, and the meeting of that demand in each age produces the great mass of any nation's drama. So far from lowering the standard of dramatic writing, it is a necessary impulse in the development of any drama. It is only when the school goes on blindly without seeing a change in the popular taste that the occasional man I have spoken of comes on. When the work of the school is legitimately in line with the public taste, the merely eccentric dramatist is like *Lord Dundreary's* bird with a single feather that goes in a corner and flocks all by itself. He may be a strong enough man to attract attention to his individuality, and his plays may be really great in themselves, but his work has little influence on the development of the art. In fact, there is no development of the art except in the line of popular taste. The specially great men mentioned have simply discovered the changes in the popular taste, and to a certain extent perhaps guided it.*

*** Orginally published in "The Sunday Magazine" (New York) for October 7, 1906.**

BOSTON MUSEUM

ESTABLISHED 1841

FORTY EIGHTH REGULAR SEASON. MR. R. M. FIELD, MANAGER.

COMMENCING MONDAY, NOV. 19, 1888,

Evenings at 7.45, and Wednesday and Saturday Afternoons at 2.

FIRST TIME ON ANY STAGE

OF THE

NEW MILITARY COMEDY

SHENANDOAH!

Written Expressly for the Boston Museum by

BRONSON HOWARD, Esq.

Author of THE HENRIETTA, THE BANKER'S DAUGHTER, YOUNG MRS. WINTHROP, ONE OF OUR GIRLS, OLD LOVE LETTERS, ETC.

WITH ENTIRELY NEW SCENERY BY LA MOSS,

AND THE FOLLOWING CAST:

PEACE.

COL. JOHN HAVERILL, U. S. A. . . . . Mr. THOS. L. COLEMAN
LIEUT. KERCHIVAL WEST } 1st Col. Haverill's regiment, classmates at West Point. { Mr. JOHN B. MASON
LIEUT. ROB'T ELLINGHAM } { Mr. CHAS. J. BELL
FRANK HAVERILL . . . . Mr. EDGAR L. DAVENPORT
EDW. THORNTON, a Southerner "by choice," Mr. WILLIS GRANGER
MRS. HAVERILL . . . . Miss ANNIE M. CLARKE
GERTRUDE ELLINGHAM, a Southern girl . . . . Miss VIOLA ALLEN
MADELINE WEST, a Northern girl . . . . Miss HELEN DAYNE

WAR.

MAJ.-GEN. IRENÆUS BUCKTHORN, Commander of the Nineteenth Army Corps . . . . Mr. C. LESLIE ALLEN
BRIG.-GEN. HAVERILL . } Officers of Sheridan's Cavalry. { . . Mr. THOS. L. COLEMAN
COL. KERCHIVAL WEST } { . . . . Mr. JOHN B. MASON
CAPT. HEARTSEASE . . } { . . . . Mr. HENRY M. PITT
LIEUT. FRANK BEDLOE } { Mr. EDGAR L. DAVENPORT
SERGEANT BARKET . . . . Mr. GEO. W. WILSON
COL. ROBERT ELLINGHAM, 10th Virginia, C.S.A. . Mr. CHAS. J. BELL
CAPT. THORNTON, Secret Service, C. S. A. . . . Mr. WILLIS GRANGER
LIEUT. HARDWICK, Surgeon, C. S. A. . . . . . . Mr. GEORGE BLAKE
CORPORAL DUNN . . . . Mr. JAMES NOLAN
CAPT. LOCKWOOD, Signal Officer . . . . Mr. HERBERT PATTEE
BENSON . . . . } Cavalrymen { . . . . Mr. C. S. ABBE
WILKINS . . . . } { Mr. HENRY MACDONNA
LIEUTENANTS . . . . { Cavalry. | Mr. H. P. WHITTEMORE
{ Infantry. | . . . Mr. THOS. FRANCIS
MRS. HAVERILL . . . . Miss ANNIE M. CLARKE
GERTRUDE ELLINGHAM . . . . Miss VIOLA ALLEN
MADELINE WEST . . . . Miss HELEN DAYNE
JENNY BUCKTHORN, U. S. A. . . . . Miss MIRIAM O'LEARY
MRS. EDITH HAVERILL . . . . Miss GRACE ATWELL
OLD MARGERY . . . . Miss KATE RYAN
JANNETTE . . . . Miss HARDING

There will be no intermission between Acts THIRD and FOURTH.

The Cavalry Trumpet Signals in Acts II. and IV. are given accurately for the various Commands as Provided in the U. S. Cavalry Tactics.

ACT FIRST.

Charleston Harbor in 1861.

After the Ball. Residence of the Ellinghams.

The citizens of Charleston knew almost the exact hour at which the attack on Fort Sumter would begin. The excitement of the preparations had reached even into their social gayeties; and they gathered on the shores of the harbor, in the gray twilight of this April morning, while yet the lingering night lay upon the waters of the bay, to view the bombardment as a spectacle.—*NICOLAY. Campaigns of the Civil War. Vol. I.*

"I shall open fire in one hour." *Beauregard's last message to Maj. Anderson, sent at 3.20 A. M., April 12, 1861.*

ACT SECOND.

The Ellinghams Remarried in Virginia.

When the Union Army under Gen. Sheridan, and the Confederate Army under Gen. Early, were encamped at Cedar Creek, about twenty miles south of Winchester, there was a Confederate signal station on Three Top Mountain, overlooking both camps; also another, near the summit of North Mountain, on the opposite side of the valley.—*Official Records and Maps.*

ACTS THIRD and FOURTH.

No Intermission between these Acts.

The Shenandoah Valley. Night and Morning. Three Top Mountain.

"Here is the steed that saved the day,
By carrying Sheridan into the fight,
From Winchester, twenty miles away."

While the two armies lay opposite each other, Gen. Sheridan was called to Washington. Soon after he left, a *startling despatch* was taken by our own signal officers from the Confederate signal station on Three Top Mountain.—*POND. Camp. Civ. War. Vol. XI.*

On the morning of Oct. 19th, the Union Army was taken completely by surprise. Thoburn's position was swept in an instant. The men who escaped capture fled to the rear. Gordon suddenly burst upon the left flank.—*POND. Supra.*

ACT FIFTH.

Washington, 1865. Residence of Gen. Buckthorn.

From Gen. Grant's Memoirs.

"I feel that we are on the eve of a new era, when there is to be great harmony between the Federal and Confederate."

The Orchestra, under the direction of MR. GEORGE PURDY, will perform the following selections:—

1. Overture—Le Caid . . . . Ambroise Thomas
2. Waltz—Ruby Royal . . . . Louis Uregh
3. Selection—War Songs . . . . Arr. by George Purdy
Introducing the following melodies: Kingdom Coming, When this Cruel War is Over, Babylon is Fallen, Raw Recruit, The Vacant Chair, Tramp, Tramp, Johnny Comes Marching, Who Will Care for Mother Now? Tenting on the Old Camp Ground, Rally Round the Flag.
4. Masque Music . . . . Sir Arthur Sullivan
Composed for a production of The Merchant of Venice, compressed from the original score by Geo. Purdy. First performance in this country.
Introduction. Barcarolle. Bourree.
Grotesque Dance. Waltz. Finale.
5. March—Old Regiment . . . . Gilmore

---

THANKSGIVING DAY,

EXTRA SHENANDOAH MATINEE.

SEATS SECURED TWO WEEKS IN ADVANCE DURING THE RUN OF SHENANDOAH.

ACTING AND STAGE MANAGER . . . . MR. HENRY M. PITT

SHENANDOAH

A MILITARY COMEDY IN FOUR ACTS

By BRONSON HOWARD

Reprinted from a privately printed edition, by permission of the Society of American Dramatists and Composers, from a copy furnished by Samuel French. It is here to be noted that the Society of American Dramatists and Composers reserves all rights in "Shenandoah."

ORIGINAL CAST OF CHARACTERS

First produced at the Star Theatre, New York City, September 9, 1889.

GENERAL HAVERILL	Officers of Sheridan's Cavalry	Wilton Lackaye.
COLONEL KERCHIVAL WEST		Henry Miller.
CAPTAIN HEARTSEASE		Morton Selton.
LIEUTENANT FRANK BEDLOE		G. W. Bailey.
MAJOR-GENERAL FRANCIS BUCKTHORN, Commander of the 19th Army Corps		Harry Harwood.
SERGEANT BARKET		James O. Barrows.
COLONEL ROBERT ELLINGHAM, 10th Virginia		Lucius Henderson.
CAPTAIN THORNTON, Secret Service, C. S. A.		John E. Kellard.
LIEUTENANT OF SIGNAL CORPS		Harry Thorn.
LIEUTENANT OF INFANTRY		Geo. Maxwell.
MRS. CONSTANCE HAVERILL		Dorothy Dorr.
GERTRUDE ELLINGHAM		Viola Allen.
MADELINE WEST		Nanette Comstock.
JENNY BUCKTHORN, U. S. A.		Effie Shannon.
MRS. EDITH HAVERILL		Alice B. Haines.
HARDWICK (SURGEON)		W. L. Dennison.
CAPTAIN LOCKWOOD, U. S. Signal Corps		C. C. Brandt.
CORPORAL DUNN		W. J. Cummings.
BENSON		Wm. Barnes.
OLD MARGERY		Mrs. Haslam.
JANNETTE		Esther Drew.

COSTUMES

HAVERILL.—Act 1. Full Evening Dress.—Acts 2 and 3. Uniform of Brigadier-General, U. S. Vol., 1864. Active Service, rough and war-worn.—Act 4. Civil Costume, Prince Albert, &c.

KERCHIVAL WEST.—Act 1. Full Evening Dress.—Acts 2 and 3. Uniform of Colonel of Cavalry, U. S. Vol., 1864 (with cloak in Act 3). Active Service, rough and war-worn.—Act 4. Travelling.

CAPTAIN HEARTSEASE.—Act 2. Uniform of Captain of Cavalry, 1864; as neat and precise as is consistent with Active Service.—Act 4. Afternoon; Civil.

LIEUTENANT FRANK BEDLOE.—Act 2. Lieutenant of Cavalry, 1864; Active Service. He must have a full beard.—Act 3. Same, disarranged for wounded man on stretcher.

GENERAL BUCKTHORN.—Acts 2 and 3. Major-General, 1864. Active Service.—Act 3. Same.—Act 4. Civil. Afternoon.

SERGEANT BARKET.—Acts 2 and 3. Sergeant of Cavalry, U. S. Vol., 1864. Active Service.—Act 4. Plain undress uniform, sacque or jacket.

ROBERT ELLINGHAM.—Act 1. Full Evening Dress.—Act 2. Confederate Colonel: Infantry, 1864. Active Service.—Act 4. Citizen; afternoon. Prince Albert (Gray).

EDWARD THORNTON.—Act 1. Riding, but not present English Cut.—Act 2. First, Confederate Captain of Cavalry. Active Service. Second costume, same, in shirt sleeves and without hat or cap.

HARDWICK.—Uniform of Confederate Surgeon, 1864. Active Service.

CORPORAL DUNN.—Uniform of rank, Cavalry, U. S. Vol., 1864. Active Service.

BENSON.—Uniform of 2nd Corporal, Cavalry, U. S. Vol., 1864. Active Service.

LIEUTENANT OF INFANTRY.—Uniform of rank, U. S. Vol., 1864. Active Service.

MRS. HAVERILL.—Act 1. Full evening ball dress.—Act 4. Mourning, but not too deep.

GERTRUDE ELLINGHAM.—Act 1. Riding habit.—Act 2. First costume, afternoon at home; simple enough for the South during war. Second costume, picturesque and not conventional dress and hat for riding.—Act 3. First costume of Act 2, or similar.—Act 4. Neat travelling costume.

MADELINE WEST.—Act 1. Full evening ball dress.—Act 2. Pretty afternoon costume.—Act 3. Same or walking.—Act 4. Afternoon costume at home.

JENNY BUCKTHORN.—Act 2. Pretty afternoon costume, with military cut, trimmings and general air.—Act 3. Same.—Act 4. Afternoon costume at home.

MRS. EDITH HAVERILL.—Young widow's costume.

OLD MARGERY.—Neat old family servant.

JANNETTE.—Young servant.

FOR PROGRAMME

In ACT I, just before the opening of the war, HAVERILL is a Colonel in the Regular Army. KERCHIVAL WEST and ROBERT ELLINGHAM are Lieutenants in his regiment, having been classmates at West Point.

ACT I.

CHARLESTON HARBOUR IN 1861. AFTER THE BALL.

The citizens of Charleston knew almost the exact hour at which the attack on Fort Sumter would begin, and they gathered in the gray twilight of the morning to view the bombardment as a spectacle.—NICOLAY, *Campaigns of the Civil War, Vol. I.*

"I shall open fire in one hour."—BEAUREGARD'S *last message to* MAJOR ANDERSON. *Sent at* 3:20 *A. M., April* 12, 1861.

ACTS II. AND III.

The Union Army, under General Sheridan, and the Confederate Army, under General Early, were encamped facing each other about twenty miles south of Winchester, on Cedar Creek. * * * General Sheridan was called to Washington. Soon after he left, a startling despatch was taken by our own Signal Officers from the Confederate Signal Station on Three Top Mountain.—POND, *Camp. Civ. War, Vol. XI.*

On the morning of October 19th, the Union Army was taken completely by surprise. Thoburn's position was swept in an instant. Gordon burst suddenly upon the left flank. The men who escaped capture streamed through the camps along the road to Winchester.—POND, *supra.*

Far away in the rear was heard cheer after cheer.—*Three Years in the Sixth Corps.*

ACT IV.

WASHINGTON, 1865. RESIDENCE OF GENERAL BUCKTHORN.

I feel that we are on the eve of a new era, when there is to be great harmony between the Federal and Confederate.—GEN. GRANT'S *Memoirs.*

SHENANDOAH

ACT I.

CHARLESTON HARBOUR IN 1861. "AFTER THE BALL."

SCENE. *A Southern Residence on the shore of Charleston Harbour. Interior.—Large double doors up centre, open. Large, wide window, with low sill. Veranda beyond the doors, and extending beyond window. A wide opening with corridor beyond. Furniture and appointments quaint and old-fashioned, but an air of brightness and of light; the general tone of the walls and upholstery that of the old Colonial period in its more ornamental and decorative phase, as shown in the early days of Charleston. Old candlesticks and candelabra, with lighted candles nearly burned down. Beyond the central doors and the window, there is a lawn with Southern foliage, extending down to the shores of the harbour; a part of the bay lies in the distance, with low-lying land beyond. The lights of Charleston are seen over the water along the shore. Moonlight. The gray twilight of early morning gradually steals over the scene as the Act progresses.*

DISCOVERED. *As the curtain rises* KERCHIVAL WEST *is sitting in a chair, his feet extended and his head thrown back, a handkerchief over his face.* ROBERT ELLINGHAM *strolls in on veranda, beyond window, smoking. He looks right, starts and moves to window; leans against the upper side of the window and looks across.*

ELLINGHAM. Kerchival!

KERCHIVAL. [*Under handkerchief.*] Eh? H'm!

ELLINGHAM. Can you sleep at a time like this? My own nerves are on fire.

KERCHIVAL. Fire? Oh—yes—I remember. Any more fireworks, Bob?

ELLINGHAM. A signal rocket from one of the batteries, now and then. [*Goes up beyond window.* KERCHIVAL *arouses himself, taking handkerchief from his eyes.*

KERCHIVAL. What a preposterous hour to be up. The ball was over an hour ago, all the guests are gone, and it's nearly four o'clock. [*Looks at his watch.*] Exactly ten minutes of four. [*Takes out a cigar.*] Our Southern friends assure us that General Beauregard is to open fire on Fort Sumter this morning. I don't believe it. [*Lighting cigar and rising, crosses and looks out through window.*] There lies the old fort—solemn and grim as ever, and the flagstaff stands above it, like a warning finger. If they do fire upon it—[*Shutting his teeth for a moment and looking down at the cigar in his hand.*]—the echo of that first shot will be heard above their graves, and heaven knows how many of our own, also; but the flag will still float!—over the graves of both sides.

[ELLINGHAM *enters up centre and comes down.*]

Are you Southerners all mad, Robert?

ELLINGHAM. Are you Northerners all blind? [KERCHIVAL *sits.*] We Virginians would prevent a war if we could. But your people in the North do not believe that one is coming. You do not understand the determined frenzy of my fellow-Southerners. Look! [*Pointing.*] Do you see the lights of the city, over the water? The inhabitants of Charleston are gathering, even now, in the gray, morning twilight, to witness the long-promised bombardment of Fort Sumter. It is to be a gala day for them. They have talked and dreamed of nothing else for weeks. The preparations have become a part of their social life—of their amusement—their gayeties. This very night at the ball—here—in the house of my own relatives—what was their talk? What were the jests they laughed at? Sumter! War! Ladies were betting bonbons that the United States would not dare to fire a shot in return, and pinning ribbons on the breasts of their "heroes." There was a signal rocket from one of the forts, and the young men who were dancing here left their partners standing on the floor to return to the batteries—as if it were the night before another Waterloo. The ladies themselves hurried away to watch the "spectacle" from their own verandas. You won't see the truth! I tell you, Kerchival, a war between the North and South is inevitable!

KERCHIVAL. And if it does come, you Virginians will join the rest.

ELLINGHAM. Our State will be the battle-ground, I fear. But every loyal son of Virginia will follow her flag. It is our religion!

KERCHIVAL. My State is New York. If New York should go against the old flag, New York might go to the devil. That is my religion.

ELLINGHAM. So differently have we been taught what the word "patriotism" means!

KERCHIVAL. You and I are officers in the same regiment of the United States Regular Army, Robert; we were classmates at West Point, and we have fought side by side on the plains. You saved my scalp once; I'd have to wear a wig, now, if you hadn't. I say, old boy, are we to be enemies?

ELLINGHAM. [*Laying his hand over his shoulder.*] My dear old comrade, whatever else comes, our friendship shall be unbroken!

KERCHIVAL. Bob! [*Looking up at him.*] I only hope that we shall never meet in battle!

ELLINGHAM. In battle? [*Stepping down front.*] The idea is horrible!

KERCHIVAL. [*Rising and crossing to him.*] My dear old comrade, one of us will be wrong in this great fight, but we shall both be honest in it. [*Gives hand,* ELLINGHAM *grasps it warmly, then turns away.*

ELLINGHAM. Colonel Haverill is watching the forts, also; he has been as sad to-night as we have. Next to leaving you, my greatest regret is that I must resign from his regiment.

KERCHIVAL. You are his favourite officer.

ELLINGHAM. Naturally, perhaps; he was my guardian.

Enter HAVERILL. *He walks down, stopping centre.*

HAVERILL. Kerchival! I secured the necessary passports to the North yesterday afternoon; this one is yours; I brought it down for you early in the evening. [KERCHIVAL *takes paper. Goes to window.*] I am ordered direct to Washington at once, and shall start with Mrs. Haverill this forenoon. You will report to Captain Lyon, of the 2d Regiment, in St. Louis. Robert! I have hoped for peace to the last, but it is hoping against hope. I feel certain, now, that the fatal blow will be struck this morning. Our old regiment is already broken up, and you, also, will now resign, I suppose, like nearly all your fellow-Southerners in the service.

ELLINGHAM. You know how sorry I am to leave your command, Colonel!

HAVERILL. I served under your father in Mexico; he left me, at his death, the guardian of you and your sister, Gertrude. Even since you became of age, I have felt that I stood in his place. But you must be your sister's only guardian now. Your father fell in battle, fighting for our common country, but you—

ELLINGHAM. He would have done as I shall do, had he lived. He was a Virginian!

HAVERILL. I am glad, Robert, that he was never called upon to decide between two flags. He never knew but one, and we fought under it together. [*Exit.*

ELLINGHAM. Kerchival! Something occurred in this house to-night which—which I shouldn't mention under ordinary circumstances, but I—I feel that it may require my further attention, and you, perhaps, can be of service to me. Mrs. Haverill, the wife of the Colonel—

KERCHIVAL. Fainted away in her room.

ELLINGHAM. You know?

KERCHIVAL. I was one of the actors in the little drama.

ELLINGHAM. Indeed!

KERCHIVAL. About half-past nine this evening, while the ladies were dressing for the ball, I was going up-stairs; I heard a quick, sharp cry, sprang forward, found myself at an open door. Mrs. Haverill lay on the floor inside, as if she had just reached the door to cry for help, when she fell. After doing all the unnecessary and useless things I could think of, I rushed out of the room to tell your sister, Gertrude, and my own sister, Madeline, to go and take care of the lady. Within less than twenty minutes afterwards, I saw Mrs. Haverill sail into the drawing-room, a thing of beauty, and with the glow of perfect health on her cheek. It was an immense relief to me when I saw her. Up to that time I had a vague idea that I had committed a murder.

ELLINGHAM. Murder!

KERCHIVAL. M—m. A guilty conscience. Every man, of course, does exactly the wrong thing when a woman faints. When I rushed out of Mrs. Haverill's room, I left my handkerchief soaked with water upon her face. I must ask her for it; it's a silk one. Luckily, the girls got there in time to take it off; she wouldn't have come to if they hadn't. It never occurred to me that she'd need to breathe in my absence.

That's all I know about the matter. What troubles you? I suppose every woman has a right to faint whenever she chooses. The scream that I heard was so sharp, quick and intense that—

ELLINGHAM. That the cause must have been a serious one.

KERCHIVAL. Yes! So I thought. It must have been a mouse.

ELLINGHAM. Mr. Edward Thornton has occupied the next room to that of Mrs. Haverill to-night.

KERCHIVAL. [*Crosses quickly.*] What do you mean?

ELLINGHAM. During the past month or more he has been pressing, not to say insolent, in his attentions to Mrs. Haverill.

KERCHIVAL. I've noticed that myself.

ELLINGHAM. And he is an utterly unscrupulous man; it is no fault of mine that he was asked to be a guest at this house to-night. He came to Charleston, some years ago, from the North, but if there are any vices and passions peculiarly strong in the South, he has carried them all to the extreme. In one of the many scandals connected with Edward Thornton's name, it was more than whispered that he entered a lady's room unexpectedly at night. But, as he killed the lady's husband in a duel a few days afterwards, the scandal dropped.

KERCHIVAL. Of course; the gentleman received ample satisfaction as an outraged husband, and Mr. Thornton apologized, I suppose, to his widow.

ELLINGHAM. He has repeated the adventure.

KERCHIVAL. Do—you—think—that?

ELLINGHAM. I was smoking on the lawn, and glanced up at the window; my eyes may have deceived me, and I must move cautiously in the matter; but it couldn't have been imagination; the shadow of Edward Thornton's face and head appeared upon the curtain.

KERCHIVAL. Whew! The devil!

ELLINGHAM. Just at that moment I, too, heard the stifled scream.

Enter EDWARD THORNTON.

THORNTON. Gentlemen!

ELLINGHAM. Your name was just on my tongue, Mr. Thornton.

THORNTON. I thought I heard it, but you are welcome to it. Miss Gertrude has asked me to ride over to Mrs. Pinckney's with her, to learn if there is any further news from the batteries. I am very glad the time to attack Fort Sumter has come at last!

ELLINGHAM. I do not share your pleasure.

THORNTON. You are a Southern gentleman.

ELLINGHAM. And you are a Northern "gentleman.'

THORNTON. A Southerner by choice; I shall join the cause.

ELLINGHAM. We native Southerners will defend our own rights, sir; you may leave them in our keeping. It is my wish, Mr. Thornton, that you do not accompany my sister.

THORNTON. Indeed!

ELLINGHAM. Her groom, alone, will be sufficient.

THORNTON. As you please, sir. Kindly offer my excuses to Miss Gertrude. You and I can chat over the subject later in the day, when we are alone. [*Moving up stage.*

ELLINGHAM. By all means, and another subject, also, perhaps.

THORNTON. I shall be entirely at your service.

[*Exit and down on veranda.*

ELLINGHAM. Kerchival, I shall learn the whole truth, if possible, to-day. If it is what I suspect—what I almost know—I will settle with him myself. He has insulted our Colonel's wife and outraged the hospitality of my friends. [*Walking right.*

KERCHIVAL. [*Walking left.*] I think it ought to be my quarrel. I'm sure I'm mixed up in it enough.

MADELINE. [*Without, calling.*] Kerchival!

ELLINGHAM. Madeline. [*Aside, starting,* KERCHIVAL *looks across at him sharply.*

KERCHIVAL. [*Aside.*] I distinctly saw Bob give a start when he heard Madeline. Now, what can there be about my sister's voice to make a man jump like that?

GERTRUDE. [*Without.*] Brother Robert!

KERCHIVAL. Gertrude! [*Aside, starting,* ELLINGHAM *looks at him sharply.*] How the tones of a woman's voice thrill through a man's soul!

Enter MADELINE.

MADELINE. Oh, Kerchival—here you are.

Enter GERTRUDE *from apartment, in a riding habit, with whip, etc.*

GERTRUDE. Robert, dear! [*Coming down to* ROBERT; *they converse in dumb show.*

MADELINE. Where are your field-glasses? I've been rummaging all through your clothes, and swords, and sashes, and things. I've turned everything in your room upside down.

KERCHIVAL. Have you?

MADELINE. I can't find your glasses anywhere. I want to look at the forts. Another rocket went up just now. [*Runs and stands on piazza, looking off right.*

KERCHIVAL. A sister has all the privileges of a wife to upset a man's things, without her legal obligation to put them straight again. [*Glances at* GERTRUDE.] I wish Bob's sister had the same privileges in my room that my own has.

GERTRUDE. Mr. Thornton isn't going with me, you say?

ELLINGHAM. He requested me to offer you his apologies.

KERCHIVAL. May *I* accompany you? [ELLINGHAM *turns to window.*

GERTRUDE. My groom, old Pete, will be with me, of course; there's no particular need of anyone else. But you may go along, if you like. I've got my hands full of sugar-plums for Jack. Dear old Jack—he always has his share when we have company. I'm going over to Mrs. Pinckney's to see if she's had any more news from General Beauregard; her son is on the General's staff.

MADELINE. [*Looking off right.*] There's another rocket from Fort Johnson; and it is answered from Fort Moultrie. Ah! [*Angrily.*] General Beauregard is a bad, wicked man! [*Coming down.*

GERTRUDE. Oh! Madeline! You are a bad, wicked Northern girl to say such a thing.

MADELINE. I *am* a Northern girl.

GERTRUDE. And I am a Southern girl. [*They face each other.*

KERCHIVAL. The war has begun. [*Dropping into chair.* ELLINGHAM *has turned from window; he strolls across, watching the girls.*

GERTRUDE. General Beauregard is a patriot.

MADELINE. He is a Rebel.

GERTRUDE. So am I.

MADELINE. Gertrude!—You—you—

GERTRUDE. Madeline!—You—

MADELINE. I—I—

GERTRUDE. I—

BOTH. O—O-h! [*Bursting into tears and rushing into each other's arms, sobbing, then suddenly kissing each other vigorously.*

KERCHIVAL. I say, Bob, if the North and South do fight, that will be the end of it.

GERTRUDE. I've got something to say to you, Madeline, dear. [*Confidentially and turning with her arms about her waist. The girls sit, talking earnestly.*

ELLINGHAM. Kerchival, old boy! There's—there's something I'd like to say to you before we part to-day.

KERCHIVAL. I'd like a word with you, also!

MADELINE. You don't really mean that, Gertrude—with me?

ELLINGHAM. I'm in love with your sister Madeline.

KERCHIVAL. The devil you are!

ELLINGHAM. I never suspected such a thing until last night.

GERTRUDE. Robert was in love with you six weeks ago. [MADELINE *kisses her.*

KERCHIVAL. *I've* made a discovery, too, Bob.

MADELINE. *I've* got something to say to *you*, Gertrude.

KERCHIVAL. I'm in love with *your* sister.

ELLINGHAM. [*Astonished.*] You are?

MADELINE. Kerchival has been in love with you for the last three months. [GERTRUDE *offers her lips—they kiss.*

KERCHIVAL. I fell in love with her the day before yesterday. [*The two gentlemen grasp each other's hand warmly.*

ELLINGHAM. We understand each other, Kerchival. [*He turns up centre, and stops at door.*] Miss Madeline, you said just now that you wished to watch the forts. Would you like to walk down to the shore?

MADELINE. Yes! [*Rising and going up to him. He takes one of her hands in his own and looks at her earnestly.*

ELLINGHAM. This will be the last day that we shall be together for the present. But we shall meet again—sometime—if we both live.

MADELINE. If we both live! You mean—if *you* live. You must go into this dreadful war, if it comes.

ELLINGHAM. Yes, Madeline, I must. Come, let us watch for our fate. [*Exeunt on veranda.*

KERCHIVAL. [*Aside.*] I must leave Charleston to-day. [*Sighs.*] Does she love me?

GERTRUDE. I am ready to start, Mr. West, when you are.

KERCHIVAL. Oh! Of course, I forgot. [*Rising.*] I shall be delighted to ride at your side.

GERTRUDE. At my side! [*Rising.*] There isn't a horse in America that can keep by the side of my Jack, when I give him his head, and I'm sure to do it. You may follow us. But you can hardly ride in that costume; while you are changing it, I'll give Jack his bonbons. [*Turning to window.*] There he is, bless him! Pawing the ground, and impatient for me to be on his back. Let him come, Pete. [*Holding up bonbons at window*]. I love you.

KERCHIVAL. Eh? [*Turning suddenly.*

GERTRUDE. [*Looking at him.*] What?

KERCHIVAL. You were saying—

GERTRUDE. Jack! [*Looking out. The head of a large black horse appears through the window.*] You dear old fellow! [*Feeds with bonbons.*] Jack has been my boy ever since he was a little colt. I brought you up, didn't I, Jack? He's the truest, and kindest, and best of friends; I wouldn't be parted from him for the world, and I'm the only woman he'll allow to be near him.

KERCHIVAL. [*Earnestly.*] You are the only woman, Miss Gertrude, that I—

GERTRUDE. Dear Jack!

KERCHIVAL. [*Aside.*] Jack embarrasses me. He's a third party.

GERTRUDE. There! That will do for the present, Jack. Now go along with Pete! If you are a very good boy, and don't let Lieutenant Kerchival West come within a quarter of a mile of me, after the first three minutes, you shall have some more sugar-plums when we get to Mrs. Pinckney's. [*An old negro leads the horse away.* GERTRUDE *looks around at* KERCHIVAL.] You haven't gone to dress yet; we shall be late. Mrs. Pinckney asked a party of friends to witness the bombardment this morning, and breakfast together on the piazza while they are looking at it. We can remain and join them, if you like.

KERCHIVAL. I hope they won't wait for breakfast until the bombardment begins.

GERTRUDE. I'll bet you an embroidered cigar-case, Lieutenant, against a box of gloves, that it will begin in less than an hour.

KERCHIVAL. Done! You will lose the bet. But you shall have the gloves; and one of the hands that go inside them shall be— [*Taking one of her hands; she withdraws it.*

GERTRUDE. My own—until some one wins it. You don't believe that General Beauregard will open fire on Fort Sumter this morning?

KERCHIVAL. No; I don't.

GERTRUDE. Everything is ready.

KERCHIVAL. It's so much easier to get everything ready to do a thing than it is to do it. I have been ready a dozen times, this very night, to say to you, Miss Gertrude, that I—that I —[*Pauses.*

GERTRUDE. [*Looking down and tapping skirt with her whip.*] Well?

KERCHIVAL. But I didn't.

GERTRUDE. [*Glancing up at him suddenly.*] I dare say, General Beauregard has more nerve than you have.

KERCHIVAL. It is easy enough to set the batteries around Charleston Harbour, but the man who fires the first shot at a woman——

GERTRUDE. Woman!

KERCHIVAL. At the American flag—must have nerves of steel.

GERTRUDE. You Northern men are so slow to—

KERCHIVAL. I have been slow; but I assure you, Miss Gertrude, that my heart—

GERTRUDE. What subject are we on now?

KERCHIVAL. You were complaining because I was too slow.

GERTRUDE. I was doing nothing of the kind, sir!—let me finish, please. You Northern men are so slow to believe that our Southern heroes—Northern *men* and Southern *heroes*—you recognize the distinction I make—you won't believe that they will keep their promises. They have sworn to attack Fort Sumter this morning, and—they—will do it. This "American Flag" you talk of is no longer our flag: it is foreign to us!—It is the flag of an enemy!

KERCHIVAL. [*Tenderly and earnestly.*] Am I your enemy?

GERTRUDE. You have told me that you will return to the North, and take the field.

KERCHIVAL. Yes, I will. [*Decisively.*

GERTRUDE. You will be fighting against my friends, against my own brother, against me. We *shall* be enemies.

KERCHIVAL. [*Firmly.*] Even that, Gertrude—[*She looks around at him; he looks squarely into her eyes as he proceeds.*]—if you will have it so. If my country needs my services, I shall not refuse them, though it makes us enemies! [*She wavers a moment, under strong emotion, and turns away; sinks upon the seat, her elbow on the back of it, and her tightly-clenched fist against her cheek, looking away from him.*

GERTRUDE. I will have it so! I am a Southern woman!

KERCHIVAL. We have more at stake between us, this morning, than a cigar-case and a box of gloves. [*Turning up stage.*

Enter MRS. HAVERILL *from apartment.*

MRS. HAVERILL. Mr. West! I've been looking for you. I have a favour to ask.

KERCHIVAL. Of me?—with pleasure.

MRS. HAVERILL. But I am sorry to have interrupted you and Gertrude. [*Apart.*] There are tears in your eyes, Gertrude, dear!

GERTRUDE. [*Apart.*] They have no right there.

MRS. HAVERILL. [*Apart.*] I'm afraid I know what has happened. A quarrel! and you are to part with each other so soon. Do not let a girl's coquetry trifle with her heart until it is too late. You remember the confession you made to me last night?

GERTRUDE. [*Apart.*] Constance! [*Starting.*] That is my secret; more a secret now than ever.

MRS. HAVERILL. [*Apart.*] Yes, dear; but you do love him. [GERTRUDE *moves away.*

GERTRUDE. You need not ride over with me, Mr. West.

KERCHIVAL. I can be ready in one moment.

GERTRUDE. I choose to go alone! Old Pete will be with me; and Jack, himself, is a charming companion.

KERCHIVAL. If you prefer Jack's company to mine—

GERTRUDE. I do. [*Exit on veranda and down right.*

KERCHIVAL. Damn Jack! But you will let me assist you to mount. [*Exit after her.*

MRS. HAVERILL. We leave for the North before noon, but every hour seems a month. If my husband should learn what happened in my room to-night, he would kill that man. What encouragement could I have given him? Innocence is never on its guard—but, [*Drawing up.*] the last I remember before I fell unconscious, he was crouching before me like a whipped cur! [*Starts as she looks out of the window.*] There is Mr. Thornton now—Ah! [*Angrily.*] No,—I must control my own indignation. I must keep him and Colonel Haverill from meeting before we leave Charleston. Edward Thornton would shoot my husband down without remorse. But poor Frank! I must not forget him, in my own trouble. I have but little time left to care for his welfare.

Re-enter KERCHIVAL.

KERCHIVAL. You said I could do you a favour, Mrs. Haverill?

MRS. HAVERILL. Yes, I wanted to speak with you about General Haverill's son, Frank. I should like you to carry a message to Charleston for me, as soon as it is light. It is a sad errand. You know too well the great misfortune that has fallen upon my husband in New York.

KERCHIVAL. His only son has brought disgrace upon his family name, and tarnished the reputation of a proud soldier. Colonel Haverill's fellow-officers sympathize with him most deeply.

MRS. HAVERILL. And poor young Frank! I could hardly have loved the boy more if he had been my own son. If he had not himself confessed the crime against the bank, I could not have believed him guilty. He has escaped from arrest. He is in the city of Charleston. I am the only one in all the world he could turn to. He was only a lad of fourteen when his father and I were married, six years ago; and the boy has loved me from the first. His father is stern and bitter now in his humiliation. This note from Frank was handed to me while the company were here last evening. I want you to find him and arrange for me to meet him, if you can do it with safety. I shall give you a letter for him.

KERCHIVAL. I'll get ready at once; and I will do all I can for the boy. [*Turning.*

MRS. HAVERILL. And—Mr. West! Gertrude and Madeline have told me that—that—I was under obligations to you last evening.

KERCHIVAL. Don't mention it. I merely ran for them, and I—I'm very glad you didn't choke—before they reached you. I trust you are quite well now?

MRS. HAVERILL. I am entirely recovered, thank you. And I will ask another favour of you, for we are old friends. I desire very much that General Haverill should not know that—that any accident occurred to me to-night—or that my health has not been perfect.

KERCHIVAL. Certainly, madam!

MRS. HAVERILL. It would render him anxious without cause.

KERCHIVAL [*Aside.*] It looks as if Robert was right; she doesn't want the two men to meet.

Enter HAVERILL. *A white silk handkerchief is in his hand.*

HAVERILL. Constance, my dear, I've been all over the place looking for you. I thought you were in your room. But—by the way, Kerchival, this is your handkerchief; your initials are on it. [KERCHIVAL *turns and stares at him a second.* MRS. HAVERILL *starts slightly and turns front.* HAVERILL *glances quickly from one to the other, then extends his hands toward* KERCHIVAL, *with the handkerchief.* KERCHIVAL *takes it.* MRS. HAVERILL *drops into chair.*

KERCHIVAL. Thank you. [*He exits with a quick glance back.* HAVERILL *looks at* MRS. HAVERILL, *who sits nervously looking away. He then glances after* KERCHIVAL. *A cloud comes over his face, and he stands a second in thought. Then, with a movement as if brushing away a passing suspicion, he smiles pleasantly and approaches* MRS. HAVERILL; *leans over her.*

HAVERILL. My fair Desdemona! [*Smiling.*] I found Cassio's handkerchief in your room. Have you a kiss for me? [*She looks up; he raises her chin with a finger and kisses her.*] That's the way I shall smother you.

MRS. HAVERILL. [*Rising and dropping her head upon his breast.*] Husband!

HAVERILL. But what is this they have been telling me?

MRS. HAVERILL. What have they said to you?

HAVERILL. There was something wrong with you in the early part of the evening; you are trembling and excited, my girl!

MRS. HAVERILL. It was nothing, John; I—I—was ill, for a few moments, but I am well now.

HAVERILL. You said nothing about it to me.

MRS. HAVERILL. Do not give it another thought.

HAVERILL. Was there anything besides your health involved in the affair? There was. [*Aside.*] How came this handkerchief in her room?

MRS. HAVERILL. My husband! I do not want to say anything more—at—at present—about what happened to-night. There has never been a shadow between us—will you not trust me?

HAVERILL. Shadow! You stand in a bright light of your own, my wife; it shines upon my whole life—there can be no shadow there. Tell me as much or as little as you like, and in your own time. I am sure you will conceal nothing from me that I ought to know. I trust my honour and my happiness to you, absolutely.

MRS. HAVERILL. They will both be safe, John, in my keeping. But there is something else that I wish to speak with you about; something very near to your heart—your son!

HAVERILL. My son!

MRS. HAVERILL. He is in Charleston.

HAVERILL. And not—in prison? To me he is nowhere. I am childless.

MRS. HAVERILL. I hope to see him to-day; may I not take him some kind word from you?

HAVERILL. My lawyers in New York had instructions to provide him with whatever he needed.

MRS. HAVERILL. They have done so, and he wants for nothing; he asks for nothing, except that I will seek out the poor young wife—only a girl herself—whom he is obliged to desert, in New York.

HAVERILL. His marriage was a piece of reckless folly, but I forgave him that.

MRS. HAVERILL. I am sure that it was only after another was dependent on him that the debts of a mere spendthrift were changed to fraud—and crime.

HAVERILL. You may tell him that I will provide for her.

MRS. HAVERILL. And may I take him no warmer message from his father?

HAVERILL. I am an officer of the United States Army. The name which my son bears came to me from men who had borne it with honour, and I transmitted it to him without a blot. He has disgraced it, by his own confession.

MRS. HAVERILL. *I* cannot forget the poor mother who died when he was born; her whose place I have tried to fill, to both

Frank and to you. I never saw her, and she is sleeping in the old graveyard at home. But I am doing what she would do to-day, if she were living. No pride—no disgrace—could have turned her face from him. The care and the love of her son has been to me the most sacred duty which one woman can assume for another.

HAVERILL. You have fulfilled that duty, Constance. Go to my son! I would go with you, but he is a man now; he could not look into my eyes, and I could not trust myself. But I will send him something which a man will understand. Frank loves you as if you were his own mother; and I—I would like him to—to think tenderly of me, also. He will do it when he looks at this picture. [*Taking a miniature from his pocket.*

MRS. HAVERILL. Of me!

HAVERILL. I have never been without it one hour, before, since we were married. He will recognize it as the one that I have carried through every campaign, in every scene of danger on the Plains; the one that has always been with me. He is a fugitive from justice. At times, when despair might overcome him, this may give him nerve to meet his future life manfully. It has often nerved me, when I might have failed without it. Give it to him, and tell him that I send it. [*Giving her the miniature.*] I could not send a kinder message, and he will understand it. [*Turning, stands a moment in thought.* THORNTON *appears at window, looking at them quietly over his shoulder, a cigar in his hand.* MRS. HAVERILL *sees him and starts with a suppressed breath, then looks at* HAVERILL, *who moves left. Aside.*] My son! My son! We shall never meet again! [*Exit in thought.*

MRS. HAVERILL *looks after him earnestly, then turns and looks at* THORNTON, *drawing up to her full height.* THORNTON *moves up stage, beyond window.*

MRS. HAVERILL. Will he dare to speak to me again? [*Enter* THORNTON*; he comes down quietly. He has thrown away cigar.*

THORNTON. Mrs. Haverill! I wish to offer you an apology.

MRS. HAVERILL. I have not asked for one, sir!

THORNTON. Do you mean by that, that you will not accept one?

MRS. THORNTON. [*Aside.*] What can I say? [*Aloud.*] Oh, Mr. Thornton!—for my husband's sake, I—

THORNTON. Ah! You are afraid that your husband may become involved in an unpleasant affair. Your solicitude for his safety, madame, makes me feel that my offense to-night was indeed unpardonable. No gentleman can excuse himself for making such a mistake as I have made. I had supposed that it was Lieutenant Kerchival West, who—

MRS. HAVERILL. What do you mean, sir?

THORNTON. But if it is your husband that stands between us—

MRS. HAVERILL. Let me say this, sir: whatever I may fear for my husband, he fears nothing for himself.

THORNTON. He knows? [*Looking at her, keenly.*]

[*Enter* KERCHIVAL WEST, *now in riding suit.*]

[*He stops, looking at them.*] You are silent. Your husband does know what occurred to-night; that relieves my conscience. [*Lightly.*] Colonel Haverill and I can now settle it between us.

MRS. HAVERILL. No, Mr. Thornton! My husband knows nothing, and, I beg of you, do not let this horrible affair go further. [*Sees* KERCHIVAL.

KERCHIVAL. Pardon me. [*Stepping forward.*] I hope I am not interrupting you. [*Aside.*] It *was* Thornton. [*Aloud.*] You said you would have a letter for me to carry, Mrs. Haverill.

MRS. HAVERILL. Yes, I—I will go up and write it at once. [*Crosses; stops and looks back. Aside.*] I wonder how much he overheard.

KERCHIVAL. [*Quietly.*] I suppose eight o'clock will be time enough for me to go?

MRS. HAVERILL. Oh, yes! [*Glancing at him a moment.*]—quite. [*Exit, through apartment.*

KERCHIVAL. [*Quietly.*] Mr. Thornton! you are a scoundrel! Do I make myself plain?

THORNTON. You make the fact that you desire to pick a quarrel with me quite plain, sir; but I choose my own quarrels and my own enemies.

KERCHIVAL. Colonel Haverill is my commander, and he is beloved by every officer in the regiment.

THORNTON. On what authority, may I ask, do you—

KERCHIVAL. The honour of Colonel Haverill's wife is under our protection.

THORNTON. Under your protection? You have a better claim than that, perhaps, to act as her champion. Lieutenant Kerchival West is Mrs. Haverill's favourite officer in the regiment.

KERCHIVAL. [*Approaching him.*] You dare to suggest that I—

THORNTON. If I accept your challenge, I shall do so not because you are her protector, but my rival.

KERCHIVAL. Bah! [*Striking him sharply on the cheek with glove. The two men stand facing each other a moment.*] Is it my quarrel now?

THORNTON. I think you are entitled to my attention, sir.

KERCHIVAL. My time here is limited.

THORNTON. We need not delay. The Bayou La Forge is convenient to this place.

KERCHIVAL. I'll meet you there, with a friend, at once.

THORNTON. It will be light enough to see the sights of our weapons in about one hour. [*They bow to each other, and* THORNTON *goes out.*

KERCHIVAL. I've got ahead of Bob.

GERTRUDE. [*Without.*] Whoa! Jack! Old boy! Steady, now—that's a good fellow.

KERCHIVAL. She has returned. I *must* know whether Gertrude Ellingham loves me—before Thornton and I meet. He is a good shot.

GERTRUDE. [*Without, calling.*] O-h! Pete! You may take Jack to the stable. Ha—ha—ha! [*Appears at window. To* KERCHIVAL.] Old Pete, on the bay horse, has been doing his best to keep up with us; but Jack and I have led him such a race! Ha—ha—ha—ha! [*Disappearing beyond the window.*

KERCHIVAL. Does she love me?

GERTRUDE. [*Entering and coming down.*] I have the very latest news from the headquarters of the Confederate Army in South Carolina. At twenty minutes after three this morning General Beauregard sent this message to Major Anderson in Fort Sumter: "I shall open fire in one hour!" The time is up!—and he will keep his word! [*Turning and looking out of the window.* KERCHIVAL *moves across to her.*

KERCHIVAL. Gertrude! I must speak to you; we may never meet again; but I must know the truth. I love you. [*Seizing her hand.*] Do you love me? [*She looks around at him as if about to speak; hesitates.*] Answer me! [*She looks down with a coquettish smile, tapping her skirt with her riding whip.*] Well? [*A distant report of a cannon, and low rumbling reverberations over the harbour.* GERTRUDE *turns suddenly, looking out.* KERCHIVAL *draws up, also looking off.*

GERTRUDE. A low—bright—line of fire—in the sky! It is a shell. [*A second's pause; she starts slightly.*] It has burst upon the fort. [*Looks over her shoulder at* KERCHIVAL, *drawing up to her full height.*] Now!—do you believe that we Southerners are in deadly earnest?

KERCHIVAL. We Northerners are in deadly earnest, too. I have received my answer. We are—enemies! [*They look at each other for a moment.* [*Exit* KERCHIVAL.

GERTRUDE. Kerchival! [*Moving quickly half across stage, looking after him eagerly; stops.*] Enemies! [*She drops into chair, sobbing bitterly. Another distant report, and low, long reverberations as the curtain descends.*

CURTAIN.

ACT II.

SCENE. *The Ellingham Homestead in the Shenandoah Valley. Exterior. Three Top Mountain in the distance. A corner of the house, with projecting end of veranda. Low wall extending up from veranda. A wide opening in the wall, with a low, heavy stone post, with flat top, on each side. Beyond the wall and opening, a road runs across stage. At the back of this road, elevation of rock and turf. This slopes up behind wood wing. It is level on the top about twelve feet; slopes down to road, and also out behind wood wings. The level part in the centre rises to about four feet above the stage. Beyond this elevation the distance is a broad valley, with Three Top Mountain rising on the right. Foliage appropriate to northern Virginia—walnut, cottonwood, &c. Rustic seats and table. Seat near veranda. A low rock near the stone post. Sunset when curtain rises. As the act proceeds this fades into twilight and then bright moonlight. The number references for the trumpet signals, in this and the next act, are to the official book, entitled "Cavalry Tactics, United States Army," published by D. Appleton & Co., N. Y., 1887. The number references for the Torch Signals, in this act, are to the General Service Code. This code may be found, with illustrations and instructions, in a book entitled "Signal Tactics," by Lieutenant Hugh T. Reed, U. S. Army, published by John Riley & Sons, N. Y., 1880. At rise of curtain, Trumpet Signal No. 34 or No. 35 is heard very distant.* GERTRUDE *and* MADELINE *discovered on elevation up center.* GERTRUDE *is shading her eyes with her hand and looking off.* MADELINE *stands a little below her, on the incline, resting her arm about* GERTRUDE'S *waist, also looking off.*

GERTRUDE. It is a regiment of Union Cavalry. The Federal troops now have their lines three miles beyond us, and only a month ago the Confederate Army was north of Winchester. One army or the other has been marching up and down the Shenandoah Valley for three years. I wonder what the next change will be. We in Virginia have had more than our share of the war. [*Looking off.*

MADELINE. You have, indeed, Gertrude. [*Walking down to seat.*] And we at home in Washington have pitied you so much. But everybody says that there will be peace in the Valley after this. [*Dropping into seat.*

GERTRUDE. Peace! [*Coming down.*] That word means something very different to us poor Southerners from what it means to you.

MADELINE. I know, dear; and we in the North know how you have suffered, too. We were very glad when General Buckthorn was appointed to the command of the Nineteenth Army Corps, so that Jenny could get permission for herself and me to come and visit you.

GERTRUDE. The old General will do anything for Jenny, I suppose.

MADELINE. Yes. [*Laughing.*] We say in Washington that Jenny is in command of the Nineteenth Army Corps herself.

GERTRUDE. I was never more astonished or delighted in my life than when you and Jenny Buckthorn rode up, this morning, with a guard from Winchester; and Madeline, dear, I—I only wish that my brother Robert could be here, too. Do you remember in Charleston, darling—that morning—when I told you that —that Robert loved you?

MADELINE. He—[*Looking down.*]—he told me so himself only a little while afterwards, and while we were standing there, on the shoreof the bay—the—the shotwas fired which compelled him to enter this awful war—and me to return to my home in the North.

GERTRUDE. I was watching for that shot, too. [*Turning.*

MADELINE. Yes—[*Rising.*]—you and brother Kerchival—

GERTRUDE. We won't talk about that, my dear. We were speaking of Robert. As I told you this morning, I have not heard from him since the battle of Winchester, a month ago. Oh, Madeline! the many, many long weeks, like these, we have suffered, after some terrible battle in which he has been engaged. I do not know, now, whether he is living or dead.

MADELINE. The whole war has been one long suspense to me. [*Dropping her face into her hands.*

GERTRUDE. My dear sister! [*Placing her arm about her waist and moving left.*] You are a Northern girl, and I am a Rebel—but we are sisters. [*They go up veranda and out. An* OLD COUNTRYMAN *comes in on a cane. He stops and glances back, raises a broken portion of the capstone of post, and places a letter under it.* GERTRUDE *has stepped back on veranda and is watching him. He raises his head sharply, looking at her and bringing his finger to his lips. He drops his head again, as with age, and goes out.* GERTRUDE *moves down to stage and up to road, looks right and left, raises the broken stone, glancing back as she does so; takes letter and moves down.*] Robert is alive! It is his handwriting! [*Tears open the wrapper.*] Only a line from him! and this—a despatch—and also a letter to me! Why, it is from Mrs. Haverill—from Washington—with a United States postmark. [*Reads from a scrap of paper.*]

"The enclosed despatch must be in the hands of Captain Edward Thornton before eight o'clock to-night. We have signaled to him from Three Top Mountain, and he is waiting for it at the bend in Oak Run. Our trusty scout at the Old Forge will carry it if you will put it in his hands."

The scout is not there, now; I will carry it to Captain Thornton myself. I—I haven't my own dear horse to depend on now; Jack knew every foot of the way through the woods about here; he could have carried a despatch himself. I can't bear to think of Jack; it's two years since he was captured by the enemy—and if he is still living—I—I suppose he is carrying one of their officers. No! Jack wouldn't fight on that side. He was a Rebel—as I am. He was one of the Black Horse Cavalry—his eyes always flashed towards the North. Poor Jack! my pet. [*Brushing her eyes.*] But this is no time for tears. I must do the best I can with the gray horse. Captain Thornton shall have the despatch. [*Reads from note.*]

"I also enclose a letter for you. I found it in a United States mail-bag which we captured from the enemy."

Oh—that's the way Mrs. Haverill's letter came—ha—ha—ha—by way of the Rebel Army! [*Opens it; reads.*]

"My Darling Gertrude: When Colonel Kerchival West was in Washington last week, on his way from Chattanooga, to serve under Sheridan in the Shenandoah Valley, he called upon me. It was the first time I had seen him since the opening of the war. I am certain that he still loves you, dear." [*She kisses the letter eagerly, then draws up.*]

It is quite immaterial to me whether Kerchival West still loves me or not. [*Reads.*]

"I have kept your secret, my darling."—Ah! my secret!—"but I was sorely tempted to betray the confidence you reposed in me at Charleston. If Kerchival West had heard you say, as I did, when your face was hidden in my bosom, that night, that you loved him with your whole heart—"—Oh! I could bite my tongue out now for making that confession—[*Looks down at letter with a smile.*] "I am certain that he still loves you." [*Trumpet Signal No.* 41. *Kisses the letter repeatedly. Trumpet Signal No.* 41, *louder than at first. She starts, listening.*

JENNY BUCKTHORN *runs in on the veranda.*

JENNY. Do you hear, Gertrude, they are going to pass this very house. [*Military band. "John Brown" playing in the distance. Chorus of Soldiers.*] I've been watching them through my glass; it is Colonel Kerchival West's regiment.

GERTRUDE. [*Eagerly, then coldly.*] Colonel West's! It is perfectly indifferent to me whose regiment it is.

JENNY. Oh! Of course. [*Coming down.*] It is equally indifferent to me; Captain Heartsease is in command of the first troop. [*Trumpet Signal No.* 52.] Column right! [*She runs up to road. Looks.*] They are coming up the hill.

GERTRUDE. At my very door! And Kerchival West in command! I will not stand here and see them pass. The despatch for Captain Thornton! I will carry it to him as soon as they are gone. [*Exit up veranda, the band and chorus increasing in volume.*

JENNY. Cavalry! That's the branch of the service I was born in; I was in a fort at the time—on the Plains. Sergeant Barket always said that my first baby squall was a command to the garrison; if any officer or soldier, from my father down, failed to obey my orders, I court-martialed him on the spot. I'll make 'em pass in review. [*Jumping up on the rustic seat.*] Yes! [*Looking off.*] There's Captain Heartsease himself, at the head of the first troop. Draw sabre! [*With parasol.*] Present! [*Imitating the action. Music. The band and chorus now full and loud; she swings parasol in time. Trumpet Signal No.* 40. *Band and chorus suddenly cease.*] Halt! Why, they are stopping here. [*Trumpet Signal No.* 38.] Dismount! I—I wonder if they are going to—I do believe—[*Looking left eagerly. Trumpet Signal No.* 17.] Assembly of Guard Details! As sure as fate, they are going into camp here. We girls will have a jolly time. [*Jumping down.*] Ha—ha—ha—ha! Let me see. How shall I receive Captain Heartsease? He deserves a court-martial, for he stole my lace handkerchief—at Mrs. Grayson's reception—in Washington. He was called away by orders to the West that very night, and we haven't met since. [*Sighs.*] He's been in lots of battles since then; I suppose he's forgotten all about the handkerchief. We girls, at home, don't forget such things. We aren't in battles. All we do is to—to scrape lint and flirt with other officers.

Enter CAPTAIN HEARTSEASE, *followed by* COLONEL ROBERT ELLINGHAM; *stops at gate.*

HEARTSEASE. This way, Colonel Ellingham. [*They enter. As they come down,* HEARTSEASE *stops suddenly, looking at* JENNY; *puts up his glasses.*] Miss Buckthorn!

JENNY. Captain Heartsease!

HEARTSEASE. [*Very quietly and with perfect composure.*] I am thunderstruck. The unexpected sight of you has thrown me into a fever of excitement.

JENNY. Has it? [*Aside.*] If he gets so excited as that in battle, it must be awful. [*Aloud.*] Colonel Ellingham! [*Crossing to him.*

ELLINGHAM. Miss Buckthorn! You are visiting my sister? I am what may be called a visitor—by force—myself.

JENNY. Oh! You're a prisoner!

ELLINGHAM. I ventured too far within the Union lines tonight, and they have picked me up. But Major Wilson has kindly accepted my parole, and I shall make the best of it.

JENNY. Is Major Wilson in command of the regiment?

HEARTSEASE. Yes. Colonel West is to join us at this point, during the evening.

ELLINGHAM. I am very glad you are here, Miss Buckthorn, with Gertrude.

JENNY. Somebody here will be delighted to see you, Colonel.

ELLINGHAM. My sister can hardlv be pleased to see me as a prisoner.

JENNY. Not your sister. [*Passing him and crossing to veranda, turns and beckons to him. She motions with her thumb over her shoulder. He goes up the steps of the veranda and turns.*

ELLINGHAM. What do you mean?

JENNY. I mean this—[*Reaching up her face, he leans down, placing his ear near her lips.*]—somebody else's sister! When she first sees you, be near enough to catch her.

ELLINGHAM. I understand you! Madeline! [*Exit on veranda.* JENNY *runs up steps after him, stops and looks back at* HEARTEASE *over the railing.* HEARTSEASE *takes a lace handkerchief from his pocket.*

JENNY. I do believe that's my handkerchief. [*A* GUARD OF SENTRIES *marches in and across stage in road. The* CORPORAL *in command orders halt and a* SENTRY *to post, then marches* GUARD *out. The* SENTRY *stands with his back to audience, afterwards moving out, appearing and disappearing during Act.*

HEARTSEASE. Miss Buckthorn! I owe you an apology. After I left your side, the last time we met, I found your handkerchief in my possession. I assure you, it was an accident.

JENNY. [*Aside, pouting.*] I thought he *intended* to steal it. [*Aloud.*] That was more than a year ago. [*Then brightly.*] Do you always carry it with you?

HEARTSEASE. Always; there. [*Indicating his left breast pocket.*

JENNY. Next to his heart!

HEARTSEASE. Shall I return it to you?

JENNY. Oh, if a lace handkerchief can be of any use to you, Captain, during the hardships of a campaign—you—you may keep that one. You soldiers have so few comforts—and it's real lace.

HEARTSEASE. Thank you. [*Returning handkerchief to his pocket.*] Miss Buckthorn, your papa is in command of the Nineteenth Army Corps. He doesn't like me.

JENNY. I know it.

HEARTSEASE. But you are in command of him.

JENNY. Yes; I always have been.

HEARTSEASE. If ever you decide to assume command of any other man, I—I trust you will give *me* your orders.

JENNY. [*Aside, starting back.*] If that was intended for a proposal, it's the queerest-shaped one I ever heard of. [*Aloud.*] Do you mean, Captain, that—that you—I must command myself now. [*Shouldering her parasol.*] 'Bout—face! March! [*Turning squarely around, marches up and out on veranda.*

HEARTSEASE. I have been placed on waiting orders. [*Stepping up and looking after her; then very quietly and without emotion.*] I am in an agony of suspense. The sight of that girl always arouses the strongest emotions of my nature.

[*Enter* COLONEL KERCHIVAL WEST, *looking at paper in his hand. The* SENTINEL, *in road, comes to a salute.*]

Colonel West!

KERCHIVAL. Captain!

HEARTSEASE. You have rejoined the regiment sooner than we expected.

KERCHIVAL. [*Looking at paper.*] Yes; General Haverill is to meet me here at seven o'clock. Major Wilson tells me that some of your company captured Colonel Robert Ellingham, of the Tenth Virginia.

HEARTSEASE. He is here under parole.

KERCHIVAL. And this is the old Ellingham homestead. [*Aside.*] Gertrude herself is here, I suppose; almost a prisoner to me, like her brother; and my troops surround their home. She must, indeed, feel that I am her enemy now. Ah, well, war is war. [*Aloud.*] By the bye, Heartsease, a young Lieutenant, Frank Bedloe, has joined our troop?

HEARTSEASE. Yes; an excellent young officer.

KERCHIVAL. I sent for him as I came through the camp. Lieutenant Frank "Bedloe" is the son of General Haverill.

HEARTSEASE. Indeed! Under an assumed name!

KERCHIVAL. He was supposed to have been killed in New Orleans more than a year ago; but he was taken prisoner instead. [*Looking left.*

HEARTSEASE. He is here.

KERCHIVAL. I should never have known him—with his full beard and bronzed face. His face was as smooth as a boy's when I last met him in Charleston.

Enter LIEUTENANT FRANK BEDLOE; *he stops, saluting.*

FRANK. You wished me to report to you, Colonel?

KERCHIVAL. You have been assigned to the regiment during my absence.

FRANK. Yes, sir. [KERCHIVAL *moves to him and grasps his hand; looks into his eyes a moment before speaking.*

KERCHIVAL. Frank Haverill.

FRANK. You—you know me, sir?

KERCHIVAL. I saw Mrs. Haverill while I was passing through Washington on Saturday. She told me that you had escaped from prison in Richmond, and had re-entered the service. She did not know then that you had been assigned to my regiment. I received a letter from her, in Winchester, this morning, informing me of the fact, and asking for my good offices in your behalf. But here is the letter. [*Taking letter from wallet and giving it to him.*] It is for you rather than for me. I shall do everything I can for you, my dear fellow.

FRANK. Thank you, sir. [*Opens letter, dropping the envelope upon the table.*] Kind, thoughtful and gentle to my faults, as ever—[*Looking at the letter.*]—and always thinking of my welfare. My poor little wife, too, is under her protection. Gentlemen, I beg of you not to reveal my secret to my father.

KERCHIVAL. General Haverill shall know nothing from us, my boy; you have my word for that.

HEARTSEASE. Nothing.

KERCHIVAL. And he cannot possibly recognize you. What with your full beard, and thinking as he does, that you are—

FRANK. That I am dead. I am dead to him. It would have been better if I had died. Nothing but my death—not even that—can wipe out the disgrace which I brought upon his name.

HEARTSEASE. [*Looking right.*] General Haverill has arrived.

Enter GENERAL HAVERILL *with a* STAFF OFFICER.

FRANK. My father!

HAVERILL. [*Exchanging salutes with the three officers. He turns to the* STAFF OFFICER, *giving him a paper and brief instructions in dumb show. The* OFFICER *goes out over the incline. Another* STAFF OFFICER *enters, salutes and hands him a paper, then stands up stage.*] Ah! The men are ready. [*Looking at the paper.*

Then to KERCHIVAL.] Colonel! I have a very important matter to arrange with you; there is not a moment to be lost. I will ask Captain Heartsease to remain. [FRANK *salutes and starts up stage;* HAVERILL *looks at him, starting slightly; raises his hand to detain him.*] One moment; your name!

HEARTSEASE. Lieutenant Bedloe, General, of my own troop, and one of our best officers. [HAVERILL *steps to* FRANK, *looking into his face a moment.*

HAVERILL. Pardon me! [*Stepping down stage.* FRANK *moves up, stops and looks back at him.* HAVERILL *stands a moment in thought, covers his face with one hand, then draws up.*] Colonel West! We have a most dangerous piece of work for a young officer—[FRANK *starts joyfully.*]—to lead a party of men, whom I have already selected. I cannot *order* an officer to undertake anything so nearly hopeless; he must be a volunteer.

FRANK. Oh, sir, General! Let me be their leader.

HAVERILL. I thought you had passed on.

FRANK. Do not refuse me, sir. [HAVERILL *looks at him a moment.* HEARTSEASE *and* KERCHIVAL *exchange glances.*

HAVERILL. You are the man we need, my young friend. You shall go. Listen! We wish to secure a key to the cipher despatches, which the enemy are now sending from their signal station on Three Top Mountain. There is another Confederate Signal Station in the Valley, just beyond Buckton's Ford. [*Pointing.*] Your duty will be this: First, to get inside the enemy's line; then to follow a path through the woods, with one of our scouts as your guide; attack the Station suddenly, and secure their code, if possible. I have this moment received word that the scout and the men are at the fort, now, awaiting their leader. Major McCandless, of my staff, will take you to the place. [*Indicating the* STAFF OFFICER. FRANK *exchanges salutes with him.*] My young friend! I do not conceal from you the dangerous nature of the work on which I am sending you. If—if you do not return, I—I will write, myself, to your friends. [*Taking out note-book.*] Have you a father living?

FRANK. My—father—is—is—he is—

HAVERILL. I understand you. A mother? Or—

KERCHIVAL. I have the address of Lieutenant Bedloe's friends, General.

HAVERILL. I will ask you to give it to me, if necessary. [*Extends his hand.*] Good-bye, my lad. [FRANK *moves to him.*

HAVERILL *grasps his hand, warmly.*] Keep a brave heart and come back to us. [FRANK *moves up stage. Exit* STAFF OFFICER.

FRANK. He is my father still. [*Exit.*

HAVERILL. My dead boy's face! [*Dropping his face into both hands.*

HEARTSEASE. [*Apart to* KERCHIVAL.] He shall not go alone. [*Aloud.*] General! Will you kindly give me leave of absence from the command?

HAVERILL. Leave of absence! To an officer in active service —and in the presence of the enemy?

KERCHIVAL. [*Taking hand of* HEARTSEASE. *Apart.*] God bless you, old fellow! Look after the boy.

HAVERILL. A—h—[*With a sudden thought, turns.*] I think I understand you, Captain Heartsease. Yes; you may have leave of absence.

HEARTSEASE. Thank you. [*Salutes.* HAVERILL *and* KERCHIVAL *salute. Exit* HEARTSEASE.

KERCHIVAL. Have you any further orders for me, General?

HAVERILL. I wish you to understand the great importance of the duty to which I have just assigned this young officer. General Sheridan started for Washington this noon, by way of Front Royal. Since his departure, we have had reason to believe that the enemy are about to move, and we must be able to read their signal despatches, if possible. [*Sitting.*] I have ordered Captain Lockwood, of our own Signal Corps, to report to you here, with officers and men. [*Takes up the empty envelope on table, unconsciously, as he speaks, tapping it on the table.*] If Lieutenant Bedloe succeeds in getting the key to the enemy's cipher, we can signal from this point—[*Pointing to elevation.*]—to our station at Front Royal. Men and horses are waiting there now, to carry forward a message, if necessary, to General Sheridan himself. [*He starts suddenly, looking at the envelope in his hand; reads address. Aside.*] "Colonel Kerchival West"—in my wife's handwriting.

KERCHIVAL. I'll attend to your orders.

HAVERILL. Postmarked at Washington, yesterday. [*Reads.*] "Private and confidential." [*Aloud.*] Colonel West! I found a paragraph, to-day, in a paper published in Richmond, taken from a prisoner. I will read it to you. [*Takes newspaper slip from his wallet and reads.*]

"From the Charleston *Mercury*. Captain Edward Thornton, of the Confederate Secret Service, has been assigned to duty in the Shenandoah Valley. Our gallant Captain still bears upon his face the mark of his meeting, in 1861, with Lieutenant, now Colonel Kerchival West, who is also to serve in the Valley, with Sheridan's Army. Another meeting between these two men would be one of the strange coincidences of the war, as they were at one time, if not indeed at present, interested in the same beautiful woman." [*Rises.*]

I will ask you to read the last few lines, yourself. [*Hands* KERCHIVAL *the slip.*

KERCHIVAL. [*Reading.*] "The scandal connected with the lovely wife of a Northern officer, at the opening of the war, was overshadowed, of course, by the attack on Fort Sumter; but many Charlestonians will remember it. The lady in defense of whose good name Captain Thornton fought the duel"—he defending her good name!—"is the wife of General Haverill, who will be Colonel West's immediate commander." [*He pauses a moment, then hands back the slip.*] General! I struck Mr. Thornton, after a personal quarrel.

HAVERILL. And the cause of the blow? There is much more in this than I have ever known of. I need hardly say that I do not accept the statement of this scandalous paragraph as correct. I will ask you to tell me the whole story, frankly, as man to man.

KERCHIVAL. [*After a moment's thought.*] I will tell you—all—frankly, General.

Enter SERGEANT BARKET.

BARKET. Colonel Wist? Adjutant Rollins wishes to report—a prisoner—just captured.

HAVERILL. We will meet again later, to-night, when the camp is at rest. We are both soldiers, and have duties before us, at once. For the present, Colonel, be on the alert; we must watch the enemy. [*He moves up stage.* BARKET *salutes.* HAVERILL *stops and looks at envelope in his hands, reading.*] "Private and confidential." [*Exit.*

KERCHIVAL. Sergeant Barket! Lieutenant Bedloe has crossed the enemy's line, at Buckton's Ford, with a party of men. I wish you to ride to the Ford yourself, and remain there, with your horse in readiness and fresh. As soon as any survivor of the party returns, ride back with the first news at full speed.

BARKET. Yes, sir. [*Starting.*

KERCHIVAL. You say a prisoner has been captured? Is it a spy?

BARKET. Worse—a petticoat.

KERCHIVAL. A female prisoner! [*Dropping into seat.*

BARKET. I towld the byes your honour wouldn't thank us fer the catchin' of her. The worst of it is she's a lady; and what's worse still, it's a purty one.

KERCHIVAL. Tell Major Wilson, for me, to let her take the oath, and everything else she wants. The Government of the United States will send her an apology and a new bonnet.

BARKET. The young lady is to take the oath, is it? She says she'll see us damned first.

KERCHIVAL. A lady, Barket?

BARKET. Well! she didn't use thim exact words. That's the way I understand her emphasis. Ivery time she looks at me, I feel like getting under a boom-proof. She was dashing through the woods on a gray horse, sur; and we had the divil's own chase. But we came up wid her, at last, down by the bend in Oak Run. Just at that moment we saw the figure of a Confederate officer, disappearing among the trays on the ither side.

KERCHIVAL. A—h!

BARKET. Two of us rayturned wid the girl; and the rist wint after the officer. Nothing has been heard of thim yet.

KERCHIVAL. Have you found any despatches on the prisoner?

BARKET. Well!—yer honour, I'm a bachelor, meself; and I'm not familar with the jayography of the sex. We byes are in mortal terror for fear somebody might order us to go on an exploring expedition.

KERCHIVAL. Tell them to send the prisoner here, Barket, and hurry to Buckton's Ford yourself, at once.

BARKET. As fast as me horse can carry me, sir, and it's a good one. [*Exit.*

KERCHIVAL. I'd rather deal with half the Confederate Army than with one woman, but I must question her. They captured her down by the Bend in Oak Run. [*Taking out map; looks at it.*] I see. She had just met, or was about to meet, a Confederate officer at that point. It is evident that she was either taking him a despatch or was there to receive one. Oak Run. [CORPORAL DUNN *and* TWO SOLDIERS enter, *with* GERTRUDE *as a prisoner.*

They stop; KERCHIVAL *sits studying map.* GERTRUDE *glances at him and marches down with head erect; stops, with her back to him.*

CORPORAL DUNN. The prisoner, Colonel West!

KERCHIVAL. Ah! Very well, Corporal; you can go. [*Rising; he motions the* GUARD *to retire.* CORPORAL DUNN *gives the necessary orders and exit with* GUARD.] Be seated, madam. [GERTRUDE *draws up, folding her arms and planting her foot, spitefully.* KERCHIVAL *shrugs his shoulder. Aside.*] I wish they'd capture a tigress for me, or some other female animal that I know how to manage better than I do a woman. [*Aloud.*] I am very sorry, madam, but, of course, my duty as a military officer is paramount to all other considerations. You have been captured within the lines of this army, and under circumstances which lead me to think that you have important despatches upon your person. I trust that you will give me whatever you have at once. I shall be exceedingly sorry if you compel me to adopt the extreme—and the very disagreeable course—for both of us—of having—you—I—I hesitate even to use the word, madam—but military law is absolute—having you—

GERTRUDE. Searched! If you dare, Colonel West! [*Turning to him suddenly and drawing up to her full height.*

KERCHIVAL. Gertrude Ellingham! [*Springs across to her, with his arms extended.*] My dear Gertrude!

GERTRUDE. [*Turning her back upon him.*] Not "dear Gertrude" to you, sir!

KERCHIVAL. Not?—Oh! I forgot.

GERTRUDE. [*Coldly.*] I am your prisoner.

KERCHIVAL. Yes. [*Drawing up firmly, with a change of manner.*] We will return to the painful realities of war. I am very sorry that you have placed yourself in a position like this, and, believe me, Gertrude—[*With growing tenderness.*]—I am still more sorry to be in such a position myself. [*Resting one hand on her arm, and his other arm about her waist.*

GERTRUDE. [*After looking down at his hands.*] You don't like the position? [*He starts back, drawing up with dignity.*] Is that the paramount duty of a military officer?

KERCHIVAL. You will please hand me whatever despatches or other papers may be in your possession.

GERTRUDE. [*Looking away.*] You will *force* me, I suppose. I am a woman; you have the power. Order in the guard! A corporal and two men—you'd better make it a dozen—I am dangerous! Call the whole regiment to arms! Beat the long roll! I won't give up, if all the armies of the United States surround me.

Enter GENERAL BUCKTHORN.

KERCHIVAL. General Buckthorn! [*Saluting.*

BUCKTHORN. Colonel West.

GERTRUDE. [*Aside.*] Jenny's father! [BUCKTHORN *glances at* GERTRUDE, *who still stands looking away. He moves down to* KERCHIVAL.

BUCKTHORN. [*Apart, gruffly.*] I was passing with my staff, and I was informed that you had captured a woman bearing despatches to the enemy. Is this the one?

KERCHIVAL. Yes, General.

BUCKTHORN. Ah! [*Turning, looks at her.*

GERTRUDE. I wonder if he will recognize me. He hasn't seen me since I was a little girl. [*Turns toward him.*

BUCKTHORN. [*Turning to* KERCHIVAL; *punches him in the ribs.*] Fine young woman!—[*Turns and bows to her very gallantly, removing his hat. She bows deeply in return.*] A-h-e-m! [*Suddenly pulling himself up to a stern, military air; then gruffly to* KERCHIVAL, *extending his hand.*] Let me see the despatches.

KERCHIVAL. She declines positively to give them up.

BUCKTHORN. Oh! Does she? [*Walks thoughtfully; turns.*] My dear young lady! I trust you will give us no further trouble. Kindly let us have those despatches.

GERTRUDE. [*Looking away.*] I have no despatches, and I would not give them to you if I had.

BUCKTHORN. What! You defy my authority? Colonel West, I command you! Search the prisoner! [GERTRUDE *turns suddenly towards* KERCHIVAL, *facing him defiantly. He looks across at her aghast. A moment's pause.*

KERCHIVAL. General Buckthorn—I decline to obey that order.

BUCKTHORN. You—you decline to obey my order! [*Moves down to him fiercely.*

KERCHIVAL. [*Apart.*] General! It is the woman I love.

BUCKTHORN. [*Apart.*] Is it? Damn you, sir! I wouldn't have an officer in my army corps who *would* obey me, under such circumstances. I'll have to look for those despatches myself.

KERCHIVAL. [*Facing him, angrily.*] If you dare, General Buckthorn!

BUCKTHORN. [*Apart.*] Blast your eyes! I'd kick you out of the army if you'd *let* me search her; but it's my military duty to swear at you. [*To* GERTRUDE.] Colonel West has sacrificed his life to protect you.

GERTRUDE. His life!

BUCKTHORN. I shall have him shot for insubordination to his commander, immediately. [*Gives* KERCHIVAL *a huge wink, and turns.*

GERTRUDE. Oh, sir! General! I have told you the truth. I have no despatches. Believe me, sir, I haven't so much as a piece of paper about me, except—

BUCKTHORN. Except? [*Turning sharply.*

GERTRUDE. Only a letter. Here it is. [*Taking letter from the bosom of her dress.*] Upon my soul, it is all I have. Truly it is.

BUCKTHORN. [*Taking letter.*] Colonel West, you're reprieved. [*Winks at* KERCHIVAL, *who turns away, laughing.* BUCKTHORN *reads letter.*] "Washington"—Ho!—ho! From within our own lines!—"Colonel Kerchival West—"

KERCHIVAL. Eh?

GERTRUDE. Please, General!—Don't read it aloud.

BUCKTHORN. Very well! I won't.

KERCHIVAL. [*Aside.*] I wonder what it has to do with me?

BUCKTHORN. [*Reading. Aside.*] "If Kerchival West had heard you say, as I did—m—m——that you loved him with your whole heart—" [*He glances up at* GERTRUDE, *who drops her head coyly.*] This is a very important military document. [*Turns to last page.*] "Signed, Constance Haverill." [*Turns to front page.*] "My dear Gertrude!" Is this Miss Gertrude Ellingham?

GERTRUDE. Yes, General.

BUCKTHORN. I sent my daughter, Jenny, to your house, with an escort, this morning.

GERTRUDE. She is here.

BUCKTHORN. [*Tapping her under the chin.*] You're an arrant little Rebel, my dear; but I like you immensely. [*Draws up suddenly, with an* "Ahem!" *Turns to* KERCHIVAL.] Colonel West, I leave this dangerous young woman in your charge. [KERCHIVAL *approaches.*] If she disobeys you in any way, or attempts to escape—read that letter! [*Giving him the letter.*

GERTRUDE. Oh! General!

BUCKTHORN. But not till then.

KERCHIVAL. [*Tenderly, taking her hand.*] My—prisoner!

GERTRUDE. [*Aside.*] I could scratch my own eyes out—or his, either—rather than have him read that letter.

Enter CORPORAL DUNN, *with* GUARD *of four soldiers and* CAPTAIN EDWARD THORNTON *as a prisoner.*

KERCHIVAL. Edward Thornton!

GERTRUDE. They have taken him also! He has the despatch!

CORPORAL DUNN. The Confederate Officer, Colonel, who was pursued by our troops at Oak Run, after they captured the young lady.

BUCKTHORN. The little witch has been communicating with the enemy!

KERCHIVAL. [*To* GERTRUDE.] You will give me your parole of honour until we next meet?

GERTRUDE. Yes. [*Aside.*] That letter! I *am* his prisoner. [*She walks up the steps and looks back at* THORNTON. *Exit.*

KERCHIVAL. [*To* BUCKTHORN.] We will probably find the despatches we have been looking for now, General.

BUCKTHORN. Prisoner! You will hand us what papers you may have.

THORNTON. I will hand you nothing.

BUCKTHORN. Colonel! [KERCHIVAL *motions to* THORNTON, *who looks at him sullenly.*

KERCHIVAL. Corporal Dunn!—search the prisoner. [DUNN *steps to* THORNTON, *taking him by the shoulder and turning him rather roughly.* THORNTON'S *back to the audience.* DUNN *throws open his coat, takes paper from his breast, hands it to* KERCHIVAL, *who gives it to* BUCKTHORN.] Proceed with the search. [DUNN *continues the search.* BUCKTHORN *drops upon seat, lights a match, looks at the paper.*

BUCKTHORN. [*Reading.*] "General Rosser will rejoin General Early with all the cavalry in his command, at——" This is important. [*Continues to read with matches. The* CORPORAL *hands a packet to* KERCHIVAL. *He removes the covering.*

KERCHIVAL. [*Starting.*] A portrait of Mrs. Haverill! [*He touches* CORPORAL DUNN *on the shoulder quickly and motions him to retire.* DUNN *falls back to the* GUARD. KERCHIVAL *speaks apart to* THORNTON, *who has turned front.*] How did this portrait come into your possession?

THORNTON. That is my affair, not yours!

BUCKTHORN. Anything else, Colonel?

KERCHIVAL. [*Placing the miniature in his pocket.*] Nothing!

THORNTON. [*Apart, over* KERCHIVAL'S *shoulder.*] A time will come, perhaps, when I can avenge the insult of this search, and also this scar. [*Pointing to a scar on his face.*] Your aim was better than mine in Charleston, but we shall meet again; give me back that picture.

KERCHIVAL. Corporal! Take your prisoner!

THORNTON. Ah! [*Viciously springing at* KERCHIVAL; CORPORAL DUNN *springs forward, seizes* THORNTON, *throws him back to the* GUARD *and stands with his carbine levelled at* THORNTON; *looks at* KERCHIVAL, *who quietly motions him out.* CORPORAL DUNN *gives the orders to the men and marches out with* THORNTON.

BUCKTHORN. Ah! [*Still reading with matches.*] Colonel! [*Rising.*] The enemy has a new movement on foot, and General Sheridan has left the army! Listen! [*Reads from despatches with matches.*] "Watch for a signal from Three Top Mountain to-night."

KERCHIVAL. We hope to be able to read that signal ourselves.

BUCKTHORN. Yes, I know. Be on your guard. I will speak with General Haverill, and then ride over to General Wright's headquarters. Keep us informed.

KERCHIVAL. I will, General. [*Saluting.* BUCKTHORN *salutes and exit.*] "Watch for a signal from Three Top Mountain to-night." [*Looking up at mountain.*] We shall be helpless to read it unless Lieutenant Bedloe is successful. I only hope the poor boy is not lying dead, already, in those dark woods beyond the Ford. [*Looking off; turns down stage, taking the miniature from his pocket.*] How came Edward Thornton to have this portrait of Mrs. Haverill in his possession? [GERTRUDE *runs in on veranda.*

GERTRUDE. Oh, Colonel West! He's here! [*Looks back.*] They are coming this way with him.

KERCHIVAL. Him! Who?

GERTRUDE. Jack.

KERCHIVAL. Jack!

GERTRUDE. My own horse!

KERCHIVAL. Ah, I remember! He and I were acquainted in Charleston.

GERTRUDE. Two troopers are passing through the camp with him.

KERCHIVAL. He is not in your possession?

GERTRUDE. He was captured at the battle of Fair Oaks, but I recognized him the moment I saw him; and I am sure he knew me, too, when I went up to him. He whinnied and looked so happy. You are in command here—[*Running down.*]—you will compel them to give him up to me?

KERCHIVAL. If he is in my command, your pet shall be returned to you. I'll give one of my own horses to the Government as a substitute, if necessary.

GERTRUDE. Oh, thank you, my dear Kerchival! [*Going to him; he takes her hand, looking into her eyes.*] I—I could almost—

KERCHIVAL. Can you almost confess, at last, Gertrude, that you—love me? [*Tenderly; she draws back, hanging her head, but leaving her hand in his.*] Have I been wrong? I felt that that confession was hovering on your tongue when we were separated in Charleston. Have I seen that confession in your eyes since we met again to-day—even among the angry flashes which they have shot out at me? During all this terrible war—in the camp and the trench—in the battle—I have dreamed of a meeting like this. You are still silent? [*Her hand is still in his. She is looking down. A smile steals over her face, and she raises her eyes to his, taking his hand in both her own.*

GERTRUDE. Kerchival! I—[*Enter* BENSON. *She looks around over her shoulder.* KERCHIVAL *looks up stage. A* TROOPER, *leading the large black horse of Act I, now caparisoned in military saddle, bridle, &c., follows* BENSON *across; another* TROOPER *follows.*] *Jack!* [*She runs up stage, meeting horse.* KERCHIVAL *turns.*

KERCHIVAL. Confound Jack! That infernal horse was always in my way!

GERTRUDE. [*With her arm about her horse's neck.*] My darling old fellow! Is he not beautiful, Kerchival? They have taken good care of him. How soft his coat is!

KERCHIVAL. Benson, explain this!

BENSON. I was instructed to show this horse and his leader through the lines, sir.

KERCHIVAL. What are your orders, my man? [*Moving up, the* TROOPER *hands him a paper. He moves a few steps down, reading it.*

GERTRUDE. You are to be mine again, Jack, mine! [*Resting her cheek against the horse's head and patting it.*] The Colonel has promised it to me.

KERCHIVAL. Ah! [*With a start, as he reads the paper.* GERTRUDE *raises her head and looks at him.*] This is General Sheridan's horse, on his way to Winchester, for the use of the General when he returns from Washington.

GERTRUDE. General Sheridan's horse? He is mine!

KERCHIVAL. I have no authority to detain him. He must go on.

GERTRUDE. I have hold of Jack's bridle, and you may order your men to take out their sabres and cut my hand off.

KERCHIVAL. [*Approaches her and gently takes her hand as it holds the bridle.*] I would rather have my own hand cut off, Gertrude, than bring tears to your eyes, but there is no alternative! [GERTRUDE *releases the bridle and turns front, brushing her eyes, her hand still held in his, his back to the audience. He returns order, and motions* TROOPERS *out; they move out with horse.* GERTRUDE *starts after the horse;* KERCHIVAL *turns quickly to check her.*] You forget—that—you are my prisoner.

GERTRUDE. I *will* go!

KERCHIVAL. General Buckthorn left me special instructions—[*Taking out wallet and letter.*]—in case you declined to obey my orders—

GERTRUDE. Oh, Colonel! Please don't read that letter. [*She stands near him, dropping her head. He glances up at her from the letter. She glances up at him and drops her eyes again.*] I will obey you.

KERCHIVAL. [*Aside.*] What the deuce can there be in that letter?

GERTRUDE. Colonel West! Your men made me a prisoner this afternoon; to-night you have robbed me, by your own orders, of—of—Jack is only a pet, but I love him; and my brother is also a captive in your hands. When we separated in Charleston you said that we were enemies. What is there lacking to make those words true to-day? You *are* my enemy! A few moments ago you asked me to make a confession to you. You can judge for yourself whether it is likely to be a confession of—love—or of hatred!

KERCHIVAL. Hatred!

GERTRUDE. [*Facing him.*] Listen to my confession, sir! From the bottom of my heart—

KERCHIVAL. Stop!

GERTRUDE. I will not stop!

KERCHIVAL. I command you.

GERTRUDE. Indeed! [*He throws open the wallet in his hand and raises the letter.*] Ah! [*She turns away; turns again, as if to speak. He half opens the letter. She stamps her foot and walks up steps of the veranda. Here she turns again.*] I tell you, I— [*He opens the letter. She turns, and exits with spiteful step.*

KERCHIVAL. I wonder if that document orders me to cut her head off! [*Returning it to wallet and pocket.*] Was ever lover in such a position? I am obliged to cross the woman I love at every step.

Enter CORPORAL DUNN, *very hurriedly.*

CORPORAL DUNN. A message from Adjutant Rollins, sir! The prisoner, Captain Thornton, dashed away from the special guard which was placed over him, and he has escaped. He had a knife concealed, and two of the guard are badly wounded. Adjutant Rollins thinks the prisoner is still within the lines of the camp—in one of the houses or the stables.

KERCHIVAL. Tell Major Wilson to place the remainder of the guard under arrest, and to take every possible means to recapture the prisoner. [CORPORAL DUNN *salutes, and exits.*] So! Thornton has jumped his guard, and he is armed. I wonder if he is trying to get away, or to find me. From what I know of the man, he doesn't much care which he succeeds in doing. That scar which I gave him in Charleston is deeper in his heart than it is in his face. [*A signal light suddenly appears on Three Top Mountain. The "Call."*] Ah!—the enemy's signal! [*Enter* CAPTAIN LOCKWOOD, *followed by* LIEUTENANT OF SIGNAL CORPS.] Captain Lockwood! You are here! Are your Signalmen with you?

LOCKWOOD. Yes, Colonel; and one of my Lieutenants. [*The* LIEUTENANT *is looking up at signal with glass.* CAPTAIN LOCKWOOD *does the same.* HAVERILL *enters, followed by two* STAFF OFFICERS.

HAVERILL. [*As he enters.*] Can you make anything of it, Captain?

LOCKWOOD. Nothing, General! Our services are quite useless unless Lieutenant Bedloe returns with the key to their signals.

HAVERILL. A—h! [*Coming down stage.*] We shall fail. It is time he had returned, if successful.

SENTINEL. [*Without.*] Halt! Who goes there? [KERCHIVAL *runs up stage, and half way up incline, looking off.*] Halt! [*A shot without.*

BARKET. [*Without.*] Och!—Ye murtherin spalpeen!

KERCHIVAL. Sentinel! Let him pass; it is Sergeant Barket.

SENTINEL. [*Without.*] Pass on.

KERCHIVAL. He didn't give the countersign. News from Lieutenant Bedloe, General!

BARKET. [*Hurrying in, up slope.*] Colonel Wist, our brave byes wiped out the enemy, and here's the papers.

KERCHIVAL. [*Taking papers.—Then to* LOCKWOOD.] Is that the key?

LOCKWOOD. Yes. Lieutenant! [LIEUTENANT *hurries up to elevation, looking through his glass.* LOCKWOOD *opens book.*

HAVERILL. What of Lieutenant Bedloe, Sergeant?

BARKET. Sayreously wounded, and in the hands of the inimy!

HAVERILL. [*Sighing.*] A—h.

BARKET. [*Coming down stone steps.*] It is reported that Captain Heartsease was shot dead at his side.

KERCHIVAL. Heartsease dead!

LIEUTENANT OF SIGNAL CORPS. [*Reading signals.*] Twelve—Twenty-two—Eleven.

BARKET. Begorra! I forgot the Sintinil entirely, but he didn't forget me. [*Holding his left arm.*

HAVERILL. Colonel West! We must make every possible sacrifice for the immediate exchange of Lieutenant Bedloe, if he is still living. It is due to him. Colonel Robert Ellingham is a prisoner in this camp; offer him his own exchange for young Bedloe.

KERCHIVAL. He will accept, of course. I will ride to the front with him myself, General, and show him through the lines.

HAVERILL. At once! [KERCHIVAL *crosses front and exit on veranda.* HAVERILL *crosses.*] Can you follow the despatch, Captain?

LOCKWOOD. Perfectly; everything is here

HAVERILL. Well!

LIEUTENANT OF SIGNAL CORPS. Eleven—Twenty-two—One—Twelve.

LOCKWOOD. [*From book.*] "General Longstreet is coming with—"

HAVERILL. Longstreet!

LIEUTENANT OF SIGNAL CORPS. One—Twenty-one.

LOCKWOOD. "With eighteen thousand men."

LIEUTENANT OF SIGNAL CORPS. Two—Eleven—Twenty-two.

LOCKWOOD. "Sheridan is away!"

HAVERILL. They have discovered his absence!

LIEUTENANT OF SIGNAL CORPS. Two—Twenty-two—Eleven—One—Twelve—One.

LOCKWOOD. "We will crush the Union Army before he can return."

HAVERILL. Signal that despatch from here to our Station at Front Royal. [*Pointing.*] Tell them to send it after General Sheridan—and ride for their lives. [LOCKWOOD *hurries out.*] Major Burton! We will ride to General Wright's headquarters at once—our horses! [*Noise of a struggle without.*

BARKET. [*Looking.*] What the devil is the row out there? [*Exit. Also one of the* STAFF OFFICERS.

HAVERILL. [*Looking off.*] What is this? Colonel West wounded!

Enter KERCHIVAL WEST, *his coat thrown open, with* ELLINGHAM, BARKET *assisting.*

ELLINGHAM. Steady, Kerchival, old boy! You should have let us carry you.

KERCHIVAL. Nonsense, old fellow! It's a mere touch with the point of the knife. I—I'm faint—with the loss of a little blood—that's all. Bob!—I—[*Reels suddenly and is caught by* ELLINGHAM *as he sinks to the ground, insensible.*

ELLINGHAM. Kerchival! [*Kneeling at his side.*

HAVERILL. Go for the surgeon! [*To* STAFF OFFICER, *who goes out quickly on veranda.*] How did this happen? [*Enter* CORPORAL DUNN *and* GUARD, *with* THORNTON. *He is in his shirt sleeves and disheveled, his arms folded. They march down.*] Captain Thornton!

ELLINGHAM. We were leaving the house together; a hunted animal sprang suddenly across our path, like a panther. [*Looking over his shoulder.*] There it stands. Kerchival!—my brother!

CORPORAL DUNN. We had just brought this prisoner to bay, but I'm afraid we were too late.

HAVERILL. This is assassination, sir, not war. If you have killed him—

THORNTON. Do what you like with me; we need waste no words. I had an old account to settle, and I have paid my debt.

ELLINGHAM. General Haverill! I took these from his breast when he first fell. [*Handing up wallet and miniature to* HAVERILL. HAVERILL *starts as he looks at the miniature.* THORNTON *watches him.*

HAVERILL. [*Aside.*] My wife's portrait!

THORNTON. If I have killed him—your honour will be buried in the same grave.

HAVERILL. Her picture on his breast! She gave it to him—not to my son! [*Dropping into seat.* CAPTAIN LOCKWOOD *enters with a* SIGNALMAN, *who has a burning torch on a long pole; he hurries up the elevation.* CAPTAIN LOCKWOOD *stands below, facing him. Almost simultaneously with the entrance of the* SIGNALMAN, GERTRUDE *runs in on veranda.*

GERTRUDE. They are calling for a surgeon! Who is it? Brother!—you are safe,—ah! [*Uttering a scream, as she sees* KERCHIVAL, *and falling on her knees at his side.*] Kerchival! Forget those last bitter words I said to you. Can't you hear my confession? I do love you. Can't you hear me? I love you! [*The* SIGNALMAN *is swinging the torch as the curtain descends,* LOCKWOOD *looking right.*

CURTAIN.

ACT III.

SCENE. *Same. It is now bright daylight, with sunshine flecking the foreground and bathing the distant valley and mountains.*

DISCOVERED. JENNY, *on low stone post, looking left. As the curtain rises, she imitates Trumpet Signal No.* 19 *on her closed fists.*

JENNY. What a magnificent line! [*Looking.*] Guides-posts! Every man and every horse is eager for the next command. There comes the flag! [*Trumpet Signal without, No.* 30.] To the standard! [*As the signal begins.*] The regiment is going to the front. Oh! I do wish I could go with it. I always do, the moment I hear the trumpets. Boots and saddles! [*Imitates No.* 16.] Mount! [*Imitates No.* 37.] I wish I was in command of the regiment. It was born in me. [*Trumpet Signal No.* 48, *without.*] Fours right! There they go! Look at those horses' ears! [*Trumpet Signal No.* 39, *without.*] Forward. [*Military band heard without—"The Battle Cry of Freedom."* JENNY *takes attitude of holding bridle and trotting.*] Rappity—plap—plap—plap, etc. [*She imitates the motions of a soldier on horseback, stepping down to rock at side of post; thence to ground and about stage, with the various curvettings of a spirited horse. Chorus of soldiers without, with the band. The music becomes more and more distant.* JENNY *gradually stops as the music is dying away, and stands, listening. As it dies entirely away, she suddenly starts to an enthusiastic attitude.*] Ah! If I were only a man! The enemy! On Third Battalion, left, front, into line, march! Draw sabres! Charge! [*Imitates Trumpet Signal No.* 44. *As she finishes, she rises to her full height, with both arms raised, and trembling with enthusiasm.*] Ah! [*She suddenly drops her arms and changes to an attitude and expression of disappointment—pouting.*] And the first time Old Margery took me to papa, in her arms, she had to tell him I was a girl. Papa was as much disgusted as I was. But he'd never admit it; he says I'm as good a soldier as any of 'em—just as I am.

Enter BARKET *on veranda, his arm in a sling.*

BARKET. [*On veranda.*] Miss Jenny!

JENNY. Barket! The regiment has marched away to the front, and we girls are left here, with just you and a corporal's guard to look after us.

BARKET. I've been watching the byes mesilf. [*Coming down.*] If a little milithary sugar-plum like you, Miss Jenny, objects to not goin' wid' 'em, what do you think of an ould piece of hard tack like me? I can't join the regiment till I've taken you and Miss Madeline back to Winchester, by your father's orders. But it isn't the first time I've escorted you, Miss Jenny. Many a time, when you was a baby, on the Plains, I commanded a special guard to accompany ye's from one fort to anither, and we gave the command in a whisper, so as not to wake ye's up.

JENNY. I told you to tell papa that I'd let him know when Madeline and I were ready to go.

BARKET. I tould him that I'd as soon move a train of army mules.

JENNY. I suppose we must start for home again to-day?

BARKET. Yes, Miss Jenny, in charge of an ould Sargeant wid his arm in a sling and a couple of convalescent throopers. This department of the United States Army will move to the rear in half an hour.

JENNY. Madeline and I only came yesterday morning.

BARKET. Whin your father got ye's a pass to the front, we all thought the fightin' in the Shenandoey Valley was over. It looks now as if it was just beginning. This is no place for women, now. Miss Gertrude Ellingham ought to go wid us, but she won't.

JENNY. Barket! Captain Heartsease left the regiment yesterday, and he hasn't rejoined it; he isn't with them, now, at the head of his company. Where is he?

BARKET. I can't say where he is, Miss Jenny. [*Aside.*] Lyin' unburied in the woods, where he was shot, I'm afraid.

JENNY. When Captain Heartsease does rejoin the regiment, Barket, please say to him for me, that—that I—I may have some orders for him, when we next meet. [*Exit on veranda.*

BARKET. Whin they nixt mate. They tell us there is no such thing as marriage in Hiven. If Miss Jenny and Captain Heartsease mate there, they'll invint somethin' that's mighty like it. While I was lyin' wounded in General Buckthorn's house at Washington, last summer, and ould Margery was taking care of me, Margery tould me, confidentially, that they was in love wid aitch ither; and I think she was about right. I've often seen Captain Heartsease take a sly look at a little lace handkerchief, just before we wint into battle. [*Looks off.*] Here's General Buckthorn himself. He and I must make it as aisy as we can for Miss Jenny's poor heart.

Enter GENERAL BUCKTHORN.

BUCKTHORN. Sergeant Barket! You haven't started with those girls yet?

BARKET. They're to go in half an hour, sir.

BUCKTHORN. Be sure they do go. Is General Haverill here?

BARKET. Yes, sir; in the house with some of his staff, and the Surgeon.

BUCKTHORN. Ah! The Surgeon. How is Colonel West, this morning, after the wound he received last night?

BARKET. He says, himself, that he's as well as iver he was; but the Colonel and Surgeon don't agray on that subject. The dochter says he mustn't lave his room for a month. The knife wint dape; and there's somethin' wrong inside of him. But the Colonel, bein' on the outside himsilf, can't see it. He's as cross as a bear, baycause they wouldn't let him go to the front this morning, at the head of his regiment. I happened to ray-mark that the Chaplain was prayin' for his raycovery. The Colonel said he'd court-martial him if he didn't stop that—quick; there's more important things for the Chaplain to pray for in his official capacity. Just at that moment the trumpets sounded, "Boots and Saddles." I had to dodge one of his boots, and the Surgeon had a narrow escape from the ither one. It was lucky for us both his saddle wasn't in the room.

BUCKTHORN. That looks encouraging. I think Kerchival will get on.

BARKET. Might I say a word to you, sur, about Miss Jenny?

BUCKTHORN. Certainly, Barket. You and old Margery and myself have been a sort of triangular mother, so to speak, to the little girl—since her own poor mother left her to our care, when she was only a baby, in the old fort on the Plains. [*At his side and unconsciously resting his arm over* BARKET'S *shoulder, familiarly. Suddenly draws up.*] Ahem! [*Then gruffly.*] What is it? Proceed.

BARKET. Her mother's bosom would have been the softest place for her poor little head to rest upon, now, sur.

BUCKTHORN. [*Touching his eyes.*] Well!

BARKET. Ould Margery tould me in Washington that Miss Jenny and Captain Heartsease were in love wid aitch ither.

BUCKTHORN. [*Starting.*] In love!

BARKET. I approved of the match.

BUCKTHORN. What the devil! [BARKET *salutes quickly and starts up stage and out.* BUCKTHORN *moves up after him; stops at post.* BARKET *stops in road.*

BARKET. So did ould Margery.

BUCKTHORN. March! [*Angrily.* BARKET *salutes suddenly, and exits.*] Heartsease! That young jackanapes! A mere fop; he'll never make a soldier. My girl in love with—bah! I don't believe it; she's too good a soldier, herself.

[*Enter* HAVERILL, *on veranda.*]

Ah, Haverill!

HAVERILL. General Buckthorn! Have you heard anything of General Sheridan since I sent that despatch to him last evening?

BUCKTHORN. He received it at midnight and sent back word that he considers it a ruse of the enemy. General Wright agrees with him. The reconnaissance yesterday showed no hostile force, on our right, and Crook reports that Early is retreating up the Valley. But General Sheridan may, perhaps, give up his journey to Washington, and he has ordered some changes in our line, to be executed this afternoon at four o'clock. I rode over to give you your instructions in person. You may order General McCuen to go into camp on the right of Meadow Brook, with the second division. [HAVERILL *is writing in his note-book.*

Enter JENNY, *on veranda.*

JENNY. Oh, papa! I'm so glad you've come. I've got something to say to you. [*Running down and jumping into his arms, kissing him. He turns with her, and sets her down, squarely on her feet and straight before him.*

BUCKTHORN. And I've got something to say to you—about Captain Heartsease.

JENNY. Oh! That's just what I wanted to talk about.

BUCKTHORN. Fall in! Front face! [*She jumps into military position, turning towards him.*] What's this I hear from Sergeant Barket? He says you've been falling in love.

JENNY. I have. [*Saluting.*

BUCKTHORN. Young woman! Listen to my orders. Fall out! [*Turns sharply and marches to* HAVERILL.] Order the Third Brigade of Cavalry, under Colonel Lowell, to occupy the left of the pike.

JENNY. Papa! [*Running to him and seizing the tail of his coat.*] Papa, dear!

BUCKTHORN. Close in Colonel Powell on the extreme left—[*Slapping his coat-tails out of* JENNY'S *hands, without looking around.*]—and hold Custer on the second line, at Old Forge Road. That is all at present. [*Turns to* JENNY.] Good-bye, my darling! [*Kisses her.*] Remember your orders! You little pet! [*Chuckling, as he taps her chin; draws up suddenly; turns to* HAVERILL.] General! I bid you good-day.

HAVERILL. Good-day, General Buckthorn. [*They salute with great dignity.* BUCKTHORN *starts up stage;* JENNY *springs after him, seizing his coat-tails.*

JENNY. But I want to talk with you, papa; I can't fall out. I—I haven't finished yet. [*Etc., clinging to his coat, as* BUCKTHORN *marches out rapidly, in road,—holding back with all her might.*

HAVERILL. It may have been a ruse of the enemy, but I hope that General Sheridan has turned back from Washington.

[*Looking at his note-book.*] We are to make changes in our line at four o'clock this afternoon. [*Returns book to pocket and stands in thought.*] The Surgeon tells me that Kerchival West will get on well enough if he remains quiet; otherwise not. He shall not die by the hand of a common assassin; he has no right to die like that. My wife gave my own picture of herself to him—not to my son—and she looked so like an angel when she took it from my hand! They were both false to me, and they have been true to each other. I will save his life for myself.

Enter GERTRUDE, *on veranda.*

GERTRUDE. General Haverill! [*Anxiously, coming down.*] Colonel West persists in disobeying the injunctions of the Surgeon. He is preparing to join his regiment at the front. Give him your orders to remain here. Compel him to be prudent!

HAVERILL. [*Quickly.*] The honour of death at the front is not in reserve for him.

GERTRUDE. Eh? What did you say, General?

HAVERILL. Gertrude! I wish to speak to you, as your father's old friend; and I was once your guardian. Your father was my senior officer in the Mexican War. Without his care I should have been left dead in a foreign land. He, himself, afterwards fell fighting for the old flag.

GERTRUDE. The old flag. [*Aside.*] My father died for it, and he—[*Looking left.*]—is suffering for it—the old flag!

HAVERILL. I can now return the kindness your father did to me, by protecting his daughter from something that may be worse than death.

GERTRUDE. What do you mean?

HAVERILL. Last night I saw you kneeling at the side of Kerchival West; you spoke to him with all the tender passion of a Southern woman. You said you loved him. But you spoke into ears that could not hear you. Has he ever heard those words from your lips? Have you ever confessed your love to him before?

GERTRUDE. Never. Why do you ask?

HAVERILL. Do not repeat those words. Keep your heart to yourself, my girl.

GERTRUDE. General! Why do you say this to me? And at such a moment—when his life—

HAVERILL. His life! [*Turning sharply.*] It belongs to me!

GERTRUDE. Oh!

KERCHIVAL. Sergeant! [*Without. He steps in from road, looking back.*] See that my horse is ready at once. General! [*Saluting.*] Are there any orders for my regiment, beyond those given to Major Wilson, in my absence, this morning? I am about to ride on after the troops and re-assume my command.

HAVERILL. [*Quietly.*] It is my wish, Colonel, that you remain here under the care of the Surgeon.

KERCHIVAL. My wound is a mere trifle. This may be a critical moment in the campaign, and I cannot rest here. I must be with my own men.

HAVERILL. [*Quietly.*] I beg to repeat the wish I have already expressed. [KERCHIVAL *walks to him, and speaks apart, almost under his breath, but very earnest in tone.*

KERCHIVAL. I have had no opportunity, yet, to explain certain matters, as you requested me to do yesterday; but whatever there may be between us, you are now interfering with my duty and my privilege as a soldier; and it is my right to be at the head of my regiment.

HAVERILL. [*Quietly.*] It is my positive order that you do not reassume your command.

KERCHIVAL. General Haverill, I protest against this—

HAVERILL. [*Quietly.*] You are under arrest, sir.

KERCHIVAL. Arrest!

GERTRUDE. Ah! [KERCHIVAL *unclasps his belt and offers his sword to* HAVERILL.

HAVERILL. [*Quietly.*] Keep your sword; I have no desire to humiliate you; but hold yourself subject to further orders from me. [KERCHIVAL *goes up veranda.*

KERCHIVAL. My regiment at the front!—and I under arrest! [*Exit.*

HAVERILL. Gertrude! If your heart refuses to be silent—if you feel that you must confess your love to that man—first tell him what I have said to you, and refer him to me for an explanation. [*Exit into road.*

GERTRUDE. What can he mean? He would save me from something worse than death, he said. "His life—it belongs to me!" What can he mean? Kerchival told me that he loved me—it seems many years since that morning in Charleston—and when we met again, yesterday, he said that he had never ceased to love me. I will not believe that he has told me a falsehood.

I have given him my love, my whole soul and my faith. [*Drawing up to her full height.*] My perfect faith!

JENNY *runs in from road, and up the slope. She looks down the hill, then enters.*

JENNY. A flag of truce, Gertude . And a party of Confederate soldiers, with an escort, coming up the hill. They are carrying someone; he is wounded.

Enter up the slope, a LIEUTENANT OF INFANTRY *with an escort of Union soldiers, their arms at right shoulder, and a party of Confederate soldiers bearing a rustic stretcher.* LIEUTENANT FRANK BEDLOE *lies on the stretcher.* MAJOR HARDWICK, *a Confederate Surgeon, walks at his side.* MADELINE *appears at veranda, watching them.* GERTRUDE *stands with her back to audience. The* LIEUTENANT *gives orders in a low tone, and the front escort moves to right, in road. The Confederate bearers and the* SURGEON *pass through the gate. The rear escort moves to left, in road, under* LIEUTENANT'S *orders. The bearers halt, front; on a sign from the* SURGEON, *they leave the stretcher on the ground, stepping back.*

MAJOR HARDWICK. Is General Haverill here?

GERTRUDE. Yes; what can we do, sir?

MADELINE. The General is just about mounting with his staff, to ride away. Shall I go for him, sir?

MAJOR. Say to him, please, that Colonel Robert Ellingham, of the Tenth Virginia, sends his respects and sympathy. He instructed me to bring this young officer to this point, in exchange for himself, as agreed upon between them last evening. [*Exit* MADELINE.

JENNY. Is he unconscious or sleeping, sir?

MAJOR. Hovering between life and death. I thought he would bear the removal better. He is waking. Here, my lad! [*Placing his canteen to the lips of* FRANK, *who moves, reviving.*] We have reached the end of our journey.

FRANK. My father!

MAJOR. He is thinking of his home. [FRANK *rises on one arm, assisted by the* SURGEON.

FRANK. I have obeyed General Haverill's orders, and I have a report to make.

GERTRUDE. We have already sent for him. [*Stepping to him.*] He will be here in a moment.

FRANK. [*Looking into her face, brightly.*] Is not this—Miss—Gertrude Ellingham?

GERTRUDE. You know me? You have seen me before?

FRANK. Long ago! Long ago! You know the wife of General Haverill?

GERTRUDE. I have no dearer friend in the world.

FRANK. She will give a message for me to the dearest friend *I* have in the world. My little wife! I must not waste even the moment we are waiting. Doctor! My note-book! [*Trying to get it from his coat. The* SURGEON *takes it out. A torn and blood-stained lace handkerchief also falls out.* GERTRUDE *kneels at his side.*] Ah! I—I—have a message from another—[*Holding up handkerchief.*]—from Captain Heartsease. [JENNY *makes a quick start towards him.*] He lay at my side in the hospital, when they brought me away; he had only strength enough to put this in my hand, and he spoke a woman's name; but I—I—forgot what it is. The red spots upon it are the only message he sent. [GERTRUDE *takes the handkerchief and looks back at* JENNY, *extending her hand.* JENNY *moves to her, takes the handkerchief and turns back, looking down on it. She drops her face into her hands and goes out sobbing.*

Enter MADELINE *on veranda.*

MADELINE. General Haverill is coming. I was just in time. He was already on his horse.

FRANK. Ah! He is coming. [*Then suddenly.*] Write! Write! [GERTRUDE *writes in the note-book as he dictates.*] "To—my wife—Edith:—Tell our little son, when he is old enough to know—how his father died; not how he lived. And tell her who filled my own mother's place so lovingly—she is your mother, too—that my father's portrait of her, which she gave to me in Charleston, helped me to be a better man!" And—oh! I must not forget this—"It was taken away from me while I was a prisoner in Richmond, and it is in the possession of Captain Henry Thornton, of the Confederate Secret Service. But her face is still beside your own in my heart. My best—warmest, last—love—to you, darling." I will sign it. [GERTRUDE *holds the book, and he signs it, then sinks back very quietly, supported by the* SURGEON. GERTRUDE *rises and walks right.*

MADELINE. General Haverill is here. [*The* SURGEON *lays the fold of the blanket over* FRANK'S *face and rises.*

GERTRUDE. Doctor!

MAJOR. He is dead. [MADELINE, *on veranda, turns and looks left. The* LIEUTENANT *orders the guard,* "Present Arms". *Enter* HAVERILL, *on veranda. He salutes the guard as he passes. The* LIEUTENANT *orders,* "Carry Arms." HAVERILL *comes down.*

HAVERILL. I am too late?

MAJOR. I'm sorry, General. His one eager thought as we came was to reach here in time to see you. [HAVERILL *moves to the bier, looks down at it, then folds back the blanket from the face. He starts slightly as he first sees it.*

HAVERILL. Brave boy! I hoped once to have a son like you. I shall be in your father's place, to-day, at your grave. [*He replaces the blanket and steps back.*] We will carry him to his comrades in the front. He shall have a soldier's burial, in sight of the mountain-top beneath which he sacrificed his young life; that shall be his monument.

MAJOR. Pardon me, General. We Virginians are your enemies, but you cannot honour this young soldier more than we do. Will you allow my men the privilege of carrying him to his grave? [HAVERILL *inclines his head. The* SURGEON *motions to the Confederate soldiers, who step to the bier and raise it gently.*

HAVERILL. Lieutenant! [*The* LIEUTENANT *orders the guard,* "Left Face." *The Confederate bearers move through the gate, preceded by* LIEUTENANT HARDWICK. HAVERILL *draws his sword, reverses it, and moves up behind the bier with bowed head. The* LIEUTENANT *orders* "Forward March," *and the cortège disappears. While the girls are still watching it, the heavy sound of distant artillery is heard, with booming reverberations among the hills and in the Valley.*

MADELINE. What is that sound, Gertrude?

GERTRUDE. Listen! [*Another and more prolonged distant sound, with long reverberations.*

MADELINE. Again! Gertrude! [GERTRUDE *raises her hand to command silence; listens. Distant cannon again.*

GERTRUDE. It is the opening of a battle.

MADELINE. Ah! [*Running down stage. The sounds again. Prolonged rumble.*

GERTRUDE. How often have I heard that sound. [*Coming down.*] This is war, Madeline! You are face to face with it now.

MADELINE. And Robert is there! He may be in the thickest of the danger—at this very moment.

GERTRUDE. Yes. Let our prayers go up for him; mine do, with all a sister's heart. [KERCHIVAL *enters on veranda, without coat or vest, his sash about his waist, looking back as he comes in.*] Kerchival!

KERCHIVAL. Go on! Go on! Keep the battle to yourselves. I'm out of it. [*The distant cannon and reverberations rising in volume. Prolonged and distant rumble.*

MADELINE. I pray for Robert Ellingham—and for the *cause* in which he risks his life! [KERCHIVAL *looks at her, suddenly; also* GERTRUDE.] Heaven forgive me if I am wrong, but I am praying for the enemies of my country. His people are my people, his enemies are my enemies. Heaven defend him and his, in this awful hour.

KERCHIVAL. Madeline! My sister!

MADELINE. Oh, Kerchival! [*Turning and dropping her face on his breast.*] I cannot help it—I cannot help it!

KERCHIVAL. My poor girl! Every woman's heart, the world over, belongs not to any country or any flag, but to her husband—and her lover. Pray for the man you love, sister—it would be treason not to. [*Passes her before him to left. Looks across to* GERTRUDE.] Am I right? [GERTRUDE *drops her head.* MADELINE *moves up veranda and out.*] Is what I have said to Madeline true?

GERTRUDE. Yes! [*Looks up.*] Kerchival!

KERCHIVAL. Gertrude! [*Hurries across to her, clasps her in his arms. He suddenly staggers and brings his hand to his breast.*

GERTRUDE. Your wound! [*Supporting him as he reels and sinks into seat.*

KERCHIVAL. Wound! I have no wound! You do love me! [*Seizing her hand.*

GERTRUDE. Let me call the Surgeon, Kerchival.

KERCHIVAL. You can be of more service to me than he can. [*Detaining her. Very heavy sounds of the battle; she starts, listening.*] Never mind that! It's only a battle. You love me!

GERTRUDE. Be quiet, Kerchival, dear. I do love you. I I told you so, when you lay bleeding here, last night. But you could not hear me. [*At his side, resting her arm about him, stroking his head.*] I said that same thing—to—to—another, more than three years ago. It is in that letter that General Buckthorn gave you. [KERCHIVAL *starts.*] No—no—you must be very quiet, or I will not say another word. If you obey me, I will repeat that part of the letter, every word; I know it by heart, for I read it a dozen times. The letter is from Mrs. Haverill.

KERCHIVAL. [*Quietly.*] Go on.

GERTRUDE. "I have kept your secret, my darling, but I was sorely tempted to betray the confidence you reposed in me at Charleston. If Kerchival West—[*She retires backward from him as she proceeds.*]—had heard you say, as I did, when your face was hidden in my bosom, that night, that you loved him with your whole heart—"

KERCHIVAL. Ah! [*Starting to his feet. He sinks back. She springs to support him.*

GERTRUDE. I will go for help.

KERCHIVAL. Do not leave me at such a moment as this. You have brought me a new life. [*Bringing her to her knees before him and looking down at her.*] Heaven is just opening before me. [*His hands drops suddenly and his head falls back. Battle.*

GERTRUDE. Ah! Kerchival! You are dying! [*Musketry. A sudden sharp burst of musketry, mingled with the roar of artillery near by.* KERCHIVAL *starts, seizing* GERTRUDE'S *arm and holding her away, still on her knees. He looks eagerly.*

KERCHIVAL. The enemy is close upon us!

BARKET *runs in, up the slope.*

BARKET. Colonel Wist! The devils have sprung out of the ground. They're pouring over our lift flank like Noah's own flood. The Union Army has started back for Winchester, on its way to the North Pole; our own regiment, Colonel, is coming over the hill in full retrate.

KERCHIVAL. My own regiment! [*Starting up.*] Get my horse, Barket. [*Turns.*] Gertrude, my life! [*Embraces* GERTRUDE.

BARKET. Your horse, is it? I'm wid ye! There's a row at Finnegan's ball, and we're in it. [*Springs to road, and out.*

KERCHIVAL. [*Turns away. Stops.*] I am under arrest. [*Retreat. Fugitives begin to straggle across stage.*

GERTRUDE. You must not go, Kerchival; it will kill you.

KERCHIVAL. Arrest be damned! [*Starts up stage, raises his arms above his head with clenched fist, rising to full height.*] Stand out of my way, you cowards! [*They cower away from him as he rushes out among them. The stream of fugitives passing across stage swells in volume.* GERTRUDE *runs through them and up to the elevation, turning.*

GERTRUDE. Men! Are you soldiers? Turn back! There is a leader for you! Turn back! Fight for your flag—and mine!—the flag my father died for! Turn back! [*She looks out and turns front.*] He has been marked for death already, and I—I can only pray. [*Dropping to her knees.*

The stream of fugitives continues, now over the elevation also. Rough and torn uniforms, bandaged arms and legs; some limping and supported by others, some dragging their muskets after them, others without muskets, others using them as crutches. Variety of uniforms, cavalry, infantry, etc.; flags draggled on the ground, the rattle of near musketry and roar of cannon continue; two or three wounded fugitives drop down beside the hedge. BENSON *staggers in and drops upon rock or stump near post. Artillerists, rough, torn and wounded, drag and force a field-piece across.* CORPORAL DUNN, *wounded, staggers to the top of elevation. There is a lull in the sounds of the battle. Distant cheers are heard without.*

CORPORAL DUNN. Listen, fellows! Stop! Listen! Sheridan! General Sheridan is coming! [*Cheers from those on stage.* GERTRUDE *rises quickly. The wounded soldiers rise, looking over hedge. All on stage stop, looking eagerly. The cheers without come nearer, with shouts of* "Sheridan! Sheridan!"] The horse is down; he is worn out.

GERTRUDE. No! He is up again! He is on my Jack! Now, for your life, Jack, and for me! You've never failed me yet. [*The cheers without now swell to full volume and are taken up by those on the stage. The horse sweeps by with* GENERAL SHERIDAN.] Jack! Jack!! Jack!!! [*Waving her arms as he passes. She throws up her arms and falls backward, caught by* DUNN. *The stream of men is reversed and surges across stage to road and on elevation, with shouts, throwing up hats, etc. The field-piece is forced up the slope with a few bold, rough movements; the artillerists are loading it, and the stream of returning fugitives is still surging by in the road as the curtain falls.*

CURTAIN.

ACT IV.

SCENE. *Residence of* GENERAL BUCKTHORN, *in Washington. Interior. Fireplace slanting upward. Small alcove. Opening to hall, with staircase beyond, and also entrance from out left.*

Door up stage. A wide opening, with portières to apartment. Upright piano down stage. Armchair and low stool before fireplace. Small table for tea, etc. Ottoman. Other chairs, ottomans, etc., to taste.

TIME. *Afternoon.*

DISCOVERED. MRS. HAVERILL, *in armchair, resting her face upon her hand, and looking into the fire.* EDITH *is on a low stool at her side, sewing a child's garment.*

EDITH. It seems hardly possible that the war is over, and that General Lee has really surrendered. [*Fife and drum, without.*] There is music in the streets nearly all the time, now, and everybody looks so cheerful and bright. [*Distant fife and drums heard playing "Johnnie Comes Marching Home."* EDITH *springs up and runs up to window, looking out.*] More troops returning! The old tattered battle-flag is waving in the wind, and people are running after them so merrily. [*Music stops.*] Every day, now, seems like a holiday. [*Coming down.*] The war is over. All the women ought to feel very happy, whose—whose husbands are—coming back to them.

MRS. HAVERILL. Yes, Edith; those women whose—husbands are coming back to them. [*Still looking into fire.*

EDITH. Oh! [*Dropping upon the stool, her head upon the arm of the chair.*

MRS. HAVERILL. [*Resting her arm over her.*] My poor little darling! *Your* husband will not come back.

EDITH. Frank's last message has never reached me.

MRS. HAVERILL. No; but you have one sweet thought always with you. Madeline West heard part of it, as Gertrude wrote it down. His last thought was a loving one, of you.

EDITH. Madeline says that he was thinking of you, too. He knew that you were taking such loving care of his little one, and of me. You have always done that, since you first came back from Charleston, and found me alone in New York.

MRS. HAVERILL. I found a dear, sweet little daughter. [*Stroking her head.*] Heaven sent you, darling! You have been a blessing to me. I hardly know how I should have got through the past few months at all without you at my side.

EDITH. What is your own trouble, dear? I have found you in tears so often; and since last October, after the battle of Cedar Creek, you— you have never shown me a letter from— from my

—Frank's father. General Haverill arrived in Washington yesterday, but has not been here yet. Is it because I am here? He has never seen me, and I feel that he has never forgiven Frank for marrying me.

MRS. HAVERILL. Nonsense, my child; he did think the marriage was imprudent, but he told me to do everything I could for you. If General Haverill has not been to see either of us, since his arrival in Washington, it is nothing that you need to worry your dear little head about. How are you getting on with your son's wardrobe?

EDITH. Oh! Splendidly! Frankie isn't a baby any longer; he's a man, now, and he has to wear a man's clothes. [*Holding up a little pair of trousers, with maternal pride.*] He's rather young to be dressed like a man, but I want Frank to grow up as soon as possible. I long to have him old enough to understand me when I repeat to him the words in which General Haverill told the whole world how his father died! [*Rising.*] And yet, even in his official report to the Government, he only honoured him as Lieutenant Bedloe. He has never forgiven his son for the disgrace he brought upon his name.

MRS. HAVERILL. I know him so well—[*Rising.*]—the unyielding pride, that conquers even the deep tenderness of his nature. He can be silent, though his own heart is breaking. [*Aside.*] He can be silent, too, though *my* heart is breaking. [*Dropping her face in her hand.*

EDITH. *Mother!* [*Putting her arm about her.*

Enter JANNETTE.

JANNETTE. A letter for you, Madam.

MRS. HAVERILL. [*Taking note. Aside.*] He has answered me. [*Opens and reads; inclines her head to* JANNETTE, *who goes out to hall. Aloud.*] General Haverill will be here this afternoon, Edith. [*Exit up the stairs.*

EDITH. There is something that she cannot confide to me, or to anyone. General Haverill returned to Washington yesterday, and he has not been here yet. He will be here to-day. I always tremble when I think of meeting him.

GENERAL BUCKTHORN *appears in hall.*

BUCKTHORN. Come right in; this way, Barket. Ah, Edith!

BARKET. [*Entering.*] As I was saying, sur—just after the battle of Sayder Creek began—

BUCKTHORN. [*To* EDITH.] More good news! The war is, indeed, over, now!

BARKET. Whin Colonel Wist rode to the front to mate his raytrating rigiment—

BUCKTHORN. General Johnson has surrendered his army, also; and that, of course, does end the war.

EDITH. I'm very glad that all the fighting is over.

BUCKTHORN. So am I; but my occupation, and old Barket's, too, is gone. Always at work on new clothes for our little soldier?

EDITH. He's growing so, I can hardly make them fast enough for him. But this is the time for his afternoon nap. I must go now, to see if he is sleeping soundly.

BUCKTHORN. Our dear little mother! [*Tapping her chin.*] I always claim the privilege of my white hair, you know. [*She puts up her lips; he kisses her. She goes out.*] The sweetest young widow I ever saw! [BARKET *coughs.* BUCKTHORN *turns sharply;* BARKET *salutes.*] Well! What the devil are you thinking about now?

BARKET. The ould time, sur. Yer honour used to claim the same privilege for brown hair.

BUCKTHORN. You old rascal! What a memory you have! You were telling me for the hundredth time about the battle of Cedar Creek; go on. I can never hear it often enough. Kerchival West was a favourite of mine, poor fellow!

BARKET. Just afther the battle of Sayder Creek began, when the Colonel rode to the front to mate his raytrating rigiment—

BUCKTHORN. I'll tell Old Margery to bring in tea for both of us, Barket.

BARKET. For both of us, sur?

BUCKTHORN. Yes; and later in the evening we'll have something else, together. This is a great day for all of us. I'm not your commander to-day, but your old comrade in arms—[*Laying his arm over* BARKET'S *shoulder.*]—and I'm glad I don't have to pull myself up now every time I forget my dignity. Ah! you and I will be laid away before long, but we'll be together again in the next world, won't we, Barket?

BARKET. Wid yer honour's permission. [*Saluting.*

BUCKTHORN. Ha-ha-ha! [*Laughing.*] If we do meet there I'm certain you'll salute me as your superior officer. There's old Margery, now. [*Looking to door. Calls.*] Margery! Tea for two!

MARGERY. [*Without.*] The tay be waiting for ye, sur; and it be boilin' over wid impatience.

BUCKTHORN. Bring up a chair, Barket. [*Sitting in arm-chair.*

BARKET. [*Having placed table and drawing up a chair.*] Do you know, Gineral, I don't fale quite aisy in my moind. I'm not quite sure that Margery will let us take our tay together. [*Sits down, doubtfully.*

BUCKTHORN. I hadn't thought of that. I—[*Glancing right.*]—I hope she will, Barket. But, of course, if she won't—she's been commander-in-chief of my household ever since Jenny was a baby.

BARKET. At Fort Duncan, in Texas.

BUCKTHORN. You and Old Margery never got along very well in those days; but I thought you had made it all up; she nursed you through your wound, last summer, and after the battle of Cedar Creek, also.

BARKET. Yis, sur, bliss her kind heart, she's been like a wife to me; and that's the trouble. A man's wife is such an angel when he's ill that he dreads to get well; good health is a misfortune to him. Auld Margery and I have had anither misunderstanding.

BUCKTHORN. I'll do the best I can for both of us, Barket. You were telling me about the battle of—

BARKET. Just afther the battle of Sayder Creek began, whin Colonel Wist rode to the front to mate his raytrating rigiment—

Enter OLD MARGERY, *tray, tea, &c. She stops abruptly, looking at* BARKET. *He squirms in his chair.* BUCKTHORN *rises and stands with his back to the mantel.* OLD MARGERY *moves to the table, arranges things on it, glances at* BARKET, *then at* BUCKTHORN, *who looks up at ceiling, rubbing his chin, &c.* OLD MARGERY *takes up one of the cups, with saucer.*

OLD MARGERY. I misunderstood yer order, sur. I see there's no one here but yerself. [*Going right.*

BUCKTHORN. Ah, Margery! [*She stops.*] Barket tells me that there has been a slight misunderstanding between you and him.

OLD MARGERY. Day before yisterday, the ould Hibernian dhrone had the kitchen upside down, to show anither old milithary vagabone loike himself how the battle of Sayder Creek was fought. He knocked the crame pitcher into the basket of clane clothes, and overturned some raspberry jam and the flat-irons into a pan of fresh eggs. There *has* been a misunderstanding betwane us.

BUCKTHORN. I see there has. I suppose Barket was showing his friend how Colonel Kerchival West rode forward to meet his regiment, when he was already wounded dangerously.

OLD MARGERY. Bliss the poor, dear young man! He and I was always good frinds, though he was somethin' of a devil in the kitchen himself, whin he got there. [*Wiping her eye with one corner of her apron.*] And bliss the young Southern lady that was in love wid him, too. [*Changing the cup and wiping the other eye with the corner of her apron.*] Nothing was iver heard of ayther of thim after that battle was over, to this very day.

BUCKTHORN. Barket was at Kerchival's side when he rode to the front. [OLD MARGERY *hesitates a moment, then moves to the table, sets down the cup and marches out.* BUCKTHORN *sits in the arm-chair again, pouring tea.*] I could always find some way to get Old Margery to do what I wanted her to do.

BARKET. You're a great man, Ginerel; we'd niver have conquered the South widout such men.

BUCKTHORN. Now go on, Barket; you were interrupted.

BARKET. Just afther the battle of Sayder Creek began, whin—

Enter JANNETTE *with card, which she hands to* BUCKTHORN.

BUCKTHORN. [*Reading card.*] Robert Ellingham! [*Rises.*] I will go to him. [*To* JANNETTE.] Go upstairs and tell Madeline to come down.

JANNETTE. Yes, sir. [*Going.*

BUCKTHORN. And, Jannette, simply say there is a caller; don't tell her who is here. [*Exit* JANNETTE *upstairs.* BUCKTHORN *follows her out to hall.*] Ellingham! My dear fellow! [*Extending his hand and disappearing.*

BARKET. Colonel Ellingham and Miss Madeline—lovers! That's the kind o' volunteers the country nades now!

Enter BUCKTHORN *and* ELLINGHAM.

BUCKTHORN. [*As he enters.*] We've been fighting four years to keep you out of Washington, Colonel, but we are delighted to see you within the lines, now.

ELLINGHAM. I am glad, indeed, General, to have so warm a welcome. But can you tell me anything about my sister, Gertrude?

BUCKTHORN. About your sister? Why, can't you tell us? And have you heard nothing of Kerchival West on your side of the line?

ELLINGHAM. All I can tell you is this: As soon as possible after our surrender at Appomatox, I made my way to the Shenandoah Valley. Our home there is utterly deserted. I have hurried down to Washington in the hopes that I might learn something of you. There is no human being about the old homestead; it is like a haunted house—empty, and dark, and solitary. You do not even know where Gertrude is?

BUCKTHORN. We only know that Kerchival was not found among the dead of his own regiment at Cedar Creek, though he fell among them during the fight. The three girls searched the field for him, but he was not there. As darkness came on, and they were returning to the house, Gertrude suddenly seized the bridle of a stray horse, sprang upon its back and rode away to the South, into the woods at the foot of Three Top Mountain. The other two girls watched for her in vain. She did not return, and we have heard nothing from her since.

ELLINGHAM. Poor girl! I understand what was in her thoughts, and she was right. We captured fourteen hundred prisoners that day, although we were defeated, and Kerchival must have been among them. Gertrude rode away, alone, in the darkness, to find him. I shall return to the South at once and learn where she now is.

JANNETTE *has re-entered, down the stairs.*

JANNETTE. Miss Madeline will be down in a moment. [*Exit in hall.*

BARKET. [*Aside.*] That name wint through his chist like a rifle ball.

BUCKTHORN. Will you step into the drawing-room, Colonel? I will see Madeline myself, first. She does not even know that you are living.

ELLINGHAM. I hardly dared asked for her. [*Passing; turns.*] Is she well?

BUCKTHORN. Yes; and happy—or soon will be.

ELLINGHAM. Peace, at last! [*Exit to apartment.* BUCKTHORN *closes portières.*

BUCKTHORN. I ought to prepare Madeline a little, Barket; you must help me.

BARKET. Yis, sur, I will.

Enter MADELINE *down the stairs.*

MADELINE. Uncle! Jannette said you wished to see me; there is a visitor here. Who is it?

BARKET. Colonel Robert Ellingham.

MADELINE. Ah! [*Staggering.*

BUCKTHORN. [*Supporting her.*] You infernal idiot! I'll put you in the guard-house!

BARKET. You wanted me to help ye, Gineral.

MADELINE. Robert is alive—and here? [*Rising from his arms, she moves to the portières, holds them aside, peeping in; gives a joyful start, tosses aside the portières and runs through.*

BUCKTHORN. Barket! There's nothing but that curtain between us and Heaven.

BARKET. I don't like stayin' out o' Hivin, myself, sur. Gineral! I'll kiss Ould Margery—if I die for it! [*Exit.*

BUCKTHORN. Kiss Old Margery! I'll give him a soldier's funeral. [*Enter* JENNY *from hall, demurely.*] Ah! Jenny, my dear! I have news for you. Colonel Robert Ellingham is in the drawing-room.

JENNY. Oh! I am delighted. [*Starting.*

BUCKTHORN. A-h-e-m!

JENNY. Oh!—exactly. I see. I have some news for *you*, papa. Captain Heartsease has arrived in Washington.

BUCKTHORN. Oh! My dear! I have often confessed to you how utterly mistaken I was about that young man. He is a soldier—as good a soldier as you are. I'll ask him to the house.

JENNY. [*Demurely.*] He is here now.

BUCKTHORN. Now?

JENNY. He's been here an hour; in the library.

BUCKTHORN. Why! Barket and I were in the library fifteen minutes ago.

JENNY. Yes, sir. We were in the bay-window; the curtains were closed.

BUCKTHORN. Oh! exactly; I see. You may tell him he has my full consent.

JENNY. He hasn't asked for it.

BUCKTHORN. Hasn't he? And you've been in the bay-window an hour? Well, my darling—I was considered one of the best Indian fighters in the old army, but it took me four years to propose to your mother. I'll go and see the Captain.

[*Exit to hall.*

JENNY. I wonder if it will take Captain Heartsease four years to propose to me. Before he left Washington, nearly two years ago, he told everybody in the circle of my acquaintance, except me, that he was in love with me. I'll be an old lady in caps before our engagement commences. Poor, dear mother! The idea of a girl's waiting four years for a chance to say "Yes." It's been on the tip of my tongue so often, I'm afraid it'll pop out, at last, before he pops the question.

Enter BUCKTHORN *and* HEARTSEASE *from hall.*

BUCKTHORN. Walk right in, Captain; this is the family room. You must make yourself quite at home here.

HEARTSEASE. Thank you. [*Walking down.*

BUCKTHORN. My dear! [*Apart to* JENNY.] The very first thing he said to me, after our greeting, was that he loved my daughter.

JENNY. Now he's told my father!

BUCKTHORN. He's on fire!

JENNY. Is he? [*Looking at* HEARTSEASE, *who stands quietly stroking his mustache.*] Why doesn't he tell *me?*

BUCKTHORN. You may have to help him a little; your mother assisted me. [*Turning up stage.*] When you and Jenny finish your chat, Captain—[*Lighting a cigar at the mantel.*]—you must join me in the smoking-room.

HEARTSEASE. I shall be delighted. By the way, General—I have been in such a fever of excitement since I arrived at this house—

JENNY. [*Aside.*] Fever? Chills!

HEARTSEASE. That I forgot it entirely. I have omitted a very important and a very sad commission. I have brought with me the note-book of Lieutenant Frank Bedloe—otherwise Haverill—in which Miss Gertrude Ellingham wrote down his last message to his young wife.

JENNY. Have you seen Gertrude?

BUCKTHORN. [*Taking book.*] How did this note-book come into your possession?

HEARTEASE. Miss Ellingham visited the prison in North Carolina where I was detained. She was going from hospital to hospital, from prison to prison, and from burial-place to burial-place, to find Colonel Kerchival West, if living—or some record of his death.

BUCKTHORN. Another Evangeline! Searching for her lover through the wilderness of this great war!

HEARTSEASE. I was about to be exchanged at the time, and she requested me to bring this to her friends in Washington. She had not intended to carry it away with her. I was not exchanged, as we then expected, but I afterwards escaped from prison to General Sherman's army.

BUCKTHORN. I will carry this long-delayed message to the widowed young mother. [*Exit.*

JENNY. I remember so well, when poor Lieutenant Haverill took out the note-book and asked Gertrude to write for him. He—he brought me a message at the same time. [*Their eyes meet. He puts up his glasses. She turns away, touching her eyes.*

HEARTSEASE. I—I remember the circumstances you probably allude to; that is—when he left my side—I—I gave him my—I mean your—lace handkerchief.

JENNY. It is sacred to me!

HEARTSEASE. Y-e-s—I would say—is it?

JENNY. [*Wiping her eyes.*] It was stained with the life-blood of a hero!

HEARTSEASE. I must apologize to you for its condition. I hadn't any chance to have it washed and ironed.

JENNY. [*Looking around at him, suddenly; then, aside.*] What could any girl do with a lover like that? [*Turning up stage.*

HEARTSEASE. [*Aside.*] She seems to remember that incident so tenderly! My blood boils!

JENNY. Didn't you long to see your—your friends at home—when you were in prison, Captain?

HEARTSEASE. Yes—especially—I longed especially, Miss Buckthorn, to see—

JENNY. *Yes!—to see—*

HEARTSEASE. But there were lots of jolly fellows in the prison. [JENNY *turns away.*] We had a dramatic society, and a glee club, and an orchestra. I was one of the orchestra. I had a banjo, with one string; I played one tune on it, that I used to play on the piano with one finger. But, Miss Buckthorn, I am a prisoner again, to-night—your prisoner.

JENNY. [*Aside.*] At last!

HEARTSEASE. I'll show you how that tune went. [*Turns to piano; sits.*

JENNY. [*Aside.*] Papa said I'd have to help him, but I don't see an opening. [HEARTSEASE *plays part of an air with one finger; strikes two or three wrong notes.*

HEARTSEASE. There are two notes down there, somewhere, that I never could get right. The fellows in prison used to dance while I played—[*Playing.*]—that is, the lame ones did; those that weren't lame couldn't keep the time.

JENNY. You must have been in great danger, Captain, when you escaped from prison.

HEARTSEASE. Y-e-s. I was badly frightened several times. One night I came face to face, on the road, with a Confederate officer. It was Captain Thornton.

JENNY. Oh! What did you do?

HEARTSEASE. I killed him. [*Very quietly, and trying the tune again at once. Enter* JANNETTE, *from in hall; she glances into the room and goes up the stairs.*] I used to skip those two notes on the banjo. It's very nice for a soldier to come home from the war, and meet those—I mean the one particular person—that he—you see, when a soldier loves a woman, as—as—

JENNY. [*Aside.*] As he loves me. [*Approaches him.*

HEARTSEASE. As soldiers often do—[*Plays; she turns away, petulantly; he plays the tune through correctly.*] That's it!

JENNY. [*Aside.*] I'm not going to be made love to by piecemeal, like this, any longer. [*Aloud.*] Captain Heartsease! Have you anything in particular to say to me? [*He looks up.*

HEARTSEASE. Y-e-s. [*Rising.*

JENNY. Say it! You told my father, and all my friends, that you were in love with me. Whom are you going to tell next?

HEARTSEASE. I *am* in love with you.

JENNY. It was my turn.

HEARTSEASE. [*Going near to her.*] Do you love me?

JENNY. [*Laying her head quietly on his breast.*] I must take time to consider.

HEARTSEASE. [*Quietly.*] I assume that this means "Yes."

JENNY. It isn't the way a girl says "No."

HEARTSEASE. My darling!

JENNY. Why! His heart is beating as fast as mine is!

HEARTSEASE. [*Quietly.*] I am frantic with joy. [*He kisses her. She hides her face on his breast. Enter* MRS. HAVERILL, *down-stairs, followed by* JANNETTE. MRS. HAVERILL *stops suddenly.* JANNETTE *stands in the doorway.* HEARTSEASE *inclines his head to her, quietly looking at her over* JENNY.] I am delighted to see you, after so long an absence; I trust that we shall meet more frequently hereafter.

JENNY. [*Looking at him.*] Eh?

HEARTSEASE. [*Looking down at her.*] I think, perhaps, it might be as well for us to repair to another apartment, and continue our interview, there!

JENNY. [*Dropping her head on his breast again.*] This room is very comfortable.

MRS. HAVERILL. Jenny, dear! [JENNY *starts up; looks from* MRS. HAVERILL *to* HEARTSEASE.

JENNY. Constance! I—'Bout face! March! [*Turns and goes out.*

MRS. HAVERILL. I am glad to see you again, Captain, and happy as well as safe.

HEARTSEASE. Thank you, Madam. I am happy. If you will excuse me, I will join—my father—in the smoking-room. [MRS. HAVERILL *inclines her head, and* HEARTSEASE *walks out.*

MRS. HAVERILL. Jannette! You may ask General Haverill to come into this room. [*Exit* JANNETTE. MRS. HAVERILL *walks down, reading a note.*] "I have hesitated to come to you personally, as I have hesitated to write to you. If I have been silent, it is because I could not bring my hand to write what was in my mind and in my heart. I do not know that I can trust my tongue to speak it, but I will come."

Enter HAVERILL *from hall; he stops.*

HAVERILL. Constance!

MRS. HAVERILL. My husband! May I call you husband? After all these months of separation, with your life in almost daily peril, and my life—what? Only a weary longing for one loving word—and you are silent.

HAVERILL. May I call you wife? I do not wish to speak that word except with reverence. You have asked me to come to you. I am here. I will be plain, direct and brief. Where is the portrait of yourself, which I gave you, in Charleston, for my son?

MRS. HAVERILL. Your son is dead, sir; and my portrait lies upon his breast, in the grave. [HAVERILL *takes the miniature from his pocket and holds it towards her in his extended hand. She starts back.*] He gave it to you? And you ask me where it is?

HAVERILL. It might have lain in the grave of Kerchival West!

MRS. HAVERILL. Ah!

HAVERILL. Not in my son's. I found it upon *his* breast. [*She turns front, dazed.*] Well! I am listening! It was not I that sought this interview, Madam; and if you prefer to remain silent, I will go. You know, now, why I have been silent so long.

MRS. HAVERILL. My only witnesses to the truth are both dead. I shall remain silent. [*Turning towards him.*] We stand before each other, living, but not so happy as they. We are parted, forever. Even if you should accept my unsupported word—if I could so far forget my pride as to give it to you—suspicion would still hang between us. I remain silent. [HAVERILL *looks at her, earnestly, for a moment; then approaches her.*

HAVERILL. I cannot look into your eyes and not see truth and loyalty there. Constance!

MRS. HAVERILL. No, John! [*Checking him.*] I will not accept your blind faith!

HAVERILL. [*Looking down at the picture in his hand.*] My faith is blind; blind as my love! I do not wish to see! [*Enter* EDITH. *She stops; looks at* HAVERILL. *He raises his head and looks at her.*

EDITH. This is General Haverill? [*Dropping her eyes.*] I am Edith, sir.

HAVERILL. [*Gently.*] My son's wife. [*Kisses her forehead.*] You shall take the place he once filled in my heart. His crime and his disgrace are buried in a distant grave.

EDITH. And you have not forgiven him, even yet?

MRS. HAVERILL. Is there no atonement for poor Frank's sin—not even his death? Can you only bury the wrong and forget the good?

HAVERILL. The good?

MRS. HAVERILL. Your own words to the Government, as his commander!

HAVERILL. What do you mean?

MRS. HAVERILL. "The victory of Cedar Creek would have been impossible without the sacrifice of this young officer."

HAVERILL. My own words, yes—but—

EDITH. "His name must take its place, forever, in the roll of names which his countrymen honour."

HAVERILL. Lieutenant Bedloe!

MRS. HAVERILL. Haverill! You did not know?

HAVERILL. My—son.

EDITH. You did not receive mother's letter?—after his death?

HAVERILL. My son! [*Sinking upon chair or ottoman.*] I left him alone in his grave, unknown; but my tears fell for him then, as they do now. He died before I reached him.

EDITH. Father! [*Laying her hand gently on his shoulder.*] You shall see Frank's face again. His little son is lying asleep upstairs; and when he wakes up, Frank's own eyes will look into yours. I have just received his last message. I will read it to you. [*Note-book. Reads.*] "Tell our little son how his father died, not how he lived. And tell her who filled my own mother's place so lovingly." [*She looks at* MRS. HAVERILL, *moves to her and hides her face in her bosom.*] My mother!

MRS. HAVERILL. Edith—my child! Frank loved us both.

EDITH. [*Reading.*] "Father's portrait of her, which she gave to me in Charleston—[HAVERILL *starts.*]—helped me to be a better man."

HAVERILL. [*Rising to his feet.*] Constance!

EDITH. [*Reading.*] "It was taken from me in Richmond, and it is in the possession of Captain Edward Thornton."

HAVERILL. One moment! Stop! Let me think! [EDITH *looks at him; retires up stage.*] Thornton was a prisoner—and to Kerchival West. A despatch had been found upon him—he was searched! [*He moves to her and takes both her hands in his own, bowing his head over them.*] My head is bowed in shame.

MRS. HAVERILL. Speak to me, John, as you used to speak! Tell me you still love me!

HAVERILL. The—the words will come—but they are—choking me—now. [*Presses her hand to his lips.*

MRS. HAVERILL. We will think no more of the past, except of what was bright in it. Frank's memory, and our own love, will be with us always.

Enter BUCKTHORN, *followed by* HEARTSEASE.

BUCKTHORN. Haverill! You are back from the war, too. It begins to look like peace in earnest.

HAVERILL. Yes. Peace and home. [*Shaking hands with him.* MRS. HAVERILL *joins* EDITH.

Enter BARKET.

BARKET. Gineral! [BUCKTHORN *moves to him.* HAVERILL *joins* MRS. HAVERILL *and* EDITH. BARKET *speaks apart, twisting one side of his face.*] I kissed her!

BUCKTHORN. Have you sent for a surgeon?

BARKET. I felt as if the inimy had surprised us agin, and Sheridan was sixty miles away.

HAVERILL. This is old Sergeant Barket. [BARKET *salutes.*] You were the last man of us all that saw Colonel West.

BARKET. Just afther the battle of Sayder Creek began—whin Colonel Wist rode to the front to mate his retreating rigiment—the byes formed in line, at sight of him, to raysist the victorious inimy. It was just at the brow of a hill—about there, sur—[*Pointing with his cane.*] and—here! [*He takes tray from table and sets it on the carpet. Lays the slices of bread in a row.*] That be the rigiment. [*All interested.* MADELINE *and* ELLINGHAM *enter, and look on.* BARKET *arranges the two cups and saucers in a row.*] That be the inimy's batthery, sur. [*Enter* MARGERY. *She goes to the table; then looks around, sharply, at* BARKET.

MARGERY. Ye ould Hibernian dhrone! What are yez doin' wid the china on the floor? You'll break it all!

BUCKTHORN. Ah—Margery! Barket is telling us where he last saw Colonel Kerchival West.

MARGERY. The young Colonel! The tay-cups and saucers be's the inimy's batthery? Yez may smash 'em, if ye loike!

BUCKTHORN. Go on, Barket. [JENNY *and* HEARTSEASE *have entered as* BARKET *proceeds; the whole party lean forward, intensely interested.* GERTRUDE *enters in hall, looks in, beckons out left.* KERCHIVAL *follows. They move up stage, back of the rest and unseen, listening.*

BARKET. Just as the rigiment was rayformed in line, and Colonel Wist was out in front—widout any coat or hat, and wid only a shtick in his hand—we heard cheers in the rear. Gineral Sheridan was coming! One word to the men—and we swept over the batthery like a whirlwind! [*Slashing his cane through the cups and saucers.*

MARGERY. Hoo—roo!

BARKET. The attack on the lift flank was checked. But when we shtopped to take breath, Colonel Wist wasn't wid us. [GERTRUDE *turns lovingly to* KERCHIVAL. *He places his arm about her.*] Heaven knows where he is now. Afther the battle was over, poor Miss Gertrude wint off by hersilf into the wilderness to find him.

KERCHIVAL. My wife! You saved my life, at last! [*Embracing her.*

BARKET. They'll niver come together in this world. I saw Miss Gertrude, myself, ride away into the woods and disappear behind a school-house on the battle-field, over there.

GERTRUDE. No, Barket—[*All start and look.*]—it was the little church; we were married there this morning!

CURTAIN.

IN MIZZOURA

A PLAY IN FOUR ACTS

Augustus Thomas

AUGUSTUS THOMAS

(Born, St. Louis, Mo., January 8, 1859)

It is not a new thing for a dramatic author to write prefaces to his plays. We are fortunate in possessing a series of personal opinions in this form that constitute a valuable asset in determining individual attitude and technical purpose. Read Schiller's opening remarks to "The Robbers," Victor Hugo's famous opinions affixed to "Cromwell" and his equally enlightening comments introducing "Hernani," and you can judge the value autobiographically and philosophically.

The American dramatist has not been given, as a general rule, to such self-examination; he has contented himself with supplying the fashions of the day in the theatre, and has left to the ubiquitous press-agent the special prerogative of whetting public curiosity as to what manner of man he is and as to the fabric from which his play has been cut. There has been no effort, thus far, on the part of literary executors, in the cases, for example, of Bronson Howard or James A. Herne, to preserve the correspondence of these men, so much of which dealt with the circumstances surrounding them while writing or the conditions affecting them while rehearsing. These data would be invaluable in preserving a perspective which the modern historian of the American theatre so wofully lacks.

All the more significant, therefore, is the edition of Mr. Augustus Thomas's works, now being issued by Messrs. Samuel French. Thus far the "autobiographies" of six plays have been prepared by the dramatist in a charming, reminiscent vein. The present Editor is privileged to make use of one, describing the evolution of "In Mizzoura," and this inclusion removes from him the necessity of commenting too lengthily on that play, for fear of creating an anti-climax.

Read consecutively, the prefaces suggest Mr. Thomas's mental equipment, his charm and distinction of personality, the variety of his experiences which have given him a man's observation of people and of things. The personalia are dropped in casually, here and there, not so much for the purpose of specific biography, as to illustrate the incentives which shaped his thought and enriched his invention as a playwright. His purpose in writing these forewords is just a little didactic; he addresses the novice who may be befuddled after reading various "Techniques of the Drama," and who looks to the established and successful dramatist for the secrets of his workshop. These prefaces reveal Thomas as working more with chips than with whole planks from a virgin forest. He confesses as much, when he talks of "Mrs. Leffingwell's Boots." It was "salvage," he writes, "it was the marketing of odds and ends and remnants, utterly useless for any other purpose." Yet, with the technical dexterity, which is Mr. Thomas's strongest point, he pieced a bright comedy picture together—a very popular one, too. In the course of his remarks, he says, "When I had the art department on the old St. Louis *Republican*;" "There is an avenue of that name [Leffingwell] in St. Louis, near a hill where I used to report railroad strikes." Similar enlightening facts dot the preface to "In Mizzoura," suggesting his varied employment in the express and railroad business. Thus, with personal odds and ends, we can build a picture of Thomas before he started on his regular employment as a playwright, in 1884, with "Editha's Burglar," in conjunction with Mrs. Frances Hodgson Burnett.

There is an autobiographical comment published, written presumably at the request of the late Hamilton Wright Mabie, which is not only worth preserving as a matter of record, but as measuring a certain facility in anecdote and felicity of manner which have always made Thomas a welcome chairman of gatherings and a polished after-dinner speaker.

"After Farragut ran the New Orleans blockade," he states, "my father took direction of the St. Charles Theatre, New Orleans, then owned by Ben De Bar. When he returned to St. Louis, in 1865, I was in my seventh year, and my earliest recollections are tinged with his stories of Matilda Herron, John Wilkes Booth, and others who played in that theatre. Father was an orator of considerable ability, and I remember him, for the amusement of my mother, reciting long speeches from Kotzebue, Schiller, and Shakespeare. In his association with the theatre he took me very early to plays, and I have always been an attendant; consequently dialogue seemed the most natural literary vehicle. I found later that this impression was justified when I discovered that the most telling things in Homer and later Greek poets and philosophy were in dialogue—that this was true of Confucius and of Christ.

"I began writing plays when I was about fourteen years of age. When I was sixteen and seventeen, an amateur company that I organized played in certain railway centres on the old North Missouri Railway, for the benefit of local unions of the working men. In 1882, I made a dramatization of Mrs. Burnett's 'Editha's Burglar'. With this as a curtain-raiser, and a rather slap-stick farce called 'Combustion', I made a tour of the country with a company I organized, and with which I ran in debt several thousand dollars. In 1889, a four-act version of 'The Burglar', arranged by me, was played in New York, and was successful, and since that time my royalties have enabled me to give my attention on the business side exclusively to play-writing.

"You ask why everybody who knows me is my friend? I might answer laconically that it was because they did not know me thoroughly, but, dismissing that defensive assumption of modesty, and making such self-inquiry as I can, I think I have a capacity for companionship from the fact that I was painfully poor as a kid. My consecutive schooling stopped when I was ten. I gave up all attempt to attend school even irregularly, when I was thirteen. Between that age and my twenty-second year, I worked in various sections of the freight departments of railways. Most of the mid-day meals of that time I took from a tin-bucket. This meal was in the company of freight-handlers on the platform, men recruited almost exclusively from the Irish at that time in the middle West; or the meal was with the brakemen in the switch shanties, these brakemen generally Americans rather near the soil; or was with the engineers and firemen in their cabs, or on the running-boards of boxcars with trainmen. Without knowing it, I acquired the ability of getting the other fellow's point of view, and, when I got old enough not to be overwrought by sympathy that was inclined to be too partisan, I found an immense intellectual enjoyment in watching the interplay between temperament and environment. I think this answers your question. I have retained a gossip's ability to be interested in most anybody else's affairs."

It is a strange combination—this democratic sympathy, with a later developed French finesse of technique, so clearly felt in comparing one of his "soil" plays, like "Alabama," with a more finished product, like "As a Man Thinks." The word "robustness" has been applied to Thomas, which recalls that when 10-cent melodrama was in flower on the American stage, the writer of "Convict 999" was called the Augustus Thomas of melodrama, and the inventor of "Jennie, the Sewing Machine Girl" was regarded as the Clyde Fitch of melodrama. Thomas is as careful in observing the small psychologies of men as Fitch ever was of women. There is a neatness, a finish to his small scenes that hint at a depth and largeness which he has never given rein to in any play he has thus far written. The consequence is, when he aimed at mental effect, the result was nearly always pompous, as when *Dr. Seelig*, in "As a Man Thinks," tries to explain the psychological matrix of the piece, and as when *Jack Brookfield*, in "The Witching Hour," explains the basis of telepathy. But when he aimed nowhere, yet gave us living, breathing flashes of character, as dominate "The Other Girl" and are typified in the small rôle of *Lew Ellinger*, in "The Witching Hour," Thomas was happiest in his humour, most unaffected in his inventions, most ingenious in his "tricks." The man on the street is his special *metier*, and his skill in knitting bones together gives one the impression of an organic whole, though, on closer examination, as in "As a Man Thinks," the skeleton is made up of three or four unrelated stories. Only skilful surgery on Thomas's part carries the play to success, for we are nearly always irritated by the degree to which he falls short of real meat in spite of all the beautiful architectonics. He "thinks things," declares one critic, —"that anybody can see; and sporadically he says things; but he does not say them connectedly and as part of some definite dramatic theme."

Thomas's interesting prefaces suggest this limitation in him, whether it be a psychic subject he is to handle or an historical period he is to cover. His manner of cogitating a theme has always been in terms of the theatre, and he is willing to curtail any part of his theme for a "point." His explanation, therefore, of the growth of detail, while lacking in the high seriousness of Poe's explanation how he conceived "The Raven," has nevertheless the same mathematical precision about it. In other words, Thomas plays the theatre as Steinitz played chess, with certain recognized openings and certain stated values to the characters. We doubt whether, if the truth were told, many changes ever occur, once a Thomas scenario is planned. His whole game is to capture as many of his audience as he can by strategy, to checkmate them by any legitimate theatrical move, regardless of tenability of subject, and in despite of truth. Hence, when he fitted up "Arizona" in clothes to suit recent Mexican complications, and called his play "Rio Grande," he found he had lost the early sincerity of "Alabama," and his raciness was swamped in an apparent sophistication which only added to his artificial method of conceiving a plot.

He has, therefore, played the theatrical game with love for it, with thorough understanding of it—and though political preferment in the Democratic Party has been offered him many times, he has thus far not deserted the theatre. As the years advance, he does not seem to lose any of his dexterity; on the other hand, he does not show inclination to be stirred in his plays by the social problems of the day. When "The Witching Hour" showed a departure into realms of subtle psychology, we thought Thomas, as a playwright, had passed into the realm of wisdom; but his introduction to that play reveals the fact that, once, he was press-agent for a thought-reader. So it was the "showman" aspect of the subject which led him to read up on auto-hypnosis. It was not so much conviction as picturesqueness which prompted him to write, in 1890, the one-act psychic sketch which afterwards became the longer play. His enthusiasm was of considerable duration; it passed from one play to another, and among his "subtle" pieces on the same theme were "The Harvest Moon" and "As a Man Thinks."

Apart from these—the nearest approach of Thomas to the so-called "intellectual" drama—and apart from the racy territorial pieces like "Alabama," "In Mizzoura," "Arizona," and "Colorado," his plays came from a desire to suit the eccentricities of "stars," like Lawrence D'Orsey in "The Earl of Pawtucket" and "The Embassy Ball"—blood-cousins in humour to *Dundreary*—or "On the Quiet" for the dry unctuousness of William Collier. In these plays, his purpose was as deep as a sheet of plate glass, as polished on the surface, and as quick to reflect the rays of smiles.

What one may say of Augustus Thomas with truth is that by temperament he is American; his dramas have a native atmosphere about them. I have never read "The Capitol" or "The Hoosier Doctor," but it is easy to imagine his treatment of such themes. All of his work bears the Thomas technique. He was more successful than Fitch in dramatization; his "Colonel Carter of Cartersville," from F. Hopkinson Smith's novel, and his "Soldiers of Fortune," from Richard Harding Davis's story, were adequate stage vehicles,—whereas Fitch failed in his handling of Mrs. Edith Wharton's "The House of Mirth" and Alfred Henry Lewis's "Wolfville Stories." And the reason for Thomas's success is that he is better equipped for mosaic work in characterization, than for large sweeps of personality. Not one of his plays contains a dominant figure worth remembering afterwards for its distinguishing marks. He has never painted a full portrait; he has only taken snap-shots. His plays have been written as houses are built. More than likely he approaches a subject as he approached "Oliver Goldsmith," as "largely a scissors and paste-pot undertaking." But over it, when finished, there is a high polish which denotes guaranteed workmanship. That same care for finish which marks his plays marks his work with the actors, at rehearsal, who have been selected by him with the unerring eye of the illustrator.

It is significant that Thomas began his career as page boy in the 41st Congress; that, after his railroad experience, he studied law; and that, after his subordinate work with the newspapers, he became editor and proprietor of the Kansas City *Mirror*. Since the death of Bronson Howard, he has been regarded as the Dean of playwrights, and once held the presidency of the Society of American Dramatists. Professor Brander Matthews, Mr. William Gillette, and he represent the theatre in the American Academy of Arts and Letters.

IN MIZZOURA

A PLAY IN FOUR ACTS

By AUGUSTUS THOMAS

REVISED 1916 BY AUGUSTUS THOMAS

Reprinted by permission of Mr. Augustus Thomas and Samuel French. The Editor wishes to record here his appreciation of their courtesy. Messrs. Samuel French have also allowed the inclusion of the preface.

PREFACE.

This preface is one of a number[1] trying to show, each for its particular play, the manner of the play's conception, whether starting from a theme, a character, or a situation; the difficulty of the start and the larger problems of the story's development, together with the ways considered and chosen to answer them. It has been thought that such accounts might be of interest, and, in some instances, perhaps, helpful to others beginning on the same kind of work.

In the spring of 1891, Mr. Nat Goodwin was one of the most popular and successful, as well as one of the most skilful, of American actors. He had played lively and slight farces almost exclusively; but, having the ability for serious work as well, he was ambitious to try it. In a comedy by Brander Matthews and George H. Jessop, called "A Gold Mine," he had given one or two dramatic scenes most convincingly; and one sentimental soliloquy with a rose in exquisite tenderness. In person he is under the average height[2]; and then, was slight, graceful, and with a face capable of conveying the subtlest shades of feeling. The forehead was ample; the eyes were large and blue, clear and steady. The nose was mildly Roman; the hair was the colour of new hay. His voice was rich and modulated. These points are reported because they helped form the equipment of the "star," who wanted a serious play in which he should be the hero. The order was without other conditions; the play might be of any period and of any land.

My own ignorance fixed certain limitations. At that time I had acquaintance with no other countries than the United States and Canada. These I knew fairly well. I had travelled them with one-night theatrical companies; and also in newspaper assignments; and over restricted districts I had worked in the employment of a railroad company. I didn't care to write from books; so my Goodwin hero was to be perforce an American. It seemed best to make him an American of 1891. Other times and places were excluded and dismissed from mind.

[1] The Witching Hour; Mrs. Leffingwell's Boots; The Earl of Pawtucket; The Harvest Moon; Oliver Goldsmith [Published by Samuel French].

[2] Written before the death of Mr. Goodwin.

Now, a blond hero five feet seven inches tall and weighing under one hundred and fifty-pounds—a Roman nose, and a steady, steel blue gaze!

I stood the Goodwin photograph on my table and looked at it until it talked to me. The slight physique couldn't explain the solid confidence of that look except there was behind it a gun. We were doing more man to man shooting in the country then than now; and my Western friendships made me more tolerant of the gun than some others were. Goodwin and a gun sent me searching mentally over the West from Colorado to the Coast, and through all occupations from bandit to fighting parson; and then my potential gallery, quite apart from any conscious effort of my own, divided itself into two kinds of gunpackers: the authorized and the others. I concluded that there would be less trouble, less "lost motion"—that was a phrase learned, and an idea applied in the old-fashioned composing-room—less lost motion, in portraying a lawful gun toter than in justifying an outlaw; and the Goodwin part was therefore to be either a soldier or a sheriff. I have said that he was thin, graceful—and he was, but he wasn't particularly erect. He was especially free from any suggestion of "setting-up:" sheriff was the way of least resistance.

My hero was a sheriff. You see how that clears the atmosphere. When you must, or may, write for a "star," it is a big start to have the character agreeably and definitely chosen.

There must be love interest, of course.

A sheriff would presumably be a bit of the rough diamond; *contrast* wherein "lieth love's delight" prompted a girl apparently of a finer strain than himself; and *conflict* necessitated a rival. The girl should be delicate and educated, the *rival* should be attractive but unworthy; and to make him doubly opposed to Goodwin I decided to have him an outlaw—someone whom it would be the sheriff's duty and business—*business* used in the stage sense—to arrest.

Four or five years before the Goodwin contract, I had been one of the *Post-Dispatch* reporters on the "Jim Cummings" express robbery. That celebrated and picturesque case was of a man who presented to an express messenger at the side door of his express car, just as the train was pulling from the St. Louis station, a forged order to carry the bearer, dead-head, to a certain distant point on the run. The messenger helped the dead-head into his car, and chummed with him, until about an hour later, when, as he was on his knees arranging some of his cargo, he found a pistol muzzle against his cheek, and his smiling visitor prepared to bind and gag him. Having done this, the stranger packed one hundred and twenty thousand dollars into a valise; and dropped off into the dark, when the train made its accustomed stop at a water-tank. The whole enterprise was so gentle, that the messenger was arrested and held as an accomplice, while the Pinkertons looked for the man with the money.

The robber was a kind-hearted person; and, being really grieved over the detention of an innocent man, wrote several exculpating letters to the papers, enclosing rifled express envelopes to prove his peripatetic identity. These letters were signed "Jim Cummings," a *nom de guerre* borrowed from an older and an abler offender of the Jesse James vintage.

After he was arrested and in his cell in the St. Louis jail, "Jim Cummings" and I became friends, as criminals and newspaper men sometimes do, and as criminals and I always have done, everywhere, most easily. The details of his arrangements, both before and after his draft on the company, were minutely in my mind, and were so very vital that, with the first need for a drama criminal, I took him. Goodwin's rival should be Jim Cummings; a glorified and beautiful and matinée Cummings, but substantially he.

This adoption rescued the girl and the sheriff from the hazy geography of the mining camps, and fixed the trio in Missouri.

After Cummings had dropped from the express car, he had walked some fifteen miles to the Missouri River, near St. Charles, and had then gone north on a train through Pike County. I had more than once made the same trip on freight trains; and I had a liking for the county as the home district of Champ Clark, a politico-newspaper comrade of several legislative sessions and conventions. Newspaper experience in those days, before the "flimsy" and the "rewrite," emphasized the value of going to the place in order to report the occurrence; and I knew that, aside from these three characters and their official and sentimental relationships, the rest of my people and my play were waiting for me in Bowling Green.

In those days, Mrs. Thomas and I used to hold hands on our evening promenades; but I think it was really our foolish New York clothes that made the blacksmith smile. At any rate, we stopped at his door and talked with him. He knew Champ Clark and Dave Ball—another Missouri statesman—and had the keenest interest in the coming convention for the legislative nomination. It was fine to hear him pronounce the state name, *Mizzoura*, as it was originally spelt on many territorial charts, and as we were permitted to call it in the public schools until we reached the grades where imported culture ruled. The blacksmith's helper, who was finishing a wagon shaft with a draw knife, was younger and less intelligent, and preferred to talk to Mrs. Thomas. It is distracting to listen at the same time to three persons; but I learned that "You kin make anything that's made out o' wood with a draw knife;" and over the bench was the frame for an upholstered chair. A driver brought in a two-horse, side seated, depot wagon on three wheels and a fence rail. The fourth wheel and its broken tire were in the wagon; and the blacksmith said he'd weld the tire at five-thirty the next morning.

We went without breakfast to see him do it. He was my heroine's father by that time; a candidate for the legislature; and I was devising for him a second comedy daughter, to play opposite to the boy with a draw knife. That day I also found the drugstore window and the "lickerish" boxes that Cummings should break through in his attempted escape; and I recovered the niggers, the "dog fannell," the linen dusters, and the paper collars which, in my recent prosperity, I'd forgotten. I also nominated Goodwin for the legislature, which increased his importance, and gave him something to sacrifice for the girl's father. But it was all so poverty-stricken, as I glimpsed it through the blacksmith shop and the little house I'd chosen for its consort. I yearned for some money; not much, but enough to afford "a hired girl," and for some means of bringing the money into the story. When we left Bowling Green, I had given Goodwin a substantial reward for the robber's capture; but he wouldn't accept it. That was a mere dramatist's device; and my quiet sheriff was already above it; besides, he wasn't sure that he'd hold the fellow. His wish to please the girl was already debating the matter with his duty.

On the way back to St. Louis, the conductor, who took our tickets, recognized me. Charlie Church had been a freight brakeman when I was in the St. Louis yards. He was proud of his advancement to a passenger conductorship—proud of his train—proud of the new Wabash road-bed on the single track line. This road-bed was made of macadam-looking metal, clean and red as the painted bricks in the local Dutch women's gardens, and hard as flint. When we gave the right-of-way, and ran in on a siding, Church brought us up a few pieces to the back platform; and with one of them scratched my initials on the glass window. "What was it, iron ore?—no, that mud that the river leaves when it rises—'Gumbo' the people call it. Some fellow found by accident that it became red flint when fired, and was making a fortune selling it to the railroad." To burn it, he used the slack coal from the Jonesburg mines nearby, which until then had also been waste. I put a handful of the stuff in my pocket; and, after the conductor left us, I turned the whole enterprise over to the Goodwin part. When the play ended, the audience should feel sure that he and Kate need never want for a dollar. I knew also where he had accidentally burnt his first sample, and made his discovery; in the blacksmith shop.

But what accident brought the raw gumbo there? Perhaps the wheels of the stage-coach; but that wasn't definitely Goodwin. The soft gumbo is not unlike putty; it would make a fair cushion for a broken limb: but I didn't want to halt my story with anybody crippled to that extent; and then I remembered the yellow dog drinking from the blacksmith's tub. I broke *his* leg and had Goodwin carry him miles in the stage, with his poor paw in a poultice of gumbo. It was a counter-pointing touch to a sheriff with two guns; it gave him an effective entrance; and it coupled in a continuous train, the sheriff, the bad man who sneered at it, the blacksmith and his motherly wife who sympathized and helped in a better dressing, the forge where a piece of the discarded gumbo should fall amongst the coke, the helper who should pump the bellows for another and verifying bake: and last, and best of all, it gave me a "curtain" for a second act; when, perturbed and adrift after being temporarily rejected by the girl, Goodwin should turn in an undefined but natural sympathy to the crippled dog in his box under the helper's bench.

That illustrates one of the dramatist's discovered rules: "If you use a *property* once use it again and again if you can." It is a *visual* thing that binds together your stuff of speech like a dowel in a mission table.

There are few better places than a railroad train for building stories; the rhythmic click of the wheels past the fish-plates makes your thoughts march as a drum urges a column of soldiers. A tentative layout of the story established in the first act, the educated Kate, discontented in her blacksmith father's surroundings; the flash fascination of our transient robber; the robber's distinct lead over Goodwin's accustomed and older blandishments. The second act saw Goodwin turned down and the robber preferred. The third act should see the robber's apprehension and arrest. I milled around the question of his identification as Illinois and Indiana went past the Pullman window; and then the one sure and unfailing witness for that purpose volunteered—the express messenger himself. There was no reason why this young man shouldn't be a native of Bowling Green, and come home from St. Louis at the end of certain runs. He would know Goodwin and the blacksmith's family; but, to put him nearer to them, more "into the story" sentimentally, I gave Goodwin a little sister, and made the messenger her accepted lover, with his arrest and detention postponing the wedding. This need to free his sister's fiancé gave the sheriff hero a third reason for getting the real robber; the other two being his official duty and the rivalry for Kate. The messenger and the sheriff's sister, the helper and the comedy daughter, and Goodwin and Kate, made three pairs of young lovers. This number might easily lead to a disastrous diffusion of interest unless the playwright were careful always to make the work of each couple, even when apparently about their own personal affairs, really to the forward trend of the story.

I doubt if the production of novels, even to the writer temperamentally disposed to that form of expression, is as absorbing as play-making. The difference between the novel and the play is the difference between *was* and *is*. Something has happened for the writer of the novel and for his people. He describes it as it was; and them as they were. In the play something *is happening*. Its form is controversial—and the playwright, by force of this controversy, is in turn each one of his characters, and not merely a witness of their doings. When they begin to take hold of him, their possession is more and more insistent—all interests in real life become more and more secondary and remote until the questions in dispute are not only decided, but there is also a written record of the debates and the decision.

By the time our train pulled into New York, I was impatient to make a running transcript of speeches of my contending people. But that is a relief that must be deferred. Like over-anxious litigants, the characters are disposed to talk too much, and must be controlled and kept in bounds by a proportioned scenario, assigning order, and respective and progressive values to them. That was the work of a day by that time, and then, with the material gathered, and the intimacy with the people and the places, the play was one that wrote itself.

AUGUSTUS THOMAS.

HOOLEY'S THEATRE,

TWENTY-THIRD SEASON

R. M. HOOLEY . . . . . . Proprietor and Manager.
HARRY J. POWERS Business Manager.

COMMENCING MONDAY EVENING, AUGUST 7th, 1893,

Every Evening and Saturday (Only) Matinee

MR. NAT C GOODWIN

AND COMPANION PLAYERS

Under the direction of Mr. Geo. J. Appleton, will produce for the first time on any stage, a drama of character, entitled

"IN MIZZOURA"

By MR. AUGUSTUS THOMAS, author of "Alabama," etc.

CAST OF CHARACTERS.

JIM RADBURN..MR. NAT C. GOODWIN
ROBERT TRAVERS..MR. FRANCIS CARLYLE
JO VERNON..MR BURR McINTOSH
COLONEL BOLLINGER..MR. WM. G BEACH
BILL SARBER..MR. ROBT. G. WILSON
SAM FOWLER..MR. ARTHUR HOOPS
DAVE..MR. LOUIS PAYNE
ESROM..MR. J W. McANDREWS
KELLY..MR. LOUIS BARRETT
CAL..MR CHARLES MILLER
KATE VERNON..MISS BELLE ARCHER
MRS. JO VERNON..MRS. JEAN CLARA WALTERS
'LIZBETH VERNON..MISS MINNIE DUPREE
EM'LY RADBURN..MISS MAE E. WOOD

Virginia Students Quartette and Villagers

SYNOPSIS OF SCENERY.

ACT I.—Living room of Jo Vernon's house, Bowling Green, Pike County, Missouri. Time—Evening in June.

ACT II.—Blacksmith shop of Jo Vernon adjoining his residence. Time—Morning of the second day.

ACT III.—Living room of Jo Vernon. Time—Evening of the second day.

ACT IV.—Home and door yard of Jim Radburn. Time—The next Morning.

The scenery painted from sketches made of the exact locality, by Albert and Burridge.

EXECUTIVE STAFF

Mr. Charles E. Power	FOR MR. GOODWIN.	Business Manager
Mr. Louis Barrett		Stage Manager
Mr. Darriel Cronin		Master Carpenter
Mr. Charles Miller		Properties

CAST.

As given at the Fifth Avenue Theatre, New York, on Monday Evening, September 4, 1893.

Jim Radburn	Mr. Nat C. Goodwin.
Robert Travers	Mr. Emmett Corrigan.
Jo Vernon	Mr. Burr McIntosh.
Colonel Bollinger	Mr. William G. Beach.
Bill Sarber	Mr. Robert G. Wilson.
Sam Fowler	Mr. Arthur Hoops.
Dave	Mr. Louis Payne.
Esrom	Mr. J. W. McAndrews.
Kelly	Mr. Louis Barrett.
Cal	Mr. Charles Miller.
Mrs. Jo Vernon	Mrs. Jean Clara Walters.
'Lizbeth Vernon	Miss Minnie Dupree.
Em'ly Radburn	Miss Mae E. Wood.
Kate Vernon	Miss Mabel Amber.

IN MIZZOURA.

ACT I.

Music at rise of curtain. The old "Forty-nine" tune, "My name is Joe Bowers."

SCENE: *Pike Co., dining-room, living-room and kitchen combined. A line of broken plaster and unmatched wall-papers marks the ceiling and back flat a little left of center. Doors right and left in 3. Door in right flat. Old-fashioned table. Dresser, low window with many panes, window-sash sliding horizontally—outside of door is pan of leaves burning to smoke off mosquitoes.*

DISCOVERED: MRS. VERNON *and* LIZBETH. MRS. VERNON *ironing;* LIZBETH *at pan of fire.*

MRS. VERNON. Lizbeth!

LIZBETH. Ma—?

MRS. VERNON. Move that pan a little furder off. The smoke's a durnation sight worse'n the skeeters.

LIZBETH. [*Rising and coming in.*] Well, we couldn't sleep fur 'em last night, and it's just as well to smoke 'em good.

MRS. VERNON. But such an all fired smell—what're you burnin'?

LIZBETH. Dog fannel—

MRS. VERNON. I thought so. It's nearly turned my stomich—come, hurry with this ironin' now.

LIZBETH. [*Coming down right of table.*] Let's leave it till mornin', ma—

MRS. VERNON. Can't, Lizbeth, it's bin put off since Wednesday, an' the furst thing we know we'll be havin' it to do Sunday—get me another iron. [LIZBETH *goes left.*] I'm reg'lar tuckered out.

LIZBETH. Me too. [*Sound of sledge hammer from door left.* LIZBETH *exits.*

MRS. VERNON *sits on rocker and fans herself with frayed-out palm leaf.*

MRS. VERNON. Lor'—to think o' this weather in June. It's jis' terrible.

Enter KATE. *She is neatly gowned and is of a superior clay.*

KATE. Mother—

MRS. VERNON. Well, Kate?

KATE. Must we have this awful odour again to-night?

MRS. VERNON. Got to have somethin', Kate, to drive off the skeeters. [*Enter* LIZBETH.] I ain't slep' none for two nights.

KATE. They might be kept out some other way. [*She sits in chair.*

MRS. VERNON. [*Taking the fresh iron and resuming work.*] I ruined my best pillar-slips an' nearly smothered myself with coal oil last night. I'll try my own way now. It's all very well fur you, Kate, whose got the only muskeeter bar in the family—

LIZBETH. [*In the rocker.*] Yes, and won't let your sister sleep with you—

KATE. I'll gladly *give* you the mosquito bar, Lizbeth, but two grown-up people can't sleep in a narrow single bed.

LIZBETH. I hope you don't s'pose I'd take it.

KATE. I gave you one to make the window frames.

MRS. VERNON. Well, kin the poor girl help that, Kate? Didn't the dogs jump through 'em? [*She indicates the ragged netting on the frame.*

KATE. Why do you have the dogs about?

MRS. VERNON. Well, when you've lived as long as I have in Pike County, you'll know you got to have dogs if you leave your winders open. There—I've ironed another pearl button in two—yes, an' it's pulled a piece right out o' one o' yer pa's bosoms. That's 'cause I'm so tired, I can't see. Lizbeth, where's them prescriptions?

LIZBETH. In the yeast-powder box.

MRS. VERNON. Well, get one for me. [LIZBETH *gets box from over the stove.*] I can't go on with this ironin' without some beer.

LIZBETH. Who'll go for it?

MRS. VERNON. Ask Dave—

LIZBETH. [*At door. Calls.*] Dave!

DAVE. [*Off.*] Yes, Lizbeth.

LIZBETH. Ma wants you to—

MRS. VERNON. Now, don't yawp it out to the whole neighbourhood, Lizbeth—tell Dave to come here.

LIZBETH. [*In a lower tone.*] Come here!

MRS. VERNON. Give me the prescription. [LIZBETH *arranges the linen in the basket. Enter* DAVE.] Dave, the ironin' an' the heat an' everything jes' about floored me—won't you go to the drug-store with this prescription, an' get me a quart bottle of St. Louis beer?

DAVE. [*Taking the prescription.*] Certainly.

MRS. VERNON. I can't send the girls after dark.

DAVE. Oh, that's all right. [*Exits to street.*

MRS. VERNON. [*Ironing again.*] If your pa ever does get into the Legislature, I hope he'll defeat this blamed local auction business. It's all well enough for those Salvation women who ain't got a thing to do but pound tambourines, but if they had the washin', and ironin', an' cookin' to do for a fambly of six—an' three dogs—they'd need something to keep body an' soul together.

KATE. [*Going to street door.*] How much longer shall you iron to-night?

MRS. VERNON. Why? Do you want the room?

KATE. Oh, no—but—

LIZBETH. Is Travers coming to-night, Kate? [*Sits in rocker.*

KATE. I don't know who may come.

MRS. VERNON. What difference does it make who does come?

KATE. None, except that the room is filled with smoke and—is hot.

MRS. VERNON. Well, to my mind, Travers may as well get himself used to places that are hot and filled with smoke—fur if he ain't one of Old Nick's own ones, I never see any—

KATE. Mother!! Mr. Travers is a gentleman!

MRS. VERNON. How do you know? Four years to a female seminary don't make you a better judge of gentlemen than us who stay to home here. Your pa's a gentleman if he is a wheelwright—so is Jim Radburn—

LIZBETH. And Dave—

MRS. VERNON. Yes, and Dave—

KATE. But none of them is like Mr. Travers.

MRS. VERNON. No, thank God they ain't. Travers, Kate—[*Pause.*] Travers—[*Pause.*] and, mind you, I've seen men before you was born—Travers is as much like a gambler as any I ever saw.

KATE. [*Coming down.*] Look here, mother—I've heard you say you had to run away from home with father because your people didn't like him—but that didn't make him any worse, did it?

MRS. VERNON. Well, it didn't make him any better, Kate, and I've regretted it from the bottom of my heart a hundred times—I want you to understand—[*Looks uneasily at door.*] I've told it to him often enough—[*Lowering voice.*] And if he was here I'd tell him again now—that I could ha' married a doctor.

LIZBETH. You're not calculatin' to run away with Travers, are you, Kate?

KATE. You know I'm not, Lizbeth—but I think you and mother might be a little more considerate in what you say. I try to make the place tidy and nice for your evenings with Dave, don't I?

LIZBETH. Well, I didn't mean nothin', Kate.

KATE. And I do my share of the housework. [*Goes to window. As her voice trembles,* MRS. VERNON *signals silence to* LIZBETH.

MRS. VERNON. Of course you do, dear. Lizbeth, you oughtn't to be so thoughtless in what you say.

Enter DAVE *with beer.*

DAVE. Here you are, Mrs. Vernon.

MRS. VERNON. Thank you, Dave—ask that old man in there if he'll have a glass.

DAVE. Yes'm. [*Exit to shop.*

MRS. VERNON. We'll clear the place right up, Kate—don't feel bad about it.

KATE. You needn't, mother—if Mr. Travers calls, we can go walking. [*Goes to door.*

MRS. VERNON. No, Kate, and I say it only fur your sake—I wouldn't have the people of Bowling Green see you trapsing the streets at night with a man you ain't knowed but a month, fur nothin'.

Enter JOE VERNON. JOE *is a six-footer, with full beard. He wears a leather apron and has his sleeves rolled up.*

JOE. Dave says, ma, that—

MRS. VERNON. Yes, here it is. [*Hands glass of beer.*] Nearly dead, Joe?

JOE. [*Smiling.*] Oh, no—but I kin stand this.

KATE. Is there any objection to our spending the evening at Mrs. Woods?

MRS. VERNON. Now, what's the attraction there?

KATE. She has a piano.

MRS. VERNON. Yes, with two teeth broke out of it. Why don't you ever play on the melodeon? [*Pointing to it.*

JOE. Yes, after Jim givin' it to you.

MRS. VERNON. [*Clearing up the ironing.*] I wouldn't treat a dog the way you treat Jim Radburn, Kate.

KATE *silent at doorway.*

JOE. [*At the wash-basin on the bench at back wall.*] Ma, where's the soap?

MRS. VERNON. I must a-left it in the dish-pan.

JOE *gets it and begins washing in tin basin.*

JOE. [*Calling through sputter.*] Dave!

DAVE. [*Off.*] Yes, sir.

JOE. [*At door of shop.*] Might as well shut up.

DAVE. All right.

BOLLINGER. [*Outside to the left.*] Good-evening, Katie.

KATE. Good-evening, Colonel.

BOLLINGER. Rain seems to let up. Where's pa? [*Appears window.*

JOE. [*Looking up from the basin.*] Hello, Tom.

BOLLINGER. Evening, Joe—Mrs. Vernon—Hello, Lizbeth.

LIZBETH. [*Again in the rocker.*] Hello, Colonel.

BOLLINGER. Jis' through?

JOE. Been puttin' in a little overtime.

BOLLINGER. Reckon you'll have another job.

JOE. How's that?

BOLLINGER. Louisiana stage bust a tire on the near fore-wheel to-night.

JOE. That's so? Look out—jus' a minute. [BOLLINGER *steps aside;* JOE *throws water out of the window.*] There, ma—don't say I lost it now. [*Throws soap back into dish-pan.*] How'd she come to do that?

BOLLINGER. Too big a load, I guess—then the rain's cut up the road so, and she were stuck in a rut, an' all of 'em pryin' at her with fence-rails.

JOE. Somethin' had to come.

BOLLINGER. Ye-ep.

MRS. VERNON. [*Sits at table and fans.*] Won't you come in?

BOLLINGER. No, thank you. Too hot. Down to Louisiana on business—sweat clean through two paper collars. This'n's getting mealy. [*He wipes his neck.*

JOE. 'J-ever see such weather. [*Punches* LIZBETH *to get out of rocker; sits in her place.* LIZBETH *goes to the melodeon stool.*

BOLLINGER. Not since I was born. I hope the blamed rain's over. All passenger trains holdin' down to eight mile an hour 'tween St. Charles and Jonesburg on the Wabash on 'count of the wash-outs.

JOE. Why don't they ballast that air track?

BOLLINGER. Too stingy, I reckon. Say, Joe, if you git through the convention, and they send you up to Jeff City, you'll have to jump on the corporations.

JOE. Well, how do things look for the convention?

BOLLINGER. Well, down Louisiana way looks about six and half a dozen. You wouldn't have any trouble at all, if we could get Radburn out o' the race.

JOE. Well, I ain't got no right to ask him to do that.

KATE. [*From the doorway.*] Do you mean, Colonel, that Mr. Radburn's following will be a serious opposition to father's nomination?

BOLLINGER. Well, it looks that way, Kate.

KATE. Is there a chance of Mr. Radburn's getting the nomination?

BOLLINGER. Yes, I should say it was a stand-off atween him an' the Guv'nor, but I'm a-rootin' for your pa.

MRS. VERNON. Well, I can't see what right Jim Radburn has got to be as strong with the Democracy as Joe Vernon. [*Crosses to dish-pan.*

JOE. You can't say nothin' against Jim, ma.

MRS. VERNON. I ain't. I'm just askin'.

BOLLINGER. Well, you see Jim's bein' sheriff four terms, an' never shootin' anybody—

MRS. VERNON. Why, he's shot fifty!

BOLLINGER. Well, I meant never killin' nobody, has naturally endeared him to the peaceable element in the community. Jim has always said, and stuck to it, that a sheriff who couldn't wing a prisoner without killin' him, was a nuisance—and you take his record, and go clean through it, you'll find out this one thing. If a man was runnin', Jim fetched him in the leg. If he pulled a gun on him, Jim smashed that hand. And he says, "You ain't got a right to kill another man, unless that man draws two guns at the same time."

JOE. Yes, I reckon Jim's the gamest we ever had.

BOLLINGER. He came up on the stage to-night from Louisiana.

JOE. Was he "'lectioneering" down there?

BOLLINGER. No, I ain't heerd of him makin' no canvass. He was helpin' me to collect testimony.

MRS. VERNON. Testimony? What fur?

BOLLINGER. Sam Fowler. You know that Express Co. is holdin' him prisoner yet?

JOE. Thought you was goin' to get a habus corpus?

BOLLINGER. Well, I was; only I went to St. Louis yesterday to see Sam. He's all right. They've got 'im in a comfortable room at the Southern Hotel, an' they are tryin' to make him confess that he stood in with the express robber. He's livin' on the fat of the land, so I told him to stick it out as long as the company did, 'cause the longer they hold him, the more damages we'll get for false imprisonment. So Jim Radburn an' me been fillin' in the time, gettin' witnesses to his good character.

MRS. VERNON. What's Radburn got to do with it?

BOLLINGER. Well, you know—on account o' Emily.

MRS. VERNON. Oh, yes! I reckon that'll put off their weddin', won't it?

BOLLINGER. I'm tryin' to fix it that way, so's to pile up the damages.

KATE. [*Quickly.*] Ma!

MRS. VERNON. What is it, Kate?

KATE. Why—

MRS. VERNON. Company?

KATE. Yes.

MRS. VERNON. Here, Lizbeth, take hold this basket.

They carry out basket.

KATE. Good-evening, Mr. Travers.

TRAVERS *appears at door.*

TRAVERS. Good-evening, Miss Vernon—good-evening, Colonel.

BOLLINGER. Evening.

TRAVERS. The rain seems to be over at last. [*He fans himself with his hat.*

BOLLINGER. I reckon we'll have some more of it with that ring around the moon.

TRAVERS. [*Coming into doorway.*] Anything new about the express robber?—Good-evening, Mr. Vernon.

JOE. [*Up to stove; tries bottle.*] How are you?

BOLLINGER. I ain't heard anything 'cept what's in the morning papers.

TRAVERS. What was that? I didn't see them.

BOLLINGER. Why, the blamed cuss has mailed one of the empty money-wrappers to the *Globe-Democrat* to show he's the real robber, and sent a letter sayin' Sam Fowler was innocent.

TRAVERS. Yes? Well, did that do any good?

BOLLINGER. On the contrary, sir, the express company says he wouldn't be so anxious about Sam—if Sam weren't a friend of his'n.

Re-enter MRS. VERNON *and* LIZBETH. LIZBETH *to rocker.*

MRS. VERNON. [*Pleasantly.*] Good-evening, Mr. Travers.

TRAVERS. Good-evening, Mrs. Vernon—Miss Elizabeth.

LIZBETH. Good-evening.

MRS. VERNON. Hasn't Kate had the politeness to ask you in?

TRAVERS. Well, it's a little cooler out here.

KATE. Won't you come in?

MRS. VERNON. Do come—the skeeters'll kill you out there.

TRAVERS *enters.*

JOE. Don't sit there. I just splashed some water there, an' it'ud spot them pants scandalous. [*Down to melodeon.*

MRS. VERNON. Lizbeth, give Mr. Travers the rocker.

LIZBETH *to bench.*

TRAVERS. Oh, no, I beg of you.

MRS. VERNON. Yes, it's the most comfortable. [*Places the rocker for him.*] Vernon there had to put his feet through it yesterday, fixin' the stove pipe, and they ain't been no furniture man along to mend it, though he ginerally comes Fridays.

TRAVERS. Thank you. [*Sits;* KATE *to chair at table;* MRS. VERNON *to cupboard, busy.*

JIM. [*Off.*] Hello, Bollinger, can't I shake you?

BOLLINGER. Well, looks like you was doin' the followin'—ha, ha!

JOE. Is that Jim?

BOLLINGER. Yes—comin' here—[*Calls.*] You ain't got that cripple with you yit?

JIM. Yes—where do you think I'd leave him?

Enter JIM RADBURN *from right to door, with small yellow dog in his arms. One front paw is tied up.*

JOE. Hello, Jim, what's that you got there?

JIM. Er—a—his leg's broke.

JOE. [*Laughing.*] Didn't pull a gun on you, did he?

JIM. The blamed fool dropped a fence-rail on him. Good-eve'n'g, Kate.

KATE. Good-evening, Jim.

MRS. VERNON. 'Tain't one o' Beauty's pups, is it?

JIM. No, 'tain't no dog o' mine. Jes' follered me—run after the stage—then, when she was stuck in the mud, Bill Sarber dropped a rail he was prying with, and—broke his poor little leg.

BOLLINGER. Sarber's the awkwardest cuss anyhow.

MRS. VERNON. Always was.

BOLLINGER. Then he laffed, and Jim made him 'pologize to everybody in the stage.

JIM. [*Looking about.*] What you been doin' to the room?

JOE. [*Proudly.*] Took out the partition.

JIM. I see. Makin' some improvements. Looks bully, don't it?

JOE. Makes the dinin'-room bigger, an' gives more space in the kitchen. Saves steps for ma.

MRS. VERNON. [*Approaching dog.*] What kind of a poultice's that? Flaxseed?

JIM. Gumbo.

MRS. VERNON. Gumbo?

BOLLINGER. That's what they call that soft mud the river leaves down there when it rises—gumbo.

JIM. It's only a cushion so the joltin' wouldn't hurt him. I just been with him to Clark's drug-store. [*To front.*] Clark said he wasn't a dog doctor.

JOE. Wouldn't 'tend to him, eh?

JIM. No—but I'll square it with him. He's up for coroner.

[*Starts for shop—stops.*] I told him that a man what'd see a little dumb animal suffer ought to be drummed out of town. Is Dave there?

JOE. Yes.

JIM. Well, we'll splinter this leg ourselves. [*Going.*

TRAVERS. Why don't you kill him, and put him out of misery?

JIM. [*Pause in door.*] Kill this little dog that took a fancy to me, and followed the stage when I got in it!

TRAVERS. Yes—why not?

JIM. [*After appealing look to the others; then back to* TRAVERS.] Why, I never killed a man.

[*Exit into shop;* JOE, MRS. VERNON, LIZBETH, *follow laughing.*

BOLLINGER *exits*

TRAVERS. [*Going to table.*] What did he say?

KATE. That he never killed a man.

TRAVERS. Well, neither have I. Is that an unusual reputation in Pike County?

KATE. It is for one who, like Mr. Radburn, carries seven bullets in his own body, fired there by men he was arresting.

TRAVERS. I've heard he was very fond of you.

KATE. [*Turning away.*] Don't talk of that.

TRAVERS. May I talk of *my* love for you?

KATE. [*Turning.*] Yes.

TRAVERS. You are not happy here.

KATE. I feel it is unworthy in me to say that I am not.

TRAVERS. Yet, you are not—

KATE. The narrowness of the life oppresses me. I do not live in their world of work and humble wishes—they made the mistake of sending me away to school. I have seen a bigger world than theirs. [*Turns, elbows on table; impulsively.*] I like you, Mr. Travers, because you are a part of that bigger world.

TRAVERS. You like me, Kate! Only like? No more?

KATE. I don't know.

TRAVERS. Will you go with me—away from here, into that bigger world?

KATE. Not until I am sure it is you for whom I go, and not merely for the liberty.

TRAVERS. How will you ever tell?

KATE. Some accident will teach me. It is a dreadful moment, isn't it, when we learn that kinship, the truest kinship, is not a thing of blood, but of ideas—my college mates, who thought as I did, were nearer to me than my family, who never can think as I do.

Enter MRS. VERNON.

MRS. VERNON. I never see such a hero as that little dog—he jis' seemed to know they was helpin' him when they pulled them poor bones together—jes' look how quiet he stands—whinnered a little, but didn't holler 'tall. [TRAVERS *goes up to door.*

KATE. [*Aside.*] That is enough to make the man despise me! [*Goes back to table.*

TRAVERS. [*Going up.*] Oh, yes—he knows he's among friends.

MRS. VERNON. [*Looking into shop.*] Now I say they's lots of folks of education what ain't got as much sense as that dog.

TRAVERS *comes down.*

KATE. Let us go walking. I can't breathe in here.

TRAVERS. With pleasure.

MRS. VERNON. Where you goin', Kate?

KATE. Only outside the door—[*At door.*] to the corner.

MRS. VERNON. [*Doubtingly.*] Well—[*Going centre. Exeunt,* TRAVERS *and* KATE—*positively.*] Well, I don't care who hears me—[*Looks cautiously out.*] I don't like his looks.

Enter JOE.

JOE. Ma!

MRS. VERNON. What?

JOE. Ain't you got some soup-meat or sompthin' you kin spare that little ki-yoodle?

MRS. VERNON. Well, if his leg's broke, he better not have no meat or stuff that'd feed a fever. If yew kin drink your second cup in the mornin' without milk, I kin spare him some o' that.

JOE. All right.

MRS. VERNON. [*Scolding.*] An' the milk's hangin' in the cistern. [*Takes cup from back wall.*] Plague take it! Woman's work's never done. [*Exit.*

JOE. [*After a moment.*] I s'pose I could a got it. [*Calls.*] Lizbeth!

LIZBETH. [*Off.*] Yes. [*Enters.*

JOE. [*Scolding.*] Why don't you help your poor ma? She's had to go after the milk.

LIZBETH. [*Angrily meeting* JOE'S *tone.*] Well, I didn't know it. [*Exit after* MRS. VERNON.

JOE. [*Getting alarm-clock. Calls into shop.*] Dave!

DAVE. [*Off.*] Yes.

JOE. [*At door.*] You don't need him, Jim?

JIM. [*Off.*] No.

JOE. [*Leaving door.*] See here— [*Enter* DAVE.] Kin you run one o' these machines?

DAVE. I allow I kin.

JOE. [*Hands clock to* DAVE.] Then set her an hour earlier, and have things fired up in the mornin'. We've got to weld that Louisiana tire, I reckon, afore breakfast.

DAVE. All right.

Enter MRS. VERNON *and* LIZBETH.

MRS. VERNON. Here, Joe— [*Hands cup.*] Git to feedin' it. I'll git attached to it, an' we've got too many dogs now.

JOE. [*Caressing her with rough push on the face.*] I know you, ma—you're the motherin'est old hen in Pike— [*Going.*] If he don't drink this I'll drowned him.

MRS. VERNON. [*To street door.*] Now, Lizbeth, I don't see nothin' of Kate. She's out there with Travers—you an' Dave kind o' hang round like you was with 'em.

LIZBETH. Come, Dave. [*To* MRS. VERNON.] Jes' not let on?

MRS. VERNON. Yes—purtendin'.

Exit LIZBETH.

DAVE. All right. [*Exit after* LIZBETH.

JOE. [*Entering door.*] Jes' look at him, ma—he's got his eyebrows in it.

MRS. VERNON. [*At door; leans on* JOE'S *shoulder.*] The darlin'—jes' to think, Joe, if one of our children was sufferin'—

JOE. [*With unction.*] You bet.

MRS. VERNON. [*Earnestly calls.*] Don't let him splash it on you, Jim—'t'll spot your clothes.

JOE. [*Pauses admiringly.*] Jim don't care a durn.

MRS. VERNON. There, I'll fix his bed. [*Getting coats from peg, back wall.*] What's a man know, anyhow? [*Exit to shop.*

JOE. [*Gets tobacco from shelf.*] She'll fix him all right—ha, ha!

JIM. [*Entering, looking back.*] Say, Joe, women are great, ain't they? [*Stands admiringly in doorway.*

JOE. [*Slowly coming down, filling pipe.*] Jim! [*Pause.* JIM *doesn't answer, only looks at* JOE.] You an' me— [*Turns quickly and looks at* JIM.] You an' me are goin' into the convention together? [JIM *nods once, and chews slowly.*] Agin each other. [JIM *nods and chews. Pause.*] Smoke? [*Offers pipe.*

JIM. [*Takes cud from mouth; hesitates—returns it.*] Chew.

JOE. Set down. [*They sit.* JIM *left of table*—JOE *to the right in rocker.*] There's somethin' I want to say to you jes' between ourselves.

Enter MRS. VERNON.

MRS. VERNON. [*Comes back of table between the men.*] I reckon he's comfortable.

JOE. Jim an' me's talkin' a minute, ma.

MRS. VERNON. [*Reassuredly.*] Well, I got my work. [*Exit.*

JOE. Jim—[JIM *looks at him.*] I been a figurin' an' I've calculated they's a difference of about $600 'tween you an' me.

JIM. [*Placidly.*] How?

JOE. [*Rising, and closing door. Returns.*] When my Kate got through the public school, you said she ought to go to college. [JIM *nods.*] I didn't think so—I admit now I was a durn fool. [JIM *nods.*] You said she had to go—an' she went—to Linenwood. [JIM *chews.*] When she come back she taught me everything I know—I don't think I could go afore this convention if it wasn't for what Kate's learned me—Jim, I'm ashamed to say so, but I let you pay her schoolin'—I've figured out it's a round six hundred dollars—an' I'm goin' to pay you every—

JIM. [*Impressively points at him with his whole hand.*] See here—[*After a fateful pause, rises.*] Don't you ever say that to me agen. [*Turns away.*

JOE. [*Half-rising, anxiously.*] Why, Jim?

JIM. [*Turning. Threatens.*] Never.

JOE. 'Tain't nothin' to make trouble 'tween us, Jim.

JIM. [*Pauses—growls slowly.*] Whatever I done—was done—have you ever said a word to her about it?

JOE. Nobody knows it, Jim, but you an' me.

JIM. Man to man?

JOE. Man to man.

JIM. [*Slightly relieved.*] Well, I done it fur her—an' whenever I hear her purty voice—soft an' low like verses out of a book—whenever I look at her face—purtier than them pictures they put in the cigar-boxes—and her hands soft and baby-like—I feel 'way down here that I helped do some of that. An' do you think, Joe Vernon, that I'd sell out? No, sir, not by a damned sight!

JOE. But look here, Jim, think of me. We're going in that convention together—agin each other—for the same office, and if you was to tell—

JIM. [*Sharp turn.*] *Tell!* Don't move—but jus' draw breath enough to take that back.

JOE. [*Putting out his hand.*] Jim!

JIM. [*Pause.*] Why, if anybody'd said you could a *thought* them things!

JOE. [*Pleadingly.*] *Jim!*

JIM. [*Long pause.*] Well, there— [*Takes* JOE's *hand.*

Enter MRS. VERNON.

MRS. VERNON. [*Nervously.*] Joe, I've a notion to holler to Kate to run home. I don't like her walkin' with that man.

JOE. What man?

MRS. VERNON. Why, Travers. I don't know what Kate sees in him. [*Returns to door.*

JIM. [*Comfortingly.*] Well, he's a city chap, and Kate's so smart about them things. Joe, how old is Kate?

JOE. Twenty, ain't she, ma?

MRS. VERNON. [*In street door.*] Lor, no—we ain't been *married* but nineteen.

JOE. Seems longer'n that to me.

JIM *looks at him, crossing to melodeon, shaking head.*

JIM. How old is she, Mrs. Vernon?

MRS. VERNON. They's fourteen months difference 'tween her an' Lizbeth.

JIM *looks at* JOE *again.*

JIM. Well, I've knowed her so long, she always seems jes' a little child to me—but Kate's old enough to be thinkin' o' gettin' married, ain't she?

MRS. VERNON. I was mother of two young uns when I was as old as Kate.

JIM *looks at* JOE *again.* JOE *is a mixture of pride and apology.*

JIM. [*Leans over back of chair.*] You know, if I had my way, I'd like Kate to see *everything.* Go to St. Louis, and Europe, an' travel. I've often thought I'd like to be well enough off to take Kate an' jes' do nothin' but travel for a whole summer,

MRS. VERNON. Oh, folks'd talk about it, Jim.

JIM. Why, I mean married—if Kate'd have me.

MRS. VERNON. Oh!

JOE. [*Explainingly.*] Of course—'fore they started.

JIM *looks at* JOE *in amused disgust.*

JIM. An' you know, Mrs. Vernon, I've had it on the tip of my tongue a dozen times to ask her.

MRS. VERNON. [*Reflectively.*] Well,—it might be the best thing that could happen to her. [*Pause.*] Kate's been awful restless lately.

JOE. [*Heartily.*] An' she likes you, Jim, better'n anybody.

JIM. Why, I *used* to *think* so, Joe, but since this feller's been in town—[*Slowly crosses and sits on table.*

MRS. VERNON. Pshaw—I'll bet that mustach of his'n is dyed.

JOE. Don't think about him, Jim, 'cause, if it comes to that, I'll put my foot down.

JIM. Not if Kate liked him.

JOE. Yes, no matter who liked him.

JIM. But I'd want her to like me.

JOE. Well, she does.

JIM. You think so.

JOE. Sure.

JIM. Dog gone it! I'd swap my poney for a trottin' horse, an' git one of them two-wheeled carts an' practice in it till I wasn't seasick, and me an' Kate of a Sunday—say—driving through Bowling Green!

MRS. VERNON. [*Grinning in admiration.*] Why, Jim!

JIM. [*Growing with his vision.*] An' I'd run that south pyazza all around the house,—and dog gone it—*we'd have a hired girl.*

MRS. VERNON. [*Starting something.*] That's the way to treat a woman, Joe Vernon, an' if you hadn't been brought up in Calloway County—

JOE. [*Completing.*] Why, Jim, when we was fust married she was so jealous we couldn't *keep* a hired girl.

MRS. VERNON. [*Waving a hand at him.*] I've got bravely over it. You kin *git* one now.

JOE. Well—we don't need one *now.*

Enter KATE.

KATE. No, I'm not offended, Lizbeth, but it isn't kind.

JOE. What's the matter?

LIZBETH *and* DAVE *appear outside of door and disappear slowly.*

KATE. Nothing. [*Crossing right of rocker.*] Jim—

JIM. Katie.

KATE. You and father are trying for the Legislature? [JIM *nods.*] A nomination in this county is as good as an election, isn't it?

JOE. [*Explaining.*] On our ticket.

JIM *nods.*

KATE. You have been very kind to me—kinder than any man I know—you've stood up for me; and you've given me lots of handsome presents—

JIM. Well?—

KATE. You have been *very* kind—I like your sister Emily—as well as if she were my *own* sister—but Joe Vernon's my *father*—he's an older man than you are—

MRS. VERNON. [*Butting in.*] Well, if he wasn't—

KATE. Wait, mother— [*To* JIM.] I shall work for him. [JIM *nods.*] In every possible way—I know a good many of these delegates—I know their wives—I shall see them.

JIM. [*Pause.*] Does politics make any difference to you, Kate?

KATE. His election does. It means a step out of this life, a breath away from the shop—it means a broader horizon for me — [*Turns away, overcome by her feelings.*

JIM. [*Pause.*] Well, Joe—I went in this thing to *win*—

JOE. Don't mind her, Jim.

JIM. I went in it to win—my friends kind a put it that way—an' it seems I ought to do my best for *them*—but—I wish you luck, old man,—I wouldn't take the nomination now—I didn't think Kate cared.

CURTAIN.

ACT II.

SCENE. VERNON'S *blacksmith shop, adjoining his living-room. Forge. Door to living-room above forge. Bellows down stage below forge. Bench with vise at left. Big double doors. Trusses. Tub of water back of anvil.*

DISCOVERED. JOE *and* CAL *beating weld of tire;* ESROM, *a half-witted negro, absently playing jew's-harp on trusses.*

JOE. [*Wearing boots and leather apron.*] Hand me the traveller. [HELPER *hands it, and drops tire horizontally on anvil, while* JOE *runs traveller around it inside.*] Jes' the same size—give it another heat an' we'll beat her out a quarter inch. [*Crosses to left centre.* HELPER *puts tire into fire and works bellows.*] Esrom!

ESROM. Yes, sah.

JOE. I'm purty busy now, an' that tune—can't you let up till I'm through?

ESROM. Yes, sah.

JOE. An' while you're resting you might bring another bucket o' water an' dump it in this tub.

ESROM. [*Going.*] Yes, sah—don't you really want to buy any mo' coke?

JOE. Not this morning, Esrom. [*Exit* ESROM *with jew's-harp, playing.*] Ready? [*Takes tire from fire and hammers weld out—when pounding is done, traveller runs over it as before. Enter* MRS. VERNON.

MRS. VERNON. Joe, can't you leave that now?

JOE. Course I can't, ma—it's Louisiana time now.

MRS. VERNON. Well, the breakfast's spilin'. [*Exit.*

JOE. [*Calling.*] Well, it's Dave an' his durned alarm-clock—if I'd let Kate set it—I guess she's all right now, Cal. [HELPER *puts tire in fire—last heating.* JOE *goes to trusses and lays wheel square. Enter* SARBER. SARBER *wears linen duster and boots, and carries a whip.*] Hello, Bill.

SARBER. [*Down,*] Hello, Joe—mighty nigh time. [*Looking at watch.*

JOE. Won't be a minute longer—soon as we stretch her a little and drop her over this bunch of bones—

SARBER. [*Examining wheel.*] Hello, Cal? [HELPER *nods.*] Fellers ain't hurt?

JOE. Nothin' ain't hurt. [*Enter* ESROM *with water.*] This wheel's got as purty a dish as I ever see.

SARBER. Don't know why the durned weld broke.

JOE. Them steel tires are hard to make fast sometimes—

ESROM. Right heah, Joe.

JOE. Let her go.

ESROM *pours water into tub.*

ESROM. [*Coaxingly.*] No coke dis mawnin'?

JOE. No. [ESROM *exits. To* SARBER, *pointing to dog under bench.*] Ever see that chap before?

SARBER. The dog?

JOE. Yes.

SARBER. Is that the same one I dropped the rail on?

JOE. [*Nods.*] Me an' Jim put his leg in splinters last night.

SARBER. [*Shaking head and smiling.*] Jim!

JOE. [*Pointing to coach.*] Looks like you been in the real estate business, Bill.

SARBER. Wall, yes—we took a turn or two at it.

Enter BOLLINGER.

BOLLINGER. Hello, Sarber, when's your ingine start?

SARBER. Joe's fixin' one of her drivers.

JOE. [*Looking towards forge.*] Won't be a minute, Tom.

BOLLINGER. Everybody waiting at the drug-store—we want to go 'fore it gets too hot,—folks says you're hanging back so Clark kin sell out his sody water.

SARBER. [*Looking at watch.*] Shake her up, Joe.

JOE. I guess we're ready. [*Two* NEGROES *of a quartette enter and stand idly about. Takes tire with* HELPER.] Get out of the way. [*Drops tire on wheel and adjusts it. Drives pin through one hole.* KELLY *enters, looks at coach, and nervously about.*

JOE. What's new, Tom, about Sam Fowler?

BOLLINGER. [*Looking at work.*] Papers say the company has let him go.

JOE. Scott free?

BOLLINGER. Yes.

JOE. Then he'll have to pay his own board now.

BOLLINGER. I reckon.

JOE *and* HELPER *carry wheel to tub and chill the tire.*

SARBER. Think she'll stay now?

JOE. As soon as we get the bolts in her. [*Two other* NEGROES *enter, completing the male quartette. Enter* TRAVERS.] Look out.

They lift wheel to trusses and silently adjust bolts. As this takes time, the NEGROES *fill in with songs.*

TRAVERS. [*Coming down with* KELLY.] Well, what's up?

KELLY. I'm goin' to skip on this stage.

TRAVERS. Why?

KELLY. Too hot,—see papers?

TRAVERS. No.

KELLY. Well, young Sam Fowler will know you the minute he sees you—and he's comin' back to-day.

TRAVERS. He can't get here till to-night, on account of the wash-outs—I'm going to risk it.

KELLY. Well, I quit you.

TRAVERS. I risk more than you.

KELLY. All right, but you don't risk me. You went in the car, like a blamed fool, without a thing on your face—

VILLAGERS *at door.*

TRAVERS. Be careful.

KELLY. Careful? I skip.

They turn up right. Enter JIM.

BOLLINGER. Hello, Jim—Louisiana?

JIM. No. [*Kneels by dog-box.*

SARBER. Hello, Jim?

JIM. Ain't you late?

SARBER. Joe's keeping me.

JIM. [*Pointing to door.*] Big load this mornin'?

SARBER. Yes, if they all go. [*Returns to wheel.* JIM *goes in house.*

KELLY. [*Coming down with* TRAVERS.] You'd risk your neck for that girl?

TRAVERS. I'm all right, Kelly. I'll get out to-night, but I've got to see her first.

They go up and exeunt.

BOLLINGER. Joe.

JOE. Yes.

BOLLINGER. [*Looking off carefully.*] I see Jim last night after we left here. He says he's out of the race for Legislature.

JOE. That's what he says.

BOLLINGER. Why?

JOE. Well, what did *he* say?

BOLLINGER. *Personal* reasons.

JOE. Well, that goes—all right, Cal,—put her on now, an' let 'em get out.

Wheel is done. CAL *takes it up to coach.*

BOLLINGER. Well, you're jes' as good as elected then, Joe.

JOE. Think so?

BOLLINGER. Sure. See here. [*Aside.*] Folks down in Louisiana thinks Jim will be the nominee. I'm goin' down to-day to bet fifteen or twenty dollars he won't, 'fore they hear of it.

JOE. No promises.

BOLLINGER. No, sir-ee—put up, or shut up—I've got twenty-two and a half in my pocket—some of it's Clark's, but blamed little.

Re-enter JIM *with pan of milk—kneels by dog and feeds it.*

SARBER. Now stand out of the way there.

BOLLINGER. Goin', Bill?

SARBER. Soon as we hitch.

They take wagon out. BOLLINGER, KELLY, TRAVERS *and* SARBER *go out with wagon.*

JOE. Come Cal—[CAL *turns.*] Hash! [CAL *exits.*] Breakfast, Jim.

JIM. Had it.

JOE. Come, set with us. [*Exit, followed by* JIM.

Enter TRAVERS.

TRAVERS. Kelly is right. I should go on that coach—but—I must see Kate—they're at breakfast—if I only—yes, just a minute. [*Beckons* KATE.] I wish that fellow wasn't here.

Enter KATE.

KATE. Mr. Travers.

TRAVERS. I should leave on that coach.

KATE. Do I keep you?

TRAVERS. Yes.

KATE. Why?

TRAVERS. Because when I leave Bowling Green now, I shall never come back.

KATE. You—you are jesting.

TRAVERS. In dead earnest. [*Slight clatter of dishes*—KATE *looks off.*] Do you care for that man?

KATE. [*Coming down.*] I admire him. I think he is a good and a noble character.

TRAVERS. Better than I am.

KATE. He may be,—but—I don't love him—

TRAVERS. Do you love me?

SARBER. [*Off.*] All ready; get in.

KATE. The stage is going. [*She turns.*

TRAVERS. Do you love me?

SARBER. Get in.

TRAVERS. Do you?

KATE. [*Pause.*] Yes.

TRAVERS. Then let them leave—[SARBER *calling* "git ap"—*and a whip cracks. We hear stage—voices go.*] Will you go with me—to-night?

KATE. How—go with you?

TRAVERS. As my wife.

KATE. But why such haste? Why go as if we feared anything?

TRAVERS. I must go to-night. Great interests depend upon it. I know your people don't like me, but I haven't time to humour them. Will you go?

KATE. Let me think till then.

TRAVERS. Yes,—good-bye till to-night. [*Holds her hand—she turns as if to leave.*] Kate! Kate! Good-bye. [*Impulsive turn and embrace.*] Till to-night.

Enter DAVE, *from breakfast.*

DAVE. Huh! [*Shortly; more a chuck than an exclamation. The lovers start.*] Oh! Seminary!

TRAVERS *exits.*

DAVE. [*Embarrassed—nodding off.*] Breakfast.

KATE. Thank you. [*Exits.*

DAVE. [*Going to bench and beginning work on shaft with draw knife.*] Well—Lizbeth don't know so blamed much about books —[*Shakes head.*] But—huh—[*Shakes head again.*] I tell you— [*Works hard—enter* LIZBETH *with pan, which she puts on forge.*

DAVE. [*Commanding.*] Come here, Lizbeth.

LIZBETH. [*Crosses to* DAVE. *Pause.*] What? [*Falling inflection.*

DAVE. [*Cautiously, approving her.*] Why, dog gone it— [*Shakes head.*] Huh! [*Swaggers.*] I tell you—[*Works.*

LIZBETH. [*Wonderingly.*] What's the matter?

DAVE. [*Threatening.*] If you was to say seminary to me—[*Swaggers.*] Huh! [*Works.*

LIZBETH. [*After pause.*] What?

DAVE. [*Ominously.*] Why, Lizbeth, the sooner we git married an' git out o' this, the better.

LIZBETH. [*Hopelessly.*] Well, what kin I do?

DAVE. [*Working.*] Dog gone it—if I had a stidy job!

LIZBETH. [*Understandingly.*] I know that, Dave. [*Goes back to pan.*

DAVE. [*Bragging.*] An' you bet your *father* knows it.

LIZBETH. [*Portentously.*] Well, I told *ma*—

DAVE. An' that's what he said. If I had a stidy job—

Enter EM'LY.

EM'LY. Hello—

DAVE. Why, how de do?

LIZBETH. Can't you come in?

EM'LY. Who's there? [*Indicates kitchen.*

LIZBETH. Only the folks and Jim.

EM'LY. I want Jim—say—Sam's there. [*Off.*

LIZBETH. Sam Fowler!—Oh, ma—[*Exits.*

DAVE. Sam—why, see here. Sam! [*Goes up.*

SAM *enters. Wears express blue and a cap.*

EM'LY. [*Beckoning.*] Sam!

DAVE *brings* SAM *down. Enter* JOE, *followed by* MRS. VERNON, LIZBETH *and* KATE.

JOE. [*Heartily.*] Sam, Sam, how are you?

SAM. [*Shaking hands.*] I didn't know how you'd feel about it.

MRS. VERNON. [*Shaking.*] Why, Lor', Sam—I'm glad—I'll bet Em'ly kissed him.

KATE *and* LIZBETH *shake hands with* SAM. *Enter* JIM—EM'LY *runs to him.*

EM'LY. Jim!

JIM *puts his left arm around* EM'LY *and sits on anvil.*

SAM. [*Approaching and taking* JIM'S *hand, smiling.*] *You* didn't think I done it, did you, Jim?

JIM. [*Nods at* EM'LY.] No, not while *she's* keepin' house for me—ha, ha!

EM'LY. He's *always* stood up for you, Sam.

JOE. Well, tell us 'bout it, Sam. Did the papers have it right?

They are a semi-circle about SAM.

SAM. Yes, purty near.

JOE. *Did* you help the feller into your car?

SAM. Yes, we were just pulling out of the depot when he came a-runnin' up to my side door with an order from the superintendent for me to carry him as fur as Vinita. He ran alongside and put his hand up, so of course I pulled him into the car.

EM'LY. Wasn't you scared, Sam?

SAM. Why, no—I thought he belonged to the company, and he went to work with me, sorting and fixing my express stuff.

JOE. Well, I'm durned!

SAM. [*Intensely serious.*] I joked with him—just like I'm joking with you—he was one of the nicest fellows I ever saw.

JOE. [*Wide-eyed with gossip.*] Don't that beat everything?

SAM. When we were eighteen or twenty miles out, an' I was stoopin' this way over a box—I felt him on my back, and grabbing at my arms—why, why—even then I thought he was jokin', and I looked around laughin', and here was his gun pokin' right into my face.

MRS. VERNON. [*Haunted.*] Just think of it!

JOE. Then he tied you.

SAM. What could I do? There was his gun—and I wasn't even on my feet—anybody could tie a fellow that way—I could tie *you*, couldn't I? [*To* JIM.

JIM. If you had the gun?

SAM. Yes.

JIM. Well, rather.

SAM. [*Indignantly.*] The ropes cut clean through here at my wrists, and there was a mark over one eye where I fell against the safe—and then the company said I was an accomplice.

JOE. Then I s'pose he jis' deliberately packed his little valise full of green-backs and—[*Pantomimes.*]—got out!

SAM. A hundred and twenty thousand—

JOE. Jump off?

SAM. No—got off at a water-tank.

JIM. I s'pose you'd know him agin?

SAM. Anywhere.

LIZBETH. [*With nursery alarm.*] He must a looked terrible.

SAM. [*Commonplace.*] Well, he didn't—nice a lookin' feller as you want to see. Black mustache—kind a curly hair—looked a little bit, you know, like a race-horse man.

EM'LY. The company said Sam wrote the superintendent's order himself.

SAM. Oh, yes—got an expert to swear it looked like my writing.

EM'LY. 'Tain't a bit—like it.

JIM. [*To* EMILY.] Did you see it?

SAM. No, but I showed her part of the letter he wrote to the newspaper, saying I was innocent. [*Feels in pocket.*] Ain't that strange? Seems to be a kind-hearted fellow.

MRS. VERNON. Jes' drove to it I s'pose by drink.

SAM. Here it is. [*Hands paper to* JIM.

JIM. Hello! [*Looks at* KATE.

JOE. What is it?

JIM *hands paper to* KATE.

KATE. [*After slight start—haughtily.*] What do you mean?

JIM. Oh, not you, Kate. [*Smiling, to* SAM.] 'Twasn't Kate dressed up like a man—no! [*General laugh.*] Oh, I didn't think that. [KATE *vexed, goes up-stage.* JIM *in whisper to others.*] Mad? [JOE *shakes his head;* JIM *nods interrogatively to* MRS. VERNON.

MRS. VERNON. [*Looking after* KATE.] Well, I can't see why.

Exit KATE.

JIM. [*After another look after* KATE—*to* SAM.] Well, I suppose you know you're watched.

SAM. [*Indifferently.*] How's that?

JIM. There's a Pinkerton here— come last night—had a letter to me from the Chief—sayin' they knew of me, an' hoped I'd co-operate with this fellow in watchin' you—and they'd pay well for it.

SAM. [*Smiling.*] What did you say?

JIM *shakes head—goes up centre.*

EM'LY. Why, Jim kicked him off—of our stoop.

General laugh.—LIZBETH *crosses to forge and gets pan.*
ESROM *enters playing jew's-harp.*

ESROM. What about the coke, Mistah Vernon?

JOE. [*At forge.*] Don't want none. [*Suddenly.*] See here; look at this clinker.

ESROM. Can't understand that—shouldn't ought to be no clinker in dat coke.

JOE. Well, there it is—hard as flint.

ESROM. [*Examines clinker.*] Funny clinker.

JOE. Well, there it is.

JIM. Hold on, Joe. I shouldn't wonder if that was that gumbo.

JOE. What gumbo?

JIM. The poultice. I throwed it among that coke.

JOE. Yes, here's some only half-burned.

ESROM. [*Going.*] I knowed they shouldn't ought to be no clinker.

JOE. But look at this red piece—as hard as a rock.

JIM. [*Half-startled.*] Why, Joe—[*Looks at him.*

JOE. What?

JIM. Well, nothing—

MRS. VERNON. Well, what about breakfast, everybody?

JOE. Let's finish it—come Sam—

SAM. I've had mine.

JOE. Well, come talk to us.

SAM. [*Going.*] All right—got heaps to tell you.

LIZBETH. How do you like the Southern Hotel?

Exeunt all but DAVE *and* JIM. JIM *takes clinker and turns it carefully over in his hand. Then looks through forge—goes to bench near dog, and gets on hands and knees, looking under it.*

DAVE. What you lost?

JIM. Here it is—[*Rises.*] Some more of that gumbo. [*Crosses to forge.*

DAVE. What you goin' to do?

JIM. Burn it. [*Looks about as if hunting help.*] Here—come pump this.

DAVE *crosses and takes bellows.*

DAVE. What do you want to burn it for?

JIM. [*Ignoring question.*] Say, Dave—

DAVE. [*Working bellows.*] Well?

JIM. You know them old coal mines down by Jonesburg?

DAVE. Yes.

JIM. What do they sell that slack for?

DAVE. They don't *sell* it—they *give* it to anyone that'll haul it away.

JIM. I wonder if they wouldn't deliver it if you took a good deal.

DAVE. Don't know.

JIM *whistles cheerily a moment and examines gumbo burning.*

JIM. [*Pause. Sitting on anvil.*] You seem under the weather, Dave.

DAVE. [*Moodily.*] Oh, I'd be all right, if I had a stidy job.

JIM. [*Laughing.*] A steady job!—why, you've been workin' nights ever since I knew you.

DAVE. I know—but Joe says—I—I ought to have a stidy job.

JIM. What's Joe got to do with it?

DAVE. Well—Lizbeth—

JIM. [*Amused.*] Oh!

DAVE. An' I think I could get one, only he don't gimme no time off to look fur it.

JIM. Wait a minute. [*Takes gumbo from fire.*] Yes, sir—she's gettin' hot. [*Puts it back and whistles a tune.*

DAVE. I've almost made a set o' furniture myself.

JIM. Have, eh?

DAVE. Dug it out with that little draw-knife. I tell you—you can make anything that's made out of wood—with a draw-knife.

JIM. [*On anvil again.*] Well, it seems to me, Dave, that you're going at it the wrong way.

DAVE. How's that?

JIM. The old man won't give his consent till you git a steady job.

DAVE. That's it—

JIM. And you want a steady job so's you can marry Lizbeth?

DAVE. Exactly.

JIM. Well, you marry—marry Lizbeth, and you'll have a steady job. [*Gets down.* DAVE, *absorbed with the idea, pumps vigorously.*] Hold on! [DAVE *stops;* JIM *takes gumbo from fire with tongs, and plunges it in the water.*] Yes, sir, there it is—hard as a rock—and ain't it a purty color?

DAVE. What you goin' to do with it?

JIM. I don't know but if the Wabash could get enough of it to ballast that track that washes out every spring, I think they'd take it.

DAVE. [*In admiration.*] Well, I'm durned. The raw gumbo is all along their track. Wouldn't cost you nothin', would it?

JIM. Not if I kin get that Jonesburg slack—ha, ha!

DAVE. Why, that's great!

JIM. [*Drawing watch.*] It's a half hour before train time. I'll jump to St. Louis with the scheme. [*Stands thinking.*

DAVE. [*Going.*] I got to get the leather put on this shaft—but that's great. [*Exit.*

KATE *appears in outside door.*

KATE. [*Coming toward* JIM, *who is turning gumbo thoughtfully in his hands.*] Jim!

JIM. Why, Kate—[*Gumbo.*] See here—how's this for an idea?

KATE. What did you mean—by this? [*She extends letter.*

JIM. Why, just that. I thought it looked like his writin',—same backhand, and no shadin' to it.

KATE. How could Mr. Travers have written it?

JIM. Why, no use gettin' mad, Kate. It kin *look* like his writin', can't it?

KATE. [*Going to anvil and leaning on back of it.*] You don't like him, Jim, do you?

JIM. [*Picks up old horse-shoe.*] Well—[*Mechanically pounds gumbo with horse-shoe.*

KATE. [*Pause.*] Not much—

JIM. No—not a great deal, Kate.

KATE. [*Displaying the letter.*] Do you think he's a bad enough man to have done this?

JIM. Well, a fellow who takes a risk like that—to clear another man who's been arrested in his place, ain't so bad.

KATE. A train robber!

JIM. Why, I don't *say* he done it.

KATE. But you think so.

JIM. [*Laughing.*] Oh, no, I don't—there's a ten thousand dollar reward for the right man.

KATE. Then why hand this letter to me? Why imply it?

JIM. Why, Kate, I'm a friend of—your pa's—I've known you ever since you was eight or ten years old. I don't know this man Travers—*you* don't know him. He comes to your house.

KATE. Well.

JIM. Comes to see *you*, don't he?

KATE. [*Getting in front of anvil.*] He does—what of it?

JIM. Why—I don't think I'd like a preacher of the Gospel if he was to do that. [*Pause.*] I—I never meant to say anything—but when men—*other* men—I mean anybody gets to payin' you attention, why, I'm afraid to keep still any longer—

KATE. [*Turns away.*] To keep still—

JIM. [*Advances.*] Yes, I've been sheriff here, an' whenever I've had anything to do, I've said to myself, now don't—do anything—ugly—'cause Kate—[KATE *turns toward him; he qualifies tone.*] some day, you know—Kate might think more of me if I hadn't done it. You know yourself that I quit drinkin' a year before the local option— on account of that essay you read, examination day—why, Kate, I care more for how *you* feel about anything than I do for anybody in the State of Mizzoura—that's just how it is. [*Pause.* KATE *is silent.*] You kin remember yourself when you was a little girl an' I used to take a horse-shoe an' tie it on the anvil an' make a side-saddle for you—an' I reckon I was the first fellow in Bowling Green that ever called you, *Miss* Kate when you come back from school.

KATE. [*Rather tenderly.*] I didn't want you to call me Miss Kate, Jim.

JIM. Jes' fun, you know—an' now, Kate, when you're a woman, an' it's only nature for men to like you,—I've got to ask you myself.

KATE. [*Pause.*] I'm awful sorry you did it, Jim.

JIM. Sorry!

KATE. Yes, because I like you well enough, Jim—but—[*Pause. Enter* JOE. KATE *stops.*

JOE. Say, Jim—

JIM. [*Motioning* JOE *to silence.*] Go on, Kate—I ain't ashamed of it—before Joe.

KATE. That's all there is to it—I just like you.

JIM. Well, I didn't know—you used to let me kiss you—

KATE. Yes, when I was coming home from school—I did. I thought I was going to love you then. But there was the school. [*Pauses.*] If I hadn't gone to Lindenwood I might have thought so still. But we could never be happy together, Jim—you haven't had proper advantages, I know, and it isn't your fault. My *education* has put the barrier between us. Those four years at the Seminary—

JOE. [*Indignantly.*] Why, Kate Vernon—everything you know, Jim Radburn—

JIM. [*Imperatively.*] Hold on—[*Pause.*] You've heard her say no, and—that lets you out. As far as I'm concerned—why, Kate's nearly right. I don't know any more'n the law allows—but—that's for Kate to say—

JIM *extends his hand in appeal to* KATE. KATE *turns her back to audience—leans on anvil, firmly shakes her head "No."* JIM *motions silence to* JOE; *makes a struggle, and pulls himself together—turns and kneels by dog, caressing it.*

CURTAIN.

ACT III.

SCENE. *Same as* ACT I, *but tidy. Doors closed and lamp lighted. Song in blacksmith shop before rise of curtain.*

DISCOVERED. DAVE *and* LIZBETH *playing checkers on home-made board.* EM'LY *and* SAM *looking on.* JOE *reading.* KATE *in walking dress looking out window.* MRS. VERNON *with glasses mending some garments.*

JOE. [*Annoyed by song—frets. Goes to the door.*] Here, you boys—don't hang around that shop; go up in the square an' sing.

MRS. VERNON. What you sen' 'em away fur?

JOE. Oh, it's one o' them blamed "mother" songs. Nobody ever sings anything about father—except the "Old man's drunk again," or somethin' like that.

DAVE. Your move, Lizbeth.

LIZBETH. [*Petulantly.*] Don't I know it?

SAM. Move there.

DAVE. Hold on, I can't beat both of you.

LIZBETH. Don't tell me, Sam. I'd a moved there anyway. Come on, Dave.

KATE. [*Solus.*] A whole hour longer; I cannot wait.

MRS. VERNON. What's fretting you, Kate?

KATE. Everything.

MRS. VERNON. [*Indicates the melodeon.*] Play something.

KATE. I can't play on that melodeon, mother.

MRS. VERNON. Poor old melodeon! for all the music we git out of it—might as well be a folding bed.

ESROM. [*Appearing at window.*] I knowed they oughtn't be any clinker in that coke.

JOE. [*From his paper.*] That's all right, Esrom.

ESROM. Don't want no mo' coke, Mistah?

JOE. No, no, no!

ESROM *hands* KATE *a letter.*

ESROM. [*Whispering.*] He—he wants an answer.

DAVE. Hold on!

LIZBETH. Well, it's a king!

DAVE. Yes—but I move first.

A knock at street door.

JOE. Come in.

Enter JIM.

MRS. VERNON. Good-evenin'.

JOE. [*Not turning.*] Who is it?

JIM. You're all here, are you?

JOE. [*Rising.*] Hello, Jim.

JIM. [*To* JOE.] Hello. [EM'LY *goes to him; he puts his arm about her.*] How long you been here?

EM'LY. All day.

JIM. What?

JOE *goes to the shelf at back and fills his pipe.*

EM'LY. So's Sam.

SAM. Mrs. Vernon made us stay to dinner. Then *supper.*

JOE. Sam didn't feel like seeing the town folks.

JIM. Why?

SAM. Well, I didn't know how they'd feel about it.

JIM. What, think you did do it?

SAM. I didn't know.

JIM. That's just the reason; why, if you hang back, what can they do?

MRS. VERNON. [*Explaining.*] Well, Em'ly was here.

JIM. I know, but Sam ought to have spunk to face 'em. It's got to come and you might as well know where your friends are.

JOE. That's so.

SAM. [*Starting to door.*] Well, I reckon most of 'em's up at the drug-store.

JIM. [*Emphatically.*] Walk right in amongst 'em.

SAM. Dog gone it! I ain't ashamed, but if they hint anything I'd feel like smashing 'em—huh!

JIM. You got to.

SAM. All right. [*Exit.*

JIM. Don't let me stop the game.

LIZBETH. Dave thinks all night.

EM'LY. [*To* JIM, *pulling him around.*] Where have you been?

JIM. St. Louis. Been to see the railroad people. Say, Joe!

JOE. Yes?

JIM. Sam's got the express people scared.

JOE. How's that?

JIM. Hearin' I was his friend, they hinted to me that they'd like to square it.

JOE. Compromise.

JIM. [*Nodding his head.*] I worked it up for him. Said Bollinger was a regular terror.

EM'LY. Will the express company have to pay Sam?

JIM. Well, rather. And after they do, Sam ought to go down to their president's office and kick 'em all around the back-yard.

Exit KATE.

JOE. What's ailing Kate?

MRS. VERNON. Seems out o' sorts—mebbe she'll tell me alone. [*Exit.*

DAVE. [*Protesting.*] You can't move backwards.

LIZBETH. Well?

DAVE. That's cornered.

JOE. He's got you, Lizbeth.

JIM. Dave!

DAVE. Yes?

JIM. I saw the Wabash folks.

DAVE. Have a talk with them?

JIM. [*Hands* DAVE *a paper.*] Yes—there's a memorandum agreement—they'll take all I can give 'em at thirty dollars a car-load.

JOE. What's that?

JIM *takes a piece of gumbo from pocket and hands it to* JOE.

JIM. [*To* DAVE.] Now I've got a proposition for you.

DAVE. What?

JIM. You superintend the burnin' of the stuff, and I'll take you in.

DAVE. Why, Jim—[*Rises in delight.*

JOE. What's this fur?

JIM. Ballast.

JOE. Ballast?

JIM. Yes, that road-bed that washes out. [*Pause.*] Thirty dollars a car.

JOE. What!

JIM. Me an' Dave.

DAVE. Why, Jim, I ain't got no claim on you.

JIM. You pumped the bellows this morning while I burned it.

DAVE. Well—

JIM. And you want a steady job, don't you?

DAVE. Well—["*I should say so,*" *understood; turns to him.*

JOE. But see here—[JIM *looks at him—waits.*]—You goin' into this?

JIM. Wouldn't you, if you got the contract?

JOE. But Dave—Dave's helpin' me!

JIM. You told him to git a job, didn't you?

JOE. Yes—but—

LIZBETH. [*Ready for a fight.*] An' that's what you told me.

JIM. [*Abetting* LIZBETH.] Yes.

JOE. But my business needs somebody.

JIM. Then why don't you let them git married?

JOE. An' me support them?

JIM. [*In disgust.*] Hell!—

JOE. What's the matter?

JIM. Ain't he worth his wages?

JOE. I never said he wasn't.

JIM. [*In superlative display.*] And he's made nearly a whole set of furniture.

JOE. But if I went to Jefferson, I was goin' to leave this shop with Dave.

LIZBETH. [*With pride.*] Dave!

JIM. Well, that's different. See here! You let 'em get married. I only want Dave to superintend this burnin'—it won't take two half-days a week to kind a-look it over—we kin get niggers to do the work, and Dave kin stay here.

LIZBETH. Dave!—

DAVE. [*Hushing her.*] Sh—

JOE. Well, I'll think it over and—

JIM. [*Positively.*] No!

JOE. No?

JIM. *I* can't fool with you, Joe; he gits the girl or we quit.

LIZBETH. An' the girl goes too.

JOE. What?

JIM. Yes, the girl goes too. [*Pause and smile.*] It's your say, Joe. [*Foot on chair.*] Well, Joe, it's up to you.

JOE. [*Giving up.*] Well, I can't help it.

JIM. [*Passing the approval to* DAVE *and* LIZBETH.] There's your girl. And you've got a stiddy job! [DAVE *and* LIZBETH *half embrace.*] What do you think of that? [*To* JOE, *who is mechanically looking at gumbo.*] Thirty dollars per car.

JOE. [*Glad to change the subject.*] Thirty, eh?

JIM. Every per car—and see here—Joe—

JOE. What?

JIM. [*Draws second paper from pocket.*] I've fixed up a kind of a resignation here.

JOE. Resignation?

JIM. Yes. I can't tend to this new business and do much work as sheriff, so I'm goin' to resign the sheriff part of it.

JOE. You mustn' do it, Jim—why, you've been keepin' the district like a prayer-meeting!

JIM. Well, somebody else kin sing the Doxology—you turn that into the council fur me.

Enter KATE *and* MRS. VERNON.

MRS. VERNON. I've put my foot down, Kate,—you can't go.

KATE. I *am* going.

MRS. VERNON. Joe Vernon, it's time you took a hand a-managin' this family.

JOE. What's the matter?

MRS. VERNON. I've told Kate she can't go out.

JOE. Well, ma,—Kate ain't a child.

MRS. VERNON. Your carelessness'll make her disgrace the whole family.

JOE. Hol' on, ma.

MRS. VERNON. I know what I'm talking about. I see that nigger give Kate a letter.

JOE. Why, he don't know how to write.

MRS. VERNON. You don't suppose I think the nigger wrote it! It's from someone else.

JOE. Who is it from, Kate?

KATE. I don't care to tell. I'm going out. [*Starts.*

MRS. VERNON. [*Interposes.*] No, Kate, you ain't.

JOE. Why, ma—if Kate wants to go walkin'—

MRS. VERNON. All right, she kin walk. But getting letters sneaked to her, and going out to meet a man's another thing. [*Persuasively going to her.*] Why don't you tell, Kate?

KATE. [*Down to end of table.*] No one has a right to my letters.

JOE. Of course not. No *right*, Kate, but your ma's naturally anxious, and she's only tryin' for your good.

KATE. [*Ready to weep.*] I'm awfully tired of it.

JOE. But you kin tell me—you ain't ashamed of it, air you?

KATE. No, I'm not!

MRS. VERNON. It's Travers, ain't it?

JOE. [*Coaxing.*] Is it, Kate?

KATE. Yes, it is.

JOE. Well, there, ma—see. [*Walks away as though matter were closed. Crossing left.*

MRS. VERNON. Air you losin' your senses, Joe Vernon?

JOE. [*Irritated.*] The girl's tole you, ain't she?

MRS. VERNON. And jes' what I thought, too. She's goin' to meet him.

KATE. Well, what of it? You're polite enough to his face.

MRS. VERNON. Of course, if he'll come here like a man. But when I was a gurl—it'd a been an insult fur a man to send a note askin' her to meet him after dark.

JOE. [*Loudly chaffing.*] Oh, ma—now don't forget—

MRS. VERNON. You upholdin' her? Jim, that's the way I have to fight to keep this family straight. What's *your* opinion?

JIM. Well, 'tain't no business o' mine, Mrs. Vernon, and—

MRS. VERNON. Do you like his looks?

JIM. [*Pause.*] He ain't jes' my kind—but may be he don't like mine.

MRS. VERNON. Do you uphold his sending letters to Kate?

JIM. Why, Mrs. Vernon, I can't blame other men fur likin' Kate.

MRS. VERNON. Meetin' them after dark?

JIM. Kate knows how I feel about her—[*Pause.*] And if *she* wanted my opinion I'd give it to her—but on the other hand—I've got an awful lot o' confidence in Kate.

MRS. VERNON. Why don't you answer his letter, Kate, an' say you'll be happy to receive him at your home? He won't think none the less of you.

KATE. I've promised to meet him, and I'm going to keep the appointment.

MRS. VERNON. Is she, Joe?

JOE. Well, ma, I can't tie her.

MRS. VERNON. Take Lizbeth with you.

KATE. I don't want Lizbeth with me.

LIZBETH. I won't play proprietary for her!

KATE. [*Starting up.*] I'm going alone. [*Crosses right.*

MRS. VERNON. [*With her back to street door.*] Not this door, you ain't.

KATE. Then the other. [*Exits, followed by* MRS. VERNON.

MRS. VERNON. [*As she disappears by door.*] We'll see!

Enter BOLLINGER *from street.*

BOLLINGER. [*In great excitement.*] Say, boys—man killed up at Clark's—

JOE. [*Catching the thrill.*] Man killed?

BOLLINGER. Yes.

LIZBETH *and* EM'LY. Oh!

JOE. Run over?

BOLLINGER. Shot.

ALL. Shot!

BOLLINGER. [*Revelling in the gossip.*] Travers shot him. Sam Fowler came in the drug-store, and the minute he saw him he said, "That's the man robbed my car—"

JIM. [*Quietly.*] What's he look like?

BOLLINGER. [*Impatiently.*] Why, *Travers*—Sam says that's the man—and Travers started for the window—stepped right into the perfumery case, then on the sody-water counter, and this fellow grabbed him. First we see Travers had his gun right against the fellow's neck and—bang—he turned around with both hands up, this way, and kneels down right at Bill Sarber's feet.

EM'LY. And Sam?

BOLLINGER. Oh, Sam's all right—say, kin one of you boys lend me a gun—we're huntin' fur him.

JOE. Hunting who?

BOLLINGER. [*Intolerant of* JOE'S *stupidity.*] Why, Travers.

JIM. [*In quiet contrast.*] Where'd he go?

BOLLINGER. Right through the window—knocked over both them green lights—kicked a box o' lickerish all over the side-walk—kin you spare one?

JOE. [*Bustling about.*] I ain't got but one, and I reckon I'll take a hand myself.

JIM. [*To* EM'LY.] Come, little gal, we got to go home.

JOE. [*At door. Calls.*] Ma—ma!—Say, Jim, you can't resign to-night—I knowed they'd be trouble if you quit.

JIM. Better meet at the Court House. [*Exit with* EM'LY *and passes window going left.*

Enter MRS. VERNON.

JOE. Where's my gun?

MRS. VERNON. What you want it fur?

JOE. [*Who is running a circle.*] What do you s'pose—fry eggs? Where is it?

LIZBETH. Travers killed a man.

MRS. VERNON. [*Adding her part to the hubbub.*] Lor'! Travers!

JOE. Where is it, Lizbeth?

BOLLINGER. Ain't you got anything you kin lend me?

MRS. VERNON. Here it is. [*Hands gun.*

JOE. Loaded?

MRS. VERNON. Don't pint it.

JOE. That—the butt end—come on!

BOLLINGER. A butcher-knife's better than nothing.

LIZBETH. Here! [*Hands knife to* BOLLINGER.

DAVE. [*As* LIZBETH *holds him.*] You don't think I'm scared.

Exeunt BOLLINGER *and* JOE.

MRS. VERNON. I don't want you to shoot anybody, Joe; pint it in the air.

DAVE *exits; when off calls* "Good-bye!"

MRS. VERNON. [*Impatient in doorway.*] I can't see what business it is of Dave's when they's three policemen in town; uniforms—where's Em'ly?

LIZBETH. Jim took her home.

MRS. VERNON. Did somebody say Travers?

LIZBETH. Yes.

Enter KATE.

KATE. What is it?

LIZBETH. Travers shot a man.

KATE. What man—why?

MRS. VERNON. [*Accusingly.*] Jus' natural deviltry—purty pass things is coming to!

KATE. Whom did he shoot?

LIZBETH. We don't know—shot him here, in the neck.

Enter SARBER *from street, hurriedly.*

SARBER. Hello,—where's the boys?

MRS. VERNON. Have they ketched him?

SARBER. Don't know—we're all huntin'—[*Starts off.*

KATE. [*Quickly.*] Mr. Sarber—

SARBER. Eh?

KATE. Who is hurt?

SARBER. [*Shouting.*] Don't know his name—Clark stuffed the hole full of cotton. [*Indicating neck.*] Says city'll have to pay for his green lights and lickorish.

KATE. Did Mr. Travers shoot the man?

SARBER. Yes'm—nearer than you an' me—which way'd they go?

LIZBETH. Court House.

SARBER. Been an awful hot day. [*Exit.*

KATE. [*In haunted fear.*] What have you heard about it?

MRS. VERNON. Why, it don't surprise me, Kate.

LIZBETH. They say Travers is the *train-robber*—

KATE. Lizbeth!

LIZBETH. Sam Fowler knew him the minute he saw him—that's why Travers had to shoot—to git away!

MRS. VERNON. Not Sam?

LIZBETH. No, didn't shoot Sam.

KATE. There has been some mistake—these people have never liked Mr. Travers.

MRS. VERNON. I knowed he'd bring disgrace on the whole house, Kate. [*Getting sun-bonnet.*] I'll go in through Mrs. Clark's back way—*she'll* know—come, Kate, I'm your mother, and a mother never deserts her child. [*In stage heroics.*

KATE. [*Recoiling.*] I don't care to go.

LIZBETH. Take me, ma.

MRS. VERNON. Come on. [*Exit with* LIZBETH.

KATE. [*In wild-eyed panic.*] Oh, how dreadful! This is what I have felt coming all the day. It is my fault, too. If I had said 'yes' last night, or only gone with him this morning—it couldn't have happened. How horrible!—killed a man! They didn't tell me whom. I—I wonder if my name was mentioned? They said—*Lizbeth* said—a *train-robber*—[*She leans on table for support.*] That letter! Jim thought the writing looked like his. Jim—Jim has told others his suspicion—Yes—Jim Radburn has done it! I see! I see! Jim hated him—they have persecuted him for *me*—Oh! oh! Why did I not go last night?

Enter TRAVERS, *pale and breathless—revolver in hand. He closes the door behind him.*

TRAVERS. Kate!

KATE. Oh!

TRAVERS. Who's there? [*Points toward shop.*

KATE. No one. What is the matter? Tell me what you did—that pistol!

TRAVERS. In self-defence—they would have killed *me* if they could.

KATE. You *shot* him?

TRAVERS. Yes. [*As she hides her face.*] Kate! Kate! I can't come in front of the window—where can I go?

KATE. They will find you here. [*He turns, facing door with pistol, left hand holding door shut, menacingly.*] No,—not that—you wouldn't shoot again! My father may come here!

TRAVERS. Kate! Do you believe me?

KATE. Yes.

TRAVERS. [*Pleading.*] In self-defence—they were ten—ten to one.

KATE. You are bleeding!

TRAVERS. [*Covers hand.*] The window cut me—give me a drink—I'm parching. [*She gets water in a dipper from bucket on bench.* TRAVERS *drinks with the tin rattling on his teeth. Noise of a galloping horse passes. He drops the dipper.*] I don't think they saw me come in here.

KATE. Why did you come?

TRAVERS. Where else? I ran—turned every corner till I lost them. If I can hide or get a horse!

KATE. [*Doubting him.*] Why did they try to arrest you?

TRAVERS. I—I don't know, Kate—some mistake.

KATE. They said the express robbery.

TRAVERS. It isn't so—

KATE. [*Goes to table and leans on it with her back to* TRAVERS.] Ah!

TRAVERS. Kate, [*Pause.*] Kate, [*Pause.*] you must believe me! Why should I be here [*Pause.*] in this little town—

KATE. Why did you shoot?

TRAVERS. I had to—they would have killed me—it is all a mistake—Kate, *Kate*—

KATE. What shall we do?

TRAVERS. If I had a horse—

KATE. But why?

TRAVERS. Listen!

There is again the sound of approaching hoofs.

KATE. Some one is coming—[*He turns at bay.*] No—I couldn't stand it—go in here—[*Opens closet.*] Quick!

TRAVERS. Yes! [*He enters the closet—she closes the door of the closet and throws open the street door; goes to table.*

JIM *rides into view and drops from his horse.*

JIM. [*In door.*] Hello?

KATE. [*Behind table.*] Well?

JIM. [*After looking slowly about.*] Where is he?

KATE. I—I—where is who?

JIM. [*In a matter of course way.*] Travers.

KATE. Why, how should I know?

JIM. Then why don't you jes' say you don't know?

KATE. [*Behind chair.*] Well, then, I don't know.

JIM. [*Shaking his head.*] Too late now.

KATE. Too late?

JIM. Yes—if it'd been all right, you wouldn't a-tried to dodge me.

KATE. [*Near melodeon.*] You may think as you choose.

JIM. [*Pause.*] I'm awful sorry for you, Kate.

KATE. Oh, you needn't be.

JIM. [*On the "qui vive."*] But I want to see Mr. Travers.

KATE. [*In distress.*] You—you annoy me very much. [*Sits left of table.*

JIM. [*In real tenderness.*] Why, Kate—Katie—see here—I'm your friend—they ain't anybody in the world feels as bad for you as I do—but be reasonable—it's only a question of time. I s'pose every man in Bowlin' Green that owns a gun or a bowie knife's collectin' up there at the Court House—your own pa and Dave—they'll be back here after a while—and what then?—don't you see?

KATE. It's horrible—don't tell me it is duty makes them hunt a fellow-man like that. [*Rises.*

JIM. I don't pretend to know anything about that—[*Pause. Picks up dipper; looks at* KATE.] Poor chap—thirsty—oh, well—that's your business, Kate. [*Puts dipper on the bench.*

KATE. [*At bay herself.*] You're not a man, Jim Radburn, you're a bloodhound—you *hunt* men.

JIM. Yes! [*Pause.*

KATE. Yes. [*End of rocker-chair.*

JIM. See here, Kate—I want a word or two with Mr. Travers. I think the honestest thing he ever done was liking you—I—

KATE. [*Fiercely.*] And that is why you *hate* him! You think he likes *me!* You think if it hadn't been for *him* I might have liked *you!* Well, I do like him—[*Pause.*] that's why you hunt him! It isn't your duty prompts you—it's your jealousy!

JIM. [*A pause in which he decides the question.*] He's in that closet.

KATE. [*Turning.*] He is not.

JIM. [*Straddling a chair and facing closet. Speaks in ordinary tone.*] Travers, *come out.* If you don't come out, I'll shoot through the door.

TRAVERS. [*Bursting from closet and levelling pistol.*] Throw up your hands!

JIM. [*Pause. In fateful monotone.*] You're a damn fool! The sound of a gun now would fill both them streets with pitchforks.

KATE. Don't—don't—shoot.

JIM. Oh, he won't!

TRAVERS. Do you think you can arrest me—alive?

JIM. It don't make no difference to me.

KATE. [*Anxiously pleading.*] If you are innocent, Mr. Travers—if you have acted in self-defence—

JIM. Wait, Kate—we ain't got time to *try* him now. *He* ain't got time; the boys are waiting up at the Court House. Mr. Travers, this young lady likes you—very much. [*He slowly rises.*

TRAVERS. [*Still covering him.*] I know the cause of your hatred, Mr. Radburn—I know you are here because I love her.

JIM. No, I'm here because *she* likes *you*—if she didn't like you 'twouldn't make any difference to me how quick we came to terms; but she likes you—your Pinkerton friend—[*Pause. Indicating neck.*] dead—the boys are up at the Court House. Clark is pretty hot about them Jumbo bottles, and they wouldn't be reasonable—my hoss is standing at the door—with anything like a fair start he can hold his own—Louisiana town is eleven miles away, and jist across from that is Illinois—and then you'll have to look out for yourself—now go!

KATE. [*With emotional appreciation.*] Jim!

JIM. [*With a restraining gesture.*] Never mind, Kate.

TRAVERS. You tell me to go?

JIM. [*Pause.*] Yes.

TRAVERS. Why, there's ten thousand dollars' reward—

JIM. For the man that—went—in—that—car—but you ain't that man.

TRAVERS. On your horse?

JIM. Yes.

TRAVERS. Kate—[*Starts toward her.*

KATE. [*Shrinking.*] Oh—h!

TRAVERS. [*Holds out hand.*] Jim Radburn!

JIM. No—I give you my horse, but I'm *damned* if I shake hands with you—!!

Exit TRAVERS. KATE *sinks in chair sobbing.* JIM *in doorway regards her tenderly.*

CURTAIN.

ACT IV.

SCENE. *Exterior of* JIM RADBURN'S *cabin-front, stoop and steps showing. Rail-fence partly broken down is across the stage at right and continues in painting on the panorama back-drop of rough country with stacks of cord wood. Many stumps showing. A mud road winds into the distance, a stile crosses fence.*

DISCOVERED. JIM *on step with pencil and queer note-paper, writing on a piece of broken board.*

JIM. Hello! Dropped my pencil. [*Picks it up.*] Of course fell on the "buttered side," an' I've got to whittle it agin. [*Takes enormous knife from his pocket and opens it.*

Enter EM'LY, *with milk-pails filled.*

EM'LY. Say, Jim—

JIM. [*Whets knife on boot.*] Well?

EM'LY. You let the pony out?

JIM. [*Sharpens pencil.*] No.

EM'LY. Ain't in his stall.

JIM. I know. [EM'LY *looks at* JIM *a moment and exits back of house. Looking at paper.*] I reckon that's right—Mayor and City Council—[*Writes—first wetting pencil in his mouth.*] Huh—I s'pose I ought to write it in ink—dog gone it—[*Writing through his speech.*] If it wasn't for Em'ly I wouldn't care—not a damn—[*Looks up.*] I wonder whether it's U. G. or E. G. [*Writes.*] I'll jus' kinder round off the top an' play it both ways. "Resignation," and after that, why they kin see me personally.

Re-enter EM'LY, *with pails empty.* EM'LY *sings.*

EM'LY. [*Pause.*] Who did let him out?

JIM. Who?

EM'LY. Pony.

JIM. Me.

EM'LY. Why, I thought you said you didn't.

JIM. Well, not to pasture; I give him to a feller.

EM'LY. [*Surprised.*] Give him?

JIM. Yes.

EM'LY. Why?

JIM. [*With meaning.*] He needed him awful bad. [*Writes.*

EM'LY *stands looking at him a moment; then turns to go.*

EM'LY. Say! [*Puts pails down.*

JIM. What?

EM'LY. Here comes Sam.

JIM. [*Writing and not looking up.*] Bully!

EM'LY. You want him?

JIM. No, but I reckon you will.

EM'LY. [*Smiling.*] Git out.

JIM. [*Writing.*] "P. S. This goes into effect from last night, and is a copy—Joe Vernon has the original document."

EM'LY. [*On the stile. Looking off.*] Hello!

SAM. [*Off.*] Hello!

Enter SAM.

EM'LY. Awful glad.

SAM. Hello, Jim.

JIM. Hello, Sam.

SAM. Know where your pony is?

JIM. Gone East.

SAM. He's in Louisiana.

JIM. Who's got him?

SAM. Why, ain't you heard?

JIM. Ain't heard nothing this morning.

EM'LY. What?

SAM. [*To* JIM.] Travers stole him. [*To* EMILY.] Stole Jim's pony after shootin' the Pinkerton.

EM'LY. Why, Jim—

JIM. Never mind, Em'ly. [*To* SAM.] Who told *you?*

SAM. The fellers. You know Travers was—er—

EM'LY. The train-robber—yes, you told us last night that—

SAM. Yes, but I mean you know he was—killed?

JIM. [*Rising. With some interest.*] Killed? When?

SAM. Last night—didn't you know?

JIM. No.

SAM. [*Puzzled.*] Why, I thought you did—why, the fellers said—why, dog gone it, they were blamed funny about it—they said, "Oh, I reckon Jim knows"—then stuck their tongues this way in their jaw—I thought maybe—[*Pantomimes pulling trigger.*

JIM. No, hadn't even heard of it.

SAM. Going to run an extra this morning—over a dozen goin' down just to see. Thought maybe Em'ly 'd like to go 'long and take a look at the remains.

EM'LY. [*Eagerly.*] Jim!

JIM. You're going, are you, Sam?

SAM. Why, calculated to.

JIM. Well, I wish you'd stay home this mornin' and kind a look after Em'ly.

SAM. Certainly.

JIM. I'm goin' to be pretty busy, I think, eh?

SAM. [*Willing to stay.*] Sure.

Exit JIM *into house.*

EM'LY. Something's worrying Jim. [*Crosses to porch.*

SAM. I guess this fellow's getting away last night.

EM'LY. No, something else. The operator waked me up after twelve o'clock with a telegram—an' Jim answered it, and then got up and dressed himself, and took both his guns and sat out on the porch here—oh, for an hour.

SAM. Telegrams, eh?

EM'LY. Yes.

SAM. Well, I guess some other robbery or something. A sheriff has so much of that.

EM'LY. I know. But Jim's worried.

SAM. Well, I couldn't sleep myself last night.

EM'LY. Me neither. After you left here, and a-telling me about it, it seemed I could see Travers shooting the man's neck every time I closed my eyes.

SAM. He's a good deal better this morning.

EM'LY. Who?

SAM. The Pinkerton that was shot.

Em'ly. The Pinkerton?

SAM. Yes.

EM'LY. I thought he was dead.

SAM. Oh, that's what Clark said—but the other doctor turned him over and got him breathing again.

EM'LY. I'm so glad—poor fellow—and Jim kicked him so yesterday—clean across that stile.

SAM. When he come here?

EM'LY. Yes, with that letter.

SAM. Speakin' of letters, I got one myself this morning.

EM'LY. [*Gets letter from pocket.*] Who from?

SAM. Looks like a girl wrote it.

EM'LY. What!

SAM. It's in typewritin' an' so I guess a girl did write it—but its from the company.

EM'LY. More mean things?

SAM. Nicer than pie. See *here*. [*Reads:*] "*And regretting deeply our error, we of course cannot deal with any lawyer, but would be pleased with a personal call from you—your salary awaits you for the time you have been absent—*"

EM'LY. [*Indignantly.*] Been absent!

SAM. And they having me locked up in a hotel.

EM'LY. I should say so.

SAM. [*Reading:*]—"*been absent. And we can guarantee your regular employment in our offices here or at any other station you may prefer. Yours very truly, etc.,—Superintendent.*"

EM'LY. Well, what do you think?

SAM. Not much—Bollinger says we can get twenty thousand dollars.

EM'LY. I know—that's what he told Jim too—he wanted us to put off the wedding.

SAM. Jim?

EM'LY. No—Bollinger—

SAM. Why?

EM'LY. He said it would make a stronger case.

SAM. [*Resenting the idea.*] Well, see here, Em'ly—

EM'LY. I'm only telling you what Bollinger said.

SAM. Put off our wedding?

EM'LY. He said for about two months.

SAM. What's he take me for?

EM'LY. Jim heard him.

SAM. What did Jim say?

EM'LY. He said—why, he said that was about ten thousand a month, just for waiting.

SAM. No, sir-ee.

EM'LY. An' Bollinger, tryin' to encourage me, said he'd let his wife go that long for half the money.

SAM. Well, do you think it's right?

EM'LY. What?

SAM. Why, this postponing for damages.

EM'LY. Not if you don't—only Bollinger said it wouldn't hurt any to wait.

SAM. See here, Em'ly—seems to me you ain't any too anxious you'self.

EM'LY. Well, how can a girl be, Sam—I can't just up and say I won't wait—especially when they're your damages—I haven't got any right to say I'm worth ten thousand dollars a month.

SAM. [*Embracing her.*] Well, you bet your life you are.

EM'LY. [*Acquiescing.*] Well—

Enter DAVE *and* LIZBETH.

DAVE. Hello, Sam.

SAM. Hello.

LIZBETH. [*Pleased with the example of* SAM *and* EM'LY.] Dave!

EM'LY. Why, how do you do?

DAVE. Where's Jim?

SAM. In the house.

LIZBETH. Isn't it awful, Em'ly. [*She and* EM'LY *go to the little porch.*

SAM. What's the matter?

DAVE. People don't understand it.

SAM. What do you mean?

DAVE. Why, Jim; lots of 'em thinks he did it.

SAM. Did what? Shoot Travers?

DAVE. No, give him that horse—

SAM. *Give* to him? Git out.

DAVE. Well, you bet they said so, and Bollinger and Sarber and Cal and lots of them think so.

SAM. [*Astonished.*] Git out!

DAVE. Yes, sir-ee.

SAM. They better not say that to me.

DAVE. Why, they'd say it to Jim—you ought to hear them talking at the convention—

SAM. Is this the day of the convention?

DAVE. 'Tain't come to order yit, but they're all up to the Court House,—one feller nailed the telegrams on a bulletin where everybody could read them.

SAM. What telegrams?

DAVE. Why, Jim's.

Enter JIM *from house.*

JIM. Mornin', Lizbeth.

LIZBETH. How de do, Jim.

JIM. Kate feelin' all right?

LIZBETH. Well; you know—

JIM. Oh, yes—natural enough—ain't you workin', Dave?

DAVE. Convention.

JIM. Sure. Forgot the convention.

DAVE. Me and Lizbeth come together because we thought Sam and Em'ly'd stand up with us.

JIM. At the Squire's?

DAVE. No, preacher's.

JIM. I reckon. [*Looks at* EM'LY.

EM'LY. Of course.

JIM. Convention ain't met?

DAVE. Not yit.

JIM. I think I'll go down to the Court House. [*Starts down and stops as he reaches the stile.*] Hello!

SAM. What's up?

JIM. Nothing'—some o' the boys—comin' here, I expect—Say!

SAM. What?

JIM. I mean Dave.

DAVE. How's that?

JIM. Will you do me a favour?

DAVE. Certainly.

JIM. [*Pointing off right.*] This letter—give it to the Mayor, or any of the Council—some of them's sure to be at the convention.

DAVE. All right. [*He goes onto the stile and stops.*] Bollinger's one, ain't he?

JIM. Yes.

DAVE. He's comin' with them fellers—

JIM. Well, give it to *him*—a little before he gits here.

DAVE. All right, Jim. [*Starts off—stops.*] No trouble, you don't reckon?

JIM. No, I reckon not.

Exit DAVE.

EM'LY. Jim!

JIM. I want you and Lizbeth to go in the house. Go on!

EM'LY. [*Going.*] What's the matter?

JIM. You go with them, Sam—and take care of 'em.

SAM. [*Joining the girls on the porch.*] Why, Jim, if there's goin' to be any trouble—

JIM. [*Watching the coming mob.*] I reckon they ain't—and anyway I want this side of the fence by myself. [*Exeunt* LIZBETH *and* EM'LY *to house.*] Take 'em way back to the kitchen.

SAM. [*At the door.*] All right?

JIM. Dead sure.

Exit SAM. JIM *removes his paper collar—adjusts the two guns under his coat-tails—takes a chew of tobacco, and fatefully waits. Enter back of fence,* BOLLINGER, SARBER, CAL, ESROM, DAVE, *and* SUPERS; DAVE *drifts away from them to left.* ESROM *playing jew's-harp. All enter when* JIM *gets through his preparations and leans against porch.*

BOLLINGER. [*Loudly.*] Here, stop the band.

SARBER. Stop her.

ESROM *is silent.*

BOLLINGER. [*Pause.*] Hello, Jim. [*His tone carries a nagging insinuation.*

JIM. Hello.

DAVE. I'll tell the old man, Jim. [*Going.*

JIM. Oh, no hurry, Dave.

Exit DAVE.

BOLLINGER. Well, they killed our friend down at Louisiana last night. [JIM *chews and nods once.*] Where's your pony?

JIM. [*After pause.*] Have you looked in the stable?

BOLLINGER. [*Sneering.*] No.

JIM. Well, don't.

BOLLINGER. Didn't calculate to, Jim. [*Pause.*] You know what that fellow said before they shot him.

JIM. [*Shakes his head.*] No.

SARBER. [*In quarrelsome bawl. Pointing at* JIM.] Why, he said—

BOLLINGER. [*Maintaining his leadership.*] Hold on! it was understood I was to do the talkin'.

ALL. Go on! Shut up, Sarber!

SARBER. He was takin' all day fur it.

BOLLINGER. [*Clashing.*] I'll take as long as I damn please, and I'll have the nigger play tunes between times if I want to—

ALL. Go on, Bollinger!

BOLLINGER. [*Resuming his nag of* JIM.] Know what he said?

JIM. [*Pause. Chews and shakes head.*] Don't care.

BOLLINGER. He said you *give* him the pony.

JIM. You *hear* him say so?

BOLLINGER. No, but the boys down Louisiana did; they knowed it was your pony, and they arrested him.

SARBER. [*Again intruding.*] Then they telegraphed you—

BOLLINGER. Hold on! [*Growl from* MOB.] They didn't know he was the train-robber—only thought he was a hoss thief—so they held him while they telegraphed you—[JIM *nods. Pause.*] That's the way we got on to him—the operator showed us the message—[*Pause.* JIM *nods.*] Showed us your answer, too. [*Pause.* JIM *nods.*] Here's a copy of it marked Exhibit B. "The man tells the truth. The pony is his'n.—Jim Radburn."

SARBER. And we saw the original.

JIM *nods.*

BOLLINGER. [*His anger now lifting his tone into police court tirade.*] While we were waiting up at the Court House where you told us to go—and I didn't have a durn thing but a butcher knife—you were a-standin' in with this feller and a-givin' him your hoss to git away on.

SARBER. [*In same manner.*] And durn good reason—Sam Fowler stood in with him, an' he's a-goin' to marry your sister—in the house now—I kin see him at the kitchen window. [*All growl, and half start over the stile toward kitchen.*

JIM. [*With sudden vehemence.*] Hold on! [*Impressive pause; and quiet by* CROWD.] You better talk it over with me first.

BOLLINGER. Well, you give him the pony, didn't you? [JIM *is silent.*] *Didn't* you?

JIM. What's that to you?

BOLLINGER. [*Half laughing.*] Well—what is it to us—

All laugh derisively.

ESROM. [*Emboldened to participate.*] I knew 'twasn't no clinker in de coke, 'cause he frowed de mud in it and—

BOLLINGER. Shoot that nigger.

SARBER. Shut up! [*Smashes* NIGGER *in the mouth.*

BOLLINGER. [*To* JIM.] Well, say—[*Pause.*] That was a fine way for a sheriff to do,—wasn't it?

JIM. I've resigned.

BOLLINGER. I got your letter. You hadn't resigned last night; you know there's a law for you, Mr. Radburn.

JIM. That's all right.

BOLLINGER. *You'll* have to "do time."

JIM. [*Smiling.*] When?

BOLLINGER. This session—you git a taste of the jug this morning.

JIM. Not this morning!

BOLLINGER. Well, we'll see—you go with us.

Murmur and start.

JIM. [*Again in sudden warning.*] Hold on, boys—[*Pause and recovery of calm.*] I claim everything this side of the fence. Now I know it ain't sociable, but I don't want you to come in. Whenever the District Attorney gits his witnesses together, I'll be there, but I won't go this mornin'—[*Pause.*] and *anyhow* I won't go with such a mangy lot of heelers as you've scraped up this trip.

BOLLINGER. I reckon you will, Jim.

Murmur and movement.

JIM. Hold on—[*Pause, with both hands on guns.*] I don't want to break my record, but I'll have to do it if you trespass on the lawn.

BOLLINGER. [*Discreetly on stile. After a pause.*] I hope you don't think we're scared, Jim?

JIM. No—ain't anything to be scared about, Tom—as long as you stay outside.—Keep off the grass.

BOLLINGER. [*His irritation returning. Threateningly.*] And don't you dare to draw a gun on any of us. Say, Sarber—go down to the Court House and git a warrant. If you had a warrant we could walk right in.

MRS. VERNON. [*Off.*] Now, Kate, be careful.

Enter KATE *and* MRS. VERNON *over the stile—the* MOB *parting to admit them.*

KATE. What is the matter? Jim!

JIM. Won't you come in? Howdy, Mrs. Vernon?

KATE *and* MRS. VERNON *come on.*

KATE. [*Anxiously. To* JIM.] What do these men want? [*To* BOLLINGER.] What is the trouble here?

BOLLINGER. [*Pointing at* JIM.] Malfeasance.

KATE. What?

BOLLINGER. Why, Miss Kate, he gave his horse to a man he ought to have arrested—a train-robber—a murderer—and—

JIM. Hold on, Bollinger—man's dead, and he used to be a friend to these ladies.

KATE. [*Crosses to the* MEN.] No—do not speak of him—we thought he was a friend—but why do you accuse Mr. Radburn?

JIM. No use talkin', Kate, they know.

BOLLINGER. You bet.

JIM. Lizbeth's inside—you an' Kate better go in, Mrs. Vernon.

KATE. No. Do you blame this man?

BOLLINGER. Blame him! Why, he's an accessory after the fact, and maybe before—I don't see how he can git out of it! Here's his telegram, really better than a plea of guilty—we ought to arrest him!

KATE. [*To* BOLLINGER.] He is not guilty. [*To* JIM.] Oh, Jim, Jim! Can you forgive me? [*She extends her hand.*

JIM. [*Taking her hand.*] Why, Kate, 'tain't none o' their business.

KATE. No, it is all mine. [*Murmur from* CROWD.—*To the* MEN.] Listen; all of you must know that Mr. Travers was attentive to me—I believed he was a gentleman—we thought he was a friend—[*Half crying.*] but he never was half the friend—never *could* be half the friend that Jim Radburn's been—

JIM. [*Expostulating.*] Kate!

KATE. [*To* JIM.] Yes, I know all about it now—my father has told me all—everything about my college days—I am humiliated to the dust.

JIM. Now, Kate—

KATE. You should have told me in the shop, when I presumed to speak of your disadvantages.

JIM. [*To* MEN.] See here—this is a little matter between me and Kate Vernon—none of your business—so why don't you saunter off? [MEN *start to go.*

KATE. [*To the* MEN.] No, I want them to stay. I have nothing to say of Mr. Travers' doings—we were mistaken—but Jim Radburn thought I cared for the man, and he was big enough to let him escape for *me*—I am the one at fault—he has almost given up his life to me. You, Col. Bollinger, and every one knows that he could win his nomination if he wanted to—[*Turning to* JIM.]—But he gave that up, too, because Joe Vernon, my father, wants it. Oh, Jim! Jim! [*Sinks on steps, sobbing.*

MRS. VERNON. [*Crosses to her.*] There, Kate, I knowed it would be too much fur you. [*To* JIM.] She's took on this way since daylight.

JIM. Say, you fellers ain't got spunk enough to keep hoss flies off a you. What do you want? Cold victuals?

BOLLINGER. Come on, fellers—[*The* MEN *start off.*] hold on, here's Joe. [MEN *return.*

MRS. VERNON. Joe Vernon!

Enter JOE *and* DAVE.

JOE. What's the matter, Jim? ain't nobody hurt? Why, Kate—

JIM. You made a pretty mess of it, ain't you?

JOE. What?

JIM. [*Pointing to* KATE.] Tellin' everything.

JOE. Well, that ain't all of it.

JIM. What ain't?

JOE. Why, they put them blamed telegrams up at the convention—I didn't see them till the fust ballot was over, and they'd nominated *me*—

MRS. VERNON. For Jefferson, Joe?

JOE. [*In great excitement.*] Yes, for the Legislature.

Cheers from CROWD.

JIM. There, Kate, do you hear that? Now, what's the use cryin'?

JOE. And I made a speech—

MRS. VERNON. Git out.

JOE. Git out yourself—

MRS. VERNON. Say, your pa's been nominated, and made a speech!

JOE. Well, lemme tell you—

JIM. Well, never mind the speech, Joe—you're as good as elected anyhow.

JOE. And you done every bit of it—why, I took them blamed telegrams, and I told that convention everything I knew. Everything Kate told me—about your getting off the track 'cause you liked her. Tom, you told me yourself that Jim wasn't makin' no canvass fur the nomination. Do you know why? 'Cause he liked my Kate. Last night he gimme his resignation as sheriff. Do you know why?

BOLLINGER. Afore he give him the hoss?

JOE. Long before—and Jim Radburn, I believe you knowed then who that feller was, and I told the convention so. He did give Travers the hoss, and then I said, "He give up his pony to this feller 'cause he didn't have the heart to make Kate feel bad" —and I said—"What's Mizzoura—what's Pike County comin' to if we kin persecute a man like that," and, by golly, they jus' stood on their hind legs and hollered fur you!

BOLLINGER. I'm a-comin' inside myself if he pulls both guns. [*Comes over the stile.*

JIM. Why, Tom.

They shake hands.

JOE. An' they're up there now, like a pack of howlin' idiots, unanimously re-electing you sheriff by acclamation, and "Vivy Vochy," over and over agin.

JIM. There, there, Kate—you're goin' to Jefferson soon—an' you kin forgit all about it.

KATE. I don't want to go to Jefferson, Jim—I don't want to—forget it. [*Turns, weeps on* JOE'S *breast.*

MRS. VERNON. Now, talk to her, Jim!

JIM. Not now—she feels too bad.

MRS. VERNON. But she'll get over that—she's comin' to her senses, an' *she knows she likes you.* Talk to her.

JIM. Some other time.

CURTAIN.

THE MOTH AND THE FLAME

Clyde Fitch

CLYDE FITCH

(1865–1909)

Clyde Fitch brought a vivacity to the American stage that no other American playwright has thus far succeeded in emulating. The total impression of his work leads one to believe that he also brought to the American stage a style which was at the same time literary and distinctly his own. His personality was interesting and lovable, quickly responsive to a variety of human nature. No play of his was ever wholly worthless, because of that personal equation which lent youth and spontaneity to much of his dialogue. When he attained popular fame, he threw off his dramas—whether original or adapted from the French and German—with a rapidity and ease that did much to create a false impression as to his haste and casualness. But Fitch, though a nervously quick worker, was never careless. He pondered his dramas long, he carried his characters in mind for years, he almost memorized his dialogue before he set it down on paper. And if he wrote in his little note-books with the same staccato speed that an artist sketches, it was merely because he saw the picture vividly, and because the preliminaries had been done beforehand.

The present Editor was privileged to know Fitch as a friend. And to be taken into the magic circle was to be given freely of that personal equation which made his plays so personal. This association was begun over a negative criticism of a play. An invitation followed to come and talk it over in his Fortieth Street study, the same room which—decorations, furniture, books and all—was bequeathed to Amherst College, and practically reproduces there the Fitchean flavour.

I have seen Clyde Fitch on many diverse occasions. Through incisive comment on people, contemporary manners, and plays, which was let drop in conversation, I was able to estimate the natural tendency of Fitch's mind. His interest was never concerned solely with dominant characters; he was quick rather to sense the idiosyncrasies of the average person. His observation was caught by the seemingly unimportant, but no less identifying peculiarities of the middle class. Besides which, his irony was never more happy than when aimed against that social set which he knew, and good-humouredly satirized.

To know Clyde Fitch intimately—no matter for how short a while—was to be put in possession of his real self. From early years, he showed the same tendencies which later developed more fully, but were not different. Success gave him the money to gratify his tastes for *objets d'art*, which he used to calculate closely to satisfy in the days when "Beau Brummell" and "Frédéric Lemaître" gave hint of his dramatic talent. He was a man of deep sentiment, shown to his friends by the countless graceful acts as host, and shown to his players. As soon as a Fitch play began to be a commodity, coveted by the theatrical manager, he nearly always had personal control of its production, and could dictate who should be in his casts. No dramatist has left behind him more profoundly pleasing memories of artistic association than Clyde Fitch. The names of his plays form a roster of stage associations—the identification of "Beau Brummell" with Richard Mansfield; of "Nathan Hale" with N. C. Goodwin; of "Barbara Frietchie" with Julia Marlowe; of "The Climbers" with Amelia Bingham; of "The Stubbornness of Geraldine" with Mary Mannering; of "The Truth" and "The Girl With Green Eyes" with Clara Bloodgood—to mention a few instances. Those who recall happy hours spent with Fitch at his country homes—either at "Quiet Corner," Greenwich, Connecticut, or at "The Other House," Katonah, New York, have vivid memory of his pervasive cordiality. His players, likewise, those whose identifying talent caught his fancy, had the same care and attention paid them in his playwriting. Sometimes, it may be, this graciousness of his made him cut his cloth to suit the figure. "Beau Brummell" was the very mold and fashion of Mansfield: but that was *Brummell's* fault and Mansfield's genius, to which was added the adaptability of Fitch. But there are no seams or patches to "Captain Jinks of the Horse Marines"—its freshness caught the freshness of Ethel Barrymore, and Fitch was confident of the blend. His eye was unerring as to stage effect, and he would go to all ends of trouble, partly for sentiment, partly for accuracy, and always for novelty, to create the desired results. Did he not, with his own hands, wire the apple-blossoms for the orchard scene in "Lovers' Lane?" Was he not careful to get the right colour for the dawn in "Nathan Hale," and the Southern evening atmosphere in "Barbara Frietchie?" And in such a play as "Girls," did he not delight in the accessories, like the clatter of the steam-pipe radiator, for particular New York environment which he knew so graphically how to portray?

That was the boy—the Peter Pan quality—in Clyde Fitch; it was not his love for the trivial, for he could be serious in the midst of it. His temperament in playwriting was as variable as Spring weather—it was extravagant in its responsiveness to the momentary mood. He would suggest a whole play in one scene; a real flash of philosophy or of psychology would be lost in the midst of a slight play on words for the sake of a laugh. One finds that often the case in "A Happy Marriage." He was never more at home than when squeezing all the human traits and humour out of a given situation, which was subsidiary to the plot, yet in atmosphere complete in itself. The *Hunter's* drawing-room just after the funeral, in "The Climbers;" the church scene in "The Moth and the Flame," which for jocularity and small points is the equal of Langdon Mitchell's wedding scene in "The New York Idea," though not so sharply incisive in its satire; the deck on board ship in "The Stubbornness of Geraldine" (so beautifully burlesqued by Weber and Fields as "The Stickiness of Gelatine"); and *Mr. Roland's* rooms in *Mrs. Crespigny's* flat, which almost upset, in its humourous bad taste, the tragedy of "The Truth"—these are instances of his unusual vein. One finds it is by these fine points, these obvious clevernesses that Fitch paved the way to popular success. But there was far more to him than this—there was the literary sense which gave one the feeling of reality in his plays—not alone because of novelty or familiarity of scene, but because of the uttered word.

Human foibles and frailties were, therefore, his specialty. Out of his vast product of playwriting, one remembers stories and scenes, rather than personages; one recalls characteristics rather than characters; one treasures quick interplay of words rather than the close reason for such. Because of that, some are right in attributing to him a feminine quickness of observation, or rather a minute observation for the feminine. That is why he determined, in "The City," to dispel the illusion that he could not write a man's play, or draw masculine characters. Yet was not *Sam Coast*, in "Her Own Way," almost the equal of *Georgiana Carley?*

I recall, one midnight—the week before Mr. Fitch sailed on his last trip to Europe—he read me "The City," two acts of which were in their final shape, the third in process of completion. There used to be a superstition among the managers to the effect that if you ever wished to consider a play by Fitch, he must be kept from reading it himself; for if he did, you would accept it on the spot. All the horror of that powerful arraignment of city life, and the equally powerful criticism of country life, was brought out on this evening we were together, and I was able to see just where, as a stage director, Clyde Fitch must have been the mainstay at rehearsals. He never lived to give the final touches to his manuscript of "The City,"—touches which always meant so much to him; he was dead by the time rehearsals were called, and there slipped from the performance some of the significant atmosphere he described to me.

There comes vividly to my mind his questions after the reading—trying out his effects on me, so to speak. Rapidly he reviewed the work on the third act he had planned for the morrow, consulting with me as though suddenly I had become a collaborator. In such a way he must have planned with Mansfield over *Brummell;* thus he may have worked with Julia Marlowe, telling her some of the romantic incidents he had drawn from his mother's own Maryland love story for "Barbara Frietchie." In the same naïve spirit, he consulted, by letter, with Arthur Byron for his "stardom" in "Major André"— which waned so soon after the first night.

Everything about the room that evening he read "The City" bore evidence of the playwright's personality. The paintings and bric-à-brac, the books—mostly biography and letters—the tapestries which seemed to blend with the bowls of flowers and furniture of French design, the windows looking out on lawns, gardens, and a pond with swans upon it, the moonlight on the Cupids that kept guard at intervals along the top of a snakelike stone fence—and Fitch, vital, happy in his work, happy in his friends, happy in life, as he had planned to live it in the years to come. And death waiting him across the water!

"Beau Brummell" began Clyde Fitch's career as a dramatist. It was produced at the New York Madison Square Theatre, May 17, 1890. At that time he had not evinced any determination to be a dramatist—but was writing juvenile sketches for *The Churchman,* afterwards gathered in a charming volume called "The Knighting of the Twins, and Ten Other Tales" (1891). Previous to this, he had attempted "A Wave of Life"—a novel whose chief value is autobiographic. Then he showed his clever facility at dialogue in a collection of "Six Conversations and Some Correspondence;" also in "The Smart Set." But, after the success of "Brummell," followed by "Frédéric Lemaître" (December 1, 1890) for Henry Miller, a dramatic season hardly passed that Fitch was not represented on the bill-boards by two or three comedies. It was very rarely that he rewrote his dramas under new titles; it was unusual for him to use over again material previously exploited. Exceptions to this were in the cases of "The Harvest," a one-act sketch given by the New York Theatre of Arts and Letters (January 26, 1893), afterwards (April 11, 1898) included as an act of "The Moth and the Flame;" "Mistress Betty" (October 15, 1895), for Mme. Modjeska, afterwards revamped as "The Toast of the Town" (November 27, 1905) for Viola Allen. Interest in the period of Beau Brummell stretched over into "The Last of the Dandies" for Beerbohm Tree. But otherwise the bulk of his work came each season as a Fitch novelty. He often played against himself, the popularity of one play killing the chances of the other. For instance, when "Lovers' Lane" opened in New York, there were also running "Captain Jinks of the Horse Marines," "Barbara Frietchie" and "The Climbers." When "The Cowboy and the Lady" was given in Philadelphia, "Nathan Hale" beat it in box-office receipts, and Fitch wrote to a friend: "If any play is going to beat it, I'd rather it was one of mine, eh?"

By the time he was ready to write "The Moth and the Flame," Fitch had won distinction with a variety of picturesque pieces, like "His Grace de Grammont," for Otis Skinner, and "Nathan Hale," for Goodwin and Maxine Elliott. It may be said to have come just when his vivacity was on the increase, for touches in it gave foretaste of his later society dramas, and showed his planning, in the manner of the French, for excellent theatrical effect. He was to become more expert in the use of materials, but no whit less clever in his expansion of "small talk" and society shallowness.

"The Harvest" is an early example of Fitch's method of workmanship. It was carefully planned and quickly written; in fact, it was set down on paper while Fitch was on the four o'clock train between New York and Boston; his motive was to show the dangerous power and fascination of a clever, dissipated, attractive man-of-the-world on a young girl, who, in her innocence, does not understand the warnings given her on all sides. The idea grew in his mind, and this growth resulted in "The Moth and the Flame," which entered more fully into the "fast" life of a man about town, and the dangerous ignorance of the society girl. Fitch loved to sketch the smart woman, like *Mrs. Lorrimer*, who, as someone has said, is frivolously constituted, but sharply witty and with some depth of heart. The fancy-dress party scene is autobiographic, he having attended such an occasion at Carroll Beckwith's studio, in New York. In technique, this scene is comparable with the one of similar gaiety in "Lord and Lady Algy"—both having an undercurrent of serious strain. The tragedy motive is relieved at almost calculated times by comedy, which shows that Fitch held to the old dramatic theory of comic relief. Often this was irritating, discounting the mood he was trying to maintain. He was not as skilful in the use of these varying elements as Pinero, with whom he might be compared—not for strength of characterization, for fullness of story or for the sheer art of interest, but for creative vitality and variety, as well as for literary feeling in the use of materials. But more important than all these was his desire to be true to the materials he had selected. On this subject he always had much to say, and his comments about Truth in the theatre comprise an enlightening exposition of his dramatic theory. This it is well to examine. In 1901, he adapted, from the French, "Sapho"—to the production of which was attached some unpleasant notoriety—and "The Marriage Game." And of these he wrote (in *Harper's Weekly*), in response to current criticism, as follows:

It is only fair to myself and to my work done on the two plays to say that my intention and desire in both instances were to be faithful to the French original, and to have the outcome a resultant moral—to the good. To put it mildly, I do not seem to have created that impression exactly in the minds of the public. From their verdict and yours I have picked myself up, pulled myself together, and realized my failure. I had thought I was taking a building from one country and rebuilding it in another with the same stones, but I discovered I had apparently pulled down one structure and raised no other. Believe me, no one regretted this more than I. But I think I have finally learned my lesson. I have learned another thing that I can't do, and I have added it to the list of things I sha'n't try to do. What I *am* trying to do is to reflect life of all kinds as I see it. To write, first, plays that will interest and mean something; and, after that, amuse. I would rather entertain everybody than one body.

And always and in any case with a result to the good. I am trying especially to reflect our own life of the present, and to get into the heart of the pictures made by the past. To do this I do not consider any detail too small, so long as it is not boring. Nor any method wrong which I feel to be true. I am naturally not always believed in, and I do not always make myself clear. Sometimes I think I am misunderstood through laziness. To give one instance, of one or the other: in a recent play of mine, 'The Climbers', something which I meant to be psychologically true was taken to be a theatrical trick. A man who was dishonest in business, but who loved his wife with the really strong love that such weak natures are capable of, is asked to look that wife in the face and, before a group of angry friends and relatives, confess the extent of his crime, his disgrace! I felt, and I still feel, the man couldn't look into his wife's eyes and say the whole ugly truth. And doubly he couldn't with the to him cruel environment of the outraged circle holding back the sympathy of his wife from him. He would feel and cry out to her, 'Let me tell you alone, if I must tell it, and *in the dark, in the dark!*' when he could not see the heart-breaking shame grow upon her face, nor see his own guilty face reflected in her eyes. The end of this sentence he would reiterate, grasping it, too, on the impulse, as a means to put off the ordeal. 'In the dark,—later in the dark', he would tell her everything. But there is no time to be lost if a public scandal is to be averted. The worst must be known at once. The chief friend of them all is there. It is he who is to fight hardest to save them. He knows the house well, and besides he has seen that very evening, after dinner, the lights turned on by the servant with the electric lever. He stands beside this lever. He quickly seizes the last sentence of the cornered guilty man, and, before the latter can think or retract, cries: 'Tell it in the dark, then!' and plunges the room in darkness. The natural impulse of that defaulter under those circumstances would be to blurt out with it; at least so I believe. Such was his vacillating, impulsive nature. And for the same reason the attempt to escape in the dark, which was silly, futile! It was another sudden impulse; had it been otherwise, he was far too sensible to have tried it. I developed that scene by taking the place mentally, or trying to, of each one of the persons engaged in it. I did not start with the so-called 'dark scene'. I had no idea I was going to do what I did until I reached the moment in my writing when it had to be done—at least done that way or not at all. As it occurred to me, so it would have occurred to the friend in the play. And so it did! And knowing this evolution of the scene, I cannot think myself that it was 'a theatrical trick'. In all cases I try to paint my personages from the inside instead of the out, and to cling to human nature as both my starting-point and my goal. This is what I want to do and am trying to do—in a sentence—to tell the Truth in the Theatre. I am trying honestly, and my heart is in it. That's all, except that I am glad of your belief in me.

This frankness and sincerity were typical of Fitch's correspondence with everyone who took him seriously. He went to every pains to explain himself, and no man more gratefully acknowledged earnest attention. It was his quickness to detect in others the spark of creative appreciation that made him answer letters to perfect strangers, giving them advice as to playwriting. "I like the tone of that man's note," he once said to me. "I'll send for him; he may be a good actor."

It was not often that he wrote on the theory of his work. There is an essay by him, published in 1904, and called "The Play and the Public." It is often quoted. But a good thing bears constant repetition, and the following sounds Fitch's conviction on a fundamental belief:

I feel myself very strongly the particular value—a value which, rightly or wrongly, I can't help feeling inestimable—in a modern play of reflecting absolutely and truthfully the life and environment about us; every class, every kind, every emotion, every motive, every occupation, every business, every idleness! Never was life so varied, so complex; what a choice, then! Take what strikes you most, in the hope it will interest others. Take what suits you most to do—what perhaps you can do best—and then do it better. Be truthful, and then nothing can be too big, nothing should be too small, so long as it is here, and *there!* Apart from the question of literature, apart from the question of art, reflect the real thing with true observation and with sincere feeling for what it is and what it represents, and that is art and literature in a modern play. If you inculcate an idea in your play, so much the better for your play and for you—and for your audience. In fact, there is small hope for your play *as* a play if you haven't some small idea in it somewhere and somehow, even if it is hidden—it is sometimes better for you if it is hidden, but it must of course be integral. Some ideas are mechanical. Then they are no good. These are the ideas for which the author does all the work, instead of letting the ideas do the work for him. One should write what one sees, but observe under the surface. It is a mistake to look at the reflection of the sky in the water of theatrical convention. Instead, look up and into the sky of real life itself.

All sound advice, and a compressed manual of dramatic technique for the beginner! But Fitch had the darting eye of a migratory interest. He often didn't "follow through," as they say in golf. With the result that he is often scored for insufficient motivation. But my knowledge of him makes me realize he felt and saw deeper than his epigrammatic style indicated. His technique was therefore often threadbare in spots,—not of that even mesh which makes of Pinero such an exceptional designer. I would put Fitch's "Captain Jinks of the Horse Marines" above Edward Sheldon's "Romance" for the faithful reproduction of early New York atmosphere. I would put it by the side of Pinero's "Trelawney of the 'Wells'." But there is no play of Fitch's which, for strength, I would hold beside "The Thunderbolt." In his feminine analyses, too, he did not probe as deep as Pinero

Within a few months of his death, Fitch was asked to deliver an address on the theatre at Harvard and at Yale. He enlarged his magazine article on "The Play and the Public" for that purpose. It is now easily accessible, included in the fourth volume of the Memorial Edition of his plays. It was found among his many papers and unfinished manuscripts. There is no recent playwright whose "Life and Letters" are more worthy of preservation. I have looked through most of the materials; have seen letters descriptive of his childhood in Schenectady, New York, (he was born, May 2, 1865 in Elmira); have read accounts of his student days at Amherst, where vagaries of dress used to stir his associates to student pranks; have relished an illustrated diary he kept while tutoring in his early years of struggle, his father refusing to countenance playwriting instead of architecture. These early years were filled with the same vivacity, affection and sympathy which later made him such a rare friend. It bears repeating what has been often said before—he had a genius for friendship, and an equal genius for losing those he did not want.

Such a biography as should be written of his picturesque popularity as a playwright would mostly be autobiographic. For a letter from Fitch had rare flavour, more personal than his plays but of the same Fitchean quality. It would, as well, be a personal record of the stage, and would set at rest many myths that have floated around his name—such as William Winter wilfully circulated about "Beau Brummell."*

* Since this was written, it has been announced that a volume, "Clyde Fitch and his Letters," is being prepared by the Editors of the "Memorial Edition" of Fitch's plays.

"The Moth and the Flame" is here reproduced because it has never before been issued, and should be made available to the student of American Drama. To say that it is typically Fitchean does not mean that, in technique or in characterization, it is his best. But it is confession that whatever he wrote bore that incommunicable touch which gives him a unique position—a position no American playwright thus far has been able to usurp.

LYCEUM THEATRE. 12th Season.

NEW YORK THEATRE CO., - - - - - - - - - - - - - PROPRIETORS
DANIEL FROHMAN, - - - - - - - - - - - - - MANAGER

WEEK COMMENCING MONDAY EVENING, APRIL 11, 1898.
Evenings at 8.30. Thursday and Saturday Matinees, at 2 15.

DANIEL FROHMAN takes pleasure in presenting

THE KELCEY-SHANNON

COMPANY,

Herbert Kelcey, Effie Shannon, Wm. J. LeMoyne, Sarah Cowell LeMoyne and their organization, under the management of SAMUEL F. KINGSTON, presenting

THE MOTH AND THE FLAME

an Original Play, in Three Acts.

By CLYDE FITCH.

CAST OF CHARACTERS.

EDWARD FLETCHER ..... Mr. KELCEY
MR. DAWSON ..... Mr. WM. J. LEMOYNE
MR. WOLTON ..... Mr. E. W. THOMAS
DOUGLAS RHODES ..... Mr. BRUCE McRAE
JOHNSTONE ..... Mr. EDWARD SEE
FANSHAW ..... Mr. DAVID TORRENCE
TRIMMINS ..... Mr. EDW. H. WILKINSON
CLERGYMAN ..... Mr. SYLVESTER DEEHAN
HOWES ..... Mr. EDWIN JAMES
MARION WOLTON ..... Miss SHANNON
MRS. LORRIMER ..... Mrs. SARAH COWELL LEMOYNE
MRS WOLTON ..... Mrs. ISABEL WALDRON
JEANNETTE GROSS ..... Miss ELEANOR MORETTI
ETHEL ..... Miss LEILA ELLIS
KITTY ..... Miss EDNA PHILLIPS
GERTRUDE ..... Miss ETHEL KINGSTON
BLANCHE ..... Miss MARY HANSON
BESSY ..... Miss MAMIE DUNN
MRS. FLETCHER, SR. ..... Mrs. FRANCES FERREN
MAID ..... Miss EMMA JANVIER

Guests, Bridesmaids, etc., by Pupils of the Stanhope-Wheatcroft School.

Produced under the stage direction of the Author.

Costumes for Act I. from special designs executed by Maurice Herrmann.

Programme continued on second page following.

ACT I.—

Mr. and Mrs. Lawrence Wolton
At Home
Tuesday Evening, January ———
at Ten O'clock.

Children's Costumes de rigueur.

——*East 69th Street.*

ACT II.—One year later—

Mrs. Lawrence Wolton
requests the honor of your presence
at the Marriage of her Daughter,
Marion,
to
Mr. Edward Houghton Fletcher,
Thursday, February 10th,
at Five o'clock,
St. Hubert's Chapel, New York.

ACT III.—THE FOLLOWING DAY.

THE MOTH AND THE FLAME

By CLYDE FITCH

[The Editor wishes to record here, in memoriam, his grateful appreciation of the desire shown by the late Mrs. Fitch to have in the present Collection a hitherto unpublished play by her son, Clyde Fitch. Through her courtesy, "The Moth and the Flame" is here included.]

CAST OF CHARACTERS

Edward Fletcher
Mr. Dawson
Mr. Wolton
Douglas Rhodes
Johnstone
Fanshaw
Trimmins
Clergyman
Howes
Marion Wolton
Mrs. Lorrimer
Mrs. Wolton
Jeanette Gross
Ethel
Kitty
Gertrude
Blanche
Maid
Mrs. Fletcher

Guests, Bridesmaids, Choristers, Servants and others.

ACT I.

SCENE. *The First Act takes place in the* WOLTON'S *house during a large fancy ball. All the guests are in children's costumes—that being insisted upon in the invitations. The stage represents a reception-room; the end of a conservatory, or ball-room, being seen through a large archway. In the upper right hand corner of the stage is a small stage built with curtains and foot-lights, for an amateur vaudeville performance, which is taking place.*

At rise of curtain the room is filled with guests in costume, on chairs before improvised stage, and the curtain of stage is just falling, as one of the Lady Guests—who, dressed (and blacked) as a small Darky Girl, has been singing a popular negro ballad ("Warmest Baby.") The mimic curtain rises again, owing to the applause of the mimic audience. The chorus of song is repeated and the curtain again falls to applause. There is a general movement among guests—with laughter and conversation.

DISCOVERED. MARION WOLTON, *dressed in Empire Child's gown, is sitting in one of the third row of chairs next the foot-lights. Up to now her back is partly turned toward the audience.* KITTY RAND, *dressed in short skirts, is just behind her.*

FANSHAW. [*Leaning over to* MARION.] I think, Marion, this was really a most amusing idea of yours, having us all come as children.

Enter DOUGLAS RHODES, *in white sailor costume. He meets* MRS. WOLTON *who enters. They talk.*

MARION. [*To* KITTY.] Your costume, Kitty, is charming.

KITTY. [*With a ball on rubber cord.*] My dear, I'm sure I look a sight. I feel as if it were bathing hour at Narragansett.

MARION. Here's Bessie. How splendid she was. [*Rises.*] [*Enter* BESSIE. *She laughs as she is greeted by shouts of laughter and applause by guests. She joins* MARION, *who shakes her hand.*] You were too funny, Bessie. [*A guest rises and offers seat to* BESSIE. *She accepts it and sits.*

JOHNSTONE. [*Monkey; white kilt suit.*] [*To* BESSIE *as she sits.*] Yes. Isn't this an awfully lovely party? [*To* FANSHAW.] Here, Fanshaw, it's your turn.

GUESTS *and* ALL. Yes, come on Fanshaw, etc. [FANSHAW *exits.*

RHODES *comes from* MRS. WOLTON, *nodding pleasantly to guests as he passes round behind them, to* MARION. *He shakes her hand.*

MARION. Why so late, Douglas?

DOUGLAS. I was dining with Mrs. Lorrimer; but I hope you've saved me a seat by you. [BLANCHE *exits, ready for stage.*

MARION. I'm sorry, but I haven't. There's the curtain.

She sits and DOUGLAS *takes a place back of guests, shaking hands with* TRIMMINS *as he does so. Mimic curtain rises, music begins, all interrupt with "Sh-h."* FANSHAW *enters on mimic stage, dressed as Little Lord Fauntleroy, and sings. Mimic curtain falls to applause. Curtain is raised. Black rag-baby thrown to him during song.* FANSHAW *enters, bows, and, as he does so,* BLANCHE *throws a small bouquet of flowers to him. This he catches and makes entrance upon stage by jumping over mimic foot-lights. He is congratulated and thanked by* MARION *and resumes his seat.*

Music begins. All interrupt again with "Sh-h." Curtain is raised, and enter ETHEL, *dressed as a child of* 1840, *in white and green. She comes forward and sings ("Henrietta"), with orchestral accompaniment, a flute obligato being a feature of the latter, which, every little while, indulges in loud variations, entirely drowning the singer's voice, much to her annoyance, and the only half-suppressed amusement of the guests. As she reaches the chorus all (at* MARION'S *suggestion) join in with her and finish the song.* MARION *rises, giving the signal that the entertainment is over. Servants come in and take away most of the chairs, leaving one in centre of stage and three up toward the left centre. All rise and form groups; those of guests near the door move into ball-room and off.* ETHEL *enters, and* MARION *at once greets her,* KITTY *and* JOHNSTONE *joining them.*

MARION. Thank you ever so much.

JOHNSTONE. Yes, indeed. Isn't this an awfully lovely party.

ETHEL. [*With large hoople and stick; quickly, much put out.*] My dear Marion, I could choke that flute player.

MARION. Don't be selfish, Ethel; the man wanted to be heard. [*Goes up to* DOUGLAS.

ETHEL. If I were a witch, I'd curse him with asthma. Mr. Johnstone, go and curse him for me.

JOHNSTONE. With pleasure.

ETHEL. Just give him a piece of my mind. [*Enter* GIRL.

JOHNSTONE. [*Flatteringly.*] He doesn't deserve such a gift. But isn't this a lovely party? Will you excuse me? [*He goes up stage to* BLANCHE, *offers his arm, which she takes, and they exit.* KITTY *and* ETHEL *watch* BLANCHE *and* JOHNSTONE, *amused.*

KITTY. [*To* ETHEL.] Just look at Blanche. Do you suppose she's going to—

ETHEL. She's going to with all her might and main, if he will only ask her.

KITTY. A large if— [*Laughing.* FANSHAW *and* GERTRUDE *join* ETHEL *and* KITTY *down stage.*

FANSHAW. Looks as if Johnny were getting pretty stuck on Blanche, doesn't it? [*Goes to* KITTY. TRIMMINS *moves up centre.*

ETHEL. Yes, or just the other way round. [*All laugh.*

GERTRUDE. Who are you dancing the cotillon with, Ethel?

ETHEL. Don't know. I've promised two men, but I haven't made up my mind who I'll dance with yet.

FANSHAW. A nice person to engage for a partner. [*Calling.*] Trimmins!

ETHEL. Sh-h! He's one of the men I've promised.

FANSHAW. [*Laughing.*] Never mind. I'm the other. [*All laugh.* GERTRUDE *says,* "Oh, Ethel!" GERTRUDE *goes toward* MARION, ETHEL *and* KITTY *at same time.* MARION *exits.*

FANSHAW. [*To* TRIMMINS.] Who are you dancing the cotillon with, Trimmins?

TRIMMINS. Ethel Stevens!

FANSHAW. Who?

TRIMMINS. Ethel Stevens!

FANSHAW. I'll bet a fiver you're not. She's dancing with me.

TRIMMINS. [*Very pleased.*] Delighted! I owe you the five with joy. [*Rushes* FANSHAW *out of the way. Crossing to* GERTRUDE.] Will you give me the pleasure? [DOUGLAS *out at back, exits.*] Thank you. [*Offers his arm, which* GERTRUDE *takes, and they go out at back.*

FANSHAW. Well!

MARION. Are you going to stand perfectly still and be robbed in that manner? [*Laughing.*

FANSHAW. Well, but what am I— [*Interrupted by one of the girl guests, who says,* "I'm here!"] Oh, so you are. [*Puts his arm in hers, and they run off together.*

ETHEL. Marion, isn't Mr. Ned Fletcher coming to-night?

MARION. Yes. [*Exit.*

KITTY. I'm so glad; he's quite the most amusing man in town this winter. [*Sitting on chair which servant left.*

ETHEL. And so many people won't ask him to their houses, you know. Mamma won't.

KITTY. Well, you know, your mother's a ridiculous person; she asks lots of awfully fast men!

ETHEL. Yes, but they are all relatives.

KITTY. [*Putting arm around* ETHEL, *pricks her finger.*] I don't believe Net Fletcher is as bad as people hint. He's too good looking. [*Fixing dress.*

ETHEL. And I don't care whether he's bad or not, he's charming enough to make up for it. Besides, I suppose all men are bad.

KITTY. Oh—I don't know.

ETHEL. I mean all nice men.

KITTY. Where has Mr. Fletcher been before this winter?

ETHEL. My dear, he's one of those men who live all over the place—most of the time in Europe—but he's been here always off and on—and in Newport and in Lenox he has yachts and things, don't you know! [*Exits down right.*

MARION. [*Enters.*] Girls, will you go into the ball-room, till the men get the tables ready here? [*She speakes aside to one of the servants, and exits. Servants bring on small table and place it with bottles, lunch, etc., a broken glass covered with napkins to fall on stage. Place seven chairs about table. Exit.*

ETHEL. *Of course.* [*To* KITTY, *crossing to her.*] Do you notice how she won't talk about Fletcher and won't listen to any one else either?

KITTY. My dear, she's heels over head.

ETHEL. Poor Douglas Rhodes! [*Half smiling, in part satire.*

KITTY. Serves him right for hanging around her all his life! Why didn't he flirt with one of us girls for a time, if only to make her jealous! [ETHEL *sees* DOUGLAS *enter, and tries to warn* KITTY. ETHEL *gives* KITTY *a violent pull of the arm to warn her to stop speaking of* DOUGLAS.

ETHEL. [*To* DOUGLAS.] You can't stay here; we're driven out.

KITTY. Come, help us make fun of the other people.

DOUGLAS. In a few minutes. I must give you a chance to make fun of me!

KITTY. Oh, we've been doing that for years! [ETHEL *blows* DOUGLAS' *whistle which he has suspended from neck, pulling it out of his pocket.* ETHEL *and* KITTY *smile coquettishly at* DOUGLAS *and exit into ball-room, arm in arm. Distant music off stage.* DOUGLAS *follows up centre. A pause. Enter* MARION. DOUGLAS, *up stage, looks admiringly at her, and smiles. Then, smiling and putting himself into a boyish attitude, he says boyishly.*

DOUGLAS. Hello, Molly!

MARION. [*Smiling back, catching his mood, speaks girlishly.*] Hello, Dug! It does take one back to old days, doesn't it!

DOUGLAS. That was what I was thinking of, Marion, the days of dancing-school. How good you were to always be my partner, even though I couldn't reverse without treading on your toes!

MARION. [*Smiling.*] You were a bad dancer—and death to slippers.

DOUGLAS. And the children's parties, with the old games, "Post Office," "Copenhagen," "Kiss in the Ring."

MARION. [*Smiling mischievously.*] You were good enough at "Kiss in the Ring" to make up for your not reversing.

DOUGLAS. [*With real sentiment, crosses to her.*] Do you remember it all as well as I do?

MARION. [*Realizing his sentiment, and trying to change their mood, but pleasantly.*] Of course I do! We were great friends then, as we are now, and as I hope we always will be, Douglas.

DOUGLAS. But if we played the old games again, would it be the same?

MARION. No, no, things are never the same.

DOUGLAS. But would you let me choose you always? Would you pretend not to see me coming, so I could slap your hands on the Copenhagen rope and take my reward? If we played "Post Office," would *I* have all my letters from *your* lips! Would you mind if, in "bow to the wittiest, kneel to the prettiest, and kiss the one you loved best," I choose you again, openly, for all three? Would you give me *all* your dances?

MARION. [*More serious, though still smiling kindly, sweetly.*] That's just it, Douglas! You can reverse now, and there are so many other girls wanting partners!

DOUGLAS. But— [*Interrupted.*

MARION. Besides, after all, we're only children *outside* to-night; our *hearts* have come of age!

DOUGLAS. Yes, Marion, but, boy's and man's, my heart's the same. I want the same partner I did then, only I want her for the game of life!

MARION. I am so sorry!

DOUGLAS. Sorry? Then you won't let your hands lie on the rope for me any more?

MARION. I am very fond of you, Douglas, and I always was, but— [*She hesitates.*

DOUGLAS. [*A little bitterly, disappointed.*] I know what you mean. I was all right for dancing-school, but life is a more serious matter— [MARION *goes to chair and sits down.*] I know I'm not like you, Marion—I know what an intellectual woman you are, and what an ordinary sort of fellow I am. But I *love* you! and I hoped— [*He breaks off and continues with his first idea.*] You went to a woman's college, and I *only* to a *man's*—You made a study of sociology—I, [*Smiling.*] principally of athletics. I know I never read books, and you seem to read everything. But I love you. You have your clubs for working girls, your charities; I know the busy, helpful life you lead. You have so much in it, I was in hopes that what room was left for a *husband* was so little, even *I* could fill it. And somehow or other I've always taken it for granted you more or less understood, and were—willing.

MARION. I was—once—

DOUGLAS. You were?

MARION. There was no one in the world I liked so much to be with as you, and I think I, too, believed my happiness was in your hands, and that some day we would decide together it was so. But I lately— [*She hesitates.*

DOUGLAS. Some one else?

MARION. I don't like you one bit less, Douglas, only—[*Rises.*

DOUGLAS. Only you liked some one else more! I was afraid so. I've heard whispers and guesses—

MARION. Don't let it make any difference with *us*, Douglas!

DOUGLAS. You love him?

MARION. Yes.

DOUGLAS. Very much?

MARION. You see, every one is against him, and I feel that I have a chance to save him.

DOUGLAS. You believe in him?

MARION. [*Shortly.*] Yes.

DOUGLAS. Would you believe anything against him?

MARION. [*On the defensive, indignant.*] *No!*

DOUGLAS. If some one told you of something dishonourable this man had done?

MARION. I would suspect the motive of the person who told me. Do you think I haven't heard plenty of gossip against him? Every girl I know has done her best to take away his character, and *begged me to introduce him to her* in the same breath.

DOUGLAS. And if I spoke against him?

MARION. [*Leaning on back of chair.*] I know I couldn't help it, after what you have told me; I should have to feel you might be influenced by jealousy.

DOUGLAS. To *unjustly* accuse a man?

MARION. Oh, Douglas, no, of course you would believe what you said, but I wouldn't trust your judgment. Don't I know every one is down on him. Even you men; are all the men in New York so proud of their past lives—not to mention the *present* of several I know?—Well, if men turn a cold shoulder, then we women must give him our hands.

DOUGLAS. You girls don't understand.

MARION. Oh, girls understand a good deal nowadays. Society and some of the newspapers attend to that. He doesn't pretend to be a saint to me—I find him perfectly frank—and I am afraid he has been rather fast! But I don't believe he is capable of an outright dishonourable action, and nothing would make me believe it!

DOUGLAS. No proof?

MARION. Only the proof of my own eyes. When I see him do something contemptible, then I'll believe *half* the stories I hear of him! [*Moving a little up centre.*

DOUGLAS. I see you *do* love him.

MARION. I do, though you are the only person I have confessed it to,—not even to him—and forgive me, [*Down a little.*] but I never liked you less than I do now when you have spoken against him. [*Up to arch.*

DOUGLAS. [*Following her.*] No, tell me you will forget it, and keep me the same old friend, and I'll promise not to speak against him to you again.

MARION. [*Smiling.*] Very well— [*They shake hands.*] Why, I want you two to be the best of friends—you *must* be—

DOUGLAS. [*Also smiling.*] Oh, I don't promise that—I haven't given you up yet, and I sha'n't until—

MARION. [*Smiling.*] When—?

DOUGLAS. [*Smiling.*] Until I see you going into the church to be married.

MARION. You'll say nothing more against Ned?

DOUGLAS. Not to you. [*Moving down, right centre.*

MARION. Oh, but you will to others? [*Follows.*

DOUGLAS. I will say what I have to say to—*him.*

MARION. To *him?*

Enter MRS. WOLTON *and* FLETCHER. FLETCHER *is dressed in dark sailor clothes.*

MRS. WOLTON. Marion, here's another little boy. [MARION *turns and greets* FLETCHER, *going to him.* DOUGLAS *and* FLETCHER *see each other and say* "Good evening" *pleasantly.*

MARION. It's too bad you missed the vaudeville.

FLETCHER. Did *you* do anything. [MARION *laughs and exits with* FLETCHER.

DOUGLAS *turns around quickly, annoyed, to speak to* MRS. WOLTON, *but, in his quick turning and in his movement of annoyance, keeping his eyes on* MARION *and* FLETCHER, *he has struck glasses and a bottle on the little supper-table beside them. They crash on the floor. He and* MRS. WOLTON *both start.*

DOUGLAS. Oh! Mrs. Wolton, forgive me; how clumsy! [*Starts to pick up.*

MRS. WOLTON. No, never mind. [*As* SERVANT *enters.*] Here is Howes— [*To* SERVANT.] Howes, see to this, please, at once.

SERVANT. Yes, m'm. Please, Mr. Dawson is here to see Mr. Wolton.

MRS. WOLTON. Mr. Dawson, my brother! Why, he's in Boston, Howes.

SERVANT. Beg pardon, m'm, but he must have returned today. Most important, he says, m'm. Where shall I show him? The ladies and gentlemen are playing "Blind Man's Buff" in Mr. Wolton's room.

MRS. WOLTON. This is the quietest place. Show Mr. Dawson in here. Where is Mr. Wolton?

SERVANT. [*Trying not to smile.*] He's blind-folded, m'm!

MRS. WOLTON. [*Smiling.*] Tell him.

SERVANT. Yes, m'm. [*Exits.*

DOUGLAS. Shall we join the game?

MRS. WOLTON. Yes, come, I will take Mr. Wolton's place! I haven't played Blind Man's Buff for— [*She calculates a moment, and then speaks amusedly.*] Good gracious!—*never mind how many years!!*

DOUGLAS. Oh, not so many as all that, I am sure! [*They go out at back.*

Enter SERVANT *with* DAWSON *in cutaway coat and vest and usual trousers.* SERVANT *at once begins to pick up the debris made by* DOUGLAS.

DAWSON. What's going on here, Howes?

SERVANT. A children's party, sir.

DAWSON. A what?

SERVANT. A children's party, sir.

DAWSON. Who are the children?

SERVANT. Mr. Wolton and Miss Wolton, sir, and her friends. Mr. Wolton's playing games now, sir, but he said he would join you in a minute.

DAWSON. [*Out loud, involuntarily, but speaking to himself—very seriously, almost tragically.*] Playing games! My God!

SERVANT. Yes, sir—one don't know what rich folks'll do next, sir. *We're* in hopes, in the kitchen, they'll take to pretending they're the servants, sir, and turn us loose in the ballroom. [*Smiling. Exits.*

DAWSON. [*Who hardly hears* SERVANT.] Playing games, with ruin and disgrace staring him in the face. [*Enter* MR. WOLTON.

MR. WOLTON. [*Flushed and gay—an elderly man in knickerbockers and evening coat, a sort of English Court costume. The handkerchief, which was tied around his eyes in the game, has slipped, and lies about his neck.*] Well, Fred, what's the good news?

DAWSON. The worst there could be!

MR. WOLTON. [*Half whispers.*] What do you mean!!

DAWSON. [*Dragging off the Blind Man's Buff handkerchief from* WOLTON'S *neck.*] What do you mean by going in for all this tomfoolery, to-night, with ruin and disgrace ready for you in the morning?

MR. WOLTON. So soon—?

DAWSON. How much longer did you think you could stave it off?

MR. WOLTON. [*Sinks exhausted into a chair.*] I didn't know.

DAWSON. Why didn't you tell me your credit was as exhausted in Boston as here? [*Taking chair from table, and sitting right of* WOLTON.

MR. WOLTON. I thought, with you doing the negotiating, it mightn't be!

DAWSON. Well, it is; do you hear me, you haven't any such thing as *credit there* nor *here!* nor anywhere, for aught I know! To-morrow is the last day of grace. Your sister-in-law has to pay this money?

MR. WOLTON. Yes.

DAWSON. What did you let her buy that house for?

MR. WOLTON. [*Testily.*] How could I help it! My brother didn't appoint me her guardian! He simply left her money in trust in my hands!

DAWSON. "In trust in your hands!" [*Laughs cruelly.*

MR. WOLTON. Don't do that!

DAWSON. And you speculated with it, and lost every cent!

MR. WOLTON. Yes.

DAWSON. What a scoundrel you are! [WOLTON *squirms miserably in his chair.* DAWSON *adds quietly.*] And yet I don't suppose there's at this moment a more popular man in New York, socially, than you.

MR. WOLTON. No, I don't believe there is!—but a damned lot of good it does me!

DAWSON. Will your sister-in-law accept her ruin quietly?

MR. WOLTON. No, she's never liked me; she'll take pleasure in exposing me!

DAWSON. But for your *wife* and *child's* sake!

MR. WOLTON. You know very well she *hates them!* They have never taken her up; she wasn't possible, socially. [DAWSON *laughs again bitterly.*] *Don't* do that!

DAWSON. Well, then, after ruining yourself and your brother's wife, you must ruin your *own!*

MR. WOLTON. [*Alarmed, uneasy.*] What do you mean?

DAWSON. I mean that my sister's own money is enough to pay for your sister's silence. Don't you understand? Your sister mustn't know, of course, that you've stolen her fortune.

Instead, your wife must be told,—poor Laura—and for her daughter's sake, she must consent to beggar herself. Her bonds will about meet the payment of the house to-morrow—they must be sold the first thing—I will see to it.—— [*As he speaks, he is looking* WOLTON *straight in the face. Something in* WOLTON'S *face grows upon him with conviction as he speaks his last few words. He breaks off suddenly.*] What! you've taken hers, too! [*He leans over* WOLTON *in the chair, his hands on his shoulders, close to his neck, in a rage. Rises.*] You've beggared *my sister*, your wife and child! You— [*Interrupted.*

MR. WOLTON. [*With a big effort, rises, throwing off* DAWSON'S *hands.*] Sh!—For God's sake, lower your voice! You'll be heard!

DAWSON. [*With a change of tone, but speaking with utter contempt.*] By a couple hundred fools! To-morrow *thousands* will hear of your dirty dishonour!! [*Going toward right a little.*

MR. WOLTON. [*To* DAWSON.] But *you*, you have money—won't you come to my rescue?

DAWSON. I couldn't if I would. You have borrowed half a fortune of me already. What I have left must go to take care of my sister and niece. Do you think I'd support *you!* No, the *State* will do that.

MR. WOLTON. That!! You'd let me go to—?

DAWSON. You'll get twenty years at least!

MR. WOLTON. You won't help me *escape!*

DAWSON. No.

MR. WOLTON. But Laura? she loves me, and Marion. *They* will suffer for me; I may be weakly dishonourable, but I've always loved them, and they me. Besides, any public dishonour which comes to my name must touch theirs too.

DAWSON. I'm not so sure about that—I think there is material for a divorce here.

MR. WOLTON. A divorce! My God, must I lose everything! Show a little pity, Fred! Remember the old days at school; was I a bad boy? We were chums for years, you know it!—You were my best man when I married Laura, and you were the gayest at the wedding! It's only been this curse of gambling with the stocks that has driven me to the devil,—that and my cursed luck.

DAWSON. *Luck* has nothing to do with *honour*.

MR. WOLTON. You don't know—oftener than you think, it has everything! [*Enter* SERVANT.

SERVANT. Supper is ready, sir. Can we have this room?

DAWSON. Yes, Howes, I'm going!

SERVANT. Thank you, sir. [*Exits.*

MR. WOLTON. Give me a word of hope, Fred!—something What are you going to do?

DAWSON. Nothing till to-morrow morning.

MR. WOLTON. And that's all you have to say?

DAWSON. All. [*The two men stand looking at each other a moment in a sort of grim embarrassment, then* DAWSON *exits. Music. It must be evident to the audience, though not to the hysterically excited* WOLTON, *that* DAWSON *has a little, a very little, pity, but doesn't wish to show it,—at any rate not yet.* WOLTON, *who has stood a moment lost in thought, an expression of despair in his face, shudders and comes to himself. He looks around to see that he is alone. He grasps his forehead tight a moment in his right hand, drops his hand, and with compressed lips nods his head determinedly. He is standing by one of the smaller supper-tables; he looks down at it and takes up a silver knife at one of the places, feels its dull edge, and throws it down sneering.* A SERVANT *appears.*

MR. WOLTON. Howes?

SERVANT. [*Coming into the room and going to* WOLTON.] Yes, sir.

MR. WOLTON. I am going up to my room. [*With a motion of his head, indicating upstairs.*] I am not feeling well. If my absence should be noticed, explain to Mrs. Wolton, but do not disturb me—do you understand?

SERVANT. Yes, sir.

MR. WOLTON. *On no account am I to be disturbed.* No one is to come to me until *after* the party is entirely over. *Don't make any mistake about that.*

SERVANT. No, sir.

WOLTON, *who is half way between centre and door right, turns for a moment, looking about the room. He is seized with a nervous twitching of his muscles. He clenches his fists, grinds his teeth to control himself, and, bowing his head, goes from the room by door.* KITTY *and* JOHNSTONE *appear in ball-room doorway, at exit of* WOLTON.

KITTY. [*Looking into room on stage.*] Here's a dear table, all by itself. [*Speaks as she appears in the doorway. The two turn and look off right at* ETHEL *and* FANSHAW *who are following them slowly.*

JOHNSTONE. Come along, Fanshaw, here's a lovely, quiet table, where we can say just what we like about everybody! [*They stand in doorway a moment, looking off right, waiting for the other couple with their backs to* WOLTON *and room.* ETHEL *and* FANSHAW *join the first couple, and all come forward, speaking. The following speeches are made as they come forward to table.*

JOHNSTONE. [*To* FANSHAW *and* ETHEL.] How you dawdle.

ETHEL. Jack Wright tore my lace.

FANSHAW. Trying to kiss her in Copenhagen. [*They are about the table.* JOHNSTONE *at once sits down first in the chair the* SERVANT *was holding for one of the ladies.* SERVANT *then opens a bottle of champagne and pours in the glasses.*

JOHNSTONE. [*Sitting.*] Come on.

KITTY. Look at him!

ETHEL. What a rude little beast you are, Johnny!

FANSHAW. Get up! [*Pushing him.*

JOHNSTONE. Well, you girls dawdle so! [KITTY and ETHEL *sit. Enter* MRS. LORRIMER *from ball-room, dressed as a Watteau Shepherdess. She is greeted by a chorus of four. Carries lamb and crook.*

ETHEL, KITTY, JOHNSTONE, FANSHAW. Oh, look at Mrs. Lorrimer!

MRS. LORRIMER. [*Pirouettes once around, and makes a bob curtsy.*] Good evening. [*Laughing.*] Well, I don't want to throw bouquets at myself, but I don't think it's bad.

ETHEL *and* KITTY. You're splendid!

JOHNSTONE. Love—— [*Sits.*]

KITTY. Get Mrs. Lorrimer a chair. [*They all move to make more room for her, and* FANSHAW *gets an extra chair from arch.*

MRS. LORRIMER. I'm afraid I'm a fifth spoke in your wheel! [*She sits. A* SERVANT *passes them bouillon which they take and eat.*

ETHEL. Don't be foolish; girls at a ball nowadays can't expect to have a man apiece. [JOHNSTONE *lights a cigarette and smokes. A* SERVANT *in ball-room is seen taking away the bouillon cups, while a second passes Bouches à la Reine there.* FANSHAW *sits above* ETHEL *left of table, after taking lamb and crook from* MRS. LORRIMER *and placing them down left corner*

MRS. LORRIMER. How is the party?

JOHNSTONE. Awfully lovely party!

KITTY. A tearing success!

ETHEL. You ought to have seen the vaudeville!

Mrs. Lorrimer. How did your stunt go, Ethel?

Fanshaw. Great.

Ethel. Oh, my dear, a brute of a flute player ruined it. I felt like thirty cents.

Fanshaw. No one could spend much more money on a party than old Wolton is doing to-night.

Mrs. Lorrimer. Does Marion show her age in a child's dress?

Kitty. She looks charmingly, but then Marion isn't so old.

Ethel. Perhaps not so old as she usually looks.

Johnstone. Aren't you a Kitty cat?

Mrs. Lorrimer. Why doesn't she paint a little?

Johnstone. What!

Kitty. *Marion?* Paint! Her *face!*

Ethel. My dear, she'd die first! [*All laugh, saying* "Marion".

Mrs. Lorrimer. [*Grandiloquently.*] Not that I approve of painting! [*Music stops.*

All. [*Laughing.*] Oh, no!

Ethel. Nor I!

All. [*Laughing.*] Oh, no!

Mrs. Lorrimer. Who's here?

Johnstone. Everybody.

Mrs. Lorrimer. Anyone I can marry?

Kitty. Oh, Mrs. Lorrimer, do be decent. You haven't been divorced a year yet.

Mrs. Lorrimer. My dear, divorce isn't like death—you don't have to go into mourning! Besides, that's what I want to get married for! I find I've a perfect passion for divorce! Just like men have it for drink. The more I get the more I want! [*Laugh.*] I've only had two divorces, and I want another!

Johnstone. You must be damned careful—I beg your pardon—

Mrs. Lorrimer. Oh, don't apologize, I say it myself!—careful about what?

Johnstone. What sort of *husband you choose.*

Mrs. Lorrimer. Exactly! None of your *ideal* men for me! I want a man with a bad record! [*Laugh.*] Plenty of proof concealed about his person, or not buried too deep in his past for me and my lawyer to ferret out. I've a perfect duck of a lawyer! He made up every bit of evidence about my last husband; that won me my case, and, my dears, it just *happened* to turn out to be true! [*Laugh.*

ETHEL. Speaking of records, who do you think is here to-night?

MRS. LORRIMER. *Ned* Fletcher—!!

KITTY. Yes.

MRS. LORRIMER. Girls—I'll tell you a secret—

JOHNSTONE. I don't want to hear it. [*Takes a chair left centre, sits and lights cigarette.*

MRS. LORRIMER. I'm crazy about him! Where is he? [*Glancing over her shoulder.*

KITTY. You've no chance; he's going to marry Marion, if she'll have him.

MRS. LORRIMER. What a shame! And will she?

ETHEL. She's mad about him!

MRS. LORRIMER. The moth and the flame! What a pity! because he'd be simply *ideal* for me! Why, do you know I hear that he— [*Stops suddenly, looking at* JOHNSTONE *and* FANSHAW.

JOHNSTONE. What do you hear? I'm in this.

MRS. LORRIMER. I forgot Johnny and Mr. Fanshaw—there are certain things you mustn't talk about before innocent little boys!

FANSHAW. You couldn't tell *us anything about Ned Fletcher!*

MRS. LORRIMER. [*Laughing.*] I don't want to! But I thought Marion was always going to marry Douglas Rhodes.

KITTY. Oh, that's all off now. It's Ned Fletcher or nothing with Marion.

ETHEL. [*Laughing.*] I believe she thinks she's going to reform him! [*All laugh.*

KITTY. There's one thing, he isn't after Marion's money.

ETHEL. Is he so rich?

JOHNSTONE. Oh, rotten! [KITTY *slaps* JOHNSTONE.

MRS. LORRIMER. Very well, do you know what I shall do? I shall take Douglas.

ETHEL. [*Hastily.*] Yes, catch his heart on the rebound; they say it's easier that way!

JOHNSTONE. That's one on you, Mrs. Lorrimer. [*Party gag.*]

MRS. LORRIMER. Oh, I'm not so very old, and have had two splendid husbands already. I don't think I have to bother about the easiest way.

JOHNSTONE. Philopene, Ethel? That's one on *you.*

MRS. LORRIMER. Has it been your method, my dear, because if so I can't congratulate you on the result. You must look out for a stronger rebound next time! Try a divorced man; I hear they come back with a terrific force! I'll be generous; try one of mine. [*All laugh. As they stop laughing there is the sound of something heavy falling in the room above. The chandelier trembles slightly, the lustres sound. All four lift their heads and listen a moment. A short pause.*

KITTY. What was that!

MRS. LORRIMER. The servants probably, upstairs! [*Enter* MARION *from ball-room, smiling at the table of people as she passes.*

JOHNSTONE. [*As she comes.*] Here's Miss Wolton.

MRS. LORRIMER. My dear Marion, pardon me for not rising, but I assure you I look much better sitting down! [MARION *stops by* MRS. LORRIMER.

JOHNSTONE. Not at all, Mrs. Lorrimer, they're awfully lovely!

MRS. LORRIMER. Well, I'm sure they don't compare with yours.

JOHNSTONE. Oh, I don't know, there are others. [MARION *goes down centre.*

MRS. LORRIMER. Marion, is Mr. Dawson here?

MARION. No, he's in Boston.—Why?

MRS. LORRIMER. Oh, nothing, only he's an unmarried man, so I thought I'd ask. [SERVANT *in ball-room takes away plates, and second* SERVANT *passes ices.*

MARION. [*To* MRS. LORRIMER.] Why are you so late, Emily? [*Back to* MRS. LORRIMER.

MRS. LORRIMER. My little girl was seedy, and I couldn't get away until I saw her asleep comfortably. It's an awful care for a young woman, my dear, having a *posthumous* child!

MARION. A what?

MRS. LORRIMER. A *posthumous* child!

MARION. [*Laughing.*] *How do you mean, Emily?*

MRS. LORRIMER. Why, born after it's father's divorce!

MARION. Are you girls going to have coffee?

MRS. LORRIMER. No.

ETHEL. Nor I.

MARION. Very well, then; join us for another game— [*She makes a movement of starting.*] Unless you men want to smoke. In that case, take your coffee in the library, where you'll find cigarettes and other smoking materials.

JOHNSTONE. [*Who has a cigarette in his mouth, and has been smoking all through the supper.*] I say! Oughtn't I to have smoked here?

MARION. [*Smiling.*] No! [*She starts to go out through ball-room.*

JOHNSTONE. I beg your pardon. Well, any way it's an awfully lovely party.

MRS. LORRIMER. Marion, is it true you're going to be divorced —I mean married?

MARION. [*By doorway.*] Married? I hope so, some day. [*Smiling, exits into ball-room.* JOHNSTONE *is eating ice.* MRS. LORRIMER *crosses to him.* KITTY *in front of table.* ETHEL *takes up lamb.* FANSHAW *exits.*

MRS. LORRIMER. Haven't you finished your ice, Johnny?

JOHNSTONE. No. I like to squash mine all up, and eat it soft.

MRS. LORRIMER. Johnny, who made your bow?

JOHNSTONE. Mother. [KITTY *drives* JOHNNY *out of room by hitting him with her ball.* MRS. LORRIMER *crosses to* ETHEL *and takes lamb.*

ETHEL. [*Who has looked back over her shoulder into the ball-room, goes up to arch.*] Mr. Fletcher has joined Marion.

MRS. LORRIMER. Oh, that's why Marion wished us to hurry! She wanted this room for herself and Fletcher!

ETHEL. *Probably.*

MRS. LORRIMER. Let's go—as if we were gone for good, and then stroll back *casually* in a few minutes, and see how we find them!

KITTY. Isn't that eavesdropping?

MRS. LORRIMER. Don't be absurd! There isn't any such thing as eavesdropping nowadays. Everybody listens to everything they can, and everyone more or less knows they're being listened to.

KITTY. But what good will it do?

MRS. LORRIMER. Why, if we—come back and catch them with his arm around her, we can take it for granted they are engaged.

ETHEL. I don't think that follows. I'm sure if I were engaged to every man I let— [*She stops quickly. All laugh.*

KITTY. [*Laughing.*] You gave yourself away that time, Ethel! [*They move out by door into ball-room. As they do so,* SERVANT *enters from right, and* MARION *enters, meeting girls and* MRS. LORRIMER.

MARION. Going to dance?—

GIRLS. Yes.

MRS. LORRIMER. No, play games. Kissing games. [*All laugh and exeunt.*

MARION. Oh, Mrs. Lorrimer! [*Enter* FLETCHER.

FLETCHER. Why did you run away?

MARION. I was afraid if I didn't the servants would never get this room ready.

FLETCHER. Have you a partner?

MARION. No.

FLETCHER. [*Pleased to be with her and yet embarrassed.*] May I —will you—that is—won't you dance with me?

MARION. Yes.

FLETCHER. [*Near her.*] I wonder why I feel so diffident with you. I think I never was diffident before! [*Smiling.*

MARION. [*Smiling.*] No, you haven't that reputation.

FLETCHER. [*Smiling apologetically, but humourously.*] Dear me, I hope you don't know what my reputation isn't—or *is.*

MARION. [*Seriously.*] I don't judge a man by his reputation.

FLETCHER. [*Involuntarily half under his breath, humourously.*] Thank heaven! [MARION *looks at him, hearing him. There is a pause. She waits willingly for him to speak, hoping he will.*] I've been a very bad fellow.

MARION. Some of the best men in the world have begun that way.

FLETCHER. They probably had some one to help—to believe in them.

MARION. And haven't you?

FLETCHER. Will you believe in me enough to—[*Looks off in ball-room up a little;* MARION *follows. He loses his control and speaks passionately.*] Don't you understand,—I love you— [*He embraces her; she allows him. The embrace lasts a moment.*] You can be my salvation! Will you be?

MARION. [*In his arms, looking up at him.*] I will—if I can—

FLETCHER. [*Whose eyes never quite look into* MARION'S, *loosening the embrace.*] You will marry me?

MARION. Yes. [*Kisses him, then quickly moves down right.*

FLETCHER. [*Following her. Not looking at her.*] People say I'm a blackguard!

MARION. People say a great many things that aren't true. What can a man do with all the world against him! "People" can force him into being as bad as they say he is.

FLETCHER. Then you won't believe them.

MARION. No, not if you deny what they say. [*He holds out his hand; she takes it. At this moment,* MRS. LORRIMER *and*

ETHEL *appear in ball-room, ostentatiously counting the chairs and making small calculation about the cotillion, but really watching slyly* MARION *and* FLETCHER. MARION *sees it and speaks to* FLETCHER *quickly under her breath.*] Don't move! Don't drop my hand, but shake it as if we'd been making a bet, and follow my lead! [*Aloud.*] It's settled then! You take my bet?

FLETCHER. [*Shaking her hand and then dropping it casually.* A box of cigars, against a box of gloves! [*Sotto voce.*] What is it?

MARION [*Sotto voce.*] Mrs. Lorrimer in the next room watching us. [*Speaks in low voce satirically to* FLETCHER *as if she were speaking to* MRS. LORRIMER.] Oh, no, Emily! I am going to marry Mr. Fletcher, but *I* intend to be the one to announce that fact, and not you. [MRS. LORRIMER *and* ETHEL *turn. They see* MARION *and* FLETCHER *and pretend surprise; they remain in the ball-room.*]

MRS. LORRIMER. [*With trumpet.*] Oh! Marion! are *you* here?

MARION. Ahem! [*With a quick, amused side glance to* FLETCHER.] We've been watching you for some time; what was the matter with the chairs?

MRS. LORRIMER. [*Embarrassed.*] Nothing—we were merely choosing places!

ETHEL. They lead from the other end, don't they? [*Joining* FLETCHER.

MARION. Yes, you know Kitty is leading for me. [*Enter* DOUGLAS. *He joins them.*] Who are you dancing with, Douglas?

DOUGLAS. No one; I'm stagging it.

MRS. LORRIMER. You don't mean to say, Marion, you have more men than women to-night!

MARION. [*With mock pride.*] Who says I don't know how to give a party?

MRS. LORRIMER. [*To* DOUGLAS.] Damn it! I wish I hadn't said I'd dance with little Johnny, or I'd come to your rescue. [DOUGLAS, *secretly amused, bows his thanks.* ETHEL *and* MARION *exchange an amused glance.*

ETHEL. [*To* MARION.] Douglas ought to give Johnny a vote of thanks.

MARION. Come, they are taking their places. [*A movement of all to go off.* DOUGLAS *touches* FLETCHER *on the arm.*

DOUGLAS. [*To* FLETCHER.] May I speak to you just a moment?

FLETCHER. Certainly— [*All go but* MARION.] Excuse me one moment, Miss Wolton,—Rhodes wants a word with me. [MARION *starts slightly, and, turning quickly, looks questioningly at* DOUGLAS. *He answers her gaze seriously and unflinchingly. She turns to* FLETCHER.

MARION. [*To* FLETCHER.] No—I won't excuse you. [*Assuming a more or less coquettish air.*] You must come with me at once. [FLETCHER *looks surprised, but moves as if to obey her.*

DOUGLAS. But why won't you trust Mr. Fletcher with me? [FLETCHER *laughs amused.*

MARION. [*Nonplussed for a moment; then she changes her mind.*] I was only jesting. [*To* FLETCHER.] But you won't— [*To* DOUGLAS, *looking at him meaningly and seriously.*]—keep us waiting long, will you? I warn you, Mr. Fletcher, I shall let them begin without us. [*Exits through ball-room as* FLETCHER *quickly kisses her hand.* DOUGLAS *waits till they are quite alone.* FLETCHER *moves down right.*

DOUGLAS. [*Following. Quietly.*] Are you going to ask Miss Wolton to marry you?

FLETCHER. I am not.

DOUGLAS. [*Momentary surprise—doubt, then relief—a sigh.*] In that case I've nothing more to say; let's join the others. [*Both make a move to go.*

FLETCHER. [*Who cannot resist saying it.*] You see, Rhodes, I *have* asked her already.

DOUGLAS. [*Stops and, turning, faces* FLETCHER, *whose back is toward audience.*]

FLETCHER. [*Turning leisurely.*] About fifteen minutes ago—but I can't see what business it is of yours.

DOUGLAS. I love her.

FLETCHER. That's no news to anybody!

DOUGLAS. And I don't intend she shall marry a— [*He stops. Short pause.*

FLETCHER. What? Why don't you finish?

DOUGLAS. [*More quietly.*] A man like you.

FLETCHER. Oh, I'm not so very unique; lots of girls run the risk of marrying a man like me!

DOUGLAS. I suppose you told her she is more to you than any one in the world.

FLETCHER. No. "Men like me" don't talk that rot. I put my arms around her— [*Stops, interrupted by the movement of* DOUGLAS, *expressive of rage, controlled instantaneously; he clenches his fists. Finishes with a half-smile at* DOUGLAS.] And told her I loved her.

DOUGLAS. [*Suppressed anger.*] You *couldn't* say she was more than any one else to you, because it would have been a lie!

FLETCHER. [*Smiling.*] You flatter me. [*Crosses to left.*

DOUGLAS. The one that is *most* to *you* is YOUR CHILD. [FLETCHER *starts; is surprised.*] You can't deny the child—

FLETCHER. I "can!" I can deny anything.

DOUGLAS. The lie could be proved to your face. In May, 1893, at Lenox, a young kindergarten teacher,—you blackguard, you!

FLETCHER. [*A little angry.*] Who told you that story?

DOUGLAS. [*Sneers.*] I'm not the only man who knows it! That sort of thing never lies buried!

FLETCHER. The girl's all right now!

DOUGLAS. Oh, I know, you sent her abroad, and pay for the child. Well, that's the mother's lookout, and not mine. But I don't believe she's the only case. One has only to look at your life now.—It was fortunate for you this winter that Mrs. Clipton's divorce trial didn't come off.

FLETCHER. [*A little more angry. Back to* DOUGLAS.] Still, what has all this to do with you, and I'll deny it all besides, if I feel like it, or need to.

DOUGLAS. You know you're not fit to marry Marion Wolton!

FLETCHER. I know I love her.

DOUGLAS. For how long?

FLETCHER. I can't say, but neither can you.—And besides, *she loves me!*

DOUGLAS. Would she if she knew you?

FLETCHER. [*Smilingly.*] Oh, come, Rhodes, drop it! I don't care a damn what I have done. I'm going to marry her! I haven't made any bones about myself. I've told her I've been a bad lot!

DOUGLAS. Oh, yes, I know, you've confessed probably to having been "fast;" that nearly always appeals to a woman, heaven knows why; I suppose it's the instinct for reformation in them. But how much of your life does that word "fast" convey to a pure girl like Marion?

FLETCHER. [*Smiling.*] Quite enough! [*Serious.*] But if she did know all there was to be known, Love forgives a great deal.

DOUGLAS. But not *everything.* There are certain things Marion would never accept. She would refuse to take the place that was the right of another.

FLETCHER. [*Down to him.*] Oh, that's your point, is it! Well, hunt out Jeannette Gros if you can; it'll do you no good! [*Crosses.*

DOUGLAS. [*Follows quickly. Angry.*] You can't prove that, because it's *not true!*

FLETCHER. [*Facing* DOUGLAS. *Angry too.*] I'll prove she had other lovers before me. Good God, man, you don't know what Marion Wolton's love means to me! I've never loved like this before! Why, if it were possible for me to treat her as I have—the other, I *couldn't.* I want to marry Marion Wolton—I *want* to make *her my wife!* and I *will!* I've had all there can be got out of my old life, and I'm sick of it. Here's my chance at a new life, and do you think I'm going to give it up? No! [*Forgetting and raising his voice.*] Do you hear me, No!!

DOUGLAS. [*Softly.*] Not so loud!

FLETCHER. [*Lowered voice.*] No! I'll fight for it with my last breath.

DOUGLAS. Then I say again, you're a blackguard!

FLETCHER. [*Laughs, turns back to audience.*] What do you want to do, fight? You know we can't here. I give you liberty to say to her all you can against me.

DOUGLAS. She won't believe me.

FLETCHER. Exactly—she loves me—

DOUGLAS. But there is one other I can tell the truth to, who may believe me.

FLETCHER. Look out you don't make yourself ridiculous, going about—the jilted lover, trying to take away the character of the accepted man! [*Leisurely following him a little.*

DOUGLAS. I don't have to do any "going about!" You are well enough known in our world to keep most of our doors closed against you. Few people are as blind as the Woltons, and I will open *his* eyes!

FLETCHER. You'll tell her father?

DOUGLAS. He is the one person she would listen to, and he can verify what I say.

FLETCHER. [*Change of tone, showing he fears this.*] Damn it! I mean to be a decent man.

DOUGLAS. [*Goes close to him and looks straight in his face.*] Then go to Jeannette Gros and marry her!

FLETCHER. [*Angry again.*] Go to H—. [*Change of tone.*] You think if I'm out of the way you'll get her?

DOUGLAS. She's told me she doesn't love me, and she proved to me that she won't believe the truth of you without extraordinary proof. There is only one person in the world who could naturally interfere and give her anything like that proof, and that's her father; and I shall tell him to-night, before I leave this house, before you can announce your engagement!

FLETCHER. With Miss Wolton's permission, I will announce our engagement to-night, in spite of you, and her father. [*Music stops. Enter* MRS. LORRIMER, *with a favour, lamb and trumpet.*

MRS. LORRIMER. Oh, here you men are! If you think this is going to be allowed, you are very much mistaken! What do men think we ask them to parties for? Eh? Anyway, a cotillion is a leap-year dance; on such an occasion you are our natural prey! Come, sir! [*Pretending to blow trumpet.*

DOUGLAS. No. [*Smiling apologetically.*] Postpone my pleasure till a little later in the evening, will you? Don't be angry with me; I want to have a few words with Mr. Wolton,—then I'll come and give *all* my favours to you!

MRS. LORRIMER. That sounds attractive; I'll let you off. [*Makes lamby squeak. Smiling, turns to* FLETCHER.] But I won't let you off.

FLETCHER. [*Smiling.*] *Don't,* please! I'm very happy to be your *consolation* prize. [*Takes lamb. Music.*

MRS. LORRIMER. I'm a dangerous woman to make that remark to. You'd better be careful, or I might take you literally at your word.

FLETCHER. Oh, if you only would! [*Pulls lamb's head.*

MRS. LORRIMER. What a charming speech. [*She and* FLETCHER *go into ball-room and off.* FLETCHER *makes lamb squeak.* MRS. WOLTON, *her arms full of a set of gay favours, crosses the ball-room;* DOUGLAS *sees her and takes a step or two towards her, then waits till she has finished speaking to the girl.* MRS. WOLTON *turns, and* DOUGLAS *addresses her.*

DOUGLAS. Mrs. Wolton, is Mr. Wolton in the ball-room?

MRS. WOLTON. No, I think he's in the smoking-room.—Aren't you going to dance? [*Coming into room.*

DOUGLAS. Not just yet—later— [*Half bows apologetically. At the same moment, the music swells and the procession of dancers, in couples, dance in five or six couples into the front room, the line curving away to right to suggest that there are very many more couples in the ball-room out of sight. As they dance, they are laughing and talking—the first couple turns, the other couples making bridges under which the first couple goes, and passes into ball-room and off, followed by each couple the same. Music softens.* MRS. WOLTON *has drawn to one side, when the dancers came in. In this dance, scarfs are used by dancers.*

DOUGLAS. Mr. Wolton there?

MRS. WOLTON. [*Mildly surprised.*] He?

DOUGLAS. I want to see Mr. Wolton very much to-night—*now.* It is a matter of the greatest importance. [*Enter* SERVANT *from ball-room.*

MRS. WOLTON. Where is Mr. Wolton, Howes?

SERVANT. He has gone to his bedroom, m'm. [*Crosses behind* MRS. WOLTON.

MRS. WOLTON. [*Surprised, but not too much so.*] What?

SERVANT. He said he was on no account to be disturbed until the party was over.

MRS. WOLTON. [*A little anxious.*] Was he ill?

SERVANT. He didn't appear so, m'm.

DOUGLAS. [*To* MRS. WOLTON.] Was he feeling ill to-night?

MRS. WOLTON. [*With a relieved voice, showing no anxiety.*] No, not at all. He was in splendid spirits. Probably he was bored and thought he would be quieter upstairs.

DOUGLAS. I don't want to be offensive, but I must, if possible, see him to-night.

MRS. WOLTON. [*Speaking very casually.*] Howes, you might go and say to Mr. Wolton, Mr. Rhodes wants to speak to him about something very urgent. [*To* DOUGLAS.] If he doesn't want to come down stairs again, he can send for you to come up.

SERVANT. Beg pardon, m'm, but he was so very strong with me that I shouldn't under any circumstances go to him, I don't quite like to— [*He hesitates, embarrassed at having not to obey* MRS. WOLTON'S *request at once.*

MRS. WOLTON. Really, he made such a point of it! Oh, very well then, you needn't go, Howes. [*With a nod of dismissal.* SERVANT *exits into ball-room and off.*

MRS. WOLTON. [*Lowers her voice so that* HOWES *sha'n't hear her, as he goes.*] Mr. Wolton is rather hard on the servants if they fail to obey his orders to the letter. I'll go myself and see if he won't see you. [*Enter* MARION *from ball-room, as her mother starts.*

MARION. Mother, where are you going with the favours?

MRS. WOLTON. To your father for a moment.

MARION. But you can't; we need them. [*Crosses. Music stops.*] I'll go for you. [MRS. WOLTON *exits centre as* MARION *exits right.* FANSHAW *appears from ball-room, enters.*

FANSHAW. Come on, Rhodes, we need your help. [*Seizing* DOUGLAS.

DOUGLAS. How long will it take?

FANSHAW. Oh, only a couple of minutes. [RHODES *and* FANSHAW *exeunt, followed by* MRS. WOLTON.

TRIMMINS. [*Off stage.*] Mrs. Lorrimer! Mrs. Lorrimer! [*Enters.*] Oh, Mrs. Lorrimer, won't you dance through with me? [TRIMMINS *does this.*

MRS. LORRIMER. Do excuse me. [*Adds a little sotto voce and coaxingly.*] And as a favour to me, go and take out poor Susie Woodruff. You know it's only "snap the whip" figure, so it won't make much difference to you if she is a bit heavy. [TRIMMINS *makes a bored grimace, and goes up stage.* MRS. LORRIMER *catches him.*] Yes, to please me! It isn't as if it were a waltz and you had to get her around all by yourself!

TRIMMINS. [*Smiling.*] Very well, to please you! But Susan Woodruff, she's the limit. [*Doubles up his arm and feels his muscles meaningly, and exits.* MARION *enters tragically. White, frightened, she staggers quickly into the room and, stopping for a second, gasps in a horrified whisper.*

MARION. Mother! [*Crosses to arch.*] Mother!! [*Music, "Won't You Come And Play With Me." Singing heard.* MARION *turns, frightened, goes down. Her mother comes to her. They meet.*

MRS. WOLTON. [*Frightened, puzzled.*] What is it? What's the matter?

MARION. [*For a moment, can't speak. She opens her lips, but the words refuse to come. Then she manages to gasp out:*] Father!

MRS. WOLTON. Your father—what? [*Starts and looks at her questioningly, frightened, as the music swells, and is joined in by the voices of the dancers.*

MARION. He is dead!

MRS. WOLTON. Dead!! [*She makes a movement towards door.* MARION *stops her.*

MARION. It's too horrible!—he has killed himself— [*Adds the latter in lower tone, almost fainting. The dancers appear in the ball-room, hand in hand in single file, led by* FANSHAW, *and dance wildly in—all singing "Won't You Come And Play With Me." They make a big circle about* MARION *and* MRS. WOLTON, *dancing out through the ball-room, the music and singing becoming fainter as they disappear. The two women are left alone. Re-enter* DOUGLAS *from ball-room.*

DOUGLAS. May I go up? [*He sees the condition of* MRS. WOLTON *and the expression of* MARION.] Is your mother ill?

MARION. Help me take her to—my room—I will tell you. [*Dancers cross as they exit. Music changes to waltz. All go out.* MRS. LORRIMER, *on end, drops their hands.* MRS. WOLTON *and* MARION *shudder as they go out.*

MRS. LORRIMER. Where is Mr. Rhodes?

FANSHAW. He was here a moment ago. [*Enter* SERVANT. *He has his overcoat on and carries his hat.* MRS. LORRIMER *turns.*

MRS. LORRIMER. Have you seen Mr. Rhodes?

SERVANT. He is just coming, m'm.

MRS. LORRIMER. [*Looking at* SERVANT *and seeing something in his face and manner.* SERVANT *crosses hurriedly.*] Is there anything the matter? Where is Mrs. Wolton? [DOUGLAS *enters before* SERVANT *can answer.* MRS. LORRIMER *at once turns to him, ignoring* SERVANT, *who, on a run, bows slightly and exits.*

MRS. LORRIMER. [*To* DOUGLAS.] What's the matter?

DOUGLAS. A most terrible thing has happened.

MRS. LORRIMER. What?

DOUGLAS. You must help me to get rid of all the guests!

MRS. LORRIMER. To get rid— [*Interrupted.*

DOUGLAS. [*Interrupting.*] Mr. Wolton has committed suicide.

MRS. LORRIMER. [*Starts and shudders; speaks very rapidly.*] Mr.—how awful! What are you going to do? You can't tell the people now. What in the world did the man mean by not waiting till the party was over! If it isn't like you men! Your own comfort before anybody else's.—Well—the only thing is to pretend it hasn't happened at all—make some excuse for Marion and her mother—the guests needn't know anything about it, —and finish the party!

DOUGLAS. Mrs. Lorrimer! Impossible!

MRS. LORRIMER. It would be sort of uncomfortable for us who know, [*She adds sincerely.*]—and the poor Woltons, of course,—it is awful for them.

DOUGLAS. I thought if you spoke to Fanshaw and stopped the cotillion and told a few of the guests— [*Interrupted.*

MRS. LORRIMER. [*Aghast.*] What! The truth?

DOUGLAS. No, say Mr. Wolton has been taken suddenly and most dangerously ill—

MRS. LORRIMER. [*To* DOUGLAS.] Very well, I'll do what I can.

DOUGLAS. Stop! [*Music stops.* DOUGLAS *goes to doorway into ball-room and draws the heavy portières, shutting out the ball-room.* MARION *enters.*

MARION. [*To* DOUGLAS, *who stays at curtains.*] They are going?

DOUGLAS. Yes.

MARION. They know?

DOUGLAS. Not the truth!

MARION. Thank you.

DOUGLAS. Mrs. Lorrimer is arranging it. [FOOTMAN *off stage calls* "43." *The numbers are repeated in another voice and farther away. A moment's pause.*

DOUGLAS. I wish I could comfort you.

MARION. [*Smiling strainedly at him.*] Thank you. [FOOTMAN *calls* "56!—56!—89!" "32!—32!—61!" DOUGLAS *holds back the portière into ball-room.*

MARION. I'd better go back to mother. How good you are to us—believe me, I appreciate it all, Douglas, *all.* [*Enter* DAWSON *hurriedly. Shows excitement and emotion. At the same moment enter* FLETCHER *from ball-room at back. The two men speak the word* "Marion" *at the same time, and turning, see each other.* DAWSON *also observes the presence of* DOUGLAS.] Uncle Fred! [*Crosses to him.* FOOTMAN *calls* "115!"] [*To* DAWSON.] You know!

FLETCHER. [*Gently, persuasively joining her.*] Why didn't you send for me at once?

DAWSON. Gentlemen, you will forgive me if I thank you both and say the guests are leaving. The family would like to be alone.

DOUGLAS. I understand, but if I can be of any use?

DAWSON. Thank you.

DOUGLAS. Shall we go, Fletcher?

FLETCHER. Good-night, Rhodes. [*Politely.*] My place is here; it is my privilege to stay by Miss Wolton. [DAWSON *looks up, surprised.* RHODES *looks angry.* FLETCHER *continues, to* MARION.] May I speak? [MARION *bows her head in assent.*] Mr. Dawson, your niece has promised to-night to be my wife. At such a terrible moment as this, I claim the right of membership of the family, to be with you and help all I can. You will accept my offices? [*Holding out his hand.*

DAWSON. [*Shaking his hand.*] Certainly. You have won a wife in a thousand. But you may be called on to do more perhaps than you imagine.

FLETCHER. I am entirely at your service.

DOUGLAS. [*Near doorway back, to all. At curtains, leaves curtains open.*] Good-night! [*All turn slightly.* DOUGLAS *bows and exits.* FLETCHER *going to* MARION.

DAWSON. [*Watching them.*] Thank God! His money will save them! [SERVANT *enters; speaks softly to* DAWSON.

SERVANT. Mr. Dawson! [DAWSON *starts, nods to* SERVANT, *who holds door open.*

DAWSON. I'm coming. [*Slowly, seriously, meaningly.*] Fletcher, I want a long talk with you to-night before you go.

FLETCHER. Very well, sir. [DAWSON *sighs heavily and exits.* SERVANT *leaves door open. The two,* MARION *and* FLETCHER, *hear the door shut behind them, and make a movement; they realize they are alone. A heavy front door slams. Lights out. There is silence. Taking* MARION *in his arms.*] My poor little girl!—My poor little girl!—Cry, for God's sake, cry!

MARION. [*With an outburst.*] Oh, it is so horrible! [*She sobs loud and hysterically in* FLETCHER'S *arms, her own arms about his neck.*]—so—horrible—

CURTAIN.

ACT II.

SCENE. *A church. At left are the steps leading to the chancel and the chancel rails. Beyond the rails are palms, grouped, which conceal the altar. Past the chancel, up stage, is the exit into the choir. Down stage is the exit to the vestry and robing-room. To right of centre begin the pews of the church on each side of a broad centre aisle. The stage is set a little diagonally so that the aisle runs from upper right toward centre stage. This will make a row or two more pews above the aisle than below it. White satin ribbons are stretched above the aisle on each side, across the entrances to the pews; this ribbon the ushers lift aside as they seat the guests. The exit right is made by the centre aisle.*

DISCOVERED. *Three ushers,* JOHNSTONE, FANSHAW *and* TRIMMINS. JOHNSTONE *is sitting in the first pew,* FANSHAW *standing outside and leaning over its front, talking to* JOHNSTONE. TRIMMINS *is leaning with his back against the side of the first pew across the aisle up stage. They are dressed in long frock coats, with buttonholes of white orchids. They are engaged in putting on white kid gloves.*

FANSHAW. Is Fletcher in the vestry yet?

JOHNSTONE. Heavens, no! How long do you want him to hang around? But he won't be late; he's serious this time.

TRIMMINS. I'm glad to hear it, because he's going to marry a splendid girl. [*A short pause.*] I hope to goodness he really loves her.

JOHNSTONE. Oh, he does, I'm sure. I'll bet you, if you like; will you put up a silk hat on it? [*Rises.*

FANSHAW. Yes, I'll take you!

JOHNSTONE. All right. [*Exit from pew. Holding out his hand which* FANSHAW *takes, and they shake.*] Done!

FANSHAW. And I hope I'll lose. And if I were he, I'd tremble in my boots with a past like his, and the present getting so conspicuously favourable.

JOHNSTONE. Oh, I don't believe in your boomerang pasts!

FANSHAW. And I don't believe Fletcher can have one single memory of his own which he wouldn't rather forget since he has come to care for Marion Wolton. [*Crosses to pew.* JOHNSTONE *crosses.*

TRIMMINS. Yes, but don't you think a fellow can sow his wild oats and be done with them, and become a good man and an honest citizen.

FANSHAW. Of course I do, else, good Lord, where'd I be! We can't all be ideal chaps like Douglas Rhodes. But there are oats and *oats*, and Fletcher's are—oats!

JOHNSTONE. Well, he's sorry for them. [*Crosses to pew. As* DOUGLAS RHODES *enters,* TRIMMINS *exits.* RHODES *is also dressed as an usher and comes up the aisle in time to hear* JOHNSTONE'S *speech, as he joins them.*

DOUGLAS. Who's sorry for what?

JOHNSTONE. Fletcher for—for—for—everything!

DOUGLAS. Hum— [*He goes up left.*

FANSHAW. If he's *honestly* sorry, he's no business marrying Marion Wolton.

JOHNSTONE. Why not?

FANSHAW. He has a debt to be paid. He can't wash his hands of the kind of things he's done; if he were in earnest in regretting his old life, he would do something to make up for it.

JOHNSTONE. Well, isn't he? He's going to marry a nice girl and settle down.

FANSHAW. If he were in earnest he'd marry, instead, one of at least two girls I know of—not this one.

JOHNSTONE. Oh, come, there's no reason why he should do a quixotic thing like that, he has a future before him.

FANSHAW. He has their futures before him.

JOHNSTONE. Don't preach. Why should he be dragged down—

FANSHAW. [*Interrupting.*] To where he dragged them?

JOHNSTONE. Exactly; Fletcher's no fool. And then there's Mr. Dawson. He swears by Fletcher now; they're regular pals.

FANSHAW. Ever since Mr. Wolton's death. I don't understand it.

DOUGLAS. [*Coming down left.*] Yes, Dawson really believes in Fletcher—well, perhaps he's right. There must be some good in everybody, and perhaps Fletcher is just beginning to come to the top. Let's hope so.

JOHNSTONE. Hang it, fellows, brace up anyway. This isn't a funeral, you know. Hello, there's the organ. [*Organ music begins, and selections appropriate and usual on such occasions continue uninterruptedly.*] The people will be coming now. [*He exits.*] *Two other ushers make a movement, throwing off a certain lazy, nonchalant manner, and getting themselves into more dignified readiness for their duties.*

DOUGLAS. [*Rises, crosses to left.*] I tell you, Fanshaw, this is a hard day for me.

FANSHAW. But I'm glad you decided to come. It would have made all sorts of gossip if you hadn't.

DOUGLAS. [*Sighs.*] Yes. Anyway, as it's got to be now, we must all make the best of it.

FANSHAW. No one besides me dreams your life is still wrapped up in Marion Wolton.

DOUGLAS. [*Embarrassed, but pleasantly. With a half laugh.*] And I suppose that ought to be some consolation, but I don't know as it is. However, I shall never be able to thank you enough for the comfort you've been. A man must have some one to talk to. And it isn't every fellow who can have a friend like you.

FANSHAW. [*Embarrassed, but pleased.*] Shut up! Here's Fletcher's mother; she came on from Richmond yesterday. [*He goes down aisle to meet her.*] And behind are those girls they want put into the front pews. [FANSHAW *and* DOUGLAS *exeunt. At the same moment that the two disappear,* MRS. FLETCHER *appears on the arm of the third usher,* TRIMMINS.

MRS. FLETCHER. [*To* TRIMMINS, *as he shows her into the first pew left.*] You know Mrs. Wolton, of course?

TRIMMINS. The bride's mother? [*Bows in affirmative.*

MRS. FLETCHER. When she comes, won't you show her in here with me, please? [TRIMMINS *bows and exits.* MRS. FLETCHER *sits, then kneels a moment, and then reseats herself with a touch to the trimming of the waist of her gown somewhere. Enter* FANSHAW *with* MRS. LORRIMER, JOHNSTONE *with* KITTY, *and* TRIMMINS *with* ETHEL; *ladies outside. Ushers exeunt as soon as guests are seated.*

MRS. LORRIMER. [*On being shown into the first pew down stage.*] Is this the farthest front you can seat us? [*In a dissatisfied tone.*

FANSHAW. [*Goes off right.*] This is the *front* pew.

MRS. LORRIMER. [*Laughing.*] Of course, so it is. How silly of me! [*She passes to the end of the pew nearest to the audience.*

KITTY. [*As she follows into the pew, to* JOHNSTONE.] Are we late?

JOHNSTONE. [*Off left.*] No, you're awfully early. [TRIMMINS *off right.*

ETHEL. [*Following into pew.*] Oh, I say, girls. Isn't that a shame, we're early. [*The three women are standing in the pew; they all turn around to glance back into the church, which is supposed to be filling with guests, every once in a while some one being seated by an usher in one of the pews visible to the audience. After a glance round, the three sit down.*] What do you think of Douglas Rhodes being an usher?

MRS. LORRIMER. Oh, my dear, it doesn't take these men long to get over a hopeless passion!

KITTY. If he is over it.

GERTRUDE. Of course he's over it, or he wouldn't be here, would he?

MRS. LORRIMER. Every time I've tried to make love to him, he has seemed to me awfully in love with her still. [*Laugh. Enter guests.*

KITTY. I was wondering this morning where in the world Marion met Mr. Fletcher?

ETHEL. Perhaps it was at that Christian thing-a-may-gig she's interested in.

KITTY. You mean the Young Men's Christian Association?

ETHEL. Yes, I'd bet on it's being the Young Men's. [*Laughs.*

MRS. LORRIMER. Oh, my dear, you know he isn't that sort of a man at all. He's much more my style!

KITTY. Well, you know none of us ever met him till he began to go to the Woltons. [*Enter ushers and guests. A new selection is started on the organ and all half rise and turn, but turn back again at once into their places complacently.*

ETHEL. I think Marion's been getting to be a perfect stick anyway, these last few years, with all the plain covered books she reads and all her "university settlement" stuff in the slums, and her working-girls' clubs and things. But that makes it all the funnier for her to marry a man she's really not known very long, don't you think so?

GERTRUDE. Where did he come from anyway?

ETHEL. Everywhere—which you know is as good as nowhere. He's that sort of a man.

MRS. LORRIMER. Oh, no, his family comes from Virginia. And he's a Harvard man. [*Enter* TRIMMINS *with guest to pew.*] Was in the fastest set there, so he must have some position! [*Laughs.*

ETHEL. And he's rich.

KITTY. But Marion wouldn't marry for money.

ETHEL. Then why is she marrying him?

MRS. LORRIMER. I don't know. I think she must be in love with him.

ETHEL. [*With a laugh.*] Ha! And then everyone says she's so sensible! [*Door slams. Another different selection is started on the organ and a door is shut off stage. The three women all half rise and turn again.*

KITTY. Here they come!

GERTRUDE. No, not yet. [*The three sit again with a murmur of disappointment.*

GERTRUDE. Well. I only hope Marion will be happy,—she's taught so many others how to enjoy the best of life.

ETHEL. I don't see how you can sympathize with her in her philanthropic fads! I believe in being charitable, but there's a right and a wrong way!

KITTY. [*Quietly.*] Yes, I don't suppose there's a fashionable subscription list in town that hasn't your name on it.

ETHEL. *Not one!* And as near the top as I can get.

MRS. LORRIMER. [*Leaning over to speak to* ETHEL.] I agree with you! I went down to one of Marion's working women's evening meetings—and, really, I was bored to death.

ETHEL. Isn't the church trimmed horribly; looks as if they did it themselves. It would be just like Marion to have some silly sentiment about it. [*Organ stops.*

KITTY. [*Strongly.*] I like Marion for her sentiment. I only hope she isn't marrying Fletcher because of it, in the hope that she will make his life, and perhaps have to spoil her own.

BLANCHE. [*Leaning over and speaking to the three women in front.*] Doesn't the church look lovely!

ETHEL. [*Who said it looked horridly.*] Perfectly lovely!

MRS. LORRIMER. Girls, who is that doddy looking creature?

ALL. [*Turning and looking back into the church.*] Where?

MRS. LORRIMER. On the left-hand side of the aisle with a last winter's coat, don't you see, with the huge sleeves!

ETHEL. Oh, yes, with the cheap fur trimming and the mangy muff—who is it?

BLANCHE. Oh, that! It's one of the groom's country relatives.

MRS. LORRIMER. She looks it. The kind that gets cards *only* to the church. [*All laugh. They rise again, excitedly, showing an increase of excitement over the first time they rose, and looking back.*

ETHEL. Are they coming?

BLANCHE. No— [*General murmur of disappointment.*] It's the bride's mother. [*All sit again.* MRS. WOLTON *enters on the arm of* DOUGLAS. *She is very handsomely dressed in black velvet and white lace. She is shown into the pew with* MRS. FLETCHER. *They exchange greetings.* DOUGLAS *exits, at the same time the* CLERGYMAN *enters behind the chancel rail and goes back behind the palms, &c. Meanwhile the following dialogue is taking place.*

MRS. LORRIMER. [*Leaning over.*] You mean how it doesn't.

KITTY. [*Half turning to look back.*] Susie Printly's Baltimore cousin has just come in—do you think she's a beauty?

ETHEL. You mean that *awfully* blonde girl.

MRS. LORRIMER. [*Laughingly.*] Yes, that's she. Fifty cents the small bottle, seventy-five the larger size! [*All three laugh. Short pause.*

ETHEL. I suppose you've heard she's engaged?

MRS. LORRIMER. No, to whom?

ETHEL. Oh, only an American. [*Pause.*

MRS. LORRIMER. Weddings always give me a homesick feeling. I like them so.

KITTY. Well, you've had your share of them, you know.

MRS. LORRIMER. Not at all. I've only been married *twice.* Do you know who I have my eyes on now?

KITTY. No, who is it?

MRS. LORRIMER. *Mr. Dawson!*

ETHEL. What?

KITTY. You're serious . . . to marry him.

MRS. LORRIMER. Yes! Everyone will tell you he's one of the best men in the world.

ETHEL. But my dear, that's a change for you! How'll you ever get him into the divorce court?

MRS. LORRIMER. Nonsense! I don't want to. Haven't you heard . . . my house in Dakota's for sale. I don't belong to the Divorce Club any more . . . the membership is getting entirely too mixed! [*They look back into the church at the people.* MRS. WOLTON *leans over to* MRS. FLETCHER.

MRS. WOLTON. I am so nervous I could almost cry out! Oh, I shall be so relieved . . . really, I can't tell you . . . when the ceremony's over. [*Organ. Wedding march.* FLETCHER *and his groomsman enter in front of the chancel rails. Guests all rise, showing excitement and turning half-way face off the stage, looking down the centre aisle.* MRS. WOLTON *and* MRS. FLETCHER *stand facing the altar.* MRS. FLETCHER *takes* MRS. WOLTON'S *arm affectionately and holds it tight in friendly sympathy. The faint sound is heard of boys' and men's voices singing with the organ the wedding hymn. All watch off the stage, as if following the slow movement of a procession coming up the aisle. Meanwhile the following dialogue occurs.*

ETHEL. The Trimmins boys are the second ushers.

MRS. LORRIMER. Which is the one you were engaged to?

ETHEL. I forget, I've flirted with them both so long, but I think it's the right hand one! [*The head of the wedding pro-*

cession appears. The choristers singing, followed by the six ushers, DOUGLAS *and* FANSHAW *leading, followed by four bridesmaids. The bride enters, leaning on the arm of* MR. DAWSON; *the choristers exit, and continue singing off stage softly until time indicated for them to stop. The bridesmaids and ushers take their places, grouped properly about the chancel steps.* MARION *stands at the centre of chancel rail, where she is joined by* FLETCHER, *the groomsmen standing to one side of him.* DAWSON *stands on the opposite side of* MARION. *The* CLERGYMAN *has come forward and stands facing them on the other side of the chancel railing. The guests open their prayer-books with a flutter of the leaves.* MARION *gives bouquet to* DAWSON. *Music stops for a moment.*]

MRS. LORRIMER. Look! do you see how charming Mr. Dawson appears by the chancel rails. I never saw him in a more becoming place, and if it's a *possible* thing I shall make a rendezvous to *meet* him there one day! [*Music begins again softly, and accompanies the service. At first it is heard quite distinctly while the* CLERGYMAN *is going through, unheard, the first part of the marriage ceremony. A short pause in the dialogue.*

ETHEL. [*Whispers to* KITTY *and* MRS. LORRIMER.] How composed she is.

MRS. LORRIMER. [*Whispering back.*] One would think she was a widow! I couldn't do better myself! [*A short pause in the dialogue.* CLERGYMAN *looks up and raises his voice a little, addressing the congregation in the church . . . but not too loud so as to be too evident.*

CLERGYMAN. "If any man . . . [*A door is shut heavily off stage. At sound of door slam,* DOUGLAS *exits and returns after* JEANNETTE'S *entrance, going directly to* MRS. WOLTON, *who seems overcome.*] can show just cause why these two persons should not lawfully be joined together . . . [*A commotion among the guests, who turn away from the altar, to look back into the church.*] . . . let him now speak. [DOUGLAS *goes top of aisle, to block the passage.*] or else hereafter forever hold his peace. . ."

JEANNETTE *enters, going to the foot of the chancel steps, cries* "Stop!" *She is a young and attractive looking woman, fashionably, but quietly dressed. All in the church are stunned. The groom, turning, sees her, and starts, but controls himself, glaring at* JEANNETTE. MARION *gazes in terror and horror at her; her bouquet drops unnoticed by her.* MRS. WOLTON *starts to leave her pew, but is held back and persuaded by* MRS. FLETCHER *to remain quietly where she is.* MR. DAWSON *steps down one step toward* JEANNETTE.

DAWSON. [*To* JEANNETTE.] Who are you?

JEANNETTE. [*With a gesture toward* FLETCHER.] *Ask him!*

DAWSON. What right have you to interrupt this ceremony?

JEANNETTE. [*With a gesture as before.*] *Ask him!*

FLETCHER. She has *no* right! [JEANNETTE *makes an exclamation of denial aloud.*

MARION. Swear that, Ned, swear it to me before this altar.

FLETCHER. [*Hesitates a moment.*] I swear it.

MARION. [*To* CLERGYMAN.] Go on with the ceremony. [DAWSON *steps back to his place. The* CLERGYMAN *takes up his prayer-book.* JEANNETTE *comes up one of the chancel steps.*

JEANNETTE. Stop!

FLETCHER. Is there no one here to put this woman out? [*He speaks to the groomsman.* DAWSON *speaks to* FANSHAW, *who exits, and immediately after the music ceases. Meanwhile the following dialogue.*

KITTY. Isn't this perfectly awful! I'm going! [*Going.*

ETHEL. I'm not. I'm going to stay.

MRS. LORRIMER. There may be something we can do. [KITTY *and* GERTRUDE *exeunt with several of the other guests.*

CLERGYMAN. [*To* JEANNETTE.] Can you show any reason why this marriage should not . . . [*Interrupted.*

JEANNETTE. [*Interrupting.*] I can.

CLERGYMAN. Then do so.

JEANNETTE. *I will.* [*She exits quickly.* MRS. WOLTON *goes to the two bridesmaids up stage, who at the same time are joined by the two bridesmaids down stage. Guests go out.*

MRS. WOLTON. [*As she goes.*] Henry! [DAWSON *joins them.*] Take them into the choir-rooms, please. [*She motions off stage.* DAWSON *with bouquet exits. Maids exeunt. As they go,* MRS. WOLTON *and* DOUGLAS *meet and speak. The* CLERGYMAN *has been speaking to* MARION. *Ushers urge guests to leave and exeunt with guests after* JEANNETTE *returns.*

FLETCHER. [*To* CLERGYMAN.] I say that woman *cannot stop* this ceremony. Go on!

MARION. [*To* CLERGYMAN.] You heard him give me his word . . . go on.

CLERGYMAN. I am very sorry, but the church does not allow me to. I must give her the chance to prove herself. [FLETCHER *speaks to his groomsman,* JOHNSTONE, *who exits into vestry. At the same time* JEANNETTE *re-enters, bringing by the hand a small child,* EDWARD, *with her. She leads him straight to the foot of the chancel steps, and, pointing to* FLETCHER, *speaks. All through the rest of this scene, the child keeps hold of the skirts of the mother . . . standing close to her side.*

JEANNETTE. This is that man's child . . . and mine. [MRS. LORRIMER *exits; also* ETHEL. *Re-enter* DAWSON *without bouquet.* FLETCHER *speaks to the* CLERGYMAN. MRS. FLETCHER *leaves the pew and joins* MRS. WOLTON. DOUGLAS *joins* MRS. LORRIMER, *and all the guests and ushers leave the church quietly.* MARION *starts to go to* MRS. WOLTON.

MARION. Mother!

JEANNETTE. [*Turning and facing* MARION.] Ah! . . . you go to *her*, in what must be the greatest sorrow of your life . . . well, so will he . . . [*With her arms around the child.*] come to me when he begins to understand, and *that's* why I am here.

FLETCHER. [*To* CLERGYMAN.] Ask her for proofs! She won't have them! It is a question of her word or mine, and surely there can be no such question, when the woman is that sort of thing! [*Turns to* MARION.] Marion! [*The* CLERGYMAN *goes to* JEANNETTE, *up stage, with whom he talks.* MARION *joins* FLETCHER, *and they come down the steps, but she does not look at him.* MRS. WOLTON *starts to go to* MARION. FLETCHER *stops her.*

FLETCHER. [*To* MRS. WOLTON.] No. I wish to speak to Marion alone. [MRS. WOLTON *and* MRS. FLETCHER *speak together up stage.* MRS. WOLTON, *turning back, faints.* DAWSON *and* MRS. FLETCHER *take her out.*

FLETCHER. [*To* MARION.] Do you despise me?

MARION. I can't . . . I love you.

FLETCHER. I didn't deceive you, did I? You will remember I confessed that before we met my life had not been fit to be lived in the same world with you.

MARION. I know, but I didn't imagine anything so bad as this.

FLETCHER. Yes, I realize that now, as it is only since I have known you that I have realized how low I was. Yet, Marion, this sort of thing exists all around us; I am not the only one. . . . [*Interrupted.*

MARION. [*Interrupting.*] *Don't*—don't try to excuse it.

FLETCHER. At any rate . . . it was before I knew you.

MARION. [*Looking up in his face for the first time, slowly.*] Since you've known me have you been good and honest?

FLETCHER. [*Without any hesitation, looks back at her, honestly.*] Yes. [*They hold this position for a moment.* CLERGYMAN *leaves* JEANNETTE. *She speaks after him, following.*

JEANNETTE. This is not *legal* proof, you say?

CLERGYMAN. It is not sufficient.

JEANNETTE. But it's moral proof. [MARION *turns and goes back to her place . . . motions* FLETCHER *to follow. He does so but almost timidly.* CLERGYMAN *turns from* JEANNETTE.] Listen! So long as he remains as he is, there's a chance that the world won't always be able to fling my boy's shame in his face. And I tell you, sir, the agony she would suffer now is nothing . . . *nothing* to what her life with him would be. And think what it is to . . . [*Her emotion racks her.*] watch your child, your own flesh and blood, day and night, all its life, terror-stricken . . . [*She controls her emotions.*] lest you find some trace of his father in him!

MARION. [*Turns to* CLERGYMAN.] We are waiting.

CLERGYMAN. But . . . [*Interrupted.*

MARION. [*Interrupting.*] I love him; I am not willing to give him up for that woman!

CLERGYMAN. But she swears a compact of marriage was made.

MARION. Has she proofs? [FLETCHER *glares at* JEANNETTE; *his muscles grow rigid.*

CLERGYMAN. *No.* [FLETCHER *relaxes.*

MARION. Very well,—I have his word against hers,—that is enough.

CLERGYMAN. [*To* FLETCHER.] But I believe you do not deny the child?

FLETCHER. [*Tentatively.*] Yes . . . yes, I *do* deny it.

MARION. [*Quickly.*] This man's past, sir, is not yours, nor mine. But his present does belong to me, and his future shall be mine too, to *make*, not *hers to mar.*

FLETCHER. [*Impatient.*] Come! We've lost enough time, let's finish this. [CLERGYMAN *goes to his proper place behind the chancel rails.*

JEANNETTE. [*Coming up one of the chancel steps.*] You shall not go on with this marriage.

FLETCHER. [*Half angry.*] She has shown what she is by the way she has chosen to stop it.

JEANNETTE. That's a cowardly lie! And it was only when I saw by the papers that my letters had been useless that I decided to humiliate myself in this way. Do you think I would so degrade my womanhood for the sake of anything on God's earth, but *one* . . . my child? [*To* MARION.] Do you think I could do anything but loathe *him!* . . . [*With a gesture toward* FLETCHER.

MARION. But I love him.

JEANNETTE. So did I *once.* And now I'd save you if I could from all I know you'll have to suffer. Once you're his, he'll tire of you. . .

MARION. [*Interrupting.*] You forget one thing . . . he is going to place a wedding-ring on my hand.

JEANNETTE. Well, look at that! [*She rips her glove off violently, and shows a wedding-ring.*] He placed it there! and said he'd take me to a church and make our compact binding.

FLETCHER. [*Who has started, frightened, at first, has controlled himself and speaks with intense quiet.*] This woman's from the streets. She's up to all the tricks.

JEANNETTE. [*Outraged.*] How dare you! I am not what he calls me! I swear that here in this holy place. *He* dragged me through the streets, and any dirt upon my skirts *his* feet have left there.

FLETCHER. Be silent. [*To* CLERGYMAN.] If you will not finish the service, we will find some one who will.

MARION. [*To* CLERGYMAN.] No, I will not leave here till we are married. I will not insult the man I have chosen for my husband by doubting his word for hers. I won't believe he made her what she is.

FLETCHER. Marion!

MARION. Ned! [*To* CLERGYMAN.] Go on! Go on with the ceremony!

JEANNETTE. You shall not go on! He's done his best to make me what he says I am . . . and God knows he might have succeeded . . . [*Emotion.*] but for my boy's sake I fought the fight for honour . . . [*Completely controlling her emotion.*] The day he tricked me . . . [*With a look of scorn at* FLETCHER.] I stood before him as pure a woman as *you* stand now, and since he left me, there has never been an hour when I couldn't look straight into my child's eyes, not one minute I couldn't feel his two arms about my neck without a shudder.

FLETCHER. [*More angry.*] I won't stand this!

JEANNETTE. [*To* MARION, *continuing in the same key and tone as her former speech . . . and pleadingly.*] *Don't* make vows that will take away this innocent boy's name.

MARION. You must answer to your child for his name and honour.

FLETCHER. [*Enraged, to* JEANNETTE.] If you don't go now I'll . . . [*Stops himself.*

JEANNETTE. Before God, yours, [*To* MARION.] mine, . . . [*Clasping her hands on her breast.*] and *his* God [*With a look of scornful warning at* FLETCHER.], that man is *his* father, and *my* husband.

FLETCHER. [*In a fearful rage.*] You lie! [*Enter* MRS. WOLTON *and* MRS. FLETCHER.

MARION. [*Surprised . . . pained.*] Sh-h . . . go on.

JEANNETTE. [*Coming between* MARION *and* FLETCHER, *she cries out . . . a wild, heart-broken, desperate cry.*] No! you shall not write Bastard on the forehead of *my child!*

FLETCHER. [*Beside himself.*] By God! [*He strikes* JEANNETTE *a blow . . . which sounds. . . .* MARION *cries out and recoils. The two mothers step forward with exclamations of fright and anger.* DAWSON *comes from the choir, brought by the sound of the cry, and goes to* MARION. JEANNETTE *falls when struck. The child clings with both arms about its mother's waist.*

MARION. [*After a moment, drawing in a long breath, to* FLETCHER.] Coward! [*Her uncle takes a step forward to her . . . he carries her wedding bouquet. She seizes it from him and dashes it at the feet of* FLETCHER, *and then, throwing back her head with an expression of scorn, turns from him, takes the arm of her uncle with determination, and goes down the chancel steps out of the church.* FLETCHER *stands crestfallen.* MRS. WOLTON *and* MRS. FLETCHER *look at each other, horrified, speechless.*

CURTAIN.

ACT III.

SCENE. *The library at the* WOLTONS. *A handsomely and luxuriously furnished room, somewhat disarranged by the preparations for the wedding. It is here that the wedding presents are displayed; along the two sides and partly across the end are placed long and narrow improvised tables, covered with all sorts of gifts—silver, glass, &c. &c. There are five piano lamps grouped together at the upper corner of table. There are faded flowers about.*

TIME. *The following day.*

DISCOVERED. MRS. LORRIMER *at left of table, a maid and man servant are busy wrapping up and addressing some of the wedding presents.*

MRS. LORRIMER. [*Who has just finished writing an address on a parcel.*] This is one to go by express, Howes.

SERVANT. [*Taking it.*] Yes, m'm. [*Placing it to one side where are others tied up and addressed.*] Beg pardon, m'm, but it's a great pity Miss Marion should lose a husband and all the wedding presents as well.

MRS. LORRIMER. Oh, it isn't always a pity, Howes, to lose a husband—it's very often a very good thing. [MAID *gives* MRS. LORRIMER *another parcel to address, which she does—copying from a card which the maid gives her with the parcel. Maid exits.*

SERVANT. [*Giving* MRS. LORRIMER *a visiting card.*] This is the address, m'm—still, if you'll excuse me for saying so, Mrs. Lorrimer—if it was me, I'd keep the presents just by way of a kind of consolation. [*She and the* SERVANT *tie up another box.*

MRS. LORRIMER. [*Addressing.*] Ah, but you see their associations would be painful. I have had two husbands and I have each time moved out of the house I occupied with each on the day after losing him.

SERVANT. You know what trouble is, m'm, to have lost two husbands. Grippe, m'm? [*Giving her another parcel.* HOWES *to table up stage.*

MRS. LORRIMER. Not exactly. Another kind of epidemic. The law, Howes. [HOWES *gives parcel.* MRS. LORRIMER *addresses it from a visiting card. Enter* MAID *with* ETHEL *and* FANSHAW.

MAID. I will tell Miss Wolton. [*Exit.* FANSHAW, ETHEL *and* MRS. LORRIMER *greet each other.*

FANSHAW. How do you do? [*Shakes hands.* MRS. LORRIMER *motions with her head a dismissal to the* SERVANT, *and he gets boxes and goes out.*

ETHEL. [*Goes to sofa and sits.*] Do you think Marion will see us?

MRS. LORRIMER. I don't know, I'm sure. She is with her mother.

ETHEL. You don't mean—

MRS. LORRIMER. Yes, but she isn't a bit like she was yesterday. She's crying like a child, poor thing,—what she's gone through!

FANSHAW. Have you seen the papers? [*Has large bundle of them.*

MRS. LORRIMER. No.

FANSHAW. It's in all of them, and some have big pictures.

ETHEL. Yes, my dear, with all of us in. Marion in a low-necked dress. You're a sight, but my picture's rather good.

FANSHAW. [*Who has gotten papers from coat-tail pocket.*] Perhaps you'd like to see them.

MRS. LORRIMER. No, no; put them away quick. I'll see them home. I take every blessed paper. [FANSHAW *up to table where he puts hat and papers.*

ETHEL. What are you doing—sending back wedding presents? [*Crosses.*

FANSHAW. Oh, I say, is that necessary?

ETHEL. I don't believe I would; there are lots of things she's been dying to have.

MRS. LORRIMER. My dear Ethel!

FANSHAW. Yes, why couldn't she—er—forget—er—overlook—er—any old thing with some of them—I mean those she wants? [*Turns up, looking at presents on table.*

MRS. LORRIMER. Well, there are some things I should think she'd be glad to send back. After all, twelve dozen oyster forks are too many for a small family like a newly married couple.

ETHEL. How many sugar spoons did she get?

MRS. LORRIMER. Thirteen, which to say the least, is an unlucky number . . . [*Rises, puts arm about* ETHEL *and comes left.*] and there's that bankrupt stock of piano lamps. [*Crosses to sofa; sits on sofa with* ETHEL. FANSHAW *comes down.*

ETHEL. [*Half laughing.*] That's true! By the way, have you sent back Mrs. Bayley's presents yet?

MRS. LORRIMER. Yes, why?

ETHEL. Go on, tell her, Fanshaw. [*Rises and goes to centre.* MRS. LORRIMER *and* FANSHAW *sit on sofa.*

FANSHAW. [*Laughing.*] Oh it's nothing, only I sent it to Mrs. Bayley myself three Christmases ago as a philopene. I suppose she thought I wouldn't remember, but she forgot both our initials are marked on the bottom.

ETHEL. [*At table, examining presents. Laughing.*] Yes, my dear, and Marion found them. People really ought to be more careful.

MRS. LORRIMER. Think of a woman with all Mrs. Bayley's money— [*Interrupted.*

ETHEL. My dear, it is the rich who do these sort of things. Every year all my second-hand Christmas cards and calendars come from my wealthiest friends! And there's that thing— [*Lifting a vase.*] Isn't it hideous? I don't know who sent it, but— [*Interrupted.*

MRS. LORRIMER. *I* do.

ETHEL. [*Innocently.*] Who?

MRS. LORRIMER. I did.

ETHEL. Good gracious. [*Laughs.*] I assure you I haven't any taste. [ETHEL *down centre.* FANSHAW *rises.*

FANSHAW. No, not a bit. [*Goes back of sofa and up to table.* ETHEL *up stage by table.*

ETHEL. How many presents did Marion get, anyway? [*Looking among the things on the table.*

MRS. LORRIMER. I don't know. [*Satirically.*] I didn't count them.

ETHEL. I don't believe she got very many—Marion has always taken up so many poor people. I'm sure I never can tell what she sees in them! [ETHEL *crosses right of table.*

MRS. LORRIMER. Oh, yes, Ethel, I know how you choose your friends. The other day I heard you were running after the Lloyds—that settles it, I said—they are either going to have a box at the Opera this year, or give a series of dinners, or a big ball. Ethel knows what she's about.

FANSHAW. Exactly—Ethel knows her business, but you left out one thing—they have the best cook in town, too.

ETHEL. [*Taking up a box with a large silver fish knife in it.*] Who gave her this fish knife?

MRS. LORRIMER. The Conrads, didn't they. . . [ETHEL *bursts out laughing.*

ETHEL. Ha! ha! ha! If that isn't appropriate! You know the old man Conrad made all his money out of imitation sardines!

FANSHAW. And very bad imitations, too.

MRS. LORRIMER. Well, if I could make as much as Conrad, I'd be willing to imitate codfish!

ETHEL. [*Takes up a small box at which she has been looking.*] Here's my present. I might as well take it home with me and save you the trouble. [*Puts it in her pocket. She looks at silver hand-glass.*

MRS. LORRIMER. [*Dryly.*] Thank you! Was that your present in a Tiffany box—a small diamond pin?

ETHEL. Yes, wasn't it sweet?

MRS. LORRIMER. Rather. I saw those pins marked down at Wanamaker's Christmas time.

ETHEL. For heaven's sake, don't tell Marion. [*Re-enter* MAID.

MAID. Mrs. Wolton will be down at once, madam— [MAID *exits at back.* FANSHAW *crosses to table.*

ETHEL. [*Who goes back to* MRS. LORRIMER.] Wasn't it awful yesterday—in the church! [*Crosses.*

MRS. LORRIMER. [*With a sigh.*] Awful. [*Rises and crosses to centre.*

ETHEL. [*Kneeling, with one knee on the sofa.*] Still, I will say one thing, I've always been dying to have it happen.

MRS. LORRIMER. Ethel! What a little beast you are.

FANSHAW. Oh, she didn't mean to Marion particularly. Did you, Ethel?

ETHEL. No; if I had my choice I'd rather see it happen to Kitty; she's always pretending she's so sincere and all that.

MRS. LORRIMER. Marion is well rid of a man like Fletcher.

ETHEL. Oh, I don't know—I believe I'd take him to-morrow if he asked me.

MRS. LORRIMER. Well, I wish he would—it would serve you just right.

FANSHAW. Oh, but you couldn't, to-morrow, even if he did ask you—you forget.

ETHEL. Oh, of course I did. My dear, I meant to tell you when I came in that I'm announcing my engag ment to-day.

MRS. LORRIMER. Good gracious, to whom?

ETHEL. To Mr. Fanshaw.

MRS. LORRIMER. Good heavens. Allow me to condole— [*Crosses to* FANSHAW.] I mean congratulate you. And so you're going to be married! [ETHEL *crosses. They shake hands.*

ETHEL. Oh, no, only engaged for a little while,—just for fun. [MRS. WOLTON *enters.*

MRS. WOLTON. Good morning, Ethel. I'm going to ask you to excuse Marion. She isn't seeing *any* one this morning.

ETHEL. I understand—of course—give her my love and tell her not to mind—every one's on her side and,—she looked perfectly lovely. Tell her she had the prettiest wedding dress anyway of the season. [*She goes to kiss* MRS. WOLTON, *who draws back. Both* MRS. WOLTON *and* MRS. LORRIMER *are aghast at the flippant manner of* ETHEL. ETHEL *raises her eyebrows, shrugs her shoulders.*] Good-bye, good-bye. Come along, Fanshaw. [*Exit.*

FANSHAW. [*Crossing to* MRS. WOLTON.] Oh, Mrs. Wolton, don't mind Ethel. She doesn't mean what she sounds like. She never does mean what she sounds like. Besides, she's a little rattled this morning. You see she's engaged again.

MRS. WOLTON. Engaged?

FANSHAW. Yes, not to Johnny. I'm it. [ETHEL *re-enters.*

ETHEL. Come along, Fanshaw.

FANSHAW. All right, I'm coming. [*Takes up hat and papers.* ETHEL *motions for him to leave papers—he does so and exits with* ETHEL.

MRS. LORRIMER. How is Marion?

MRS. WOLTON. In the same extraordinary frame of mind—I'm afraid she'll be ill.

MRS. LORRIMER. You mean, so composed?

MRS. WOLTON. Yes, so hard—she hasn't shed a tear—the only person she's at all human with is that poor creature upstairs. And you know she's sent for *him.*

MRS. LORRIMER. [*Surprised.*] She's going to see him?

MRS. WOLTON. She insists upon doing so.

MRS. LORRIMER. I wonder why? I never want to see any of my husbands again—[*Crosses to* MRS. WOLTON.] after they've once disappointed me.

MRS. WOLTON. I suspect—I don't know—Marion refuses to talk about it, but her sending for this Mrs.—er—Miss—er—dear me, I don't know what to call her—but you know who I mean—I think Marion has an idea she can help her to—er—[*She hesitates.*

MRS. LORRIMER. You don't mean to marry Fletcher? [MRS. WOLTON *nods her head. Incredulously.*] She still wants to?

MRS. WOLTON. Anything for her child's future.

MRS. LORRIMER. [*Very seriously reflecting.*] Well, I can understand that. [*She rouses herself and finishes in her old manner.*] But, my dear, I can sympathize with her, too, poor thing. I know what's before her—you see, both mine were brutes.

MRS. WOLTON. [*Rises and crosses to* MRS. LORRIMER.] Will you mind if I say something very frank to you?

MRS. LORRIMER. [*Tentatively.*] Well—frank things are always disagreeable.

MRS. WOLTON. Anyway, I am going to run the risk. You know you are considered—rather—er—

MRS. LORRIMER. I suppose you want to say heartless?

MRS. WOLTON. Oh, no!

MRS. LORRIMER. Well—then frivolous—

MRS. WOLTON. Yes—perhaps—and—a few other things—but you aren't.

MRS. LORRIMER. Yes, I am.

MRS. WOLTON. No, you're not.—These qualities are all only on the surface. [*Both sit on sofa.*] They are the rouge and powder of your character—underneath, I believe you are plain and sincere.

MRS. LORRIMER. [*Laughing.*] I'm not so mad about being plain, but sincere I would like to be.

MRS. WOLTON. It's your wretched luck in your married life that has made you what you are!

MRS. LORRIMER. [*Sincerely, with much feeling, and almost breaking down.*] You're right. It was a case of hardening my heart and laughing in the world's face, or—or having it laugh in mine perhaps.

MRS. WOLTON. What you need now as you did in the beginning is a *good* husband—like mine was.

MRS. LORRIMER. Good men don't grow on bushes, and besides, good men don't seem to care about me.

MRS. WOLTON. I know just the man, and I believe he's been in love with you for years, though he may not know it himself! [MRS. LORRIMER *looks at her questioningly.* MRS. WOLTON *goes to her and, putting her arm around her neck, whispers in her ear.*] I want you for a *sister*-in-law.

MRS. LORRIMER. [*Embarrassed, pleased.*] Mrs. Wolton!

MRS. WOLTON. Call me "Laura," and I shall feel as if matters had progressed a little. [*Enter* DAWSON—*suddenly and un-*

ceremoniously. Both women start slightly and exchange a quick, covert, meaning glance. Rise.

DAWSON. Ah, Laura—I attended to that for you at once. Has she come?

MRS. WOLTON. Yes, she's upstairs.

DAWSON. Good. [MRS. LORRIMER *coughs.*] Mrs. Lorrimer — [*Shaking her hand.*] I have followed you here—they told me at your house.

MRS. WOLTON. [*Rather hopefully.*] You want to see Mrs. Lorrimer?

MRS. LORRIMER. [*Very quickly, aside to* MRS. WOLTON *with humour.*] Say "Emily"—that may help a little, too!

MRS. WOLTON. You want to see Emily?

DAWSON. [*A momentary surprise at the name.*] Emily, sweet name—er—yes, if you will allow me, alone. [*Goes right, takes out handkerchief, and mops brow.*

MRS. WOLTON. Alone!—very well! [*Aside to* MRS. LORRIMER.] I'd no idea it would come so soon. It must be *that.*

MRS. LORRIMER. [*Blushing.*] No, no, it's something else— [*Believing though that it is.*

MRS. WOLTON. [*Still aside.*] One thing delights me, you're as much in love as he is— [*Aloud.*] Good-bye, *Emily.*

MRS. LORRIMER. [*Aloud, with emphasis.*] Good-by, *Laura!* [MRS. WOLTON *exits.*

DAWSON. Mrs. Lorrimer— [*Crosses centre.*] I want to speak to you on a matter of the greatest privacy.

MRS. LORRIMER. Yes. [*Very quietly.*

DAWSON. You are the only woman in the world who can help me.

MRS. LORRIMER. [*Seriously.*] I consider that a true compliment, Mr. Dawson.

DAWSON. I hesitate because I do not know if I have the right to ask you to share my secret with me.

MRS. LORRIMER. As far as I am concerned, I *give* you that right.

DAWSON. You will help me at no matter what inconvenience to yourself?

MRS. LORRIMER. Yes—but I may not—er—consider it an "inconvenience" to myself. [*Smiling.*

DAWSON. Very well then—the terrible trouble of yesterday is not the only calamity that may happen to my sister and her daughter.

MRS. LORRIMER. [*Rising—surprised, disappointed, but still affected seriously by his serious manner.*] It is of them you wish to speak to me?

DAWSON. Yes.

MRS. LORRIMER. It is for them you wish my help?

DAWSON. Yes.

MRS. LORRIMER. [*With one sigh, dismisses her disappointment and holds out her hand—crosses to right of table.*] It is yours for the asking.

DAWSON. Thank you! [*Presses her hand.*] Mr. Wolton killed himself to escape being convicted of a crime. [*Sits left of table.*

MRS. LORRIMER. [*Withdraws her hand slowly from his, and whispers in tremulous surprise and horror.*] What!!!

DAWSON. He had misappropriated funds entrusted to his care,—exposure became inevitable—you know the rest.

MRS. LORRIMER. But Marion, Mrs. Wolton?

DAWSON. They know nothing!

MRS. LORRIMER. Nothing! [*Looks puzzled.*] But how—

DAWSON. The night of the catastrophe, Fletcher announced his engagement to Marion, and claimed his right to bear a share of the family's trouble. I took him at his word by asking him to come to the rescue of his future wife's name and honour with—money!

MRS. LORRIMER. And he did!

DAWSON. Yes—willingly! He was splendid that night.

MRS. LORRIMER. That's why you suddenly became his champion!

DAWSON. Yes, I couldn't believe the tales against him, when he had proved his love for Marion by such a big act of generosity.

MRS. LORRIMER. He knows everything?

DAWSON. Everything, that same night.

MRS. LORRIMER. And he has never breathed a word?

DAWSON. That was only natural up to yesterday, but now — [*Interrupted.*

MRS. LORRIMER. He doesn't threaten to tell?

DAWSON. He does, unless Marion marries him. He's mad about her. The good in him has loved her up to now; now it's the devil in him. He's not the same man!

MRS. LORRIMER. And what do you want me to do?

DAWSON. Advise me.

MRS. LORRIMER. *I.* Advise *you?*

DAWSON. Yes. Shall we tell Marion?

MRS. LORRIMER. About her father?

DAWSON. Yes.

MRS. LORRIMER. No, no! Not if we can help it!

DAWSON. But— [*Interrupted.*

MRS. LORRIMER. And Fletcher must be paid every cent he gave.

DAWSON. Not easily done. Of course you will understand I have nothing; what I had went at the first, and I shall need all my income now for Laura and Marion.

MRS. LORRIMER. You will borrow this money in your name.

DAWSON. I have no security. [*A moment's pause; both think —rise.*

MRS. LORRIMER. Do you carry a life insurance? [*Crosses left.*

DAWSON. Yes, quite a heavy one.

MRS. LORRIMER. Why not borrow on your life insurance this sum?

DAWSON. [*Pleased.*] Of course, of course! What a fool I've been not to think of that! How clever you are! But again, it must be borrowed privately for many reasons. [*Again a moment's pause, while both think.*

MRS. LORRIMER. [*Showing decision and determination.*] I think I know some one.

DAWSON. Who?

MRS. LORRIMER. Don't ask me till I've seen him and found out—I will go now—[*Crossing up centre.*]—at once, and make a beginning, and you must go to Fletcher and keep him from coming here.

DAWSON. That won't be necessary, for surely Marion wouldn't see him.

MRS. LORRIMER. On the contrary she has *sent* for him!

DAWSON. [*Astonished.*] She isn't still in love with him! I'll go to him and say I've come to talk business; I think that's the best way to put it.

MRS. LORRIMER. Yes, and now, go right away!

DAWSON. [*With a world of appreciation and sentiment in his voice and manner.*] *Without thanking you?*

MRS. LORRIMER. Yes, please, because I don't want you to thank me in a hurry—I want you to take a good long time over it. [*A moment's pause; they look at each other.* DAWSON *seizes her hand, half shamefacedly, and kisses it. He starts for hat, which he placed on table as he entered.*

MRS. LORRIMER. [*Drawing him back—half shyly.*] Oh—answer me just one question. . . .

DAWSON. A dozen.

MRS. LORRIMER. What have you—a nice man—I mean—a man like you. . . [*Interrupted.*

DAWSON. [*Interrupting.*] What kind of a man?

MRS. LORRIMER. A "nice" man—you *are* a nice man, aren't you? [*Smiling sweetly and rather archly at him.*

DAWSON. [*Embarrassed.*] Well—I—I'm afraid I shall have to leave the answer with you—am I?

MRS. LORRIMER. Yes, I think you are—and why have you never married?

DAWSON. Well, you see, *some* people marry so often, some others of us don't marry at all, just to strike a sort of balance!

MRS. LORRIMER. [*Laughing.*] That's mean of you to say to me! Come, answer my question honestly.

DAWSON. Well, I've only known one woman in the world who wouldn't bore me.

MRS. LORRIMER. There are such things as happy marriages, aren't there?

DAWSON. I should like to risk one, only—[*He hesitates and stops.*

MRS. LORRIMER. This "one woman in the world?"

DAWSON. Oh, she's absurd, impossible!

MRS. LORRIMER. Why? . . .

DAWSON. She wants to divorce all her husbands.

MRS. LORRIMER. Well, but don't give her a chance!

DAWSON. Eh, what?

MRS. LORRIMER. Don't give her a chance—any reason.

DAWSON. By George! I never thought of that.

MRS. LORRIMER. [*Delighted.*] You stupid!

DAWSON. [*Delighted.*] Don't you know who I mean?

MRS. LORRIMER. [*Very self-consciously.*] No—how should I?

DAWSON. Can't you guess?

MRS. LORRIMER. I don't want to guess, I want to know for *certain.*

DAWSON. You are "the only woman in the world!" [*He bows low before her, his right arm bent, his hand on his chest.*

MRS. LORRIMER. [*Takes his arm.*] Well, I am ready to run the risk if you are. [MRS. LORRIMER *and* DAWSON *cross right.*] But now we mustn't lose any more time—take a cable-car; I will, it'll be quicker than a cab. Perhaps you won't approve of cable-cars for me, though. They are the most emotional mode of convenience I've ever tried.—This morning, in two curves I sat in three men's laps!

DAWSON. *Ah.* [*Laughing.*] Don't let those curves get to be a habit, or I'll sue the company for alienating your affections.

MRS. LORRIMER. [*Laughing.*] Come! [*Takes his arm again and they meet* MARION, *who enters.*

MARION. [*As she comes.*] Tired out, Emily? [DAWSON *goes up stage to door.*

MRS. LORRIMER. Tired! I never felt so rested in all my life! I haven't tied up very many. [*With a look and gesture toward the table of presents.*] I've been interrupted—and now you must excuse me for a little while, but I'll come back and do some more.

DAWSON. I'll go at once— [*To* MARION.]—an errand for Emily—Mrs. Lorrimer. [*Emphasis on the name and a meaning look.*] Good-bye— [*Going. Both women say* "Good-bye," *but* MRS. LORRIMER *follows him.* MARION'S *back is turned.* MRS. LORRIMER *quickly gives* DAWSON *a large bunch of violets she carries in exchange for a small rose-bud he wears in his button-hole. He cannot get it into his coat. There is amused confusion.* MARION *turns and* DAWSON *quickly exits.* MRS. LORRIMER *down left of table.*

MARION. [*Right of table.*] It's like the death of someone, isn't it? This is the death of my marriage, and these gifts are its clothes.

MRS. LORRIMER. Has—er—she gone?

MARION. No—she's waiting up in my room.

MRS. LORRIMER. What for?

MARION. [*Quietly.*] I mean to make him marry her if I can, here, to-day.

MRS. LORRIMER. [*Doubtfully.*] Do you think you can?

MARION. If he loves me, I think so. I shall ask him to prove his love by doing the one honourable, honest thing there is for him to do. [*To sofa.*

MRS. LORRIMER. You believe in this woman?

MARION. He has practically acknowledged that what she says is true.

MRS. LORRIMER. [*Tenderly.*] And *you,* dear, and your love — [*Crosses to* MARION. *Interrupted.*

MARION. *My* love—for *him.* [*Sits on sofa.*] The blow he struck Jeannette fell on my heart and killed my love. A man who would strike a woman will do most anything,—and think where he did it, and *why?* Because she was pleading and fighting for the rights of his child!

MRS. LORRIMER. I am glad, dear, you can take it so calmly.

MARION. [*Calmly.*] Oh, no, it isn't exactly that—I am reasonable; I see I've escaped a great misery and I'm grateful — [*Enter* SERVANT.] But I suffer terribly, for the moment I close my eyes, I see only the dreadful scene of yesterday.

SERVANT. Mr. Fletcher, ma'am.

MRS. LORRIMER. Oh! He's missed him!

MARION. What? [*Rises.*] Who's missed who?

MRS. LORRIMER. Nothing. Nobody!

MARION. [*To* SERVANT.] Show him in, Howes. [SERVANT *bows slightly and exits.*

MRS. LORRIMER. [*Quickly.*] Let me go the other way. [*Reaches door.*

MARION. You're coming back?

MRS. LORRIMER. Yes. [*Kisses* MARION.

MARION. What a sweet rose that is. [*Touching* DAWSON'S *rose in* MRS. LORRIMER'S *dress.*

MRS. LORRIMER. Yes, it's the loveliest rose I've ever seen. [*Exit quickly as* FLETCHER *enters.*

FLETCHER. [*Speaking seriously but pleasantly, evidently expecting that everything is to be made all right between them.*] Thank you for sending for me, but I would have come without your message!

MARION. [*Looks at him, surprised at his tone. Speaks quietly.*] Jeannette is upstairs waiting.

FLETCHER. [*Starts; his whole manner changes; he realizes now that he has to fight for what he wants and against what he doesn't want.*] Why?

MARION. I've promised her you shall marry her, if I can make you.

FLETCHER. You can't. No, no, Marion. [*Pleading.*] You won't throw me over for yesterday. I lost my temper, I know, and I'm sorry for it, but I love you— [*Interrupted.*

MARION. [*Interrupting.*] Prove it by doing what I ask.

FLETCHER. [*Angry.*] Never! [*Goes right.*

MARION. [*Follows him.*] If you make the reparation there is in your power, it would save you from being utterly contemptible in my eyes!

FLETCHER. *You* say that!!!

MARION. Yes,—will you do what I ask?

FLETCHER. [*Angry.*] No!

MARION. [*Angry.*] Then I do *right* to despise you!

FLETCHER. No, because it is *my love* for *you* that keeps me back. [MARION *laughs a bitter, satirical laugh.*] I will marry only *you.*

MARION. Me! Ha! [*Laughs again.*

FLETCHER. [*Angrily—close to her.*] And I *will* marry you.

MARION. No, you'll not! [*Faces him.*

FLETCHER. I will *force* you to marry me.

MARION. How dare you to take that tone with me.

FLETCHER. I dare more than that.

MARION. [*Goes to bell.*] Take care, or I'll have the servants turn you out of the house! [FLETCHER *laughs an ironical laugh.*] *Will* you marry Jeannette Gros!

FLETCHER. [*More angry.*] No! [*He follows her.*] And I won't leave this house, either. [*Takes her hand.*

MARION. Don't touch me!

FLETCHER. I won't leave the house because it's *mine.* And so will *you* be!

MARION. No!

FLETCHER. Yes, you will, because I'll buy you with your father's reputation!

MARION. With what!

FLETCHER. With your father's good name.

MARION. You—scoundrel.

FLETCHER. We are well mated, for you are the daughter of one! [MARION *immediately touches the bell, which is heard ringing in the distance.*] You had better dismiss the servant when he comes; I am sure you would rather he didn't hear all I have to say.

MARION. [*Almost under her breath.*] *You* cannot injure my father!

FLETCHER. Ask your uncle, Mr. Dawson! [MARION *looks up questioningly, as if she suddenly remembered something.* SERVANT *enters.*

MARION. Ask Mrs. Wolton to please come here at once.

SERVANT. Yes, m'm. [*Crosses room and exits.*

FLETCHER. You remember the night of your fancy-dress ball and your father's—death— [*He pauses*—MARION *doesn't answer, but looks troubled.*] He took his life to save it from being—disgraced, because he was a *thief!*

MARION. Stop! [*She draws herself up and looks* FLETCHER *in the face. He stops. She goes to door left and opens it. He goes right. Enter* MRS. WOLTON, *a little frightened.* MARION *takes her hand and leads her down stage.* MRS. WOLTON *sees* FLETCHER, *but does not bow.* FLETCHER *bows.* MARION *takes* MRS. WOLTON'S *hand and the two women stand, facing* FLETCHER *who stands.*

MARION. You repeat, if you dare, the vile slander of my father!

MRS. WOLTON. Your father?

FLETCHER. All that I said is true, and more!

MRS. WOLTON. What is true? What did he say? [*A pause.* FLETCHER *remains doggedly silent.*

MARION. Ah! You daren't repeat it before my mother! [FLETCHER *sneers.*] You know she would prove the lie in your face! Did you think you would frighten me into marrying you! Do you think a man with a reputation like yours, could injure the reputation of a man like my father, loved by everyone!

FLETCHER. And who cheated those very people who loved him—that's only what *I* did. He was no better than I— [MRS. WOLTON *makes a movement and an effort to interrupt him.*

MARION. [*To* MRS. WOLTON.] Let him finish, mother. [*Holding her back.*

FLETCHER. He left you both beggars, and robbed his own sister besides.

MRS. WOLTON. *It is not true!*

MARION. [*Not believing him.*] How is it, then, that we have everything, everything we could wish for! How is it we have lived in our old home, lived our old life, if we were beggars!

FLETCHER. How?—thanks to *my* money, *I've* paid for it all! [MARION *opens her lips to speak, but cannot; a short pause.*

MRS. WOLTON. You! [MARION *stops her with her hand on her arm.* MARION *and* MRS. WOLTON *cross to sofa.*

FLETCHER. [*Quietly.*] It is true! This is *my* house you're in! [*A pause—the two women are stunned, speechless, unable to comprehend and believe, yet unable to contradict. Re-enter* DAWSON.

FLETCHER. Ah! [*Relieved, as* DAWSON *is his proof.* DAWSON, *looking from one person to the other, realizes the situation. He looks a little frightened at the two women. An awkward moment's pause.*] Question *him* if you doubt my word.

MARION. My father! Is what he says true? [*The women are afraid to question.*

DAWSON. [*To* FLETCHER.] Have you told them?

FLETCHER. The truth? *Yes!*

DAWSON. [*To* FLETCHER.] Your reason?

FLETCHER. I didn't come here to do it; she made me angry. She drove me to it.

MARION. [*In a hard, tuneless voice.*] He says my father was not honest—is that *true?*

DAWSON. [*Answers with difficulty.*] Yes. [*A sob comes into* MARION'S *throat and she almost breaks down, but she at once controls herself.*

MARION. He says *his* money has been supporting us since—since—

DAWSON. [*To* FLETCHER.] A *manly* way to put it!

FLETCHER. [*Crosses left. Bursting out again.*] I wanted you to feel an obligation to me—I don't want to lose you.—You loved me yesterday; if you were once bound to me, you'd love me again—you can't change like that over night.

MARION. If yesterday had left any love in my heart for you, you would have destroyed it by what you have done to-day.

MRS. WOLTON. [*Who has gained control of herself.*] But I don't understand how it was his money—

DAWSON. [*Interrupts.*] At the time of your husband's death a large sum of money was needed to keep his wrong-doing from being made public. I took Fletcher into my confidence, and he lent us this sum.

MARION. You should have *told* me.

DAWSON. I wanted to save you.

MARION. No! no! It was placing me in a terribly false position. It was placing all of us! Well, *I* take the debt now on *my* shoulders! Between us three we will manage to pay it up in time—I am ready to give up the rest of my life to it. [*Crosses to* FLETCHER.] Don't be afraid, you will be paid!

FLETCHER. And you still persist in your refusal to marry me?

MARION. Yes! Yes! Yes!! A thousand times now more than ever.

FLETCHER. And do you think all those years you are trying to scrape up the money, I'll hold my tongue? I don't care about the money, I only care about you.—If I can't have you, do you think I'm going to accept the disgrace you helped heap upon me yesterday? Not I, if I know it! Throw me over, and I'll make public your father's record—every dishonest bit of it! [*Strikes table.*

MRS. WOLTON. [*Cries out.*] No! No! [*Crosses to* DAWSON.

DAWSON. You dare threaten?

MARION. No, no! He can't mean it.

MRS. WOLTON. [*Taking* DAWSON'S *arm.*] No, no! He wouldn't bring this disgrace upon us! What good would it do him?

FLETCHER. Then persuade her to marry me.

DAWSON. No. Rather the disgrace!

MARION. [*To* FLETCHER.] I never thought I would humble myself before you, but I do, now, and I beg you, for the love you say you have for me, spare the name of a man, who at least never harmed you! Don't dishonour my father's memory. Isn't it enough revenge for you that my mother and I know it! [*With tears.* FLETCHER *is a little affected, but* DAWSON *does not see this, and interrupts. He pulls* MARION *away from before* FLETCHER.

DAWSON. No—I won't have you pleading to him! [*Places her to left and* MARION *puts arms about her mother.*

FLETCHER. I know who I have to thank for all this—Rhodes!

MARION. There is no need to mention his name. [*Arms about her mother.*

FLETCHER. Isn't there! It was he who brought Jeannette here—it was he we both have to thank for yesterday's ordeal.

MARION. [*To* DAWSON, *half-heartedly.*] What? [*She places* MRS. WOLTON *on sofa.*

FLETCHER. You didn't believe me when I told you of your father! But this is as true as that was. And the night you promised to marry me, Rhodes threatened to do this very thing.

MARION. It isn't possible! He wouldn't have submitted me to yesterday's humiliation!

FLETCHER. How else could she—living quietly in a little town in Switzerland—know of our affairs here?

DAWSON. I confess Rhodes tried to prejudice me, but I was too much impressed with Fletcher's generosity.

FLETCHER. That money was nothing. I'd do it all over again to-morrow if Marion would only marry me.

MARION. Douglas tried to influence me, too.

FLETCHER. He wants you himself, that's why!

MARION. [*In despair.*] Then I have no one—no friend to believe in! Not even you, Uncle Fred, for you should have told me about my father in the beginning.

FLETCHER. [*To* MARION.] You have me!

MARION. Oh! Can't I make you understand, *you* least of all! [SERVANT *enters and announces*—"Mrs. Lorrimer—Mr. Rhodes." *Those on the stage look up surprised.*

MRS. WOLTON. Oh! this is more than I will bear! Mr. Rhodes, I must beg you to excuse us.

DOUGLAS. To excuse you?

MRS. LORRIMER. I have brought Mr. Rhodes— [*Interrupted.*

MRS. WOLTON. Then, I must ask you to take him away if he is unwilling to leave without you!

DAWSON. No, Laura, wait— [*Interrupted.*

MARION. Mother is right. It should have been enough for Mr. Rhodes to have witnessed our humiliation yesterday. It is adding another insult for him to come here to-day.

MRS. LORRIMER. Marion, you don't know what you're saying—

DOUGLAS. [*Stops* MRS. LORRIMER.] No! Miss Wolton is doubtless right— [*Movement from* MARION.] You did not tell me Mr. Fletcher was here, or I shouldn't have been persuaded to come. I prefer to go—

MRS. LORRIMER. No, not without my telling why you came.

DOUGLAS. No, I must ask you to keep the reason entirely to yourself—and Mr. Dawson. [*Starts to go.*

DAWSON. [*Stops him.*] Not yet. I understand now why you have come with Mrs. Lorrimer. It is not fair that your reason for coming should not be known.

FLETCHER. We know it; Miss Wolton has sufficiently explained. His presence here at this moment is only another insult.

DOUGLAS. Oh, you wish me to go? [MRS. LORRIMER *begins to cross back of* DOUGLAS *to right of table.*] That puts another colour on the matter. I am at a loss to imagine how Mrs. Wolton could accuse me of the sentiments she did. I will stay and wait for an explanation from her.

MARION. I will give it to you if you will excuse me for a moment. [*Going,*

DAWSON. [*Meeting her.*] What are you going to do?

MARION. Bring her here—she is in my room——

FLETCHER. [*Uneasy.*] Jeannette!

MARION. [*Ignoring* FLETCHER, *speaks to* DAWSON *in reply to* FLETCHER'S *question.*] She will tell us who brought her to New York, and that will answer—Mr. Rhodes. [*She exits.*

FLETCHER. [*To* DAWSON.] I refuse to remain to see this woman. [*Takes his hat.*

DAWSON. I have no wish to detain you—but kindly give your address that I may communicate with you.

FLETCHER. My bankers you know,—that is all that is necessary, as I shall very likely sail—what day is this?

DAWSON. Friday.

FLETCHER. [*Bitterly.*] Oh, yes, of course, my wedding-day was on Thursday! I think I shall sail in to-morrow's steamer. [MARION *re-enters. Sees* FLETCHER *going, her voice stops him.*

MARION. You are going—wait. This gentleman has asked me a question, which I think you can answer for me, by answering a question of mine to you. How did you know of my marriage to—of my marriage of yesterday?

JEANNETTE. From a friend who wrote me and sent me the newspapers.

MARION. [*Meaningly.*] A man or woman friend?

JEANNETTE. A woman!

MARION. [*Starts—it is the first shock of doubt she has had.*] Douglas Rhodes had nothing to do with your appearance yesterday in the church?

DOUGLAS. [*Astonished—hurt.*] *You thought that?*

JEANNETTE. Oh, no, Miss Wolton, he had nothing in the world to do with it.

MARION. [*Stands up as if shot, her face full of shame and grief—turns slowly toward* DOUGLAS, *bows her head, half whispers.*] I beg your pardon.

DAWSON. [*To* FLETCHER.] You see you were wrong, Mr. Fletcher.

FLETCHER. Possibly. Good-bye.

MRS. WOLTON. And our secret, my husband's— [*Hesitates, searching for a word—does not finish.*

FLETCHER. Oh, I was only trying to bully your daughter into marrying me—a drowning man, you know—I thought I could make her love me again if I once had a good chance—that's all. Well—I've bought lots of pleasure at the cost of other people's; now I'm going to pay my debt, I suppose, with some misery on my own account, but—well,—I sha'n't disturb Wolton's memory. [MRS. WOLTON *whispers aloud to herself involuntarily*— "Thank God!" FLETCHER *continues speech.*] Because, because— [*A sob comes in his throat.*] I can't help it, I still love his daughter. [*After a long look at* MARION, *exits.* MARION *has turned from* DOUGLAS *and listened to the end of* FLETCHER'S *speech. As he goes,* JEANNETTE *involuntarily seizes* MARION'S *hand.* MARION *frees herself from* JEANNETTE *with an encouraging look at her, and follows* FLETCHER *out.*

MRS. LORRIMER. Well, bad as he is, there is something about that man that takes right hold of me. [*To* DAWSON.] It's lucky I've fallen in love with you, or I might have had one more inning in the divorce club.

DAWSON. I'm only afraid there's a little danger of you trying it again, anyway.

MRS. LORRIMER. With *you?* Oh, no! The day we are married I'm going to begin writing letters to the newspapers in favour of abolishing the institution.

MARION. [*Enters.* JEANNETTE *goes to her quickly, calm and hopefully.*] Go to him, he is waiting. [JEANNETTE *gives an exclamation of emotional relief and joy.*] Be tactful; he wants to sail on to-morrow's steamer—don't . . . [*Interrupted.*

JEANNETTE. I understand—he shall sail alone, if he will only leave his name behind for my boy.

MARION. That he will do—he said so. [*As* MARION *turns,* JEANNETTE *takes her hand and leaves the room.*

MRS. LORRIMER. [*Crosses to* MARION.] Now, Marion, I want you to know why Douglas came.

DOUGLAS. [*Rises, comes center.*] Please— [*He shakes his head.*

DAWSON. But she *must* know some time.

DOUGLAS. Not before me.

DAWSON. Have you forgotten, Marion, our debt to Fletcher?

MARION. [*Realizes what it is. To* DOUGLAS.] *You* would —Oh no, rather leave the debt with him to repay.

DOUGLAS. Why?

MARION. Because I owe you now more than I can ever repay, for the wonderful friendship you have given me all my life! I haven't the right to accept anything more from you.

DOUGLAS. Let me be the judge of that—

MARION. Still, after all that's gone by, you don't hate me?

DOUGLAS. [*Forgetting himself.*] Hate you? No. I—[MARION *crosses to sofa, sits.* MRS. LORRIMER, *as he begins to speak, has touched* DAWSON'S *arm meaningly.* DAWSON *moves quickly and softly to* DOUGLAS, *and, with a quiet, soft, firm touch on his arm, stops him before he can say "I love you."*

DAWSON. [*Aside to* DOUGLAS.] Wait—trust to me who love you both, and wait.

DOUGLAS. [*To* MARION.] You'll leave the debt with me?

MARION. Yes! [MRS. LORRIMER, MRS. WOLTON *and* DAWSON *all exchange happy, hopeful glances.* DOUGLAS *and* MARION *look at each other.*

CURTAIN.

THE NEW YORK IDEA

Langdon Mitchell

LANGDON MITCHELL

(Born Philadelphia, Pa., February 17, 1862)

The performance of "The New York Idea" at the Lyric Theatre, New York, on November 19, 1906, was one of the rare, distinguished events in the American Theatre. It revealed the fact that at last an American playwright had written a drama comparable with the very best European models, scintillating with clear, cold brilliancy, whose dialogue carried with it an exceptional literary style. It was a play that showed a vitality which will serve to keep it alive for many generations, which will make it welcome, however often it is revived; for there is a universal import to its satire which raises it above the local, social condition it purports to portray. And though there is nothing of an ideal character about its situations, though it seems to be all head, with a minimum of apparent heart, it none the less is universal in the sense that Restoration comedy is universal. It presents a type of vulgarity, of sporting spirit, that is common in every generation, whether in the time of Congreve and Wycherley, whether in the period of Sheridan or Oscar Wilde. Its wit is not dependent on local colour, though ostensibly it is written about New York. On its first presentment, it challenged good writing on the part of the critics. High Comedy always does that—tickles the brain and stimulates it, drives it at a pace not usually to be had in the theatre. Is it comedy or is it farce, the critics queried? Is Mr. Mitchell sincere, and does he flay the evil he so photographically portrays? Does he treat the sacred subject of matrimony too flippantly? And should the play, in order to be effective, have a moral tag, or should it be, what on the surface it appears to be, a series of realistic scenes about people whom one cannot admire and does not want to know intimately? Some of the writers found the picture not to their liking—that is the effect good satire sometimes has when it strikes home. Yet when Grace George revived "The New York Idea" in a spirit so different from Mrs. Fiske's, nine years after, on September 28, 1915, at the Playhouse, New York, the *Times* was bound to make the following confession: "A vast array of American authors have turned out plays innumerable, but not one of them has quite matched in sparkling gayety and wit this work of Langdon Mitchell's. And the passing years have left its satire still pointed. They have not dimmed its polish nor so much as scratched its smart veneer."

The play was written expressly for Mrs. Fiske. Its hard, sharp interplay of humour was knowingly cut to suit her hard, sharp method of acting. Her interpretation was a triumph of head over heart. Grace George tried to read into *Cynthia Karslake* an element of romance which is suggested in the text, but which was somewhat over-sentimentalized by her soft portrayal. There is some element of relationship between "The New York Idea" and Henry Arthur Jones' "Mary Goes First;" there is the same free air of sporting life, so graphically set forth in "Lord and Lady Algy." But the American play is greater than these because of its impersonal strain.

In a letter to the present Editor, Mr. Mitchell has broken silence regarding the writing of "The New York Idea." Never before has he tried to analyze its evolution. He says:

The play was written for Mrs. Fiske. The choice of subject was mine. I demanded complete freedom in the treatment, and my most wise manager, Mr. Harrison Grey Fiske, accorded this. The play was produced and played as written, with the exception of one or two short scenes, which were not acceptable to Mrs. Fiske; that is, she felt, or would have felt, somewhat strained or unnatural in these scenes. Accordingly, I cut them out, or rather rewrote them. The temperament of the race-horse has to be considered—much more, that of the 'star'.

When I was writing the play, I had really no idea of satirizing divorce or a law or anything specially temperamental or local. What I wanted to satirize was a certain extreme frivolity in the American spirit and in our American life—frivolity in the deep sense—not just a girl's frivolity, but that profound, sterile, amazing frivolity which one observes and meets in our churches, in political life, in literature, in music; in short, in every department of American thought, feeling and action. The old-fashioned, high-bred family in "The New York Idea" are solemnly frivolous, and the fast, light-minded, highly intelligent hero and heroine are frivolous in their own delightful way—frivolity, of course, to be used for tragedy or comedy. Our frivolity is, I feel, on the edge of the tragic. Indeed, I think it entirely tragic, and there are lines, comedy lines, in "The New York Idea," that indicate this aspect of the thing.

Of course, there is more than merely satire or frivolity in the play: there is the Englishman who appears to Americans to be stupid on account of his manner, but who is frightfully intelligent; and there are also the energy and life and vigor of the two men characters. There is, too, throughout the play, the conscious humour of these two characters, and of the third woman, *Vida*. The clergyman is really more frivolous often and far less conscious of his frivolity—enough, that I rather thought one of the strongest things about the play was the consciousness of their own humour, of the three important characters.

The characters were selected from that especial class, or set, in our Society, whose ancestors and traditions go back to colonial times. They are not merely *society* characters, for, of course, people in society may lack all traditions. I mention this merely because my selection of characters from such a set of people gives the play a certain mellowness and a certain air which it otherwise would not have. If *Jack* and *Cynthia* were both completely self-made, or the son and daughter of powerful, self-made people, their tone could not be the same.

The piece was played in England as a farce; and it was given without the permission of the author or American manager. It was given for a considerable number of performances in Berlin, after the Great War began. In the German translation it was called "Jonathan's Daughter."* Our relations with Germany at the time were strained on account of 'certain happenings', but, notwithstanding, the play was extraordinarily well received.

When "The New York Idea" was first published by the Walter Baker Co., of Boston, it carried as an introduction a notice of the play written by William Archer, and originally published in the London *Tribune* of May 27, 1907. This critique follows the present foreword, as its use in the early edition represents Mr. Mitchell's choice.

The writing of "The New York Idea" was not Mr. Mitchell's first dramatic work for Mrs. Fiske. At the New York Fifth Avenue Theatre, on September 12, 1899, she appeared in "Becky Sharp," his successful version of Thackeray's "Vanity Fair," which held the stage for some time, and was later revived with considerable renewal of its former interest. Two years after, rival versions were presented in London, one by David Balsillie (Theatre Royal, Croydon, June 24, 1901) and the other by Robert Hichens and Cosmo Gordon Lennox (Prince of Wales's Theatre, August 27, 1901)—the latter play used during the

* At the Kammerspiel Theatre, Berlin, under the direction of Max Reinhardt, October 7, 1916. There are translations in Danish, Swedish and Hungarian.

existence of the New Theatre (New York). Most of Mr. Mitchell's attempts in play-writing have been in dramatization, first of his father's "The Adventures of François," and later of Thackeray's "Pendennis," Atlantic City, October 11, 1916. He was born February 17, 1862, at Philadelphia, the son of Silas Weir Mitchell, and received his education largely abroad. He studied law at Harvard and Columbia, and was admitted to the bar in 1882. He was married, in 1892, to Marion Lea, of London, whose name was connected with the early introduction of Ibsen to the English public; she was in the initial cast of "The New York Idea," and to her the play is dedicated.

Mr. William Archer's Notice of "The New York Idea."

* * * * * * * * * * * *

. . . This play, too, I was unable to see, but I have read it with extraordinary interest. It is a social satire so largely conceived and so vigorously executed that it might take an honourable place in any dramatic literature. We have nothing quite like it on the latter-day English stage. In tone and treatment it reminds one of Mr. Carton; but it is far broader in conception and richer in detail than "Lord and Lady Algy" or "Lady Huntworth's Experiment." In France, it might perhaps be compared to "La Famille Benoiton" or "Le Monde ou l'on s'ennuie," or better, perhaps, to a more recent, but now almost forgotten satire of the 'nineties, "Paris Fin-de-Siècle."

I find it very hard to classify "The New York Idea" under any of the established rubrics. It is rather too extravagant to rank as a comedy; it is much too serious in its purport, too searching in its character-delineation and too thoughtful in its wit, to be treated as a mere farce. Its title—not, perhaps, a very happy one—is explained in this saying of one of the characters: "Marry for whim and leave the rest to the divorce court—that's the New York idea of marriage." And again: "The modern American marriage is like a wire fence—the woman's the wire—the posts are the husbands. One—two—three! And if you cast your eye over the future, you can count them, post after post, up hill, down dale, all the way to Dakota."

Like all the plays, from Sardou's "Divorçons" onward, which deal with a too facile system of divorce, this one shows a discontented woman, who has broken up her home for a caprice, suffering agonies of jealousy when her ex-husband proposes to make use of the freedom she has given him, and returning to him at last with the admission that their divorce was at least "premature." In this central conception there is nothing particularly original. It is the wealth of humourous invention displayed in the details both of character and situation that renders the play remarkable.

It is interesting to note, by the way, a return on Mr. Mitchell's part to that convenient assumption of the Restoration and eighteenth century comedy writers that any one in holy orders could solemnize a legal marriage at any time or place, without the slightest formality of banns, witnesses, registration or anything of the sort. One gathers that in New York the entrance to and the exit from the holy estate of matrimony are equally prompt and easy; or that, as one of the characters puts it, "the church is a regular quick-marriage counter."

I presume there is some exaggeration in this, and that a marriage cannot actually be celebrated at midnight, over a champagne-and-lobster supper, by a clergyman who happened to drop in. But there can be no doubt that whatever the social merits or demerits of the system, facility of divorce and remarriage is an immense boon to the dramatist. It places within his reach an inexhaustible store of situations and complications which are barred to the English playwright, to whom divorce always means an ugly and painful scandal. The moralist may insist that this ought always to be the case; and indeed that is the implication which Mr. Mitchell, as a moralist, conveys to us.

He sacrifices the system of divorce for every trivial flaw of temper which prevails in the society he depicts; but he no doubt realizes that his doctrine as a satirist is hostile to his interest as a dramatist. Restrict the facilities of divorce and you at once restrict the possibilities of matrimonial comedy. Marriage becomes no longer a comic, but a tragic institution.

In order to keep his theme entirely on the comic plane, Mr. Mitchell has given no children to either of the two couples whom he puts through such a fantastic quadrille. Law or no law, the separation of its parents is always a tragedy to the child; which is not to say, of course, that their remaining together may not in some cases be the more tragic of the two alternatives. Be this as it may, Mr. Mitchell has eluded the issue.

Nor has he thereby falsified his problem, for his characters belong to that class of society in which, as Mr. Dooley points out, the multiplication of automobiles is preferred to that of progeny. But he has not omitted to hint at the problem of the children, and, as it were, confess his deliberate avoidance of it. He does so in a touch of exquisite irony. *John* and *Cynthia Karslake* are a couple devoted, not to automobiles, but to horses. Even their common passion for racing cannot keep them together; but their divorce is so "premature," and leaves *John* so restless and dissatisfied, that he actually neglects the cares of the stable. His favourite mare, Cynthia K, falls ill, and when his trainer brings him the news he receives it with shocking callousness. Then the trainer meets *Cynthia* and complains to her of her ex-husband's indifference. "Ah, ma'am," he says, "when husband and wife splits, it's the horses that suffers." I know not where to look for a speech of profounder ironic implication. More superficial, but still a good specimen of Mr. Mitchell's wit, is *William Sudley's* remark as to *John Karslake:* 'Oh, yes, he comes of a very respectable family, though I remember his father served a term in the Senate."

Altogether "The New York Idea" is, from the intellectual point of view, the most remarkable piece of work I have encountered in America. It is probably too true to the details of American life to have much success in England; but the situation at the end of the third act could not fail to bring down the house even here. It would take too long to describe it in detail. Suffice it to say that just at the point where *Cynthia Karslake* dismisses her second bridegroom, to return to her first, the choir assembled for the marriage ceremony, mistaking a signal, bursts forth with irresistibly ludicrous effect into "The Voice That Breathed O'er Eden."*

** The Editor takes the occasion to express his thanks to Mr. William Archer for his kind permission to quote this analysis of the play.*

LYRIC THEATRE

REGINALD DeKOVEN, - - - - - - - Proprietor
SAM S. and LEE SHUBERT (Inc.), - - - Lessees and Managers

NINTH AND LAST WEEK.
BEGINNING MONDAY EVENING, JANUARY 14, 1907.
Matinee Saturday.

Under the Direction of HARRISON GREY FISKE

MRS. FISKE

—AND—

THE MANHATTAN COMPANY

Presenting a Play in Four Acts, Entitled

THE NEW YORK IDEA

BY LANGDON MITCHELL

Cast of Characters.

Philip Phillimore......................................Charles Harbury
Mrs. Phillimore, his mother......................................Ida Vernon
The Reverend Mathew Phillimore, his brother..............Dudley Clinton
Grace Phillimore, his sister..............................Emily Stevens
Miss Heneage, his aunt..................................Blanche Weaver
William Sudley, his cousin................................Dudley Digges
Mrs. Vida Phillimore, his divorced wife......................Marion Lea
Brooks, her footman......................................Frederick Kerby
Benson, her maid..Belle Bohn
Sir Wilfrid Cates-Darby....................................George Arliss
John Karslake..John Mason
Mrs. Cynthia Karslake, his divorced wife....................Mrs. Fiske
Nogam, his valet..James Morley
Tim Fiddler..Robert V. Ferguson
Thomas, the Phillimore's family servant....................Richard Clarke

ACT I—Drawing-Room in the Phillimore house, Washington Square.
Wednesday afternoon, at five o'clock.

ACT II—Mrs. Vida Phillimore's Boudoir, Fifth Avenue.
Thursday morning, at eleven.

ACT III—Same as Act I.
Thursday evening, at ten.

ACT IV—John Karslake's House, Madison Avenue.
Thursday, at midnight.

Scene—New York. Time—The Present.

The production staged by Mr. and Mrs. Fiske.

THE NEW YORK IDEA

A COMEDY IN FOUR ACTS

By LANGDON MITCHELL

[This play, copyrighted in 1907, 1908, and published originally by Walter H. Baker and Co., of Boston, Mass., is fully protected and the right of representation is reserved. Application for the right of performing this play may be made to Alice Kauser, 1402 Broadway, New York, N. Y. The Editor takes this opportunity of thanking Mr. Langdon Mitchell for his great interest in the compilation of this Collection, and for his permission to have "The New York Idea" used in it. The complete revision of the stage directions, especially for this volume, makes it possible to regard the play, here printed, as the only authentic version.]

THE PEOPLE.

PHILIP PHILLIMORE, *a Judge on the bench, age 50.*
GRACE PHILLIMORE, *his sister, age 20.*
MRS. PHILLIMORE, *his mother, age 70.*
MISS HENEAGE, *his aunt, age 60.*
MATTHEW PHILLIMORE, *his brother—a bishop, age 45.*
WILLIAM SUDLEY, *his cousin, age 50.*
MRS. VIDA PHILLIMORE, *his divorced wife, age 35.*
SIR WILFRID CATES-DARBY.
JOHN KARSLAKE, *lawyer, politician and racing-man, age 35.*
MRS. CYNTHIA KARSLAKE, *his divorced wife, age 25.*
BROOKS, MRS. PHILLIMORE'S *footman.*
TIM FIDDLER, MR. KARSLAKE'S *trainer.*
NOGAM, *his valet.*
THOMAS, *the family servant of the* PHILLIMORES, *age 45.*
BENSON, MRS. VIDA PHILLIMORE'S *maid, age 20.*

The following is the Cast for the evening performance at the Lyric Theatre, New York, Monday, November 19, 1906.

PHILIP PHILLIMORE	Charles Harbury.
MRS. PHILLIMORE, *his mother*	Ida Vernon.
THE REVEREND MATTHEW PHILLIMORE, *his brother*	Dudley Clinton.
GRACE PHILLIMORE, *his sister*	Emily Stevens.
MISS HENEAGE, *his aunt*	Blanche Weaver.
WILLIAM SUDLEY, *his cousin*	William B. Mack.
MRS. VIDA PHILLIMORE, *his divorced wife*	Marion Lea.
BROOKS, *her footman*	George Harcourt.
BENSON, *her maid*	Belle Bohn.
SIR WILFRID CATES-DARBY	George Arliss.
JOHN KARSLAKE	John Mason.
MRS. CYNTHIA KARSLAKE, *his divorced wife*	Mrs. Fiske.
NOGAM, *his valet*	Dudley Digges.
TIM FIDDLER	Robert V. Ferguson.
THOMAS, the PHILLIMORE'S *family servant*	Richard Clarke.

Scene—New York. Time—The Present.

Revived in New York at The Playhouse, Tuesday Evening, September 28, 1915, with the following Cast.

PHILIP PHILLIMORE	Lumsden Hare.
GRACE PHILLIMORE	Norah Lamison.
MRS. PHILLIMORE	Eugenie Woodward.
MISS HENEAGE	Josephine Lovett.
MATTHEW PHILLIMORE	Albert Reed.
WILLIAM SUDLEY	John Cromwell.
MRS. VIDA PHILLIMORE	Mary Nash.
SIR WILFRID CATES-DARBY	Ernest Lawford.
JOHN KARSLAKE	Conway Tearle.
MRS. CYNTHIA KARSLAKE	Grace George.
BROOKS	Selwyn Joyce.
TIM FIDDLER	Tracy Barrow.
NOGAM	G. Guthrie McClintic.
THOMAS	Richard Clarke.
BENSON	Anita Wood.

To Marion Lea

THE NEW YORK IDEA

ACT I.

SCENE. *Living-room in the house of* PHILIP PHILLIMORE. *Five* P. M. *of an afternoon of May. The general air and appearance of the room is that of an old-fashioned, decorous, comfortable interior. There are no electric lights and no electric bells. Two bell ropes as in old-fashioned houses. The room is in dark tones inclining to sombre and of old-fashioned elegance.*

Seated in the room are MISS HENEAGE, MRS. PHILLIMORE *and* THOMAS. MISS HENEAGE *is a solidly built, narrow-minded woman in her sixties. She makes no effort to look younger than she is, and is expensively but quietly dressed, with heavy elegance. She commands her household and her family connection, and on the strength of a large and steady income feels that her opinion has its value.* MRS. PHILLIMORE *is a semi-professional invalid, refined and unintelligent. Her movements are weak and fatigued. Her voice is habitually plaintive and she is entirely a lady without a trace of being a woman of fashion.* THOMAS *is an easy-mannered, but respectful family servant, un-English both in style and appearance. He has no deportment worthy of being so called, and takes an evident interest in the affairs of the family he serves.*

MISS HENEAGE *is seated at the tea-table, facing the footlights.* MRS. PHILLIMORE *is seated at the table on the right.* THOMAS *stands near by. Tea things on table. Decanter of sherry in coaster. Bread and butter on plate. Vase with flowers. Silver match-box. Large old-fashioned tea urn. Guard for flame. "The Evening Post" on tea-table.* MISS HENEAGE *and* MRS. PHILLIMORE *both have cups of tea.* MISS HENEAGE *sits up very straight, and pours tea for* GRACE, *who enters from door. She is a pretty and fashionably dressed girl of twenty. She speaks superciliously, coolly, and not too fast. She sits on the sofa gracefully and without lounging. She wears a gown suitable for spring visiting, hat, parasol, and gloves.*

GRACE. [*As she moves to the sofa.*] I never in my life walked so far and found so few people at home. [*Pauses. Takes off gloves. Somewhat querulously.*] The fact is the nineteenth of May is ridiculously late to be in town.

MISS HENEAGE. Thomas, Mr. Phillmore's sherry?

THOMAS. [*Indicating the particular table.*] The sherry, ma'am.

MISS HENEAGE. Mr. Phillimore's *Post?*

THOMAS. [*Pointing to "The Evening Post" on the tea-table.*] The *Post,* ma'am.

MISS HENEAGE. [*Indicating cup.*] Miss Phillimore.

THOMAS *takes cup of tea to* GRACE. *Silence. They all sip tea.* THOMAS *goes back, fills sherry glass, remaining round and about the tea-table. They all drink tea during their entire conversation.*

GRACE. The Dudleys were at home. They wished to know when my brother Philip was to be married, and where and how?

MISS HENEAGE. If the Dudleys were persons of breeding, they'd not intrude their curiosity upon you.

GRACE. I like Lena Dudley.

MRS. PHILLIMORE. [*Speaking slowly and gently.*] Do I know Miss Dudley?

GRACE. She knows Philip. She expects an announcement of the wedding.

MRS. PHILLIMORE. I trust you told her that my son, my sister and myself are all of the opinion that those who have been divorced should remarry with modesty and without parade.

GRACE. I told the Dudleys Philip's wedding was here, tomorrow.

MISS HENEAGE. [*To* MRS. PHILLIMORE, *picking up a sheet of paper from the table.*] I have spent the afternoon, Mary, in arranging and listing the wedding gifts, and in writing out the announcements of the wedding. I think I have attained a proper form of announcement. [*Taking the sheet of note-paper and giving it to* THOMAS.] Of course the announcement Philip himself made was quite out of the question. [GRACE *smiles.*] However, there is mine. [*She points to the paper.* THOMAS *gives the list to* MRS. PHILLMORE *and moves away.*

GRACE. I hope you'll send an announcement to the Dudleys.

MRS. PHILLIMORE. [*Prepared to make the best of things, plaintively reads.*] "Mr. Philip Phillimore and Mrs. Cynthia Dean Karslake announce their marriage, May twentieth, at three o'clock, Nineteen A, Washington Square, New York." [*Replacing the paper on* THOMAS'S *salver.*] It sounds very nice.

[THOMAS *returns the paper to* MISS HENEAGE.

MISS HENEAGE. In my opinion it barely escapes sounding nasty. However, it is correct. The only remaining question is—to whom the announcement should not be sent. [THOMAS *goes out.*] I consider an announcement of the wedding of two divorced persons to be in the nature of an intimate communication. It not only announces the wedding—it also announces the divorce. [*Returning to her teacup.*] The person I shall ask counsel of is cousin William Sudley. He promised to drop in this afternoon.

GRACE. Oh! We shall hear all about Cairo.

MRS. PHILLIMORE. William is judicious. [THOMAS *returns.*

MISS HENEAGE. [*With finality.*] Cousin William will disapprove of the match unless a winter in Cairo has altered his moral tone.

THOMAS. [*Announcing.*] Mr. Sudley.

He ushers in WILLIAM SUDLEY, *a little oldish gentleman. He is and appears thoroughly insignificant. But his opinion of the place he occupies in the world is enormous. His manners, voice, presence, are all those of a man of breeding and self-importance.*

MRS. PHILLIMORE *and* MISS HENEAGE. [*Rising and greeting* SUDLEY; *a little tremulously.*] My dear William!

[THOMAS *withdraws.*

SUDLEY. [*Shakes hands with* MRS. PHILLIMORE, *soberly glad to see them.*] How d'ye do, Mary? [*Greeting* MISS HENEAGE.] A very warm May you're having, Sarah.

GRACE. [*Coming forward to welcome him.*] Dear Cousin William!

MISS HENEAGE. Wasn't it warm in Cairo when you left?

She will have the strict truth, or nothing; still, on account of SUDLEY'S *impeccable respectability, she treats him with more than usual leniency.*

SUDLEY. [*Sitting down.*] We left Cairo six weeks ago, Grace, so I've had no news since you wrote in February that Philip was engaged. [*After a pause.*] I need not to say I consider Philip's engagement excessively regrettable. He is a judge upon the Supreme Court bench with a divorced wife—and such a divorced wife!

GRACE. Oh, but Philip has succeeded in keeping everything as quiet as possible.

SUDLEY. [*Acidly.*] No, my dear! He has not succeeded in keeping his former wife as quiet as possible. We had not been in Cairo a week when who should turn up but Vida Phillimore. She went everywhere and did everything no woman should!

GRACE. [*With unfeigned interest.*] Oh, what did she do?

SUDLEY. She "did" Cleopatra at the tableaux at Lord Errington's! She "did" Cleopatra, and she did it robed only in some diaphanous material of a nature so transparent that—in fact she appeared to be draped in moonshine. [MISS HENEAGE *indicates the presence of* GRACE *and rises.*] That was only the beginning. As soon as she heard of Philip's engagement, she gave a dinner in honour of it! Only divorcées were asked! And she had a dummy —yes, my dear, a dummy!—at the head of the table. He stood for Philip—that is he sat for Philip!

[*Rising and moving to the table.*

MISS HENEAGE. [*Irritated and disgusted.*] Ah!

MRS. PHILLIMORE. [*With dismay and pain.*] Dear me!

MISS HENEAGE. [*Confident of the value of her opinion.*] I disapprove of Mrs. Phillimore.

SUDLEY. [*Taking a cigarette.*] Of course you do, but has Philip taken to Egyptian cigarettes in order to celebrate my winter at Cairo?

GRACE. Those are Cynthia's.

SUDLEY. [*Thinking that no one is worth knowing whom he does not know.*] Who is "Cynthia?"

GRACE. Mrs. Karslake—She's staying here, Cousin William. She'll be down in a minute.

SUDLEY. [*Shocked.*] You don't mean to tell me—? —!

MISS HENEAGE. Yes, William, Cynthia is Mrs. Karslake—Mrs. Karslake has no New York house. I disliked the publicity of a hotel in the circumstances, and, accordingly, when she became engaged to Philip, I invited her here.

SUDLEY. [*Suspicious and distrustful.*] And may I ask *who* Mrs. Karslake is?

MISS HENEAGE. [*With confidence.*] She was a Deane.

SUDLEY. [*Walking about the room, sorry to be obliged to concede good birth to any but his own blood.*] Oh, oh—well, the Deanes are extremely nice people. [*Approaching the table.*] Was her father J. William Deane?

MISS HENEAGE. [*Nodding, still more secure.*] Yes.

SUDLEY. [*Giving in with difficulty.*] The family is an old one. J. William Deane's daughter? Surely he left a very considerable—

MISS HENEAGE. Oh, fifteen or twenty millions.

SUDLEY. [*Determined not to be dazzled.*] If I remember rightly she was brought up abroad.

MISS HENEAGE. In France and England—and I fancy brought up with a very gay set in very gay places. In fact she is what is called a "sporty" woman.

SUDLEY. [*Always ready to think the worst.*] We might put up with that. But you don't mean to tell me Philip has the—the—assurance to marry a woman who has been divorced by—

MISS HENEAGE. Not at all. Cynthia Karslake divorced her husband.

SUDLEY. [*Gloomily, since he has less fault to find than he expected.*] She divorced him! Ah!

[*He seeks the consolation of his tea.*

MISS HENEAGE. The suit went by default. And, my dear William, there are many palliating circumstances. Cynthia was married to Karslake only seven months. There are no—[*Glancing at* GRACE] no hostages to Fortune! Ahem!

SUDLEY. [*Still unwilling to be pleased.*] Ah! What sort of a young woman is she?

GRACE. [*With the superiority of one who is not too popular.*] Men admire her.

MISS HENEAGE. She's not conventional.

MRS. PHILLIMORE. [*Showing a faint sense of justice.*] I am bound to say she has behaved discreetly ever since she arrived in this house.

MISS HENEAGE. Yes, Mary—but I sometimes suspect that she exercises a degree of self-control—

SUDLEY. [*Glad to have something against some one.*] She claps on the lid, eh? And you think that perhaps some day she'll boil over? Well, of course fifteen or twenty millions—but who's Karslake?

GRACE. [*Very superciliously.*] He owns Cynthia K. She's the famous mare.

MISS HENEAGE. He's Henry Karslake's son.

SUDLEY. [*Beginning to make the best of fifteen millions-in-law.*] Oh!—Henry!—Very respectable family. Although I remember his father served a term in the Senate. And so the wedding is to be to-morrow?

MRS. PHILLIMORE. [*Assenting.*] To-morrow.

SUDLEY. [*Rising, his respectability to the front when he thinks of the ceremony.* GRACE *rises.*] To-morrow. Well, my dear Sarah, a respectable family with some means. We must accept her. But on the whole, I think it will be best for me not to see the young woman. My disapprobation would make itself apparent.

GRACE. [*Whispering to* SUDLEY.] Cynthia's coming.

[*He doesn't hear.*

CYNTHIA *comes in, absorbed in reading a newspaper. She is a young creature in her twenties, small and high-bred, full of the love of excitement and sport. Her manner is wide-awake and keen, and she is evidently in no fear of the opinion of others. Her dress is exceedingly elegant, but with the elegance of a woman whose chief interests lie in life out of doors. There is nothing hard or masculine in her style, and her expression is youthful and ingenuous.*

SUDLEY. [*Sententious and determinately epigrammatic.*] The uncouth modern young woman, eight feet high, with a skin like a rhinoceros and manners like a cave-dweller—an habitué of the race-track and the divorce court—

GRACE. [*Aside to* SUDLEY.] Cousin William!

SUDLEY. Eh, oh!

CYNTHIA. [*Reading her newspaper, advances into the room, immersed, excited, trembling. She lowers paper to catch the light.*] "Belmont favourite—six to one—Rockaway—Rosebud, and Flying Cloud. Slow track—raw wind—h'm, h'm, h'm— At the half, Rockaway forged ahead, when Rosebud under the lash made a bold bid for victory—neck by neck—for a quarter—when Flying Cloud slipped by the pair and won on the post by a nose in one forty nine!" [*Speaking with the enthusiasm of a sport.*] Oh, I wish I'd seen the dear thing do it. Oh, it's Mr. Sudley! You must think me very rude. How do you do, Mr. Sudley?

[*Going over to* SUDLEY.

SUDLEY. [*Bowing without cordiality.*] Mrs. Karslake.

[CYNTHIA *pauses, feeling he should say something. As he says nothing, she speaks again.*

CYNTHIA. I hope Cairo was delightful? Did you have a smooth voyage?

SUDLEY. [*Pompously.*] You must permit me, Mrs. Karslake—

CYNTHIA. [*With good temper, somewhat embarrassed, and talking herself into ease.*] Oh, please don't welcome me to the family. All that formal part is over, if you don't mind. I'm one of the tribe now! You're coming to our wedding to-morrow?

SUDLEY. My dear Mrs. Karslake, I think it might be wiser—

CYNTHIA. [*Still with cordial good temper.*] Oh, but you must come! I mean to be a perfect wife to Philip and all his relations! That sounds rather miscellaneous, but you know what I mean.

SUDLEY. [*Very sententious.*] I am afraid—

CYNTHIA. [*Gay and still covering her embarrassment.*] If you don't come, it'll look as if you were not standing by Philip when he's in trouble! You'll come, won't you—but of course you will.

SUDLEY. [*After a self-important pause.*] I will come, Mrs. Karslake. [*Pausing.*] Good-afternoon. [*In a tone of sorrow and light compassion.*] Good-bye, Mary. Good-afternoon, Sarah. [*Sighing.*] Grace, dear. [*To* MISS HENEAGE.] At what hour did you say the alimony commences?

MISS HENEAGE. [*Quickly and commandingly to cover his slip.*] The ceremony is at three P. M., William.

[SUDLEY *walks toward the door.*

MRS. PHILLIMORE. [*With fatigued voice and manner as she rises.*] I am going to my room to rest awhile.

[*She trails slowly from the room.*

MISS HENEAGE. [*To* SUDLEY.] Oh, William, one moment—I entirely forgot! I've a most important social question to ask you! [*She accompanies him slowly to the door.*] in regard to the announcements of the wedding—who they shall be sent to and who not. For instance—the Dudleys—[*Deep in their talk,* SUDLEY *and* MISS HENEAGE *pass out together.*

CYNTHIA. [*From the sofa.*] So that's Cousin William?

GRACE. [*From the tea-table.*] Don't you like him?

CYNTHIA. [*Calmly sarcastic.*] Like him? I love him. He's so generous. He couldn't have received me with more warmth if I'd been a mulatto.

THOMAS *comes in, preceded by* PHILLIMORE. PHILIP PHILLIMORE *is a self-centered, short-tempered, imperious member of the respectable fashionables of New York. He is well and solidly dressed, and in manner and speech evidently a man of family. He is accustomed to being listened to in his home circle and from the bench, and it is practically impossible for him to believe that he can make a mistake.*

GRACE. [*Outraged.*] Really you know— [CYNTHIA *moves to the table.*] Philip!

PHILIP *nods to* GRACE *absent-mindedly. He is in his working suit and looks tired. He walks into the room silently; goes over to the tea-table, bends over and kisses* CYNTHIA *on the forehead. Goes to his chair, which* THOMAS *has moved to suit him. He sits, and sighs with satisfaction.*

PHILIP. [*As if exhausted by brain work.*] Ah, Grace! [GRACE *immediately sails out of the room.*] Well, my dear, I thought I should never extricate myself from the court-room. You look very debonnair!

CYNTHIA. The tea's making. You'll have your glass of sherry?

PHILIP. [*The strain of the day evidently having been severe.*] Thanks! [*Taking it from* THOMAS *and sighing.*] Ah!

CYNTHIA. I can see it's been a tiring day with you.

PHILIP. [*His great tussle with the world leaving him unworsted but utterly spent.*] H'm! [*He gratefully sips his tea.*

CYNTHIA. Were the lawyers very long-winded?

PHILIP. [*Almost too tired for speech.*] Prolix to the point of somnolence. It might be affirmed without inexactitude that the prolixity of counsel is the somnolence of the judiciary. I am fatigued, ah! [*A little suddenly, awaking to the fact that his orders have not been carried out to the letter.*] Thomas! My *Post* is not in its usual place!

CYNTHIA. It's here, Philip. [THOMAS *gets it.*

PHILIP. Thanks, my dear. [*Opening "The Post."*] Ah! This hour with you—is—is really the—the—[*Absently.*] the one vivid moment of the day. [*Reading.*] H'm—shocking attack by the President on vested interests. H'm—too bad—but it's to be expected. The people insisted on electing a desperado to the presidential office—they must take the hold-up that follows. [*After a pause, he reads.*] H'm! His English is lacking in idiom, his spelling in conservatism, his mind in balance, and his character in repose.

CYNTHIA. [*Amiable but not very sympathetic.*] You seem more fatigued than usual. Another glass of sherry, Philip?

PHILIP. Oh, I ought not to—

CYNTHIA. I think you seem a little more tired than usual.

PHILIP. Perhaps I am. [*She pours out sherry.* PHILIP *takes glass but does not sip.*] Ah, this hour is truly a grateful form of restful excitement. [*After an inspired interval.*] You, too, find it—eh? [*He looks at* CYNTHIA.

CYNTHIA. [*With veiled sarcasm.*] Decidedly.

PHILIP. Decidedly what, my dear?

CYNTHIA. [*Her sarcasm still veiled.*] Restful.

PHILIP. H'm! Perhaps I need the calm more than you do. Over the case to-day I actually—eh—[*Sipping his tea.*] slumbered. I heard myself do it. That's how I know. A dressmaker sued on seven counts. [*Reading his newspaper.*] Really, the insanity of the United States Senate—you seem restless, my dear. Ah—um—have you seen the evening paper? I see there has been a lightning change in the style or size of hats which ladies—

[*Sweeping a descriptive motion with his hand, he gives the paper to* CYNTHIA, *then moves his glass, reads, and sips.*

CYNTHIA. The lamp, Thomas.

THOMAS *blows out the alcohol lamp on the tea-table with difficulty. Blows twice. Movement of* PHILIP *each time. Blows again.*

PHILIP. [*Irritably.*] Confound it, Thomas! What are you puffing and blowing at—?

THOMAS. It's out, ma'am—yes, sir.

PHILIP. You're excessively noisy, Thomas!

THOMAS. [*In a fluster.*] Yes, sir—I am.

CYNTHIA. [*Soothing* THOMAS'S *wounded feelings.*] We don't need you, Thomas.

THOMAS. Yes, ma'am.

PHILIP. Puffing and blowing and shaking and quaking like an automobile in an ecstasy! [THOMAS *meekly withdraws.*

CYNTHIA. [*Not unsympathetically.*] Too bad, Philip! I hope my presence isn't too agitating?

PHILIP. Ah—it's just because I value this hour with you, Cynthia—this hour of tea and toast and tranquillity. It's quite as if we were married—happily married—already.

CYNTHIA. [*Admitting that married life is a blank, begins to look through paper.*] Yes, I feel as if we were married already.

PHILIP. [*Not recognizing her tone.*] Ah! It's the calm, you see.

CYNTHIA. [*Without warmth.*] The calm? Yes—yes, it's—it's the calm.

PHILIP. [*Sighs.*] Yes, the calm—the Halcyon calm of—of second choice. H'm! [*He reads and turns over the leaves of the paper.* CYNTHIA *reads. There is a silence.*] After all, my dear—the feeling which I have for you—is—is—eh—the market is in a shocking condition of plethora! H'm—h'm—and what are you reading?

CYNTHIA. [*Embarrassed.*] Oh, eh—well—I—eh—I'm just running over the sporting news.

PHILIP. Oh! [*He looks thoughtful.*

CYNTHIA. [*Beginning to forget* PHILIP *and to remember more interesting matters.*] I fancied Hermes would come in an easy winner. He came in nowhere. Nonpareil was ridden by Henslow—he's a rotten bad rider. He gets nervous.

PHILIP. [*Still interested in his newspaper.*] Does he? H'm! I suppose you do retain an interest in horses and races. H'm—I trust some day the—ah—law will attract— Oh [*Turning a page.*], here's the report of my opinion in that dressmaker's case—Haggerty *vs.* Phillimore.

CYNTHIA. [*Puzzled.*] Was the case brought against you?

PHILIP. Oh—no. The suit was brought by Haggerty, Miss Haggerty, a dressmaker, against the—in fact, my dear, against the former Mrs. Phillimore. [*After a pause, he returns to his reading.*

CYNTHIA. [*Curious about the matter.*] How did you decide it?

PHILIP. I was obliged to decide in Mrs. Phillimore's favour. Haggerty's plea was preposterous.

CYNTHIA. Did you—did you meet the—the—former—?

PHILIP. No.

CYNTHIA. I often see her at afternoon teas.

PHILIP. How did you recognize—

CYNTHIA. Why—[*Opening the paper.*] because Mrs. Vida Phillimore's picture appears in every other issue of most of the evening papers. And I must confess I was curious. But, I'm sure you find it very painful to meet her again.

PHILIP. [*Slowly, considering.*] No,—would you find it so impossible to meet Mr.—

CYNTHIA. [*Much excited and aroused.*] Philip! Don't speak of him. He's nothing. He's a thing of the past. I never think of him. I forget him!

PHILIP. [*Somewhat sarcastic.*] That's extraordinarily original of you to forget him.

CYNTHIA. [*Gently, and wishing to drop the subject.*] We each of us have something to forget, Philip—and John Karslake is to me— Well, he's dead!

PHILIP. As a matter of fact, my dear, he *is* dead, or the next thing to it—for he's bankrupt.

CYNTHIA. [*After a pause.*] Bankrupt? [*Excited and moved.*] Let's not speak of him. I mean never to see him or think about him or even hear of him! [*He assents. She reads her paper. He sips his tea and reads his paper. She turns a page, starts and cries out.*

PHILIP. God bless me!

CYNTHIA. It's a picture of—of—

PHILIP. John Karslake?

CYNTHIA. Picture of him, and one of me, and in the middle between us "Cynthia K!"

PHILIP. "Cynthia K!"

CYNTHIA. [*Excited.*] My pet riding mare! The best horse he has! She's an angel even in a photograph! Oh! [*Reading.*] "John Karslake drops a fortune at Saratoga." [*Rises and walks up and down excitedly.* PHILIP *takes the paper and reads.*

PHILIP. [*Unconcerned, as the matter hardly touches him.*] Hem —ah— Advertises country place for sale—stables, famous mare "Cynthia K"—favourite riding-mare of former Mrs. Karslake, who is once again to enter the arena of matrimony with the well-known and highly respected judge of—

CYNTHIA. [*Sensitive and much disturbed.*] Don't! Don't, Philip, please don't!

PHILIP. My dear Cynthia—take another paper—here's my *Post!* You'll find nothing disagreeable in *The Post.*

[CYNTHIA *takes paper.*

CYNTHIA. [*After reading, near the table.*] It's much worse in *The Post.* "John Karslake sells the former Mrs. Karslake's jewels—the famous necklace now at Tiffany's, and the sporty ex-husband sells his wife's portrait by Sargent!" Philip, I can't stand this. [*Puts paper on the table.*

PHILIP. Really, my dear, Mr. Karslake is bound to appear occasionally in print—or even you may have to meet him.

[THOMAS *comes in.*

CYNTHIA. [*Determined and distressed.*] I won't meet him! I won't meet him. Every time I hear his name or "Cynthia K's" I'm so depressed.

THOMAS. [*Announcing with something like reluctance.*] Sir, Mr. Fiddler. Mr. Karslake's trainer.

FIDDLER *walks in. He is an English horse trainer, a wide-awake, stocky, well-groomed little cockney. He knows his own mind and sees life altogether through a stable door. Well-dressed for his station, and not too young.*

CYNTHIA. [*Excited and disturbed.*] Fiddler? Tim Fiddler? His coming is outrageous!

FIDDLER. A note for you, sir.

CYNTHIA. [*Impulsively.*] Oh, Fiddler—is that you?

FIDDLER. Yes'm!

CYNTHIA. [*In a half whisper, still speaking on impulse.*] How is she! Cynthia K? How's Planet II and the colt and Golden Rod? How's the whole stable? Are they well?

FIDDLER. No'm—we're all on the bum. [*Aside.*] Ever since you kicked us over!

CYNTHIA. [*Reproving him, though pleased.*] Fiddler!

FIDDLER. The horses is just simply gone to Egypt since you left, and so's the guv'nor.

CYNTHIA. [*Putting an end to* FIDDLER.] That will do, Fiddler.

FIDDLER. I'm waiting for an answer, sir.

CYNTHIA. What is it, Philip?

PHILIP. [*Uncomfortable.*] A mere matter of business. [*Aside to* FIDDLER.] The answer is, Mr. Karslake can come. The—the coast will be clear. [FIDDLER *goes out.*

CYNTHIA. [*Amazed; rising.*] You're not going to see him?

PHILIP. But Karslake, my dear, is an old acquaintance of mine. He argues cases before me. I will see that you do not have to meet him.

[CYNTHIA *walks the length of the room in excited dejection.*

MATTHEW *comes in. He is a High-church clergyman to a highly fashionable congregation. His success is partly due to his social position and partly to his elegance of speech, but chiefly to his inherent amiability, which leaves the sinner in happy peace and smiles on the just and unjust alike.*

MATTHEW. [*Most amiably.*] Ah, my dear brother!

PHILIP. [*Greeting him.*] Matthew.

MATTHEW. [*Nodding to* PHILIP.] Good afternoon, my dear Cynthia. How charming you look! [CYNTHIA *sits down at the tea-table. To* CYNTHIA.] Ah, why weren't you in your pew yesterday? I preached a most original sermon.

[*He lays his hat and cane on the divan.*

THOMAS. [*Aside to* PHILIP.] Sir, Mrs. Vida Phillimore's maid called you up on the telephone, and you're to expect Mrs. Phillimore on a matter of business.

PHILIP. [*Astonished and disgusted.*] Here, impossible! [*To* CYNTHIA.] Excuse me, my dear! [PHILIP, *much embarrassed, goes out, followed by* THOMAS.

MATTHEW. [*Approaching* CYNTHIA'S *chair, happily and pleasantly self-important.*] No, really, it was a wonderful sermon, my dear. My text was from Paul—"It is better to marry than to burn." It was a strictly logical sermon. I argued—that, as the grass withereth, and the flower fadeth,—there is nothing final in Nature; not even Death! And, as there is nothing final in Nature, not even Death;—so then if Death is not final—why should marriage be final? [*Gently.*] And so the necessity of—eh—divorce! You see? It was an exquisite sermon! All New York was there! And all New York went away happy! Even the sinners—if there were any! I don't often meet sinners—do you?

CYNTHIA. [*Indulgently, in spite of his folly, because he is kind.*] You're such a dear, delightful Pagan! Here's your tea!

MATTHEW. [*Taking the tea.*] Why, my dear—you have a very sad expression!

CYNTHIA. [*A little bitterly.*] Why not?

MATTHEW. [*With sentimental sweetness.*] I ıeel as if I were of no use in the world when I see sadness on a young face. Only sinners should feel sad. You have committed no sin!

CYNTHIA. [*Impulsively.*] Yes, I have!

MATTHEW. Eh?

CYNTHIA. I committed the unpardonable sin—whe—when I married for love!

MATTHEW. One must not marry for anything else, my dear!

CYNTHIA. Why am I marrying your brother?

MATTHEW. I often wonder why? I wonder why you didn't choose to remain a free woman.

CYNTHIA. [*Going over the ground she has often argued with herself.*] I meant to; but a divorcée has no place in society. I felt horridly lonely! I wanted a friend. Philip was ideal as a friend—for months. Isn't it nice to bind a friend to you?

MATTHEW. [*Setting down his teacup.*] Yes—yes!

CYNTHIA. [*Growing more and more excited and moved as she speaks.*] To marry a friend—to marry on prudent, sensible grounds—a man—like Philip? That's what I should have done first, instead of rushing into marriage—because I had a wild, mad, sensitive, sympathetic—passion and pain and fury—of, I don't know what—that almost strangled me with happiness!

MATTHEW. [*Amiable and reminiscent.*] Ah—ah—in my youth—I,—I too!

CYNTHIA. [*Coming back to her manner of every day.*] And besides—the day Philip asked me I was in the dumps! And now—how about marrying only for love? [PHILIP *comes back.*

MATTHEW. Ah, my dear, love is not the only thing in the world!

PHILIP. [*Half aside.*] I got there too late, she'd hung up.

CYNTHIA. Who, Philip?

PHILIP. Eh—a lady—eh—

[THOMAS, *flurried, comes in with a card on a salver.*

THOMAS. A card for you, sir. Ahem—ahem—Mrs. Phillimore—that was, sir.

PHILIP. Eh?

THOMAS. She's on the stairs, sir. [*He nods backward, only to find* VIDA *at his side. He announces her as being the best way of meeting the difficulty.*] Mrs. Vida Phillimore!

VIDA *comes in slowly, with the air of a spoiled beauty. She stops just inside the door and speaks in a very casual manner. Her voice is languorous and caressing. She is dressed in the excess of the French fashion and carries a daring parasol. She smiles and comes in, undulating, to the middle of the room. Tableau.* THOMAS *withdraws.*

VIDA. How do you do, Philip. [*After a pause.*] Don't tell me I'm a surprise! I had you called up on the 'phone and I sent up my card—and, besides, Philip dear, when you have the—the—habit of the house, as unfortunately I have, you can't treat yourself like a stranger in a strange land. At least, I can't—so here I am. My reason for coming was to ask you about that B. & O. stock we hold in common. [*To* MATTHEW, *condescendingly, the clergy being a class of unfortunates debarred by profession from the pleasures of the world.*] How do you do? [*Pause. She then goes to the real reason of her visit.*] Do be polite and present me to your wife-to-be.

PHILIP. [*Awkwardly.*] Cynthia—

CYNTHIA. [*Cheerfully, with dash, putting the table between* VIDA *and herself.*] We're delighted to see you, Mrs. Phillimore. I needn't ask you to make yourself at home, but will you have a cup of tea? [MATTHEW *sits near the little table.*

VIDA. [*To* PHILIP.] My dear, she's not in the least what I expected. I heard she was a dove! She's a very dashing kind of a dove! [*To* CYNTHIA, *who moves to the tea-table.*] My dear, I'm paying you compliments. Five lumps and quantities of cream. I find single life very thinning. [*To* PHILIP, *calm and ready to be agreeable to any man.*] And how well you're looking! It must be the absence of matrimonial cares—or is it a new angel in the house?

CYNTHIA. [*Outraged at* VIDA'S *intrusion, but polite though delicately sarcastic.*] It's most amusing to sit in your place. And how at home you must feel here in this house where you have made so much trouble—I mean tea. [*Rises.*] Do you know it would be in much better taste if you would take the place you're accustomed to?

VIDA. [*As calm as before.*] My dear, I'm an intruder only for a moment; I sha'n't give you a chance to score off me again! But I must thank you, dear Philip, for rendering that decision in my favour—

PHILIP. I assure you—

VIDA. [*Unable to resist a thrust.*] Of course, you would like to have rendered it against me. It was your wonderful sense of justice, and that's why I'm so grateful—if not to you, to your Maker!

PHILIP. [*Feels that this is no place for his future wife. Rises quickly. To* CYNTHIA.] Cynthia, I would prefer that you left us. [MATTHEW *moves to the sofa and sits down.*

CYNTHIA. [*Determined not to leave the field first, remains seated.*] Certainly, Philip!

PHILIP. I expect another visitor who—

VIDA. [*With flattering insistence, to* CYNTHIA.] Oh, my dear—don't go! The truth is—I came to see you! I feel most cordially towards you—and really, you know, people in our position should meet on cordial terms.

CYNTHIA. [*Taking it with apparent calm, but pointing her remarks.*] Naturally. If people in our position couldn't meet, New York society would soon come to an end. [THOMAS *comes in.*

VIDA. [*Calm, but getting her knife in too.*] Precisely. Society's no bigger than a band-box. Why, it's only a moment ago I saw Mr. Karslake walking—

CYNTHIA. Ah!

THOMAS. [*Announcing clearly. Everyone changes place, in consternation, amusement or surprise.* CYNTHIA *moves to leave the room, but stops for fear of attracting* KARSLAKE'S *attention.*] Mr. John Karslake!

Enter KARSLAKE. *He is a powerful, generous personality, a man of affairs, breezy, gay and careless. He gives the impression of being game for any fate in store for him. His clothes indicate sporting propensities and his taste in waistcoats and ties is brilliant.* KARSLAKE *sees first* PHILIP *and then* MATTHEW. THOMAS *goes out.*

PHILIP. How do you do?

JOHN. [*Very gay and no respecter of persons.*] Good-afternoon, Mr. Phillimore. Hello—here's the church! [*Crossing to* MATTHEW *and shaking hands. He slaps him on the back.*] I hadn't the least idea—how are you? By George, your reverence, that was a racy sermon of yours on Divorce! What was your text? [*Sees* VIDA *and bows, very politely.*] Galatians 4: 2, "The more the merrier," or "Who next?" [*Smiles.*] As the whale said after Jonah! [CYNTHIA *makes a sudden movement, upsetting her tea-cup.* JOHN *faces about quickly and they face each other.* JOHN *gives a frank start. A pause holds them.*

JOHN. [*Astounded, in a low voice.*] Mrs. Karslake—[*Bowing.*] I was not aware of the pleasure in store for me. I understood you were in the country. [*Recovering and moving to her chair.*] Perhaps you'll be good enough to make me a cup of tea?—that is if the teapot wasn't lost in the scrimmage. [*There is another pause.* CYNTHIA, *determined to equal him in coolness, returns to the tea-tray.*] Mr. Phillimore, I came to get your signature in that matter of Cox *vs.* Keely.

PHILIP. I shall be at your service, but pray be seated.

[*He indicates a chair by the tea-table.*

JOHN. [*Sitting beyond but not far from the tea-table.*] And I also understood you to say you wanted a saddle-horse.

PHILIP. You have a mare called—eh—"Cynthia K?"

JOHN. [*Promptly.*] Yes—she's not for sale.

PHILIP. Oh, but she's just the mare I had set my mind on.

JOHN. [*With a touch of humour.*] You want her for yourself?

PHILIP. [*A little flustered.*] I—eh—I sometimes ride.

JOHN. [*Now sure of himself.*] She's rather lively for you, Judge. Mrs. Karslake used to ride her.

PHILIP. You don't care to sell her to me?

JOHN. She's a dangerous mare, Judge, and she's as delicate and changeable as a girl. I'd hate to leave her in your charge!

CYNTHIA. [*Eagerly but in a low voice.*] Leave her in mine, Mr. Karslake!

JOHN. [*After a slight pause.*] Mrs. Karslake knows all about a horse, but— [*Turning to* CYNTHIA.] Cynthia K's got rather tricky of late.

CYNTHIA. [*Haughtily.*] You mean to say you think she'd chuck me?

JOHN. [*With polite solicitude and still humourous. To* PHILIP.] I'd hate to have a mare of mine deprive you of a wife, Judge. [*Rises.* CYNTHIA *shows anger.*] She goes to Saratoga next week, C. W.

VIDA. [*Who has been sitting and talking to* MATTHEW *for lack of a better man, comes to talk to* KARSLAKE.] C. W.?

JOHN. [*Rising as she rises.*] Creditors willing.

VIDA. [*Changing her seat for one near the tea-table.*] I'm sure your creditors are willing.

JOHN. Oh, they're a breezy lot, my creditors. They're giving me a dinner this evening.

VIDA. [*More than usually anxious to please.*] I regret I'm not a breezy creditor, but I do think you owe it to me to let me see your Cynthia K! Can't you lead her around to my house?

JOHN. At what hour, Mrs. Phillimore?

VIDA. Say eleven? And you, too, might have a leading in my direction—771 Fifth Avenue.

[JOHN *bows.* CYNTHIA *hears and notes this.*

CYNTHIA. Your cup of tea, Mr. Karslake.

JOHN. Thanks. [*Taking his tea and sipping it.*] I beg your pardon—you have forgotten, Mrs. Karslake—very naturally, it has slipped your memory, but I don't take sugar. [CYNTHIA, *furious with him and herself. He hands the cup back. She makes a second cup.*

CYNTHIA. [*Cheerfully; in a rage.*] Sorry!

JOHN. [*Also apparently cheerful.*] Yes, gout. It gives me a twinge even to sit in the shadow of a sugar-maple! First you riot, and then you diet!

VIDA. [*Calm and amused; aside to* MATTHEW.] My dear Matthew, he's a darling! But I feel as if we were all taking tea on the slope of a volcano! [MATTHEW *sits down.*

PHILIP. It occurred to me, Mr. Karslake, you might be glad to find a purchaser for your portrait by Sargent?

JOHN. It's not *my* portrait. It's a portrait of Mrs. Karslake, and to tell you the truth—Sargent's a good fellow—I've made up my mind to keep it—to remember the artist by.

[CYNTHIA *is wounded by this.*

PHILIP. H'm!

[CYNTHIA *hands a second cup to* JOHN.

CYNTHIA. [*With careful politeness.*] Your cup of tea, Mr. Karslake.

JOHN. [*Rising and taking the tea with courteous indifference.*] Thanks—sorry to trouble you.

[*He drinks the cup of tea standing by the tea-table.*

PHILIP. [*To make conversation.*] You're selling your country place?

JOHN. If I was long of hair—I'd sell that.

CYNTHIA. [*Excited. Taken out of herself by the news.*] You're not really selling your stable?

JOHN. [*Finishes his tea, places the empty cup on the tea-table, and reseats himself.*] Every gelding I've got—seven foals and a donkey! I don't mean the owner.

CYNTHIA. [*Still interested and forgetting the discomfort of the situation.*] How did you ever manage to come such a cropper?

JOHN. Streak of blue luck!

CYNTHIA. [*Quickly.*] I don't see how it's possible—

JOHN. You would if you'd been there. You remember the head man? [*Sitting down.*] Bloke?

CYNTHIA. Of course!

JOHN. Well, his wife divorced him for beating her over the head with a bottle of Fowler's Solution, and it seemed to prey on his mind. He sold me—

CYNTHIA. [*Horrified.*] Sold a race?

JOHN. About ten races, I guess.

CYNTHIA. [*Incredulous.*] Just because he'd beaten his wife?

JOHN. No. Because she divorced him.

CYNTHIA. Well, I can't see why that should prey on his mind! [*Suddenly remembers.*

JOHN. Well, I have known men that it stroked the wrong way. But he cost me eighty thousand. And then Urbanity ran third in the thousand-dollar stakes for two-year-olds at Belmont.

CYNTHIA. [*Throws this remark in.*] I never had faith in that horse.

JOHN. And, of course, it never rains monkeys but it pours gorillas! So when I was down at St. Louis on the fifth, I laid seven to three on Fraternity—

CYNTHIA. Crazy! Crazy!

JOHN. [*Ready to take the opposite view.*] I don't see it. With her record she ought to have romped it an easy winner.

CYNTHIA. [*Her sporting instinct asserting itself.*] She hasn't the stamina! Look at her barrel!

JOHN. Well, anyhow, Geranium finished me!

CYNTHIA. You didn't lay odds on Geranium!

JOHN. Why not? She's my own mare—

CYNTHIA. Oh!

JOHN. Streak o' bad luck—

CYNTHIA. [*Plainly anxious to say "I told you so."*] Streak of poor judgment! Do you remember the day you rode Billy at a six-foot stone wall, and he stopped and you didn't, and there was a hornet's nest [MATTHEW *rises.*] on the other side, and I remember you were hot just because I said you showed poor judgment? [*She laughs at the memory. A general movement of disapproval. She remembers the situation.*] I beg your pardon.

MATTHEW. [*Rises to meet* VIDA. *Hastily.*] It seems to me that horses are like the fourth gospel. Any conversation about them becomes animated almost beyond the limits of the urbane! [VIDA, *disgusted by such plainness of speech, rises and goes to* PHILIP *who waves her to a chair.*

PHILIP. [*Formally.*] I regret that you have endured such reverses, Mr. Karslake. [JOHN *quietly bows.*

CYNTHIA. [*Concealing her interest and speaking casually.*] You haven't mentioned your new English horse—Pantomime. What did he do at St. Louis?

JOHN. [*Sitting down.*] Fell away and ran fifth.

CYNTHIA. Too bad. Was he fully acclimated? Ah, well—

JOHN. We always differed—you remember—on the time needed—

MATTHEW. [*Coming over to* CYNTHIA, *and speaking to carry off the situation as well as to get a tip.*] Isn't there a—eh—a race to-morrow at Belmont Park?

JOHN. Yes. I'm going down in my auto.

CYNTHIA. [*Evidently wishing she might be going too.*] Oh!

MATTHEW. And what animal shall you prefer?

[*Covering his personal interest with amiable altruism.*

JOHN. I'm backing Carmencita.

CYNTHIA. [*With a gesture of despair.*] Carmencita! Carmencita! [MATTHEW *returns to* VIDA'S *side.*

JOHN. You may remember we always differed on Carmencita.

CYNTHIA. [*Disgusted at* JOHN'S *dunderheadedness.*] But there's no room for difference. She's a wild, headstrong, dissatisfied, foolish little filly. The deuce couldn't ride her—she'd shy at her own shadow—"Carmencita." Oh, very well then, I'll wager you—and I'll give you odds too—"Decorum" will come in first, and I'll lay three to one he'll beat Carmencita by five lengths! How's that for fair?

JOHN. [*Never forgetting the situation.*] Sorry I'm not flush enough to take you.

CYNTHIA. [*Impetuously.*] Philip, dear, you lend John enough for the wager.

MATTHEW. [*As nearly horrified as so soft a soul can be.*] Ahem! Really—

JOHN. It's a sporty idea, Mrs. Karslake, but perhaps in the circumstances—

CYNTHIA. [*Her mind on her wager.*] In what circumstances?

PHILIP. [*With a nervous laugh.*] It does seem to me there is a certain impropriety—

CYNTHIA. [*Remembering the conventions, which, for a moment, had actually escaped her.*] Oh, I forgot. When horses are in the air—

MATTHEW. [*Pouring oil on troubled waters. Moving, he speaks to* VIDA *from the back of her armchair.*] It's the fourth gospel, you see. [THOMAS *comes in with a letter on a salver, which he hands to* PHILIP.

CYNTHIA. [*Meekly.*] You are quite right, Philip. [PHILIP *goes up.*] The fact is, seeing Mr. Karslake again [*Laying on her indifference with a trowel.*] he seems to me as much a stranger as if I were meeting him for the first time.

MATTHEW. [*Aside to* VIDA.] We are indeed taking tea on the slope of a volcano.

VIDA. [*About to go, but thinking she will have a last word with* JOHN.] I'm sorry your fortunes are so depressed, Mr. Karslake.

PHILIP. [*Looking at the card that* THOMAS *has just brought in.*] Who in the world is Sir Wilfrid Cates-Darby?

[*There is a general stir.*

JOHN. Oh—eh—Cates-Darby? [PHILIP *opens the letter which* THOMAS *has brought with the card.*] That's the English chap I bought Pantomime of.

PHILIP. [*To* THOMAS.] Show Sir Wilfrid Cates-Darby in.

THOMAS *goes out. The prospect of an Englishman with a handle to his name changes* VIDA'S *plans and, instead of leaving the house, she goes to sofa, and poses there.*

JOHN. He's a good fellow, Judge. Place near Epsom. Breeder. Over here to take a shy at our races.

THOMAS. [*Opening the door and announcing.*] Sir Wilfrid Cates-Darby.

Enter SIR WILFRID CATES-DARBY. *He is a high-bred, sporting Englishman. His manner, his dress and his diction are the perfection of English elegance. His movements are quick and graceful. He talks lightly and with ease. He is full of life and unsmiling good temper.*

PHILIP. [*To* SIR WILFRID *and referring to the letter of introduction in his hand.*] I am Mr. Phillimore. I am grateful to Stanhope for giving me the opportunity of knowing you, Sir Wilfrid. I fear you find it warm?

SIR WILFRID. [*Delicately mopping his forehead.*] Ah, well—ah—warm, no—hot, yes! Deuced extraordinary climate yours, you know, Mr. Phillimore.

PHILIP. [*Conventionally.*] Permit me to present you to—[*The unconventional situation pulls him up short. It takes him a moment to decide how to meet it. He makes up his mind to pretend that everything is as usual, and presents* CYNTHIA *first.*] Mrs. Karslake.

[SIR WILFRID *bows, surprised and doubtful.*

CYNTHIA. How do you do?

PHILIP. And to Mrs. Phillimore. [VIDA *bows nonchalantly, but with a view to catching* SIR WILFRID'S *attention.* SIR WILFRID *bows, and looks from her to* PHILIP.] My brother—and Mr. Karslake you know.

SIR WILFRID. How do, my boy. [*Half aside, to* JOHN.] No idea you had such a charming little wife— What?— Eh? [KARSLAKE *moves to speak to* MATTHEW *and* PHILIP *in the further room.*

CYNTHIA. You'll have a cup of tea, Sir Wilfrid?

SIR WILFRID. [*At the table.*] Thanks, awfully. [*Very cheerfully.*] I'd no idea old John had a wife! The rascal never told me!

CYNTHIA. [*Pouring tea and facing the facts.*] I'm not Mr. Karslake's wife!

SIR WILFRID. Oh!— Eh?— I see—

[*He is evidently trying to think this out.*

VIDA. [*Who has been ready for some time to speak to him.*] Sir Wilfrid, I'm sure no one has asked you how you like our country?

SIR WILFRID. [*Going to* VIDA *and standing by her at the sofa.*] Oh, well, as to climate and horses, I say nothing. But I like your American humour. I'm acquiring it for home purposes.

VIDA. [*Getting down to love as the basis of conversation.*] Aren't you going to acquire an American girl for home purposes?

SIR WILFRID. The more narrowly I look the agreeable project in the face, the more I like it. Oughtn't to say that in the presence of your husband. [*He casts a look at* PHILIP, *who has gone into the next room.*

VIDA. [*Cheerful and unconstrained.*] He's not my husband!

SIR WILFRID. [*Completely confused.*] Oh—eh?—my brain must be boiled. You are—Mrs.—eh—ah—of course, now I see! I got the wrong names! I thought you were Mrs. Phillimore. [*Sitting down by her.*] And that nice girl, Mrs. Karslake! You're deucedly lucky to be Mrs. Karslake. John's a prime sort. I say, have you and he got any kids? How many?

VIDA. [*Horrified at being suspected of maternity, but speaking very sweetly.*] He's not my husband.

SIR WILFRID. [*His good spirits all gone, but determined to clear things up.*] Phew! Awfully hot in here! Who the deuce is John's wife?

VIDA. He hasn't any.

SIR WILFRID. Who's Phillimore's wife?

VIDA. He hasn't any.

Sir Wilfrid. Thanks, fearfully! [*To* Matthew, *whom he approaches; suspecting himself of having lost his wits.*] Would you excuse me, my dear and Reverend Sir—you're a churchman and all that—would you mind straightening me out?

Matthew. [*Most graciously.*] Certainly, Sir Wilfrid. Is it a matter of doctrine?

Sir Wilfrid. Oh, damme—beg your pardon,—no, it's not words, it's women.

Matthew. [*Ready to be outraged.*] Women!

Sir Wilfrid. It's divorce. Now, the lady on the sofa—

Matthew. *Was* my brother's wife; he divorced her—incompatibility—Rhode Island. The lady at the tea-table *was* Mr. Karslake's wife; she divorced him—desertion—Sioux Falls. One moment—she is about to marry my brother.

Sir Wilfrid. [*Cheerful again.*] I'm out! Thought I never would be! Thanks!

[Vida *laughs.*

Vida. [*Not a whit discountenanced and ready to please.*] Have you got me straightened out yet?

Sir Wilfrid. Straight as a die! I say, you had lots of fun, didn't you? [*Returning to his position by the sofa.*] And so *she's* Mrs. John Karslake?

Vida. [*Calm, but secretly disappointed.*] Do you like her?

Sir Wilfrid. My word!

Vida. [*Fully expecting personal flattery.*] Eh?

Sir Wilfrid. She's a box o' ginger!

Vida. You haven't seen many American women!

Sir Wilfrid. Oh, haven't I?

Vida. If you'll pay me a visit to-morrow—at twelve, you shall meet a most charming young woman, who has seen you once, and who admires you—ah!

Sir Wilfrid. I'm there—what!

Vida. Seven hundred and seventy-one Fifth Avenue.

Sir Wilfrid. Seven seventy-one Fifth Avenue—at twelve.

Vida. At twelve.

Sir Wilfrid. Thanks! [*Indicating* Cynthia.] She's a thoroughbred—you can see that with one eye shut. Twelve. [*Shaking hands.*] Awfully good of you to ask me. [*He joins* John.] I say, my boy, your former's an absolute certainty. [*To* Cynthia.] I hear you're about to marry Mr. Phillimore, Mrs. Karslake?

KARSLAKE *crosses to* VIDA *and together they move to the sofa and sit down.*

CYNTHIA. To-morrow, 3 P. M., Sir Wilfrid.

SIR WILFRID. [*Much taken with* CYNTHIA.] Afraid I've run into a sort of family party, eh? [*Indicating* VIDA.] The Past and the Future—awfully chic way you Americans have of asking your divorced husbands and wives to drop in, you know—celebrate a christenin', or the new bride, or—

CYNTHIA. Do you like your tea strong?

SIR WILFRID. Middlin'.

CYNTHIA. Sugar?

SIR WILFRID. One!

CYNTHIA. Lemon?

SIR WILFRID. Just torture a lemon over it. [*He makes a gesture as of twisting a lemon peel. She hands him his tea.*] Thanks! So you do it to-morrow at three?

CYNTHIA. At three, Sir Wilfrid.

SIR WILFRID. Sorry!

CYNTHIA. Why are you sorry?

SIR WILFRID. Hate to see a pretty woman married. Might marry her myself.

CYNTHIA. Oh, but I'm sure you don't admire American women.

SIR WILFRID. Admire you, Mrs. Karslake—

CYNTHIA. Not enough to marry me, I hope.

SIR WILFRID. Marry you in a minute! Say the word. Marry you now—here.

CYNTHIA. You don't think you ought to know me a little before—

SIR WILFRID. Know you? Do know you.

CYNTHIA. [*Covering her hair with her handkerchief.*] What colour is my hair?

SIR WILFRID. Pshaw!

CYNTHIA. You see! You don't know whether I'm a chestnut or a strawberry roan! In the States we think a few months of friendship is quite necessary.

SIR WILFRID. Few months of moonshine! Never was a friend to a woman—thank God, in all my life.

CYNTHIA. Oh—oh, oh!

SIR WILFRID. Might as well talk about being a friend to a whiskey-and-soda.

CYNTHIA. A woman has a soul, Sir Wilfrid.

SIR WILFRID. Well, good whiskey is spirits—dozens o' souls!

CYNTHIA. You are so gross!

SIR WILFRID. [*Changing his seat for one at the tea-table.*] Gross? Not a bit! Friendship between the sexes is all fudge! I'm no friend to a rose in my garden. I don't call it friendship—eh—eh—a warm, starry night, moonbeams and ilex trees, "and a spirit who knows how" and all that—eh— [*Getting closer to her.*] You make me feel awfully poetical, you know— [PHILIP *comes toward them, glances nervously at* CYNTHIA *and* SIR WILFRID, *and walks away again.*] What's the matter? But, I say—poetry aside—do you, eh—— [*Looking around to place* PHILIP.] Does he—y'know—is he—does he go to the head?

CYNTHIA. Sir Wilfrid, Mr. Phillimore is my sober second choice.

SIR WILFRID. Did you ever kiss him? I'll bet he fined you for contempt of court. Look here, Mrs. Karslake, if you're marryin' a man you don't care about—

CYNTHIA. [*Amused and excusing his audacity as a foreigner's eccentricity.*] Really!

SIR WILFRID. Well, I don't offer myself—

CYNTHIA. Oh!

SIR WILFRID. Not this instant—

CYNTHIA. Ah!

SIR WILFRID. But let me drop in to-morrow at ten.

CYNTHIA. What country and state of affairs do you think you have landed in?

SIR WILFRID. New York, by Jove! Been to school, too. New York is bounded on the North, South, East and West by the state of Divorce! Come, come, Mrs. Karslake, I like your country. You've no fear and no respect—no cant and lots of can. Here you all are, you see—your former husband, and your new husband's former wife—sounds like Ollendoff! Eh? So there you are, you see! But, jokin' apart—why do you marry him? Oh, well, marry him if you must! You can run around the corner and get a divorce afterwards—

CYNTHIA. I believe you think they throw one in with an ice-cream soda!

SIR WILFRID. [*Rising.*] Damme, my dear lady, a marriage in your country is no more than a—eh—eh—what do you call 'em?

A thank you, ma'am. That's what an American marriage is—a thank you, ma'am. Bump—bump—you're over it and on to the next.

CYNTHIA. You're an odd fish! What? I believe I like you!

SIR WILFRID. 'Course you do! You'll see me when I call to-morrow—at ten? We'll run down to Belmont Park, eh?

CYNTHIA. Don't be absurd!

VIDA. [*Has finished her talk with* JOHN, *and breaks in on* SIR WILFRID, *who has hung about* CYNTHIA *too long to suit her.*] To-morrow at twelve, Sir Wilfrid!

SIR WILFRID. Twelve!

VIDA. [*Shaking hands with* JOHN.] Don't forget, Mr. Karslake—eleven o'clock to-morrow.

JOHN. [*Bowing assent.*] I won't!

VIDA. [*Coming over to* CYNTHIA.] Oh, Mrs. Karslake, I've ordered Tiffany to send you something. It's a sugar-bowl to sweeten the matrimonial lot! I suppose nothing would induce you to call?

CYNTHIA. [*Distantly and careless of offending.*] Thanks, no—that is, is "Cynthia K" really to be there at eleven? I'd give a gold mine to see her again.

VIDA. Do come!

CYNTHIA. If Mr. Karslake will accommodate me by his absence.

VIDA. Dear Mr. Karslake, you'll have to change your hour.

JOHN. Sorry, I'm not able to.

CYNTHIA. I can't come later for I'm to be married.

JOHN. It's not as bad as that with me, but I am to be sold up—Sheriff, you know. Can't come later than eleven.

VIDA. [*To* CYNTHIA.] Any hour but eleven, dear.

CYNTHIA. [*Perfectly regardless of* VIDA, *and ready to vex* JOHN *if possible.*] Mrs. Phillimore, I shall call on you at eleven—to see Cynthia K. I thank you for the invitation. Good-afternoon.

VIDA. [*Aside to* JOHN, *crossing to speak quietly to him.*] It's mere bravado; she won't come.

JOHN. You don't know her.

There is a pause and general embarrassment. SIR WILFRID *uses his eye-glass.* JOHN *angry.* CYNTHIA *triumphant.* MATTHEW *embarrassed.* VIDA *irritated.* PHILIP *puzzled. Everybody is at odds.*

SIR WILFRID. [*For the first time a witness to the pretty complications of divorce. To* MATTHEW.] Do you have it as warm as this ordinarily?

MATTHEW. [*For whom these moments are more than usually painful, and wiping his brow.*] It's not so much the heat as the humidity.

JOHN. [*Looks at watch and, relieved, glad to be off.*] I shall be late for my creditors' dinner.

SIR WILFRID. [*Interested and walking toward* JOHN.] Creditors' dinner.

JOHN. [*Reading the note.*] Fifteen of my sporting creditors have arranged to give me a blow-out at Sherry's, and I'm expected right away or sooner. And, by the way, I was to bring my friends—if I had any. So now's the time to stand by me! Mrs. Phillimore?

VIDA. Of course!

JOHN. [*Ready to embarrass* CYNTHIA, *if possible, and speaking as if he had quite forgotten their former relations.*] Mrs. Karslake—I beg your pardon. Judge? [PHILIP *declines.*] No? Sir Wilfrid?

SIR WILFRID. I'm with you!

JOHN. [*To* MATTHEW.] Your Grace?

MATTHEW. I regret—

SIR WILFRID. Is it the custom for creditors—

JOHN. Come on, Sir Wilfrid! [THOMAS *opens door.*] Good-night, Judge—Your Grace—

SIR WILFRID. Is it the custom—

JOHN. Hang the custom! Come on—I'll show you a gang of creditors worth having!

SIR WILFRID *and* JOHN *go out, arm in arm, preceded by* VIDA. MATTHEW *crosses the room, smiling, as if pleased, in a Christian way, with this display of generous gaiety. He stops short suddenly and looks at his watch.*

MATTHEW. Good gracious! I had no idea the hour was so late. I've been asked to a meeting with Maryland and Iowa, to talk over the divorce situation. [*He leaves the room quickly and his voice is heard in the hall.*] Good-afternoon! Good-afternoon!

CYNTHIA *is evidently much excited. The outer door slams.* PHILIP *comes down slowly.* CYNTHIA *stands, her eyes wide, her breathing visible, until* PHILIP *speaks, when she seems suddenly to realize her position. There is a long pause.*

PHILIP. [*With a superior air.*] I have seldom witnessed a more amazing cataclysm of jocundity! Of course, my dear, this has all been most disagreeable for you.

CYNTHIA. [*Excitedly.*] Yes, yes, yes!

PHILIP. I saw how much it shocked your delicacy.

CYNTHIA. [*Distressed and moved.*] Outrageous.

[PHILIP *sits down.*

PHILIP. Do be seated, Cynthia. [*Taking up the paper. Quietly.*] Very odd sort of an Englishman—that Cates-Darby!

CYNTHIA. Sir Wilfrid?—Oh, yes! [PHILIP *settles down to the paper. To herself.*] Outrageous! I've a great mind to go at eleven—just as I said I would!

PHILIP. Do sit down, Cynthia!

CYNTHIA. What? What?

PHILIP. You make me so nervous—

CYNTHIA. Sorry—sorry. [*She sits down and, seeing the paper, takes it, looking at the picture of* JOHN KARSLAKE.

PHILIP. [*Sighing with content.*] Ah! now that I see him, I don't wonder you couldn't stand him. There's a kind of—ah—spontaneous inebriety about him. He is incomprehensible! If I might with reverence cross-question the Creator, I would say to him: "Sir, to what end or purpose did you create Mr. John Karslake?" I believe I should obtain no adequate answer! However, [*Sighs.*] at last we have peace—and *The Post!* [PHILIP, *settling himself, reads his paper;* CYNTHIA, *glancing at her paper, occasionally looks across at* PHILIP.] Forget the dust of the arena—the prolixity of counsel—the involuntary fatuity of things in general. [*After a pause, he goes on with his reading.*] Compose yourself!

MISS HENEAGE, MRS. PHILLIMORE *and* GRACE *come in.* CYNTHIA *sighs without letting her sigh be heard. She tries to compose herself. She glances at the paper and then, hearing* MISS HENEAGE, *starts slightly.* MISS HENEAGE *and* MRS. PHILLIMORE *stop at the table.*

MISS HENEAGE. [*Carrying a sheet of paper.*] There, my dear Mary, is the announcement as I have now reworded it. I took William's suggestion. [MRS. PHILLIMORE *takes and casually reads it.*] I also put the case to him, and he was of the opinion that the announcement should be sent *only* to those people who are really *in* society. [*She sits near the table.* CYNTHIA *braces herself to bear the* PHILLIMORE *conversation.*

GRACE. I wish you'd make an exception of the Dudleys.

[CYNTHIA *rises and moves to the chair by the table.*

MISS HENEAGE. And, of course, that excludes the Oppenheims—the Vance-Browns.

MRS. PHILLIMORE. It's just as well to be exclusive.

GRACE. I do wish you'd make an exception of Lena Dudley.

MISS HENEAGE. We might, of course, include those new Girardos, and possibly—possibly the Paddingtons.

GRACE. I do wish you would take in Lena Dudley.

[*They are now sitting.*

MRS. PHILLIMORE. The mother Dudley is as common as a charwoman, and not nearly as clean.

PHILIP. [*Sighing, his own feelings, as usual, to the fore.*] Ah! I certainly am fatigued!

CYNTHIA *begins to slowly crush the newspaper she has been reading with both hands, as if the effort of self-repression were too much for her.*

MISS HENEAGE. [*Making the best of a gloomy future.*] We shall have to ask the Dudleys sooner or later to dine, Mary—because of the elder girl's marriage to that dissolute French Marquis.

MRS. PHILLIMORE. [*Plaintively.*] I don't like common people any more than I like common cats, and of course in my time—

MISS HENEAGE. I think I shall include the Dudleys.

MRS. PHILLIMORE. You think you'll include the Dudleys?

MISS HENEAGE. Yes, I think I will include the Dudleys!

Here CYNTHIA'S *control breaks down. Driven desperate by their chatter, she has slowly rolled her newspaper into a ball, and at this point tosses it violently to the floor and bursts into hysterical laughter.*

MRS. PHILLIMORE. Why, my dear Cynthia— Compose yourself.

PHILIP. [*Hastily.*] What is the matter, Cynthia?

[*They speak together.*

MISS HENEAGE. Why, Mrs. Karslake, what is the matter?

GRACE. [*Coming quickly forward.*] Mrs. Karslake!

CURTAIN.

ACT II.

SCENE. MRS. VIDA PHILLIMORE'S *boudoir. The room is furnished to please an empty-headed, pleasure-loving and fashionable woman. The furniture, the ornaments, what pictures there are, all witness to taste up-to-date. Two French windows open on to a balcony, from which the trees of Central Park can be seen. There is a table between them; a mirror, a scent bottle, &c., upon it. On the right, up stage, is a door; on the right, down stage, another door. A lady's writing-table stands between the two, nearer centre of stage. There is another door up stage; below it, an open fireplace, filled with potted plants, andirons, &c., not in use. Over it is a tall mirror; on the mantel-piece are a French clock, candelabra, vases, &c. On a line with the fireplace is a lounge, gay with silk pillows. A florist's box, large and long, filled with American Beauty roses, rests on a low table near the head of the lounge. Small tables and light chairs where needed.*

BENSON, *alone in the room, is looking critically about her. She is a neat and pretty little English lady's maid in black silk and a thin apron. Still surveying the room, she moves here and there, and, her eyes lighting on the box of flowers, she goes to the door of* VIDA'S *room and speaks to her.*

BENSON. Yes, ma'am, the flowers have come.

She holds open the door through which VIDA, *in a morning gown, comes in slowly. She is smoking a cigarette in as æsthetic a manner as she can, and is evidently turned out in her best style for conquest.*

VIDA. [*Faces the balcony as she speaks, and is, as always, even and civil, but a bit disdainful toward her servant.*] Terribly garish light, Benson. Pull down the— [BENSON, *obeying, partly pulls down the shade.*] Lower still—that will do. [*As she speaks she goes about the room, giving the tables a push here and the chairs a jerk there, and generally arranging the vases and ornaments.*] Men hate a clutter of chairs and tables. [*Stopping and taking up a hand mirror from the table, she faces the windows.*] I really think I'm too pale for this light.

BENSON. [*Quickly, understanding what is implied.*] Yes, ma'am. [BENSON *goes out for the rouge, and* VIDA *seats herself at the table. There is a knock at the door.*] Come! [BROOKS *comes in.*

BROOKS. [*An ultra-English f otman, in plush and calves.*] Any horders, m'lady?

VIDA. [*Incapable of remembering the last man, or of considering the new one.*] Oh,—of course! You're the new—

BROOKS. Footman, m'lady.

VIDA. [*As a matter of form.*] Your name?

BROOKS. Brooks, m'lady. [BENSON *returns with the rouge.*

VIDA. [*Carefully giving instructions while she keeps her eyes on the glass and is rouged by* BENSON.] Brooks, I am at home to Mr. Karslake at eleven; not to any one else till twelve, when I expect Sir Wilfrid Cates-Darby.

[BROOKS, *watching* BENSON, *is inattentive.*

BROOKS. Yes, m'lady.

VIDA. [*Calm, but wearied by the ignorance of the lower classes.*] And I regret to inform you, Brooks, that in America there are no ladies, except salesladies!

BROOKS. [*Without a trace of comprehension.*] Yes, m'lady.

VIDA. I am at home to no one but the two names I have mentioned. [BROOKS *bows and exits. She dabs on rouge while* BENSON *holds glass.*] Is the men's club-room in order?

BENSON. Perfectly, ma'am.

VIDA. Whiskey and soda?

BENSON. Yes, ma'am, and the ticker's been mended. The British sporting papers arrived this morning.

VIDA. [*Looking at her watch which lies on the dressing-table.*] My watch has stopped.

BENSON. [*Glancing at the French clock on the chimney-piece.*] Five to eleven, ma'am.

VIDA. [*Getting promptly to work.*] H'm, h'm, I shall be caught. [*Rising.*] The box of roses, Benson! [BENSON *brings the box of roses, uncovers the flowers and places them at* VIDA'S *side.*] My gloves—the clippers, and the vase! [*Each of these things* BENSON *places in turn within* VIDA'S *range where she sits on the sofa. She has the long box of roses at her side on a small table, a vase of water on the floor by her side. She cuts the stems and places the roses in the vase. When she feels that she has reached a picturesque position, in which any onlooker would see in her a creature filled with the love of flowers and of her fellow man, she says:*] There! [*The door opens and* BROOKS *comes in;* VIDA *nods to* BENSON.

BROOKS. [*Announcing stolidly.*] Sir John Karslake.

JOHN, *dressed in very nobby riding togs, comes in gaily and forcibly.* BENSON *withdraws as he enters, and is followed by* BROOKS. VIDA, *from this moment on, is busied with her roses.*

VIDA. [*Languorously, but with a faint suggestion of humour.*] Is that really you, Sir John?

JOHN. [*Lively and far from being impressed by* VIDA.] I see now where we Americans are going to get our titles. Good-morning! You look as fresh as paint. [*He lays his gloves and riding crop on the table, and takes a chair.*

VIDA. [*Facing the insinuation with gentle pain.*] I hope you don't mean that? I never flattered myself for a moment you'd come. You're riding Cynthia K?

JOHN. Fiddler's going to lead her round here in ten minutes!

VIDA. Cigars and cigarettes! Scotch?

[*Indicating a small table.*

JOHN. Scotch! [*Goes up quickly to table and helps himself to Scotch and seltzer.*

VIDA. And now *do* tell me all about *her!* [*Putting in her last roses; she keeps one rosebud in her hand, of a size suitable for a man's buttonhole.*

JOHN. [*As he drinks.*] Oh, she's an adorable creature—delicate, high-bred, sweet-tempered—

VIDA. [*Showing her claws for a moment.*] Sweet-tempered? Oh, you're describing the horse! By "her," I meant—

JOHN. [*Irritated by the remembrance of his wife.*] Cynthia Karslake? I'd rather talk about the last Tornado.

[*He drops moodily into a chair.*

VIDA. [*With artful soothing.*] There is only one thing I want to talk about, and that is, *you!* Why were you unhappy?

JOHN. [*Still cross.*] Why does a dollar last such a short time?

VIDA. [*Curious.*] Why did you part?

JOHN. Did you ever see a schooner towed by a tug? Well, I parted from Cynthia for the same reason that the hawser parts from the tug—I couldn't stand the tug.

VIDA. [*Sympathizing.*] Ah!

JOHN. [*After a pause, and still cross.*] Awful cheerful morning chat.

VIDA. [*Excusing her curiosity and coming back to love as the only subject for serious conversation.*] I must hear the story, for I'm anxious to know why I've taken such a fancy to you!

JOHN. [*Very nonchalantly.*] Why do *I* like you?

VIDA. [*Doing her best to charm.*] I won't tell you—it would flatter you too much.

JOHN. [*Not a bit impressed by* VIDA, *but humanly ready to flirt.*] Tell me!

VIDA. There's a rose for you.

[*Giving him the one she has in her hand.*

JOHN. [*Saying what is plainly expected of him.*] I want more than a rose—

VIDA. [*Passing over this insinuation.*] You refuse to tell me—?

JOHN. [*Once more reminded of* CYNTHIA, *speaks with sudden feeling.*] There's nothing to tell. We met, we loved, we married, we parted; or at least we wrangled and jangled. [*Sighs.*] Ha! Why weren't we happy? Don't ask me, why! It may have been *partly* my fault!

VIDA. [*With tenderness.*] Never!

JOHN. [*His mind on* CYNTHIA.] But I believe it's all in the way a girl's brought up. Our girls are brought up to be ignorant of life—they're ignorant of life. Life is a joke, and marriage is a picnic, and a man is a shawl-strap— 'Pon my soul, Cynthia Deane—no, I can't tell you! [*In great irritation, he rises abruptly, and strides up and down the room.*

VIDA. [*Gently.*] Please tell me!

JOHN. Well, she was an heiress, an American heiress—and she'd been taught to think marriage meant burnt almonds and moonshine and a yacht and three automobiles, and she thought—I don't know what she thought, but I tell you, Mrs. Phillimore, marriage is three parts love and seven parts forgiveness of sins. [*He continues restlessly to pace the floor as he speaks of* CYNTHIA.

VIDA. [*Flattering him as a matter of second nature.*] She never loved you.

JOHN. [*On whom she has made no impression at all.*] Yes, she did. For six or seven months there was not a shadow between us. It was perfect, and then one day she went off like a pistol-shot! I had a piece of law work and couldn't take her to see Flashlight race the Maryland mare. The case meant a big fee, big Kudos, and in sails Cynthia, Flashlight-mad! And will I put on my hat and take her? No—and bang she goes off like a stick o' dynamite—what did I marry her for?—and words—pretty high words, until she got mad, when she threw over a chair, and said, oh, well,

—marriage was a failure, or it was with me, so I said she'd better try somebody else. She said she would, and marched out of the room.

VIDA. [*Gently sarcastic.*] But she came back!

JOHN. She came back, but not as you mean. She stood at the door and said, "Jack, I shall divorce you." Then she came over to my study-table, dropped her wedding ring on my law papers, and went out. The door shut, I laughed; the front door slammed, I damned. [*After a silence, moving abruptly to the window.*] She never came back. [*He turns away and then, recovering, moves toward* VIDA, *who catches his hands.*

VIDA. [*Hoping for a contradiction.*] She's broken your heart.

JOHN. [*Taking a chair by the lounge.*] Oh, no!

VIDA. [*Encouraged, begins to play the game again.*] You'll never love again!

JOHN. [*Speaking to her from the foot of the sofa.*] Try me! Try me! Ah, no, Mrs. Phillimore, I shall laugh, live, love and make money again! And let me tell you one thing—I'm going to rap her one over the knuckles. She had a stick of a Connecticut lawyer, and he—well, to cut a legal story short, since Mrs. Karslake's been in Europe, I have been quietly testing the validity of the decree of divorce. Perhaps you don't understand?

VIDA. [*Displaying her innate shrewdness.*] Oh, about a divorce, everything!

JOHN. I shall hear by this evening whether the divorce will stand or not.

VIDA. But it's to-day at three she marries—you won't let her commit bigamy?

JOHN. [*Shaking his head.*] I don't suppose I'd go as far as that. It may be the divorce will hold, but anyway I hope never to see her again.

[*He sits down beside her so that their faces are now directly opposite. Taking advantage of the close range, her eyes, without loss of time, open a direct fire.*

VIDA. Ah, my poor boy, she has broken your heart. [*Believing that this is her psychological moment, she lays her hand on his arm, but draws it back as soon as he attempts to take it.*] Now don't make love to me.

JOHN. [*Bold and amused, but never taken in.*] Why not?

VIDA. [*With immense gentleness.*] Because I like you too much! [*More gaily.*] I might give in, and take a notion to like you still more!

JOHN. Please do!

VIDA. [*With gush, and determined to be womanly at all hazards.*] Jack, I believe you'd be a lovely lover!

JOHN. [*Immensely diverted.*] Try me!

VIDA. [*Not hoping much from his tone.*] You charming, tempting, delightful fellow, I could love you without the least effort in the world,—but, no!

JOHN. [*Playing the game.*] Ah, well, now *seriously!* Between two people who have *suffered* and made their own mistakes—

VIDA. [*Playing the game too, but not playing it well.*] But you see, you don't *really* love me!

JOHN. [*Still ready to say what is expected.*] Cynthia—Vida, no man can sit beside you and look into your eyes without feeling—

VIDA. [*Speaking the truth as she sees it, seeing that her methods don't succeed.*] Oh! That's not love! That's simply—well, my dear Jack, it's beginning at the wrong end. And the truth is you hate Cynthia Karslake with such a whole-hearted hate, that you haven't a moment to think of any other woman.

JOHN. [*With sudden anger.*] I hate her!

VIDA. [*Very softly and most sweetly.*] Jack—Jack, I could be as foolish about you as—oh, as foolish as anything, my dear! And perhaps some day—perhaps some day you'll come to me and say, Vida, I am totally indifferent to Cynthia—and then—

JOHN. And then?

VIDA. [*The ideal woman in mind.*] Then, perhaps, you and I may join hands and stroll together into the Garden of Eden. It takes two to find the Garden of Eden, you know—and once we're on the inside, we'll lock the gate.

JOHN. [*Gaily, and seeing straight through her veneer.*] And lose the key under a rose-bush!

VIDA. [*Agreeing very softly.*] Under a rose-bush! [*There is a very soft knock at which* JOHN *starts up quickly.*] Come! [BROOKS *comes in, with* BENSON *close at his heels.*

BROOKS. [*Stolid, announces.*] My lady—Sir Wilf—[BENSON *stops him with a sharp movement and turns toward* VIDA.

BENSON. [*With intention.*] Your dressmaker, ma'am. [BENSON *waves* BROOKS *to go and* BROOKS *very haughtily complies.*

VIDA. [*Wonderingly.*] My dressmaker, Benson? [*With quick intelligence.*] Oh, of course, show her up. Mr. Karslake, you won't mind for a few minutes using my men's club-room? Benson will show you! You'll find cigars and the ticker, sporting papers, whiskey; and, if you want anything special, just 'phone down to my "chef."

JOHN. [*Looking at his watch.*] How long?

VIDA. [*Very anxious to please.*] Half a cigar! Benson will call you.

JOHN. [*Practically-minded.*] Don't make it too long. You see, there's my sheriff's sale on at twelve, and those races this afternoon. Fiddler will be here in ten minutes, remember!

[*The door opens.*

VIDA. [*To* JOHN.] Run along! [JOHN *leaves and* VIDA, *instantly practical, makes a broad gesture to* BENSON.] Everything just as it was, Benson! [BENSON *whisks the roses out of the vase and replaces them in the box. She gives* VIDA *scissors and empty vases, and, when* VIDA *finds herself in precisely the same position which preceded* JOHN'S *entrance, she says:*] There!

[BROOKS *comes in as* VIDA *takes a rose from basket.*

BROOKS. [*With characteristic stolidness.*] Your ladyship's dressmaker! M'lady! [*Enter* SIR WILFRID *in morning suit, boutonnière, &c.*

VIDA. [*With tender surprise and busy with the roses.*] Is that really you, Sir Wilfrid! I never flattered myself for an instant that you'd remember to come.

SIR WILFRID. [*Moving to the head of the sofa.*] Come? 'Course I come! Keen to come see you. By Jove, you know, you look as pink and white as a huntin' mornin'.

VIDA. [*Ready to make any man as happy as possible.*] You'll smoke?

SIR WILFRID. Thanks! [*He watches her as she trims and arranges the flowers.*] Awfully long fingers you have! Wish I was a rose, or a ring, or a pair of shears! I say, d' you ever notice what a devil of a fellow I am for originality, what? [*Unlike* JOHN, *is evidently impressed by her.*] You've got a delicate little den up here! Not so much low livin' and high thinkin', as low lights and no thinkin' at all, I hope—eh?

[*By this time* VIDA *has filled a vase with roses and rises to sweep by him and, if possible, make another charming picture to his eyes.*

VIDA. [*Gliding gracefully past him.*] You don't mind my moving about?

SIR WILFRID. [*Impressed.*] Not if you don't mind my watchin'. [*Sitting down on the sofa.*] And sayin' how wel you do it.

VIDA. It's most original of you to come here this morning. I don't quite see why you did.

She places the roses here and there, as if to see their effect, and leaves them on a small table near the door through which her visitors entered.

SIR WILFRID. Admiration.

VIDA. [*Sauntering slowly toward the mirror as she speaks.*] Oh, I saw that you admired her! And of course, she did say she was coming here at eleven! But that was only bravado! She won't come, and besides, I've given orders to admit no one!

SIR WILFRID. [*Attempting to dam the stream of her talk which flows gently but steadily on.*] May I ask you—

VIDA. And, indeed, if she came now, Mr. Karslake has gone, and her sole object in coming was to make him uncomfortable. [*She moves toward the table, stopping a half minute at the mirror to see that she looks as she wishes to look.*] Very dangerous symptom, too, that passionate desire to make one's former husband unhappy! But, I can't believe that your admiration for Cynthia Karslake is so warm that it led you to pay me this visit a half hour too early in the hope of seeing—

SIR WILFRID. [*Rising; most civil, but speaking his mind like a Briton.*] I say, would you mind stopping a moment! [*She smiles.*] I'm not an American, you know; I was brought up not to interrupt. But you Americans, it's different with you! If somebody didn't interrupt you, you'd go on forever.

VIDA. [*Passing him to tantalize.*] My point is you come to see Cynthia—

SIR WILFRID. [*Believing she means it.*] I came hopin' to see—

VIDA. [*Provokingly.*] Cynthia!

SIR WILFRID. [*Perfectly single-minded and entirely taken in.*] But I would have come even if I'd known—

VIDA. [*Evading him, while he follows.*] I don't believe it!

SIR WILFRID. [*Protesting whole-heartedly.*] Give you my word I—

VIDA. [*Leading him on.*] You're here to see *her!* And of course—

SIR WILFRID. [*Determined to be heard because, after all, he's a man.*] May I have the—eh—the floor? [VIDA *sits down in a chair.*] I was jolly well bowled over with Mrs. Karslake, I admit that, and I hoped to see her here, but—

VIDA. [*Talking nonsense and knowing it.*] You had another object in coming. In fact, you came to see Cynthia, and you came to see me! What I really long to know is, why you wanted to see *me!* For, of course, Cynthia's to be married at three! And, if she wasn't she wouldn't have you!

SIR WILFRID. [*Not intending to wound; merely speaking the flat truth.*] Well, I mean to jolly well ask her.

VIDA. [*Indignant.*] To be your wife?

SIR WILFRID. Why not?

VIDA. [*Still indignant.*] And you came here, to my house—in order to ask her—

SIR WILFRID. [*Truthful even on a subtle point.*] Oh, but that's only my first reason for coming, you know.

VIDA. [*Concealing her hopes.*] Well, now I *am* curious—what is the second?

SIR WILFRID. [*Simply.*] Are you feelin' pretty robust?

VIDA. I don't know!

SIR WILFRID. [*Crosses to the buffet.*] Will you have something, and then I'll tell you!

VIDA. [*Gaily.*] Can't I support the news without—

SIR WILFRID. [*Trying to explain his state of mind, a feat which he has never been able to accomplish.*] Mrs. Phillimore, you see it's this way. Whenever you're lucky, you're too lucky. Now, Mrs. Karslake is a nipper and no mistake, but as I told you, the very same evenin' and house where I saw her—

[*He attempts to take her hand.*

VIDA. [*Gently rising and affecting a tender surprise.*] What!

SIR WILFRID. [*Rising with her.*] That's it!—You're over! [*He suggests with his right hand the movement of a horse taking a hurdle.*

VIDA. [*Very sweetly.*] You don't really mean—

SIR WILFRID. [*Carried away for the moment by so much true womanliness.*] I mean, I stayed awake for an hour last night, thinkin' about you.

VIDA. [*Speaking to be contradicted.*] But, you've just told me—that Cynthia—

SIR WILFRID. [*Admitting the fact.*] Well, she did—she did bowl my wicket, but so did you—

VIDA. [*Taking him very gently to task.*] Don't you think there's a limit to—

[*She sits down.*

SIR WILFRID. [*Roused by so much loveliness of soul.*] Now, see here, Mrs. Phillimore! You and I are not bottle babies, eh, are we? You've been married and—I—I've knocked about, and we both know there's a lot of stuff talked about—eh, eh, well, you know:—the one and only—that a fellow can't be awfully well smashed by two at the same time, don't you know! All rubbish! You know it, and the proof of the puddin's in the eatin', I am!

VIDA. [*With gentle reproach.*] May I ask where I come in?

SIR WILFRID. Well, now, Mrs. Phillimore, I'll be frank with you, Cynthia's my favourite, but you're runnin' her a close second in the popular esteem!

VIDA. [*Laughing, determined not to take offense.*] What a delightful, original, fantastic person you are!

SIR WILFRID. [*Frankly happy that he has explained everything so neatly.*] I knew you'd take it that way!

VIDA. And what next, pray?

SIR WILFRID. Oh, just the usual,—eh,—thing,—the—eh—the same old question, don't you know. Will you have me if she don't?

VIDA. [*A shade piqued, but determined not to risk showing it.*] And you call that the same old usual question?

SIR WILFRID. Yes, I know, but—but will you? I sail in a week; we can take the same boat. And—eh—eh—my dear Mrs. —mayn't I say Vida, I'd like to see you at the head of my table.

VIDA. [*With velvet irony.*] With Cynthia at the foot?

SIR WILFRID. [*Practical, as before.*] Never mind Mrs. Karslake,—I admire her—she's—but you have your own points! And you're here, and so'm I!—damme I offer myself, and my affections, and I'm no icicle, my dear, tell you that for a fact, and,—and in fact what's your answer!—[VIDA *sighs and shakes her head.*] Make it, yes! I say, you know, my dear Vida—

[*He catches her hands.*

VIDA. [*Drawing them from his.*] Unhand me, dear villain! And sit further away from your second choice! What can I say? I'd rather have *you* for a lover than any man I know! You must be a lovely lover!

SIR WILFRID. I am!

[*He makes a second effort to catch her fingers.*

VIDA. Will you kindly go further away and be good!

SIR WILFRID. [*Quite forgetting* CYNTHIA.] Look here, if you say yes, we'll be married—

VIDA. In a month!

SIR WILFRID. Oh, no—this evening!

VIDA. [*Incapable of leaving a situation unadorned.*] This evening! And sail in the same boat with *you?* And shall we sail to the Garden of Eden and stroll into it and lock the gate on the inside and then lose the key—under a rose-bush?

SIR WILFRID. [*After a pause and some consideration.*] Yes; yes, I say—that's too clever for me! [*He draws nearer to her to bring the understanding to a crisis.*

VIDA. [*Interrupted by a soft knock.*] My maid—come!

SIR WILFRID. [*Swinging out of his chair and moving to the sofa.*] Eh?

BENSON. [*Coming in and approaching* VIDA.] The new footman, ma'am—he's made a mistake. He's told the lady you're at home.

VIDA. What lady?

BENSON. Mrs. Karslake; and she's on the stairs, ma'am.

VIDA. Show her in.

SIR WILFRID *has been turning over the roses. On hearing this, he faces about with a long stemmed one in his hand. He subsequently uses it to point his remarks.*

SIR WILFRID. [*To* BENSON, *who stops.*] One moment! [*To* VIDA.] I say, eh—I'd rather not see her!

VIDA. [*Very innocently.*] But you came here to see her.

SIR WILFRID. [*A little flustered.*] I'd rather not. Eh,—I fancied I'd find you and her together—but her—[*Coming a step nearer.*] findin' me with you looks so dooced intimate,—no one else, d'ye see, I believe she'd—draw conclusions—

BENSON. Pardon me, ma'am—but I hear Brooks coming!

SIR WILFRID. [*To* BENSON.] Hold the door!

VIDA. So you don't want her to know—?

SIR WILFRID. [*To* VIDA.] Be a good girl now—run me off somewhere!

VIDA. [*To* BENSON.] Show Sir Wilfrid the men's room.

[BROOKS *comes in.*

SIR WILFRID. The men's room! Ah! Oh! Eh!

VIDA. [*Beckoning him to go at once.*] Sir Wil— [*He hesitates; then as* BROOKS *advances, he flings off with* BENSON.

BROOKS. Lady Karslake, milady!

VIDA. Anything more inopportune! I never dreamed she'd come— [CYNTHIA *comes in veiled. As she walks quickly into the room,* VIDA *greets her languorously.*] My dear Cynthia, you don't mean to say—

CYNTHIA. [*Rather short, and visibly agitated.*] Yes, I've come.

VIDA. [*Polite, but not urgent.*] Do take off your veil.

CYNTHIA. [*Complying.*] Is no one here?

VIDA. [*As before.*] Won't you sit down?

CYNTHIA. [*Agitated and suspicious.*] Thanks, no— That is, yes, thanks. Yes! You haven't answered my question?

[CYNTHIA *waves her hand through the haze; glances suspiciously at the smoke, and looks about for the cigarette.*

VIDA. [*Playing innocence in the first degree.*] My dear, what makes you imagine that any one's here!

CYNTHIA. You've been smoking.

VIDA. Oh, puffing away! [CYNTHIA *sees the glasses.*

CYNTHIA. And drinking—a pair of drinks? [*Her eyes lighting on* JOHN'S *gloves on the table at her elbow.*] Do they fit you, dear? [VIDA *smiles;* CYNTHIA *picks up the crop and looks at it and reads her own name.*] "Jack, from Cynthia."

VIDA. [*Without taking the trouble to double for a mere woman.*] Yes, dear; it's Mr. Karslake's crop, but I'm happy to say he left me a few minutes ago.

CYNTHIA. He left the house? [VIDA *smiles.*] I wanted to see him.

VIDA. [*With a shade of insolence.*] To quarrel?

CYNTHIA. [*Frank and curt.*] I wanted to see him.

VIDA. [*Determined to put* CYNTHIA *in the wrong.*] And I sent him away because I didn't want you to repeat the scene of last night in my house.

CYNTHIA. [*Looks at crop and is silent.*] Well, I can't stay. I'm to be married at three, and I had to play truant to get here!

[BENSON *comes in.*

BENSON. [*To* VIDA.] There's a person, ma'am, on the sidewalk.

VIDA. What person, Benson?

BENSON. A person, ma'am, with a horse.

CYNTHIA. [*Happily agitated.*] It's Fiddler with Cynthia K!

[*She walks rapidly to the window and looks out.*

VIDA. [*To* BENSON.] Tell the man I'll be down in five minutes.

CYNTHIA. [*Looking down from the balcony with delight.*] Oh, there she is!

VIDA. [*Aside to* BENSON.] Go to the club-room, Benson, and say to the two gentlemen I can't see them at present—I'll send for them when—

BENSON. [*Listening.*] I hear some one coming.

VIDA. Quick! [BENSON *leaves the door which opens and* JOHN *comes in slowly, carelessly.* VIDA *whispers to* BENSON.

BENSON. [*Moving close to* JOHN *and whispering.*] Beg par—

VIDA. [*Under her breath.*] Go back!

JOHN. [*Not understanding.*] I beg pardon!

VIDA. [*Scarcely above a whisper.*] Go back!

JOHN. [*Dense.*] Can't! I've a date! With the sheriff!

VIDA. [*A little cross.*] Please use your eyes.

JOHN. [*Laughing and flattering* VIDA.] I am using my eyes.

VIDA. [*Fretted.*] Don't you see there's a lovely creature in the room?

JOHN. [*Not knowing what it is all about, but taking a wicked delight in seeing her customary calm ruffled.*] Of course there is.

VIDA. Hush!

JOHN. [*Teasingly.*] But what I want to know is—

VIDA. Hush!

JOHN. [*Enjoying his fun.*] —is when we're to stroll in the Garden of Eden—

VIDA. Hush!

JOHN. —and lose the key. [*To put a stop to this, she lightly tosses her handkerchief into his face.*] By George, talk about attar of roses!

CYNTHIA. [*At window, excited and moved at seeing her mare once more.*] Oh, she's a darling! [*Turning.*] A perfect darling! [JOHN *starts up; he sees* CYNTHIA *at the same instant that she sees him.*] Oh! I didn't know you were here. [*After a pause, with "take-it-or-leave-it" frankness.*] I came to see *you!* [JOHN *looks entremely dark and angry;* VIDA *rises.*

VIDA. [*To* CYNTHIA, *most gently, and seeing there's nothing to be gained of* JOHN.] Oh, pray feel at home, Cynthia, dear! [*Stopping by the door to her bedroom; to* JOHN.] When I've a nice street frock on, I'll ask you to present me to Cynthia K. [VIDA *opens the door and goes out.* CYNTHIA *and* JOHN *involuntarily exchange glances.*

CYNTHIA. [*Agitated and frank.*] Of course, I told you yesterday I was coming here.

JOHN. [*Irritated.*] And I was to deny myself the privilege of being here?

CYNTHIA. [*Curt and agitated.*] Yes.

JOHN. [*Ready to fight.*] And you guessed I would do that?

CYNTHIA. No.

JOHN. What?

CYNTHIA. [*Speaks with agitation, frankness and good will.*] Jack—I mean, Mr. Karslake,—no, I mean, Jack! I came because—well, you see, it's my wedding day!—and—and—I—I—was rude to you last evening. I'd like to apologize and make peace with you before I go—

JOHN. [*Determined to be disagreeable.*] Before you go to your last, long home!

CYNTHIA. I came to apologize.

JOHN. But you'll remain to quarrel!

CYNTHIA. [*Still frank and kind.*] I will not quarrel. No!—and I'm only here for a moment. I'm to be married at three, and just look at the clock! Besides, I told Philip I was going to Louise's shop, and I did—on the way here; but, you see, if I stay too long he'll telephone Louise and find I'm not there, and he might guess I was here. So you see I'm risking a scandal. And now, Jack, see here, I lay my hand on the table, I'm here on the square, and,—what I want to say is, why—Jack, even if we have made a mess of our married life, let's put by anger and pride. It's all over now and can't be helped. So let's be human, let's be reasonable, and let's be kind to each other! Won't you give me your hand? [JOHN *refuses.*] I wish you every happiness!

JOHN. [*Turning away, the past rankling.*] I had a client once, a murderer; he told me he murdered the man, and he told me, too, that he never felt so kindly to anybody as he did to that man after he'd killed him!

CYNTHIA. Jack!

JOHN. [*Unforgiving.*] You murdered my happiness!

CYNTHIA. I won't recriminate!

JOHN. And now I must put by anger and pride! I do! But not self-respect, not a just indignation—not the facts and my clear memory of them!

CYNTHIA. Jack!

JOHN. No!

CYNTHIA. [*With growing emotion, and holding out her hand.*] I give you one more chance! Yes, I'm determined to be generous. I forgive everything you ever did to me. I'm ready to be friends. I wish you every happiness and every—every—horse in the world! I can't do more than that! [*She offers it again.*] You refuse?

JOHN. [*Moved but surly.*] I like wildcats and I like Christians, but I don't like Christian wildcats! Now I'm close hauled, trot out your tornado! Let the Tiger loose! It's the tamer, the man in the cage that has to look lively and use the red hot crowbar! But, by Jove, I'm out of the cage! I'm a mere spectator of the married circus! [*He puffs vigorously.*

CYNTHIA. Be a game sport then! Our marriage was a wager; you wagered you could live with me. You lost; you paid with a divorce; and now is the time to show your sporting blood. Come on, shake hands and part friends.

JOHN. Not in this world! Friends with you, no! I have a proper pride. I don't propose to put my pride in my pocket.

CYNTHIA. [*Jealous and plain spoken.*] Oh, I wouldn't ask you to put your pride in your pocket while Vida's handkerchief is there. [JOHN *looks angered.*] Pretty little bijou of a handkerchief! [*Pulling out the handkerchief.*] And she is charming, and divorced, and reasonably well made up.

JOHN. Oh, well, Vida is a woman. [*Toying with the handkerchief.*.] I'm a man, a handkerchief is a handkerchief, and, as some old Aristotle or other said, whatever concerns a woman, concerns me!

CYNTHIA. [*Not oblivious of him, but in a low voice.*] Insufferable! Well, yes. [*She sits down. She is too much wounded to make any further appeal.*] You're perfectly right. There's no possible harmony between divorced people! I withdraw my hand and all good feeling. No wonder I couldn't stand you. Eh? However, that's pleasantly past! But at least, my dear Karslake, let us have some sort of beauty behaviour! If we cannot be decent, let us endeavour to be graceful. If we can't be moral, at least we can avoid being vulgar.

JOHN. Well—

CYNTHIA. If there's to be no more marriage in the world—

JOHN. [*Cynically.*] Oh, but that's not it; there's to be more and more and more!

CYNTHIA. [*With a touch of bitterness.*] Very well! I repeat then, if there's to be nothing but marriage and divorce, and remarriage, and re-divorce, at least, at least, those who *are* divorced can avoid the vulgarity of meeting each other here, there, and everywhere!

JOHN. Oh, that's where you come out!

CYNTHIA. I thought so yesterday, and to-day I know it. It's an insufferable thing to a woman of any delicacy of feeling to find her husband—

JOHN. Ahem—former!

CYNTHIA. *Once* a husband always—

JOHN. [*In the same cynical tone.*] Oh, no! Oh, dear, no.

CYNTHIA. To find her—to find the man she has once lived with —in the house of—making love to—to find you here! [JOHN *smiles and rises.*] You smile,—but I say, it should be a social axiom, no woman should have to meet her former husband.

JOHN. [*Cynical and cutting.*] Oh, I don't know; after I've served my term I don't mind meeting my jailor.

CYNTHIA. [*As* JOHN *takes chair near her.*] It's indecent—at the horse-show, the opera, at races and balls, to meet the man who once— It's not civilized! It's fantastic! It's half baked! Oh, I never should have come here! [*He sympathizes, and she grows irrational and furious.*] But it's entirely your fault!

JOHN. My fault?

CYNTHIA. [*Working herself into a rage.*] Of course. What business have you to be about—to be at large. To be at all!

JOHN. Gosh!

CYNTHIA. [*Her rage increasing.*] To be where I am! Yes, it's just as horrible for you to turn up in my life as it would be for a dead person to insist on coming back to life and dinner and bridge!

JOHN. Horrid idea!

CYNTHIA. Yes, but it's *you* who behave just as if you were not dead, just as if I'd not spent a fortune on your funeral. You do; you prepare to bob up at afternoon teas,—and dinners—and embarrass me to death with your extinct personality!

JOHN. Well, of course we *were* married, but it didn't quite kill me.

CYNTHIA. [*Angry and plain spoken.*] You killed yourself for me—I divorced you. I buried you out of my life. If any human soul was ever dead, you are! And there's nothing I so hate as a gibbering ghost.

JOHN. Oh, I say!

CYNTHIA. [*With hot anger.*] Go gibber and squeak where gibbering and squeaking are the fashion!

JOHN. [*Laughing and pretending to a coldness he does not feel.*] And so, my dear child, I'm to abate myself as a nuisance! Well, as far as seeing you is concerned, for my part it's just like seeing a horse who's chucked you once. The bruises are O. K., and you see him with a sort of easy curiosity. Of course, you know, he'll jolly well chuck the next man!—Permit me! [JOHN *picks up her gloves, handkerchief and parasol, and gives her these as she drops them one by one in her agitation.*] There's pleasure in the thought.

CYNTHIA. Oh!

JOHN. And now, may I ask you a very simple question? Mere curiosity on my part, but, why did you come here this morning?

CYNTHIA. I have already explained that to you.

JOHN. Not your real motive. Permit me!

CYNTHIA. Oh!

JOHN. But I believe I have guessed your real—permit me—your real motive!

CYNTHIA. Oh!

JOHN. [*With mock sympathy.*] Cynthia, I am sorry for you.

CYNTHIA. H'm?

JOHN. Of course we had a pretty lively case of the fever—the mutual attraction fever, and we *were* married a very short time. And I conclude that's what's the matter with *you!* You see, my dear, seven months of married life is too short a time to cure a bad case of the fancies.

CYNTHIA. [*In angry surprise.*] What?

JOHN. [*Calm and triumphant.*] That's my diagnosis.

CYNTHIA. [*Slowly and gathering herself together.*] I don't think I understand.

JOHN. Oh, yes, you do; yes, you do.

CYNTHIA. [*With blazing eyes.*] What do you mean?

JOHN. Would you mind not breaking my crop! Thank you! I mean [*With polite impertinence.*] that ours was a case of premature divorce, and, ahem, you're in love with me still.

He pauses. CYNTHIA *has one moment of fury, then she realizes at what a disadvantage this places her. She makes an immense effort, recovers her calm, thinks hard for a moment more, and then, has suddenly an inspiration.*

CYNTHIA. Jack, some day you'll get the blind staggers from conceit. No, I'm not in love with you, Mr. Karslake, but I shouldn't be at all surprised if she were. She's just your sort, you know. She's a man-eating shark, and you'll be a toothsome mouthful. Oh, come now, Jack, what a silly you are! Oh, yes, you are, to get off a joke like that; me—in love with—

[*She looks at him.*

JOHN. Why are you here? [*She laughs and begins to play her game.*] Why are you here?

CYNTHIA. Guess! [*She laughs.*

JOHN. Why are you—

CYNTHIA. [*Quickly.*] Why am I here! I'll tell you. I'm going to be married. I had a longing, an irresistible longing to see you make an ass of yourself just once more! It happened!

JOHN. [*Uncertain and discomfited.*] I know better!

CYNTHIA. But I came for a serious purpose, too. I came, my dear fellow, to make an experiment on myself. I've been with you thirty minutes; and— [*She sighs with content.*] It's all right!

JOHN. What's all right?

CYNTHIA. [*Calm and apparently at peace with the world.*] I'm immune.

JOHN. Immune?

CYNTHIA. You're not catching any more! Yes, you see, I said to myself, if I fly into a temper—

JOHN. You did!

CYNTHIA. If I fly into a temper when I see him, well, that shows I'm not yet so entirely convalescent that I can afford to have Jack Karslake at my house. If I remain calm I shall ask him to dinner.

JOHN. [*Routed.*] Ask me if you dare! [*He rises.*

CYNTHIA. [*Getting the whip hand for good.*] Ask you to dinner? Oh, my dear fellow. [JOHN *rises.*] I'm going to do much more than that. [*She rises.*] We must be friends, old man! We must meet, we must meet often, we must show New York the way the thing should be done, and, to show you I mean it— I want you to be my best man, and give me away when I'm married this afternoon.

JOHN. [*Incredulous and impatient.*] You don't mean that!

[*He pushes back his chair.*

CYNTHIA. There you are! Always suspicious!

JOHN. You don't mean that!

CYNTHIA. [*Hiding her emotion under a sportswoman's manner.*] Don't I? I ask you, come! And come as you are! And I'll lay my wedding gown to Cynthia K that you won't be there! If you're there, you get the gown, and if you're not, I get Cynthia K!—

JOHN. [*Determined not to be worsted.*] I take it!

CYNTHIA. Done! Now, then, we'll see which of us two is the real sporting goods! Shake! [*They shake hands on it.*] Would you mind letting me have a plain soda? [JOHN *goes to the table, and, as he is rattled and does not regard what he is about, he fills the glass three-fourths full with whiskey. He gives this to* CYNTHIA *who looks him in the eye with an air of triumph.*] Thanks. [*Maliciously, as* VIDA *enters.*] Your hand is a bit shaky. I think *you* need a little King William. [JOHN *shrugs his shoulders, and, as* VIDA *immediately speaks,* CYNTHIA *defers drinking.*

VIDA. [*To* CYNTHIA.] My dear, I'm sorry to tell you your husband—I mean, my husband—I mean Philip—he's asking for you over the 'phone. You must have said you were coming here. Of course, I told him you were not here, and hung up.

BENSON. [*Entering hurriedly and at once moving to* VIDA.] Ma'am, the new footman's been talking with Mr. Phillimore on the wire. [VIDA, *gesture of regret.*] He told Mr. Phillimore that his lady was here, and, if I can believe my ears, ma'am, he's got Sir Wilfrid on the 'phone now!

SIR WILFRID. [*Making his appearance, perplexed and annoyed.*] I say, y' know—extraordinary country; that old chap, Phillimore, he's been damned impertinent over the wire! Says I've run off with Mrs. Karslake—talks about "Louise!" Now, who the dooce is Louise? He's comin' round here, too—I said Mrs. Karslake wasn't here— [*Seeing* CYNTHIA.] Hello! Good job! What a liar I am!

BENSON. [*Coming to the door. To* VIDA.] Mr. Fiddler, ma'am, says the mare is gettin' very restive.

[JOHN *hears this and moves at once.* BENSON *withdraws.*

JOHN. [*To* VIDA.] If that mare's restive, she'll break out in a rash.

VIDA. [*To* JOHN.] Will you take me?

JOHN. Of course. [*They go to the door.*

CYNTHIA. [*To* JOHN.] Tata, old man! Meet you at the altar! If I don't, the mare's mine!

[SIR WILFRID *looks at her amazed.*

VIDA. [*To* CYNTHIA.] Do the honours, dear, in my absence!

JOHN. Come along, come along, never mind them! A horse is a horse!

JOHN *and* VIDA *go out gaily and in haste. At the same moment* CYNTHIA *drinks what she supposes to be her glass of plain soda. As it is whiskey straight, she is seized with astonishment and a fit of coughing.* SIR WILFRID *relieves her of the glass.*

SIR WILFRID. [*Indicating the contents of the glass.*] I say, do you ordinarily take it as high up—as seven fingers and two thumbs.

CYNTHIA. [*Coughing.*] Jack poured it out. Just shows how groggy he was! And now, Sir Wilfrid—

[*She gets her things to go.*

SIR WILFRID. Oh, you can't go!

[BROOKS *appears at the door.*

CYNTHIA. I am to be married at three.

SIR WILFRID. Let him wait. [*Aside to* BROOKS, *whom he meets near the door.*] If Mr. Phillimore comes, bring his card up.

BROOKS. [*Going.*] Yes, Sir Wilfrid.

SIR WILFRID. To me! [*Tipping him.*

BROOKS. [*Bowing.*] To you, Sir Wilfrid. [BROOKS *goes.*

SIR WILFRID. [*Returning to* CYNTHIA.] I've got to have my innings, y' know! [*Looking at her more closely.*] I say, you've been crying!—

CYNTHIA. King William!

SIR WILFRID. You *are* crying! Poor little gal!

CYNTHIA. [*Tears in her eyes.*] I feel all shaken and cold.

[BROOKS *returns with a card.*

SIR WILFRID. [*Astonished and sympathetic.*] Poor little gal.

CYNTHIA. [*Her eyes wet.*] I didn't sleep a wink last night. [*With disgust.*] Oh, what is the matter with me?

SIR WILFRID. Why, it's as plain as a pikestaff! You— [BROOKS *has carried in the card to* SIR WILFRID, *who picks it up and says aside, to* BROOKS:] Phillimore? [BROOKS *assents. Aloud to* CYNTHIA, *calmly deceitful.*] Who's Waldorf Smith? [CYNTHIA *shakes her head. To* BROOKS, *returning card to salver.*] Tell the gentleman Mrs. Karslake is not here! [BROOKS *leaves the room.*

CYNTHIA. [*Aware that she has no business where she is.*] I thought it was Philip!

SIR WILFRID. [*Telling the truth as if it were a lie.*] So did I! [*With cheerful confidence.*] And now, Mrs. Karslake, I'll tell you why you're cryin'. [*Sitting down beside her.*] You're marryin' the wrong man! I'm sorry for you, but you're such a goose. Here you are, marryin' this legal luminary. What for? You don't know! He don't know! But I do! You pretend you're marryin' him because it's the sensible thing; not a bit of it. You're marryin' Mr. Phillimore because of all the other men you ever saw he's the least like Jack Karslake.

CYNTHIA. That's a very good reason.

SIR WILFRID. There's only one good reason for marrying, and that is because you'll die if you don't!

CYNTHIA. Oh, I've tried that!

SIR WILFRID. The Scripture says: "Try! try! again!" I tell you, there's nothing like a w'im!

CYNTHIA. What's that? W'im? Oh, you mean a *whim!* Do please try and say W*h*im!

SIR WILFRID. [*For the first time emphasizing his H in the word.*] W*h*im. You must have a w'im—w'im for the chappie you marry.

CYNTHIA. I had—for Jack.

SIR WILFRID. Your w'im wasn't wimmy enough, my dear! If you'd had more of it, and tougher, it would ha' stood, y'know! Now, I'm not proposin'!

CYNTHIA. [*Diverted at last from her own distress.*] I hope not!

SIR WILFRID. Oh, I will later! It's not time yet! As I was saying—

CYNTHIA. And pray, Sir Wilfrid, when will it be time?

SIR WILFRID. As soon as I see you have a w'im for me! [*Rising, looks at his watch.*] And now, I'll tell you what we'll do! We've got just an hour to get there in, my motor's on the corner, and in fifty minutes we'll be at Belmont Park.

CYNTHIA. [*Her sporting blood fired.*] Belmont Park!

SIR WILFRID. We'll do the races, and dine at Martin's—

CYNTHIA. [*Tempted.*] Oh, if I only could! I can't! I've got to be married! You're awfully nice; I've almost got a "w'im" for you already.

SIR WILFRID. [*Delighted.*] There you are! I'll send a telegram! [*She shakes her head. He sits and writes at the table.*

CYNTHIA. No, no, no!

SIR WILFRID. [*Reading what he has written.*] "Off with Cates-Darby to Races. Please postpone ceremony till seven-thirty."

CYNTHIA. Oh, no, it's impossible!

SIR WILFRID. [*Accustomed to have things go his way.*] No more than breathin'! You can't get a w'im for me, you know, unless we're together, so together we'll be! [JOHN KARSLAKE *opens the door, and, unnoticed, walks into the room.*] And to-morrow you'll wake up with a jolly little w'im— , [*Reading.*] "Postpone ceremony till seven-thirty." There. [*He puts on her cloak and turning, sees* JOHN.] Hello!

JOHN. [*Surly.*] Hello! Sorry to disturb you.

SIR WILFRID. [*Cheerful as possible.*] Just the man! [*Giving him the telegraph form.*] Just step round and send it, my boy. Thanks! [JOHN *reads it.*

CYNTHIA. No, no, I can't go!

SIR WILFRID. Cockety-coo-coo-can't. I say, you must!

CYNTHIA. [*Positively.*] *No!*

JOHN. [*Astounded.*] Do you mean you're going—

SIR WILFRID. [*Very gay.*] Off to the races, my boy!

JOHN. [*Angry and outraged.*] Mrs. Karslake can't go with you there!

CYNTHIA *starts, amazed at his assumption of marital authority, and delighted that she will have an opportunity of outraging his sensibilities.*

SIR WILFRID. Oho!

JOHN. An hour before her wedding!

SIR WILFRID. [*Gay and not angry.*] May I know if it's the custom—

JOHN. [*Jealous and disgusted.*] It's worse than eloping—

SIR WILFRID. Custom, y' know, for the husband, that was, to dictate—

JOHN. [*Thoroughly vexed.*] By George, there's a limit!

CYNTHIA. What? What? What? [*Gathering up her things.*] What did I hear you say?

SIR WILFRID. Ah!

JOHN. [*Angry.*] I say there's a limit—

CYNTHIA. [*More and more determined to arouse and excite* JOHN.] Oh, there's a limit, is there?

JOHN. There is! I bar the way! It means reputation—it means—

CYNTHIA. [*Enjoying her opportunity.*] We shall see what it means!

SIR WILFRID. Aha!

JOHN. [*To* CYNTHIA.] I'm here to protect your reputation—

SIR WILFRID. [*To* CYNTHIA.] We've got to make haste, you know.

CYNTHIA. Now, I'm ready—

JOHN. [*To* CYNTHIA.] Be sensible. You're breaking off the match—

CYNTHIA. [*Excitedly.*] What's that to you?

SIR WILFRID. It's boots and saddles!

JOHN. [*Taking his stand between them and the door.*] No thoroughfare!

SIR WILFRID. Look here, my boy—!

CYNTHIA. [*Catching at the opportunity of putting* JOHN *in an impossible position.*] Wait a moment, Sir Wilfrid! Give me the wire! [*Facing him.*] Thanks! [*Taking the telegraph form from him and tearing it up.*] There! Too rude to chuck him by wire! But you, Jack, you've taken on yourself to look after my interests, so I'll just ask you, old man, to run down to the Supreme Court and tell Philip—nicely, you know—I'm off with Sir Wilfrid and where! Say I'll be back by seven, if I'm not later! And make it clear, Jack, I'll marry him by eight-thirty or nine at the latest! And mind *you're* there, dear! And now, Sir Wilfrid, we're off.

JOHN. [*Staggered and furious, giving way as they pass him.*] I'm not the man to—to carry—

CYNTHIA. [*Quick and dashing.*] Oh, yes, you are.

JOHN. —a message from you.

CYNTHIA. [*Triumphant.*] Oh, yes, you are; you're just exactly the man! [CYNTHIA *and* SIR WILFRID *whirl out.*

JOHN. Great miracles of Moses!

CURTAIN.

ACT III.

SCENE. *The same as that of Act I, but the room has been cleared of superfluous furniture, and arranged for a wedding ceremony.* MRS. PHILLIMORE *is reclining on the sofa at the right of the table,* MISS HENEAGE *at its left.* SUDLEY *is seated at the right of the table.* GRACE *is seated on the sofa. There is a wedding-bell of roses, an arch of orange blossoms, and, girdled by a ribbon of white, an altar of calla lilies. There are cushions of flowers, alcoves of flowers, vases of flowers—in short, flowers everywhere and in profusion and variety. Before the altas are two cushions for the couple to kneel on and, on pedestals, at each side of the arch, are twin candelabra. The hangings are pink and white.*

The room, first of all, and its emblems, holds the undivided attention; then slowly engaging it, and in contrast to their gay surroundings, the occupants. About each and everyone of them, hangs a deadly atmosphere of suppressed irritation.

SUDLEY. [*Impatiently.*] All very well, my dear Sarah. But you see the hour. Twenty to ten! We have been here since half-past two.

MISS HENEAGE. You had dinner?

SUDLEY. I did not come here at two to have dinner at eight, and be kept waiting until ten! And, my dear Sarah, when I ask where the bride is—

MISS HENEAGE. [*With forced composure.*] I have told you all I know. Mr. John Karslake came to the house at lunch time, spoke to Philip, and they left the house together.

GRACE. Where is Philip?

MRS. PHILLIMORE. [*Feebly, irritated.*] I don't wish to be censorious or to express an actual opinion, but I must say it's a bold bride who keeps her future mother-in-law waiting for eight hours. However, I will not venture to— [MRS. PHILLIMORE *reclines again and fades away into silence.*

GRACE. [*Sharply and decisively.*] I do! I'm sorry I went to the expense of a silver ice-pitcher.

MRS. PHILLIMORE *sighs.* MISS HENEAGE *keeps her temper with an effort which is obvious.* THOMAS *opens the door.*

SUDLEY. [*To* MRS. PHILLIMORE.] For my part, I don't believe Mrs. Karslake means to return here or to marry Philip at all!

THOMAS. [*Coming in, and approaching* MISS HENEAGE.] Two telegrams for you, ma'am! The choir boys have had their supper. [*A slight movement ripples the ominous calm of all.* THOMAS *steps back.*

SUDLEY. [*Rising.*] At last we shall know!

MISS HENEAGE. From the lady! Probably!

MISS HENEAGE *opens the first telegram and reads it at a glance, laying it on the salver again with a look at* SUDLEY. THOMAS *passes the salver to* SUDLEY, *who takes the telegram.*

GRACE. There's a toot now.

MRS. PHILLIMORE. [*Feebly, confused.*] I don't wish to intrude, but really I cannot imagine Philip marrying at midnight. [*As* SUDLEY *reads,* MISS HENEAGE *opens the second telegram, but does not read it.*

SUDLEY. [*Reading.*] "Accident, auto struck" —something! "Gasoline"—did something—illegible, ah! [*Reads.*] "Home by nine forty-five! Hold the church!"

[*A general movement sets in.*

MISS HENEAGE. [*Profoundly shocked.*] "Hold the church!" William, she still means to marry Philip! and to-night, too!

SUDLEY. It's from Belmont Park.

GRACE. [*Making a great discovery.*] She went to the races!

MISS HENEAGE. This is from Philip! [*Reading the second telegram.*] "I arrive at ten o'clock. Have dinner ready." [MISS HENEAGE *motions to* THOMAS, *who, obeying, retires. Looking at her watch.*] They are both due now. [*Movement.*] What's to be done? [*She rises and* SUDLEY *shrugs his shoulders.*

SUDLEY. [*Rising.*] After a young woman has spent her wedding day at the races? Why, I consider that she has broken the engagement,—and when she comes, tell her so.

MISS HENEAGE. I'll telephone Matthew. The choir boys can go home—her maid can pack her belongings—and when the lady arrives—

Impudently, the very distant toot of an auto-horn breaks in upon her words, producing, in proportion to its growing nearness, an increasing pitch of excitement and indignation. GRACE *flies to the door and looks out.* MRS. PHILLIMORE, *helpless, does not know what to do or where to go or what to say.* SUDLEY *moves about excitedly.* MISS HENEAGE *stands ready to make herself disagreeable.*

GRACE. [*Speaking rapidly and with excitement.*] I hear a man's voice. Cates-Darby and brother Matthew.

A loud and brazenly insistent toot outrages afresh. Laughter and voices outside are heard faintly. GRACE *looks out of the door, and, as quickly withdraws.*

MISS HENEAGE. Outrageous!

SUDLEY. Disgraceful!

MRS. PHILLIMORE. Shocking! [*Partly rising as the voices and horn are heard.*] I shall not take any part at all, in the—eh—
[*She fades away.*

MISS HENEAGE. [*Interrupting her.*] Don't trouble yourself.

Through the growing noise of voices and laughter, CYNTHIA'S *voice is heard.* SIR WILFRID *is seen in the outer hall. He is burdened with wraps, not to mention a newspaper and parasol, which in no wise check his flow of gay remarks to* CYNTHIA, *who is still outside.* CYNTHIA'S *voice, and now* MATTHEW'S, *reach those inside, and, at last, both join* SIR WILFRID, *who has turned at the door to wait for them. As she reaches the door,* CYNTHIA *turns and speaks to* MATTHEW, *who immediately follows her. She is in automobile attire, wearing goggles, a veil, and an exquisite duster of latest Paris style. They come in with a subdued bustle and noise. As their eyes light on* CYNTHIA, SUDLEY *and* MISS HENEAGE *exclaim, and there is a general movement.*

SUDLEY. 'Pon my word!

GRACE. Hah!

MISS HENEAGE. [*Bristling up to her feet, her sensibilities outraged.*] Shocking!

GRACE *remains standing above sofa.* SUDLEY *moves toward her,* MISS HENEAGE *sitting down again.* MRS. PHILLIMORE *reclines on sofa.* CYNTHIA *begins to speak as soon as she appears and speaks fluently to the end.*

CYNTHIA. No! I never was so surprised in my life, as when I strolled into the paddock and they gave me a rousing reception—old Jimmy Withers, Debt Gollup, Jack Deal, Monty Spiffles, the Governor and Buckeye. All of my old admirers! They simply fell on my neck, and, dear Matthew, what do you think I did? I turned on the water main! [*There are movements and murmurs of disapprobation from the family.* MATTHEW *indicates a desire to go.*] Oh, but you can't go!

MATTHEW. I'll return in no time!

CYNTHIA. I'm all ready to be married. Are they ready? [MATTHEW *waves a pious, polite gesture of recognition to the family.*] I beg everybody's pardon! [*Taking off her wrap and putting it on the back of a chair.*] My goggles are so dusty, I can't see who's who! [*To* SIR WILFRID.] Thanks! You *have* carried it well! [*She takes the parasol from* SIR WILFRID.

SIR WILFRID. [*Aside to* CYNTHIA.] When may I—?

CYNTHIA. See you next Goodwood!

SIR WILFRID. [*Imperturbably.*] Oh, I'm coming back!

CYNTHIA. [*Advancing a bit toward the family.*] Not a bit of use in coming back! I shall be married before you get here! Ta! Ta! Goodwood!

SIR WILFRID. [*Not in the least affected.*] I'm coming back. [*He goes out quickly. There are more murmurs of disapprobation from the family. There is a slight pause.*

CYNTHIA. [*Beginning to take off her goggles, and moving nearer "the family."*] I do awfully apologize for being so late!

MISS HENEAGE. [*Importantly.*] Mrs. Karslake—

SUDLEY. [*Importantly.*] Ahem! [CYNTHIA *lays down goggles, and sees their severity.*

CYNTHIA. Dear me! [*Surveying the flowers and for a moment speechless.*] Oh, good heavens! Why, it looks like a smart funeral!

MISS HENEAGE *moves; then speaks in a perfectly ordinary natural tone, but her expression is severe.* CYNTHIA *immediately realizes the state of affairs in its fullness.*

MISS HENEAGE. [*To* CYNTHIA.] After what has occurred, Mrs. Karslake—

CYNTHIA. [*Glances quietly toward the table, and then sits down at it, composed and good-tempered.*] I see you got my wire—so you know where I have been.

MISS HENEAGE. To the race-course!

SUDLEY. With a rowdy Englishman. [CYNTHIA *glances at* SUDLEY, *uncertain whether he means to be disagreeable, or whether he is only naturally so.*

MISS HENEAGE. We concluded you desired to break the engagement!

CYNTHIA. [*Indifferently.*] No! No! Oh! No!

MISS HENEAGE. Do you intend, despite of our opinion of you—

CYNTHIA. The only opinion that would have any weight with me would be Mrs. Phillimore's.

[*She turns expectantly to* MRS. PHILLIMORE.

MRS. PHILLIMORE. I am generally asleep at this hour, and, accordingly, I will not venture to express any—eh—any—actual opinion. [*She fades away.* CYNTHIA *smiles.*

MISS HENEAGE. [*Coldly.*] You smile. We simply inform you that as regards *us*, the alliance is not grateful.

CYNTHIA. [*Affecting gaiety and unconcern.*] And all this because the gasoline gave out.

SUDLEY. My patience has given out!

GRACE. So has mine. I'm going.

[*She makes good her word.*

SUDLEY. [*Vexed beyond civility. To* CYNTHIA.] My dear young lady: You come here, to this sacred—eh—eh—spot—altar!—[*Gesture.*] odoriferous of the paddock!—speaking of Spiffles and Buckeye,—having practically eloped!—having created a scandal, and disgraced our family!

CYNTHIA. [*Affecting surprise at this attitude.*] How does it disgrace you? Because I like to see a high-bred, clean, nervy, sweet little four-legged gee play the antelope over a hurdle!

MISS HENEAGE. Sister, it is high time that you—

[*She turns to* CYNTHIA *with a gesture.*

CYNTHIA. [*With quiet irony.*] Mrs. Phillimore is generally asleep at this hour, and accordingly she will not venture to express—

SUDLEY. [*Spluttering with irritation.*] Enough, madam—I *venture* to—to—to—to say, you are leading a fast life.

CYNTHIA. [*With powerful intention.*] Not in this house! For six heavy weeks have I been laid away in the grave, and I've found it very slow indeed trying to keep pace with the dead!

SUDLEY. [*Despairingly.*] This comes of horses!

CYNTHIA. [*Indignant.*] Of what?

SUDLEY. C-c-caring for horses!

MISS HENEAGE. [*With sublime morality.*] What Mrs. Karslake cares for is—men.

CYNTHIA. [*Angry and gay.*] What would you have me care for? The Ornithorhyncus Paradoxus? or Pithacanthropus Erectus? Oh, I refuse to take you seriously. [SUDLEY *begins to prepare to leave; he buttons himself into respectability and his coat.*

SUDLEY. My dear madam, I take myself seriously—and madam, I—I retract what I have brought with me [*Feeling in his waistcoat pocket.*] as a graceful gift,—an Egyptian scarab—a—a—sacred beetle, which once ornamented the person of a—eh—mummy.

CYNTHIA. [*Scoring in return.*] It should never be absent from your pocket, Mr. Sudley! [SUDLEY *walks away in a rage.*

MISS HENEAGE. [*Rising, to* SUDLEY.] I've a vast mind to withdraw my— [CYNTHIA *moves.*

CYNTHIA. [*Interrupts; maliciously.*] Your wedding present? The little bronze cat!

MISS HENEAGE. [*Moves, angrily.*] Oh! [*Even* MRS. PHILLIMORE *comes momentarily to life, and expresses silent indignation.*

SUDLEY. [*Loftily.*] Sarah, I'm going.

GRACE, *who has met* PHILIP, *takes occasion to accompany him into the room.* PHILIP *looks dusty and grim. As they come in,* GRACE *speaks to him. and* PHILIP *shakes his head. They pause near the door.*

CYNTHIA. [*Emotionally.*] I shall go to my room! However, all I ask is that you repeat to Philip—[*As she moves toward the door, she comes suddenly upon* PHILIP, *and speaks to him in a low voice.*

SUDLEY. [*To* MISS HENEAGE, *determined to win.*] As I go out, I shall do myself the pleasure of calling a hansom for Mrs. Karslake— [PHILIP *moves slightly from the door.*

PHILIP. As you go out, Sudley, have a hansom called, and when it comes, get into it.

SUDLEY. [*Furious.*] Eh,—eh,—my dear sir, I leave you to your fate. [PHILIP *angrily points him the door and* SUDLEY *leaves in great haste.*

MISS HENEAGE. [*With weight.*] Philip, you've not heard—

PHILIP. [*Interrupting.*] Everything—from Grace! My sister has repeated your words to me—and her own! I've told her what I think of *her.* [PHILIP *looks witheringly at* GRACE.

GRACE. I sha'n't wait to hear any more.

[*She flounces out of the room.*

PHILIP. Don't make it necessary for me to tell you what I think of you. [PHILIP *moves to the right, toward his mother, to whom he gives his arm.* MISS HENEAGE *immediately seeks the opposite side.*] Mother, with your permission, I desire to be alone. I expect both you and Grace, Sarah, to be dressed and ready for the ceremony a half hour from now. [*As* PHILIP *and* MRS. PHILLIMORE *are about to go out,* MISS HENEAGE *speaks.*

MISS HENEAGE. I shall come or not as I see fit. And let me add, my dear brother, that a fool at forty is a fool indeed. [MISS HENEAGE, *high and mighty, goes out, much pleased with her quotation.*

MRS. PHILLIMORE. [*Stupid and weary as usual, to* PHILIP, *as he leads her to the door.*] My dear son—I won't venture to express— [CYNTHIA, *in irritation, moves to the table.*

PHILIP. [*Soothing a silly mother.*] No, mother, don't! But I shall expect you, of course, at the ceremony. [MRS. PHILLIMORE *languidly retires.* PHILIP *strides to the centre of the room, taking the tone, and assuming the attitude of, the injured husband.*] It is proper for me to tell you that I followed you to Belmont. I am aware—I know with whom—in fact, *I know all!* [*He punctuates his words with pauses, and indicates the whole censorious universe.*] And now let me assure you—I am the last man in the world to be jilted on the very eve of—of—everything with you. I won't be jilted. [CYNTHIA *is silent.*] You understand? I propose to marry you. I won't be made ridiculous.

CYNTHIA. [*Glancing at* PHILIP.] Philip, I didn't mean to make you—

PHILIP. Why, then, did you run off to Belmont Park with that fellow?

CYNTHIA. Philip, I—eh—

PHILIP. [*Sitting down at the table.*] What motive? What reason? On our wedding day? Why did you do it?

CYNTHIA. I'll tell you the truth. I was bored.

PHILIP. [*Staggered.*] Bored? In my company?

CYNTHIA. I was bored, and then—and besides, Sir Wilfrid asked me to go.

PHILIP. Exactly, and that was why you went. Cynthia, when you promised to marry me, you told me you had forever done with love. You agreed that marriage was the rational coming together of two people.

CYNTHIA. I know, I know!

PHILIP. Do you believe that now?

CYNTHIA. I don't know what I believe. My brain is in a whirl! But, Philip, I am beginning to be—I'm afraid—yes, I am afraid that one can't just select a great and good man [*Indicating him.*] and say: I will be happy with him.

PHILIP. [*With complacent dignity.*] I don't see why not. You must assuredly do one or the other: You must either let your heart choose or your head select.

CYNTHIA. [*Gravely.*] No, there's a third scheme: Sir Wilfrid explained the theory to me. A woman should marry whenever she has a whim for the man, and then leave the rest to the man. Do you see?

PHILIP. [*Furious.*] Do I see? Have I ever seen anything else? Marry for whim! That's the New York idea of marriage.

CYNTHIA. [*Observing cynically.*] New York ought to know.

PHILIP. Marry for whim and leave the rest to the divorce court! Marry for whim and leave the rest to the man. That was the former Mrs. Phillimore's idea. Only she spelled "whim" differently; she omitted the "w." [*He rises in his anger.*] And now you—*you* take up with this preposterous— [CYNTHIA *moves uneasily.*] But, nonsense! It's impossible! A woman of your mental calibre— No. Some obscure, primitive, female *feeling* is at work corrupting your better judgment! What is it you *feel?*

CYNTHIA. Philip, you never felt like a fool, did you?

PHILIP. No, never.

CYNTHIA. [*Politely.*] I thought not.

PHILIP. No, but whatever your feelings, I conclude you are ready to marry me.

CYNTHIA. [*Uneasy.*] Of course, I came back. I am here, am I not?

PHILIP. You are ready to marry me?

CYNTHIA. [*Twisting in the coils.*] But you haven't had your dinner.

PHILIP. Do I understand you refuse?

CYNTHIA. Couldn't we defer—?

PHILIP. You refuse?

CYNTHIA. [*Desperately thinking of an escape from her promise, and finding none.*] No, I said I'd marry you. I'm a woman of my word. I will.

PHILIP. [*Triumphant.*] Ah! Very good, then. Run to your room. [CYNTHIA *turns to* PHILIP.] Throw something over you. In a half hour I'll expect you here! And Cynthia, my dear, remember! I cannot cuculate like a wood-pigeon, but—I esteem you!

CYNTHIA. [*Hopelessly.*] I think I'll go, Philip.

PHILIP. I may not be fitted to play the love-bird, but—

CYNTHIA. [*Spiritlessly.*] I think I'll go, Philip.

PHILIP. I'll expect you,—in half an hour.

CYNTHIA. [*With leaden despair.*] Yes.

PHILIP. And, Cynthia, don't think any more about that fellow, Cates-Darby.

CYNTHIA. [*Amazed and disgusted by his misapprehension.*] No. [*As* CYNTHIA *leaves,* THOMAS *comes in from the opposite door.*

PHILIP. [*Not seeing* THOMAS, *and clumsily defiant.*] And if I had that fellow, Cates-Darby, in the dock—!

THOMAS. Sir Wilfrid Cates-Darby.

PHILIP. Sir what—what—wh-who? [SIR WILFRID *enters in evening dress.* PHILIP *looks* SIR WILFRID *in the face and speaks to* THOMAS.] Tell Sir Wilfrid Cates-Darby I am not at home to him. [THOMAS *is embarrassed.*

SIR WILFRID. [*Undaunted.*] My dear Lord Eldon—

PHILIP. [*Again addressing* THOMAS.] Show the gentleman the door. [*There is a pause.* SIR WILFRID, *with a significant gesture, glances at the door.*

SIR WILFRID. [*Moving to the door, he examines it and returns to* PHILIP.] Eh,—I admire the door, my boy! Fine, old carved mahogany panel; but don't ask me to leave by it, for Mrs. Karslake made me promise I'd come, and that's why I'm here. [THOMAS *does not wait for further orders.*

PHILIP. Sir, you are—impudent—!

SIR WILFRID. [*Interrupting.*] Ah, you put it all in a nutshell, don't you?

PHILIP. To show your face here, after practically eloping with my wife!

SIR WILFRID. [*Affecting ignorance.*] When were you married?

PHILIP. We are as good as married.

SIR WILFRID. Oh, pooh, pooh! You can't tell me that grace before soup is as good as a dinner! [*He takes out his cigar-case and, in the absence of a match, enjoys a smokeless smoke.*

PHILIP. Sir—I—demand—

SIR WILFRID. [*Calmly carrying the situation.*] Mrs. Karslake is *not* married. *That's* why I'm here. I am here for the same purpose *you* are; to ask Mrs. Karslake to be my wife.

PHILIP. Are you in your senses?

SIR WILFRID. [*Pricking his American cousin's pet vanity.*] Come, come, Judge—you Americans have no sense of humour. [*Taking a small jewel-case from his pocket.*] There's my regards for the lady—and [*Reasonably.*], if I must go, I will. Of course, I would like to see her, but—if it isn't your American custom—

THOMAS. [*Opens the door and announces.*] Mr. Karslake.

SIR WILFRID. Oh, well, I say; if he can come, I can!

JOHN KARSLAKE, *in evening dress, comes in quickly, carrying a large and very smart bride's bouquet, which he hands to* PHILIP, *who stands transfixed. Because it never occurs to him to refuse it or chuck it away,* PHILIP *accepts the bouquet gingerly, but frees himself of it at the first available moment.* JOHN *walks to the centre of the room. Deep down he is feeling wounded and unhappy. But, as he knows his coming to the ceremony on whatever pretext is a social outrage, he carries it off by assuming an air of its being the most natural thing in the world. He controls the expression of his deeper emotion, but the pressure of this keeps his face grave, and he speaks with effort.*

JOHN. My compliments to the bride, Judge.

PHILIP. [*Angry.*] And you, too, have the effrontery?

SIR WILFRID. There you are!

JOHN. [*Pretending ease.*] Oh, call it friendship—

[THOMAS *leaves.*

PHILIP. [*Puts bouquet on table. Ironically.*] I suppose Mrs. Karslake—

JOHN. She wagered me I wouldn't give her away, and of course—

Throughout his stay JOHN *hides the emotions he will not show behind a daring irony. Under its effects,* PHILIP, *on his right, walks about in a fury.* SIR WILFRID, *sitting down on the edge of the table, is gay and undisturbed.*

PHILIP. [*Taking a step toward* JOHN.] You will oblige me—both of you—by immediately leaving—

JOHN. [*Smiling and going to* PHILIP.] Oh, come, come, Judge—suppose I *am* here? Who has a better right to attend his wife's obsequies! Certainly, I come as a mourner—for *you!*

SIR WILFRID. I say, is it the custom?

JOHN. No, no—of course it's not the custom, no. But we'll make it the custom. After all,—what's a divorced wife among friends?

PHILIP. Sir, your humour is strained!

JOHN. Humour,—Judge?

PHILIP. It is, sir, and I'll not be bantered! Your both being here is—it is—gentlemen, there is a decorum which the stars in their courses do not violate.

JOHN. Now, Judge, never you mind what the stars do in their divorces! Get down to earth of the present day. Rufus Choate and Daniel Webster are dead. You must be modern. You must let peroration and poetry alone! Come along now. Why shouldn't I give the lady away?

SIR WILFRID. Hear! Hear! Oh, I beg your pardon!

JOHN. And why shouldn't we both be here? American marriage is a new thing. We've got to strike the pace, and the only trouble is, Judge, that the judiciary have so messed the thing up that a man can't be sure he *is* married until he's divorced. It's a sort of marry-go-round, to be sure! But let it go at that! Here we all are, and we're ready to marry my wife to you, and start her on her way to him!

PHILIP. [*Brought to a standstill.*] Good Lord! Sir, you cannot trifle with monogamy!

JOHN. Now, now, Judge, monogamy is just as extinct as knee-breeches. The new woman has a new idea, and the new idea is—well, it's just the opposite of the old Mormon one. Their idea is one man, ten wives and a hundred children. Our idea is one woman, a hundred husbands and one child.

PHILIP. Sir, this is polyandry.

JOHN. Polyandry? A hundred to one it's polyandry; and that's it, Judge! Uncle Sam has established consecutive polyandry,—but there's got to be an interval between husbands! The fact is, Judge, the modern American marriage is like a wire fence. The woman's the wire—the posts are the husbands. [*He indicates himself, and then* SIR WILFRID *and* PHILIP.] One—two—three! And if you cast your eye over the future you can count them, post after post, up hill, down dale, all the way to Dakota!

PHILIP. All very amusing, sir, but the fact remains—

JOHN. [*Going to* PHILIP *who at once moves away.*] Now, now, Judge, I like you. But you're asleep; you're living in the dark ages. You want to call up Central. "Hello, Central! Give me the present time, 1906, New York!"

SIR WILFRID. Of course you do, and—there you are!

PHILIP. [*Heavily.*] There I am not, sir! And—[*To* JOHN.] as for Mr. Karslake's ill-timed jocosity,—sir, in the future—

SIR WILFRID. Oh, hang the future!

PHILIP. I begin to hope, Sir Wilfrid, that in the future I shall have the pleasure of hanging you! [*To* JOHN.] And as to you, sir, your insensate idea of giving away your own—your former—

my—your—oh! Good Lord! This is a nightmare! [*He turns to go in despair.* MATTHEW, *coming in, meets him, and stops him at the door.*

MATTHEW. [*To* PHILIP.] My dear brother, Aunt Sarah Heneage refuses to give Mrs. Karslake away, unless you yourself,—eh—

PHILIP. [*As he goes out.*] No more! I'll attend to the matter! [*The* CHOIR BOYS *are heard practising in the next room.*

MATTHEW. [*Mopping his brow.*] How do you both do? My aunt has made me very warm. [*Ringing the bell.*] You hear our choir practising—sweet angel boys! H'm! H'm! Some of the family will not be present. I am very fond of you, Mr. Karslake, and I think it admirably Christian of you to have waived your—eh—your—eh—that is, now that I look at it more narrowly, let me say, that in the excitement of pleasurable anticipation, I forgot, Karslake, that your presence might occasion remark—[THOMAS *responds to his ring.*] Thomas! I left, in the hall, a small hand-bag or satchel containing my surplice.

THOMAS. Yes, sir. Ahem!

MATTHEW. You must really find the hand-bag at once.

[THOMAS *turns to go, when he stops startled.*

THOMAS. Yes, sir. [*Announcing in consternation.*] Mrs. Vida Phillimore. [VIDA PHILLIMORE, *in full evening dress, steps gently up to* MATTHEW.

MATTHEW. [*Always piously serene.*] Ah, my dear child! Now this is just as it should be! That is, eh— [*He walks to the centre of the room with her*, VIDA, *the while, pointedly disregarding* SIR WILFRID.] That is, when I come to think of it—your presence might be deemed inauspicious.

VIDA. But, my dear Matthew,—I had to come. [*Aside to him.*] I have a reason for being here.

[THOMAS, *who has left the room, again appears.*

MATTHEW. [*With a helpless gesture.*] But, my dear child—

THOMAS. [*With sympathetic intention.*] Sir, Mr. Phillimore wishes to have your assistance, sir—with Miss Heneage *immediately!*

MATTHEW. Ah! [*To* VIDA.] One moment! I'll return. [*To* THOMAS.] Have you found the bag with my surplice?

He goes out with THOMAS, *speaking.* SIR WILFRID *moves at once to* VIDA. JOHN, *moving to a better position, watches the door.*

SIR WILFRID. [*To* VIDA.] You're just the person I most want to see!

VIDA. [*With affected iciness.*] Oh, no, Sir Wilfrid, Cynthia isn't here yet! [*She moves to the table, and* JOHN, *his eyes on the door, coming toward her, she speaks to him with obvious sweetness.*] Jack, dear, I never was so ravished to see any one.

SIR WILFRID. [*Taken aback.*] By Jove!

VIDA. [*Very sweet.*] I knew I should find you here!

JOHN. [*Annoyed but civil.*] Now don't do that!

VIDA. [*Sweeter than ever.*] Jack! [*They sit down.*

JOHN. [*Civil but plain spoken.*] Don't do it!

VIDA. [*In a voice dripping with honey.*] Do what, Jack?

JOHN. Touch me with your voice! I have troubles enough of my own. [*He sits not far from her; the table between them.*

VIDA. And I know *who* your troubles are! Cynthia!

[*From this moment* VIDA *abandons* JOHN *as an object of the chase and works him into her other game.*

JOHN. I hate her. I don't know why I came.

VIDA. You came, dear, because you couldn't stay away—you're in love with her.

JOHN. All right, Vida, what I feel may be *love*—but all I can say is, if I could get even with Cynthia Karslake—

VIDA. You can, dear—it's as easy as powdering one's face; all you have to do is to be too nice to me!

JOHN. [*Looking at her inquiringly.*] Eh!

VIDA. Don't you realize she's jealous of you? Why did she come to my house this morning? She's jealous—and all you have to do—

JOHN. If I can make her wince, I'll make love to you till the Heavenly cows come home!

VIDA. Well, you see, my dear, if you make love to me it will [*Delicately indicating* SIR WILFRID.] cut both ways at once!

JOHN. Eh,—what! Not Cates-Darby? [*Starting.*] Is that Cynthia?

VIDA. Now don't get rattled and forget to make love to me.

JOHN. I've got the jumps. [*Trying to follow her instructions.*] Vida, I adore you.

VIDA. Oh, you must be more convincing; that won't do at all.

JOHN. [*Listening.*] Is that she now?

[MATTHEW *comes in and passes to the inner room.*

VIDA. It's Matthew. And, Jack, dear, you'd best get the hang of it before Cynthia comes. You might tell me all about your divorce. That's a sympathetic subject. Were you able to undermine it?

JOHN. No. I've got a wire from my lawyer this morning. The divorce holds. She's a free woman. She can marry whom she likes. [*The organ is heard, very softly played.*] Is that Cynthia? [*He rises quickly.*

VIDA. It's the organ!

JOHN. [*Overwhelmingly excited.*] By George! I should never have come! I think I'll go.

[*He makes a movement toward the door.*

VIDA. [*Rises and follows him remonstratingly.*] When I need you?

JOHN. I can't stand it.

VIDA. Oh, but, Jack—

JOHN. Good-night!

VIDA. I feel quite ill. [*Seeing that she must play her last card to keep him, pretends to faintness; sways and falls into his arms.*] Oh!

JOHN. [*In a rage, but beaten.*] I believe you're putting up a fake.

The organ swells as CYNTHIA *enters sweepingly, dressed in full evening dress for the wedding ceremony.* JOHN, *not knowing what to do, keeps his arms about* VIDA *as a horrid necessity.*

CYNTHIA. [*Speaking as she comes in, to* MATTHEW.] Here I am. Ridiculous to make it a conventional thing, you know. Come in on the swell of the music, and all that, just as if I'd never been married before. Where's Philip? [*She looks for* PHILIP *and sees* JOHN *with* VIDA *in his arms. She stops short.*

JOHN. [*Uneasy and embarrassed.*] A glass of water! I beg your pardon, Mrs. Karslake— [*The organ plays on.*

CYNTHIA. [*Ironical and calm.*] Vida!

JOHN. She has fainted.

CYNTHIA. [*Cynically.*] Fainted? [*Without pausing.*] Dear, dear, dear, terrible! So she has. [SIR WILFRID *takes the flowers from a vase and prepares to sprinkle* VIDA'S *forehead with the water it contains.*] No, no, not her forehead, Sir Wilfrid, her frock! Sprinkle her best Paquin! If it's a real faint, she will not come to!

VIDA. [*Coming quickly to her senses as her Paris importation is about to suffer.*] I almost fainted.

CYNTHIA. Almost!

VIDA. [*Using the stock phrase as a matter of course, and reviving rapidly.*] Where am I? [JOHN *glances at* CYNTHIA *sharply.*] Oh, the bride! I beg every one's pardon. Cynthia, at a crisis like this, I simply couldn't stay away from Philip!

CYNTHIA. Stay away from Philip?

[JOHN *and* CYNTHIA *exchange glances.*

VIDA. Your arm, Jack; and lead me where there is air.

JOHN *and* VIDA *go into the further room. The organ stops.* SIR WILFRID *nad* CYNTHIA *are practically alone in the room.* JOHN *and* VIDA *are barely within sight. He is first seen to take her fan and give her air; then to pick up a book and read to her.*

SIR WILFRID. I've come back.

CYNTHIA. [*To* SIR WILFRID.] Asks for air and goes to the greenhouse. [CYNTHIA *crosses the room and* SIR WILFRID *offers her a seat.*] I know why you are here. It's that intoxicating little whim you suppose me to have for you. My regrets! But the whim's gone flat! Yes, yes, my gasoline days are over. I'm going to be garaged for good. However, I'm glad you're here; you take the edge off—

SIR WILFRID. Mr. Phillimore?

CYNTHIA. [*Sharply.*] No, Karslake. I'm just waiting to say the words [THOMAS *comes in unnoticed.*] "love, honour and obey" to Phillimore—[*Looking back.*] and *at* Karslake! [*Seeing* THOMAS.] What is it? Mr. Phillimore?

THOMAS. Mr. Phillimore will be down in a few minutes, ma'am. He's very sorry, ma'am [*Lowering his voice and coming nearer to* CYNTHIA, *mindful of the respectabilities*], but there's a button off his waistcoat.

CYNTHIA. [*Rising. With irony.*] Button off his waistcoat!

[THOMAS *goes out.*

SIR WILFRID. [*Delightedly.*] Ah! So much the better for me. [CYNTHIA *looks into the other room.*] Now, then, never mind those two! [CYNTHIA *moves restlessly.*] Sit down.

CYNTHIA. I can't.

SIR WILFRID. You're as nervous as—

CYNTHIA. Nervous! Of course I'm nervous! So would you be nervous if you'd had a runaway and smash up, and you were going to try it again. [*She is unable to take her eyes from* VIDA *and* JOHN, *and* SIR WILFRID, *noting this, grows uneasy.*] And if some one doesn't do away with those calla lilies—the odor makes me faint! [SIR WILFRID *moves.*] No, it's not the lilies! It's the orange blossoms!

SIR WILFRID. Orange blossoms.

CYNTHIA. The flowers that grow on the tree that hangs over the abyss! [SIR WILFRID *promptly confiscates the vase of orange blossoms.*] They smell of six o'clock in the evening. When Philip's fallen asleep, and little boys are crying the winners outside, and I'm crying inside, and dying inside and outside and everywhere.

SIR WILFRID. [*Returning to her side.*] Sorry to disappoint you. They're artificial. [CYNTHIA *shrugs her shoulders.*] That's it! They're emblematic of artificial domesticity! And I'm here to help you balk it. [*He sits down and* CYNTHIA *half rises and looks toward* JOHN *and* VIDA.] Keep still now, I've a lot to say to you. Stop looking—

CYNTHIA. Do you think I can listen to you make love to me when the man who—who—whom I most despise in all the world, is reading poetry to the woman who—who got me into the fix I'm in!

SIR WILFRID. [*Leaning over her chair.*] What do you want to look at 'em for? [CYNTHIA *moves.*] Let 'em be and listen to me! Sit down; for damme, I'm determined.

CYNTHIA. [*Now at the table and half to herself.*] I won't look at them! I won't think of them. Beasts! [SIR WILFRID *interposes between her and her view of* JOHN. THOMAS *opens the door and walks in.*

SIR WILFRID. Now, then— [*He sits down.*

CYNTHIA. Those two *here!* It's just as if Adam and Eve should invite the snake to their golden wedding. [*Seeing* THOMAS.] What is it, what's the matter?

THOMAS. Mr. Phillimore's excuses, ma'am. In a very short time— [THOMAS *goes out.*

SIR WILFRID. I'm on to you! You hoped for more buttons!

CYNTHIA. I'm dying of the heat; fan me.

[SIR WILFRID *fans* CYNTHIA.

SIR WILFRID. Heat! No! You're dying because you're ignorin' nature. Certainly you are! You're marryin' Phillimore! [CYNTHIA *appears faint.*] Can't ignore nature, Mrs. Karslake.

Yes, you are; you're forcin' your feelin's. [CYNTHIA *glances at him.*] And what you want to do is to let yourself go a bit—up anchor and sit tight! I'm no seaman, but that's the idea! [CYNTHIA *moves and shakes her head.*] So just throw the reins on nature's neck, jump this fellow Phillimore and marry me!

[*He leans toward* CYNTHIA.

CYNTHIA. [*Naturally, but with irritation.*] You propose to me here, at a moment like this? When I'm on the last lap—just in sight of the goal—the gallows—the halter—the altar, I don't know what its name is! No, I won't have you! [*Looking toward* KARSLAKE *and* VIDA.] And I won't have you stand near me! I won't have you talking to me in a low tone! [*Her eyes glued on* JOHN *and* VIDA.] Stand over there—stand where you are.

SIR WILFRID. I say—

CYNTHIA. I can hear you—I'm listening!

SIR WILFRID. Well, don't look so hurried and worried. You've got buttons and buttons of time. And now my offer. You haven't yet said you would—

CYNTHIA. Marry you? I don't even know you!

SIR WILFRID. [*Feeling sure of being accepted.*] Oh,—tell you all about myself. I'm no duke in a pickle o' debts, d'ye see? I can marry where I like. Some o' my countrymen are rotters, ye know. They'd marry a monkey, if poppa-up-the-tree had a corner in cocoanuts! And they do marry some queer ones, y' know. [CYNTHIA *looks beyond him, exclaims and turns.* SIR WILFRID *turns.*

CYNTHIA. Do they?

SIR WILFRID. Oh, rather. That's what's giving your heiresses such a bad name lately. If a fellah's in debt he can't pick and choose, and then he swears that American gals are awfully fine lookers, but they're no good when it comes to continuin' the race! Fair dolls in the drawin'-room, but no good in the nursery.

CYNTHIA. [*Thinking of* JOHN *and* VIDA *and nothing else.*] I can see Vida in the nursery.

SIR WILFRID. You understand when you want a brood mare, you don't choose a Kentucky mule.

CYNTHIA. I think I see one.

SIR WILFRID. Well, that's what they're saying over there. They say your gals run to talk [*He plainly remembers* VIDA'S *volubility.*] and I have seen gals here that would chat life into a wooden Indian! That's what you Americans call being clever.—All brains and no stuffin'! In fact, some of your American gals are the nicest boys I ever met.

CYNTHIA. So that's what you think?

SIR WILFRID. Not a bit what *I* think—what my countrymen think!

CYNTHIA. Why are you telling me?

SIR WILFRID. Oh, just explaining my character. I'm the sort that can pick and choose—and what I want is heart.

CYNTHIA. [VIDA *and* JOHN *ever in mind.*] No more heart than a dragon-fly! [*The organ begins to play softly.*

SIR WILFRID. That's it, dragon-fly. Cold as stone and never stops buzzing about and showin' off her colours. It's that American dragon-fly girl that I'm afraid of, because, d'ye see, I don't know what an American expects when he marries; yes, but you're not listening!

CYNTHIA. I am listening. I am!

SIR WILFRID. [*Speaking directly to her.*] An Englishman, ye see, when he marries expects three things: love, obedience, and five children.

CYNTHIA. Three things! I make it seven!

SIR WILFRID. Yes, my dear, but the point is, will you be mistress of Traynham?

CYNTHIA. [*Who has only half listened to him.*] No, Sir Wilfrid, thank you, I won't. [*She turns to see* JOHN *walk across the drawing-room with* VIDA, *and apparently absorbed in what she is saying.*] It's outrageous!

SIR WILFRID. Eh? Why you're cryin'?

CYNTHIA. [*Almost sobbing.*] I am not.

SIR WILFRID. You're not crying because you're in love with me?

CYNTHIA. I'm not crying—or if I am, I'm crying because I love my country. It's a disgrace to America—cast-off husbands and wives getting together in a parlour and playing tag under a palm-tree. [JOHN, *with intention and determined to stab* CYNTHIA, *kisses* VIDA'S *hand.*

SIR WILFRID. Eh! Oh! I'm damned! [*To* CYNTHIA.] What do you think that means?

CYNTHIA. I don't doubt it means a wedding here, at once—after mine! [VIDA *and* JOHN *leave the drawing-room and walk slowly toward them.*

VIDA. [*Affecting an impossible intimacy to wound* CYNTHIA *and tantalize* SIR WILFRID.] Hush, Jack—I'd much rather no one should know anything about it until it's all over!

CYNTHIA. [*Starting and looking at* SIR WILFRID.] What did I tell you?

VIDA. [*To* CYNTHIA.] Oh, my dear, he's asked me to champagne and lobster at *your* house—his house! Matthew is coming! [CYNTHIA *starts, but controls herself.*] And you're to come, Sir Wilfrid. [*Intending to convey the idea of a sudden marriage ceremony.*] Of course, my dear, I would like to wait for your wedding, but something rather—rather important to me is to take place, and I know you'll excuse me. [*The organ stops.*

SIR WILFRID. [*Piqued at being forgotten.*] All very neat, but you haven't given me a chance, even.

VIDA. Chance? You're not serious?

SIR WILFRID. I am!

VIDA. [*Striking while the iron is hot.*] I'll give you a minute to offer yourself.

SIR WILFRID. Eh?

VIDA. Sixty seconds from now.

SIR WILFRID. [*Uncertain.*] There's such a thing as bein' silly.

VIDA. [*Calm and determined.*] Fifty seconds left.

SIR WILFRID. I take you—count fair. [*He hands her his watch and goes to where* CYNTHIA *stands.*] I say, Mrs. Karslake—

CYNTHIA. [*Overwhelmed with grief and emotion.*] They're engaged; they're going to be married to-night, over champagne and lobster at my house!

SIR WILFRID. Will you consider your—

CYNTHIA. [*Hastily, to get rid of him.*] No, no, no, no! Thank you, Sir Wilfrid, I will not.

SIR WILFRID. [*Calm, and not to be laid low.*] Thanks awfully. [CYNTHIA *walks away. Returning to* VIDA.] Mrs. Phillimore—

VIDA. [*Returning his watch.*] Too late! [*To* KARSLAKE.] Jack, dear, we must be off.

SIR WILFRID. [*Standing and making a general appeal for information.*] I say, is it the custom for American girls—that sixty seconds or too late? Look here! Not a bit too late. I'll take you around to Jack Karslake's, and I'm going to ask you the same old question again, you know. [*To* VIDA.] By Jove, you know in your country it's the pace that kills.

[SIR WILFRID *follows* VIDA *out the door.*

JOHN. [*Gravely to* CYNTHIA, *who has walked away.*] Good-night, Mrs. Karslake, I'm going; I'm sorry I came.

CYNTHIA. Sorry? Why are you sorry? [JOHN *looks at her; she winces a little.*] You've got what you wanted. [*After a pause.*] I wouldn't mind your marrying Vida—

JOHN. [*Gravely.*] Oh, wouldn't you?

CYNTHIA. But I don't think you showed good taste in engaging yourselves *here.*

JOHN. Of course, I should have preferred a garden of roses and plenty of twilight.

CYNTHIA. [*Rushing into speech.*] I'll tell you what you *have* done—you've thrown yourself away! A woman like that! No head, no heart! All languor and loose—loose frocks—she's the typical, worst thing America can do! She's the regular American marriage worm!

JOHN. I have known others—

CYNTHIA. [*Quickly.*] Not me. I'm not a patch on that woman. Do you know anything about her life? Do you know the things she did to Philip? Kept him up every night of his life—forty days out of every thirty—and then, without his knowing it, put brandy in his coffee to make him lively at breakfast.

JOHN. [*Banteringly.*] I begin to think she is just the woman—

CYNTHIA. [*Unable to quiet her jealousy.*] She is *not* the woman for *you!* A man with your bad temper—your airs of authority—your assumption of—of—everything. What you need is a good, old-fashioned, bread-poultice woman!

[CYNTHIA *comes to a full stop and faces him.*

JOHN. [*Sharply.*] Can't say I've had any experience of the good old-fashioned bread-poultice.

CYNTHIA. I don't care what you say! If you marry Vida Phillimore—you sha'n't do it. [*Tears of rage choking her.*] No, I liked your father and, for *his* sake, I'll see that his son doesn't make a donkey of himself a second time.

JOHN. [*Too angry to be amused.*] Oh, I thought I was divorced. I begin to feel as if I had you on my hands still.

CYNTHIA. You have! You shall have! If you attempt to marry her, I'll follow you—and I'll find her—I'll tell Vida—[*He turns to her.*] I will. I'll tell Vida just what sort of a dance you led me.

JOHN. [*Quickly on her last word but speaking gravely.*] Indeed! Will you? And *why* do you care what happens to me?

CYNTHIA. [*Startled by his tone.*] I—I—ah—

JOHN. [*Insistently and with a faint hope.*] *Why* do you *care?*

CYNTHIA. I don't. Not in your sense—

JOHN. How dare you then pretend—

CYNTHIA. I don't pretend.

JOHN. [*Interrupting her; proud, serious and strong.*] How dare you look me in the face with the eyes that I once kissed, and pretend the least regard for me? [CYNTHIA *recoils and looks away. Her own feelings are revealed to her clearly for the first time.*] I begin to understand our American women now. Fire-flies—and the fire they gleam with is so cold that a midge couldn't warm his heart at it, let alone a man. You're not of the same race as a man! You married me for nothing, divorced me for nothing, because you *are* nothing!

CYNTHIA. [*Wounded to the heart.*] Jack! What are you saying?

JOHN. [*With unrestrained emotion.*] What,—you feigning an interest in me, feigning a lie—and in five minutes—[*With a gesture, indicating the altar.*] Oh, you've taught me the trick of your sex—you're the woman who's not a woman!

CYNTHIA. [*Weakly.*] You're saying terrible things to me.

JOHN. [*Low and with intensity.*] You haven't been divorced from me long enough to forget—what you should be ashamed to remember.

CYNTHIA. [*Unable to face him and pretending not to understand him.*] I don't know what you mean?

JOHN. [*More forcibly and with manly emotion.*] You're not able to forget me! You know you're not able to forget me; ask yourself if you are able to forget me, and when your heart, such as it is, answers "no," then— [*The organ is plainly heard.*] Well, then, prance gaily up to the altar and marry that, if you can!

He abruptly quits the room and CYNTHIA, *moving to an armchair, sinks into it, trembling.* MATTHEW *comes in and is joined by* MISS HENEAGE *and* PHILIP. *They do not see* CYNTHIA *buried deeply in her chair. Accordingly,* MISS HENEAGE *moves over to the sofa and waits. They are all dressed for an evening reception and* PHILIP *is in the tradional bridegroom's rig.*

MATTHEW. [*As he enters.*] I am sure you will do your part, Sarah—in a spirit of Christian decorum. [*To* PHILIP.] It was impossible to find my surplice, Philip, but the more informal the better.

PHILIP. [*With pompous responsibility.*] Where's Cynthia?

[MATTHEW *gives a glance around the room.*

MATTHEW. Ah, here's the choir! [*He moves forward to meet it.* CHOIR BOYS *come in very orderly; divide and take their places, an even number on each side of the altar of flowers.* MATTHEW *vaguely superintends.* PHILIP *gets in the way of the bell and moves out of the way.* THOMAS *comes in.*] Thomas, I directed you— One moment, if you please. [*He indicates the tables and chairs which* THOMAS *hastens to push against the wall.*

PHILIP. [*Walking forward and looking around him.*] Where's Cynthia? [CYNTHIA *rises, and, at the movement,* PHILIP *sees her and moves toward her. The organ grows suddenly silent.*

CYNTHIA. [*Faintly.*] Here I am.

[MATTHEW *comes down. Organ plays softly.*

MATTHEW. [*To* CYNTHIA.] Ah, my very dear Cynthia, I knew there was something. Let me tell you the words of the hymn I have chosen:

"Enduring love; sweet end of strife!
Oh, bless this happy man and wife!"

I'm afraid you feel—eh—eh!

CYNTHIA. [*Desperately calm.*] I feel awfully queer—I think I need a scotch.

Organ stops. PHILIP *remains uneasily at a little distance.* MRS. PHILLIMORE *and* GRACE *enter back slowly, as cheerfully as if they were going to hear the funeral service read. They remain near the doorway.*

MATTHEW. Really, my dear, in the pomp and vanity—I mean—ceremony of this—this unique occasion, there should be sufficient exhilaration.

CYNTHIA. [*With extraordinary control.*] But there isn't!

[*Feeling weak, she sits down.*

MATTHEW. I don't think my Bishop would approve of—eh—anything *before!*

CYNTHIA. [*Too agitated to know how much she is moved.*] I feel very queer.

MATTHEW. [*Piously sure that everything is for the best.*] My dear child—

CYNTHIA. However, I suppose there's nothing for it—now—but—to—to—

MATTHEW. Courage!

CYNTHIA. [*Desperate and with a sudden explosion.*] Oh, don't speak to me. I feel as if I'd been eating gunpowder, and the very first word of the wedding service would set it off!

MATTHEW. My dear, your indisposition is the voice of nature. [CYNTHIA *speaks more rapidly and with growing excitement.* MATTHEW *makes a movement toward the* CHOIR BOYS.

CYNTHIA. Ah,—that's it—nature! [MATTHEW *shakes his head.*] I've a great mind to throw the reins on nature's neck.

PHILIP. Matthew! [*He moves to take his stand for the ceremony.*

MATTHEW. [*Looks at* PHILIP. *To* CYNTHIA.] Philip is ready. [PHILIP *comes forward and the organ plays the wedding march.*

CYNTHIA. [*To herself, as if at bay.*] Ready? Ready? Ready?

MATTHEW. Cynthia, you will take Miss Heneage's arm. [MISS HENEAGE *moves stiffly nearer to the table.*] Sarah! [*He waves* MISS HENEAGE *in the direction of* CYNTHIA, *at which she advances a joyless step or two.* MATTHEW *goes over to give the choir a low direction.*] Now please don't forget, my boys. When I raise my hands so, you begin, "Enduring love, sweet end of strife," etc. [CYNTHIA *has risen. On the table by which she stands is her long lace cloak.* MATTHEW *assumes sacerdotal importance and takes his position inside the altar of flowers.*] Ahem! Philip! [*He signs to* PHILIP *to take his position.*] Sarah! [CYNTHIA *breathes fast, and supports herself against the table.* MISS HENEAGE, *with the silent air of a martyr, goes toward her and stands for a moment looking at her.*] The ceremony will now begin.

The organ plays Mendelssohn's wedding march. CYNTHIA *turns and faces* MISS HENEAGE. MISS HENEAGE *slowly reaches* CYNTHIA *and extends her hand in her readiness to lead the bride to the altar.*

MISS HENEAGE. Mrs. Karslake!

PHILIP. Ahem! [MATTHEW *walks forward two or three steps.* CYNTHIA *stands as if turned to stone.*

MATTHEW. My dear Cynthia. I request you—to take your place. [CYNTHIA *moves one or two steps as if to go up to the altar. She takes* MISS HENEAGE'S *hand and slowly they walk toward* MATTHEW.] Your husband to be—is ready, the ring is in my pocket. I have only to ask you the—eh—necessary questions,—and—eh—all will be blissfully over in a moment.

[*The organ grows louder.*

CYNTHIA. [*At this moment, just as she reaches* PHILIP, *stops, faces round, looks him,* MATTHEW, *and the rest in the face, and cries out in despair.*] Thomas! Call a hansom! [THOMAS *goes out, leaving the door open.* MISS HENEAGE *crosses the room quickly;* MRS. PHILLIMORE, *shocked into action, rises.* CYNTHIA *catches up her cloak from the table.* PHILIP *turns and* CYNTHIA *comes forward and stops.*] I can't, Philip—I can't. [*Whistle of hansom is heard off; the organ stops.*] It is simply a case of throwing the reins on nature's neck—up anchor—and sit tight! [MATTHEW *moves to* CYNTHIA.] Matthew, don't come near me! Yes, yes, I distrust you. It's your business, and you'd marry me if you could.

PHILIP. [*Watching her in dismay as she throws on her cloak.*] Where are you going?

CYNTHIA. I'm going to Jack.

PHILIP. What for?

CYNTHIA. To stop his marrying Vida. I'm blowing a hurricane inside, a horrible, happy hurricane! I know myself—I know what's the matter with me. If I married you and Miss Heneage—what's the use of talking about it—he mustn't marry that woman. He sha'n't. [CYNTHIA *has now all her wraps on and walks toward the door rapidly. To* PHILIP.] Sorry! So long! Good-night and see you later.

Reaching the door, she goes out in blind haste and without further ceremony. MATTHEW, *in absolute amazement, throws up his arms.* PHILIP *is rigid.* MRS. PHILLIMORE *sinks into a chair.* MISS HENEAGE *stands supercilious and unmoved.* GRACE, *the same. The choir, at* MATTHEW'S *gesture, mistakes it for the concerted signal, and bursts lustily into the Epithalamis:*

"Enduring love—sweet end of strife!
Oh, bless this happy man and wife!"

CURTAIN.

ACT IV.

SCENE. *The scene is laid in* JOHN KARSLAKE'S *study and smoking-room. There is a bay window on the left. A door on the left leads to stairs and the front of the house, while a door at the back leads to the dining-room. A fireplace and a mantel are on the right. A bookcase contains law and sporting books. On the wall is a full-length portrait of* CYNTHIA. *Nothing of this portrait is seen by audience except the gilt frame and a space of canvas. A large table with writing materials is littered over with law books, sporting books, papers, pipes, crops, a pair of spurs, &c. A wedding ring lies on it. There are three very low easy-chairs. The general appearance of the room is extremely gay and garish in colour. It has the easy confusion of a man's room. There is a small table on which, lying open, is a woman's sewing-basket, and, beside it, a piece of rich fancy work, as if a lady had just risen from sewing. Laid on the further end of it are a lady's gloves. On a chair-back is a lady's hat. It is a half hour later than the close of Act III. Curtains are drawn over the window. A lamp on the table is lighted, as are, too, the various electric lights. One chair is conspicuously standing on its head.*

NOGAM *is busy at the larger table. The door into the dining-room is half open.*

SIR WILFRID. [*Coming in from the dining-room.*] Eh—what did you say your name was?

NOGAM. Nogam, sir.

SIR WILFRID. Nogam? I've been here thirty minutes. Where are the cigars? [NOGAM *motions to a small table near the entrance door.*] Thank you. Nogam, Mr. Karslake was to have followed us here, immediately. [*He lights a cigar.*

NOGAM. Mr. Karslake just now 'phoned from his club [SIR WILFRID *walks toward the front of the room.*], and he's on his way home, sir.

SIR WILFRID. Nogam, why is that chair upside down?

NOGAM. Our orders, sir.

VIDA. [*Speaking as she comes in.*] Oh, Wilfrid! [SIR WILFRID *turns.* VIDA *coming slowly toward him.*] I can't be left longer alone with the lcbster! He reminds me too much of Phillimore!

SIR WILFRID. Karslake's coming; stopped at his club on the way! [*To* NOGAM.] You haven't heard anything of Mrs. Karslake—?

NOGAM. [*Surprised.*] No, sir!

SIR WILFRID. [*In an aside to* VIDA, *as they move right to appear to be out of* NOGAM'S *hearing.*] Deucedly odd, ye know—for the Reverend Matthew declared she left Phillimore's house before *he* did,—and she told them she was coming here!

[NOGAM *evidently takes this in.*

VIDA. Oh, she'll turn up.

SIR WILFRID. Yes, but I don't see how the Reverend Phillimore had the time to get here and make us man and wife, don't y' know—

VIDA. Oh, Matthew had a fast horse and Cynthia a slow one—or she's a woman and changed her mind! Perhaps she's gone back and married Phillimore. And besides, dear, Matthew wasn't in the house four minutes and a half; only just long enough to hoop the hoop. [*She twirls her new wedding ring gently about her finger.*] Wasn't it lucky he had a ring in his pocket?

SIR WILFRID. Rather.

VIDA. And are you aware, dear, that Phillimore bought and intended it for Cynthia? Do come [*Going toward the door through which she has just entered.*], I'm desperately hungry! Whenever I'm married that's the effect it has! [VIDA *goes out and* SIR WILFRID, *following, stops to talk to* NOGAM.

SIR WILFRID. We'll give Mr. Karslake ten minutes, Nogam. If he does not come then, you might serve supper.

[*He joins* VIDA.

NOGAM. [*To* SIR WILFRID.] Yes, sir. [*The outside door opens and* FIDDLER *walks in.*

FIDDLER. [*Easy and business-like.*] Hello, Nogam, where's the guv'nor? That mare's off her oats, and I've got to see him.

NOGAM. He'll soon be here.

FIDDLER. Who was the parson I met leaving the house?

NOGAM. [*Whispering.*] Sir Wilfrid and Mrs. Phillimore have a date with the guv'nor in the dining-room, and the reverend gentleman—[*He makes a gesture as of giving an ecclesiastical blessing.*

FIDDLER. [*Amazed.*] He hasn't spliced them? [NOGAM *assents.*] He has? They're married? Never saw a parson could resist it!

NOGAM. Yes, but I've got another piece of news for you. Who do you think the Rev. Phillimore expected to find *here?*

FIDDLER. [*Proud of having the knowledge.*] Mrs. Karslake? I saw her headed this way in a hansom with a balky horse only a minute ago. If she hoped to be in at the finish—

[FIDDLER *is about to set the chair on its legs.*

NOGAM. [*Quickly.*] Mr. Fiddler, sir, please to let it alone.

FIDDLER. [*Putting the chair down in surprise.*] Does it live on its blooming head?

NOGAM. Don't you remember? *She* threw it on its head when she left here, and he won't have it up. Ah, that's it—hat, sewing-basket and all,—the whole rig is to remain as it was when she handed him his knock-out. [*A bell rings ouside.*

FIDDLER. There's the guv'nor—I hear him!

NOGAM. I'll serve the supper. [*Taking a letter from his pocket and putting it on the mantel.*] Mr. Fiddler, would you mind giving this to the guv'nor? It's from his lawyer—his lawyer couldn'. find him and left it with me. He said it was very importantt [*The bell rings again. Speaking from the door to* SIR WILFRID.] I'm coming, sir!

NOGAM *goes out, shutting the door.* JOHN KARSLAKE *comes in. His hat is pushed over his eyes; his hands are buried in his pockets, and his appearance generally is one of weariness and utter discouragement. He walks into the room slowly and heavily. He sees* FIDDLER, *who salutes, forgetting the letter.* JOHN *slowly sinks into the arm-chair near his study table.*

JOHN. [*As he walks to his chair.*] Hello, Fiddler! [*After a pause,* JOHN *throws himself into a chair, keeping his hat on. He throws down his gloves, sighing.*

FIDDLER. Came in to see you, sir, about Cynthia K.

JOHN. [*Drearily.*] Damn Cynthia K!—

FIDDLER. Couldn't have a word with you?

JOHN. [*Grumpy.*] No!

FIDDLER. Yes, sir.

JOHN. Fiddler.

FIDDLER. Yes, sir.

JOHN. Mrs. Karslake— [FIDDLER *nods.*] You used to say she was our mascot?

FIDDLER. Yes, sir.

JOHN. Well, she's just married herself to a—a sort of a man—

FIDDLER. Sorry to hear it, sir.

JOHN. Well, Fiddler, between you and me, we're a pair of idiots.

FIDDLER. Yes, sir!

JOHN. And now it's too late!

FIDDLER. Yes, sir—oh, beg your pardon, sir—your lawyer left a letter. [JOHN *takes letter; opens it and reads it, indifferently at first.*

JOHN. [*As he opens the letter.*] What's he got to say, more than what his wire said?—Eh—[*Dumbfounded as he reads.*] what?—Will explain.—Error in wording of telegram.—Call me up.—[*Turning quickly to the telephone.*] The man can't mean that she's still— Hello! Hello! [JOHN *listens.*

FIDDLER. Would like to have a word with you, sir—

JOHN. Hello, Central!

FIDDLER. That mare—

JOHN. [*Consulting the letter, and speaking into the 'phone.*] 33246a 38! Did you get it?

FIDDLER. That mare, sir, she's got a touch of malaria—

JOHN. [*At the 'phone.*] Hello, Central—33246a—38!—Clayton Osgood—yes, yes, and say, Central—get a move on you!

FIDDLER. If you think well of it, sir, I'll give her a tonic—

JOHN. [*Still at the 'phone.*] Hello! Yes—yes—Jack Karslake. Is that you, Clayton? Yes—yes—well—

FIDDLER. Or if you like, sir, I'll give her—

JOHN. [*Turning on* FIDDLER.] Shut up! [*To 'phone.*] What was that? Not you—not you—a technical error? You mean to say that Mrs. Karslake is still—my— Hold the wire, Central—get off the wire! Get off the wire! Is that you, Clayton? Yes, yes—she and I are still— I got it! Good-bye! [*He hangs up the receiver; falls back into a chair. For a moment he is overcome. He takes up telephone book.*

FIDDLER. All very well, Mr. Karslake, but I must know if I'm to give her—

JOHN. [*Turning over the leaves of the telephone book in hot haste.*] What's Phillimore's number?

FIDDLER. If you've no objections, I think I'll give her a—

JOHN. L—M—N—O—P— It's too late! She's married by this! Married!—and—my God—I—I am the cause. Phillimore—

FIDDLER. I'll give her—

JOHN. Give her wheatina!—give her grape-nuts—give her away! [FIDDLER, *biding his time, walks toward the window.*] Only be quiet! Phillimore!

[SIR WILFRID *comes in.*

SIR WILFRID. Hello! We'd almost given you up!

JOHN. [*In his agitation unable to find* PHILLIMORE'S *number.*] Just a moment! I'm trying to get Phillimore on the 'phone to—to tell Mrs. Karslake—

SIR WILFRID. No good, my boy—she's on her way here! [JOHN *drops the book and looks up dumbfounded.*] The Reverend Matthew was here, y' see—and he said—

JOHN. [*Rising, turns.*] Mrs. Karslake is coming here? [SIR WILFRID *nods.*] To this house? Here?

SIR WILFRID. That's right.

JOHN. Coming here? You're sure? [SIR WILFRID *nods assent.*] Fiddler, I want you to stay here, and if Mrs. Karslake comes, don't fail to let me know! Now then, for heaven's sake, what did Matthew say to you?

SIR WILFRID. Come along in and I'll tell you.

JOHN. On your life now, Fiddler, don't fail to let me—

[SIR WILFRID *carries* JOHN *off with him.*

VIDA. [*From the dining-room.*] Ah, here you are!

FIDDLER. Phew!

A moment's pause, and CYNTHIA *opens the front door, and comes in very quietly, almost shyly, as if she were uncertain of her welcome.*

CYNTHIA. Fiddler! Where is he? Has he come? Is he here? Has he gone?

FIDDLER. [*Rattled.*] Nobody's gone, ma'am, except the Reverend Matthew Phillimore.

CYNTHIA. Matthew? He's been here and gone? [FIDDLER *nods assent.*] You don't mean I'm too late? He's married them already?

FIDDLER. Nogam says he married them!

CYNTHIA. He's married them! Married! Married before I could get here! [*Sinking into an armchair.*] Married in less time than it takes to pray for rain! Oh, well, the church—the church is a regular quick marriage counter. [VIDA *and* JOHN *are heard in light-hearted laughter.*] Oh!

FIDDLER. I'll tell Mr. Karslake—

CYNTHIA. [*Rising and going to the dining-room door, turns the key in the lock and takes it out.*] No—I wouldn't see him for the world! [*Moving to the work-table with the key.*] If I'm too late, I'm too late! and that's the end of it! [*Laying the key on the table, she remains standing near it.*] I've come, and now I'll go! [*There is a long pause during which* CYNTHIA *looks slowly about the room, then sighs and changes her tone.*] Well, Fiddler, it's all a good deal as it used to be in my day.

FIDDLER. No, ma'am—everything changed, even the horses.

CYNTHIA. [*Absent-mindedly.*] Horses—how are the horses?

[*Throughout her talk with* FIDDLER *she gives the idea that she is saying good-bye to her life with* JOHN.

FIDDLER. Ah, when husband and wife splits, ma'am, it's the horses that suffer. Oh, yes, ma'am, we're all changed since you give us the go-by,—even the guv'nor.

CYNTHIA. How's he changed?

FIDDLER. Lost his sharp for horses, and ladies, ma'am —gives 'em both the boiled eye.

CYNTHIA. I can't say I see any change; there's my portrait—I suppose he sits and pulls faces at me.

FIDDLER. Yes, ma'am, I think I'd better tell him of your bein' here.

CYNTHIA. [*Gently but decidedly.*] No, Fiddler, no! [*Again looking about her.*] The room's in a terrible state of disorder. However, your new mistress will attend to that. [*Pause.*] Why, that's not her hat!

FIDDLER. Yours, ma'am.

CYNTHIA. Mine? [*Walking to the table to look at it.*] Is that my work-basket? [*After a pause.*] My gloves? [FIDDLER *assents.*] And I suppose—[*Hurriedly going to the writing-table.*] My—yes, there it is: my wedding ring!—just where I dropped it! Oh, oh, oh, he keeps it like this—hat, gloves, basket and ring, everything just as it was that crazy, mad day when I— [*She glances at* FIDDLER *and breaks off.*] But for heaven's sake, Fiddler, set that chair on its feet!

FIDDLER. Against orders, ma'am.

CYNTHIA. Against orders?

FIDDLER. You kicked it over, ma'am, the day you left us.

CYNTHIA. No wonder he hates me with the chair in that state! He nurses his wrath to keep it warm. So, after all, Fiddler, everything *is* changed. and that chair is the proof of it. I suppose Cynthia K is the only thing in the world that cares a whinney whether I'm alive or dead. [*She breaks down and sobs.*] How is she, Fiddler?

FIDDLER. Off her oats, ma'am, this evening.

CYNTHIA. Off her oats! Well, she loves me, so I suppose she will die, or change, or—or something. Oh, she'll die, there's no doubt about that—she'll die. [FIDDLER, *who has been watching his chance, takes the key off the table while she is sobbing, tiptoes up stage, unlocks the door and goes out. After he has done so,* CYNTHIA *rises and dries her eyes.*] There—I'm a fool—I must go—before—before—he—

[*As she speaks her last word.* JOHN *comes in swiftly.*

JOHN. Mrs. Karslake!

CYNTHIA. [*Confused.*] I—I—I just heard Cynthia K was ill—[JOHN *assents.* CYNTHIA *tries to put on a cheerful and indifferent manner.*] I—I ran round—I—and—and— [*Pausing, she turns and takes a few steps.*] Well, I understand it's all over.

JOHN. [*Cheerfully.*] Yes, it's all over.

CYNTHIA. How is the bride?

JOHN. Oh, she's a wonder.

CYNTHIA. Indeed! Did she paw the ground like the war-horse in the Bible? I'm sure when Vida sees a wedding ring she smells the battle afar off. As for you, my dear Karslake, I should have thought once bitten, twice shy! But, you know best.

VIDA, *unable to keep her finger long out of a pie, saunters in.*

VIDA. Oh, Cynthia, I've just been through it again, and I feel as if I were eighteen. There's no use talking about it, my dear, with a woman it's never the second time! And how nice you were, Jack,—he never even laughed at us! [SIR WILFRID *follows her with hat and cane.* VIDA *kisses* JOHN.] That's the wages of virtue!

SIR WILFRID. [*In time to see her kiss* JOHN.] I say, is it the custom? Every time she does that, my boy, you owe me a thousand pounds. [*Seeing* CYNTHIA, *who approaches them, he looks at her and* JOHN *in turn.*] Mrs. Karslake. [*To* JOHN.] And then you say it's not an extraordinary country!

[CYNTHIA *is more and more puzzled.*

VIDA. [*To* JOHN.] See you next Derby, Jack! [*Walking to the door. To* SIR WILFRID.] Come along, Wilfrid! We really ought to be going. [*To* CYNTHIA.] I hope, dear, you haven't married him! Phillimore's a tomb! Good-bye, Cynthia—I'm so happy! [*As she goes.*] Just think of the silly people, dear, that only have this sensation once in a lifetime!

[JOHN *follows* VIDA *out the door.*

SIR WILFRID. [*To* CYNTHIA.] Good-bye, Mrs. Karslake. And I say, ye know, if you have married that dull old Phillimore fellah, why, when you've divorced him, come over and stay at Traynham! I mean, of course, ye know, bring your new husband. There'll be lots o' horses to show you, and a whole covey of jolly little Cates-Darbys. Mind you come! [*With real delicacy of feeling and forgetting his wife.*] Never liked a woman as much in my life as I did you!

VIDA. [*Outside; calling him.*] Wilfrid, dear!

SIR WILFRID. [*Loyal to the woman who has caught him.*]—except the one that's calling me!

JOHN *returns, and* SIR WILFRID, *nodding to him, goes out.* JOHN *shuts the door and crosses the room. There is a pause.*

CYNTHIA. So you're not married?

JOHN. No. But I know that you imagined I was.

CYNTHIA. [*After a pause.*] I suppose you think a woman has no right to divorce a man—and still continue to feel a keen interest in his affairs?

JOHN. Well, I'm not so sure about that, but I don't quite see how—

CYNTHIA. A woman can be divorced—and still— [JOHN *assents; she hides her embarrassment.*] Well, my dear Karslake, you've a long life before you, in which to learn how such a state of mind is possible! So I won't stop to explain. Will you be kind enough to get me a cab? [*She moves to the door.*

JOHN. Certainly. I was going to say I am not surprised at your feeling an interest in me. I'm only astonished that, having actually married Phillimore, you come here—

CYNTHIA. [*Indignantly.*] I'm not married to him!

JOHN. [*Silent for a moment.*] I left you on the brink—made me feel a little uncertain.

CYNTHIA. [*In a matter of course tone.*] I changed my mind—that's all.

JOHN. [*Taking his tone from her.*] Of course. [*After an interval.*] Are you going to marry him?

CYNTHIA. I don't know.

JOHN. Does he know you—

CYNTHIA. I told him I was coming here.

JOHN. Oh! He'll turn up here, then—eh? [CYNTHIA *is silent.*] And you'll go back with him, I suppose?

CYNTHIA. [*Talking at random.*] Oh—yes—I suppose so. I—I haven't thought much about it.

JOHN. [*Changing his tone.*] Well, sit down; do. Till he comes—talk it over. [*He places the armchair more comfortably for her.*] This is a more comfortable chair!

CYNTHIA. [*Shamefacedly.*] You never liked me to sit in that one!

JOHN. Oh, well—it's different now. [CYNTHIA *moves and sits down, near the upset chair. There is a long pause, during which* JOHN *thoughtfully paces the room.*] You don't mind if I smoke?

CYNTHIA. [*Shaking her head.*] No.

JOHN. [*Lighting his pipe and sitting down on the arm of a chair.*] Of course, if you find my presence painful, I'll—skiddoo.

He indicates the door. CYNTHIA *shakes her head.* JOHN *smokes his pipe and remains seated.*

CYNTHIA. [*Suddenly and quickly.*] It's just simply a fact, Karslake, and that's all there is to it—if a woman has once been married—that is, the first man she marries—then—she may quarrel, she may hate him—she may despise him—but she'll always be jealous of him with other women. Always! [JOHN *takes this as if he were simply glad to have the information.*

JOHN. Oh— H'm! ah—yes—yes.

CYNTHIA. [*After a pause.*] You probably felt jealous of Phillimore.

JOHN. [*Reasonably, sweetly, and in doubt.*] N-o! [*Apologetically.*] I felt simply: Let him take his medicine.

CYNTHIA. Oh!

JOHN. I beg your pardon—I meant—

CYNTHIA. You meant what you said!

JOHN. [*Moving a step toward her.*] Mrs. Karslake, I apologize —I won't do it again. But it's too late for you to be out alone—Philip will be here in a moment—and of course, then—

CYNTHIA. It isn't what you *say*—it's—it's—it's everything. It's the entire situation. Suppose by any chance I don't marry Phillimore! And suppose I were seen at two or three in the morning leaving my former husband's house! It's all wrong. I have no business to be here! I'm going! You're perfectly horrid to me, you know—and—the whole place—it's so familiar, and so—so associated with—with—

JOHN. Discord and misery—I know—

CYNTHIA. Not at all with discord and misery! With harmony and happiness—with—with first love, and infinite hope—and—and—Jack Karslake,—if you don't set that chair on its legs, I think I'll explode. [JOHN *crosses the room rapidly, and sets the chair on its legs. His tone changes.*

JOHN. [*While setting chair on its legs.*] There! I beg your pardon.

CYNTHIA. [*Nervously.*] I believe I hear Philip. [*She rises.*

JOHN. [*Going up to the window.*] N-o! That's the policeman trying the front door! And now, see here, Mrs. Karslake,—you're only here for a short minute, because you can't help yourself, but I want you to understand that I'm not trying to be disagreeable—I don't want to revive all the old unhappy—

CYNTHIA. Very well, if you don't—give me my hat. [JOHN *does so.*] And my sewing! And my gloves, please! [*She indicates the several articles which lie on the small table.*] Thanks! [CYNTHIA *throws the lot into the fireplace, and returns to the place she has left near table.*] There! I feel better! And now—all I ask is—

JOHN. [*Laughing.*] My stars, what a pleasure it is!

CYNTHIA. What is?

JOHN. Seeing you in a whirlwind!

CYNTHIA. [*Wounded by his seeming indifference.*] Oh!

JOHN. No, but I mean, a real pleasure! Why not? Time's passed since you and I were together—and—eh—

CYNTHIA. And you've forgotten what a vile temper I had!

JOHN. [*Reflectively.*] Well, you did kick the stuffing out of the matrimonial buggy—

CYNTHIA. [*Pointedly but with good temper.*] It wasn't a buggy; it was a break cart— [*She stands back of the arm-chair.*] It's all very well to blame me! But when you married me, I'd never had a bit in my mouth!

JOHN. Well, I guess I had a pretty hard hand. Do you remember the time you threw both your slippers out of the window?

CYNTHIA. Yes, and do you remember the time you took my fan from me by force?

JOHN. After you slapped my face with it!

CYNTHIA. Oh, oh! I hardly touched your face! And do you remember the day you held my wrists?

JOHN. You were going to bite me!

CYNTHIA. Jack! I never! I showed my teeth at you! And I *said* I would bite you!

JOHN. Cynthia, I never knew you to break your word! [*He laughs. Casually.*] And anyhow—they were awfully pretty teeth! [CYNTHIA, *though bolt upright, has ceased to seem pained.*] And I say—do you remember, Cyn—

[*He leans over her armchair to talk.*

CYNTHIA. [*After a pause.*] You oughtn't to call me "Cyn"—it's not nice of you. It's sort of cruel. I'm not—Cyn to you now.

JOHN. Awfully sorry; didn't mean to be beastly, Cyn. [CYNTHIA *turns quickly.* JOHN *stamps his foot.*] Cynthia! Sorry. I'll make it a commandment: thou shalt not Cyn!!

[CYNTHIA *laughs and wipes her eyes.*

CYNTHIA. How can you, Jack? How can you?

JOHN. Well, hang it, my dear child, I—I'm sorry, but you know I always got foolish with you. Your laugh 'd make a horse laugh. Why, don't you remember that morning in the park before breakfast—when you laughed so hard your horse ran away with you!

CYNTHIA. I do, I do! [*Both laugh. The door opens and* NOGAM *comes in, unnoticed by either.*] But what was it started me laughing? [*Laughing, she sits down and laughs again.*] That morning. Wasn't it somebody we met? [*Laughing afresh.*] Wasn't it a man on a horse? [*As her memory pieces the picture, she again goes off into laughter.*

JOHN. [*Laughing too.*] Of course! You didn't know him in those days! But I did! And he looked a sight in the saddle!

[NOGAM, *trying to catch their attention, moves toward the table.*

CYNTHIA. Who was it?

JOHN. Phillimore!

CYNTHIA. He's no laughing matter now. [*Seeing* NOGAM.] Jack, he's here!

JOHN. Eh? Oh, Nogam?

NOGAM. Mr. Phillimore, sir—

JOHN. In the house?

NOGAM. On the street in a hansom, sir—and he requests Mrs. Karslake—

JOHN. That'll do, Nogam. [NOGAM *goes out and there is a pause.* JOHN, *on his way to the window, looks at* CYNTHIA, *who has slowly risen and turned her back to him.*] Well, Cynthia?

[*He speaks almost gravely and with finality.*]

CYNTHIA. [*Trembling.*] Well?

JOHN. It's the hour of decision; are you going to marry him? [*Pause.*] Speak up!

CYNTHIA. Jack,—I—I—

JOHN. There he is—you can join him. [*He points to the street.*

CYNTHIA. Join Phillimore—and go home—with him—to his house, and Miss Heneage and—

JOHN. The door's open. [*He points to the door.*

CYNTHIA. No, no! It's mean of you to suggest it!

JOHN. You won't marry—

CYNTHIA. Phillimore—no; never. [*Running to the window.*] No; never, never, Jack.

JOHN. [*Opening the window and calling out.*] It's all right, Judge. You needn't wait.

There is a pause. JOHN *leaves the window and bursts into laughter. He moves toward the door and closes it.* CYNTHIA *looks dazed.*

CYNTHIA. Jack! [JOHN *laughs.*] Yes, but I'm here, Jack.

JOHN. Why not?

CYNTHIA. You'll have to take me round to the Holland House!

JOHN. Of course, I will! But, I say, Cynthia, there's no hurry.

CYNTHIA. Why, I—I—can't stay here.

JOHN. No, of course you can't stay here. But you can have a bite, though. [CYNTHIA *shakes her head.* JOHN *places the small chair, which was upset, next to the table, and the armchair close by.*] Oh, I insist. Just look at yourself—you're as pale as a sheet and —here, here. Sit right down. I insist! By George, you must do it! [CYNTHIA *moves to the chair drawn up to the table, and sits down.*

CYNTHIA. [*Faintly.*] I *am* hungry.

JOHN. Just wait a moment.

[JOHN *rushes out, leaving the door open.*

CYNTHIA. I don't want more than a nibble! [*After a pause.*] I am sorry to give you so much trouble.

JOHN. No trouble at all. [*From the dining-room comes the cheerful noise of glasses and silver.*] A hansom, of course, to take you round to your hotel? [*Speaking as he returns with a tray.*

CYNTHIA. [*To herself.*] I wonder how I ever dreamed I could marry that man.

JOHN. [*Now by the table.*] Can't imagine! There!

CYNTHIA. I am hungry. Don't forget the hansom.

[*She eats; he waits on her, setting this and that before her.*

JOHN. [*Goes to the door, opens it and calls.*] Nogam, a hansom at once.

NOGAM. [*From without.*] Yes, sir.

JOHN. [*Again at the table, shows, and from now on continues to show, his true feelings for her.*] How does it go?

CYNTHIA. [*Faintly.*] It goes all right. Thanks!

[*Hardly eating at all.*

JOHN. You always used to like anchovy. [CYNTHIA *nods and eats.*] Claret? [CYNTHIA *shakes her head.*] Oh, but you must!

CYNTHIA. [*Tremulously.*] Ever so little. [*He fills her glass and then his.*] Thanks!

JOHN. Here's to old times! [*Raising his glass.*

CYNTHIA. [*Very tremulous.*] Please not!

JOHN. Well, here's to your next husband.

CYNTHIA. [*Very tenderly.*] Don't!

JOHN. Oh, well, then, what shall the toast be?

CYNTHIA. I'll tell you—[*After a pause.*] you can drink to the relation I am to you!

JOHN. [*Laughing.*] Well—what relation are you?

CYNTHIA. I'm your first wife once removed!

JOHN. [*Laughing, drinks.*] I say, you're feeling better.

CYNTHIA. Lots.

JOHN. [*Reminiscent.*] It's a good deal like those mornings after the races—isn't it?

CYNTHIA. [*Nods.*] Yes. [*Half-rising.*] Is that the hansom?

JOHN. [*Going up to the window.*] No.

CYNTHIA. [*Sitting down again.*] What is that sound?

JOHN. Don't you remember?

CYNTHIA. No.

JOHN. That's the rumbling of the early milk wagons.

CYNTHIA. Oh, Jack.

JOHN. Do you recognize it now?

CYNTHIA. Do I? We used to hear that—just at the hour, didn't we—when we came back from awfully jolly late suppers and things!

JOHN. H'm!

CYNTHIA. It must be fearfully late. I must go.

She rises and moves to the chair where she has left her cloak. She sees that JOHN *will not help her and puts it on herself.*

JOHN. Oh, don't go—why go?

CYNTHIA. [*Embarrassed and agitated.*] All good things come to an end, you know.

JOHN. They don't need to.

CYNTHIA. Oh, you don't mean that! And, you know, Jack, if I were caught—seen at this hour, leaving this house, you know—it's the most scandalous thing any one ever did, my being here at all. Good-bye, Jack! [*After a pause and almost in tears.*] I'd like to say, I—I—I—well, I sha'n't be bitter about you hereafter, and— [*Halting.*] Thank you awfully, old man, for the fodder and all that! [*She turns to go out.*

JOHN. Mrs. Karslake—wait—

CYNTHIA. [*Stopping to hear.*] Well?

JOHN. [*Serious.*] I've rather an ugly bit of news for you.

CYNTHIA. Yes?

JOHN. I don't believe you know that I have been testing the validity of the decree of divorce which you procured.

CYNTHIA. Oh, have you?

JOHN. Yes; you know I felt pretty warmly about it.

CYNTHIA. Well?

JOHN. Well, I've been successful. [*After a pause.*] The decree's been declared invalid. Understand?

CYNTHIA. [*Looking at him for a moment; then speaking.*] Not—precisely.

JOHN. [*After a moment's silence.*] I'm awfully sorry—I'm awfully sorry, Cynthia, but, you're my wife still.

[*There is a pause.*

CYNTHIA. [*With rapture.*] Honour bright?

[*She sinks into the armchair.*

JOHN. [*Nods. Half laughingly.*] Crazy country, isn't it?

CYNTHIA. [*Nods. After an interval.*] Well, Jack—what's to be done?

JOHN. [*Gently.*] Whatever you say.

[*He moves a few steps toward her.*

NOGAM. [*Quietly coming in.*] Hansom, sir.

[*He goes out and* CYNTHIA *rises.*

JOHN. Why don't you finish your supper?

[CYNTHIA *hesitates.*

CYNTHIA. The—the—hansom—

JOHN. Why go to the Holland? After all—you know, Cyn, you're at home here.

CYNTHIA. No, Jack, I'm not—I'm not at home here—unless—unless—

JOHN. Out with it!

CYNTHIA. [*Bursting into tears.*] Unless I—unless I'm at home in your heart, Jack!

JOHN. What do you think?

CYNTHIA. I don't believe you want me to stay.

JOHN. Don't you?

CYNTHIA. No, no, you hate me still. You never can forgive me. I know you can't. For I can never forgive myself. Never, Jack, never, never!

[*She sobs and he takes her in his arms.*

JOHN. [*Very tenderly.*] Cyn! I love you! [*Strongly.*] And you've got to stay! And hereafter you can chuck chairs around till all's blue! Not a word now.

[*He draws her gently to a chair.*

CYNTHIA. [*Wiping her tears.*] Oh, Jack! Jack!

JOHN. I'm as hungry as a shark. We'll nibble together.

CYNTHIA. Well, all I can say is, I feel that of all the improprieties I ever committed this—this—

JOHN. This takes the claret, eh? Oh, Lord, how happy I am!

CYNTHIA. Now don't say that! You'll make me cry more.

She wipes her eyes. JOHN *takes out the wedding ring from his pocket; he lifts a wine-glass, drops the ring into it and offers her the glass.*

JOHN. Cynthia!

CYNTHIA. [*Looking at it and wiping her eyes.*] What is it?

JOHN. Benedictine!

CYNTHIA. Why, you know I never take it.

JOHN. Take this one for my sake.

CYNTHIA. That's not benedictine. [*With gentle curiosity.*] What is it?

JOHN. [*Slides the ring out of the glass and puts his arm about* CYNTHIA. *He slips the ring on to her finger and, as he kisses her hand, says:*] Your wedding ring!

CURTAIN.

THE EASIEST WAY

EUGENE WALTER

EUGENE WALTER

(Born, Cleveland, Ohio, November 27, 1874)

When questioned once regarding "The Easiest Way," Mr. Eugene Walter said, "Incidentally, I do not think much of it. To my mind a good play must have a tremendous uplift in thought and purpose. 'The Easiest Way' has none of this. There is not a character in the play really worth while, with the exception of the old agent. The rest, at best, are not a particular adornment to society, and the strength of the play lies in its true portrayal of the sordid type of life which it expressed. As it is more or less purely photographic, I do not think it should be given the credit of an inspiration—it is rather devilishly clever, but a great work it certainly is not."

Such was not the verdict of the first night audience, at the Stuyvesant Theatre, New York, January 19, 1909. It was found to be one of the most direct pieces of work the American stage had thus far produced—disagreeably realistic, but purging—and that is the test of an effective play—by the very poignancy of the tragic forces closing in around the heroine. Though it is not as literary a piece of dramatic expression as Pinero's "Iris," it is better in its effect; because its relentlessness is due, not so predominantly to the moral downgrade of the woman, as to the moral downgrade of a certain phase of life which engulfs those nearest the centre of it. The play roused a storm of comment; there were camps that took just the stand Mr. Walter takes in the opening quotation. But the play is included in this collection because its power, as a documentary report of a phase of American stage life, is undeniable; because, as a piece of workmanship, shorn of the usual devices called theatrical, it comes down to the raw bone of the theme, and firmly progresses to its great climax,—great in the sense of overpowering,—at the very fall of the final curtain.

Mr. Walter's various experiences in the theatre as an advance man, his star reporting on the Detroit *News*, his struggles to gain a footing in New York, contributed something to the bitter irony which runs as a dark pattern through the texture of "The

Easiest Way." He is one of the many American dramatists who have come from the newspaper ranks, having served on the Cleveland *Plain Dealer* and *Press*, the New York *Sun* and *Globe*, the Cincinnati *Post* and the Seattle *Star*. Not many will disagree with the verdict that thus far he has not excelled this play, though "Paid in Full" (February 25, 1908) contains the same sting of modern life, which drives his characters to situations dramatic and dire, making them sell their souls and their peace of minds for the benefit of worldly ease and comfort. Note this theme in "Fine Feathers" (January 7, 1913) and "Nancy Lee" (April 9, 1918). In this sense, his plays all possess a consistency which makes no compromises. Arthur Ruhl, in his "Second Nights", refers to Walter as of the "no quarter" school. He brings a certain manly subtlety to bear on melodramatic subjects, as in "The Wolf" (April 18, 1908) and "The Knife" (April 12, 1917); he seems to do as he pleases with his treatment, as he did right at the start with his first successful play. For, of "The Easiest Way" it may be said that, for the first time in his managerial career, Mr. David Belasco agreed to accept it with the condition that not a word of the manuscript should be changed.

It is interesting to note about Walter that, though he may now repudiate it, "The Easiest Way" stands distinct in its class; perhaps the dramatist has ripened more in technique—one immediately feels the surety and vital grip of dramatic expertness in Walter, much more so than in George Broadhurst, Bayard Veiller, or other American dramatists of his class. But he has not surpassed "The Easiest Way" in the burning intention with which it was written.

As a dramatist, Walter adopts an interesting method; he tries out his plays on the road, experimenting with various names, and re-casting until ready for metropolitan production. His dramas have many *aliases*, and it is a long case to prove an alibi; any student who has attempted to settle dates will soon find that out. His military play, written out of his experiences as a United States cavalryman in the Spanish American War, was called "Boots and Saddles," after it was given as "Sergeant James." "Fine Feathers," "The Knife," "The Heritage," "Nancy Lee"—were all second or third choice as to name.

In his advancement, Mr. Walter gives much credit to three American managers—Kirke LaShelle, and the Selwyn brothers,

Archie and Edgar. It was the Selwyns who, during his various ventures in the "show business," persuaded him to move to Shelter Island, and write "The Undertow." It was in their house that "Paid in Full" was finished. Let Mr. Walter continue the narrative:

The circumstances under which "The Easiest Way" was written are rather peculiar. When I was an advance-agent, ahead of second-class companies, the need of money caused me to write a one-act piece called "All the Way from Denver," which in time I was able to dispose of. Later, after having written "Paid in Full," I realized that in the play, "All the Way from Denver," there was a situation or theme that might prove exceedingly valuable in a four-act play. After discussing the possibilities with Mr. Archie Selwyn, we concluded to write it. In the meantime, the one-act piece had come into the possession of Margaret Mayo, and through her, Mr. Edgar Selwyn decided that the title should be "The Easiest Way" instead of "All the Way from Denver."

The play was then taken in its scenario form to Mr. C. B. Dillingham, and discussed with him at length. This was prior to the public presentation of "Paid in Full." I possessed no particular reputation as a dramatic writer—in fact, the Messrs. Selwyn—Archie and Edgar—were the only ones who took me seriously, and thought me a possibility. Mr. Dillingham was not particularly impressed with the piece, because he thought it was much too broad in theme, and he did not like the idea of slapping the managerial knuckles of the theatre. Further, the obvious inference in "The Easiest Way," that *Laura* was kept out of work in order to be compelled to yield herself to *Brockton*, was a point which did not appeal to him. However, we had a working agreement with him, and later, Mr. Archie Selwyn, in discussing the story of the play with Mr. David Belasco, aroused his interest. The latter saw "Paid in Full" and "The Wolf," and so he sent for me, with the result that "The Easiest Way" was first produced in Hartford, Conn., on December 31, 1908. Since its New York production, it has been presented in nearly every country of the world. It has not always met with commercial success, but it has always been regarded as a play of representative importance.

William Winter was one of the bitterest enemies of "The Easiest Way." He placed it with "Zaza" and Brieux's "Three Daughters of M. Dupont." As an opposite extreme view, we give the opinion of Mr. Walter Eaton, written in 1909, concerning the play: "It places Mr. Walter as a leader among our dramatists." In some respects, we may have surpassed it since then, in imaginative ideality; but, as an example of relentless realism, it still holds its own as a distinct contribution. The text has been edited for private circulation, and it is this text which is followed here. A few modifications, of a technical nature, have been made in the stage directions; but even with these slight changes, the directions are staccato, utilitarian in conciseness, rather than literary in the Shaw sense.

DAVID BELASCO'S

STUYVESANT THEATRE

44th STREET near BROADWAY *New York City*

Under the *sole* management of DAVID BELASCO

DAVID BELASCO

PRESENTS

FRANCES STARR

—IN—

THE EASIEST WAY

An American play concerning a peculiar phase of New York life.

In Four Acts and Four Scenes,

By EUGENE WALTER.

CHARACTERS OF THE PLAY

JOHN MADISON	EDWARD H ROBINS
WILLARD BROCKTON	JOSEPH KILCOUR
JIM WESTON	WILLIAM SAMPSON
LAURA MURDOCK	FRANCES STARR
ELFIE ST. CLAIR	LAURA NELSON HALL
ANNIE	EMMA DUNN

Program Continued on Second Page Following

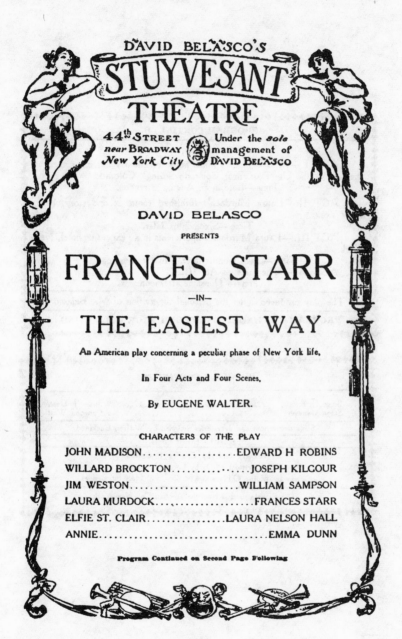

PROGRAM CONTINUED.

SYNOPSIS.

ACT I.—Mrs. William's ranch house or country home, perched on the side of the Ute Pass, near Colorado Springs, Colorado.

Time—Late in an August afternoon.

ACT II.—Laura Murdock's furnished room, second story, back. New York.

Time—Six months later.

ACT III.—Laura Murdock's apartments in an expensive hotel, New York.

Time—Two months later. In the morning.

ACT IV.—The same as Act III.

Time—The same afternoon.

The play produced under the personal supervision of Mr. Belasco.

PROGRAM CONTINUED ON SECOND PAGE FOLLOWING.

PROGRAM CONTINUED.

Stage Director.......................................William J. Dean
Stage Manager ....! angdon West

---

Stage decorations and accessories designed by Wilfred Buckland.

Scenes by Ernest Gross.

Scenery built by Charles J. Carson.

Electrical effects by Louis Hartman.

Gowns by Mollie O'Hara. Hats by Bendel.

The Pianola used is from the Aeolian Co., New York.

THE EASIEST WAY

AN AMERICAN PLAY CONCERNING A PARTICULAR PHASE OF NEW YORK LIFE

IN FOUR ACTS AND FOUR SCENES

By EUGENE WALTER

CHARACTERS.

Laura Murdock.
Elfie St. Clair.
Annie.
Willard Brockton.
John Madison.
Jim Weston.

DESCRIPTION OF CHARACTERS.

LAURA MURDOCK, twenty-five years of age, is a type not uncommon in the theatrical life of New York, and one which has grown in importance in the profession since the business of giving public entertainments has been so reduced to a commercial basis.

At an early age she came from Australia to San Francisco. She possessed a considerable beauty and an aptitude for theatrical accomplishment which soon raised her to a position of more or less importance in a local stock company playing in that city. A woman of intense superficial emotions, her imagination was without any enduring depths, but for the passing time she could place herself in an attitude of great affection and devotion. Sensually, the woman had marked characteristics, and, with the flattery that surrounded her, she soon became a favourite in the select circles which made such places as "The Poodle Dog" and "Zinkand's" famous. In general dissipation, she was always careful not in any way to indulge in excesses which would jeopardize her physical attractiveness, or for one moment to diminish her sense of keen worldly calculation.

In time she married. It was, of course, a failure. Her vacillating nature was such that she could not be absolutely true to the man to whom she had given her life, and, after several bitter experiences, she had the horror of seeing him kill himself in front of her. There was a momentary spasm of grief, a tidal wave of remorse, and then the peculiar recuperation of spirits, beauty and attractiveness that so marks this type of woman. She was deceived by other men in many various ways, and finally came to that stage of life that is known in theatrical circles as being "wised up."

At nineteen, the attention of a prominent theatrical manager being called to her, she took an important part in a New York production, and immediately gained considerable reputation. The fact that, before reaching the age of womanhood, she had had more escapades than most women have in their entire lives was not generally known in New York, nor was there a mark upon her face or a single coarse mannerism to betray it. She was soft-voiced, very pretty, very girlish. Her keen sense of worldly calculation led her to believe that in order to progress in her theatrical career she must have some influence outside of her art and dramatic accomplishment; so she attempted, with no little success, to infatuate a hard-headed, blunt and supposedly invincible theatrical manager, who, in his cold, stolid way, gave her what love there was in him. This, however, not satisfying her, she played two ends against the middle, and, finding a young man of wealth and position who could give her, in his youth, the exuberance and joy utterly apart from the character of the theatrical manager, she adopted him, and for a while lived with him. Exhausting his money, she cast him aside, always spending a certain part of the time with the theatrical manager. The young man became crazed, and, at a restaurant, tried to murder all of them.

From that time up to the opening of the play, her career was a succession of brilliant coups in gaining the confidence and love, not to say the money, of men of all ages and all walks in life. Her fascination was as undeniable as her insincerity of purpose. She had never made an honest effort to be an honest woman, although she imagined herself always persecuted, the victim of circumstances,—and was always ready to excuse any viciousness of character which led her into her peculiar difficulties. While acknowledged to be a mistress of her business—that of acting—from a purely technical point of view, her lack of sympathy, her abuse of her dramatic temperament in her private affairs, had been such as to make it impossible for her sincerely to impress audiences with real emotional power, and, therefore, despite the influences which she always had at hand, she remained a mediocre artist.

At the time of the opening of our play, she has played a summer engagement with a stock company in Denver, which has just ended. She has met JOHN MADISON, a man of about twenty-seven years of age, whose position is that of a dramatic critic on one of the local papers. LAURA MURDOCK, with her usual wisdom, started to fascinate JOHN MADISON, but has found that, for once in her life, she has met her match.

JOHN MADISON is good to look at, frank, virile, but a man of broad experience, and not to be hookwinked. For the first time LAURA MURDOCK feels that the shoe is pinching the other foot, and, without any possible indication of reciprocal affection, she has been slowly falling desperately, madly, honestly and decently in love with him. She has for the past two years been the special favourite and mistress of WILLARD BROCKTON. The understanding is one of pure friendship. He is a man who has a varied taste in the selection of his women; is honest in a general way, and perfectly frank about his amours. He has been most generous with LAURA MURDOCK, and his close relations with several very prominent theatrical managers have made it possible for him to secure her desirable engagements, generally in New York. With all her past experiences, tragic and otherwise, LAURA MURDOCK has found nothing equal to this sudden, this swiftly increasing, love for the young Western man. At first she attempted to deceive him. Her baby face, her masterful assumption of innocence and childlike devotion, made no impression upon him. He has let her know in no uncertain way that he knew her record from the day she stepped on American soil in San Francisco to the time when she had come to Denver, but still he liked her.

JOHN MADISON is a peculiar type of the Western man. Up to the time of his meeting LAURA, he had always been employed either in the mines or on a newspaper west of the Mississippi River. He is one of those itinerant reporters; to-day you might find him in Seattle, to-morrow in Butte, the next week in Denver, and then possibly he would make the circuit from Los Angeles to 'Frisco, and then all around again. He drinks his whiskey straight, plays his faro fairly, and is not particular about the women with whom he goes. He started life in the Western country at an early age. His natural talents, both in literature and in general adaptability to all conditions of life, were early exhibited, but his *alma mater* was the bar-room, and the faculty of that college its bartenders and gamblers and general habitués.

He seldom has social engagements outside of certain disreputable establishments, where a genial personality or an overburdened pocketbook gives *entrée*, and the rules of conventionality have never even been whispered. His love affairs, confined to this class of women, have seldom lasted more than a week or ten days. His editors know him as a brilliant genius, irresponsible, unreliable, but at times inestimably valuable. He cares little for personal appearance beyond a certain degree of neatness. He is quick on the trigger, and in a time of overheated argument can go some distance with his fists; in fact, his whole career is best described as "happy-go-lucky."

He realizes fully his ability to do almost anything fairly well, and some things especially well, but he has never tried to accomplish anything beyond the earning of a comfortable living. Twenty-five or thirty dollars a week was all he needed. With that he could buy his liquor, treat his women, sometimes play a little faro, sit up all night and sleep all day, and in general lead the life of good-natured vagabondage which has always pleased him and which he had chosen as a career.

The objection of safer and saner friends to this form of livelihood was always met by him with a slap on the back and a laugh. "Don't you worry about me, partner; if I'm going to hell I'm going there with bells on," was always his rejoinder; and yet, when called upon to cover some great big news story, or report some vital event, he settled down to his work with a steely determination and a grim joy that resulted in work which classified him as a genius. Any great mental effort of this character, any unusual achievement along these lines, would be immediately followed by a protracted debauch that would upset him physically and mentally for weeks at a time, but he always recovered and landed on his feet, and with the same laugh and smile again went at his work.

If there have been opportunities to meet decent women of good social standing, he has always thrown them aside with the declaration that they bore him to death, and there never had entered into his heart a feeling or idea of real affection until he met LAURA. He fell for a moment under the spell of her fascination, and then, with cold logic, he analyzed her, and found out that, while outwardly she had every sign of girlhood,—ingenuousness, sweetness of character and possibility of affection,—spiritually and mentally she was nothing more than a moral wreck. He observed keenly her efforts to win him and her disappointment at her failure—not that she cared so much for him personally, but that it hurt her vanity not to be successful with this good-for-nothing, good-natured vagabond, when men of wealth and position she made kneel at her feet. He observed her slowly-changing point of view: how from a kittenish ingenuousness she became serious, womanly, really sincere. He knew that he had awakened in her her first decent affection, and he knew that she was awakening in him his first desire to do things and be big and worth while. So together these two began to drift toward a path of decent dealing, decent ambition, decent thought, and decent love, until at last they both find themselves, and acknowledge all the wickedness of what had been, and plan for all the virtue and goodness of what is to be. It is at this point that our first act begins.

ELFIE ST. CLAIR is a type of a Tenderloin grafter in New York, who, after all, has been more sinned against than sinning; who, having been imposed upon, deceived, ill-treated and bull-dozed by the type of men who prey on women in New York, has turned the tables, and with her charm and her beauty has gone out to make the same slaughter of the other sex as she suffered with many of her sisters.

She is a woman without a moral conscience, whose entire life is dictated by a small mental operation. Coming to New York as a beautiful girl, she entered the chorus. She became famous for her beauty. On every hand were the stage-door vultures ready to give her anything that a woman's heart could desire, from clothes to horses, carriages, money and what-not; but, with a girl-like instinct, she fell in love with a man connected with the company, and, during all the time she might have profited and become a rich woman by the attentions of these outsiders, she remained true to her love, until finally her fame as the beauty of the city had waned. The years told on her to a certain extent, and there were others coming, as young as she had been and as good to look at; and, where the automobile of the millionaire had once been waiting for her, she found that, through her faithfulness to her lover, it was now there for some one else. Yet she was content with her joys, until finally the man deliberately jilted her and left her alone.

What had gone of her beauty had been replaced by a keen knowledge of human nature and of men, so she determined to give herself up entirely to a life of gain. She knows just how much champagne should be drunk without injuring one's health. She knows just what physical necessities should be indulged in to preserve to the greatest degree her remaining beauty. There is no trick of the hair-dresser, the modiste, the manicurist, or any one of the legion of people who devote their time to aiding the outward fascinations of women, which she does not know. She knows exactly what perfumes to use, what stockings to wear, how she should live, how far she should indulge in any dissipation; and all this she has determined to devote to profit. She knows that as an actress she has no future; that the time of a woman's beauty is limited. Conscious that she has already lost the youthful litheness of figure which had made her so fascinating in the past, she has laid aside every sentiment, physical and spiritual, and has determined to choose a man as her companion who has the biggest bank-roll and the most liberal nature. His age, his station in life, the fact whether she likes or dislikes him, do not enter into this scheme at all. She figures that she has been made a fool of by men, and that there is only one revenge,—the accumulation of a fortune to make her independent of them once and for all. There are, of course, certain likes and dislikes that she enjoys, and in a way she indulges them. There are men whose company she cares for, but their association is practically sexless and has come down to a point of mere good fellowship.

WILLARD BROCKTON, a New York broker, is an honest sensualist, and when one says an honest sensualist, the meaning is—a man who has none of the cad in his character, who takes advantage of no one, and who allows no one to take advantage of him. He honestly detests any man who takes advantage of a pure woman. He detests any man who deceives a woman. He believes that there is only one way to go through life, and that is to be frank with those with whom one deals. He is a master-hand in stock manipulation, and in the questionable practises of Wall Street he has realized that he has to play his cunning and craft against the cunning and craft of others. He is not at all in sympathy with this mode of living, but he thinks it is the only method by which he can succeed in life. He measures success by the accumulation of money, but he considers his business career as a thing apart from his private existence.

He does not associate, to any great extent, with what is known as "society." He keeps in touch with it simply to maintain his business position. There is always an inter-relationship among the rich in business and private life, and he gives such entertainments as are necessary to the members of New York's exclusive set, simply to make certain his relative position with other successful Wall Street men.

As far as women are concerned, the particular type of actress, such as LAURA MURDOCK and ELFIE ST. CLAIR, appeals to him. He likes their good fellowship. He loves to be with a gay party at night in a café. He likes the rather looseness of living which does not quite reach the disreputable. Behind all this, however, is a certain high sense of honour. He detests and despises the average stage-door Johnny, and he loathes the type of man who seeks to take young girls out of theatrical companies for their ruin.

His women friends are as wise as himself. When they enter into an agreement with him there is no deception. In the first place he wants to like them; in the second place he wants them to like him; and finally, he wants to fix the amount of their living expenses at a definite figure, and have them stand by it. He wants them to understand that he reserves the right, at any time, to withdraw his support, or transfer it to some other woman, and he gives them the same privilege.

He is always ready to help anyone who is unfortunate, and he has always hoped that some of these girls whom he knew would finally come across the right man, marry and settle down; but he insists that such an arrangement can be possible only by the honest admission on the woman's part of what she has done and been, and by the thorough understanding of all these things by the man involved. He is gruff in his manner, determined in his purposes, honest in his point of view. He is a brute, almost a savage, but he is a thoroughly good brute and a pretty decent savage.

At the time of the opening of this play, he and LAURA MURDOCK have been friends for two years. He knows exactly what she is and what she has been, and their relations are those of pals. She has finished her season in Denver, and he has come out there to accompany her home. He has always told her, whenever she felt it inconsistent with her happiness to continue her relations with him, it is her privilege to quit, and he has reserved the same condition.

JIM WESTON, between forty-five and fifty years of age, is the type of the semi-broken-down showman. In the evolution of the theatrical business in America, the old circus and minstrel men have gradually been pushed aside, while younger men, with more advanced methods, have taken their place. The character is best realized by the way it is drawn in the play.

ANNIE. The only particular attention that should be called to the character of the negress, ANNIE, who is the servant of

LAURA, is the fact that she must not in any way represent the traditional smiling coloured girl or "mammy" of the South. She is the cunning, crafty, heartless, surly, sullen Northern negress, who, to the number of thousands, are servants of women of easy morals, and who infest a district of New York in which white and black people of the lower classes mingle indiscriminately, and which is one of the most criminal sections of the city. The actress who plays this part must keep in mind its innate and brutal selfishness.

SYNOPSIS.

Act I. Mrs. Williams' Ranch House or Country Home, perched on the side of Ute Pass, near Colorado Springs, Colorado.

Time. Late in an August afternoon.

Act II. Laura Murdock's furnished Room, second story back, New York.

Time. Six months later.

Act III. Laura Murdock's Apartments in an expensive Hotel.

Time. Two months later. In the morning.

Act IV. Laura Murdock's Apartments. The same as Act III.

Time. The afternoon of the same day.

THE EASIEST WAY

ACT I.

SCENE. *The scene is that of the summer country ranch house of* MRS. WILLIAMS, *a friend of* LAURA MURDOCK'S, *and a prominent society woman of Denver, perched on the side of Ute Pass, near Colorado Springs. The house is one of unusual pretentiousness, and, to a person not conversant with conditions as they exist in this part of Colorado, the idea might be that such magnificence could not obtain in such a locality. At the left of stage the house rises in the form of a turret, built of rough stone of a brown hue, two stories high, and projecting a quarter of the way out on the stage. The door leads to a small elliptical terrace built of stone, with heavy benches of Greek design, strewn cushions, while over the top of one part of this terrace is suspended a canopy made from a Navajo blanket. The terrace is supposed to extend almost to the right of stage, and here it stops. The stage must be cut here so that the entrance of* JOHN *can give the illusion that he is coming up a steep declivity or a long flight of stairs. There are chairs at right and left, and a small table at left. There are trailing vines around the balustrade of the terrace, and the whole setting must convey the idea of quiet wealth. Up stage is supposed to be the part of the terrace overlooking the cañon, a sheer drop of two thousand feet, while over in the distance, as if across the cañon, one can see the rolling foot-hills and lofty peaks of the Rockies, with Pike's Peak in the distance, snow-capped and colossal. It is late in the afternoon, and, as the scene progresses, the quick twilight of a cañon, beautiful in its tints of purple and amber, becomes later pitch black, and the curtain goes down on an absolutely black stage. The cyclorama, or semi-cyclorama, must give the perspective of greater distances, and be so painted that the various tints of twilight may be shown.*

AT RISE. LAURA MURDOCK *is seen leaning a bit over the balustrade of the porch and shielding her eyes with her hand from the late afternoon sun, as she seemingly looks up the Pass to the left, as if expecting the approach of someone. Her gown is simple, girlish and attractive, and made of summery, filmy stuff. Her hair is done up in the simplest fashion, with a part in the centre, and there is about her every indication of an effort to assume that girlishness of demeanour which has been her greatest asset through life.* WILLARD BROCKTON *enters; he is a man six feet or more in height, stocky in build, clean-shaven and immaculately dressed. He is smoking a cigar, and upon entering takes one step forward and looks over toward* LAURA *in a semi-meditative manner.*

WILL. Blue?

LAURA. No.

WILL. What's up?

LAURA. Nothing.

WILL. A little preoccupied.

LAURA. Perhaps.

WILL. What's up that way?

LAURA. Which way?

WILL. The way you are looking.

LAURA. The road from Manitou Springs. They call it the trail out here.

WILL. I know that. You know I've done a lot of business west of the Missouri.

LAURA. [*With a half-sigh.*] No, I didn't know it.

WILL. Oh, yes; south of here in the San Juan country. Spent a couple of years there once.

LAURA. [*Still without turning.*] That's interesting.

WILL. It was then. I made some money there. It's always interesting when you make money. Still—

LAURA. [*Still leaning in an absent-minded attitude.*] Still what?

WILL. Can't make out why you have your eyes glued on that road. Someone coming?

LAURA. Yes.

WILL. One of Mrs. Williams' friends, eh? [WILL *crosses, and sits on seat.*

LAURA. Yes.

WILL. Yours too?

LAURA. Yes.

WILL. Man?

LAURA. Yes, a *real* man.

WILL. [*Catches the significance of this speech. He carelessly throws the cigar over the balustrade. He comes down and leans on chair with his back to* LAURA. *She has not moved more than to place her left hand on a cushion and lean her head rather wearily against it, looking steadfastly up the Pass.*] A real man. By that you mean—

LAURA. Just that—a real man.

WILL. Any difference from the many you have known?

LAURA. Yes, from all I have known.

WILL. So that is why you didn't come into Denver to meet me to-day, but left word for me to come out here?

LAURA. Yes.

WILL. I thought that I was pretty decent to take a dusty ride half-way across the continent in order to keep you company on your way back to New York, and welcome you to our home; but maybe I had the wrong idea.

LAURA. Yes, I think you had the wrong idea.

WILL. In love, eh?

LAURA. Yes, just that,—in love.

WILL. A new sensation.

LAURA. No; the first conviction.

WILL. You have had that idea before. Every woman's love is the real one when it comes. [*Crosses up to* LAURA.] Do you make a distinction in this case, young lady?

LAURA. Yes.

WILL. For instance, what?

LAURA. This man is poor—absolutely broke. He hasn't even got a [*Crosses to armchair, leans over and draws with parasol on ground.*] good job. You know, Will, all the rest, including yourself, generally had some material inducement.

WILL. What's his business? [*Crosses to table and sits looking at magazine.*

LAURA. He's a newspaper man.

WILL. H'm-m. Romance?

LAURA. Yes, if you want to call it that,—romance.

WILL. Do I know him?

LAURA. How could you? You only came from New York to-day, and he has never been there.

He regards her with a rather amused, indulgent, almost paternal expression, in contrast to his big, bluff, physical personality, with his iron-gray hair and his bulldog expression. LAURA *looks more girlish than ever. This is imperative in order to thoroughly understand the character.*

WILL. How old is he?

LAURA. Twenty-seven. You're forty-five.

WILL. No, forty-six.

LAURA. Shall I tell you about him? Huh?

[*Crosses to* WILL, *placing parasol on seat.*

WILL. That depends.

LAURA. On what?

WILL. Yourself.

LAURA. In what way?

WILL. If it will interfere in the least with the plans I have made for you and for me.

LAURA. And have you made any particular plans for me that have anything particularly to do with you?

WILL. Yes, I have given up the lease of our apartment on West End Avenue, and I've got a house on Riverside Drive. Everything will be quiet and decent, and it'll be more comfortable for you. There's a stable near by, and your horses and car can be kept over there. You'll be your own mistress, and besides I've fixed you up for a new part.

LAURA. A new part! What kind of a part?

WILL. One of Charlie Burgess's shows, translated from some French fellow. It's been running over in Paris, Berlin, and Vienna, and all those places, for a year or more, and appears to be an awful hit. It's going to cost a lot of money. I told Charlie he could put me down for a half interest, and I'd give all the money providing you got an important rôle. Great part, I'm told. Kind of a cross between a musical comedy and an opera. Looks as if it might stay in New York all season. So that's the change of plan. How does it strike you?

[LAURA *crosses to door, meditating; pauses in thought.*

LAURA. I don't know.

WILL. Feel like quitting? [*Turns to her.*

LAURA. I can't tell.

WILL. It's the newspaper man, eh?

LAURA. That would be the only reason.

WILL. You've been on the square with me this summer, haven't you? [*Crosses to table.*

LAURA. [*Turns, looks at* WILL.] What do you mean by "on the square?"

WILL. Don't evade. There's only one meaning when I say that, and you know it. I'm pretty liberal. But you understand where I draw the line. You've not jumped that, have you, Laura?

LAURA. No, this has been such a wonderful summer, such a wonderfully different summer. Can you understand what I mean by that when I say "wonderfully different summer?"

[*Crossing to* WILL.

WILL. Well, he's twenty-seven and broke, and you're twenty-five and pretty; and he evidently, being a newspaper man, has that peculiar gift of gab that we call romantic expression. So I guess I'm not blind, and you both think you've fallen in love. That it?

LAURA. Yes, I think that's about it; only I don't agree to the "gift of gab" and the "romantic" end of it. [*Crosses to table.*] He's a man and I'm a woman, and we both have had our experiences. I don't think, Will, that there can be much of that element of what some folks call hallucination.

[*Sits on chair; takes candy-box on lap; selects candy.*

WILL. Then the Riverside Drive proposition and Burgess's show is off, eh?

LAURA. I didn't say that.

WILL. And if you go back on the Overland Limited day after to-morrow, you'd just as soon I'd go to-morrow or wait until the day after you leave? [LAURA *places candy-box back on table.*

LAURA. I didn't say that, either.

WILL. What's the game?

LAURA. I can't tell you now.

WILL. Waiting for him to come? [*Crosses, sits on seat.*

LAURA. Exactly.

WILL. Think he is going to make a proposition, eh?

LAURA. I know he is.

WILL. Marriage?

LAURA. Possibly.

WILL. You've tried that once, and taken the wrong end. Are you going to play the same game again?

LAURA. Yes, but with a different card.

[*Picks up magazine off table.*

WILL. What's his name?

LAURA. Madison—John Madison.

[*Slowly turning pages of magazine.*

WILL. And his job?

LAURA. Reporter.

WILL. What are you going to live on,—the extra editions?

LAURA. No, we're young, there's plenty of time. I can work in the meantime, and so can he; and then with his ability and my ability it will only be a matter of a year or two when things will shape themselves to make it possible.

WILL. Sounds well—a year off.

LAURA. If I thought you were going to make fun of me, Will, I shouldn't have talked to you.

[*Throws down magazine, crosses to door of house.*

WILL. [*Crossing down in front of table.*] I don't want to make fun of you, but you must realize that after two years it isn't an easy thing to be dumped with so little ceremony. Maybe you have never given me any credit for possessing the slightest feeling, but even I can receive shocks from other sources than a break in the market.

LAURA. [*Crosses to* WILL.] It isn't easy for me to do this. You've been awfully kind, awfully considerate, but when I went to you it was just with the understanding that we were to be pals. You reserved the right then to quit me whenever you felt like it, and you gave me the same privilege. Now, if some girl came along who really captivated you in the right way, and you wanted to marry, it would hurt me a little,—maybe a lot,—but I should never forget that agreement we made, a sort of two weeks' notice clause, like people have in contracts.

WILL. [*Is evidently very much moved. Walks up stage to right end of seat, looks over the cañon.* LAURA *looks after him.* WILL *has his back to the audience. Long pause.*] I'm not hedging, Laura. If that's the way you want it to be, I'll stand by just exactly what I said [*Turns to* LAURA.], but I'm fond of you, a damn sight fonder than I thought I was, now that I find you slipping away; but if this young fellow is on the square [LAURA *crosses to* WILL, *taking his right hand.*] and he has youth and ability, and you've been on the square with him, why, all right. Your life hasn't had much in it to help you get a diploma from any celestial college, and if you can start out now and be a good girl, have a good husband, and maybe some day good children [LAURA *sighs.*], why, I'm not going to stand in the way. Only I don't want you to make any of those mistakes that you made before.

LAURA. I know, but somehow I feel that this time the real thing has come, and with it the real man. I can't tell you, Will, how much different it is, but everything I felt before seems so sort of earthly—and somehow this love that I have for this man is so different. It's made me want to be truthful and sincere and humble for the first time in my life. The only other thing I ever had that I cared the least bit about, now that I look back, was your friendship. We have been good pals, haven't we?

[*Puts arms about* WILL.

WILL. Yes, it's been a mighty good two years for me. I was always proud to take you around, because I think you one of the prettiest things in New York [LAURA *crosses and girlishly jumps into armchair.*], and that helps some, and you're always jolly, and you never complained. You always spent a lot of money, but it was a pleasure to see you spend it; and then you never offended me. Most women offend men by coming around looking untidy and sort of unkempt, but somehow you always knew the value of your beauty, and you always dressed up. I always thought that maybe some day the fellow would come along, grab you, and make you happy in a nice way, but I thought that he'd have to have a lot of money. You know you've lived a rather extravagant life for five years, Laura. It won't be an easy job to come down to cases and suffer for the little dainty necessities you've been used to.

LAURA. I've thought all about that, and I think I understand.

[*Facing audience; leaning elbows on lap.*

WILL. You know if you were working without anybody's help, Laura, you might have a hard time getting a position. As an actress you're only fair.

LAURA. You needn't remind me of that. That part of my life is my own. [*Crosses up to seat.*] I don't want you to start now and make it harder for me to do the right thing. It isn't fair; it isn't square; and it isn't right. You've got to let me go my own way. [*Crosses to* WILL; *puts right hand on his shoulder.*] I'm sorry to leave you, in a way, but I want you to know that if I go with John it changes the spelling of the word comradeship into love, and mistress into wife. Now please don't talk any more. [*Crosses to post; takes scarf off chair.*

WILL. Just a word. Is it settled?

LAURA. [*Impatiently.*] I said I didn't know. I would know to-day—that's what I'm waiting for. Oh, I don't see why he doesn't come. [WILL *turns up to seat looking over Pass.*

WILL. [*Pointing up the Pass.*] Is that the fellow coming up here?

LAURA. [*Quickly running toward the balustrade of seat, saying as she goes:*] Where? [*Kneels on seat.*

WILL. [*Pointing.*] Up the road there. On that yellow horse.

LAURA. [*Looking.*] Yes, that's John. [*She waves her handkerchief, and putting one hand to her mouth cries:*] Hello!

JOHN. [*Off stage with the effect as if he was on the road winding up toward the house.*] Hello yourself!

LAURA. [*Same effect.*] Hurry up, you're late.

JOHN. [*Same effect, a little louder.*] Better late than never.

LAURA. [*Same effect.*] Hurry up.

JOHN. [*Little louder.*] Not with this horse.

LAURA. [*To* WILL, *with enthusiastic expression.*] Now, Will, does he look like a yellow reporter?

WILL. [*With a sort of sad smile.*] He *is* a good-looking chap.

LAURA. [*Looking down again at* JOHN.] Oh, he's just simply more than that. [*Turns quickly to* WILL.] Where's Mrs. Williams?

WILL. [*Motioning with thumb toward left side of ranch house.*] Inside, I guess, up to her neck in bridge.

LAURA. [*Goes hurriedly over to door.*] Mrs. Williams! Oh, Mrs. Williams!

MRS. WILLIAMS. [*Heard off stage.*] What is it, my dear?

LAURA. Mr. Madison is coming up the path.

MRS. WILLIAMS. [*Off stage.*] That's good.

LAURA. Sha'n't you come and see him?

MRS. WILLIAMS. [*Same.*] Lord, no! I'm six dollars and twenty cents out now, and up against an awful streak of luck.

LAURA. Shall I give him some tea?

MRS. WILLIAMS. [*Same.*] Yes, do, dear; and tell him to cross his fingers when he thinks of me.

In the meantime WILL *has leaned over the balustrade, evidently surveying the young man, who is supposed to be coming up the path, with a great deal of interest. Underneath his stolid, businesslike demeanour of squareness, there is undoubtedly within his heart a very great affection for* LAURA. *He realizes that during her whole career he has been the only one who has influenced her absolutely. Since the time they lived together, he has always dominated, and he has always endeavoured to lead her along a path that meant the better things of a Bohemian existence. His coming all the way from New York to Denver to accompany* LAURA *home was simply another example of his keen interest in the woman, and he suddenly finds that she has drifted away from him in a manner to which he could not in the least object, and that she had been absolutely fair and square in her agreement with him.* WILL *is a man who, while rough and rugged in many ways, possesses many of the finer instincts of refinement, latent though they may be, and his meeting with* JOHN *ought, therefore, to show much significance, because on his impressions of the young man depend the entire justification of his attitude in the play.*

LAURA. [*Turning toward* WILL *and going to him, slipping her hand involuntarily through his arm, and looking eagerly with him over the balustrade in almost girlish enthusiasm.*] Do you like him?

WILL. [*Smiling.*] I don't know him.

LAURA. Well, do you think you'll like him?

WILL. Well, I hope I'll like him.

LAURA. Well, if you hope you'll like him you ought to think you like him. He'll turn the corner of that rock in just a minute and then you can see him. Do you want to see him?

WILL. [*Almost amused at her girlish manner.*] Why, yes—do you?

LAURA. Do I? Why, I haven't seen him since last night! There he is. [*Waves her hand.*] Hello, John!

[*Gets candy-box, throws pieces of candy at* JOHN.

JOHN. [*His voice very close now.*] Hello, girlie! How's everything?

LAURA. Fine! Do hurry.

JOHN. Just make this horse for a minute. Hurry is not in his dictionary.

LAURA. I'm coming down to meet you.

JOHN. All—right.

LAURA. [*Turns quickly to* WILL.] You don't care. You'll wait, won't you?

WILL. Surely.

LAURA *hurriedly exits.* WILL *goes down centre of the stage. After a short interval* LAURA *comes in, more like a sixteen-year-old girl than anything else, pulling* JOHN *after her. He is a tall, finely built type of Western manhood, a frank face, a quick, nervous energy, a mind that works like lightning, a prepossessing smile, and a personality that is wholly captivating. His clothes are a bit dusty from the ride, but are not in the least pretentious, and his leggins are of canvas and spurs of brass, such as are used in the Army. His hat is off, and he is pulled on to the stage, more like a great big boy than a man. His hair is a bit tumbled, and he shows every indication of having had a rather long and hard ride.*

LAURA. Hello, John!

JOHN. Hello, girlie!

Then she suddenly recovers herself and realizes the position she is in. Both men measure each other for a moment in silence, neither flinching the least bit. The smile has faded from JOHN'S *face, and the mouth droops into an expression of firm determination.* LAURA *for a moment loses her ingenuousness. She is the least bit frightened at finally placing the two men face to face, and in a voice that trembles slightly from apprehension:*

LAURA. Oh, I beg your pardon! Mr. Madison, this is Mr. Brockton, a friend of mine from New York. You've often heard me speak of him; he came out here to keep me company when I go home.

JOHN. [*Comes forward, extends a hand, looking* WILL *right in the eye.*] I am very glad to know you, Mr. Brockton.

WILL. Thank you.

JOHN. I've heard a great deal about you and your kindness to Miss Murdock. Anything that you have done for her in a spirit of friendliness I am sure all her friends must deeply appreciate, and I count myself in as one.

WILL. [*In an easy manner that rather disarms the antagonistic attitude of* JOHN.] Then we have a good deal in common, Mr. Madison, for I also count Miss Murdock a friend, and when two friends of a friend have the pleasure of meeting, I dare say that's a pretty good foundation for them to become friends too.

JOHN. Possibly. Whatever my opinion may have been of you, Mr. Brockton, before you arrived, now I have seen you—and I'm a man who forms his conclusions right off the bat—I don't mind telling you that you've agreeably surprised me. That's just a first impression, but they run kind o' strong with me.

WILL. Well, young man, I size up a fellow in pretty short order, and all things being equal, I think you'll do.

LAURA. [*Radiantly.*] Shall I get the tea?

JOHN. Tea!

LAURA. Yes, tea. You know it must be tea—nothing stronger.
[*Crosses to door.*

JOHN. [*Looking at* WILL *rather comically.*] How strong are you for that tea, Mr. Brockton?

WILL. I'll pass; it's your deal, Mr. Madison.

JOHN. Mine! No, deal me out this hand.

LAURA. I don't think you're at all pleasant, but I'll tell you one thing—it's tea this deal or no game.

[*Crosses up stage to seat, picks up magazine, turns pages.*

WILL. No game then [*Crosses to door.*], and I'm going to help Mrs. Williams; maybe she's lost nearly seven dollars by this time, and I'm an awful dub when it comes to bridge. [*Exit.*

LAURA. [*Tossing magazine on to seat, crosses quickly to* JOHN, *throws her arms around his neck in the most loving manner.*] John!

As the Act progresses the shadows cross the Pass, and golden light streams across the lower hills and tops the snow-clad peaks. It becomes darker and darker, the lights fade to beautiful opalescent hues, until, when the curtain falls on the act, with JOHN *and* WILL *on the scene, it is pitch dark, a faint glow coming out of the door. Nothing else can be seen but the glow of the ash on the end of each man's cigar as he puffs it in silent meditation on their conversation.*

JOHN. Well, dear?

LAURA. Are you going to be cross with me?

JOHN. Why?

LAURA. Because he came?

JOHN. Brockton?

LAURA. Yes.

JOHN. You didn't know, did you?

LAURA. Yes, I did.

JOHN. That he was coming?

LAURA. He wired me when he reached Kansas City.

JOHN. Does he know?

LAURA. About us?

JOHN. Yes.

LAURA. I've told him.

JOHN. When?

LAURA. To-day.

JOHN. Here?

LAURA. Yes.

JOHN. With what result?

LAURA. I think it hurt him.

JOHN. Naturally.

LAURA. More than I had any idea it would.

JOHN. I'm sorry. [*Sits in armchair.*

LAURA. He cautioned me to be very careful and to be sure I knew my way.

JOHN. That was right.

LAURA *gets a cushion in each hand off seat; crosses down to left of armchair, throws one cushion on ground, then the other on top of it, and kneels beside his chair. Piano in house playing a Chopin Nocturne.*

LAURA. John.

JOHN. Yes.

LAURA. We've been very happy all summer.

JOHN. Very.

LAURA. [*Rises, sits on left arm of chair, her arm over back.*] And this thing has gradually been growing on us?

JOHN. That's true.

LAURA. I didn't think that, when I came out here to Denver to play in a little stock company, it was going to bring me all this happiness, but it has, hasn't it?

JOHN. Yes.

LAURA. [*Changing her position, sits on his lap, arms around his neck.*] And now the season's over and there is nothing to keep me in Colorado, and I've got to go back to New York to work.

JOHN. I know; I've been awake all night thinking about it.

LAURA. Well?

JOHN. Well?

LAURA. What are we going to do?

JOHN. Why, you've got to go, I suppose.

LAURA. Is it good-bye?

JOHN. For a while, I suppose—it's good-bye.

LAURA. What do you mean by a while?

[LAURA *turns* JOHN'S *face to her, looks at him searchingly.*

JOHN. Until [*Piano plays crescendo, then softens down.*] I get money enough together, and am making enough to support you, then come and take you out of the show business and make you Mrs. Madison.

LAURA *tightens her arm around his neck, her cheek goes close to his own, and all the wealth of affection the woman is capable of at times is shown. She seems more like a dainty little kitten purring close to its master. Her whole thought and idea seem to be centred on the man whom she professes to love.*

LAURA. John, that is what I want above everything else.

JOHN. But, Laura, we must come to some distinct understanding before we start to make our plans. We're not children.

LAURA. No, we're not.

JOHN. Now in the first place [LAURA *rises, crosses to centre.*] we'll discuss you, and in the second place we'll discuss me. We'll keep nothing from each other [LAURA *picks up cushions, places them on seat.*], and we'll start out on this campaign [LAURA *turns back to centre, facing audience.*] of decency and honour, fully understanding its responsibilities, without a chance of a come-back on either side.

LAURA. [*Becoming very serious.*] You mean that we should tell each other all about each other, so, no matter what's ever said about us by other people, *we'll* know it first?

JOHN. [*Rising.*] That's precisely what I'm trying to get at.

LAURA. Well, John, there are so many things I don't want to speak of even to you. It isn't easy for a woman to go back and dig up a lot of ugly memories and try to excuse them. [*Crosses to front of table, picks up magazine, places it on table.*

JOHN. I've known everything from the first; how you came to San Francisco as a kid and got into the show business, and how you went wrong, and then how you married, still a kid, and how your husband didn't treat you exactly right, and then how, in a fit of drunkenness, he came home and shot himself. [LAURA *buries her head in her hands, making exclamations of horror.* JOHN *crosses to her as if sorry for hurting her; touches her on shoulder.*] But that's all past now, and we can forget that. And I know how you were up against it after that, how tough it was for you to get along. Then finally how you've lived, and—and that you and this man Brockton have been—well—never mind. I've known it all for months, and I've watched you. Now, Laura, the habit of life is a hard thing to get away from. You've lived in this way for a long time. If I ask you to be my wife you'll have to give it up; you'll have to go back to New York and struggle on your own hook until I get enough to come for you. I don't know how long that will be, but it *will* be. Do you love me enough to stick out for the right thing?

LAURA *crosses to him, puts her arms around him, kisses him once very affectionately, looks at him very earnestly.*

LAURA. Yes. I think this is my one great chance. I do love you and I want to do just what you said.

JOHN. I think you will. I'm going to make the same promise. Your life, dear girl, has been an angel's compared with mine. I've drank whiskey, played bank, and raised hell ever since the time I could develop a thirst; and ever since I've been able to earn my own living I've abused every natural gift God gave me. The women I've associated with aren't good enough to touch the hem of your skirt, but they liked me, and [JOHN *crosses to armchair, turns up stage, then faces her.*] well—I must have liked them. My life hasn't been exactly loose, it's been all in pieces. I've never done anything dishonest. I've always gone wrong just for the fun of it, until I met you. [*Crosses to her, takes her in his arms.*] Somehow then I began to feel that I was making an awful waste of myself.

LAURA. John!

JOHN. Some lovers place a woman on a pedestal and say, "She never has made a mistake." [*Taking her by each arm he playfully shakes her.*] Well, we don't need any pedestals. I just know you never will make a mistake.

LAURA. [*Kissing him.*] John, I'll never make you take those words back. [*Arms around his neck.*

JOHN. That goes double. You're going to cut out the cabs and cafés, and I'm going to cut out the whiskey and all-night sessions [LAURA *releases him; he backs slightly away.*]; and you're going to be somebody and I'm going to be somebody, and if my hunch is worth the powder to blow it up, we're going to show folks things they never thought were in us. Come on now, kiss me.

She kisses him; tears are in her eyes. He looks into her face with a quaint smile.

JOHN. You're on, ain't you, dear?

LAURA. Yes, I'm on.

JOHN. Then [*Points toward door with his left arm over her shoulder.*] call him.

LAURA. Brockton?

JOHN. Yes, and tell him you go back to New York without any travelling companion this season.

LAURA. Now?

JOHN. Sure.

LAURA. You want to hear me tell him?

JOHN. [*With a smile.*] We're partners, aren't we? I ought to be in on any important transaction like that, but it's just as you say.

LAURA. I think it would be right you should. I'll call him now.

JOHN. All right. [*Crossing to stairway.* LAURA *crosses to door; twilight is becoming very much more pronounced.*

LAURA. [*At door.*] Mr. Brockton! Oh, Mr. Brockton!

WILL. [*Off stage.*] Yes.

LAURA. Can you spare a moment to come out here?

WILL. Just a moment.

LAURA. You must come now.

WILL. All right. [*She waits for him and after a reasonable interval he appears at door.*] Laura, it's a shame to lure me away from that mad speculation in there. I thought I might make my fare back to New York if I played until next summer. What's up?

LAURA. Mr. Madison wants to talk to you, or rather I do, and I want him to listen.

WILL. [*His manner changing to one of cold, stolid calculation.*] Very well. [*Comes down off step of house.*

LAURA. Will.

WILL. Yes?

LAURA. I'm going home day after to-morrow on the Overland Limited.

WILL. I know.

LAURA. It's awfully kind of you to come out here, but under the circumstances I'd rather you'd take an earlier or a later train.

WILL. And may I ask what circumstances you refer to?

LAURA. Mr. Madison and I are going to be married. [*Pause.*] He [WILL *looks inquiringly at* JOHN.] knows of your former friendship for me, and he has the idea that it must end.

WILL. Then the Riverside Drive proposition, with Burgess's show thrown in, is declared off, eh?

LAURA. Yes; everything is absolutely declared off.

WILL. Can't even be friends any more, eh?

JOHN *crosses, and, taking* LAURA'S *arm, passes her over to seat; his back is partly to audience.*

JOHN. You could hardly expect Miss Murdock to be friendly with you under the circumstances. You could hardly expect me to [LAURA *puts scarf across her shoulders.*] sanction any such friendship.

WILL. I think I understand your position, young man, and I perfectly agree with you, that is—if your plans come out successfully.

JOHN. Thank you.

LAURA. Then everything is settled [*Crossing in front of* JOHN *and facing* WILL, *back to audience.*] just the way it ought to be—frankly and aboveboard?

WILL. Why, I guess so. If I was perfectly confident that this new arrangement was going to result happily for you both, I think it would be great, only I'm somewhat doubtful, for when people become serious and then fail, I know how hard those things hit, having *been* hit once myself.

JOHN. So you think we're making a wrong move and there isn't a chance of success!

WILL. No, I don't make any such gloomy prophecy. If you make Laura a good husband, and she makes you a good wife, and together you win out, I'll be mighty glad. As far as I am concerned I shall absolutely forget every thought of Laura's friendship for me.

LAURA. I thought you'd be just that way.

[*Crosses to* WILL, *shakes hands.*

WILL. [*Rising.*] And now I must be off. [*Takes her by both hands and shakes them.*] Good-bye, girlie! Madison, good luck. [*Crosses to* JOHN. *Shakes* JOHN'S *hands; looks into his eyes.*] I think you've got the stuff in you to succeed if your foot don't slip.

JOHN. What do you mean by my foot slipping, Mr. Brockton?

WILL. You want me to tell you?

JOHN. I sure do.

WILL. [*Turns to Laura.*] Laura, run into the house and see if Mrs. Williams has won another quarter. [LAURA *sinks fearfully into chair.*] Madison and I are going to smoke a cigar and have a friendly chat, and when we get through I think we'll both be better off.

LAURA. You are sure that everything will be all right?

WILL. Sure.

LAURA *looks at* JOHN *for assurance, and exits; he nods reassuringly.*

WILL. Have a cigar?

[SERVANT *places lamp on table inside house.*

JOHN. No, I'll smoke my own.

[*Crosses down right; sits in armchair.*

WILL. What is your business? [*Crosses up to seat centre; sits.*

JOHN. What's yours?

WILL. I'm a broker.

JOHN. I'm a reporter, so I've got something on you.

WILL. What kind?

JOHN. General utility, dramatic critic on Sunday nights.

WILL. Pay you well?

JOHN. [*Turns, looking at* WILL.] That's pretty fresh. What's the idea?

WILL. I'm interested. I'm a plain man, Mr. Madison, and I do business in a plain way. Now, if I ask you a few questions and discuss this matter with you in a frank way, don't get it in your head that I'm jealous or sore, but simply I don't want either of you people to make a move that's going to cost you a lot of pain and trouble. If you want me to talk sense to you, all right. If you don't we'll drop it now. What's the answer?

JOHN. I'll take a chance, but before you start I want to tell you that the class of people that you belong to I have no use for—they don't speak my language. You are what they call a manipulator of stocks; that means that you're living on the weaknesses of other people, and it almost means that you get your daily bread, yes, and your cake and your wine, too, from the production of others. You're a "gambler under cover." Show me a man who's dealing bank, and he's free and aboveboard. You can figure the percentage against you, and then, if you buck the tiger and get stung, you do it with your eyes open. With your financiers the game is crooked twelve months of the year, and, from a business point of view, I think you are a crook. Now I guess we understand each other. If you've got anything to say, why, spill it.

WILL *rises, comes down toward* JOHN, *showing anger in his tones.*

WILL. We are not talking business now, but women. How much money do you earn?

[*Crosses to chair left of table; gets it.*

JOHN. Understand I don't think it is any of your damn business, but I'm going through with you on this proposition, just to see how the land lays. But take my tip, you be mighty careful how you speak about the girl if you're not looking for trouble.

WILL. All right, but how much did you say you made?

[*Crosses over to centre of stage, carrying chair; sits.*

JOHN. Thirty dollars a week.

WILL. Do you know how much Laura could make if she just took a job on her own merits?

JOHN. As I don't intend to share in her salary, I never took the trouble to inquire.

WILL. She'd get about forty dollars.

JOHN. That laps me ten.

WILL. How are you going to support her? Her cabs cost more than your salary, and she pays her week's salary for an every-day walking-hat. She's always had a maid; her simplest gown flirts with a hundred-dollar note; her manicurist and her hair-dresser will eat up as much as you pay for your board. She never walks when it's stormy, and every afternoon there's her ride in the park. She dines at the best places in New York, and one meal costs her more than you make in a day. Do you imagine for a moment that she's going to sacrifice these luxuries for any great length of time?

JOHN. I intend to give them to her.

WILL. On thirty dollars a week?

JOHN. I propose to go out and make a lot of money.

WILL. How?

JOHN. I haven't decided yet, but you can bet your sweet life that if I ever try and make up my mind that it's got to be, it's got to be.

WILL. Never have made it, have you?

JOHN. I have never tried.

WILL. Then how do you know you can?

JOHN. Well, I'm honest and energetic. If you can get great wealth the way you go along, I don't see why I can't earn a little.

WILL. There's where you make a mistake. Money-getting doesn't always come with brilliancy. I know a lot of fellows in New York who can paint a great picture, write a good play, and, when it comes to oratory, they've got me lashed to a pole; but they're always in debt. They never get anything for what they do. In other words, young man, they are like a sky-rocket without a stick,—plenty of brilliancy, but no direction, and they blow up and fizzle all over the ground.

JOHN. That's New York. I'm in Colorado, and I guess you know there is a difference.

WILL. I hope you'll make your money, because I tell you frankly that's the only way you can hold this girl. She's full of heroics now, self-sacrifice, and all the things that go to make up the third act of a play, but the minute she comes to darn her stockings, wash out her own handkerchiefs and dry them on the window, and send out for a pail of coffee and a sandwich for lunch, take it from me it will go Blah! [*Rises, crosses to front of table with chair, places it with back to him, braces his back on it, facing* JOHN.] You're in Colorado writing her letters once a day with no checks in them. That may be all right for some girl who hasn't tasted the joy of easy living, full of the good things of life, but one who for ten years has been doing very well in the way these women do is not going to let up for any great length of time. So take my advice if you want to hold her. Get that money quick, and don't be so damned particular how you get it either.

JOHN'S *patience is evidently severely tried. He approaches* WILL, *who remains impassive.*

JOHN. Of course you know you've got the best of me.

WILL. How?

JOHN. We're guests.

WILL. No one's listening.

JOHN. 'Tisn't that. If it was anywhere but here, if there was any way to avoid all the nasty scandal, I'd come a shootin' for you, and you know it.

WILL. Gun-fighter, eh?

JOHN. Perhaps. Let me tell you this. I don't know how you make your money, but I know what you do with it. You buy yourself a small circle of sycophants; you pay them well for feeding your vanity; and then you pose,—pose with a certain frank admission of vice and degradation. And those who aren't quite as brazen as you call it manhood. Manhood? [*Crossing slowly to armchair, sits.*] Why, you don't know what the word means. It's the attitude of a pup and a cur.

WILL. [*Angrily.*] Wait a minute [*Crosses to* JOHN.], young man, or I'll—

JOHN *rises quickly. Both men stand confronting each other for a moment with fists clenched. They are on the very verge of a personal encounter. Both seem to realize that they have gone too far.*

JOHN. You'll what?

WILL. Lose my temper and make a damn fool of myself. That's something I've not done for—let me see—why, it must be nearly twenty years—oh, yes, fully that.

[*He smiles;* JOHN *relaxes and takes one step back.*

JOHN. Possibly it's been about that length of time since you were human, eh?

WILL. Possibly—but you see, Mr. Madison, after all, you're at fault.

JOHN. Yes?

WILL. Yes, the very first thing you did was to lose your temper. Now people who always lose their temper will never make a lot of money, and you admit that that is a great necessity—I mean now—to you.

JOHN. I can't stand for the brutal way you talk. [*Crosses up to seat, picks up newspaper, slams it down angrily on seat, and sits with elbow on balustrade.*

WILL. But you have got to stand it. The truth is never gentle. [*Crosses up and sits left of* JOHN.] Most conditions in life are unpleasant, and, if you want to meet them squarely, you have got to realize the unpleasant point of view. That's the only way you can fight them and win.

JOHN [*Turns to* WILL.] Still, I believe Laura means what she says, in spite of all you say and the disagreeable logic of it. I think she loves me. If she should ever want to go back to the old way of getting along, I think she'd tell me so. So you see, Brockton, all your talk is wasted, and we'll drop the subject.

[*Crosses down and sits in armchair.*

WILL. And if she should ever go back and come to me, I am going to insist that she let you know all about it. It'll be hard enough to lose her, caring for her the way you do, but it would hurt a lot more to be double-crossed.

JOHN. [*Sarcastically.*] That's very kind. Thanks!

WILL. Don't get sore. It's common sense and it goes, does it not?

JOHN. [*Turns to* WILL.] Just what goes?

WILL. If she leaves you first, you are to tell me, and if she comes to me I'll make her let you know just when and why.

JOHN *is leaning on arm, facing* WILL; *his hand shoots out in a gesture of warning to* WILL.

JOHN. Look out!
WILL. I said common sense.
JOHN. All right.
WILL. Agreed? [*A pause.*
JOHN. You're on.

By this time the stage is black and all that can be seen is the glow of the two cigars. Piano in the next room is heard. JOHN *crosses slowly and deliberately to door, looks in, throws cigar away over the terrace, exits into house, closes doors, and, as* WILL *is seated on terrace, puffing cigar, the red coal of which is alone visible, a slow curtain.*

CURTAIN.

ACT II.

SCENE. *Six months have elapsed. The furnished room of* LAURA MURDOCK, *second story back of an ordinary, cheap theatrical lodging-house in the theatre district of New York. The house is evidently of a type of the old-fashioned brown-stone front, with high ceilings, dingy walls, and long, rather insecure windows. The woodwork is depressingly dark. The ceiling is cracked, the paper is old and spotted and in places loose. There is a door leading to the hallway. There is a large old-fashioned wardrobe in which are hung a few old clothes, most of them a good deal worn and shabby, showing that the owner*—LAURA MURDOCK—*has had a rather hard time of it since leaving Colorado in the first act. The doors of this wardrobe must be equipped with springs so they will open outward, and also furnished with wires so they can be controlled from the back. This is absolutely necessary, owing to "business" which is done during the progress of the act. The drawer in the bottom of the wardrobe is open at rise. This is filled with a lot of rumpled tissue-paper and other rubbish. An old pair of shoes is seen at the upper end of the wardrobe on the floor. There is an armchair over which is thrown an ordinary kimono, and on top of the wardrobe are a number of magazines and old books, and an unused parasol wrapped up in tissue paper.*

The dresser, which is upstage, against the wall, is in keeping with the general meanness, and its adornment consists of old post-cards stuck in between the mirror and its frame, with some well-worn veils and ribbons hung on the side. On the dresser is a pin-cushion, a bottle of cheap perfume, purple in colour and nearly empty; a common crockery match-holder, containing matches, which must be practicable; a handkerchief-box, powder-box and puff, rouge-box and rouge paw, hand mirror, small alcohol curling-iron heater, which must also be practicable, as it is used in the "business" of the act; scissors, curling-tongs, hair comb and brush, and a small cheap picture of JOHN MADISON; *a small work-box containing a thimble and thread,—and stuck in the pincushion are a couple of needles, threaded. Directly to the left of the bureau, with the door to the outside closet intervening, is a broken-down washstand, on which is a basin half full of water, a bottle of tooth-powder, tooth brushes and holder, soap and soap-dish, and other cheap toilet articles, and a small drinking-glass. Hung on the corner of the washstand is a soiled towel. Hung on the rack across the top of the washstand one can see a pair of stockings. On the floor in front of the washstand is a pitcher half full of water; also a large waste-water jar of the cheapest type.*

Below the washstand, and with the head against the wall, is a three-quarter old wooden bed, also showing the general decay of the entire room. Tacked on the head of this bed is a large photo of JOHN MADISON, *with a small bow of dainty blue ribbon at the top, covering the tack. Under the photo are arranged half a dozen cheap, artificial violets, in pitiful recognition of the girl's love for her absent sweetheart.*

Under the mattress at the head of the bed is a heavy cardboard box, about thirty inches long, seven inches wide and four inches deep, containing about one hundred and twenty-five letters and eighty telegrams, tied in about eight bundles with dainty ribbon. One bundle must contain all practical letters of several closely written pages each, each letter having been opened. They must be written upon business paper and envelopes, such as are used in newspaper offices and by business men.

Under the pillow at the head of the bed is carelessly thrown a woman's night-dress. On the bed is an old book, open, with face downward, and beside it is an apple which some one has been nibbling. Across the foot of the bed is a soiled quilt, untidily folded. The pillows are hollow in the centre, as if having been used lately. At the foot of the bed is a small table, with soiled and ink-stained cover, upon which are a cheap pitcher, containing some withered carnations, and a desk-pad, with paper, pen, ink, and envelopes scattered around.

Against the wall below the bed is an old mantel-piece and fireplace with iron grate, such as are used in houses of this type. On the mantel-piece are photos of actors and actresses, an old mantel clock in the centre, in front of which is a box of cheap peppermint candy in large pieces, and a plate with two apples upon it; some cheap pieces of bric-à-brac and a little vase containing joss-sticks, such as one might burn to improve the atmosphere of these dingy, damp houses. Below the mantel-piece is a thirty-six inch theatre trunk, with theatre labels on it, in the tray of which are articles of clothing, a small box of thread, and a bundle of eight pawn tickets. Behind the trunk is a large cardboard box. Hanging from the ceiling directly over the table is a single arm gas-jet, from which is hung a turkey wish-bone. On the jet is a little wire arrangement to hold small articles for heating. Beside the table is a chair. Under the bed are a pair of bedroom slippers and a box. Between the bed and the mantel is a small tabourette on which are a book and a candle-stick with the candle half burned. On the floor in front of the door is a slipper,—also another in front of the dresser,—as if they had been thrown carelessly down. On the wardrobe door, on the down-stage side, is tacked another photo of JOHN MADISON.

In an alcove off left is a table on which is a small oil stove, two cups, saucers and plates, a box of matches, tin coffee-box, and a small Japanese teapot. On a projection outside the window is a pint milk bottle, half filled with milk, and an empty benzine bottle, which is labelled. Both are covered with snow.

The backing shows a street snow-covered. In arranging the properties it must be remembered that in the wardrobe is a box of Uneeda biscuits, with one end torn open. There is a door down right, opening inward, leading into the hallway. The window is at back, running from floor nearly to the ceiling. This window does not rise, but opens in the manner of the French or door window.

On the outside of the window covering the same is an iron guard such as is used in New York on the lower back windows. The rods running up and down are about four inches apart. There is a projection outside the window such as would be formed by a storm door in the basement; running the full length of the window and about thirty inches wide, raised about a foot from the floor in front and about nine inches in the back, there is opening inward a door at left back, leading into a small alcove, as has been mentioned before. The door is half glass, the glass part being the upper half, and is ajar when the curtain rises. A projection at fireplace such as would be made for a chimney is in the wall which runs from left centre diagonally to left first entrance.

AT RISE *the stage is empty. After a pause* LAURA *enters, passes the dresser, places umbrella at the right, end of it against wall, crosses to back of armchair, removes gloves, lays them over back of chair, takes off coat and hat, hangs hat on end of wardrobe, and puts coat inside; notices old slipper in front of dresser and one on the extreme right, and with impatience picks them up and puts them in the wardrobe drawer. Then crosses to dresser, gets needle and thread off pincushion, and mends small rip in glove, after which she puts gloves in top drawer of dresser, crosses to extreme end of dresser, and gets handkerchief out of box, takes up bottle containing purple perfume, holds it up so she can see there is only a small quantity left, sprinkles a drop on handkerchief carefully, so as not to use too much, looks at bottle again to see how much is left, places it on dresser; goes to up-stage side of bed, kneels on head of the bed and looks lovingly at photo of* JOHN MADISON, *and finally pulls up the mattress, takes out box of letters, and opens it. She then sits down in Oriental fashion, with her feet under her, selects a bundle of letters, unties the ribbon, and takes out a letter such as has been hereinbefore described, glances it over, puts it down in her lap, and again takes a long look at the picture of* JOHN MADISON. ANNIE *is heard coming upstairs.* LAURA *looks quickly towards the door, puts the letters back in box, and hurriedly places box under mattress, and replaces pillow.* ANNIE *knocks on door.* LAURA *rises and crosses to door.*

LAURA. Come in.

ANNIE, *a chocolate-colored negress, enters. She is slovenly in appearance, but must not in any way denote the "mammy." She is the type one encounters in cheap theatrical lodging-houses. She has a letter in her hand,—also a clean towel folded,—and approaches* LAURA.

LAURA. Hello, Annie.

ANNIE. Heah's yo' mail, Miss Laura.

LAURA. [*Taking letter.*] Thank you!

[*She looks at the address and does not open it.*

ANNIE. One like dat comes every mornin', don't it? Used to all be postmahked Denver. Must 'a' moved. [*Trying to look over* LAURA'S *shoulder;* LAURA *turns and sees her;* ANNIE *looks away.*] Where is dat place called Goldfield, Miss Laura?

LAURA. In Nevada.

ANNIE. In *Nevada?*

LAURA. Yes, Nevada.

ANNIE. [*Draws her jacket closer around her as if chilly.*] Must be mighty smaht to write yuh every day. De pos'man brings it 'leven o'clock mos' always, sometimes twelve, and again sometimes tehn; but it comes every day, don't it?

LAURA. I know.

ANNIE. [*Crosses to right of armchair, brushes it off and makes an effort to read letter, leaning across chair.*] Guess must be from yo' husban', ain't it?

LAURA. No, I haven't any.

ANNIE. [*Crossing to centre triumphantly.*] Dat's what Ah tole Mis' Farley when she was down talkin' about you dis morning. She said if he all was yo' husban' he might do somethin' to help you out. Ah told her Ah didn't think you had any husban'. Den she says you ought to have one, you're so pretty.

LAURA. Oh, Annie!

ANNIE. [*Sees door open; goes and bangs it shut.*] Der ain't a decent door in dis old house. Mis' Farley said yo' might have mos' any man you [*Hangs clean towel on washstand.*] wanted just for de askin', but Ah said yuh [*Takes newspaper and books off bed, and places them on table.*] was too particular about the man yo' 'd want. Den she did a heap o'talking.

LAURA. About what? [*Places letter open on table, looks at hem of skirt, discovers a rip, rises, crosses up to dresser, gets needle, crosses down to trunk; opens and takes thimble out; closes lid of tray, sits on it, and sews skirt during scene.*

ANNIE. [*At bed, fussing around, folds nightgown and places it under pillow.*] Well, you know, Mis' Farley she's been havin' so much trouble wid her roomers. Yestuhday dat young lady on de second flo' front, she lef'. She's goin' wiv some troupe on the road. She owed her room for three weeks and jus' had to leave her trunk. [*Crosses and fusses over table.*] My! how Mis' Farley did scold her. Mis' Farley let on she could have paid dat money if she wanted to, but somehow Ah guess she couldn't—

[*Reads letter on table.*

LAURA. [*Sees her, angrily exclaims.*] Annie!

ANNIE. [*In confusion, brushing off table.*]—for if she could she wouldn't have left her trunk, would she, Miss Laura?

[*Crosses to armchair, and picks up kimono off back.*

LAURA. No, I suppose not. What did Mrs. Farley say about me?

ANNIE. Oh! nothin' much. [*Crosses left and stands.*

LAURA. Well, what?

ANNIE. She kinder say somethin' 'bout yo' being three weeks behind in yo' room rent, and she said she t'ought it was 'bout time yuh handed her somethin', seein' as how yuh must o' had some stylish friends when yuh come here.

LAURA. Who, for instance?

ANNIE. Ah don't know. Mis' Farley said some of 'em might slip yo' enough jest to help yuh out. [*Pause.*] Ain't yo' got nobody to take care of you at all, Miss Laura?

[*Hangs kimono over back of armchair.*

LAURA. No! No one.

ANNIE. Dat's too bad.

LAURA. Why?

ANNIE. [*Crossing again.*] Mis' Farley says yuh wouldn't have no trouble at all gettin' any man to take care of yuh if yuh wanted to.

LAURA. [*With sorrowful shudder.*] Please [*Doors of wardrobe open very slowly.*] don't, Annie.

ANNIE. Dere's a gemman [*Playing with corner of tablecloth.*] dat calls on one of de ladies from the Hippodrome, in de big front room downstairs. He's mighty nice, and he's been askin' 'bout you.

LAURA. [*Exasperated.*] Oh, shut up!

ANNIE. [*Sees doors of wardrobe have swung open; she crosses, slams them shut, turns to* LAURA.] Mis' Farley says—[*Doors have *swung open again; they hit her in the back. She turns and bangs them to with all her strength.*] Damn dat door! [*Crosses to washstand, grabs basin which is half full of water, empties same into waste-jar, puts basin on washstand, and wipes it out with soiled towel.*] Mis' Farley says if she don't get someone in the house dat has reg'lar money soon, she'll have to shut up and go to the po'house.

LAURA. I'm sorry; I'll try again to-day. [*Rises, crosses up to mantel, gets desk-pad, &c., crosses to right of table, sits.*

ANNIE. [*Crosses to back of bed, wiping basin with towel.*] Ain't yo' got any job at all?

LAURA. No.

ANNIE. When yuh come here yuh had lots of money and yo' was mighty good to me. You know Mr. Weston?

LAURA. Jim Weston?

ANNIE. Yassum, Mr. Weston what goes ahead o' shows and lives on the top floor back; he says nobody's got jobs now. Dey're so many actors and actoresses out o' work. Mis' Farley says she don't know how she's goin' to live. She said you'd been mighty nice up until three weeks ago, but yuh ain't got much left, have you, Miss Laura?

LAURA. [*Rising and going to the bureau.*] No. It's all gone.

ANNIE. Mah sakes! All dem rings and things? You ain't done sold them? [*Sinks on bed.*

LAURA. They're pawned. What did Mrs. Farley say she was going to do?

ANNIE. Guess maybe Ah'd better not tell.

[*Crosses to door hurriedly, carrying soiled towel.*

LAURA. Please do. [*Crosses to chair, left side.*

ANNIE. Yuh been so good to me, Miss Laura. Never was nobody in dis house what give me so much, and Ah ain't been gettin' much lately. And when Mis' Farley said yuh must either pay yo' rent or she would ask yuh for your room, Ah jest set right down on de back kitchen stairs and cried. Besides, Mis' Farley don't like me very well since you've ben havin' yo' breakfasts and dinners brought up here.

LAURA. Why not? [*Takes kimono off chair-back, crosses up to dresser, puts kimono in drawer, takes out purse.*

ANNIE. She has a rule in dis house dat nobody can use huh chiny or fo'ks or spoons who ain't boa'ding heah, and de odder day when yuh asked me to bring up a knife and fo'k she ketched me coming upstairs, and she says, "Where yuh goin' wid all dose things, Annie?" Ah said, "Ah'm just goin' up to Miss Laura's room with dat knife and fo'k." Ah said, "Ah'm goin' up for nothin' at all, Mis' Farley, she jest wants to look at them, Ah guess." She said, "She wants to eat huh dinner wid 'em, Ah guess." Ah got real mad, and Ah told her if she'd give me mah pay Ah'd brush right out o'here; dat's what Ah'd do, Ah'd brush right out o'here. [*Violently shaking out towel.*

LAURA. I'm sorry, Annie, if I've caused you any trouble. Never mind, I'll be able to pay the rent to-morrow or next day anyway. [*She fumbles in purse, takes out a quarter, and turns to* ANNIE.] Here!

ANNIE. No, ma'm, Ah don' want dat.

[*Making a show of reluctance.*

LAURA. Please take it.

ANNIE. No, ma'am, Ah don' want it. You need dat. Dat's breakfast money for yuh, Miss Laura.

LAURA. Please take it, Annie. I might just as well get rid of this as anything else.

ANNIE. [*Takes it rather reluctantly.*] Yuh always was so good, Miss Laura. Sho' yuh don' want dis?

LAURA. Sure.

ANNIE. Sho' yo' goin' to get planty mo'?

LAURA. Sure.

MRS. FARLEY'S VOICE. [*Downstairs.*] Annie! Annie!

ANNIE. [*Going to door, opens it.*] Dat's Mis' Farley. [*To* MRS. FARLEY.] Yassum, Mis' Farley.

SAME VOICE. Is Miss Murdock up there?

ANNIE. Yassum, Mis' Farley, yassum!

MRS. FARLEY. Anything doin'?

ANNIE. Huh?

MRS. FARLEY. Anything doin'?

ANNIE. [*At door.*] Ah—Ah—hain't asked, Missy Farley.

MRS. FARLEY. Then do it.

LAURA. [*Coming to the rescue at the door. To* ANNIE.] I'll answer her. [*Out of door to* MRS. FARLEY.] What is it, Mrs. Farley?

MRS. FARLEY. [*Her voice softened.*] Did ye have any luck this morning, dearie?

LAURA. No; but I promise you faithfully to help you out this afternoon or to-morrow.

MRS. FARLEY. Sure? Are you certain?

LAURA. Absolutely.

MRS. FARLEY. Well, I must say these people expect me to keep— [*Door closed.*

LAURA *quietly closes the door, and* MRS. FARLEY'S *rather strident voice is heard indistinctly.* LAURA *sighs and walks toward table; sits.* ANNIE *looks after her, and then slowly opens the door.*

ANNIE. Yo' sho' dere ain't nothin' I can do fo' yuh, Miss Laura?

LAURA. Nothing.

ANNIE *exits.* LAURA *sits down and looks at letter, opening it. It consists of several pages closely written. She reads some of them hurriedly, skims through the rest, and then turns to the last page without reading; glances at it; lays it on table; rises.*

LAURA. Hope, just nothing but hope.

She crosses to bed, falls face down upon it, burying her face in her hands. Her despondency is palpable. As she lies there a hurdy-gurdy in the street starts to play a popular air. This arouses her and she rises, crosses to wardrobe, takes out box of crackers, opens window, gets bottle of milk off sill outside, places them on table, gets glass off washstand, at the same time humming the tune of the hurdy-gurdy, when a knock comes; she crosses quickly to dresser; powders her nose. The knock is timidly repeated.

LAURA. [*Without turning, and in a rather tired tone of voice.*] Come in.

JIM WESTON, *a rather shabby theatrical advance-agent of the old school, enters timidly, halting at the door and holding the knob in his hand. He is a man of about forty years old, dressed in an ordinary manner, of medium height, and in fact has the appearance of a once prosperous clerk who has been in hard luck. His relations with* LAURA *are those of pure friendship. They both live in the same lodging-place, and, both having been out of employment, they have naturally become acquainted.*

JIM. Can I come in?

LAURA. [*Without turning.*] Hello, Jim Weston. [*He closes door and enters.*] Any luck?

JIM. Lots of it.

LAURA. That's good. Tell me,

JIM. It's bad luck. Guess you don't want to hear.

LAURA. I'm sorry. Where have you been?

JIM. I kind o' felt around up at Burgess's office. I thought I might get a job there, but he put me off until to-morrow. Somehow those fellows always do business to-morrow.

[*Hurdy-gurdy dies out.*

LAURA. Yes, and there's always to-day to look after.

JIM. I'm ready to give up. I've tramped Broadway for nine weeks until every piece of flagstone gives me the laugh when it sees my feet coming. Got a letter from the missis this morning. The kids got to have some clothes, there's measles in the town, and mumps in the next village. I've just got to raise some money or get some work, or the first thing you'll know I'll be hanging around Central Park on a dark night with a club.

LAURA. I know just how you feel. Sit down, Jim. [JIM *crosses and sits in chair right of table.*] It's pretty tough for me [*Offers* JIM *glass of milk; he refuses; takes crackers.*], but it must be a whole lot worse for you with a wife and kids.

JIM. Oh, if a man's alone he can generally get along—turn his hand to anything; but a woman—

LAURA. Worse, you think?

JIM. I was just thinking about you and what Burgess said?

LAURA. What was that?

[*Crosses to bed; sits on up-stage side, sipping milk.*

JIM. You know Burgess and I used to be in the circus business together. He took care of the grafters when I was boss canvas man. I never could see any good in shaking down the rubes for all the money they had and then taking part of it. He used to run the privilege car, you know.

LAURA. Privilege car?

JIM. Had charge of all the pickpockets,—dips we called 'em—sure-thing gamblers, and the like. Made him rich. I kept sort o' on the level and I'm broke. Guess it don't pay to be honest—

LAURA. [*Turns to him and in a significant voice:*] You don't really think that?

JIM. No, maybe not. Ever since I married the missis and the first kid come, we figured the only good money was the kind folks worked for and earned; but when you can't get hold of that, it's tough.

LAURA. I know.

JIM. Burgess don't seem to be losing sleep over the tricks he's turned. He's happy and prosperous, but I guess he ain't any better now than he was then.

LAURA. Maybe not. I've been trying to get an engagement from him. There are half a dozen parts in his new attractions that I could do, but he has never absolutely said "no," but yet somehow he's never said "yes."

JIM. He spoke about you.

LAURA. In what way? [*Rising, stands behind* JIM's *chair.*

JIM. I gave him my address and he seen it was yours, too. Asked if I lived in the same place.

LAURA. Was that all?

JIM. Wanted to know how you was getting on. I let him know you needed work, but I didn't tip my hand you was flat broke. He said something about you being a damned fool.

LAURA. [*Suddenly and interested.*] How? [*She crosses.*

JIM. Well, Johnny Ensworth—you know he used to do the fights on the *Evening Journal;* now he's press-agent for Burgess; nice fellow and way on the inside—he told me where you were in wrong.

LAURA. What have I done? [*Sits in armchair.*

JIM. Burgess don't put up the money for any of them musical comedies—he just trails. Of course he's got a lot of influence, and he's always Johnny-on-the-Spot to turn any dirty trick that they want. There are four or five rich men in town who are there with the bank-roll, providing he engages women who ain't so very particular about the location of their residence, and who don't hear a curfew ring at 11:30 every night.

LAURA. And he thinks I am too particular?

JIM. That's what was slipped me. Seems that one of the richest men that is in on Mr. Burgess's address-book is a fellow named Brockton from downtown some place. He's got more money than the Shoe and Leather National Bank. He likes to play show business.

LAURA. [*Rises quickly.*] Oh! [*Crosses to wardrobe, gets hat; crosses to dresser, gets scissors with intention of curling feathers.*

JIM. I thought you knew him. I thought it was just as well to tell you where he and Burgess stand. They're pals.

LAURA. [*Coming over to* JIM *and with emphasis crosses to down-stage side of bed; puts hat and scissors on bed.*] I don't want you to talk about him or any of them. I just want you to know that

I'm trying to do everything in my power to go through this season without any more trouble. I've pawned everything I've got; I've cut every friend I knew. But where am I going to end? That's what I want to know—where am I going to end? [*To bed and sits.*] Every place I look for a position something interferes. It's almost as if I were blacklisted. I know I could get jobs all right if I wanted to pay the price, but I won't. I just want to tell you, I won't. No!

[*Rises, crosses to mantel, rests elbow.*

JIM. That's the way to talk. [*Rises.*] I don't know you very well, but I've watched you close. I'm just a common, ordinary showman who never had much money, and I'm going out o' date. I've spent most of my time with nigger-minstrel shows and circuses, but I've been on the square. That's why I'm broke. [*Rather sadly.*] Once I thought the missis would have to go back and do her acrobatic act, but she couldn't do that, she's grown so damn fat. [*Crosses to* LAURA.] Just you don't mind. It'll all come out right.

LAURA. It's an awful tough game, isn't it?

JIM. [*During this speech* LAURA *gets cup, pours milk back into bottle, closes biscuit-box, puts milk on shed outside, and biscuits into wardrobe, cup in alcove.*] It's hell forty ways from the Jack. It's tough for me, but for a pretty woman with a lot o' rich fools jumping out o' their automobiles and hanging around stage doors, it must be something awful. I ain't blaming the women. They say "self-preservation is the first law of nature," and I guess that's right; but sometimes when the show is over and I see them fellows with their hair plastered back, smoking cigarettes in a [LAURA *crosses to chair right of table and leans over back.*] holder long enough to reach from here to Harlem, and a bankroll that would bust my pocket and turn my head, I feel as if I'd like to get a gun and go a-shooting around this old town.

LAURA. Jim!

JIM. Yes, I do—you bet.

LAURA. That wouldn't pay, would it?

JIM. No, they're not worth the job of sitting on that throne in Sing Sing, and I'm too poor to go to Matteawan. But all them fellows under nineteen and over fifty-nine ain't much use to themselves or anyone else.

LAURA. [*Rather meditatively.*] Perhaps all of them are not so bad.

JIM. [*Sits on bed.*] Yes, they are,—angels and all. Last season I had one of them shows where a rich fellow backed it on account of a girl. We lost money and he lost his girl; then we got stuck in Texas. I telegraphed: "Must have a thousand, or can't move." He just answered: "Don't move." We didn't.

LAURA. But that was business.

JIM. Bad business. It took a year for some of them folks to get back to Broadway. Some of the girls never did, and I guess never will.

LAURA. Maybe they're better off, Jim. [*Sits right of table.*

JIM. Couldn't be worse. They're still in Texas. [*To himself.*] Wish I knew how to do something else, being a plumber or a walking delegate; they always have jobs.

LAURA. Well, I wish I could do something else too, but I can't, and we've got to make the best of it.

JIM. I guess so. I'll see you this evening. I hope you'll have good news by that time. [*Starts to exit, about to open door; then retreats a step, with hand on door-knob, crosses and in a voice meant to be kindly*:] If you'd like to go to the theatre to-night, and take some other woman in the house, maybe I can get a couple of tickets for some of the shows. I know a lot of fellows who are working.

LAURA. No, thanks. I haven't anything to wear to the theatre, and I don't—

JIM. [*With a smile crosses to* LAURA, *puts arm around her.*] Now you just cheer up! Something's sure to turn up. It always has for me, and I'm a lot older than you, both in years and in this business. There's always a break in hard luck sometime—that's sure.

LAURA. [*Smiling through her tears.*] I hope so. But things are looking pretty hopeless now, aren't they?

JIM. I'll go down and give Mrs. F. a line o' talk and try to square you for a couple of days more anyway. But I guess she's laying pretty close to the cushion herself, poor woman.

LAURA. Annie says a lot of people owe her.

JIM. Well, you can't pay what you haven't got. And even if money was growing on trees, it's winter now. [JIM *goes towards door.*] I'm off. Maybe to-day is lucky day. So long!

LAURA. Good-bye.

JIM. Keep your nerve. [*Exit*

LAURA. I will. [*She sits for a moment in deep thought, picks up the letter received, as if to read it, and then throws it down in anger. She buries her head in hands.*] I can't stand it—I just simply can't stand it.

MRS. FARLEY'S VOICE. [*Off stage.*] Miss Murdock—Miss Murdock.

LAURA. [*Brushing away tears, rises, goes to door, and opens it.*] What is it?

SAME VOICE. There's a lady down here to see you.

ELFIE'S VOICE. [*Off stage.*] Hello, dearie, can I come up?

LAURA. Is that you, Elfie?

ELFIE. Yes; shall I come up?

LAURA. Why, certainly.

She waits at the door for a moment, and ELFIE ST. CLAIR *appears. She is gorgeously gowned in the rather extreme style affected by the usual New York woman who is cared for by a gentleman of wealth and who has not gone through the formality of matrimonial alliance. Her conduct is always exaggerated and her attitude vigorous. Her gown is of the latest design, and in every detail of dress she shows evidence of most extravagant expenditure. She carries a hand-bag of gold, upon which are attached such trifles as a gold cigarette-case, a gold powder-box, pencils, and the like.* ELFIE *throws her arms around* LAURA, *and both exchange kisses.*

ELFIE. Laura, you old dear [*Crossing to table.*], I've just found out where you've been hiding, and came around to see you.

LAURA. [*Who is much brightened by* ELFIE'S *appearance.*] Elfie, you're looking bully. How are you, dear?

ELFIE. Fine.

LAURA. Come in and sit down. I haven't much to offer, but—

ELFIE. Oh, never mind. It's such a grand day outside, and I've come around in my car to take you out. [*Sits right of table.*] You know I've got a new one, and it can go some.

LAURA. [*Sits on arm of chair.*] I am sorry, but I can't go out this afternoon, Elfie.

ELFIE. What's the matter?

LAURA. You see I'm staying home a good deal nowadays. I haven't been feeling very well and I don't go out much.

ELFIE. I should think not. I haven't seen you in Rector's or Martin's since you come back from Denver. Got a glimpse of you one day trailing up Broadway, but couldn't get to you—you dived into some office or other. [*For the first time she surveys the room, rises, looks around critically, crossing to mantel.*] Gee! Whatever made you come into a dump like this? It's the limit.

LAURA. [*Crossing and standing back of the table.*] Oh, I know it isn't pleasant, but it's my home, and after all—a home's a home.

ELFIE. Looks more like a prison. [*Takes candy from mantel; spits it out on floor.*] Makes me think of the old days of Child's sinkers and a hall bedroom.

LAURA. It's comfortable. [*Leaning hands on table.*

ELFIE. Not! [*Sits on bed, trying bed with comedy effect.* Say, is this here for an effect, or do you sleep on it?

LAURA. I sleep on it.

ELFIE. No wonder you look tired. Say, listen, dearie. What else is the matter with you anyway?

LAURA. Nothing.

ELFIE. Yes, there is. What happened between you and Brockton? [*Notices faded flowers in vase on table; takes them out, tosses them into fireplace, replaces them with gardenias which she wears.*] He's not broke, because I saw him the other day.

LAURA. Where?

ELFIE. In the park. Asked me out to luncheon, but I couldn't go. You know, dearie, I've got to be so careful. Jerry's so awful jealous—the old fool.

LAURA. Do you see much of Jerry nowadays, Elfie?

ELFIE. Not any more than I can help and be nice. He gets on my nerves. Of course, I've heard about your quitting Brockton.

LAURA. Then why do you ask?

[*Crosses around chair right of table; stands.*

ELFIE. Just wanted to hear from your own dear lips what the trouble was. Now tell me all about it. Can I smoke here?

[*Takes cigarette-case up, opens it, selecting cigarette.*

LAURA. Surely. [*Gets matches off bureau, puts them on table.*

ELFIE. Have one? [*Offers case.*

LAURA. No, thank you.

[*Sits in chair right of table, facing* ELFIE.

ELFIE. H'm-m, h'm-m, hah! [*Lights cigarette.*] Now go ahead. Tell me all the scandal. I'm just crazy to know.

LAURA. There's nothing to tell. I haven't been able to find work, that is all, and I'm short of money. You can't live in hotels, you know, with cabs and all that sort of thing, when you're not working.

ELFIE. Yes, you can. I haven't worked in a year.

LAURA. But you don't understand, dear. I— I— Well, you know I— well, you know—I can't say what I want.

ELFIE. Oh, yes, you can. You can say anything to me—everybody else does. We've been pals. I know you got along a little faster in the business than I did. The chorus was my limit, and you went into the legitimate thing. But we got our living just the same way. I didn't suppose there was any secret between you and me about that.

LAURA. I know there wasn't then, Elfie, but I tell you I'm different now. I don't want to do that sort of thing, and I've been very unlucky. This has been a terribly hard season for me. I simply haven't been able to get an engagement.

ELFIE. Well, you can't get on this way. Won't [*Pauses, knocking ashes off cigarette to cover hesitation.*] Brockton help you out?

LAURA. What's the use of talking to you [*Rises and crosses to fireplace.*], Elfie; you don't understand.

ELFIE. [*Puffing deliberately on cigarette and crossing her legs in almost a masculine attitude.*] No? Why don't I understand?

LAURA. Because you can't; you've never felt as I have.

ELFIE. How do you know?

LAURA. [*Turning impatiently.*] Oh, what's the use of explaining?

ELFIE. You know, Laura, I'm not much on giving advice, but you make me sick. I thought you'd grown wise. A young girl just butting into this business might possibly make a fool of herself, but you ought to be on to the game and make the best of it.

LAURA. [*Going over to her angrily.*] If you came up here, Elfie, to talk that sort of stuff to me, please don't. I was West this summer. I met someone, a real man, who did me a whole lot of good,—a man who opened my eyes to a different way of going along—a man who—Oh, well, what's the use? You don't know—you don't know. [*Sits on bed.*

ELFIE. [*Throws cigarette into fireplace.*] I don't know, don't I? I don't know, I suppose, that when I came to this town from up state,—a little burg named Oswego,—and joined a chorus, that I didn't fall in love with just such a man. I suppose I don't know that then I was the best-looking girl in New York, and everybody talked about me? I suppose I don't know that there were men, all ages and with all kinds of money, ready to give me anything for the mere privilege of taking me out to supper? And I didn't do it, did I? For three years I stuck by this good man who was to lead me in a good way toward a good life. And all the time I was getting older, never quite so pretty one day as I had been the day before. I never knew then what it was to be tinkered with by hair-dressers and manicures or a hundred and one of those other people who make you look good. I didn't have to have them then. [*Rises, crosses to right of table, facing* LAURA.] Well, you know, Laura, what happened.

LAURA. Wasn't it partly your fault, Elfie?

ELFIE. [*Speaking across table angrily.*] Was it my fault that time made me older and I took on a lot of flesh? Was it my fault that the work and the life took out the colour, and left the make-up? Was it my fault that other pretty young girls came along, just as I'd come, and were chased after, just as I was? Was it my fault the cabs weren't waiting any more and people didn't talk about how pretty I was? And was it my fault when he finally had me alone, and just because no one else wanted me, he got tired and threw me flat—cold flat [*Brings hand down on toble.*]—and I'd been on the dead level with him! [*With almost a sob, crosses up to bureau, powders nose, comes down back of table.*] It almost broke my heart. Then I made up my mind to get even and get all I could out of the game. Jerry came along. He was a has-been and I was on the road to be. He wanted to be good to me, and I let him. That's all.

LAURA. Still, I don't see how you can live that way.

[*Lies on bed.*

ELFIE. Well, you did, and you didn't kick.

LAURA. Yes, but things are different with me now. You'd be the same way if you were in my place.

ELFIE. No. I've had all the romance I want, and I'll stake you to all your love affairs. [*Crosses back of bed, touches picture over bed.*] I am out to gather in as much coin as I can in my own way, so when the old rainy day comes along I'll have a little change to buy myself an umbrella.

LAURA. [*Rising and angrily crossing to armchair.*] What did you come here for? Why can't you leave me alone when I'm trying to get along?

Elfie. Because I want to help you.

Laura. [*During speech crosses to up-stage side of bed, angrily tosses quilt to floor and sits on bed in tears.*] You can't help me. I'm all right—I tell you I am. What do you care anyway?

Elfie. [*Sits on bed, crosses down stage to lower left side of bed, sits facing* Laura.] But I do care. I know how you feel with an old cat for a landlady and living up here on a side street with a lot of cheap burlesque people. Why, the room's cold [Laura *rises, crosses to window.*], and there's no hot water, and you're beginning to look shabby. You haven't got a job—chances are you won't have one. What does [*Indicating picture on bed with thumb.*] this fellow out there do for you? Send you long letters of condolences? That's what I used to get. When I wanted to buy a new pair of shoes or a silk petticoat, he told me how much he loved me; so I had the other ones re-soled and turned the old petticoat. And look at you, you're beginning to show it. [*She surveys her carefully.*] I do believe there are lines coming in your face [Laura *crosses to dresser quickly, picks up hand mirror, and looks at herself.*], and you hide in the house because you've nothing new to wear.

Laura. [*Puts down mirror, crossing down to back of bed.*] But I've got what you haven't got. I may have to hide my clothes, but I don't have to hide my face. And you with that man—he's old enough to be your father—a toddling dote hanging on your apron-strings. I don't see how you dare show your face to a decent woman.

Elfie. [*Rises.*] You don't!—but you did once and I never caught you hanging your head. You say he's old. I know he's old, but he's good to me. He's making what's left of my life pleasant. You think I like him. I don't,—sometimes I hate him,—but he understands; and you can bet your life his check is in my mail every Saturday night or there's a new lock on the door Sunday morning. [*Crossing to fireplace.*

Laura. How can you say such things to me?

Elfie. [*Crosses to left end of table.*] Because I want you to be square with yourself. You've lost all that precious virtue women gab about. When you've got the name, I say get the game.

Laura. You can go now, Elfie, and don't come back.

Elfie. [*Gathering up muff, &c.*] All right, if that's the way you want it to be, I'm sorry. [*A knock on the door.*

Laura. [*Controlling herself after a moment's hesitation.*] Come in

ANNIE *enters with a note, crosses, and hands it to* LAURA.

ANNIE. Mis' Farley sent dis, Miss Laura.

[LAURA *takes the note and reads it. She is palpably annoyed.*

LAURA. There's no answer.

ANNIE. She tol' me not to leave until Ah got an answah.

LAURA. You must ask her to wait.

ANNIE. She wants an answah.

LAURA. Tell her I'll be right down—that it will be all right.

ANNIE. But, Miss Laura, she tol' me to get an answah.

[*Exit reluctantly.*

LAURA. [*Half to herself and half to* ELFIE.] She's taking advantage of your being here. [*Standing near door.*

ELFIE. How?

LAURA. She wants money—three weeks' room-rent. I presume she thought you'd give it to me.

ELFIE. Huh! [*Moves to left.*

LAURA. [*Crossing to table.*] Elfie, I've been a little cross; I didn't mean it.

ELFIE. Well?

LAURA. Could—could you lend me thirty-five dollars until I get to work?

ELFIE. Me?

LAURA. Yes.

ELFIE. Lend *you* thirty-five dollars?

LAURA. Yes; you've got plenty of money to spare.

ELFIE. Well, you certainly have got a nerve.

LAURA. You might give it to me. I haven't a dollar in the world, and you pretend to be such a friend to me!

ELFIE. [*Turning and angrily speaking across table.*] So that's the kind of woman you are, eh? A moment ago you were going to kick me out of the place because I wasn't decent enough to associate with you. You know how I live. You know how I get my money—the same way you got most of yours. And now that you've got this spasm of goodness I'm not fit to be in your room; but you'll take my money to pay your debts. You'll let me go out and do this sort of thing for your benefit, while you try to play the grand lady. I've got your number now, Laura. Where in hell is your virtue anyway? You can go to the devil—rich, poor, or any other way. I'm off!

ELFIE *rushes toward door; for a moment* LAURA *stands speechless, then bursts into hysterics.*

LAURA. Elfie! Elfie! Don't go now! Don't leave me now! [ELFIE *hesitates with hand on door-knob.*] I can't stand it. I can't be alone. Don't go, please; don't go.

LAURA *falls into* ELFIE'S *arms, sobbing. In a moment* ELFIE'S *whole demeanour changes and she melts into the tenderest womanly sympathy, trying her best to express herself in her crude way.*

ELFIE. There, old girl, don't cry, don't cry. You just sit down here and let me put my arms around you. [ELFIE *leads* LAURA *over to armchair, places muff, &c., in chair, and sits* LAURA *down in chair.* ELFIE *sits on right arm of chair with her left arm behind* LAURA; *hugs* LAURA *to her.* LAURA *in tears and sobbing during scene.*] I'm awful sorry—on the level, I am. I shouldn't have said it. I know that. But I've got feelings too, even if folks don't give me credit for it.

LAURA. I know, Elfie. I've gone through about all I can stand.

ELFIE. Well, I should say you have—and more than I would. Anyway a good cry never hurts any woman. I have one myself, sometimes—under cover.

LAURA. [*More seriously, recovering herself.*] Perhaps what you said was true.

ELFIE. We won't talk about it.

[*Wiping* LAURA'S *eyes and kissing her.*

LAURA. [*With persistence.*] But perhaps it was true, and, Elfie—

ELFIE. Yes.

LAURA. I think I've stood this just as long as I can. Every day is a living horror.

ELFIE. [*Looking around room.*] It's the limit.

LAURA. I've got to have money to pay the rent. I've pawned everything I have, except the clothes on my back.

ELFIE. I'll give you all the money you need, dearie. Great heavens, don't worry about that. Don't you care if I got sore and—and lost my head.

LAURA. No; I can't let you do that. [*Rises; crosses to table.*] You may have been mad,—awfully mad,—but what you said was the truth. I can't take your money. [*Sits right of table.*

ELFIE. Oh, forget that. [*Rises, crosses to centre.*

LAURA. Maybe—maybe if he knew all about it—the suffering—he wouldn't blame me.

ELFIE. Who—the good man who wanted to lead you to the good life without even a bread-basket for an advance-agent? Huh!

LAURA. Still he doesn't know how desperately poor I am.

ELFIE. He knows you're out of work, don't he?

LAURA. [*Turning to* ELFIE.] Not exactly. I've let him think that I'm getting along all right.

ELFIE. Then you're a chump. Hasn't he sent you anything?

LAURA. He hasn't anything to send.

ELFIE. Well, what does he think you're going to live on?—asphalt croquettes with conversation sauce?

LAURA. I don't know—I don't know. [*Sobbing.*

ELFIE. [*Crosses to* LAURA, *puts arms around her.*] Don't be foolish, dearie. You know there is somebody waiting for you—somebody who'll be good to you and get you out of this mess.

LAURA. You mean Will Brockton? [*Looking up.*

ELFIE. Yes.

LAURA. Do you know where he is?

ELFIE. Yes.

LAURA. Well?

ELFIE. You won't get sore again if I tell you, will you?

LAURA. No—why? [*Rises.*

ELFIE. He's downstairs—waiting in the car. I promised to tell him what you said.

LAURA. Then it was all planned, and—and—

ELFIE. Now, dearie, I knew you were up against it, and I wanted to bring you two together. He's got half of the Burgess shows, and if you'll only see him everything will be fixed.

LAURA. When does he want to see me?

ELFIE. Now.

LAURA. Here?

ELFIE. Yes. Shall I tell him to come up?

LAURA. [*After a long pause, crossing around to bed, down-stage side.*] Yes.

ELFIE. [*Suddenly becomes animated.*] Now you're a sensible dear. I'll bet he's half frozen down there. [*Goes to door.*] I'll send him up. Look at you, Laura, you're a sight. [*Crosses to* LAURA, *takes her by hand, leads her up to washstand, takes towel and wipes* LAURA'*s eyes.*] It'll never do to have him see you looking like this; come over here and let me fix your eyes. Now, Laura, I want you to promise me you won't do any more crying. [*Leads* LAURA *over to dresser, takes powder-puff and powders* LAURA'S *face.*] Come over here and let me powder your nose. Now when he comes up you tell him he has got to blow us all off to a dinner to-night at Martin's, seven-thirty. Let me look at you. Now you're all right. [*After daubing* LAURA'S *face with the rouge paw,* ELFIE *takes* LAURA'S *face in her hands and kisses her.*] Make it strong now, seven-thirty, don't forget. I'll be there. [*Crosses to armchair, gathers up muff, &c.*] So long.

[*Exit.*

After ELFIE'S *exit* LAURA *crosses slowly to wardrobe, pulls off picture of* JOHN; *crosses to dresser, takes picture of* JOHN *from there; carries both pictures over to bed; kneels on bed, pulls down picture at head of bed; places all three pictures under pillow.* WILL *is heard coming upstairs, and knocks.*

LAURA. Come in.

WILL *enters. His dress is that of a man of business, the time being about February. He is well groomed and brings with him the impression of easy luxury.*

WILL. [*As he enters.*] Hello, Laura.

There is an obvious embarrassment on the part of each of them. She rises, goes to him and extends her hand.

LAURA. I'm—I'm glad to see you, Will.

WILL. Thank you.

LAURA. Won't you sit down?

WILL. [*Regaining his ease of manner.*] Thank you again.

[*Puts hat and cane at end of wardrobe; removes overcoat and places it on back of armchair; sits in armchair.*

LAURA. [*Sits right of table.*] It's rather cold out, isn't it?

WILL. Just a bit sharp.

LAURA. You came with Elfie in the car?

WILL. She picked me up at Martin's; we lunched there.

LAURA. By appointment?

WILL. I'd asked her.

LAURA. Well?

WILL. Well, Laura.

LAURA. She told you?

WILL. Not a great deal. What do you want to tell me?

LAURA. [*Very simply, and avoiding his glance.*] Will, I'm ready to come back.

WILL. [*With an effort concealing his sense of triumph and satisfaction. Rises, crosses to* LAURA.] I'm mighty glad of that, Laura. I've missed you like the very devil.

LAURA. Do we—do we have to talk it over much?

[*Crosses to left of table in front of bed.*

WILL. Not at all unless you want to. I understand—in fact, I always have.

LAURA. [*Wearily.*] Yes, I guess you always did. I didn't.

[*Crosses and sits right of table.*

WILL. It will be just the same as it was before, you know.

LAURA. Yes.

WILL. I didn't think it was possible for me to miss anyone the way I have you. I've been lonely.

LAURA. That's nice in you to say that.

WILL. You'll have to move out of here right away. [*Crossing to back of table, surveying room.*] This place is enough to give one the colly-wabbles. If you'll be ready to-morrow I'll send my man over to help you take care of the luggage.

LAURA. To-morrow will be all right, thank you.

WILL. And you'll need some money in the meantime. I'll leave this here.

[*He takes a roll of bills and places it on the bureau.*

LAURA. You seem to have come prepared. Did Elfie and you plan this all out?

WILL. Not planned—just hoped. I think you'd better go to some nice hotel now. Later we can arrange.

[*Sits on up-stage side of bed.*

LAURA. Will, we'll always be frank. I said I was ready to go, It's up to you—when and where.

WILL. The hotel scheme is the best, but, Laura—

LAURA. Yes?

WILL. You're quite sure this is in earnest. You don't want to change? You've time enough now.

LAURA. I've quite made up my mind. It's final.

WILL. If you want to work, Burgess has a nice part for you. I'll telephone and arrange if you say so.

LAURA. Thanks. Say I'll see him in the morning.

WILL. And, Laura, you know when we were in Denver, and—

LAURA. [*Rises hurriedly; crosses right.*] Please, please, don't speak of it.

WILL. I'm sorry, but I've got to. I told [*Rises, and crosses to left.*] Madison [LAURA *turns her head.*]—pardon me, but I must do this—that if this time ever came I'd have you write him the truth. Before we go any further I'd like you to do that now.

LAURA. Say good-bye? [*Turns to* WILL.

WILL. Just that.

LAURA. I wouldn't know how to begin. It will hurt him awfully deeply.

WILL. It'll be worse if you don't. He'll like you for telling him. It would be honest, and that is what he expects.

LAURA. Must I—now?

WILL. I think you should.

LAURA. [*Goes to table and sits down.*] How shall I begin, Will?

WILL. [*Standing back of table.*] You mean you don't know what to say?

LAURA. Yes.

WILL. Then I'll dictate.

LAURA. I'll do just as you say. You're the one to tell me now.

WILL. Address it the way you want to. [*She complies.*] I'm going to be pretty brutal. In the long run I think that is best, don't you?

LAURA. It's up to you.

WILL. Ready?

LAURA. Begin.

WILL. [*Dictating.*] "All I have to say can be expressed in one word, 'good-bye.' I shall not tell you where I've gone, but remind you of what Brockton told you the last time he saw you. He is here now [*Pause.*], dictating this letter. What I am doing is voluntary—my own suggestion. Don't grieve. Be happy and successful. I do not love you"—

[*She puts pen down; looks at him.*

LAURA. Will—please.

WILL. It has got to go just that way—"I do not love you." Sign it "Laura." [*She does it.*] Fold it, put it in an envelope—seal it—address it. Now shall I mail it?

LAURA. No. If you don't mind I'd sooner. It's a sort of a last—last message.

WILL. [*Crosses to armchair; gets coat, puts it on.*] All right. You're a little upset now, and I'm going. We are all to dine at

Martin's to-night at seven-thirty. There'll be a party. Of course you'll come. [*Gets hat and cane.*

LAURA. I don't think I can. You see—

WILL. I know. I guess there's enough there [*Indicating money.*] for your immediate needs. Later you can straighten things up. Shall I send the car?

LAURA. Yes, please.

WILL. Good. It will be the first happy evening I've had in a long, long time. You'll be ready?

[*Approaches and bends over her as if to caress her.*

LAURA. [*Shrinking away.*] Please don't. Remember we don't dine until seven-thirty.

WILL. All right. [*Exit.*

For a moment LAURA *sits silent, and then angrily rises, crosses up to dresser, gets alcohol lamp, crosses to table with lamp, lights same, and starts back to dresser. Knock at door.*

LAURA. Come in. [ANNIE *enters, and stops.*] That you, Annie?

ANNIE. Yassum.

LAURA. Mrs. Farley wants her rent. There is some money. [*Tosses money on to table.*] Take it to her.

ANNIE *goes to the table, examines the roll of bills and is palpably surprised.*

ANNIE. Dey ain't nothin' heah, Miss Laura, but five great big one hunderd dollah bills.

LAURA. Take two. And look in that upper drawer. You'll find some pawn tickets there. [ANNIE *complies.*

ANNIE. Yassum. [*Aside.*] Dat's real money—dem's yellow-backs sure.

LAURA. Take the two top ones and go get my lace gown and one of the hats. The ticket is for a hundred and ten dollars. Keep ten for yourself, and hurry.

ANNIE. [*Aside.*] Ten for myself—I never see so much money. [*To* LAURA, *her astonishment nearly overcoming her.*] Yassum, Miss Laura, yassum. [*She goes toward door, and then turns to* LAURA.] Ah'm so mighty glad yo' out all yo' trouble, Miss Laura. I says to Mis' Farley now—

LAURA. [*Snapping her off.*] Don't—don't. Go do as I tell you and mind your business. [ANNIE *turns sullenly and walks toward the door. At that moment* LAURA *sees the letter, which she has thrown on the table.*] Wait a minute. I want you to mail a letter. [*By this time her hair is half down, hanging loosely over her shoulders. Her waist is open at the throat, collar off, and she has the appearance of a woman's untidiness when she is at that particular stage of her toilet. Hands letter to* ANNIE, *but snatches it away as* ANNIE *turns to go. She glances at the letter long and wistfully, and her nerve fails her.*] Never mind.

ANNIE *exits. Slowly* LAURA *puts the letter over the flame of the alcohol lamp and it ignites. As it burns she holds it in her fingers, and when half consumed throws it into waste-jar, sits on side of bed watching letter burn, then lies down across bed on her elbows, her chin in her hands, facing audience. As the last flicker is seen the curtain slowly descends.*

CURTAIN.

ACT III.

SCENE. *Two months have elapsed. The scene is at* BROCKTON'S *apartment in a hotel such as is not over particular concerning the relations of its tenants. There are a number of these hotels throughout the theatre district of New York, and, as a rule, one will find them usually of the same type. The room in which this scene is placed is that of the general living-room in one of the handsomest apartments in the building. The prevailing colour is green, and there is nothing particularly gaudy about the general furnishings. They are in good taste, but without the variety of arrangement and ornamentation which would naturally obtain in a room occupied by people a bit more particular concerning their surroundings. Down stage is a table about three feet square which can be used not only as a general centre-table, but also for service while the occupants are eating. There is a breakfast service on this table, and also a tray and stand behind it. There is a chair at either side of the table, and at right coming up stage, the room turns at a sharp angle of thirty-five degrees, and this space is largely taken up by a large doorway. This is equipped with sliding-doors and hung with green portières, which are handsome and in harmony with the general scheme of the furnishings of the room. This entrance is to the sleeping-room of the apartments.*

At the back of the stage is a lar ~ window or alcove. The window is on the ordinary plan, and the view through it shows the back of another building of New York, presumably a hotel of about the same character. Green portières are also hung on the windows. Down left is the entrance to the corridor of the hotel, and this must be so arranged that it works with a latch-key and opens upon a small hallway, which separates the apartment from the main hallway. This is necessary as the action calls for the slamming of a door, and later the opening of the direct and intimate door of the apartment with a latch-key. Left of centre is a sofa, and there is a general arrangement of chairs without over-crowding the apartment. Just below, where the right portière is hung, is a long, full-length mirror, such as women dress by. Against wall is a lady's fancy dresser.

To the immediate left of the sliding-doors, which go into the sleeping-apartment, is a lady's small writing-desk, with a drawer on the right-hand side, in which is a pearl-handled 32-calibre revolver. The front of the desk is open at rise. On top of the desk is a desk lamp and a large box of candy; inside the desk is writing material, &c. In pigeon-hole left there is a small photo and frame, which ANNIE *places on the table when she removes the breakfast set. In front of centre window in alcove is a small table on which is a parlour lamp, and some newspapers, including the "New York Sun." On the floor running between the desk and table is a large fur rug. In front of the table is a small gilt chair; in front of desk there is also a small gilt chair; there is a pianola piano, on top of which is a bundle of music-rolls. In place, ready to play, is a roll of a negro tune called "Bon-Bon Buddie, My Chocolate Drop." On top of the piano, in addition to the music-rolls, are a fancy lamp, a large basket of chrysanthemums, and two photos in frames, at the upper corner. Standing on the floor is a large piano lamp. On the sofa are cushions, and thrown over its back is a lady's opera-coat. On the sofa are also a fan and some small dinner favours.*

On the dresser are a lady's silver toilet set, including powder boxes, rouge boxes, manicuring implements, and a small plush black cat that might have been a favour at some time. Two little dolls hang on the side of the glass of the dresser, which also might have been favours. These are used later in the action, and are necessary.

AT RISE. *When the curtain rises on this scene it is noticeable that the occupants of the room must have returned rather late at night, after having dined, not wisely, but too well. In the alcove is a man's dress-coat and vest thrown on the cushions in a most careless manner; a silk hat badly rumpled is near it. Over the top of sofa is an opera-cloak, and hung on the mirror is a huge hat, of the evening type, such as women would pay handsomely for. A pair of gloves is thrown on top of the pier-glass. The curtains in the bay-window are half drawn, and the light shades are half drawn down the windows, so that when the curtain goes up the place is in a rather dim light. On the table are the remains of a breakfast, which is served in a box-like tray such as is used in hotels.* LAURA *is discovered sitting at right of table, her hair a bit untidy. She has on a very expensive negligée gown.* WILL, *in a business suit, is at the other side of the table, and both have evidently just about concluded their breakfast and are reading the newspapers while they sip their coffee.* LAURA *is intent in the scanning of her "Morning Telegraph," while* WILL *is deep in the market reports of the "Journal of Commerce," and in each instance these things must be made apparent.* WILL *throws down the paper rather impatiently.*

WILL. Have you seen the *Sun*, Laura?

LAURA. No.

WILL. Where is it?

LAURA. I don't know.

WILL. [*In a loud voice.*] Annie, Annie! [*A pause.*] Annie! [*In an undertone, half directed to* LAURA.] Where the devil is that nigger?

LAURA. Why, I suppose she's at breakfast.

WILL. Well, she ought to be here.

LAURA. Did it ever occur to you that she has got to eat just the same as you have?

WILL. She's your servant, isn't she?

LAURA. My maid.

WILL. Well, what have you got her for,—to eat or to wait on you? Annie!

LAURA. Don't be so cross. What do you want?

WILL. I want the *Sun*.

[BROCKTON *pours out one half glass of water from bottle.*

LAURA. I will get it for you.

Rather wearily she gets up and goes to the table, where there are other morning papers; she takes the "Sun," hands it to him, goes back to her seat, re-opens the "Morning Telegraph." There is a pause. ANNIE *enters from the sleeping-room.*

ANNIE. Do yuh want me, suh?

WILL. Yes, I did want you, but don't now. When I'm at home I have a man to look after me, and I get what I want.

LAURA. For heaven's sake, Will, have a little patience. If you like your man so well, you had better live at home, but don't come around here with a grouch and bulldoze everybody.

WILL. Don't think for a moment that there's much to come around here for. Annie, this room's stuffy.

ANNIE. Yassuh.

WILL. Draw those portières. Let those curtains up. [ANNIE *lets up curtain.*] Let's have a little light. Take away these clothes and hide them. Don't you know that a man doesn't want to see the next morning anything to remind him of the night before. Make the place look a little respectable.

In the meantime ANNIE *scurries around, picking up the coat and vest, opera-cloak, &c., as rapidly as possible, and throwing them over her arm without any idea of order. It is very apparent that she is rather fearful of the anger of* WILL *while he is in this mood.*

WILL. [*Looking at her.*] Be careful. You're not taking the wash off the line.

ANNIE. Yassuh. [*Exit in confusion.*

LAURA. [*Laying down paper and looking at* WILL.] Well, I must say you're rather amiable this morning.

WILL. I feel like hell.

LAURA. Market unsatisfactory?

WILL. No; head too big. [*He lights a cigar; as he takes a puff he makes an awful face.*] Tastes like punk. [*Puts cigar into cup.*

LAURA. You drank a lot.

WILL. We'll have to cut out those parties. I can't do those things any more. I'm not as young as I was, and in the morning it makes me sick. How do you feel?

LAURA. A little tired, that's all. [*Rises, and crosses to bureau.*

WILL. You didn't touch anything?

LAURA. No.

WILL. I guess you're on the safe side. It was a great old party, though, wasn't it?

LAURA. Did you think so?

WILL. Oh, for that sort of a blow-out. Not too rough, but just a little easy. I like them at night and I hate them in the morning. [*He picks up the paper and commences to glance it over in a casual manner, not interrupting his conversation.*] Were you bored?

LAURA. Yes; always at things like that.

WILL. Well, you don't have to go.

LAURA. You asked me.

WILL. Still, you could say no. [LAURA *picks up paper, puts it on table and crosses back to bureau.*

LAURA. But you asked me.

WILL. What did you go for if you didn't want to?

LAURA. *You* wanted me to.

WILL. I don't quite get you.

LAURA. Well, Will, you have all my time when I'm not in the theatre, and you can do with it just what you please. You pay for it. I'm working for you.

WILL. Is that all I've got,—just your time?

LAURA. [*Wearily.*] That and the rest. [LAURA *crosses up to desk, gets "part," crosses to sofa, turning pages of "part."*] I guess you know. [*Crosses to sofa and sits.*

WILL. [*Looking at her curiously.*] Down in the mouth, eh? I'm sorry.

LAURA. No, only if you want me to be frank, I'm a little tired. You may not believe it, but I work awfully hard over at the theatre. Burgess will tell you that. I know I'm not so very good as an actress, but I try to be. [LAURA *lies down on sofa.*] I'd like to succeed, myself. They're very patient with me. Of course they've got to be,—that's another thing you're paying for, but I don't seem to get along except this way.

WILL. Oh, don't get sentimental. If you're going to bring up that sort of talk, Laura, do it sometime when I haven't got a hang-over, and then don't forget talk never does count for much.

LAURA *crosses up to mirror, picks up hat from box, puts it on, looks in mirror. She turns around and looks at him steadfastly for a minute. During this entire scene, from the time the curtain rises, she must in a way indicate a premonition of an approaching catastrophe, a feeling, vague but nevertheless palpable, that something is going to happen. She must hold this before her audience so that she can show to them, without showing to him, the disgust she feels.* LAURA *has tasted of the privations of self-sacrifice during her struggle, and she has weakly surrendered and is unable to go back, but that brief period of self-abnegation has shown to her most clearly the rottenness of the other sort of living. There are enough sentimentality and emotion in her character to make it impossible for her to accept this manner of existence as* ELFIE *does. Hers is not a nature of careless candour, but of dreamy ideals and better living, warped, handicapped, disillusioned, and destroyed by a weakness that finds its principal force in vanity.* WILL *resumes his newspaper in a more attentive way. The girl looks at him and expresses in pantomine, by the slightest gesture or shrug of the shoulders, her growing distaste for him and his way of living. In the meantime* WILL *is reading the paper rather carefully. He stops suddenly and then looks at his watch.*

LAURA. What time is it?
WILL. After ten.
LAURA. Oh.

WILL *at this moment particularly reads some part of the paper, turns to her with a keen glance of suspicion and inquiry, and then for a very short moment evidently settles in his mind a cross-examination. He has read in this paper a despatch from Chicago, which speaks of* JOHN MADISON *having arrived there as a representative of a big Western mining syndicate which is going to open large operations in the Nevada gold-fields, and representing* MR. MADISON *as being on his way to New York with sufficient capital to enlist more, and showing him to be now a man of means. The attitude of* LAURA *and the coincidence of the despatch bring back to* WILL *the scene in Denver, and later in New York, and with that subtle intuition of the man of the world he connects the two.*

WILL. I don't suppose, Laura, that you'd be interested now in knowing anything about that young fellow out in Colorado? What was his name—Madison?

LAURA. Do you know anything?

WILL. No, nothing particularly. I've been rather curious to know how he came out. He was a pretty fresh young man and did an awful lot of talking. I wonder how he's doing and how he's getting along. I don't suppose by any chance you have ever heard from him?

LAURA. No, no; I've never heard. [*Crosses to bureau.*

WILL. I presume he never replied to that letter you wrote?

LAURA. No.

WILL. It would be rather queer, eh, if this young fellow should [*Looks at paper.*] happen to come across a lot of money—not that I think he ever could, but it would be funny, wouldn't it?

LAURA. Yes, yes; it would be unexpected. I hope he does. It might make him happy.

WILL. Think he might take a trip East and see you act. You know you've got quite a part now.

LAURA. [*Impatiently.*] I wish you wouldn't discuss this. Why do you mention it now? [*Crossing to right of table.*] Is it because you were drinking last night and lost your sense of delicacy? You once had some consideration for me. What I've done I've done. I'm giving *you* all that I can. Please, please, don't hurt me any more than you can help. That's all I ask.

[*Crossing up to mirror. Crosses back to right of table; sits.*

WILL. Well, I'm sorry. I didn't mean that, Laura. I guess I am feeling a little bad to-day. Really, I don't want to hurt your feelings, my dear.

He gets up, goes to her, puts his hands on her shoulders, and his cheek close to the back of her head. She bends forward and shudders a little bit. It is very easy to see that the life she is leading is becoming intolerable to her.

WILL. You know, dearie, I do a lot for you because you've always been on the level with me. I'm sorry I hurt you, but there was too much wine last night and I'm all upset. Forgive me.

LAURA, *in order to avoid his caresses, has leaned forward; her hands are clasped between her knees, and she is looking straight outward with a cold, impassive expression.* WILL *regards her silently for a moment. Really in the man's heart there is an affection, and really he wants to try to comfort her; but he seems to realize that she has slipped away from the old environment and conditions, and that he simply bought her back; that he hasn't any of her affection, even with his money; that she evinces toward him none of the old camaraderie; and it hurts him, as those things always hurt a selfish man, inclining him to be brutal and inconsiderate.* WILL *crosses to centre, and stands reading paper; bell rings; a pause and second bell.* WILL *seizes upon this excuse to go up-stage and over towards the door.*

WILL. [*After second bell.*] Damn that bell.

He continues on his way; he opens the door, leaves it open, and passes on to the outer door, which he opens. LAURA *remains immovable and impassive, with the same cold, hard expression on her face. He comes in, slamming the outer door with effect, which one must have at this point of the play, because it is essential to a situation coming later. Enters the room, closes the door, and holds in his hand a telegram. Looks from newspaper to telegram.*

WILL. A wire.

LAURA. For me?

WILL. Yes.

LAURA. From whom, I wonder. Perhaps Elfie with a luncheon engagement.

WILL. [*Handing telegram to her.*] I don't know. Here.

Pause; he faces her, looking at her. She opens it quickly. She reads it and, as she does, gasps quickly with an exclamation of fear and surprise. This is what the despatch says (it is dated at Buffalo and addressed to LAURA*): "I will be in New York before noon. I'm coming to marry you and I'm coming with a bank-roll. I wanted to keep it secret and have a big surprise for you, but I can't hold it any longer, because I feel just like a kid with a new top. Don't go out, and be ready for the big matrimonial thing. All my love. John."*

WILL. No bad news, I hope?

LAURA. [*Walking up stage rather hurriedly.*] No, no—not bad news.

WILL. I thought you were startled.

LAURA. No, not at all.

WILL. [*Looking at paper about where he had left off.*] From Elfie? [*Crosses to, and sits in armchair.*

LAURA. No, just a friend.

WILL. Oh!

He makes himself rather comfortable in the chair, and LAURA *regards him for a moment from up stage as if trying to figure out how to get rid of him.*

LAURA. Won't you be rather late getting down town, Will?

WILL. Doesn't make any difference. I don't feel much like the office now. Thought I might order the car and take a spin through the park. The cold air will do me a lot of good. Like to go?

LAURA. No, not to-day. I thought your business was important; you said so last night. [*Crosses to sofa, and stands.*

WILL. No hurry. Do you—er—want to get rid of me?

LAURA. Why should I?

WILL. Expecting someone?

LAURA. No—not exactly. [*Crosses up to window.*

WILL. If you don't mind, I'll stay here. [*Lets curtain fly up.*

LAURA. Just as you please. [*A pause. Crosses to piano; plays.*] Will?

WILL. Yes.

LAURA. How long does it take to come from Buffalo?

WILL. Depends on the train you take.

LAURA. About how long?

WILL. Between eight and ten hours, I think. Some one coming?

LAURA. Do you know anything about the trains?

WILL. Not much. Why don't you find out for yourself? Have Annie get the time-table?

LAURA. I will. Annie! Annie!

[*Rises from piano.* ANNIE *appears at doorway.*

ANNIE. Yassum!

LAURA. Go ask one of the hall-boys to bring me a New York Central time-table.

ANNIE. Yassum!

Crosses the stage and exits through door. LAURA *sits on left arm of sofa.*

WILL. Then you *do* expect someone, eh?

LAURA. Only one of the girls who used to be in the same company with me. But I'm not sure that she's coming here.

WILL. Then the wire was from her?

LAURA. Yes.

WILL. Did she say what train she was coming on?

LAURA. No.

WILL. Well, there are a lot of trains. About what time did you expect her in?

LAURA. She didn't say.

WILL. Do I know her?

LAURA. I think not. I met her while I worked in 'Frisco.

WILL. Oh! [*Resumes his paper.*

ANNIE *reënters with a time-table and hands it to* LAURA.

LAURA. Thanks; take those breakfast things away, Annie. [*Sits on sofa.*

ANNIE *complies; takes them across stage, opens the door leading to the corridor, exits.* LAURA *in the meantime is studying the time-table.*

LAURA. I can't make this out.

WILL. Give it here; maybe I can help you.

LAURA *crosses to right of table, sits opposite* WILL, *and hands him the time-table. He takes it and handles it as if he were familiar with it.*

WILL. Where is she coming from?

LAURA. The West; the telegram was from Buffalo. I suppose she was on her way when she sent it.

WILL. There's a train comes in here at 9:30—that's the Twentieth Century,—that doesn't carry passengers from Buffalo; then there's one at 11:41; one at 1:49; another at 3:45; another at 5:40; and another at 5:48—that's the Lake Shore Limited, a fast train; and all pass through Buffalo. Did you think of meeting her?

LAURA. No. She'll come here when she arrives.

WILL. Knows where you live?

LAURA. She has the address.

WILL. Ever been to New York before?

LAURA. I think not.

WILL. [*Passing her the time-table.*] Well, that's the best I can do for you.

LAURA. Thank you. [*Crosses and puts time-table in desk.*

WILL. [*Takes up the paper again.* LAURA *looks at clock.*] By George, this is funny.

LAURA. What?

WILL. Speak of the devil, you know.

LAURA. Who?

WILL. Your old friend Madison.

LAURA. [*Utters a slight exclamation and makes an effort to control herself.*] What—what about him?

WILL. He's been in Chicago.

LAURA. How do you know?

WILL. Here's a despatch about him.

LAURA. [*Coming quickly over to him, looks over his shoulder.*] What—where—what's it about?

WILL. Well, I'm damned if he hasn't done what he said he'd do—see! [*Holds the paper so that she can see.* LAURA *takes paper.*] He's been in Chicago, and is on his way to New York. He's struck it rich in Nevada and is coming with a lot of money. Queer, isn't it? [LAURA *puts paper on table.*] Did you know anything about it? [*Lights cigarette.*

LAURA. No, no; nothing at all. [*Crosses to bureau.*

WILL. Lucky for him, eh?

LAURA. Yes, yes; it's very nice.

WILL. Too bad he couldn't get this a little sooner, eh, Laura?

LAURA. Oh, I don't know—I don't think it's too bad. What makes you ask?

WILL. Oh, nothing. I suppose he ought to be here to-day. Are you going to see him if he looks you up?

LAURA. No, no; I don't want to see him. You know that, don't you, that I don't want to see him? What makes you ask these questions? [*Crosses to sofa and sits.*

WILL. Just thought you might meet him, that's all. Don't get sore about it.

LAURA. I'm not.

She holds the telegram crumpled in one hand. WILL *lays down the paper, and regards* LAURA *curiously. She sees the expression on his face and averts her head in order not to meet his eye.*

LAURA. What are you looking at me that way for?

WILL. I wasn't conscious that I was looking at you in any particular way—why?

LAURA. Oh, nothing. I guess I'm nervous, too. [*Lies on sofa.*

WILL. I dare say you are. [*A pause.*

LAURA. Yes, I am. [WILL *crosses to* LAURA.

WILL. You know I don't want to delve into a lot of past history at this time, but I've got to talk to you for a moment.

LAURA. Why don't you do it some other time? I don't want to be talked to now. [*Rises and crosses a little to left.*

WILL. But I've got to do it just the same.

LAURA. [*Trying to affect an attitude of resigned patience and resignation.*] Well, what is it? [*Resuming seat on sofa*

WILL. You've always been on the square with me, Laura. That's why I've liked you a lot better than the other women.

LAURA. Are you going into all that again now, this morning? I thought we understood each other.

WILL. So did I, but somehow I think that maybe we *don't* quite understand each other.

LAURA. In what way? [*Turns to* WILL.

WILL. [*Looking her straight in the eye.*] That letter I dictated to you the day that you came back to me, and left it for you to mail—did you mail it?

LAURA. Yes.

WILL. You're quite sure?

LAURA. Yes, I'm quite sure. I wouldn't say so if I wasn't.

WILL. And you didn't know Madison was coming East until you read about it in that newspaper?

LAURA. No—no, I didn't know.

WILL. Have you heard from him?

LAURA. No—no—I haven't heard from him. Don't talk to me about this thing. Why can't you leave me alone? I'm miserable enough as it is. [*Crossing to extreme right.*

WILL. [*Crossing to table.*] But I've got to talk to you. Laura, you're lying to me.

LAURA. What! [*She makes a valiant effort to become angry.*

WILL. You're lying to me, and you've been lying to me, and I've trusted you. Show me that telegram!

LAURA. No.

WILL. [*Going over towards her.*] Show me that telegram!

[LAURA *crosses up to doors leading into bedroom.*

LAURA. [*Tears telegram in half.*] You've no right to ask me.

WILL. Are you going to make me take it away [LAURA *crosses to window.*] from you? I've [*Crosses to sofa.*] never laid my hands on you yet.

LAURA. It's my business.

[*Crossing to left of sofa, around it on down-stage side.*

WILL. Yes, and it's mine.

During scene. Backing away from WILL, *who is following her,* LAURA *backs against bureau.* WILL *grabs her and attempts to take telegram from her. She has put it in the front of her waist. She slowly draws it out.*

WILL. That telegram's from Madison. Give it here!

LAURA. No.

WILL. I'm going to find out where I stand. Give me that telegram, or I'll take it away from you.

LAURA. No.

WILL. Come on!

LAURA. I'll give it to you.

[*Takes telegram out of waist, and hands it to him.*

He takes it slowly, looking her squarely in the eye. WILL *crosses to centre, and does not glance away while he slowly smoothes it out so that it can be read; when he finally takes it in both hands to read it she staggers back a step or two weakly.*

WILL. [*Reads the telegram aloud.*] "I will be in New York before noon. I'm coming to marry you, and I'm coming with a bank-roll. I wanted to keep it a secret and have a big surprise for you, but I can't hold it any longer, because I feel just like a kid with a new top. Don't go out, and be ready for the big matrimonial thing. All my love. John." Then you knew?

LAURA. Yes.

WILL. But you didn't know he was coming until this arrived?

LAURA. No.

WILL. And you didn't mail the letter [*Tossing telegram on table*], did you?

LAURA. No.

WILL. What did you do with it?

LAURA. I—I burned it.

WILL. Why?

[LAURA *is completely overcome and unable to answer.*

WILL. Why?

LAURA. I—I couldn't help it—I simply couldn't help it.

WILL. So you've been corresponding all this time.

LAURA. Yes.

WILL. And he doesn't know [*With a gesture around the room, indicating the condition in which they live.*] about us?

LAURA. No.

WILL. [*Taking a step towards her.*] By God, I never beat a woman in my life, but I feel as though I could wring your neck.

LAURA. Why don't you? You've done everything else. Why don't you?

WILL. Don't you know that I gave Madison my word that if you came back to me I'd let him know? Don't you know that I like that young fellow, and I wanted to protect him, and did everything I could to help him? And do you know what you've done to me? You've made me out a liar—you've made me lie to a man—a man—you understand. What are you going to do now? Tell me—what are you going to do now? Don't stand there as if you've lost your voice—how are you going to square me?

LAURA. I'm not thinking about squaring you. What am I going to do for him?

WILL. Not what *you* are going to do for him—what am *I* going to do for him. Why, I couldn't have that young fellow think that I tricked him into this thing for you or all the rest of the women of your kind on earth. God! I might have known that you, and the others like you, couldn't be square. [*The girl looks at him dumbly. He glances at his watch, walks up stage, looks out of the window, comes down again, goes to the table, and looks at her across it.*] You've made a nice mess of it, haven't you?

LAURA. [*Weakly.*] There isn't any mess. Please go away. He'll be here soon. Please let *me* see him—please do that.

WILL. No, I'll wait. This time I'm going to tell him myself, and I don't care how tough it is.

LAURA. [*Immediately regaining all her vitality.*] No, you mustn't do that. [*Crossing back of table to centre.*] Oh, Will, I'm not offering any excuse. I'm not saying anything, but I'm telling you the truth. I couldn't give him up—I couldn't do it. I love him.

WILL. Huh. [*Grins; crosses to front of sofa.*

LAURA. Don't you think so? I know you can't see what I see, but I do. And why can't you go away? Why can't you leave me this? It's all I ever had. He doesn't know. No one will ever tell him. I'll take him away. It's the best for him—it's the best for me. Please go.

WILL. Why—do you think that I'm going to let you trip him the way you tripped me? [*Crosses and sits in armchair.*] No. I'm going to stay right here until that young man arrives, and I'm going to tell him that it wasn't my fault. You were to blame.

LAURA. Then you are going to let him know. You're not going to give me a single, solitary chance?

WILL. I'll give you every chance that you deserve when he knows. Then he can do as he pleases, but there must be no more deception, that's flat.

[LAURA *crosses and kneels beside* WILL's *chair.*

LAURA. Then you must let me tell him—[WILL *turns away impatiently.*]—yes, you must. If I didn't tell him before, I'll do it now. You must go. If you ever had any regard for me—if you ever had any affection—if you ever had any friendship, please let me do this now. I want you to go—you can come back. Then you'll see—you'll know—only I want to try to make him understand that—that maybe if I am weak I'm not vicious. I want to let him know that I didn't want to do it, but I couldn't help it. Just give me the chance to be as good as I can be. [WILL *gives her a look.*] Oh, I promise you, I will tell him, and then—then I don't care what happens—only he must learn everything from me—please—please—let me do this—it's the last favour I shall ever—ever ask of you. Won't you?

[LAURA *breaks down and weeps.*

WILL. [*Rising, looks at her a moment as if mentally debating the best thing to do. Crosses in front of table; stands facing her with back to audience.*] All right, I won't be unkind. I'll be back early this afternoon, and just remember, this is the time you'll have to go right through to the end. Understand?

LAURA. Yes, I'll do it,—all of it. Won't you please go—now? [*Crosses; sits in armchair.*

WILL. All right. [*He exits into the bedroom and immediately enters again with overcoat on his arm and hat in hand; he goes centre, and turns.*] I am sorry for you, Laura, but remember you've got to tell the truth.

LAURA. [*Who is sitting in a chair looking straight in front of her with a set expression.*] Please go. [WILL *exits.*

LAURA *sits in a chair in a state of almost stupefaction, holding this attitude as long as possible.* ANNIE *enters, and in a characteristic manner begins her task of tidying up the room;* LAURA, *without changing her attitude, and staring straight in front of her, her elbows between her knees and her chin on her hands.*

LAURA. Annie!

ANNIE. Yassum.

LAURA. Do you remember in the boarding-house—when we finally packed up—what you did with everything?

ANNIE. Yassum.

LAURA. You remember that I used to keep a pistol?

ANNIE. Yo' all mean dat one yo' say dat gemman out West gave yuh once?

LAURA. Yes.

ANNIE. Yassum, Ah 'membuh it.

LAURA. Where is it now?

ANNIE. [*Crosses to writing-desk.*] Last Ah saw of it was in dis heah draw' in de writin'-desk. [*This speech takes her across to desk; she opens the drawer, fumbles among a lot of old papers, letters, &c., and finally produces a small thirty-two calibre, and gingerly crosses to* LAURA.] Is dis it?

LAURA. [*Slowly turns around and looks at it.*] Yes. Put it back. I thought perhaps it was lost. [ANNIE *complies, when the bell rings.* LAURA *starts suddenly, involuntarily gathering her negligée gown closer to her figure, and at once she is under a great stress of emotion, and sways upon her feet to such an extent that she is obliged to put one hand out on to the table to maintain her balance. When she speaks, it is with a certain difficulty of articulation.*] See—who—that is—and let me know.

ANNIE. [*Turning.*] Yassum. [*Crosses, opens the first door, and afterwards opens the second door.*

ELFIE'S VOICE. [*Off stage.*] Hello, Annie,—folks home?

ANNIE. Yassum, she's in.

LAURA *immediately evinces her tremendous relief, and* ELFIE, *without waiting for a reply, has shoved* ANNIE *aside and enters,* ANNIE *following and closing the door.* ELFIE *is beautifully gowned in a morning dress with an overabundance of fur trimmings and all the furbelows that would accompany the extravagant raiment generally affected by a woman of that type.* ELFIE *approaching effusively.*

ELFIE. Hello, dearie.

LAURA. Hello, Elfie.

LAURA *crosses and sits on sofa.* ELFIE *puts muff, &c., on table.*

ELFIE. It's a bully day out. [*Crossing to bureau, looking in mirror.*] I've been shopping all morning long; just blew myself until I'm broke, that's all. My goodness, don't you ever get dressed? Listen. [*Crosses left of table to centre.*] Talk about cinches. I copped out a gown, all ready made, and fits me like the paper on the wall, for $37.80. Looks like it might have cost $200. Anyway I had them charge $200 on the bill, and I kept the change. There are two or three more down town there, and I want you to go down and look them over. Models, you know, being sold out. I don't blame you for not getting up earlier. [*She sits at the table, not noticing* LAURA.] That was some party last night. I know you didn't drink a great deal, but gee! what an awful tide Will had on. How do you feel? [*Looks at her critically.*] What's the matter, are you sick? You look all in. What you want to do is this—put on your duds and go out for an hour. It's a perfectly grand day out. My Gaud! how the sun does shine! Clear and cold. [*A pause.*] Well, much obliged for the conversation. Don't I get a "Good-morning," or a "How-dy-do," or a something of that sort?

LAURA. I'm tired, Elfie, and blue—terribly blue.

ELFIE. [*Rises; crosses to* LAURA.] Well now, you just brace up and cut out all that emotional stuff. I came down to take you for a drive. You'd like it; just through the park. Will you go?

LAURA. [*Going up stage.*] Not this morning, dear; I'm expecting somebody.

ELFIE. A man?

LAURA. [*Finding it almost impossible to suppress a smile.*] No, a gentleman.

ELFIE. Same thing. Do I know him?

LAURA. You've heard of him. [*At desk, looking at clock.*

ELFIE. Well, don't be so mysterious. Who is he?

LAURA. What is your time, Elfie?

ELFIE. [*Looks at her watch.*] Five minutes past eleven.

LAURA. Oh, I'm slow. I didn't know it was so late. Just excuse me, won't you, while I get some clothes on. He may be here any moment. Annie!

[*She goes up stage towards portières.*

ELFIE. Who?

LAURA. I'll tell you when I get dressed. Make yourself at home, won't you, dear?

ELFIE. I'd sooner hear. What is the scandal anyway?

LAURA. [*As she goes out.*] I'll tell you in a moment. Just as soon as Annie gets through with me. [*Exit.*

ELFIE. [*Gets candy-box off desk, crosses, sits on arm of sofa, selecting candy. In a louder voice.*] Do you know, Laura, I think I'll go back on the stage.

LAURA. [*Off stage.*] Yes?

ELFIE. Yes, I'm afraid I'll have to. I think I need a sort of a boost to my popularity.

LAURA. How a boost, Elfie?

ELFIE. I think Jerry is getting cold feet. He's seeing a little too much of me [*Places candy-box on sofa.*] nowadays.

LAURA. What makes you think that?

ELFIE. I think he is getting a relapse of that front-row habit. There's no use in talking, Laura, it's a great thing for a girl's credit when a man like Jerry can take two or three friends to the theatre, and when you make your entrance delicately point to you with his forefinger and say, "The third one from the front on the left belongs to muh." The old fool's hanging around some of these musical comedies lately, and I'm getting a little nervous every time rent day comes.

LAURA. Oh, I guess you'll get along all right, Elfie.

ELFIE. [*With serene self-satisfaction.*] Oh, that's a cinch [*Rises; crosses to table, looking in dresser mirror at herself, and giving her hat and hair little touches.*], but I like to leave well enough alone, and if I had to make a change right now it would require a whole lot of thought and attention, to say nothing of the inconvenience, and I'm so nicely settled in my flat. [*She sees the pianola.*] Say, dearie, when did you get the piano-player? I got one of them phonographs [*Crosses to pianola, tries the levers, &c.*], but this has got that beat a city block. How does it work? What did it cost?

LAURA. I don't know.

ELFIE. Well, Jerry's got to stake me to one of these. [*Looks over the rolls on top. Mumbles to herself.*] "Tannhauser, William Tell, Chopin." [*Then louder.*] Listen, dear. Ain't you got anything else except all this high-brow stuff?

LAURA. What do you want?

ELFIE. Oh, something with a regular tune to it [*Looks at empty box on pianola.*]. Oh, here's one; just watch me tear this off. [*The roll is the tune of "Bon-Bon Buddie, My Chocolate Drop." She starts to play and moves the lever marked "Swell" wide open, increases the tempo, and is pumping with all the delight and enthusiasm of a child.*] Ain't it grand?

LAURA. Gracious, Elfie, don't play so loud. What's the matter?

ELFIE. I shoved over that thing marked "Swell." [*Stops and turns. Rises; crosses to centre and stands.*] I sure will have to speak to Jerry about this. I'm stuck on that swell thing. Hurry up. [LAURA appears.] Gee! you look pale. [*And then in a tone of sympathy:*] I'll just bet you and Will have had a fight, and he always gets the best of you, doesn't he, dearie? [LAURA *crosses to dresser, and busies herself.*] Listen. Don't you think you can ever get him trained? I almost threw Jerry down the stairs the other night and he came right back with a lot of American beauties and a check. I told him if he didn't look out I'd throw him down-stairs every night. He's getting too damned independent and it's got me nervous. Oh, dear, I s'pose I will have to go back on the stage. [*Sits in armchair.*

LAURA. In the chorus?

ELFIE. Well, I should say not. I'm going to give up my musical career. Charlie Burgess is putting on a new play, and he says he has a part in it for me if I want to go back. It isn't much, but very important,—sort of a pantomime part. A lot of people talk about me, and just at the right time I walk across the stage and make an awful hit. I told Jerry that if I went [LAURA *crosses to sofa, picks up candy-box, puts it upon desk, gets telegram from table, crosses to centre.*] on he'd have to come across with one of those Irish crochet lace gowns. He fell for it. Do you know, dearie, I think he'd sell out his business just to have me back on the stage for a couple of weeks, just to give box-parties every night for my *en*-trance and *ex*-its.

LAURA. [*Seriously.*] Elfie! [LAURA *takes* ELFIE *by the hand, and leads her over to sofa.* LAURA *sits,* ELFIE *standing.*

ELFIE. Yes, dear.

LAURA. Come over here and sit down.

ELFIE. What's up?

LAURA. Do you know what I'm going to ask of you?

ELFIE. If it's a touch, you'll have to wait until next week. [*Sits opposite* LAURA.

LAURA. No: just a little advice.

ELFIE. [*With a smile.*] Well, that's cheap, and Lord knows you need it. What's happened?

LAURA *takes the crumpled and torn telegram that* WILL *has left on the table and hands it to* ELFIE. *The latter puts the two pieces together, reads it very carefully, looks up at* LAURA *about middle of telegram, and lays it down.*

ELFIE. Well?

LAURA. Will suspected. There was something in the paper about Mr. Madison—the telegram came—then we had a row.

ELFIE. Serious?

LAURA. Yes. Do you remember what I told you about that letter—the one Will made me write—I mean to John—telling him what I had done?

ELFIE. Yes, you burned it.

LAURA. I tried to lie to Will—he wouldn't have it that way. He seemed to know. He was furious.

ELFIE. Did he hit you?

LAURA. No; he made me admit that John didn't know, and then he said he'd stay here and tell himself that I'd made him lie, and then he said something about liking the other man and wanting to save him.

ELFIE. Save—shucks! He's jealous.

LAURA. I told him if he'd only go I'd—tell John myself when he came, and now you see I'm waiting—and I've got to tell—and—and I don't know how to begin—and—and I thought you could help me—you seem so sort of resourceful, and it means—it means so much to me. If John turned on me now I couldn't go back to Will, and, Elfie,—I don't think I'd care to—stay here any more.

ELFIE. What! [*In an awestruck tone, taking* LAURA *in her arms impulsively.*] Dearie, get that nonsense out of your head and be sensible. I'd just like to see any two men who could make me think about—well—what you seem to have in your mind.

LAURA. But I don't know; don't you see, Elfie, I don't know. If I don't tell him, Will will come back and he'll tell him, and I know John and maybe—Elfie, do you know, I think John would kill him.

ELFIE. Well, don't you think anything about that. Now let's get [*Rises, crosses to armchair, draws it over a little, sits on left arm.*] down to cases, and we haven't much time. Business is business, and love is love. You're long on love and I'm long on business, and between the two of us we ought to straighten this thing out. Now, evidently John is coming on here to marry you.

LAURA. Yes.

ELFIE. And you love him?

LAURA. Yes.

ELFIE. And as far as you know the moment that he comes in here it's quick to the Justice and a big matrimonial thing.

LAURA. Yes, but you see how impossible it is—

ELFIE. I don't see anything impossible. From all you've said to me about this fellow there is only one thing to do.

LAURA. One thing?

ELFIE. Yes—get married quick. You say he has the money and you have the love, and you're sick of Brockton, and you want to switch and do it in the decent, respectable, conventional way, and he's going to take you away. Haven't you got sense enough to know that, once you're married to Mr. Madison, Will Brockton wouldn't dare go to him, and if he did Madison wouldn't believe him? A man will believe a whole lot about his girl, but nothing about his wife.

LAURA. [*Turns and looks at her. There is a long pause.*] Elfie [*Rises; crosses to right of table.*]—I—I don't think I could do like that to John. I don't think—I could deceive him.

ELFIE. You make me sick. The thing to do is to lie to all men. [*Rises; pushes chair to table.*]—they all lie to you. Protect yourself. You seem to think that your happiness depends on this. Now do it. Listen. [*Touches* LAURA *to make her sit down;* LAURA *sits right of table;* ELFIE *sits on right arm of chair left of table, with elbows on table.*] Don't you realize that you and me, and all the girls that are shoved into this life, are practically the common prey of any man who happens to come along? Don't you know that they've got about as much consideration for us as they have for any pet animal around the house, and the only way that we've got it on the animal is that we've got brains? This is a game, Laura, *not a sentiment.* Do you suppose this Madison [LAURA *turns to* ELFIE.]—now don't get sore—hasn't turned these tricks himself before he met you, and I'll gamble he's done it since! A man's natural trade is a heartbreaking business. Don't tell me about women breaking men's hearts. The only thing they can ever break is their bank roll. And besides, this is not Will's business; he has no right to interfere. You've been with him—yes, and he's been nice to you; but I don't think that he's given you any the best of it. Now if you want to leave and go your own way and marry any Tom, Dick, or Harry that you want, it's nobody's affair but yours.

LAURA. But you don't understand—it's John. I can't lie to him.

ELFIE. Well, that's too bad about you. I used to have that truthful habit myself, and the best I ever got was the worst of it. All this talk about love and loyalty and constancy is fine and dandy in a book, but when a girl has to look out for herself, take it from me, whenever you've got that trump card up your sleeve just play it and rake in the pot. [*Takes* LAURA's *hand affectionately.*] You know, dearie, you're just about the only one in the world I love.

LAURA. Elfie!

ELFIE. Since I broke away from the folks up state and they've heard things, there ain't any more letters coming to me with an Oswego postmark. Ma's gone, and the rest don't care. You're all I've got in the world, Laura, and what I'm asking you to do is because I want to see you happy. I was afraid this thing was coming off, and the thing to do now is to grab your happiness, no matter how you get it nor where it comes from. There ain't a whole lot of joy in this world for you and me and the others we know, and what little you get you've got to take when you're young, because, when those gray hairs begin to come, and the make-up isn't going to hide the wrinkles, unless you're well fixed, it's going to be hell. You know what a fellow doesn't know doesn't hurt him, and he'll love you just the same and you'll love him. As for Brockton, let him get another girl; there're plenty 'round. Why, if this chance came to me I'd tie a can to Jerry so quick that you could hear it rattle all the way down Broadway. [*Rises, crosses back of table to* LAURA, *leans over back of chair, and puts arms around her neck very tenderly.*] Dearie, promise me that you won't be a damn fool.

[*The bell rings; both start.*

LAURA. [*Rises.*] Maybe that's John.

[ELFIE *brushes a tear quickly from her eye.*

ELFIE. Oh! And you'll promise me, Laura?

LAURA. I'll try. [ANNIE *enters up stage from the adjoining room and crosses to the door.*] If that's Mr. Madison, Annie, tell him to come in.

LAURA *stands near the table, almost rigid. Instinctively* ELFIE *goes to the mirror and re-arranges her gown and hair as* ANNIE *exits.* ELFIE *turns to* LAURA.

ELFIE. If I think he's the fellow when I see him, watch me and I'll tip you the wink.

[*Kisses* LAURA; *up stage puts on coat.*

She goes up stage to centre; LAURA *remains in her position. The doors are heard to open, and in a moment* JOHN *enters. He is dressed very neatly in a business suit, and his face is tanned and weather-beaten. After he enters, he stands still for a moment. The emotion that both he and* LAURA *go through is such that each is trying to control it,* LAURA *from the agony of her position, and* JOHN *from the mere hurt of his affection. He sees* ELFIE *and forces a smile.*

JOHN. [*Quietly.*] Hello, Laura! I'm on time.

LAURA *smiles, quickly crosses the stage, and holds out her hand.*

LAURA. Oh, John, I'm so glad—so glad to see you.

[*They hold this position for a moment, looking into each other's eyes.* ELFIE *moves so as to take* JOHN *in from head to toe and is obviously very much pleased with his appearance. She coughs slightly.* LAURA *takes a step back with a smile.*] Oh, pardon me, John—one of my dearest friends, Miss Sinclair; she's heard a lot about you.

ELFIE, *with a slight gush, in her most captivating manner, goes over and holds out her gloved hand laden with bracelets, and with her sweetest smile crosses to centre.*

ELFIE. How do you do?

MADISON. I'm glad to meet you, I'm sure.

ELFIE. [*Still holding* JOHN'S *hand.*] Yes, I'm sure you are—particularly just at this time. [*To* LAURA.] You know that old stuff about two's company and three [LAURA *smiles.*] is a crowd. Here's where I vamoose. [*Crosses to door.*

LAURA. [*As* ELFIE *goes toward door.*] Don't hurry, dear.

ELFIE. [*With a grin.*] No, I suppose not; just fall down stairs and get out of the way, that's all. [*Crosses to* JOHN.] Anyway,

Mr. Madison, I'm awfully glad to have met you, and I want to congratulate you. They tell me you're rich.

JOHN. Oh, no; not rich.

ELFIE. Well, I don't believe you—anyway I'm going. Ta-ta, dearie. Good-bye, Mr. Madison.

JOHN. Good-bye.

[JOHN *crosses up to back of sofa; removes coat, puts it on sofa.*

ELFIE. [*Goes to the door, opens it and turns.* JOHN'S *back is partly toward her and she gives a long wink at* LAURA, *snapping fingers to attract* LAURA'S *attention.*] I must say, Laura, that when it comes to picking live ones, you certainly can go some.

[*After this remark both turn toward her and both smile.*

[*Exit.*

After ELFIE *exits,* JOHN *turns to* LAURA *with a pleasant smile, and jerks his head towards the door where* ELFIE *has gone out.*

JOHN. I bet she's a character.

LAURA. She's a dear.

JOHN. I can see that all right. [*Crossing to centre.*

LAURA. She's been a very great friend to me.

JOHN. That's good, but don't I get a "how-dy-do," or a handshake, or a little kiss? You know I've come a long way.

LAURA *goes to him and places herself in his arms; he kisses her affectionately. During all this scene between them the tenderness of the man is very apparent. As she releases herself from his embrace he takes her face in his hands and holds it up towards his.*

JOHN. I'm not much on the love-making business, Laura, but I never thought I'd be as happy as I am now. [JOHN *and* LAURA *cross to centre.* LAURA *kneels in armchair with back to audience,* JOHN *stands left of her.*] I've been counting mile-posts ever since I left Chicago, and it seemed like as if I had to go 'round the world before I got here.

LAURA. You never told me about your good fortune. If you hadn't telegraphed I wouldn't even have known you were coming.

JOHN. I didn't want you to. I'd made up my mind to sort of drop in here and give you a great big surprise,—a happy one, I knew,—but the papers made such a fuss in Chicago that I thought you might have read about it—did you?

LAURA. No.

JOHN. Gee! fixed up kind o' scrumptious, ain't you? [*Crosses in front of sofa, around behind it, surveying rooms.*] Maybe you've been almost as prosperous as I have.

LAURA. You can get a lot of gilt and cushions in New York at half price, and besides, I've got a pretty good part now.

JOHN. Of course I know that, but I didn't think it would make you quite so comfortable. Great, ain't it?

LAURA. Yes.

JOHN. [*Standing beside her chair, with a smile.*] Well, are you ready?

LAURA. For what, dear? [*Looking up at him.*

JOHN. You know what I said in the telegram?

LAURA. Yes. [*Leans her head affectionately on his shoulder.*

JOHN. Well, I meant it.

LAURA. I know.

JOHN. I've got to get back [JOHN *looks around; crosses behind table to chair right of table, and sits facing her across it.*], Laura, just as soon as ever I can. There's a lot of work to be done out in Nevada and I stole away to come to New York. I want to take you back. Can you go?

LAURA. Yes—when?

JOHN. This afternoon. We'll take the eighteen-hour train to Chicago, late this afternoon, and connect at Chicago with the Overland, and I'll soon have you in a home. [*Pause.*] And here's another secret.

LAURA. What, dear?

JOHN. I've got that home all bought and furnished, and while you couldn't call it a Fifth Avenue residence, still it has got something on any other one in town.

LAURA. But, John, you've been so mysterious. In all your letters you haven't told me a single, solitary thing about your good luck.

JOHN. I've planned to take you out and show you all that.

LAURA. You should have told me,—I've been so anxious.

JOHN. I waited until it was a dead-sure thing. You know it's been pretty tough sledding out there in the mining country, and it did look as if I never would make a strike; but your spirit was with me and luck was with me, and I knew if I could only hold out that something would come my way. I had two pals, both of them miners,—they had the knowledge and I had the luck,—and one day, clearing away a little snow to build a fire, I poked my toe into the dirt, and there was somethin' there, dearie, that looked suspicious. I called Jim,—that's one of the men,—and in less time than it takes to tell you there were three maniacs scratching away at old mother earth for all there was in it. We staked our claims in two weeks, and I came to Reno to raise enough money for me to come East. Now things are all fixed and it's just a matter of time. [*Taking* LAURA's *hand.*

LAURA. So you're very, very rich, dear?

JOHN. Oh, not rich [*Releasing her hand, he leans back in his chair.*], just heeled. I'm not going down to the Wall Street bargain counter and buy the Union Pacific, or anything like that; but we won't have to take the trip on tourists' tickets, and there's enough money to make us comfortable all the rest of our lives.

LAURA. How hard you must have worked and suffered.

JOHN. Nobody else ever accused me of that, but I sure will have to plead guilty to you. [*Rises; stands at upper side of table.*] Why, dear, since the day you came into my life, hell-raising took a sneak out the back door and God poked His toe in the front, and ever since then I think He's been coming a little closer to me. [*Crossing over.*] I used to be a fellow without much faith, and kidded everybody who had it, and I used to say to those who prayed and believed, "You may be right, but show me a message." You came along and you brought that little document in your sweet face and your dear love. Laura, you turned the trick for me, and I think I'm almost a regular man now.

LAURA *turns away in pain; the realization of all she is to* JOHN *weighs heavily upon her. She almost loses her nerve, and is on the verge of not going through with her determination to get her happiness at any price.*

LAURA. John, please, don't. I'm not worth it.

[*Rises, crosses to right.*

JOHN. [*With a light air.*] Not worth it? Why, you're worth [*Crossing behind table, stands behind* LAURA.] that and a whole lot more. And see how you've got on! Brockton told me you never could get along in your profession, but I knew you could. [*Crosses back of* LAURA, *takes her by the shoulders, shakes her playfully.*] I knew what you had in you, and here you are. You see, if my foot hadn't slipped on the right ground and kicked up pay-dirt, you'd been all right. You succeeded and I succeeded, but I'm going to take you away; and after a while, when things sort of smooth out, and it's all clear where the money's [*Crosses to sofa and sits.*] coming from, we're going to move back here, and go to Europe, and just have a great time, like a couple of good pals.

LAURA. [*Slowly crosses to* JOHN.] But if I hadn't succeeded and if things—things weren't just as they seem—would it make any difference to you, John?

JOHN. Not the least in the world. [*He takes her in his arms and kisses her, drawing her on to sofa beside him.*] Now don't you get blue. I should not have surprised you this way. It's taken you off your feet. [*He looks at his watch, rises, crosses behind sofa, gets overcoat.*] But we've not any time to lose. How soon can you get ready?

LAURA. [*Kneeling on sofa, leaning over back.*] You mean to go?

JOHN. Nothing else.

LAURA. Take all my things?

JOHN. All your duds.

LAURA. Why, dear, I can get ready most any time.

JOHN. [*Looking off into bedroom.*] That your maid?

LAURA. Yes,—Annie.

JOHN. Well, you and she can pack everything you want to take; the rest can follow later. [*Puts coat on.*] I planned it all out. There's a couple of the boys working down town,—newspaper men on Park Row. Telephoned them when I got in and they're waiting for me. I'll just get down there as soon as I can. I won't be gone long.

LAURA. How long?

JOHN. I don't know just how long, but we'll make that train. I'll get the license. We'll be married and we'll be off on our honeymoon this afternoon. Can you do it?

LAURA *goes up to him, puts her hands in his, and they confront each other.*

LAURA. Yes, dear, I could do anything for you.

He takes her in his arms and kisses her again. Looks at her tenderly.

JOHN. That's good. Hurry now. I won't be long. Good-bye.

LAURA. Hurry back, John.

JOHN. Yes. I won't be long. [*Exit.*

LAURA. [*Stands for a moment looking after him; then she suddenly recovers herself and walks rapidly over to the dresser, picks up large jewel-case, takes doll that is hanging on dresser, puts them on her left arm, takes black cat in her right hand and uses it in emphasizing her words in talking to* ANNIE. *Places them all on table.*] Annie, Annie, come here!

ANNIE. Yassum. [*She appears at the door.*

LAURA. Annie, I'm going away, and I've got to hurry.

ANNIE. Goin' away?

LAURA. Yes. I want you to bring both my trunks out here,—I'll help you,—and start to pack. We can't take everything [ANNIE *throws fur rug from across doorway into bedroom.*], but bring all the clothes out and we'll hurry as fast as we can. Come on.

Exit LAURA *with* ANNIE. *In a very short interval she re-appears, and both are carrying a large trunk between them. They put it down, pushing sofa back.*

ANNIE. Look out for your toes, Miss Laura.

LAURA. I can take two.

ANNIE. Golly, such excitement. [*Crosses to table; pushes it over further, also armchair.*] Wheah yuh goin', Miss Laura?

LAURA. Never mind where I'm going. I haven't any time to waste now talking. I'll tell you later. This is one time, Annie, that you've got to move. Hurry up.

LAURA *pushes her in front of her. Exeunt the same way and re-appear with a smaller trunk.*

ANNIE. Look out fo' your dress, Miss Laura.

These trunks are of the same type as those in Act II. When the trunks are put down LAURA *opens one and commences to throw things out.* ANNIE *stands watching her.* LAURA *kneels in front of trunk, working and humming "Bon-Bon Buddie."*

ANNIE. Ah nevah see you so happy, Miss Laura.

LAURA. I never was so happy. For heaven's sake, go get something. Don't stand there looking at me. I want you to hurry.

ANNIE. I'll bring out all de fluffy ones first.

LAURA. Yes, everything. [ANNIE *enters with armful of dresses and hat-box of tissue-paper; dumps tissue-paper on floor, puts dresses in trunk.*

ANNIE. [*Goes out again. Outside.*] You goin' to take dat opera-cloak? [*Enters with more dresses, puts them on sofa, takes opera-cloak, spreads it on top of dresses on trunk.*] My, but dat's a beauty. I jest love dat crushed rosey one. [*Exit.*

LAURA. Annie, you put the best dresses on the foot of the bed and I'll get them myself. You heard what I said?

ANNIE. [*Off stage.*] Yassum.

ANNIE *hangs dresses across bed in alcove.* LAURA *continues busily arranging the contents of the trunk, placing some garments here and some there, as if she were sorting them out.* WILL *quietly enters and stands at the door, looking at her. He holds this position as long as possible, and when he speaks it is in a very quiet tone.*

WILL. Going away?

LAURA. [*Starts, rises, and confronts him.*] Yes.

WILL. In somewhat of a hurry, I should say.

LAURA. Yes.

WILL. What's the plan?

LAURA. I'm just going, that's all.

WILL. Madison been here?

LAURA. He's just left.

WILL. Of course you are going with him?

LAURA. Yes.

WILL. West?

LAURA. To Nevada.

WILL. Going—er—to get married?

LAURA. Yes, this afternoon.

WILL. So he didn't care then?

LAURA. What do you mean when you say "he didn't care"?

WILL. Of course you told him about the letter, and how it was burned up, and all that sort of thing, didn't you?

LAURA. Why, yes.

WILL. And he said it didn't make any difference?

LAURA. He—he didn't say anything. We're just going to be married, that's all.

WILL. Did you mention my name and say that we'd been rather companionable for the last two months?

LAURA. I told him you'd been a very good friend to me.

During this scene LAURA *answers* WILL *with difficulty, and to a man of the world it is quite apparent that she is not telling the truth.* WILL *looks over toward her in an almost threatening way.*

WILL. How soon do you expect him back?

[*Crossing to centre.*

LAURA. Quite soon. I don't know just exactly how long he'll be.

WILL. And you mean to tell me that you kept your promise and told him the truth? [*Crossing to trunk.*

LAURA. I—I—[*Then with defiance.*] What business have you got to ask me that? What business have you got to interfere anyway? [*Crossing up to bed in alcove, gets dresses off foot, and puts them on sofa.*

WILL. [*Quietly.*] Then you've lied again. You lied to him, and you just tried to lie to me now. I must say, Laura, that you're not particularly clever at it, although I don't doubt but that you've had considerable practice.

Gives her a searching look and slowly walks over to the chair at the table and sits down, still holding his hat in his hand and without removing his overcoat. LAURA *sees* BROCKTON *sitting, stops and turns on him, laying dresses down.*

LAURA. What are you going to do?

WILL. Sit down here and rest a few moments; maybe longer.

LAURA. You can't do that.

WILL. I don't see why not. This is my own place.

LAURA. But don't you see that he'll come back here soon and find you here?

WILL. That's just exactly what I want him to do.

LAURA. [*With suppressed emotion, almost on the verge of hysteria.*] I want to tell you this. If you do this thing you'll ruin my life. You've done enough to it already. Now I want you to go. You've got to go. I don't think you've got any right to come here now, in this way, and take this happiness from me. I've given you everything I've got, and now I want to live right and decent, and he wants me to, and we love each other. Now, Will Brockton, it's come to this. You've got to leave this place, do you hear? You've got to leave this place. Please get out. [*Crossing to trunk.*

WILL. [*Rises and comes to her.*] Do you think I'm going to let a woman make a liar out of me? I'm going to stay right here. I like that boy, and I'm not going to let you put him to the bad.

LAURA. I want you to go. [*Slams trunk lid down, crosses to dresser, opens drawer to get stuff out.*

WILL. And I tell you I won't go. I'm going to show you up. I'm going to tell him the truth. It isn't you I care for—he's got to know.

LAURA. [*Slams drawer shut, loses her temper, and is almost tiger-like in her anger.*] You don't care for me?

WILL. No.

LAURA. It isn't me you're thinking of?

WILL. No.

LAURA. Who's the liar now?

WILL. Liar?

LAURA. Yes, liar. You are. You don't care for this man, and you know it.

WILL. You're foolish.

LAURA. Yes, I am foolish and I've been foolish all my life, but I'm getting a little sense now. [*Kneels in armchair, facing* WILL; *her voice is shaky with anger and tears.*] All my life, since the day you first took me away, you've planned and planned and planned to keep me, and to trick me and bring me down with you. When you came to me I was happy. I didn't have much, just a little salary and some hard work.

WILL. But like all the rest you found that wouldn't keep you, didn't you?

LAURA. You say I'm bad, but who's made me so? Who took me out night after night? Who showed me what these luxuries were? Who put me in the habit of buying something I couldn't afford? You did.

WILL. Well, you liked it, didn't you?

LAURA. Who got me in debt, and then, when I wouldn't do what you wanted me to, who had me discharged from the company, so I had no means of living? Who followed me from one place to another? Who, always entreating, tried to trap me into this life, and I didn't know any better?

WILL. You didn't know any better?

LAURA. I knew it was wrong—yes; but you told me everybody in this business did that sort of thing, and I was just as good as anyone else. Finally you got me and you kept me. Then, when I went away to Denver, and for the first time found a gleam of happiness, for the first time in my life—

WILL. You're crazy.

LAURA. Yes, I am crazy. [*Rises angrily, crosses and sweeps table-cover off table; crosses to dresser, knocks bottles, &c., off upper end; turns, faces him, almost screaming.*] You've made me crazy. You followed me to Denver, and then when I got back you bribed me again. You pulled me down, and you did the same old thing until this happened. Now I want you to get out, you understand? I want you to get out.

WILL. Laura, you can't do this. [*Starts to sit on trunk.*

LAURA. [*Screaming, crossing to* WILL; *she attempts to push him.*] No, you won't; you won't stay here. You're not going to do this thing again. I tell you I'm going to be happy. I tell you I'm going to be married. [*He doesn't resist her very strongly. Her anger and her rage are entirely new to him. He is surprised and cannot understand.*] You won't see him; I tell you, you won't tell him. You've got no business to. I hate you. I've hated you for months. I hate the sight of your face. I've wanted to go, and now I'm going. You've got to go, do you hear? You've got to get out—get out. [*Pushes him again.*

WILL. [*Throwing her off;* LAURA *staggers to armchair, rises, crosses left.*] What the hell is the use of fussing with a woman. [*Exit.*

LAURA. [*Hysterically.*] I want to be happy, I'm going to be married, I'm going to be happy.

[*Sinks down in exhausted state in front of trunk.*

CURTAIN, SLOW.

ACT IV.

SCENE. *The same scene as Act III. It is about two o'clock in the afternoon.*

AT RISE. *When the curtain rises, there are two big trunks and one small one up stage. These are marked in the usual theatrical fashion. There are grips packed, umbrellas, and the usual paraphernalia that accompanies a woman when she is making a permanent departure from her place of living. All the bric-à-brac, &c., has been removed from dresser. On down-stage end of dresser is a small alligator bag containing night-dress, toilet articles, and bunch of keys. The dresser drawers are some of them half open, and old pieces of tissue-paper and ribbons are hanging out. The writing-desk has had all materials removed and is open, showing scraps of torn-up letters, and in one pigeon-hole is a New York Central time-table; between desk and bay-window is a lady's hat-trunk containing huge picture hat. It is closed. Behind table is a suit-case with which* ANNIE *is working when curtain rises. Under desk are two old millinery boxes, around which are scattered old tissue-paper, a pair of old slippers, a woman's shabby hat, old ribbon, &c. In front of window at end of pianola is thrown a lot of old empty boxes, such as are used for stocking and shirtwaist boxes. The picture-frame and basket of flowers have been removed from pianola. The stool is on top of pianola, upside down. There is an empty White Rock bottle, with glass turned over it, standing between the legs of the stool. The big trunk is in front of sofa, and packed, and it has a swing tray under which is packed a fancy evening gown; the lid is down. On top of lid are an umbrella, lady's travelling-coat, hat and gloves. On left end of sofa are a large Gladstone bag, packed and fastened, a smaller trunk (thirty-four inch), tray with lid. In tray are articles of wearing apparel. In end of tray is revolver wrapped in tissue-paper. Trunk is closed, and supposed to be locked. Tossed across left arm of armchair are couple of violet cords. Down stage centre is a large piece of wide tan ribbon. The room has the general appearance of having been stripped of all personal belongings. There are old magazines and tissue-paper all over the place. A bearskin rug is thrown up against table in low window, the furniture is all on stage as used in Act III. At rise* LAURA *is sitting on trunk with clock in hand.* ANNIE *is on floor behind table, fastening suit-case.* LAURA *is pale and perturbed.*

ANNIE. Ain't yuh goin' to let me come to yuh at all, Miss Laura?

LAURA. I don't know yet, Annie. I don't even know what the place is like that we're going to. Mr. Madison hasn't said much. There hasn't been time.

ANNIE. Why, Ah've done ma best for yuh, Miss Laura, yes, Ah have. Ah jest been with yuh ev'ry moment of ma time, an' [*Places suit-case on table; crosses to centre.*] Ah worked for yuh an' Ah loved yuh, an' Ah doan' wan' to be left 'ere all alone in dis town 'ere New York. [LAURA *turns to door;* ANNIE *stoops, grabs up ribbon, hides it behind her back.*] Ah ain't the kind of cullud lady knows many people. Can't yuh take me along wid yuh, Miss Laura?—yuh all been so good to me.

LAURA. Why, I told you to [*Crosses to door, looks out, returns disappointed.*] stay here and get your things together [ANNIE *hides ribbon in front of her waist.*], and then Mr. Brockton will probably want you to do something. Later, I think he'll have you pack up, just as soon as he finds I'm gone. I've got the address that you gave me. I'll let you know if you can come on.

ANNIE. [*Suddenly.*] Ain't yuh goin' to give me anything at all jes' to remembuh yuh by? Ah've been so honest—

LAURA. Honest?

ANNIE. Honest, Ah have.

LAURA. You've been about as honest as most coloured [*Crosses to table; gets suit-case; crosses to sofa and puts suit-case on it.*] girls are who work for women in the position that I am in. You haven't stolen enough to make me discharge you, but I've seen what you've taken. [*Sits on end of sofa facing left.*

ANNIE. Now, Miss Laura.

LAURA. Don't try to fool me. What you've got you're welcome to, but for heaven's sake don't prate around here about loyalty and honesty. I'm sick of it.

ANNIE. Ain't yuh goin' to give me no recommendation?

LAURA. [*Impatiently looking around the room.*] What good would my recommendation do? You can always go and get another position with people who've lived the way I've lived, and my recommendation to the other kind wouldn't amount to much.

ANNIE. [*Sits on trunk.*] Ah can just see whah Ah'm goin',—back to dat boa'din'-house in 38th Street fo' me. [*Crying.*

LAURA. Now shut your noise. I don't want to hear any more. I've given you twenty-five dollars for a present. I think that's enough.

[ANNIE *assumes a most aggrieved appearance.*

ANNIE. Ah know, but twenty-five dollars ain't a home, and I'm [*Rises, crosses to rubbish heap, picks up old slippers and hat, puts hat on head as she goes out, looks into pier-glass.*] losin' my home. Dat's jest my luck—every time I save enough money to buy my weddin' clothes to get married I lose my job.

[*Exit.*

LAURA. I wonder where John is. We'll never be able to make that train. [*She crosses to window, then to desk, takes out time-table, crosses to armchair and spreads time-table on back, studies it, crosses impatiently to trunk, and sits nervously kicking her feet. After a few seconds' pause the bell rings. She jumps up excitedly.*] That must be he,—Annie—go quick. [ANNIE *crosses and opens the door in the usual manner.*

JIM'S VOICE. [*Outside.*] Is Miss Murdock in?

ANNIE. Yassuh, she's in.

LAURA *is up stage and turns to receive visitor.* JIM *enters. He is nicely dressed in black and has an appearance of prosperity about him, but in other respects he retains the old drollness of enunciation and manner. He crosses to* LAURA *in a cordial way and holds out his hand.* ANNIE *crosses, after closing the door, and exits through the portières into the sleeping-apartment.*

JIM. How-dy-do, Miss Laura?

LAURA. Jim Weston, I'm mighty glad to see you.

JIM. Looks like as if you were going to move?

LAURA. Yes, I am going to move, and a long ways, too. How well you're looking,—as fit as a fiddle.

JIM. Yes; I am feelin' fine. Where yer goin'? Troupin'?

LAURA. No, indeed.

JIM. [*Surveying the baggage.*] Thought not. What's comin' off now? [*Takes off coat, puts coat and hat on trunk.*

LAURA. [*Very simply.*] I'm going to be married this afternoon.

JIM. Married?

LAURA. And then I'm going West.

JIM. [*Leaving the trunk, walking toward her and holding out his hands.*] Now I'm just glad to hear that. Ye know when I heard how—how things was breakin' for ye—well, I ain't knockin' or anythin' like that, but me and the missis have talked ye over a lot. I never did think this feller was goin' to do the right thing by yer. Brockton never looked to me like a fellow would marry anybody, but now that he's goin' through just to make you a nice, respectable wife, I guess everything must have happened for the best. [LAURA *averts her eyes. Both sit on trunk,* JIM *left of* LAURA.] Y' see I wanted to thank you for what you did a couple of weeks ago. Burgess wrote me a letter and told me I could go ahead of one of his big shows if I wanted to come back, and offering me considerable money. He mentioned your name, Miss Laura, and I talked it over with the missis, and—well, I can tell ye now when I couldn't if ye weren't to be hooked up—we decided that I wouldn't take that job, comin' as it did from you [*Slowly.*] and the way I knew it was framed up.

LAURA. Why not?

JIM. [*Embarrassed.*] Well, ye see, there are three kids and they're all growing up, all of them in school, and the missis, she's just about forgot show business and she's playing a star part in the kitchen, juggling dishes and doing flip-flaps with pancakes; and we figgered that as we'd always gone along kinder clean-like, it wouldn't be good for the kids to take a job comin' from Brockton because you—you—well—you—

LAURA. I know. [*Rises; sits on left arm of chair.*] You thought it wasn't decent. Is that it?

JIM. Oh, not exactly, only—well, you see I'm gettin' along pretty [*Rises; crosses to* LAURA.] good now. I got a little one-night-stand theatre out in Ohio—manager of it, too. The town is called Gallipolis. [*With a smile.*

LAURA. Gallipolis?

JIM. Oh, that ain't a disease. It is the name of a town. Maybe you don't know much about Gallipolis, or where it is.

LAURA. No.

JIM. Well, it looks just like it sounds. We got a little house, and the old lady is happy, and I feel so good that I can even stand her cookin'. Of course we ain't makin' much money, but I guess I'm gettin' a little old-fashioned around theatres anyway. The fellows from newspapers and colleges have got it on me. Last time I asked a man for a job he asked me what I knew about the Greek drama, and when I told him I didn't know the Greeks had a theatre in New York he slipped me a laugh and told me to come in again on some rainy Tuesday. Then Gallipolis showed on the map, and I beat it for the West. [JIM *notices by this time the pain he has caused* LAURA, *and is embarrassed.*] Sorry if I hurt ye—didn't mean to; and now that yer goin' to be Mrs. Brockton, well, I take back all I said, and, while I don't think I want to change my position, I wouldn't turn it down for—for that other reason, that's all.

LAURA. [*With a tone of defiance in her voice.*] But, Mr. Weston, I'm not going to be Mrs. Brockton.

JIM. No? [*Crosses left a little.*

LAURA. No.

JIM. Oh—oh—

LAURA. I'm going to marry another man, and a good man.

JIM. The hell you are!

[LAURA *rises and puts hand on* JIM'S *shoulder.*

LAURA. And it's going to be altogether different. I know what you meant when you said about the missis and the kids, and that's what I want—just a little home, just a little peace, just a little comfort, and—and the man has come who's going to give it to me. You don't want me to say any more, do you? [*Crosses to door, opens it, and looks out; closes it and crosses to* JIM.

JIM. [*Emphatically, and with a tone of hearty approval.*] No, I don't, and now I'm just going to put my mit out and shake yours and be real glad. I want to tell ye it's the only way to go along. I ain't never been a rival to Rockefeller, nor I ain't never made Morgan jealous, but since the day my old woman took her make-up off for the last time, and walked out of that stage-door to give me a little help and bring my kids into the world, I knew that was the way to go along; and if you're goin' to take that road, by Jiminy, I'm glad of it, for you sure do deserve it. I wish yer luck.

LAURA. Thank you.

JIM. I'm mighty glad you side-stepped Brockton. You're young [LAURA *sits on trunk.*], and you're pretty, and you're sweet, and if you've got the right kind of a feller there ain't no reason on earth why you shouldn't jest forgit the whole business and see nothin' but laughs and a good time comin' to you, and the sun sort o' shinin' every twenty-four hours in the day. You know the missis feels just as if she knew you, after I told her about them hard times we had at Farley's boarding-house, so I feel that it's paid me to come to New York [*Picks up pin; puts it in lapel of coat.*] even if I didn't book anything but "East Lynne" and "Uncle Tom's Cabin." [*Goes over to her.*] Now I'm goin'. Don't forget Gallipolis 's [LAURA *helps him on with his coat.*] the name, and sometimes the mail does get there. I'd be awful glad if you wrote the missis a little note tellin' us how you're gettin' along, and if you ever have to ride on the Kanawha and Michigan, just look out of the window when the train passes our town, because that is about the best you'll get.

LAURA. Why?

JIM. They only stop there on signal. And make up your mind that the Weston family is with you forty ways from the Jack day and night. Good-bye, and God bless you.

LAURA. Good-bye, Jim. I'm so glad to know you're happy, for it is good to be happy. [*Kisses him.*

JIM. You bet. [*Moves toward the door. She follows him after they have shaken hands.*] Never mind, I can get out all right. [*Opens the door, and at the door:*] Good-bye again.

LAURA. [*Very softly.*] Good-bye. [*Exit* JIM *and closes the door. She stands motionless until she hears the outer door slam.*] I wonder why he doesn't come. [*She goes up and looks out of the window and turns down stage, crosses right, counting trunks; as she counts suitcase on table, bell rings; she crosses hurriedly to trunk centre.*] Hurry, Annie, and see who that is.

ANNIE *enters, crosses, opens door, exits, and opens the outer door.*

ANNIE'S VOICE. She's waitin' for yer, Mr. Madison.

LAURA *hurries down to the centre of stage.* JOHN *enters, hat in hand and his overcoat on arm, followed by* ANNIE. *He stops just as he enters and looks at* LAURA *long and searchingly.* LAURA *instinctively feels that something has happened. She shudders and remains firm.* ANNIE *crosses and exits. Closes doors.*

LAURA. [*With a little effort.* JOHN *places hat and coat on trunk.*] Aren't you a little late, dear?

JOHN. I—I was detained down town a few minutes. I think that we can carry out our plan all right.

LAURA. [*After a pause.*] Has anything happened?

JOHN. I've made all the arrangements. The men will be here in a few minutes for your trunks. [*Crosses to coat; feels in pocket.*] I've got the railroad tickets and everything else, but—

LAURA. But what, John?

He goes over to her. She intuitively understands that she is about to go through an ordeal. She seems to feel that JOHN *has become acquainted with something which might interfere with their plan. He looks at her long and searchingly. Evidently he too is much wrought up, but when he speaks to her it is with a calm dignity and force which show the character of the man.*

JOHN. Laura.

LAURA. Yes?

JOHN. You know when I went down town I said I was going to call on two or three of my friends in Park Row.

LAURA. I know.

JOHN. I told them who I was going to marry.

LAURA. Well?

JOHN. They said something about you and Brockton, and I found that they'd said too much, but not quite enough.

LAURA. What did they say?

JOHN. Just that—too much and not quite enough. There's a minister waiting for us over on Madison Avenue. You see, then you'll be my wife. That's pretty serious business, and all I want now from you is the truth.

LAURA. Well?

JOHN. Just tell me that what they said was just an echo of the past—that it came from what had been going on before that wonderful day out in Colorado. Tell me that you've been on the level. I don't want their word, Laura—I just want yours.

LAURA *summons all her courage, looks up into his loving eyes, shrinks a moment before his anxious face, and speaks as simply as she can.*

LAURA. Yes, John, I have been on the level.

JOHN. [*Very tenderly.*] I knew that, dear, I knew it. [*He takes her in his arms and kisses her. She clings to him in pitiful helplessness. His manner is changed to one of almost boyish happiness.*] Well, now everything's all ready, let's get on the job. We haven't a great deal of time. Get your duds on.

LAURA. When do we go?

JOHN. Right away. The great idea is to get away.

LAURA. All right.

[*Gets hat off trunk, crosses to bureau, puts it on.*

JOHN. Laura, you've got trunks enough, haven't you? One might think we're moving a whole colony. [*Turns to her with a smile.*] And, by the way, to me you are a whole colony—anyway you're the only one I ever wanted to settle with.

LAURA. That's good. [*Takes bag off bureau, crosses to trunk, gets purse, coat, umbrella, as if ready to leave. She hurriedly gathers her things together, adjusting her hat and the like, and almost to herself in a low tone:*] I'm so excited. [*Continues preparations.*] Come on.

In the meantime JOHN *crosses by to get his hat and coat, and while the preparations are about to be completed and* LAURA *has said "Come on," she is transfixed by the noise of the slamming of the outer door. She stops as if she had been tremendously shocked, and a moment later the rattling of a latch-key in the inner door also stops* JOHN *from going any further. His coat is half on.*

LAURA looks toward the door, paralyzed with fright, and JOHN looks at her with an expression of great apprehension. Slowly the door opens, and BROCKTON enters with coat and hat on. As he turns to close the door after him, LAURA, pitifully and terribly afraid, retreats two or three steps, and lays coat, bag, purse and umbrella down in armchair, standing dazed. BROCKTON enters leisurely, paying no attention to anyone, while JOHN becomes as rigid as a statue, and follows with his eyes every move BROCKTON makes. The latter walks leisurely across the stage, and afterwards into the rooms through the portières. There is a wait of a second. No one moves. BROCKTON finally reënters with coat and hat off, and throws back the portières in such a manner as to reveal the bed and his intimate familiarity with the outer room. He goes down stage in the same leisurely manner and sits in a chair opposite JOHN, crossing his legs.

WILL. Hello, Madison, when did you get in?

Slowly JOHN seems to recover himself. His right hand starts up toward the lapel of his coat and slowly he pulls his Colt revolver from the holster under his armpit. There is a deadly determination and deliberation in every movement that he makes. WILL jumps to his feet and looks at him. The revolver is uplifted in the air, as a Western man handles a gun, so that when it is snapped down with a jerk the deadly shot can be fired. LAURA is terror-stricken, but before the shot is fired she takes a step forward and extends one hand in a gesture of entreaty.

LAURA. [*In a husky voice that is almost a whisper.*] Don't shoot.

The gun remains uplifted for a moment. JOHN is evidently wavering in his determination to kill. Slowly his whole frame relaxes. He lowers the pistol in his hand in a manner which clearly indicates that he is not going to shoot. He quietly puts it back in the holster, and WILL is obviously relieved, although he stood his ground like a man.

JOHN. [*Slowly.*] Thank you. You said that just in time. [*A pause.*

WILL. [*Recovering and in a light tone.*] Well, you see, Madison, that what I said when I was—

JOHN. [*Threateningly.*] Look out, Brockton, I don't want to talk to you. [*The men confront.*

WILL. All right.

JOHN. [*To* LAURA.] Now get that man out of here.

LAURA. John, I—

JOHN. Get him out. Get him out before I lose my temper or they'll take him out without his help.

LAURA. [*To* WILL.] Go—go. Please go.

WILL. [*Deliberately.*] If that's the way you want it, I'm willing.

Exit WILL *into the sleeping-apartment.* LAURA *and* JOHN *stand facing each other. He enters again with hat and coat on, and passes over toward the door.* LAURA *and* JOHN *do not move. When he gets just a little to the left of the centre of the stage* LAURA *steps forward and stops him with her speech.*

LAURA. Now before you go, and to you both, I want to tell you how I've learned to despise him. John, I know you don't believe me, but it's true—it's true. I don't love anyone in the world but just you. I know you don't think that it can be explained—maybe there isn't any explanation. I couldn't help it. I was so poor, and I had to live, and he wouldn't let me work, and he's only let me live one way, and I was hungry. Do you know what that means? I was hungry and didn't have clothes to keep me warm, and I tried, oh, John, I tried so hard to do the other thing,—the right thing,—but I couldn't.

JOHN. I—I know I couldn't help much, and perhaps I could have forgiven you if you hadn't lied to me. That's what hurt. [*Turning to* WILL *and approaching until he can look him in the eyes.*] I expected you to lie, you're that kind of a man. You left me with a shake of the hand, and you gave me your word, and you didn't keep it. Why should you keep it? Why should anything make any difference with you? Why, you pup, you've no right to live in the same world with decent folks. Now you make yourself scarce, or take it from me, I'll just kill you, that's all.

WILL. I'll leave, Madison, but I'm not going to let you think that I didn't do the right thing with you. She came to me voluntarily. She said she wanted to come back. I told you that, when I was in Colorado, and you didn't believe me, and I told you that when she did this sort of thing I'd let you know. I dictated a letter to her to send to you, and I left it sealed and stamped in her hands to mail. She didn't do it. If there's been a lie, she told it. I didn't.

JOHN *turns to her. She hangs her head and averts her eyes in a mute acknowledgment of guilt. The revelation hits* JOHN *so hard that he sinks on the trunk centre, his head fallen to his breast. He is utterly limp and whipped. There is a moment's silence.*

WILL. [*Crosses to* JOHN.] You see! Why, my boy, whatever you think of me or the life I lead, I wouldn't have had this come to you for anything in the world. [JOHN *makes an impatient gesture.*] No, I wouldn't. My women don't mean a whole lot to me because I don't take them seriously. I wish I had the faith and the youth to feel the way you do. You're all in and broken up, but I wish I could be broken up just once. I did what I thought was best for you because I didn't think she could ever go through the way you wanted her to. I'm sorry it's all turned out bad. [*Pause.*] Good-bye.

He looks at JOHN *for a moment as if he was going to speak.* JOHN *remains motionless. The blow has hit him harder than he thought.* WILL *exits. The first door closes. In a moment the second door is slammed.* JOHN *and* LAURA *look at each other for a moment. He gives her no chance to speak. The hurt in his heart and his accusation are shown by his broken manner. A great grief has come into his life and he doesn't quite understand it. He seems to be feeling around for something to say, some way to get out. His head turns toward the door. With a pitiful gesture of the hand he looks at her in all his sorrow.*

JOHN. Well? [*Rises.*

LAURA. John, I— [*Takes off hat and places it on table.*

JOHN. I'd be careful what I said. Don't try to make excuses. I understand.

LAURA. It's not excuses. I want to tell you what's in my heart, but I can't; it won't speak, and you don't believe my voice.

JOHN. You'd better leave it unsaid.

LAURA. But I must tell. I can't let you go like this. [*She goes over to him and makes a weak attempt to put her arms around him. He takes her arms and puts them back to her side.*] I love you. I—how can I tell you—but I do, I do, and you won't believe me.

He remains silent for a moment and then takes her by the hand, leads her over to the chair and places her in it.

JOHN. I think you do as far as you are able; but, Laura, I guess you don't know what a decent sentiment is. [*He gathers himself together. His tone is very gentle and very firm, but it carries a tremendous conviction, even with his grief ringing through his speech.*] Laura, you're not immoral, you're just unmoral, kind o' all out of shape, and I'm afraid there isn't a particle of hope for you. When we met neither of us had any reason to be proud, but I thought that you thought that it was the chance of salvation which sometimes comes to a man and a woman fixed as we were then. What had been had been. It was all in the great to-be for us, and now, how you've kept your word! What little that promise meant, when I thought you handed me a new lease of life!

LAURA. [*In a voice that is changed and metallic. She is literally being nailed to the cross.*] You're killing me—killing me.

JOHN. Don't make such a mistake. In a month you'll recover. There will be days when you will think of me, just for a moment, and then it will be all over. With you it is the easy way, and it always will be. You'll go on and on until you're finally left a wreck, just the type of the common woman. And you'll sink until you're down to the very bed-rock of depravity. I pity you.

LAURA. [*Still in the same metallic tone of voice.*] You'll never leave me to do that. I'll kill myself.

JOHN. Perhaps that's the only thing left for you to do, but you'll not do it. It's easier to live. [*Crosses, gets hat and coat, turns and looks at her,* LAURA *rising at the same time.*

LAURA. John, I said I'd kill myself, and I mean it. If it's the only thing to do, I'll do it, and I'll do it before your very eyes. [*She crosses quickly, gets keys out of satchel, opens trunk, takes gun out of trunk, stands facing* JOHN*—waiting a moment.*] You understand that when your hand touches that door I'm going to shoot myself. I will, so help me God!

JOHN. [*Stops and looks at her.*] Kill yourself? [*Pause.*] Before me? [*Pause.*] All right. [*Raising his voice.*] Annie, Annie!

ANNIE. [*Enters.*] Yes, sir.

JOHN. [LAURA *looks at* JOHN *in bewilderment.*] You see your mistress there has a pistol in her hand?

ANNIE. [*Frightened.*] Yassuh—

JOHN. She wants to kill herself. I just called you to witness that the act is entirely voluntary on her part. Now, Laura, go ahead.

LAURA. [*Nearly collapsing, drops the pistol to the floor.*] John, I—can't—

JOHN. Annie, she's evidently changed her mind. You may go.

ANNIE. But, Miss Laura, Ah—

JOHN. [*Peremptorily.*] You may go. [*Bewildered and not understanding,* ANNIE *exits through the portières. In that same gentle tone, but carrying with it an almost frigid conviction.*] You didn't have the nerve. I knew you wouldn't. For a moment you thought the only decent thing for you to do was to die, and yet you couldn't go through. I am sorry for you,—more sorry than I can tell. [*He takes a step towards the door.*

LAURA. You're going—you're going?

JOHN. Yes.

LAURA. And—and—you never thought that perhaps I'm frail, and weak, and a woman, and that now, maybe, I need your strength, and you might give it to me, and it might be better. I want to lean on you,—lean on you, John. I know I need someone. Aren't you going to let me? Won't you give me another chance?

JOHN. I gave you your chance, Laura.

LAURA. [*Throws arms around his neck.*] Give me another.

JOHN. But you leaned the wrong way. Good-bye.

[*He pulls away and goes out, slamming both doors.*

LAURA. [*Screaming.*] John—John—I—[*She sits on trunk, weeping in loud and tearful manner; rises in a dazed fashion, starts to cross, sees gun, utters loud cry of mingled despair and anger, grabs up gun, crossing to bureau, opens up-stage drawer, throws gun in, slams drawer shut, calling:*] Annie! Annie!

ANNIE. [*Appears through the portières.*] Ain't yuh goin' away, Miss Laura?

LAURA. [*Suddenly arousing herself, and with a defiant voice.*] No, I'm not. I'm going to stay right here. [ANNIE *crosses and opens trunk, takes out handsome dress, hangs it over back of armchair, crosses up to hat-trunk, takes out hat.* LAURA *takes it from her, crosses to trunk left, starts to unpack it.*] Open these trunks, take out those clothes, get me my prettiest dress. Hurry up. [*She goes before the mirror.*] Get my new hat, dress up my body and paint up my face. It's all they've left of me. [*To herself.*] They've taken my soul away with them.

ANNIE. [*In a happy voice.*] Yassum, yassum.

LAURA. [*Who is arranging her hair.*] Doll me up, Annie.

ANNIE. Yuh goin' out, Miss Laura?

LAURA. Yes. I'm going to Rector's to make a hit, and to hell with the rest!

At this moment the hurdy-gurdy in the street, presumably immediately under her window, begins to play the tune of "Bon-Bon Buddie, My Chocolate Drop." There is something in this rag-time melody which is particularly and peculiarly suggestive of the low life, the criminality and prostitution that constitute the night excitement of that section of New York City known as the Tenderloin. The tune,—its association,—is like spreading before LAURA'S *eyes a panorama of the inevitable depravity that awaits her. She is torn from every ideal that she so weakly endeavoured to grasp, and is thrown into the mire and slime at the very moment when her emancipation seems to be assured. The woman, with her flashy dress in one arm and her equally exaggerated type of picture hat in the other, is nearly prostrated by the tune and the realization of the future as it is terrifically conveyed to her. The negress, in the happiness of serving* LAURA *in her questionable career, picks up the melody and hums it as she unpacks the finery that has been put away in the trunk.*

LAURA. [*With infinite grief, resignation, and hopelessness.*] O God—O my God. [*She turns and totters toward the bedroom. The hurdy-gurdy continues, with the negress accompanying it.*

A SLOW CURTAIN.

END OF THE PLAY.

THE RETURN OF PETER GRIMM

David Belasco

DAVID BELASCO

(Born, San Francisco, July 25, 1853)

The present Editor has had many opportunities of studying the theatre side of David Belasco. He has been privileged to hear expressed, by this Edison of our stage, diverse opinions about plays and players of the past, and about insurgent experiments of the immediate hour. He has always found a man quickly responsive to the best memories of the past, an artist naïvely childlike in his love of the theatre, shaped by old conventions and modified by new inventions. Belasco is the one individual manager to-day who has a workshop of his own; he is pre-eminently a creator, whereas his contemporaries, like Charles Frohman, were emphatically manufacturers of goods in the amusement line.

Such a man is entitled to deep respect, for the "carry-on" spirit with which he holds aloft the banner used by Boucicault, Wallack, Palmer, and Daly. It is wrong to credit him with deafness to innovation, with blindness to new combinations. He is neither of these. It is difficult to find a manager more willing to take infinite pains for effect, with no heed to the cost; it is impossible to place above him a director more successful in creating atmosphere and in procuring unity of coöperation from his staff. No one, unless it be Winthrop Ames, gives more personal care to a production than David Belasco. Considering that he was reared in the commercial theatre, his position is unique and distinctive.

In the years to come, when students enter the Columbia University Dramatic Museum, founded by Professor Brander Matthews, they will be able to judge, from the model of the stage set for "Peter Grimm," exactly how far David Belasco's much-talked-of realism went; they will rightly regard it as the high point in accomplishment before the advent of the "new" scenery, whose philosophy Belasco understands, but whose artistic spirit he cannot accept. Maybe, by that time, there will be preserved for close examination the manuscripts of Belasco's plays—models of thoroughness, of managerial foresight. The present Editor had occasion once to go through these typewritten copies; and there remains impressed on the memory the detailed exposition in "The Darling of the Gods." Here was not only indicated every shade of lighting, but the minute stage business for acting, revealing how wholly the manager gave himself over to the creation of atmosphere. I examined a mass of data—"boot plots," "light plots," "costume designs." Were the play ever published in this form, while it might confuse the general reader, it would enlighten the specialist. It would be a key to realistic stage management, in which Belasco excels. Whether it be his own play, or that of some outsider, with whom, in the final product, Belasco always collaborates, the manuscripts, constituting his producing library, are evidence of his instinctive eye for stage effect.

The details in the career of David Belasco are easily accessible. It is most unfortunate that the stupendous record of his life's accomplishment thus far, which, in two voluminous books, constituted the final labour of the late William Winter, is not more truly reflective of the man and his work. It fails to reproduce the flavour of the dramatic periods through which Belasco passed, in his association with Dion Boucicault as private secretary, in his work with James A. Herne at Baldwin's Theatre, in San Francisco, in his pioneer realism at the old New York Madison Square Theatre, when the Mallory Brothers were managers, Steele Mackaye was one of the stock dramatists, Henry DeMille was getting ready for collaboration with Belasco, Daniel Frohman was house-manager and Charles Frohman was out on the road, trying his abilities as advance-man for Wallack and Madison Square successes. Winter's life is orderly and matter-of-fact; Belasco's real life has always been melodramatic and colourful.

His early struggles in San Francisco, his initial attempts at playwriting, his intercourse with all the big actors of the golden period of the '60's—Mr. Belasco has written about them in a series of magazine reminiscences, which, if they are lacking in exact sequence, are measure of his type of mind, of his vivid memory, of his personal opinions.

Belasco has reached his position through independence which, in the '90's, brought down upon him the relentless antagonism of the Theatrical Trust—a combine of managers that feared the advent of so individualistic a playwright and manager. They feared his ability to do so many things well, and they disliked the way the public supported him. This struggle, tempestuous and prolonged, is in the records.

A man who has any supreme, absorbing interest at all is one who thrives on vagaries. Whatever Belasco has touched since his days of apprenticeship in San Francisco, he has succeeded in imposing upon it what is popularly called "the Belasco atmosphere." Though he had done a staggering amount of work before coming to New York, and though, when he went to the Lyceum Theatre, he and Henry DeMille won reputation by collaborating in "The Wife," "Lord Chumley," "The Charity Ball," and "Men and Women," he was probably first individualized in the minds of present-day theatregoers when Mrs. Leslie Carter made a sensational swing across stage, holding on to the clapper of a bell in "The Heart of Maryland." Even thus early, he was displaying characteristics for which, in later days, he remained unexcelled. He was helping Bronson Howard to touch up "Baron Rudolph," "The Banker's Daughter" and "The Young Mrs. Winthrop;" he was succeeding with a dramatization of H. Rider Haggard's "She," where William Gillette had failed in the attempt.

"The Heart of Maryland" established both Belasco and Mrs. Carter. Then he started on that extravagant period of spectacular drama, which gave to the stage such memorable pictures as "Du Barry," with Mrs. Carter, and "The Darling of the Gods," with Blanche Bates. In such pieces he literally threw away the possibilities of profit, in order to gratify his decorative sense. Out of that time came two distinctive pieces—one, the exquisitely poignant "Madame Butterfly" and the other, "The Girl of the Golden West"—both giving inspiration to the composer, Puccini, who discovered that a Belasco play was better suited for the purposes of colourful Italian opera than any other American dramas he examined.

Counting his western vicissitudes as one period, and the early New York days as a second, one might say that in the third period David Belasco exhibited those excellences and limitations which were thereafter to mark him and shape all his work. There is an Oriental love of colour and effect in all he does; but there is no monotony about it. "The Darling of the Gods" was different from "The Girl of the Golden West," and both were distinct from "The Rose of the Rancho." It is this scenic decorativeness which has enriched many a slim piece, accepted by him for presentation, and such a play has always been given that care and attention which has turned it eventually into a Belasco "offering." None of his collaborators will gainsay this genius of his. John Luther Long's novel was unerringly dramatized; Richard Walton Tully, when he left the Belasco fold, imitated the Belasco manner, in "The Bird of Paradise" and "Omar, the Tentmaker." And that same ability Belasco possesses to dissect the heart of a romantic piece was carried by him into war drama, and into parlour comedies, and plays of business condition. I doubt whether "The Auctioneer" would read well, or, for the matter of that, "The Music Master;" Charles Klein has written more coherent dialogue than is to be found in these early pieces. But they are vivid in mind because of Belasco's management, and because he saw them fitted to the unique figure of David Warfield.

But a Belasco success is furthered by the tremendous public curiosity that follows him in all he does. There is a wizardry about him which fascinates, and makes excellent reading in the press. Long before I saw the three-winged screen upon which it is his custom to sort out and pin up his random notes for a play, it was featured in the press. So were pictures of his "collection," in rooms adjoining his studio—especially his Napoleonic treasures which are a by-product of his Du Barry days. No man of the theatre is more constantly on the job than he. It is said that old John Dee, the famous astrologer whom Queen Elizabeth so often consulted, produced plays when he was a student at Cambridge University, with stage effects which only one gifted in the secrets of magic could have consummated. Belasco paints with an electric switchboard, until the emotion of his play is unmistakably impressed upon the eye. At a moment's notice he will root out his proscenium arch, and build a "frame" which obliterates the footlights; at another time he will build an "apron" to his stage, not for its historical significance, but merely to give depth and mellowness to such an ecclesiastical picture as Knoblauch's "Marie-Odile." He has spent whole nights alone in the theatre auditorium with his electrician, "feeling" for the "siesta" somnolence which carried his audience instantly into the Spanish heat of old California, in "The Rose of the Rancho;" and the moving scenery which took the onlooker from the foothills of the Sierras to the cabin of "The Girl of the Golden West" was a "trick" well worth the experiment.

Thus, no manager is more ingenious, more resourceful than David Belasco. But his care for detail is often a danger; he does not know fully the value of elimination; the eye of the observer is often worried by the multiplicity of detail, where reticence would have been more quickly effective. This is the Oriental in Belasco. His is a strange blend of realism and decorativeness.

"A young man came to me once," he said to me, "with the manuscript of a new play, which had possibilities in it. But after I had talked with him awhile, I found him preaching the doctrines of the 'new' art. So I said to him, 'My dear sir, here is your manuscript. The first scene calls for a tenement-house set. How would you mount it?' "

He smiled, maybe at the recollection of Gordon Craig's statements that "actuality, accuracy of detail, are useless on the stage," and that "all is a matter of proportion and nothing to do with actuality."

"I felt," Mr. Belasco continued, "that the young man would find difficulty in reconciling the nebulous perspectives of Mr. Craig with the squalor of a city block. I said to him, 'I have been producing for many years, and I have mounted various plays calling for differing atmospheres. I don't want to destroy your ideals regarding the 'new art', but I want you to realize that a manager has to conform his taste to the material he has in hand. I consider that one of the most truthful sets I have ever had on the stage was the one for the second act of Eugene Walter's 'The Easiest Way'. A boarding-house room on the top floor cannot be treated in any other way than as a boarding-house room. And should I take liberties with what we know for a fact exists in New York, on Seventh Avenue, just off Broadway, then I am a bad producer and do not know my business. I do not say there is no suggestion in realism; it is unwise to clutter the stage with needless detail. But we cannot idealize a little sordid ice-box where a working girl keeps her miserable supper; we cannot symbolize a broken jug standing in a wash-basin of loud design. Those are the necessary evils of a boarding-house, and I must be true to them'."

One will have to give Mr. Belasco this credit, that whatever he is, he is *it* to the bent of his powers. Had he lived in Elizabeth's day, he would have been an Elizabethan heart and soul. But his habit is formed as a producer, and he conforms the "new" art to this habit as completely as Reinhardt Reinhardtized the morality play, "Everyman," or Von Hofmannsthal Teutonized "Elektra."

"The Return of Peter Grimm" has been chosen for the present collection. It represents a Belasco interest and conviction greater than are to be found in any of his other plays. While there are no specific claims made for the fact that *Peter* materializes after his death, it is written with plausibility and great care. The psychic phenomena are treated as though real, and our sympathy for *Peter* when he returns is a human sympathy for the inability of a spirit to get his message across. The theme is not etherealized; one does not see through a mist dimly. There was not even an attempt, in the stage production of the piece, which occurred at the Belasco Theatre, New York, on October 17, 1911, to use the "trick" of gauze and queer lights; there was only one supreme thing done—to make the audience feel that *Peter* was on a plane far removed from the physical, by the ease and naturalness with which he slipped past objects, looked through people, and was unheeded by those whom he most wanted to influence. The remarkable unity of idea sustained by Mr. Belasco as manager, and by Mr. Warfield as actor, was largely instrumental in making the play a triumph. The playwright did not attempt to create supernatural mood; he did not resort to natural tricks such as Maeterlinck used in "L'Intruse," or as Mansfield employed in "Dr. Jekyll and Mr. Hyde." He reduced what to us seems, at the present moment, a complicated explanation of a psychic condition to its simple terms, and there was nothing strange to the eye or unusual in the situation. One cannot approach the theme of the psychic without a personal concern. Sardou's "Spiritisme" was the culmination of years of investigation; the subject was one with which Belasco likewise has had much to do during the past years.

It is a privilege to be able to publish "Peter Grimm." Thus far not many of the Belasco plays are available in reading form. "May Blossom" and "Madame Butterfly" are the only ones. "Peter Grimm" has been novelized—in the day, now fortunately past, when a play was novelized in preference to perpetuating its legitimate form. And excerpts from the dialogue have been used. But this is the first time the complete text has appeared and it has been carefully edited by the author himself. In addition to which Mr. Belasco has written the following account of "Peter's" evolution, to be used in this edition.

The play, "The Return of Peter Grimm," is an expression in dramatic form of my ideas on a subject which I have pondered over since boyhood: "Can the dead come back?" *Peter Grimm* did come back. At the same time, I inserted a note in my program to say that

I advanced no positive opinion; that the treatment of the play allowed the audience to believe that it had actually seen *Peter*, or that he had not been seen but existed merely in the minds of the characters on the stage. Spiritualists from all over the country flocked to see "The Return of Peter Grimm," and I have heard that it gave comfort to many. It was a difficult theme, and more than once I was tempted to give it up. But since it has given relief to those who have loved and lost, it was not written in vain. Victorian Sardou dealt with the same subject, but he did not show the return of the dead; instead, he delivered a spirit message by means of knocking on a table. His play was not a success, and I was warned by my friends to let the subject alone; but it is a subject that I never can or never have let alone; yet I never went to a medium in my life—could not bring myself to do it. My dead must come to me, and have come to me—or so I believe.

The return of the dead is the eternal riddle of the living. Although mediums have been exposed since the beginning of time, and so-called "spiritualism" has fallen into disrepute over and over again, it emerges triumphantly in spite of charlatans, and once more becomes the theme of the hour.

The subject first interested me when, as a boy, I read a story in which the dead "foretold dangers to loved ones." My mother had "premonitions" which were very remarkable, and I was convinced, at the time, that the dead gave these messages to her. She personally could not account for them. I probably owe my life to one of my mother's premonitions. I was going on a steamboat excursion with my school friends, when my mother had a strong presentiment of danger, and begged me not to go. She gave in to my entreaties, however, much against her will. Just as the boat was about to leave the pier, a vision of her pale face and tear-filled eyes came to me. I heard her voice repeating, "I wish you would not go, Davy." The influence was so strong that I dashed down the gang-plank as it was being pulled in. The boat met with disaster, and many of the children were killed or wounded. These premonitions have also come to me, but I do not believe as I did when a boy that they are warnings from the dead, although I cannot explain them, and they are never wrong; the message is always very clear.

My mother convinced me that the dead come back by coming to me at the time of her death—or so I believe. One night, after a long, hard rehearsal, I went to bed, worn out, and fell into a deep sleep. I was awakened by my mother, who stood in my bedroom and called to me. She seemed to be clothed in white. She repeated my name over and over—the name she called me in my boyhood: "Davy! Davy!" She told me not to grieve—that she was dying; that she *had* to see me. I distinctly saw her and heard her speak.

She was in San Francisco at the time—I, in New York. After she passed out of the room, I roused my family and told what I had heard and seen. I said: "My mother is dead. I know she is dead;" but I could not convince my family that I had not been dreaming. I was very restless—could not sleep again. The next day (we were rehearsing "Zaza") I went out for luncheon during the recess with a member of my company. He was a very absent-minded man, and at the table he took a telegram from his pocket which he said he had forgotten to give me: it announced the death of my mother at the time I had seen her in my room. I am aware that this could be explained as thought transference, accompanied by a dream in which my mother appeared so life-like as to make me believe the dream real. This explanation, however, does not satisfy me. I am sure that I did see her. Other experiences of a kindred nature served to strengthen my belief in the naturalness of what we call the supernatural. I decided to write a play dealing with the return of the dead: so it followed that when I was in need of a new play for David Warfield, I chose this subject. Slight of figure, unworldly, simple in all his ways, Warfield was the very man to bring a message back from the other world. Warfield has always appeared to me as a character out of one of Grimm's Fairy Tales. He was, to my mind, the one man to impersonate a spirit and make it seem real. So my desire to write a play of the dead, and my belief in Warfield's artistry culminated in "The Return of Peter Grimm." The subject was very difficult, and the greatest problem confronting me was to preserve the illusion of a spirit while actually using a living person. The apparition of the ghost in "Hamlet" and in "Macbeth," the spirits who return to haunt *Richard III*, and other ghosts of the theatre convinced me that green lights and dark stages with spot-lights would not give the illusion necessary to this play. All other spirits have been visible to someone on the stage, but *Peter* was visible to none, save the dog (who wagged his tail as his master returned from the next world) and to *Frederik*, the nephew, who was to see him but for a second. *Peter* was to be in the same room with the members of the household, and to come into close contact with them. They were to feel his influence without seeing him. He was to move among them, even appear to touch them, but they were to look past him or above him—never into his face. He must, of course, be visible to the audience. My problem, then, was to reveal a dead man worrying about his earthly home, trying to enlist the aid of anybody—everybody—to take his message. Certainly no writer ever chose a more difficult task; I must say that I was often very much discouraged, but something held me to the work in spite of myself. The choice of an occupation for my leading character was very limited. I gave *Peter* various trades and professions, none of which seemed to suit the part, until I made him a quaint old Dutchman, a nursery-man who loved his garden and perennials—the flowers that pass away and return season after season. This gave a clue to his character; gave him the right to found his belief in immortality on the lessons learned in his garden.

"God does not send us strange flowers every year,
When the warm winds blow o'er the pleasant places,
The same fair flowers lift up the same fair faces.
The violet is here . . . .
It all comes back, the odour, grace and hue,
. . . . it IS the THING WE KNEW.
So after the death winter it shall be," etc.

Against a background of budding trees, I placed the action of the play in the month of April; April with its swift transitions from bright sunlight to the darkness of passing clouds and showers. April weather furnished a natural reason for raising and lowering the lights—that the dead could come and go at will, seen or unseen. The passing rain-storms blended with the tears of those weeping for their loved ones. A man who comes back must not have a commonplace name—a name suggestive of comedy—and I think I must have read over every Dutch name that ever came out of Holland before I selected the name of "*Peter Grimm.*" It was chosen because it suggested (to me) a stubborn old man with a sense of justice—whose spirit *would* return to right a wrong and adjust his household affairs.

The stage setting was evolved after extreme care and thought. It was a mingling of the past and present. It was *Peter's* sitting-room, with a mixture of furniture and family portraits and knick-knacks, each with an association of its own. It was such a room as would be dear to all old-fashioned, home-loving people—unlike a room of the present, from which every memento of parents and grand-parents would be banished in favour of strictly modern or antique formal furniture. In this room, the things of *Peter's* father mingled with those of *Peter's* boyhood and young manhood. This was done in order that the influence of his familiar belongings might be felt by the people of the play. When his niece stood with her hand on his chair; when she saw the lilies he loved; when she touched his pipe, or any of the familiar objects dear to her because of their associations, *Peter* was brought vividly back to her mind, although she could not see him.

Peter's clothing was selected with unusual care so that it would not catch the reflection from the lights. Months of preparation and weeks of rehearsal were necessary.

One detail that was especially absorbing was the matter of lighting; catching the high lights and shadows. This was the first time the "bridge of lights" was used on any stage. Lighting has always been to me more than mere illumination. It is a revelation of the heart and soul of the story. It points the way. Lights should be to the play what the musical accompaniment is to the singer. A wordless story could be told by lights. Lights should be mixed as a painter mixes his colours—a bit of pink here, of blue there; a touch of red, a lavender or a deep purple, with shadows intervening to give the desired effect. Instead of throwing a mysterious light upon the figure of *Peter*, I decided to reverse the process and put no lights on him. The light was on the other people—the people still in life, with just enough amber to give them colour.

The play was cut and cut until there was not a superfluous line in it. Every word was necessary, although it might not have seemed so when read. It was only after the play was recalled as a whole, that the necessity for everything could be seen. The coming of the circus with the clown singing "Uncle Rat has come to town," and the noise of the drums, are instances of this. It seemed like halting the action to bring in a country circus procession, but its necessity is shown in the final scene when the little boy, *William*, passes away. It is always cruel to see a child die on the stage. The purpose of the coming of the circus was to provide a pleasant memory for the child to recall as his mind wandered away from earth, and to have his death a happy one. This was made more effective when *Peter* took up the refrain of the song as though he knew what was passing in the dying boy's mind, showing that the dead have their own world and their own understanding.

No company of players ever had situations so fraught with danger of failure. They were very nervous. Mr. Warfield appeared in the part for several weeks before he felt at ease as the living man who returns as his own spirit.

There is one memory associated with the play which will remain in my heart as long as it beats. This piece was written during the last year-and-a-half of my daughter Augusta's life. For some reason, which I could not understand then, but which was clear to me later, the subject fascinated her. She showed the greatest interest in it. The dear child was preparing to leave the world, but we did not know it. When the manuscript was finished, she kept it by her side, and, notwithstanding her illness, saw the dress rehearsal. During the writing of the play, she often said, "Yes, father, it is all true. I believe every word of it." It was as though the thought embodied in the play gave her comfort. When we discovered how ill she was, I took her to Asheville, North Carolina, thinking the climate would help her. She grew worse. Still hoping, we went to Colorado, and there I lost her.

It has seemed to me since that the inspiration compelling me to go on with "Peter Grimm," in spite of its difficulties, came from this daughter who died.

I cannot close this reminiscence of "The Return of Peter Grimm" without acknowledging the help and inspiration received from David Warfield, without whose genius and personality the play would not have been possible.

I doubt whether Mr. Belasco has ever infused so much imaginative ingenuity into the structure and picture of a play. Even in the reading, its quaint charm is instantly revealed. We quite agree with Winter in saying that the effectiveness of the rôle of *Peter* lies in its simplicity. This was the triumph of Warfield's interpretation. It may have been difficult to attain the desired effects, but once reached, technical skill did the rest. It will be noted on the program that credit is given for an idea to Mr. Cecil DeMille, son of Mr. Belasco's former collaborator. "The Return of Peter Grimm" was scheduled for production in London by Sir Herbert Tree, but plans were cut short by that actor's sudden death, July 2, 1917.

Mr. Belasco's interest in the psychic and the supernatural has been seen in other plays, notably in "The Case of Becky," by Edward Locke, and in Henry Bernstein's "The Secret"—example of Belasco's most skilled adaptation from the French, though we remember the excellence of his version of Berton and Simon's "Zaza." That he thought Warfield admirably suited to this type of play was one of the chief incentives which prompted him to write "Van Der Decken" (produced on the road, December 12, 1915), a play whose theme is "The Flying Dutchman"—and not thus far given in New York. *

* Some of Mr. Belasco's recent opinions regarding the stage have been published in book form, under the title, "The Theatre through its Stage Door" (Harper).

BELASCO THEATRE

FORTY FOURTH STREET, near BROADWAY
Under the *Sole* Management *of* DAVID BELASCO

BEGINNING TUESDAY EVENING, OCTOBER 17, 1911.
Matinees Thursday and Saturday.

DAVID BELASCO
Presents

DAVID WARFIELD

—IN—

THE RETURN OF PETER GRIMM

A PLAY, IN THREE ACTS.

By DAVID BELASCO.

"Only one thing really counts—only one thing—love. It is the only thing that tells in the long run: nothing else endures to the end."

CAST OF CHARACTERS.

PETER GRIMM	DAVID WARFIELD
FREDERIK, his nephew	JOHN SAINPOLIS
JAMES HARTMAN	THOMAS MEIGHAN
ANDREW MacPHERSON	JOSEPH BRENNAN
REV. HENRY BATHOLOMMEY	WILLIAM BOAG
COLONEL TOM LAWTON	JOHN F. WEBBER
WILLEM	PERCY HELTON
KATHRIEN	JANET DUNBAR
MRS. BATHOLOMMEY	MARIE BATES
MARTA	MARIE REICHARDT
THE CLOWN	TONY BEVAN

PROGRAM CONTINUED ON SECOND PAGE FOLLOWING

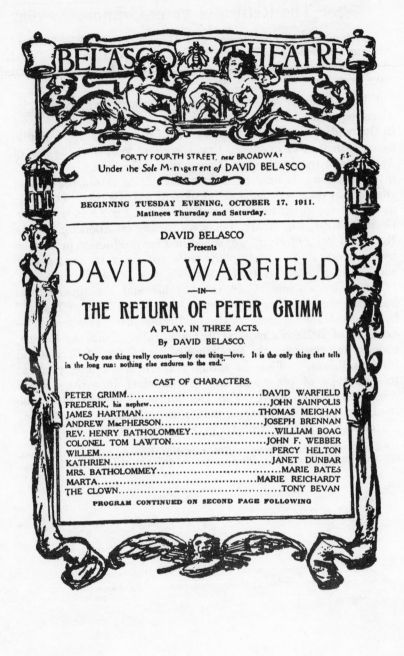

PROGRAM CONTINUED.

SYNOPSIS.

The scene of the play is laid in the living room of Peter Grimm's home at Grimm Manor, a small town in New York State, founded by early settlers from Holland.

The first act takes place at eleven o'clock in the morning, on a fine spring day.

The second act passes ten days later, towards the close of a rainy afternoon.

The third act takes place at twenty minutes to twelve on the same night.

PROGRAM CONTINUED ON SECOND PAGE FOLLOWING

PROGRAM CONTINUED.

NOTE—Mr. Belasco does not intend to advance any theory as to the probability of the return of the main character of this play. For *the many*, it may be said that he could exist only in the minds of the characters grouped about him—in their subconscious memories. For *the few*, his presence will embody the theory of the survival of persistent personal energy. This character has, so far as possible, been treated to accord with either thought. The initial idea of the play was first suggested as a dramatic possibility by Mr. Cecil DeMille, to whom Mr. Belasco acknowledges his indebtedness. A conversation with Professor James, of Harvard, and the works of Professor Hyslop of the American branch of the London Society of Psychical Research have also aided Mr. Belasco.

The play produced under the personal supervision of Mr. Belasco.

Stage Director....................................William J. Dean
Stage Manager....................................William Boag

Scene by Ernest Gros.

Scenery built by Charles J. Carson.
Electrical effects by Louis Hartman.

THE RETURN OF PETER GRIMM

A PLAY IN THREE ACTS

By DAVID BELASCO

ACT I.

The scene shows a comfortable living-room in an old house. The furniture was brought to America by PETER GRIMM'S *ancestors. The* GRIMMS *were, for the most part, frugal people, but two or three fine paintings have been inherited by* PETER.

A small, old-fashioned piano stands near the open window, a few comfortable chairs, a desk with a hanging lamp above it, and an arm-chair in front of it, a quaint old fireplace, a Dutch wall clock with weights, a sofa, a hat-rack, and mahogany flower-pot holders, are set about the room; but the most treasured possession is a large family Bible lying on a table. A door leads to a small office occupied by PETER'S *secretary.*

Stairs lead to the sleeping-rooms above. Through the window, hot-houses, beds of tulips, and other flowers, shrubs and trees are seen. "Peter Grimm's Botanic Gardens" supply seeds, plants, shrubbery and trees to the wholesale, as well as retail trade, and the view suggests the importance of the industry. An old Dutch windmill, erected by a Colonial ancestor, gives a quaint touch to the picture. Although PETER GRIMM *is a very wealthy man, he lives as simply as his ancestors.*

As the curtain is raised, the room is empty; but CATHERINE *is heard singing in the dining-room.* JAMES HARTMAN, PETER'S *secretary, opens his door to listen, a small bundle of letters in his hand. He is a well set up young man, rather blunt in his manner, and a trifle careless in his dress. After a pause, he goes back into the office, leaving the door ajar. Presently* CATHERINE *enters. In spite of her youth and girlish appearance, she is a good, thrifty housekeeper. She wears a simple summer gown, and carries a bunch of gay tulips and an old silver pitcher, from which she presently pours water into the Harlequin Delft vase on* PETER GRIMM'S *desk. She peeps into the office, retreating, with a smile on her lips, as* JAMES *appears.*

CATHERINE. Did I disturb you, James?

JAMES. [*On the threshold.*] No indeed.

CATHERINE. Do you like your new work?

JAMES. Anything to get back to the gardens, Catherine. I've always done outside work and I prefer it; but I would shovel dirt rather than work for any one else.

CATHERINE. [*Amused.*] James!

JAMES. It's true. When the train reached the Junction, and a boy presented the passengers with the usual flower and the "compliments of Peter Grimm"—it took me back to the time when that was my job; and when I saw the old sign, "Grimm's Botanic Gardens and Nurseries"—I wanted to jump off the train and run through the grounds. It seemed as though every tulip called "hello" to me.

CATHERINE. Too bad you left college! You had only one more year.

JAMES. Poor father! He's very much disappointed. Father has worked in the dirt in overalls—a gardener—all his life; and, of course, he over-estimates an education. He's far more intelligent than most of our college professors.

CATHERINE. I understand why you came back. You simply *must* live where things grow, mustn't you, James? So must I. Have you seen our orchids?

JAMES. Orchids are pretty; but they're doing wonderful things with potatoes these days. I'd rather improve the breed of a squash than to have an orchid named after me. Wonderful discovery of Luther Burbank's—creating an edible cactus. Sometimes I feel bitter thinking what I might have done with vegetables, when I was wasting time studying Greek.

CATHERINE. [*Changing suddenly.*] James: why don't you try to please Uncle Peter Grimm?

JAMES. I do; but he is always asking my opinion, and when I give it, he blows up.

CATHERINE. [*Coaxingly.*] Don't be quite so blunt. Try to be like one of the family.

JAMES. I'm afraid I shall never be like one of *this* family.

CATHERINE. Why not? I'm no relation at all; and yet—

JAMES. [*Making a resolution.*] I'll do my best to agree with him. [*Offering his hand.*] It's a promise. [*They shake hands.*

CATHERINE. Thank you, James.

JAMES. [*Still holding her hand.*] It's good to be back, Catherine. It's good to see you again.

He is still holding her hand when FREDERIK GRIMM *enters. He is the son of* PETER'S *dead sister, and has been educated by* PETER *to carry on his work. He is a graduate of Amsterdam College, Holland, and, in appearance and manner, suggests the foreign student. He has managed to pull through college creditably, making a specialty of botany.* PETER *has given him the usual trip through Europe, and* FREDERIK *has come to his rich uncle to settle down and learn his business. He has been an inmate of the household for a few months. He poses as a most industrious young man, but is, at heart, a shirker.*

FREDERIK. Where's Uncle?

JAMES. Good-morning, Frederik. Your uncle's watching father spray the plum trees. The black knot's after them again.

FREDERIK. I can hardly keep my eyes open. Uncle wakes me up every morning at five—creaking down the old stairs. [*Eyeing* CATHERINE *admiringly.*] You're looking uncommonly pretty this morning, Kitty. [CATHERINE *edges away and runs upstairs to her room.*

FREDERIK. Hartman!

JAMES. Yes?

FREDERIK. Miss Catherine and you and I are no longer children—our positions are altered—please remember that. I'm no longer a student home for the holidays from Amsterdam College. I'm here to learn the business which I am expected to carry on. Miss Catherine is a young lady now, and my uncle looks upon her as his daughter. You are here as my uncle's secretary. That's how we three stand in this house. Don't call me "Frederik," and hereafter be good enough to say, "Miss Grimm."

JAMES. [*Amiably.*] Very well.

FREDERIK. James: there's a good opportunity for a young man like you in our Florida house. I think that if I spoke for you—

JAMES. Why do you wish to ship me off to Florida?

FREDERIK. I don't understand you, Hartman. I don't wish to ship you off. I am merely thinking of your future. You seem to have changed since—

JAMES. We've all grown up, as you just said. [JAMES *has laid some mail on the desk, and is about to leave the room, when* FREDERIK *speaks again, but in a more friendly manner.*

FREDERIK. The old man's aging; do you notice it?

JAMES. Your uncle's mellowing, yes; but that's only to be expected. He's changing foliage with the years.

FREDERIK. He's growing as old-fashioned as his hats. In my opinion, this would be the time to sell.

JAMES. [*Astonished.*] Sell? Sell a business that has been in his family for—why, it's his religion!

FREDERIK. It's at the height of its prosperity. It would sell like that! [*Snapping his fingers.*] What was the last offer the old man refused from Hicks, of Rochester, Jim?

JAMES. [*Noticing the sudden friendliness—looking at* FREDERIK, *half-amused, half-disgusted.*] Can't repeat correspondence, Mr. Grimm. [*Amazed.*] Good heavens! You surprise me! Would you sell your great, great grandfather? I learned to read by studying his obituary out in the peach orchard: "Johann Grimm, of Holland, an upright settler." There isn't a day your uncle doesn't tell me that you are to carry on the work.

FREDERIK. So I am, but it's not *my* religion. [*Sarcastically.*] Every man can't be blessed like you with the soul of a market gardener—a peddler of turnips.

JAMES. [*Thinking—ignoring* FREDERIK.] He's a great old man—your uncle. It's a big name—Grimm—Peter Grimm. The old man knows his business—he certainly knows his business. [*Changing.*] God! It's an awful thought that a man must die and carry all that knowledge of orchids to the grave! I wonder if it doesn't all count somewhere. . . . I must attend to the mail.

PETER GRIMM *enters from the gardens. He is a well-preserved man of sixty, very simple and plain in his ways. He has not changed his style of dress in the past thirty years. His clothing, collar, tie, hat and shoes are all old-fashioned. He is an estimable man, scrupulously honest, gentle and sympathetic; but occasionally he shows a flash of Dutch stubbornness.*

FREDERIK. I ran over from the office, Uncle Peter, to make a suggestion.

PETER. Yes?

FREDERIK. I suggest that we insert a full-page cut of your new tulip in our mid-summer floral almanac.

PETER. [*Who has hung up his hat on his own particular peg, affably assenting.*] A good idea!

FREDERIK. The public is expecting it.

PETER. You think so, my boy?

FREDERIK. Why, Uncle, you've no idea of the stir this tulip has created. People stop me in the street to speak of it.

PETER. Well, well, you surprise me. I didn't think it so extraordinary.

FREDERIK. I've had a busy morning, sir, in the packing house.

PETER. That's good. I'm glad to see you taking hold of things, Fritz. [*Humourously, touching* FREDERIK *affectionately on the shoulder.*] We mustn't waste time; for that's the stuff life's made of. [*Seriously.*] It's a great comfort to me, Frederik, to know that when I'm in my little private room with James, or when I've slipped out to the hothouses,—you are representing me in the offices—*young* Mr. Grimm. . . . James, are you ready for me?

JAMES. Yes, sir.

PETER. I'll attend to the mail in a moment. [*Missing* CATHERINE, *he calls according to the household signal.*] Ou—oo! [*He is answered by* CATHERINE, *who immediately appears from her room, and comes running downstairs.*] Catherine, I have news for you. I've named the new rose after you: "Katie—a hardy bloomer." It's as red as the ribbon in your hair.

CATHERINE. Thank you, Uncle Peter, thank you very much. And now you must have your cup of coffee.

PETER. What a fine little housewife! A busy girl about the house, eh, Fritz? Is there anything you need to-day, Katie?

CATHERINE. No, Uncle Peter, I have everything I need, thank you.

PETER. Not everything,—not everything, my dear. [*Smiling at* FREDERIK. JAMES, *ignored, is standing in the background.*] Wait! Wait till I give you a husband. I have my plans. [*Looking from* FREDERIK *to* CATHERINE.] People don't always know what I'm doing, but I'm a great man for planning. Come, Katie, tell me, on this fine spring morning, what sort of husband would you prefer?

CATHERINE. [*Annoyed,—with girlish impatience.*] You're always speaking of weddings, Uncle Peter. I don't know what's come over you of late.

PETER. It's nesting time, . . . spring weddings are in the air; besides, my grandmother's linen-chest upstairs must be used again for you [*Impulsively drawing* CATHERINE *to him.*], my house fairy. [*Kisses her.*] There, I mustn't tease her. But I leave it to Fritz if I don't owe her a fine husband—this girl of mine. Look what she has done for *me!*

CATHERINE. Done for you? I do you the great favour to let *you* do everything for *me.*

PETER. Ah, but who lays out my linen? Who puts flowers on my desk every day? Who gets up at dawn to eat breakfast with me? Who sees that I have my second cup of coffee? But better than all that—who brings youth into my old house?

CATHERINE. That's not much—youth.

PETER. No? We'll leave it to Fritz. [FREDERIK, *amused, listens in silence.*] What should I be now—a rough old fellow—a bachelor—without youth in my house, eh? God knows! Katie has softened me towards all the ladies—er—mellowed me as time has mellowed my old pictures. [*Points to pictures.*] And I was growing hard—hard and fussy.

CATHERINE. [*Laughing.*] Ah, Uncle Peter, have I made you take a liking to all the rest of the ladies?

PETER. Yes. It's just as it is when you have a pet: you like all that breed. You can only see *your* kind of kitten.

JAMES. [*Coming down a step, impressed by* PETER'S *remark—speaking earnestly.*] That's so, sir. [*The others are surprised.*] I hadn't thought of it in that way, but it's true. You study a girl for the first time, and presently you notice the same little traits in every one of them. It makes you feel differently towards all the rest.

PETER. [*Amused.*] Why, James, what do *you* know about girls? "Bachelor" is stamped all over you—you're positively labelled.

JAMES. [*Good-naturedly.*] Perhaps. [*Goes back to the office.*

PETER. Poor James! What a life before him! When a bachelor wants to order a three-rib roast, who's to eat it? I never had a proper roast until Katie and Frederik came to make up my family; [*Rubbing his hands.*] but the roasts are not big enough. [*Giving* FREDERIK *a knowing look.*] We must find a husband.

CATHERINE. You promised not to—

PETER. I want to see a long, long table with plenty of young people.

CATHERINE. I'll leave the room, Uncle.

PETER. With myself at the head, carving, carving, carving, watching the plates come back, and back, and back. [*As she is about to go.*] There, there, not another word of this to-day.

The 'phone rings. JAMES *re-enters and answers it.*

JAMES. Hello! [*Turns.*] Rochester asks for Mr. Peter Grimm to the 'phone. Another message from Hicks' greenhouses.

PETER. Ask them to excuse me.

JAMES. [*Bluntly.*] You'll have to excuse him. [*Listens.*] No, no, the gardens are not in the market. You're only wasting your time.

PETER. Tc! Tc! James! Can't you say it politely? [JAMES *listens at 'phone.*

FREDERIK. [*Aside to* PETER.] James is so painfully blunt. [*Then changing.*] Is it—er—a good offer? Is Hicks willing to make it worth while? [*Catching his uncle's astonished eye—apologetically.*] Of course, I know you wouldn't think of—

CATHERINE. I should say not! My home? An offer? *Our* gardens? I should say not!

FREDERIK. Mere curiosity on my part, that's all.

PETER. Of course, I understand. Sell out? No indeed. We are thinking of the next generation.

FREDERIK. Certainly, sir.

PETER. We're the last of the family. The business—that's Peter Grimm. It will soon be Frederik Grimm. The love for the old gardens is in our blood.

FREDERIK. It is, sir. [*Lays a fond hand on* PETER'S *shoulder.*

PETER. [*Struck.*] I have an idea. We'll print the family history in our new floral almanac.

FREDERIK. [*Suppressing a yawn.*] Yes, yes, a very good idea.

PETER. Katie, read it to us and let us hear how it sounds.

CATHERINE. [*Reads.*] "In the spring of 1709 there settled on Quassick Creek, New York State, Johann Grimm, aged twenty-two, husbandman and vine-dresser, also Johanna, his wife."

PETER. Very interesting.

FREDERIK. Very interesting, indeed.

CATHERINE. "To him Queen Anne furnished one square, one rule, one compass, two whipping saws and several small pieces. To him was born—"

PETER. [*Interrupting.*] You left out two augurs.

CATHERINE. [*Reads.*] Oh, yes—"and two augurs. To him was born a son—"

PETER. [*Who knows the history by heart, has listened, his eyes almost suffused—repeating each word to himself, as she reads. He has lived over each generation down to the present and nods in approval as she reaches this point.*] The foundation of our house. And here we are prosperous and flourishing—after seven generations. We'll print it, eh, Fritz?

FREDERIK. Certainly, sir. By all means let us print it.

PETER. And now we are depending upon you, Frederik, for the next line in the book. [*To* CATHERINE—*slyly—as she closes the book.*] If my sister could see Frederik, what a proud mother she would be!

JAMES. [*Turning from the 'phone to* PETER.] Old man Hicks himself has come to the 'phone. Says he *must* speak to Mr. Peter Grimm.

FREDERIK. I'd make short work of him, Uncle.

PETER. [*At the 'phone.*] How are you, my old friend? . . . How are your plum trees? [*Listens.*] Bad, eh? Well, we can only pray and use Bordeaux Mixture. . . . No . . . Nonsense! This business has been in my family for seven generations. Why sell? I'll see that it stays in the family seven generations longer! [*Echoing.*] Do I propose to live that long? N—no; but my plans will. [*Looks towards* FREDERIK *and* CATHERINE.] How? Never mind. Good-morning.

[*Hangs up the receiver.*

JAMES. Sorry to disturb you, sir, but some of these letters are—

FREDERIK. I'm off.

PETER. [*Who has lifted a pot of tulips to set it in the sun—standing with the pot in his hands.*] And remember the saying: [*A twinkle in his upraised eyes.*] "Thou, O God, sellest all good things at the price of labour." [*Smells the tulips and sets them down.*

FREDERIK. [*Goes briskly towards the door.*] That's true, sir. I want to speak to you later, Uncle— [*Turning, looking at* JAMES.] on a private matter. [*He goes off looking at his watch, as though he had a hard day's work before him.*

PETER. [*Looking after* FREDERIK.] Very capable young fellow, Frederik. I was a happy man, James, when I heard that he had won the prize for botany at Amsterdam College. I had to find out the little I know by experience.

JAMES. [*Impulsively.*] Yes, and I'll wager you've forgotten more than— [*Catching a warning glance from* CATHERINE, *he pauses.*

PETER. What?

JAMES. Nothing, sir. I—

CATHERINE. [*Tugging at* PETER'S *coat—speaking to him apart, as* JAMES *busies himself at the desk.*] Uncle Peter, I think you're unfair to James. We used to have him to dinner very often before he went away. Now that he's back, you treat him like a stranger.

PETER. [*Surprised.*] Eh? I didn't know that I— [*Petting* CATHERINE.] A good, unselfish girl. She thinks of everybody. [*Aloud.*] James, will you have dinner with us to-day?

JAMES. [*Pleased and surprised.*] Thank you, sir—yes, sir.

PETER. It's a roast goose—cooked sweet, James. [*Smacks his lips.*] Fresh green herbs in the dressing and a Figaro pudding. Marta brought over that pudding receipt from Holland.

MARTA, *an old family servant, has entered with the air of having forgotten to wind the clock. She smiles happily at* PETER'S *allusion to her puddings, attends to the old clock, and passes off with* CATHERINE. PETER *sits at the desk, glancing over the mail.*

PETER. Katie's blossoming like a rose. Have you noticed how she's coming out lately, James?

JAMES. Yes, sir.

PETER. You've noticed it, too? [*Picks up another letter, looking over it.*

JAMES. Yes, sir.

PETER. [*Pausing, taking off his eye-glasses and holding them on his thumb. Philosophically.*] How prettily Nature accomplishes her will—making a girl doubly beautiful that a young man may yield his freedom the more easily. Wonderful! [*During the following, he glances over letters.*] A young girl is like a violet sheltered under a bush, James; and that is as it should be, isn't it?

JAMES. No, sir, *I* don't think so.

PETER. [*Surprised.*] What?

JAMES. I believe people should think for themselves—not be . . .

PETER. Go on.

JAMES. —er—

PETER. Well?

JAMES. [*Remembering his promise to* CATHERINE.] Nothing.

PETER. Go on, James.

JAMES. I mean swallowed up.

PETER. Swallowed up? Explain yourself, James.

JAMES. I shouldn't have mentioned it.

PETER. Certainly, certainly. Don't be afraid to express an honest opinion.

JAMES. I only meant that you can't shape another's life. We are all free beings and—

PETER. Free? Of course Katie's free—to a certain extent. Do you mean to tell me that any young girl should be freer? Nonsense! She should be happy that *I* am here to think for her —*I*! *We* must think for people who can't think for themselves; and a young girl can't. [*Signing an answer to a letter after hastily glancing over it.*] You have extraordinary ideas, James.

JAMES. Excuse me, sir; you asked my opinion. I only meant that we can't think for others—any more than we can eat or sleep for them.

PETER. [*As though accepting the explanation.*] Oh . . . I see what you mean.

JAMES. Of course, every happy being is bound by its nature to lead its own life—that it may be a free being. Evidently I didn't make my meaning clear. [*Giving* PETER *another letter to sign.*

PETER. Free? Happy? James, you talk like an anarchist! You surprise me, sir. Where do you get these extraordinary ideas?

JAMES. By reading modern books and magazines, sir, and of course—

PETER. I thought so. [*Pointing to his books.*] Read Heine. Cultivate sentiment. [*Signing the letter.*] Happy? Has it ever occurred to you that Katie is not happy?

JAMES. No, sir, I can't truthfully say that it has.

PETER. I imagine not. These are the happiest hours of her life. Young . . . in love . . . soon to be married.

JAMES. [*After a long pause.*] Is it settled, sir?

PETER. No, but I'll soon settle it. Anyone can see how she feels towards Frederik.

JAMES. [*After a shorter pause.*] Isn't she very young to marry, sir?

PETER. Not when she marries into the family; not when *I* am in the house—[*Touching his chest.*] to guard her—to watch over her. Leave it to *me.* [*Enthusiastically.*] Sit here, James. Take one of Frederik's cigars. [JAMES *politely thanks him, but doesn't take one.*] It's a pleasure to talk to some one who's interested; and you *are* interested, James?

JAMES. Yes, sir, I'm much more interested than you might think.

PETER. Good. We'll take up the mail in a minute. Now, in order to carry out my plans—

CATHERINE. [*Sticking her head in the door.*] Ready for coffee?

PETER. Er—a little later. Close the door, dear. [*She disappears, closing the door.*] In order to carry out my plans, I have had to use great diplomacy. I made up my mind to keep Katie in the family; being a rich man—everybody knows it—I've had to guard against fortune-hunters. However, I think I've done away with them, for the whole town understands that Katie hasn't a penny—doesn't it, James?

JAMES. Yes, sir.

PETER. Yes, I think I've made that very clear. My dream was to bring Catherine up to keep her in the family, and it has been fulfilled. My plans have turned out beautifully, for she is satisfied and happy.

JAMES. But did you want her to be happy simply because *you* are happy, sir? Don't you want her to be happy because *she* is happy?

PETER. If she's happy, why should I care? [*Picks up the last letter.*

JAMES. *If* she's happy.

PETER. [*Losing his temper.*] What do you mean? That's the second time you've said that. Why do you harp on—

JAMES. [*Rising.*] Excuse me, sir.

PETER. [*Angrily.*] Sit down. What do you know?

JAMES. Nothing, sir. . . .

PETER. You must know something to speak in this manner.

JAMES. No, I don't. You're a great expert in your line, Mr. Grimm, and I have the greatest respect for your opinion; but you can't mate people as you'd graft tulips. And more than once, I've—I've caught her crying and I've thought perhaps . .

PETER. [*Pooh-poohing.*] Crying? Of course! Was there ever a girl who didn't cry? . . . You amuse me . . . with your ideas of life. . . . Ha! Haven't I asked her why she was crying,—and hasn't she always said: "I don't know why—it's nothing." They love to cry. [*Signs the last letter.*] But that's what they all cry over—nothing. James, do you know how I happened to meet Katie? She was prescribed for me by Doctor MacPherson.

JAMES. [*Taking the letter.*] Prescribed?

PETER. As an antidote. I was growing to be a fussy bachelor, with queer notions. You are young, but see that you don't need the Doctor, James. Do you know how I was cured? I'll tell you. One day, when I had business in the city, the Doctor went with me, and before I knew what he was at—he had marched me into a home for babies. . . . Katie was nearest the door—the first one. Pinned over her crib was her name: "Catherine Staats, aged three months." She held out her little arms . . . so friendless—so pitiful—so alone—and I was done for. We brought her back home, the Doctor, a nurse and I. The first time I carried her up those stairs—all my fine bachelor's ideas went out of my head. I knew then that my theories were all humbug. I had missed the child in the house who was to teach me everything. I had missed many children in my house. From that day, I watched over her life. [*Rising, pointing towards the head of the stairs.*] James, I was born in this house—in the little room where I sleep; and her children shall one day play in the room in which I was born. . . . That's very pretty, eh? [*Wipes his eyes, sentimentally.*] I've always seen it that way.

JAMES. [*Coolly.*] Yes; it's *very* pretty if it turns out well.

PETER. How can it turn out otherwise?

JAMES. To me, sir, it's not a question of sentiment—of where her children shall play, so long as they play happily.

PETER. What? Her children can play anywhere—in China if they want to! Are you in your senses? A fine reward for giving a child all your affection—to live to see *her* children playing in China. No, sir! I propose to keep my household together, by your leave. [*Banging his clenched fist on the desk.*] It's my plan. [*Cleans his pipe, looking at* JAMES *from time to time.* JAMES *posts the letters in a mail-box outside the door.* PETER *goes to the window, calling off.*] Otto! Run to the office and tell Mr. Frederik he may come in now. [*The voice of a gruff Dutchman: "Het is pastoor's dag."* (It is the pastor's day.)] Ah, yes; I had forgotten. It's William's day to take flowers to the Pastor. [*A knock is heard and, as* PETER *calls "Come in,"* WILLIAM, *a delicate child of eight, stands timidly in the doorway of the dining-room, hat in hand.*] How are you to-day, William? [*Pats* WILLIAM *on the shoulder.*

WILLIAM. The Doctor says I'm well now.

PETER. Good! Then you shall take flowers to the church. [*Calls off.*] A big armful, Otto!

MARTA *has entered with a neatly folded, clean handkerchief which she tucks into* WILLIAM'S *breast pocket.*

PETER. [*In a low voice, to* JAMES.] There's your example of freedom! William's mother, old Marta's spoiled child, was free. You remember Annamarie, James?—let to come and go as she pleased. God knows where she is now . . . and here is William with the poor old grandmother. . . . Run along with the flowers, William. [*Gives* WILLIAM *some pennies as he goes.*] How he shoots up, eh, Marta?

MARTA. [*With the hopeless sorrow of the old, as she passes off.*] Poor child . . . poor child.

PETER. Give Katie more freedom, eh? Oh, no! I shall guard her as I would guard my own, for she is as dear to me as though she were mine, and, by marriage, please God, she shall be a Grimm in *name.*

JAMES. Mr. Grimm, I—I wish you would transfer me to your branch house in Florida.

PETER. What? You who were so glad to come back! James, you need a holiday. Close your desk. Go out and busy yourself with those pet vegetables of yours. Change your ideas; then come back sane and sensible, and attend to your work. [*Giving a last shot at* JAMES *as he passes into the office and* FREDERIK *re-enters.*] You don't know what you want!

FREDERIK. [*Looking after* JAMES.] Uncle Peter, when I came in this morning, I made up my mind to speak to you of James.

PETER. James?

FREDERIK. Yes, I've wondered lately if . . . it seems to me that James is interested in Catherine.

PETER. James? Impossible.

FREDERIK. I'm not so sure.

PETER. [*Good-naturedly.*] James? James Hartman?

FREDERIK. When I look back and remember him as a barefoot boy living in a shack behind our hot-houses—and see him now—in here with you—

PETER. All the more credit, Frederik.

FREDERIK. Yes; but these are the sort of fellows who dream of getting into the firm. And there are more ways than one.

PETER. Do you mean to say—He wouldn't presume to think of such a thing.

FREDERIK. Oh, wouldn't he! The class to which he belongs presumes to think of anything. I believe he has been making love to Catherine.

PETER. [*After a slight pause, goes to the dining-room door and calls.*] Katie! Katie!

FREDERIK. [*Hastily.*] Don't say that I mentioned it. [CATHERINE *enters.*

PETER. Katie, I wish to ask you a question. I— [*He laughs.*] Oh, it's absurd. No, no, never mind.

CATHERINE. What is it?

PETER. I can't ask you. It's really too absurd.

CATHERINE. [*Her curiosity aroused.*] What is it, Uncle? . . . Tell me . . . tell me . . .

PETER. Has James ever—

CATHERINE. [*Taken back and rather frightened—quickly.*] No. . . .

PETER. What? . . . How did you know what I . . . [FREDERIK *gives her a shrewd glance; but* PETER, *suspecting nothing, continues.*] I meant . . . has James shown any special interest in you?

CATHERINE. [*As though accepting the explanation.*] Oh . . . [*Flurried.*[Why, Uncle Peter! . . . Uncle Peter! . . . whatever put this notion into your head?

PETER. It's all nonsense, of course, but—

CATHERINE. I've always known James. . . . We went to school together. . . . James has shown no interest he ought not to have shown, Uncle Peter,—if that's what you mean. He has always been very respectful in a perfectly friendly way.

PETER. [*Convinced.*] Respectful in a perfectly friendly way. [*To* FREDERIK.] You can't ask more than that. Thank you, dear, that's all I wanted. Run along. [*Glad to escape,* CATHERINE *leaves the room.*] He was only respectful in a perfectly friendly way. [*Slaps* FREDERIK *on the back.*] You're satisfied now, I hope?

FREDERIK. No, I am not. If *she* hasn't noticed what he has in mind, *I* have. When I came into this room a few moments ago,—it was as plain as day. He's trying to make love to her under our very eyes. I saw him. I wish you would ask him to stay in his office and attend to his own business. [JAMES *now re-enters on his way to the gardens.*]

PETER. James, it has just occurred to me—that— [*James pauses.*] What was your reason for wanting to give up your position? Had it anything to do with my little girl?

JAMES. Yes, sir.

PETER. You mean that—you—you love her?

JAMES. [*In a low voice.*] Yes, sir.

PETER. O-ho! [FREDERIK *gives* PETER *a glance as though to say, "Now, do you believe it?"*

JAMES. But she doesn't know it, of course; she never would have known it. I never meant to say a word to her. I understand, sir.

PETER. James! Come here . . . here! . . . [*Bringing* JAMES *up before him at the desk.*] Get your money at the office. You may have that position in Florida. Good-bye, James.

JAMES. I'm very sorry that . . . Good-bye, sir.

FREDERIK. You are not to tell her that you're going. You're not to bid her good-bye.

PETER. [*To* FREDERIK.] Sh! Let me attend to—

JAMES. [*Ignoring* FREDERIK.] I'm sorry, Mr. Grimm, that— [*His voice falters.*

PETER. [*Rising.*] James, I'm sorry, too. You've grown up here and—Tc! Tc! Good fortune to you—James. Get this notion out of your head, and perhaps one day you'll come back to us. We shall see. [*Shakes hands with* JAMES, *who leaves the room too much overcome to speak.*

DR. MACPHERSON. [*Who has entered, saying carelessly to* JAMES *as he passes him.*] Hy're you, Jim? Glad Jim's back. One of the finest lads I ever brought into this world.

The DOCTOR *is a man of about* PETER'S *age, but more powerfully built. He has the bent shoulders of the student and his face is exceedingly intellectual. He is the rare type of doctor who forgets to make out his bills. He has a grizzled grey beard, and his hair is touched with grey. He wears silver-rimmed spectacles. His substantial but unpressed clothing is made by the village tailor.*

PETER. Good-morning, Andrew.

FREDERIK. Good-morning, Doctor.

DR. MACPHERSON. [*Casts a quick, professional glance at* PETER.] Peter, I've come over to have a serious word with you. Been on my mind all night. [*Brings down a chair and sits opposite* PETER.] I—er—Frederik . . . [FREDERIK, *who is not a favourite of the* DOCTOR'S, *takes the hint and leaves the room.*] Peter, have you provided for everybody in this house?

PETER. What? Have I—

DR. MACPHERSON. You're a terrible man for planning, Peter; but what have you done? [*Casually.*] Were you to die,—say to-morrow,—how would it be with— [*Making a gesture to include the household.*] —the rest of them?

PETER. What do you mean? If I were to die to-morrow . . .

DR. MACPHERSON. You won't. Don't worry. Good for a long time yet, but every one must come to it—sooner or later. I mean—what would Katie's position be in this house? I know you've set your heart upon her marrying Frederik, and all that sort of nonsense, but will it work? I've always thought 'twas a pity Frederik wasn't James and James wasn't Frederik.

PETER. What!

DR. MACPHERSON. Oh, it's all very well if she *wants* Frederik, but supposing she does not. Peter, if you mean to do something for her—do it *now.*

PETER. Now? You mean that I—You mean that I might . . . die?

DR. MACPHERSON. All can and do.

PETER. [*Studying the* DOCTOR'S *face.*] You think . . .

DR. MACPHERSON. The machinery is wearing out, Peter. Thought I should tell you. No cause for apprehension, but—

PETER. Then why tell me?

DR. MACPHERSON. When I cured you of that cold—wet flowerbeds—two days ago, I made a discovery. [*Seeing* CATHERINE *enter, he pauses. She is followed by* MARTA, *carrying a tray containing coffee and a plate of waffles.*] Coffee! I told you not to touch coffee, Peter. It's rank poison.

CATHERINE. Wouldn't you like a cup, Doctor?

PETER. Yes he'll take a cup. He won't prescribe it, but he'll drink it.

DR. MACPHERSON. [*Horrified.*] And hot waffles between meals!

PETER. Yes, he'll take hot waffles, too. [MARTA *goes to get another plate and more waffles, and* CATHERINE *follows her.*]

Now, Andrew, you can't tell me that I'm sick. I won't have it. Every day we hear of some old boy one hundred years of age who was given up by the doctors at twenty. No, sir! I'm going to live to see children in my house,—Katie's babies creeping on my old floor; playing with my old watch-dog, Toby. I've promised myself a long line of rosy Grimms.

DR. MACPHERSON. My God, Peter! That dog is fifteen years old now. Do you expect nothing to change in your house? Man, you're a home worshipper. However, I—I see no reason why—[*Lying.*] you shouldn't reach a ripe old age. [*Markedly, though feigning to treat the subject lightly.*] Er—Peter, I should like to make a compact with you . . . that whoever *does* go first—and you're quite likely to outlive me,—is to come back and let the other fellow know . . . and settle the question. Splendid test between old neighbours—real contribution to science.

PETER. Make a compact to—stuff and nonsense!

DR. MACPHERSON. Don't be too sure of that.

PETER. No, Andrew, no, positively, no. I refuse. Don't count upon *me* for any assistance in your spook tests.

DR. MACPHERSON. And how many times do you think *you've* been a spook yourself? You can't tell me that man is perfect; that he doesn't live more than one life; that the soul doesn't go on and on. Pshaw! The persistent personal energy *must* continue, or what *is* God? [CATHERINE *has re-entered with another cup, saucer and plate which she sets on the table, and pours out the coffee.*

CATHERINE. [*Interested.*] Were you speaking of—of ghosts, Doctor?

PETER. Yes, he has begun again. [*To* CATHERINE.] You're just in time to hear it. [*To* DR. MACPHERSON.] Andrew, I'll stay behind, contented in *this* life; knowing what I have here on earth, and you shall die and return with your—ha!—persistent personal whatever-it-is, and keep the spook compact. Every time a knock sounds, or a chair squeaks, or the door bangs, I shall say, "Sh! There's the Doctor!"

CATHERINE. [*Noticing a book which the* DOCTOR *has taken from his pocket, and reading the title.*] "Are the Dead Alive?"

DR. MACPHERSON. I'm in earnest, Peter. *I'll* promise and I want *you* to promise, too. Understand that I am not a so-called spiritist. I am merely a seeker after truth. [*Puts more sugar in his coffee.*

PETER. That's what they *all* are—seekers after truth. Rubbish! Do you really believe such stuff?

DR. MACPHERSON. I know that the dead are alive. They're here—here—near us—close at hand. [PETER, *in derision, lifts the table-cloth and peeps under the table—then, taking the lid off the sugar-bowl, peers into it.*] Some of the great scientists of the day are of the same opinion.

PETER. Bah! Dreamers! They accomplish nothing in the world. They waste their lives dreaming of the world to come.

DR. MACPHERSON. You can't call Sir Charles Crookes, the inventor of Crookes Tubes,—a waster? Nor Sir Oliver Lodge, the great biologist; nor Curie, the discoverer of radium; nor Doctor Lombroso, the founder of Science of Criminology; nor Doctors Maxwell, deVesmé, Richet, Professor James, of Harvard, and our own Professor Hyslop. Instead of laughing at ghosts, the scientific men of to-day are trying to lay hold of them. The frauds and cheats are being crowded from the field. Science is only just peeping through the half-opened door which was shut until a few years ago.

PETER. If ever I see a ghost, I shall lay violent hands upon it and take it to the police station. That's the proper place for frauds.

DR. MACPHERSON. I'm sorry, Peter, very sorry, to see that you, like too many others, make a jest of the most important thing in life. Hyslop is right: man will spend millions to discover the North Pole, but not a penny to discover his immortal destiny.

PETER. [*Stubbornly.*] I don't believe in spook mediums and never shall believe in them.

DR. MACPHERSON. Probably most professional mediums cheat —perhaps every one of them; but some of them are capable of real demonstrations at times.

PETER. Once a swindler, always a swindler. Besides, why can't my old friends come straight back to me and say, "Peter Grimm, here I am!" When they do—if they do—I shall be the first man to take off my hat to them and hold out my hand in welcome.

DR. MACPHERSON. You ask me why? Why can't a telegram travel on a fence instead of on a wire? Your friends *could* come back to you if you could put yourself in a receptive condition; but if you cannot, you must depend upon a medium—a sensitive.

PETER. A what? [*To* CATHERINE.] Something new, eh? He has all the names for them. Yesterday it was "apports"—flowers that fell down from nowhere and hit you on the nose. He talks like a medium's parrot. He has only to close his eyes and along comes the parade. Spooks! Spooky spooks! And now he wants me to settle my worldly affairs and join in the procession.

CATHERINE. [*Puzzled.*] Settle your worldly affairs? What do you mean, Uncle Peter?

PETER. [*Evasively.*] Just some more of his nonsense. Doctor, you've seen a good many cross to the other world; tell me—did you ever see one of them come back—one?

DR. MACPHERSON. No.

PETER. [*Sipping his coffee.*] Never have, eh? And never will. Take another cup of poison, Andrew.

The DOCTOR *gives his cup to* CATHERINE, *who fills it.* PETER *passes the waffles to the* DOCTOR, *at the same time winking at* CATHERINE *as the* DOCTOR *takes another.*

DR. MACPHERSON. There was not perhaps the intimate bond between doctor and patients to bring them back. But in my own family, I have known of a case.

PETER. [*Apart to* CATHERINE.] He's off again.

CATHERINE. [*Eager to listen.*] Please don't interrupt, Uncle. I love to hear him tell of—

DR. MACPHERSON. I have known of a return such as you mention. A distant cousin died in London and she was seen almost instantly in New York.

PETER. She must have travelled on a biplane, Andrew.

DR. MACPHERSON. If my voice can be heard from San Francisco over the telephone, why cannot a soul with a God-given force behind it dart over the entire universe? Is Thomas Edison greater than God?

CATHERINE. [*Shocked.*] Doctor!

DR. MACPHERSON. And they can't tuck it *all* on telepathy. Telepathy cannot explain the case of a spirit-message giving the contents of a sealed letter known only to the person that died. Here's another interesting case.

PETER. This is better than "Puss in Boots," isn't it, Katie? More—er—flibbertigibberty. Katie always loved fairy stories.

CATHERINE. [*Listening eagerly.*] Uncle, please.

DR. MACPHERSON. [*Ignoring* PETER, *speaking directly to* CATHERINE, *who is all attention.*] An officer on the Polar vessel, the *Jeannette*, sent to the Artic regions by the New York *Herald*, appeared at his wife's bedside. *She* was in Brooklyn—*he* was on the Polar sea. He said to her, "Count." She distinctly heard a ship's bell and the word "Count" again. She had counted six when her husband's voice said, "Six bells—and the *Jeanette* is lost." The ship was really lost at the time she saw the vision.

PETER. A bad dream. "Six bells and the"—Ha! Ha! Spirit messages! Suet pudding has brought me messages from the North Pole, and I receive messages from Kingdom Come after I've eaten a piece of mince pie.

DR. MACPHERSON. There have been seventeen thousand other cases found to be worth investigation by the London Society of Psychical Research.

PETER. [*Changing.*] Supposing, Andrew, that I did "cross over"—I believe that's what you call dying,—that I *did* want to come back to see how you and the little Katie and Frederik were getting on, how do you think I could manage to do it?

DR. MACPHERSON. When we hypnotize subjects, Peter, our thoughts take possession of them. As we enter their bodies, we take the place of a something that leaves them—a shadow-self. This self can be sent out of the room—even to a long distance. This self leaves us entirely after death on the first, second or third day, or so I believe. This is the force which you would employ to come back to earth—the astral envelope.

PETER. Yes, but what proof have you, Doctor, that I've got an—an astral envelope.

DR. MACPHERSON. [*Easily.*] De Rochas has actually photographed it by radio-photography.

PETER. Ha! Ha! Ha! Ho! Ho!

DR. MACPHERSON. Mind you—they couldn't *see* it when they photographed it.

PETER. I imagine not. See it? Ho! Ho!

DR. MACPHERSON. It stood a few feet away from the sleeper, and was located by striking at the air and watching for the corresponding portion of the sleeper's body to recoil. By pricking a certain part of this shadow-self with a pin, the cheek of the patient could be made to bleed. The camera was focussed on this part of the shadow-self for fifteen minutes. The result was the profile of a head.

PETER. [*After a pause.*] . . . You believe that?

DR. MACPHERSON. The experiment has been repeated again and again. Nobody acquainted with the subject denies it now.

PETER. Spook pictures taken by professional mediums! [*Turning away from the table as though he had heard enough.*

DR. MACPHERSON. De Rochas, who took the pictures of which I speak, is a lawyer of standing; and the room was full of scientists who saw the pictures taken.

PETER. Hypnotized—all of them. Humbug, Andrew!

DR. MACPHERSON. Under these conditions, it is quite impossible to hypnotize a room full of people. Perhaps you think the camera was hypnotized? In similar circumstances, says Lombroso, an unnatural current of cold air went through the room and lowered the thermometer several degrees. Can you hypnotize a thermometer?

CATHERINE. [*Impressed.*] That's wonderful, Doctor!

PETER. Yes, it's a very pretty fairy story; but it would sound better set to shivery music. [*Sings.*] Tol! Dol! Dol! Dol! [*Rising to get his pipe and tobacco.*] No, sir! I refuse to agree to your compact. You cannot pick the lock of heaven's gate. We don't come back. God did enough for us when he gave us life and strength to work and the work to do. He owes us no explanations. I believe in the old-fashioned paradise with a locked gate. [*He fills his pipe and lights it.*] No bogies for me.

DR. MACPHERSON. [*Rising.*] Peter, I console myself with the thought that men have scoffed at the laws of gravitation, at vaccination, magnetism, daguerreotypes, steamboats, cars, telephones, wireless telegraphy and lighting by gas. [*Showing feeling.*] I'm *very* much disappointed that you refuse my request.

PETER. [*Laying down his pipe on the table.*] Since you take it so seriously—here— [*Offers his hand.*] I'll agree. I know you're an old fool—and I'm another. Now then— [*Shakes hands.*] it's settled. Whichever one shall go first— [*He bursts into laughter—then controlling himself.*] If I *do* come back, I'll apologize, Andrew.

DR. MACPHERSON. Do you mean it?

PETER. I'll apologize. Wait [*Taking the keys from the sideboard.*], let us seal the compact in a glass of my famous plum brandy.

DR. MACPHERSON. Good!

PETER. [*As he passes off.*] We'll drink to spooks.

CATHERINE. You really do believe, Doctor, that the dead can come back, don't you?

DR. MACPHERSON. Of course I do, and why not?

CATHERINE. Do you believe that you could come back here into this room and I could see you?

DR. MACPHERSON. You might not see me; but I could come back to this room.

CATHERINE. Could you talk to me?

DR. MACPHERSON. Yes.

CATHERINE. And could I hear you?

DR. MACPHERSON. I believe so. That's what we're trying to make possible. [CATHERINE, *still wondering, passes off with the tray. From the cellar,* PETER *can be heard singing lustily.*

PETER. "If you want a bite that's good to eat,
(Tra, la, ritte, ra, la, la, la!)
Try out a goose that's fat and sweet,
(Tra, la, ritte, ra, la, la, la!")

During the song, MRS. BATHOLOMMEY *has given a quick tap on the door and entered. She is about forty years of age. Her faded brown hair is streaked with grey. She wears a plain black alpaca costume.*

MRS. BATHOLOMMEY. [*Agitated.*] Good-morning, Doctor. Fortunate that I found you alone.

DR. MACPHERSON. [*Dryly.*] Hy're you, Mrs. Batholommey?

The REV. HENRY BATHOLOMMEY *now enters. He is a man of about forty-five, wearing the frock coat, high waistcoat and square topped hat of a minister of the Dutch Reformed Church.*

REV. MR. BATHOLOMMEY. Hy're, Henry?

The REV. MR. BATHOLOMMEY *bows.* WILLIAM *has returned from his errand and entered the room,—a picture-book under his arm. He sits up by the window, absorbed in the pictures—unnoticed by the others.*

MRS. BATHOLOMMEY. [*Closing the door left open by* PETER, *shutting out the sound of his voice.*] Well, Doctor . . . [*She pauses for a moment to catch her breath and wipe her eyes.*] I suppose you've told him he's got to die.

DR. MACPHERSON. [*Eyeing* MRS. BATHOLOMMEY *with disfavour.*] Who's got to die?

MRS. BATHOLOMMEY. Why, Mr. Grimm, of course.

DR. MACPHERSON. [*Amazed.*] Does the whole damned town know it?

MRS. BATHOLOMMEY. Oh!

REV. MR. BATHOLOMMEY. Easy, Doctor. You consulted Mr. Grimm's lawyer and *his* wife told *my* wife.

DR. MACPHERSON. He gabbed, eh? Hang the professional man who tells things to his wife.

MRS. BATHOLOMMEY. Doctor!

REV. MR. BATHOLOMMEY. [*With solicitude.*] I greatly grieve to hear that Mr. Grimm has an incurable malady. His heart, I understand. [*Shakes his head.*

DR. MACPHERSON. He's not to be told. Is that clear? He may die in twenty minutes—may outlive us all—probably will.

MRS. BATHOLOMMEY. [*Pointing to* REV. MR. BATHOLOMMEY.] It seems to me, Doctor, that if *you* can't do any more, it's *his* turn. It's a wonder you Doctors don't baptize the babies.

REV. MR. BATHOLOMMEY. Rose!

MRS. BATHOLOMMEY. At the last minute, he'll want to make a will—and you know he hasn't made one. He'll want to remember the church and his charities and his friends; and if he dies before he can carry out his intentions, the minister will be blamed as usual. It's not fair.

REV. MR. BATHOLOMMEY. Sh! Sh! My dear! These private matters—

DR. MACPHERSON. I'll trouble you, Mistress Batholommey, to attend to your own affairs. Did you never hear the story of the lady who flattened her nose—sticking it into other people's business?

REV. MR. BATHOLOMMEY. Doctor! Doctor! I can't have that!

MRS. BATHOLOMMEY. Let him talk, Henry. No one in this town pays any attention to Dr. MacPherson since he took up with spiritualism.

REV. MR. BATHOLOMMEY. Rose! [*He motions to her to be silent, as* PETER, *coming up the stairs from the cellar, is heard singing.*

PETER. "Drop in the fat some apples red,
(Tra, la, ritte, ra, la, la, la!)
Then spread it on a piece of bread,
(Tra, la, ritte, ra, la, la, la!)"

[*He opens the door, carrying a big bottle in his hand; hailing the* BATHOLOMMEYS *cheerfully.*] Good-morning, good people. [*He puts the jug on the sideboard and hangs up the key. The* BATHOLOMMEYS *look sadly at* PETER. MRS. BATHOLOMMEY *in the foreground tries to smile pleasantly, but can only assume the peculiarly pained expression of a person about to break terrible news.*

REV. MR. BATHOLOMMEY. [*Rising to the occasion—warmly grasping* PETER'S *hand.*] Ah, my dear friend! Many thanks for the flowers William brought us, and the noble cheque you sent me. We're still enjoying the vegetables you generously provided. I *did* relish the squash.

PETER. [*Catching a glimpse of* MRS. BATHOLOMMEY'S *gloomy expression.*] Anything distressing you this morning, Mrs. Batholommey?

MRS. BATHOLOMMEY. No, no. . . . I hope *you're* feeling well—er—I don't mean that—I—

REV. MR. BATHOLOMMEY. [*Cheerily.*] Of course, she does; and why not, why not, dear friend?

PETER. Will you have a glass of my plum brandy?

MRS. BATHOLOMMEY. [*Stiffly.*] No, thank you. As you know, I belong to the W. C. T. U.

PETER. Pastor?

REV. MR. BATHOLOMMEY. [*Tolerantly.*] No, thank you. I am also opposed to er—

PETER. We're going to drink to spooks—the Doctor and I.

MRS. BATHOLOMMEY. [*With a startled cry.*] Oh! [*Lifts her handkerchief to her eyes.*] How can you! And at a time like this. The very idea—*you* of all people!

PETER. [*Coming down with two glasses—handing one to the* DOCTOR.] You seem greatly upset, Mrs. Batholommey. Something must have happened.

REV. MR. BATHOLOMMEY. Nothing, nothing, I assure you. My wife is a trifle nervous to-day. We must all keep up our spirits, Mr. Grimm.

PETER. Of course. Why not? [*Looking at* MRS. BATHOLOMMEY—*struck.*] I know why you're crying. You've been to a church wedding. [*To the* DOCTOR, *lifting his glass.*] To astral envelopes, Andrew. [*They drink.*

MRS. BATHOLOMMEY. [*With sad resignation.*] You were always kind to us, dear Mr. Grimm. There never *was* a kinder, better. sweeter man than you *were.*

PETER. Than *I was?*

REV. MR. BATHOLOMMEY. Rose, my dear!

MRS. BATHOLOMMEY. What *will* become of William? [*Weeps.*

PETER. William? Why should you worry over William? I am looking after him. I don't understand—

MRS. BATHOLOMMEY. [*Seeing that she has gone too far.*] I only meant—it's too bad he had such an M—

PETER. An M—?

MRS. BATHOLOMMEY. [*In pantomime—mouthing the word so that* WILLIAM *cannot hear.*] Mother . . . Annamarie.

PETER. Oh! . . .

MRS. BATHOLOMMEY. She ought to have told you or Mr. Batholommey who the F— was.

PETER. F—?

MRS. BATHOLOMMEY. [*In pantomime—as before.*] Father.

PETER. Oh. . . [*Spelling out the word.*] S-c-o-u-n-d-r-e-l—whoever he is! [*Calls.*] William. [WILLIAM *looks up from his book.*] You're very contented here with me, are you not?

WILLIAM. Yes, sir.

PETER. And you want to stay here?

WILLIAM. Yes, sir. [*At that moment, a country circus band—playing a typical parade march—blares out as it comes up some distant street.*] There's a circus in town.

PETER. A circus?

WILLIAM. Yes, sir. The parade has started. [*Opens the window and looks out towards left.*] Here it comes—

PETER. [*Hurrying to the door.*] Where? Where?

WILLIAM. [*Pointing.*] There!

PETER. [*As delighted as* WILLIAM.] You're right. It's coming this way! Here come the chariots. [*Gestures to the* BATHOLOMMEYS *to join him at the window. The music comes nearer and nearer—the parade is supposed to be passing.* WILLIAM *gives a cry of delight as a clown appears at the window with handbills under his arm.*

THE CLOWN. [*As he throws the handbills into the room.*] Billy Miller's big show and monster circus is in town this afternoon. Only one ring. No confusion. [*Seeing* WILLIAM.] Circus day comes but once a year, little sir. Come early and see the wild animals and hear the lions roar-r-r! Mind! [*Holding up his *finger to* WILLIAM.] I shall expect to see *you.* Wonderful troupe of trained mice in the side show. [*Sings.*]

"Uncle Rat has gone to town,
Ha! H'm!
Uncle Rat has gone to town
To buy Miss Mouse a—"

[*Ends the song abruptly.*] Ha! Ha! Ha! Ha! [*The* CLOWN *disappears, repeating "Billy Miller's Big Show," &c., until his voice is lost and the voices of shouting children are heard as they run after him.*

PETER. [*Putting his hand in his pocket.*] We'll go. You may buy the tickets, William—two front seats. [FREDERIK *re-enters with a floral catalogue.*

MRS. BATHOLOMMEY. [*Apart to* REV. MR. BATHOLOMMEY—*looking at* PETER.] Somebody ought to tell him.

WILLIAM. [*Getting the money from* PETER.] I'm going! I'm going! [*Dances.*] Oh, Mr. Grimm, there ain't anyone else like you in the world. When the *other boys* laugh at your funny old hat, *I* never do. [*Pointing to* PETER'S *hat on the peg.*

PETER. My hat? They laugh at my hat?

WILLIAM. We'll have such a good time at the circus. It's too bad you've got to die, Mr. Grimm.

There is a pause. PETER *stops short, looking at* WILLIAM. *The others are startled, but stand motionless, watching the effect of* WILLIAM'S *revelation.* FREDERIK *doesn't know what to make of it. There is an ominous silence in the room. Then* MRS. BATHOLOMMEY, *whose smile has been frozen on her face, takes* WILLIAM'S *hand and is about to draw him away, when* PETER *lays his hand on* WILLIAM'S *shoulder.* MRS. BATHOLOMMEY *steps back.*

PETER. [*Kindly.*] Yes, William, most people have to. . . . What made you think of it just then?

WILLIAM. [*Points to the* DOCTOR.] He said so. Perhaps in twenty minutes.

REV. MR. BATHOLOMMEY. [*Quietly but very sternly.*] William! [WILLIAM *now understands that he should not have repeated what he heard.*

PETER. Don't frighten the boy. Only children tell the truth. Tell me, William—you heard the Doctor say that? [WILLIAM *is silent. He keeps his eyes on the* CLERGYMAN *who is looking at him warningly. The tears run down his cheeks—he puts his fingers to his lips—afraid to speak.*] Don't be frightened. You heard the Doctor say that?

WILLIAM. [*His voice trembling.*] Y—es, sir.

PETER. [*Looks round the room—beginning to understand.*] . . . What did you mean, Andrew?

DR. MACPHERSON. I'll tell you, Peter, when we're alone.

PETER. But . . . [MRS. BATHOLOMMEY *shakes her finger threateningly at* WILLIAM *who whimpers.*] Never mind. It popped out, didn't it, William? Get the circus tickets and we'll have a fine time just the same. [WILLIAM *goes for the tickets.*

REV. MR. BATHOLOMMEY. I—er—good-morning, dear friend. [*Takes* PETER'S *hand.*] Any time you 'phone for me—day or night—I'll run over instantly. God bless you, sir. I've never come to you for any worthy charity and been turned away—never.

MRS. BATHOLOMMEY. [*Suddenly overcome.*] Good-bye, Mr. Grimm. [*In tears, she follows her husband. The* DOCTOR *and* PETER *look at each other.*

DR. MACPHERSON. [*Cigar in mouth—very abruptly.*] It's cardiac valvular—a little valve— [*Tapping heart.*] —here. [*Slaps* PETER *on the shoulder.*] There's my 'phone. [*As a bell is heard faintly but persistently ringing across the street.*] I'll be back. [*Catches up his hat to hasten off.*

PETER. Just a minute.

DR. MACPHERSON. [*Turning.*] Don't fret yourself, Peter. You're not to imagine you're worse than you are. [*Angrily.*] Don't funk!

PETER. [*Calmly.*] That wasn't my reason for detaining you, Andrew. [*With a twinkle in his eye.*] I merely wanted to say—

DR. MACPHERSON. Yes?

PETER. That if there is anything in that ghost business of yours, I won't forget to come back and apologize for my want of faith. [*The* DOCTOR *goes home.* FREDERIK *stands looking at his* UNCLE. *There is a long pause.* PETER *throws up both hands.*] Rubbish! Doctors are very often wrong. It's all guess work, eh, Fritz?

FREDERIK. [*Thinking of his future in case of* PETER'S *death.*] Yes, sir.

PETER. However, to be on the safe side, I'll take that nip of plum brandy. [*Then thinking aloud.*] Not yet . . . Not yet . . . I'm not ready to die yet. I have so much to live for. . . . When I'm older . . . When I'm a little old leaf ready to curl up, eh, Fritz? [*He drains the glass. Goes up to the peg, takes down his hat, looks at it as though remembering* WILLIAM'S *words, then puts it back on the peg. He shows no sign of taking* DR. MACPHERSON'S *verdict to heart—in fact, he doesn't believe it.*] Frederik, get me some small change for the circus—enough for William and me.

FREDERIK. Are you going . . . after all? . . . And with that child?

PETER. Why not?

FREDERIK. [*Suddenly showing feeling.*] That little tattler? A child that listens to everything and just told you . . . He shouldn't be allowed in this part of the house. He should be sent away.

PETER. [*Astonished.*] Why do you dislike him, Frederik? He's a fine little fellow. You surprise me, my boy . . . [CATHERINE *enters and goes to the piano, running her hands softly over the keys—playing no melody in particular.* PETER *sits in his big chair at the table and picks up his pipe.* FREDERIK, *with an inscrutable face, now strikes a match and holds it to his uncle's pipe.* PETER *thoughtfully takes one or two puffs; then speaking so as not to be heard by* CATHERINE.] Frederik, I want to think that after I'm gone, everything will be the same here . . . just as it is now.

FREDERIK. Yes, sir. [*Sitting near* PETER.

PETER. Just as it is . . . [FREDERIK *nods assent.* PETER *smokes. The room is very cheerful. The bright midday sunshine creeps through the windows,—almost causing a haze in the room—and resting on the pots and vases and bright flowers on the tables.*

CATHERINE. [*Singing.*] "The bird so free in the heavens"—

PETER. [*Looking up—still in thought—seeming not to hear the song.*] And my charities attended to. [FREDERIK *nods assent.*

CATHERINE. "Is but the slave of the nest;
For all must toil as God wills it,—
Must laugh and toil and rest."

PETER. [*Who has been thinking.*] Just as though I were here.

CATHERINE. "The rose must blow in the garden"—

PETER. William, too. Don't forget *him*, Frederik.

FREDERIK. No, Uncle.

CATHERINE. "The bee must gather its store;
The cat must watch the mouse-hole;
The dog must guard the door."

PETER. [*As though he had a weight off his mind.*] We won't speak of this again. It's understood. [*Smokes, listening with pleasure as* CATHERINE *finishes the song.*

CATHERINE. [*Repeats the chorus.*]

"The cat must watch the mouse-hole;
The dog must guard the door.
La la, La la," *&c.*

At the close of the song, PETER *puts down his pipe and beckons to* CATHERINE.

PETER. Give me the Book. [CATHERINE *brings the Bible to* PETER *as the garden bell rings outside.*

FREDERIK. Noon.

PETER. [*Opening the Book at the history of the family—points to the closely written page.*] Under my name I want to see this written: "Married: Catherine and Frederik." I want to see you settled, Katie— [*Smiling.*] settled happily for life. [*He takes her hand and draws* FREDERIK *towards his chair.* CATHERINE, *embarrassed, plays with a rose in her belt.*] Will you? . . .

CATHERINE. I . . . . I don't know. . . .

PETER. [*Taking the rose and her hand in his own.*] *I* know for you, my dear. Make me happy.

CATHERINE. There's nothing I wouldn't do to make *you* happy, Uncle, but—

FREDERIK. You know that I love you, Kitty.

PETER. Yes, yes, yes. *That's* all understood. He has always loved you. Everybody knows it.

CATHERINE. Uncle . . .

PETER. Make it a June wedding. We have ten days yet. [*Slipping her hand in* FREDERIK'S, *taking the rose, and tapping their clasped hands with the flower as he speaks.*

FREDERIK. Say yes, Kitty.

CATHERINE. [*Nervously.*] I couldn't in ten days. . . .

FREDERIK. But—

PETER. [*To* FREDERIK.] Who is arranging the marriage, you or I? Say a month, then, Katie. . . . Promise me.

CATHERINE. [*Her lips set.*] If you have set your heart on it, I will, Uncle Peter . . . I will . . . I promise.

PETER. [*Takes a ring off his hand.*] The wedding ring—my dear mother's. [*Gives it to* CATHERINE.] You've made me very happy, my dear. [*He kisses* CATHERINE. *Then, releasing her, he nods to* FREDERIK *to follow his example.* PETER *turns his back on the young people and smokes.*

FREDERIK. Catherine . . . [*Dreading his embrace, she retreats towards* PETER *and, as she touches him, his pipe falls to the floor. She looks at him, startled.* FREDERIK, *struck, looking intently at* PETER *who sits motionless.*

CATHERINE. Uncle Peter . . . Uncle! What is it? What's the matter? [*Runs to the door—calling across the street.*] Doctor! There he is—just going out. [*Calls.*] Come back. Come back, Doctor. [*To* FREDERIK.] I felt it. I felt something strange a minute ago. I felt it.

FREDERIK. [*Taking* PETER'S *hand.*] Uncle Peter!

CATHERINE. [*Coming back to* PETER *and looking at him transfixed.*] Uncle Peter! Answer me! . . . It's Katie!

The DOCTOR *enters hurriedly.*

DR. MACPHERSON. Is it . . . Peter? [*He goes quickly to* PETER *and listens to his heart.* CATHERINE *and* FREDERIK *on either side of him. The* DOCTOR *with tender sympathy takes* CATHERINE *in his arms.*

WILLIAM. [*Rushes in with two tickets in his hand, leaving the door open. The circus music is faintly heard.*] Mr. Grimm!

DR. MACPHERSON. Sh! [*A pause as though breaking the news to them all.*] He's gone.

FREDERIK. [*Questioningly—dazed.*] Dead? [CATHERINE *is overcome.*

WILLIAM. [*At* PETER'S *side—holding up the circus ticket.*] He can't be dead . . . I've got his ticket to the circus.

CURTAIN.

ACT II.

SCENE. *The second act takes place ten days later, towards the close of a rainy afternoon. A fire is burning in the grate and a basket of hickory wood stands beside the hearth.* PETER'S *hat is no longer on the peg. His pipes and jar of tobacco are missing. A number of wedding presents are set on a table, some unopened. The interior of the room, with its snapping fire, forms a pleasant contrast to the gloomy exterior. The day is fading into dusk.* MRS. BATHOLOMMEY *is at the piano, playing the wedding march from "Lohengrin." Four little girls are grouped about her, singing the words to the air.*

"Faithful and true:
We lead ye forth,
Where love triumphant
Shall lighten the way."

"Bright star of love,
Flower of the earth,
Shine on ye both
On Love's perfect day."

MRS. BATHOLOMMEY. That's better. Children, remember that this is to be a very *quiet* wedding. You're to be here at noon to-morrow. You're not to speak as you enter the room and take your places near the piano. Miss Staats will come down from her room,—at least I suppose she will—and will stand . . . [*Thinks.*] I don't know where—but you're to stop when *I* look at you. Watch me as though I were about to be married. [*She takes her place at the foot of the stairs and the children repeat the song until she has marched across the room and stationed herself in some appropriate corner. As* FREDERIK *appears from the hall, where he leaves his raincoat and umbrella,* MRS. BATHOLOMMEY *motions the children to silence.*] That will do, dears, thank you. Hurry home between showers. [*The children go as she explains to* FREDERIK.] My Sunday-school scholars. . . . I thought your dear uncle would like a song at the wedding. I know how bright and cheery he would have been—poor man. Dear, noble, charitable soul!

FREDERIK. [*In a low voice.*] Where's Catherine?

MRS. BATHOLOMMEY. [*Taking up her fancy work, seating herself.*] Upstairs.

FREDERIK. With that sick child? Tc!

MRS. BATHOLOMMEY. Catherine finds it a pleasure to sit beside the little fellow. William is very much better.

FREDERIK. [*Taking a telegram from his pocket-book.*] Well, we shall soon be off to Europe. I've just had a telegram to say a cabin has been reserved for me on the *Imperator.* To-morrow, thank God, we shall take the afternoon train to New York.

MRS. BATHOLOMMEY. I must confess that I'm very glad. Of course, I'm happy to stay and chaperone Catherine; but poor Mr. Batholommey has been alone at the parsonage for ten days . . . ever since your dear uncle . . . [*Pauses, unwinding yarn, then unburdening her mind.*] I didn't think at first that Catherine could persuade herself to marry you.

FREDERIK. [*Sharply.*] I don't understand you, Mrs. Batholommey.

MRS. BATHOLOMMEY. I mean she seemed so averse to—to an immediate marriage; but of course it was your uncle's last request, and that influenced her more than anything else. So it's to be a June wedding, after all; he has his wish. You'll be married in ten days from the time he left us. [*Remembering.*] Some more letters marked personal came for him while you were out. I put them in the drawer— [*Points to desk.*] with the rest. It seems odd to think the postman brings your uncle's letters regularly, yet *he* is not here.

FREDERIK. [*Looking towards the door of the office.*] Did Hartman come?

MRS. BATHOLOMMEY. Yes. He seemed rather surprised that you'd sent for him.

FREDERIK. Did you—er—tell him that we intend to leave to-morrow?

MRS. BATHOLOMMEY. I spoke of your wedding trip,—yes.

FREDERIK. Did he seem inclined to stay?

MRS. BATHOLOMMEY. He didn't say. He seemed very much agitated. [MARTA *enters, carrying a night lamp.*] We'll pack Miss Catherine's things to-night, Marta. [*She notices the lamp.*] The night lamp for William? [*Looks up towards the door of his room.*] Go in very quietly. He's asleep, I think. [MARTA *goes up the stairs and into* WILLIAM'S *room.*] By the way, Mr. Batholommey was very much excited when he heard that your uncle had left a personal memorandum concerning *us.* We're anxious to hear it read. [FREDERIK, *paying no attention to her words, is glancing at the wedding presents.*] We're anxious to hear it read.

JAMES. [*Entering.*] Did you wish to see me?

FREDERIK. [*Offering his hand to* JAMES.] How do you do, Hartman? I'm very glad you consented to come back. My uncle never went into his office again after you left. There is some private correspondence concerning matters of which I know nothing; it lies on your old desk. . . . I'm anxious to settle everything to-night.

MRS. BATHOLOMMEY *leaves the room.*

JAMES. Very well. I have no doubt but that I can get through with it by midnight.

FREDERIK. If you care to remain longer with the firm, I—er—

JAMES. No, thank you.

FREDERIK. I appreciate the fact that you came on my uncle's account. I have no ill-feeling against you, Hartman.

JAMES. I'm not refusing to stay because of any ill-feeling. I'm going because I know that you'll sell out before your uncle's cold in his grave. I don't care to stay to see the old place change hands.

FREDERIK. I? Sell out? My intention is to carry out every wish of my dear old uncle's.

JAMES. I hope so. I haven't forgotten that you wanted him to sell out to Hicks of Rochester on the very day he died. [*Exit into the office.*

CATHERINE *comes from* WILLIAM'S *room, simply dressed in white—no touch of mourning.* FREDERIK *goes to the foot of the stairs and calls softly.*

FREDERIK. Kitty! Here is our marriage license. I have the cabin on the *Imperator.* Everything is arranged.

CATHERINE. [*Coming downstairs.*] Yes. . . . I meant to speak to you—again.

FREDERIK. To-morrow's the day, dear.

CATHERINE. [*Very subdued.*] Yes. . . .

FREDERIK. A June wedding—just as Uncle Peter wished.

CATHERINE. [*As before.*] Yes . . . Just as he wished. *Everything* is just as he . . . . [*With a change of manner—earnestly—looking at* FREDERIK.] Frederik, I don't want to go away. I don't want to go to Europe. If only I could stay quietly here in— [*Tears in her voice as she looks round the room.*] —in my dear home.

FREDERIK. Why do you want to stay in this old cottage—with its candles and lamps and shadows? It's very gloomy, very depressing.

CATHERINE. I don't want to leave this house. . . . I don't want any home but this. [*Panic-stricken.*] Don't take me away, Frederik. I know you've never really liked it at Grimm's Manor. Are you sure you'll want to come back to live here?

FREDERIK. [*As though speaking to a child.*] Of course. I'll do anything you ask.

CATHERINE. I—I've always wanted to please . . . [*After a slight pause, finding it difficult to speak his name.*] Uncle Peter. . . . I felt that I owed everything to him. . . . If he had lived . . . if I could see *his* happiness at our marriage—it would make *me* happy; [*Pathetically.*] but he's gone . . . and . . . I'm afraid we're making a mistake. I don't feel towards you as I ought, Frederik. I've told you again and again; but I want to tell you once more: I'm willing to marry you . . . but I don't love you—I never shall.

FREDERIK. How do you know?

CATHERINE. I know . . . I know. . . . It seems so disloyal to speak like this after I promised *him;* but—

FREDERIK. Yes, you *did* promise Uncle Peter you'd marry me, didn't you?

CATHERINE. Yes.

FREDERIK. And he died believing you?

CATHERINE. Yes.

FREDERIK. Then it all comes to this: are you going to live up to your promise?

CATHERINE. That's it. That's what makes me try to live up to it. [*Wiping her eyes.*] But you know how I feel. . . . You understand. . . .

FREDERIK. Perfectly; you don't quite know your own mind. . . . Very few young girls do, I suppose. I love you and in time you'll grow to care for me. [MARTA *re-enters from* WILLIAM'S *room and closing the door comes down the stairs and passes off.*] What *are* we to do with that child?

CATHERINE. He's to stay here, of course.

FREDERIK. The child should be sent to some institution. What claim has he on you—on any of us?

CATHERINE. Why do you dislike him?

FREDERIK. I don't, but—

CATHERINE. Yes, you do. I can't understand it. I remember how angry you were when you came back from college and found him living here. You never mention his mother's name, yet you played together as children. When Uncle tried to find Annamarie and bring her back, you were the only one opposed to it.

FREDERIK. William is an uncomfortable child to have in the house. He has a way of staring at people as though he had a perpetual question on his lips. It's most annoying.

CATHERINE. What question?

FREDERIK. As for his mother—I've never seen her since she left this house and I don't care to hear her name on your lips. Her reputation is— [*The rain starts pattering on the shingled roof.*] Tc! More rain . . . the third day of it. . . . [*Going to the window—calling.*] Otto! [*Angrily.*] Otto! See what the wind has done—those trellises. [*Bangs the window shut.*] That old gardener should have been laid off years ago. . . . By the way, his son James is here for a few hours—to straighten matters out. I must see how he's getting on. [*Taking her hand, drawing her towards the table with a change of manner.*] Have you seen all the wedding presents, Kitty? I'll be back in a few minutes. [*Pats her cheek and exits.*

CATHERINE *stands over her wedding presents just as he left her—not looking at them—her eyes filled with tears. The door is suddenly opened and the* DOCTOR *enters, a tweed shawl over his shoulders, wearing a tweed cap. He has a book under his arm.*

DR. MACPHERSON. How's William? [CATHERINE *tries to hide her tears, but he sees through her. He tosses his cap, coat and book on the sofa.*] What's the matter?

CATHERINE. Nothing. . . . I was only thinking. . . . I was hoping that those we love . . . and lose . . . *can't* see us here. I'm beginning to believe there's not much happiness in *this* world.

DR. MACPHERSON. Why, you little snip. I've a notion to spank you. Talking like that with life before you! Read this book, child; [*Gesturing towards the book on the sofa.*] it proves that the dead *do* see us; they *do* come back. [*Walks to the foot of the stairs—turns.*] Catherine, I understand that you've not a penny to your name—unless you marry Frederik; that he has inherited you along with the orchids and tulips. Don't let that influence you. If Peter's plans bind you—and you look as though they did—my door's open. Think it over. It's not too late. [*Goes half-way up the stairs—then pauses.*] Don't let the neighbours' opinions and a few silver spoons— [*Pointing to the wed-*

ding presents.] stand in the way of your future. [*Exit into* WILLIAM'S *room. The rain increases. The sky grows blacker—the room darker.* CATHERINE *gives a cry and stretches out her arms, not looking up.*

CATHERINE. Uncle Peter! Uncle Peter! Why did you do it? Why did you ask it? Oh, dear! Oh, dear! If you could see me now. [*She stands rigid—her arms outstretched.* MARTA, *who has silently entered from the dining-room with fresh candles, goes to* CATHERINE. CATHERINE *suddenly buries her face on* MARTA'S *broad breast, breaking into sobs; then recovering, wipes her eyes.*] There, there . . . I mustn't cry . . . others have troubles, too, haven't they?

MARTA. Others have troubles, too.

CATHERINE. I had hoped, Marta, that Annamarie would have heard of Uncle's loss and come back to us at this time. . . .

MARTA. If it had only brought us all together once more; but no message . . . nothing . . I cannot understand.

CATHERINE. She knows that our door is open. . . .

The rain beats against the windows. A sharp double knock is heard at the door. CATHERINE *starts as though suddenly brought to herself, hastily goes into the next room, taking the* DOCTOR'S *book with her.* MARTA *has hurried towards the front door, when the* REV. MR. BATHOLOMMEY *and* COLONEL LAWTON *appear in the hall as though they had entered quickly, to escape the storm.* MARTA, *greeting them, passes off to tell* FREDERIK *of their presence. The* REV. MR. BATHOLOMMEY *wears a long, black cloth, rain-proof coat.* COLONEL LAWTON *wears a rubber poncho.* COLONEL LAWTON *is a tall man with a thin brown beard and moustache, about forty-eight. He is dressed in a Prince Albert coat, unpressed trousers, and a negligée shirt. He wears spectacles and has a way of throwing back his head and peering at people before answering them. The* REV. MR. BATHOLOMMEY *sets his umbrella in the hall and the* COLONEL *hangs his broad-brimmed hat on the handle—as though to let it drip.*

REV. MR. BATHOLOMMEY. Brr! I believe it's raining icicles.

COLONEL LAWTON. [*Taking off his overshoes.*] Gee Whillikins! What a day! Good thing the old windmill out yonder is tied up. Great weather for baptisms, Parson. [*There is a faint, far-away rumble of thunder.* FREDERIK *enters.*] Well, here we are, Frederik, my boy—at the time you mentioned.

REV. MR. BATHOLOMMEY. How are you, Frederik?

COLONEL LAWTON *crosses to the fire, followed by the* REV. MR. BATHOLOMMEY.

FREDERIK. [*Who has gone to the desk for a paper lying under a paper-weight.*] I sent for you to hear a memorandum left by my uncle. I only came across it yesterday. [*There is a louder peal of thunder. A flash of lightning illuminates the room.*

COLONEL LAWTON. I must have drawn up ten wills for the old gentleman, but he always tore 'em up. May I have a drink of his plum brandy, Frederik?

FREDERIK. Help yourself. Pastor?

REV. MR. BATHOLOMMEY. Er—er—

COLONEL LAWTON *goes to the sideboard and pours out two drinks from a decanter. A heavy roll of thunder now ends in a sharp thunderclap.* MRS. BATHOLOMMEY, *who is entering the room, gives a cry and puts her hands over her face.* COLONEL LAWTON *bolts his whiskey. The* REV. MR. BATHOLOMMEY *takes a glass and stands with it in his hand.*

MRS. BATHOLOMMEY. [*Removing her hands in time to see the brandy.*] Why, Henry! What are you doing? Are your feet wet?

REV. MR. BATHOLOMMEY. No, Rose; they're not. I want a drink and I'm going to take it. It's a bad night. [*Drinks.*

COLONEL LAWTON. [*Throws a hickory log on the fire, which presently blazes up, making the room much lighter.*] Go ahead, Frederik. [*Sits.*

REV. MR. BATHOLOMMEY *has drawn up a chair for his wife, and now seats himself before the snapping hickory fire.*

REV. MR. BATHOLOMMEY. I knew that your uncle would remember his friends and his charities. He was so liberal! One might say of him that he was the very soul of generosity. He gave in such a free-handed, princely fashion.

FREDERIK. [*Reading in a businesslike manner.*] For Mrs. Batholommey—

MRS. BATHOLOMMEY. The dear man—to think that he remembered me! I knew he'd remember the church and Mr. Batholommey, of course; but to think that he'd remember me! He knew that my income was very limited. He was so thoughtful! His purse was always open.

FREDERIK. [*Eyes* MRS. BATHOLOMMEY *for a second, then continues.*] For Mr. Batholommey— [REV. MR. BATHOLOMMEY *nods solemnly.*] and the Colonel.

COLONEL LAWTON. [*Taking out a cigar.*] He knew that I did the best I could for him . . . [*His voice breaks.*] the grand old man. [*Recovering.*] What'd he leave me? Mrs. B. —er? [*Nods inquiringly at* MRS. BATHOLOMMEY, *who bows assent, and he lights his cigar.*

FREDERIK. [*Glancing at the paper.*] Mrs. Batholommey, he wished you to have his miniature—with his affectionate regards.

MRS. BATHOLOMMEY. Dear old gentleman—and er—yes?

FREDERIK. To Mr. Batholommey—

MRS. BATHOLOMMEY. But—er—you didn't finish with me.

FREDERIK. You're finished.

MRS. BATHOLOMMEY. I'm finished?

FREDERIK. You may read it yourself if you like.

REV. MR. BATHOLOMMEY. No, no, no. She'll take your word for it. [*Firmly.*] Rose!

FREDERIK. [*Reads.*] "To Mr. Batholommey, my antique watch-fob—with my profound respects." [*Continues.*] To Colonel Lawton—

MRS. BATHOLOMMEY. His watch fob? Is *that* what he left to *Henry?* Is that all? [*As* FREDERIK *nods.*] Well! If he had no wish to make *your* life easier, Henry, he should at least have left something for the church. Oh! Won't the congregation have a crow to pick with you!

FREDERIK. [*Reading.*] "To my life-long friend, Colonel Lawton, I leave my most cherished possession." [COLONEL LAWTON *has a look on his face as though he were saying, "Ah! I'll get something worth while."*

MRS. BATHOLOMMEY. [*Angrily.*] When the church members hear that—

COLONEL LAWTON. [*Chewing his cigar.*] I don't know why he was called upon to leave anything to the church—he gave it thousands; and only last month, he put in chimes. As *I* look at it, he wished to give you something he had *used*—something personal. Perhaps the miniature and the fob *ain't* worth three whoops in Hell,—it's the sentiment of the thing that counts—[*Chewing the word with his cigar.*] the sentiment. Drive on, Fred.

FREDERIK. "To Colonel Lawton, my father's prayer-book."

COLONEL LAWTON. [*Suddenly changing—dazed.*] His prayer-book . . . me?

MRS. BATHOLOMMEY. [*Seeing* FREDERIK *lay down the paper and rise.*] Is that all?

FREDERIK. That's all.

COLONEL LAWTON. [*Still dazed.*] A prayer-book. . . . Me? Well, I'll be— [*Struck.*] Here, Parson, let's swap. You take the prayer-book—I'll take the old fob.

REV. MR. BATHOLOMMEY. [*Stiffly.*] Thank you. I already *have* a prayer-book. [*Goes to the window and looks out—his back turned to the others—trying to control his feelings.*

MRS. BATHOLOMMEY. [*Her voice trembling with vexation and disappointment.*] Well, all that I can say is—I'm disappointed in your uncle.

COLONEL LAWTON. Is it for this you hauled us out in the rain, Frederik?

MRS. BATHOLOMMEY. [*Bitterly.*] I see now . . . he only gave to the church to show off.

REV. MR. BATHOLOMMEY. Rose! . . . I myself am disappointed, but—

MRS. BATHOLOMMEY. He did! Or why didn't he *continue* his work? He was *not* a generous man. He was a hard, uncharitable, selfish old man.

REV. MR. BATHOLOMMEY. [*Horrified.*] Rose, my dear!

MRS. BATHOLOMMEY. He was! If he were here, I'd say it to his face. The congregation sicked *you* after him. Now that he's gone and you'll get nothing more, they'll call you slow—slow and pokey. You'll see! You'll see to-morrow.

REV. MR. BATHOLOMMEY. Sh!

MRS. BATHOLOMMEY. As for the Colonel, who spent half his time with Mr. Grimm, what is *his* reward? A watch-fob! [*Prophetically.*] Henry, mark my words—this will be the end of *you.* It's only a question of a few weeks. One of these new football playing ministers, just out of college, will take *your* place. It's not what you *preach* now that counts; it's what you coax out of the rich parishioners' pockets.

REV. MR. BATHOLOMMEY. [*In a low voice.*] *Mrs.* Batholommey!

MRS. BATHOLOMMEY. Religion doesn't stand where it did, Henry—there's no denying that. There was a time when people had to go to church—they weren't decent if they didn't. Now you have to wheedle 'em in. The church needs funds in these days when a college professor is openly saying that— [*Her voice breaks.*] the Star of Bethlehem was a comet. [*Weeps.*

REV. MR. BARTHOLOMMEY. Control yourself. I must insist upon it, Mrs. Batholommey.

MRS. BATHOLOMMEY. [*Breaking down—almost breathlessly.*] Oh! If I said all the things I feel like saying about Peter Grimm —well—I shouldn't be fit to be a clergyman's wife. Not to leave his dear friends a—

COLONEL LAWTON. He *wasn't* liberal; but, for God's sake, madam, pull yourself together and think what he ought to have done for me!—I've listened to his plans for twenty years. I've virtually given up my business for him, and what have I got out of it? Not a button! Not a button! A bible. Still *I'm* not complaining. Hang that chimney, Frederik, it's smoking. [COLONEL LAWTON *stirs the fire—a log falls out and the flame goes down. The room has gradually grown darker as the night approaches*

MRS. BATHOLOMMEY. [*Turning on* COLONEL LAWTON.] Oh, you've feathered your nest, Colonel! You're a rich man.

COLONEL LAWTON. [*Enraged, raising his voice.*] What? I never came here that *you* weren't begging.

FREDERIK. [*Virtuously—laying down the paper.*] Well, I'm disgusted! When I think how much more I should have if he hadn't continually doled out money to every one of you!

COLONEL LAWTON. What?

FREDERIK. He was putty in your hands.

MRS. BATHOLOMMEY. Yes, you can afford to defend his memory—you've got the money.

FREDERIK. I don't defend his memory. He was a gullible old fossil, and the whole town knew it.

MRS. BATHOLOMMEY. *You* did at any rate. I've heard you flatter him by the hour.

FREDERIK. Of course. He liked flattery and I gave him what he wanted. Why not? I gave him plenty. The rest of you were at the same thing; and I had the pleasure of watching him give you the money that belonged to me—to *me*—my money. . . What business had he to be generous with my money? [*The* COLONEL *strikes a match to light his cigar, and, as it flares up, the face of* FREDERIK *is seen—distorted with anger.*] I'll tell you this: had he lived much longer, there would have been nothing left for me. It's a fortunate thing for me that— [*He pauses, knowing that he has said too much. The room is now very dark. The rain has subsided. Everything is quiet outside. There is not a sound, save the ticking of the clock.*

REV. MR. BARTHOLOMMEY. [*Solemnly—breaking the pause.*] Young man, it might have been better had Mr. Grimm given his *all* to charity—for he has left his money to an ingrate.

FREDERIK. [*Laughing derisively.*] Ha! Ha!

MRS. BATHOLOMMEY. Sh! Someone's coming.

All is quiet. The clock ticks in the dark. The door opens.

FREDERIK. [*With a change of voice.*] Come in. [*Nobody enters.*] Where's a light? We've been sitting in the dark like owls. Come in. [*A pause. He strikes a match and holds it above his head. The light shows the open door. A wind, blowing through the doorway, causes the match to flicker, and* FREDERIK *protects it with his hand.*

COLONEL LAWTON. I'll see who's . . . [*Looks out.*] No one.

MRS. BATHOLOMMEY. Someone *must* be there. Who opened the door? [*The wind puts out the match in* FREDERIK'S *hand. The room is once more in semi-darkness.*] There . . . it closed again . . . [FREDERIK *strikes another match and holds it up. The door is seen to be closed.*

COLONEL LAWTON. [*Who is nearest to the door.*] I didn't touch it.

FREDERIK. [*Blowing out the match.*] I'll have the lamps brought in.

MRS. BARTHOLOMMEY. Curious . . .

REV. MR. BATHOLOMMEY. It was the wind—a draught.

COLONEL LAWTON. [*Returning to his chair.*] Must have been.

CATHERINE. [*Entering with a lamp.*] Did someone call me?

Without pausing, she sets the lamp on the table down right—opposite the group of characters. She turns up the wick and PETER GRIMM *is seen standing in the room—half in shadow. He is as he was in life. The clothes he wears appear to be those he wore about his house in the first act. He carries his hat in his hand. He has the same kind smile, the same deferential manner, but his face is more spiritual and years younger. The lamp, which* CATHERINE *has placed on the table, brightens the room.*

PETER. [*Whose eyes never leave* CATHERINE. Yes . . . I called you . . . I've come back.

FREDERIK. [*To* CATHERINE.] No.

PETER. Don't be frightened, Katie. It's the most natural thing in the world. You wanted me and I came.

FREDERIK. Why? What made you think someone called you?

CATHERINE. I'm so accustomed to hear Uncle Peter's voice in this room, that sometimes I forget he's not here. . . . I can't get over it! I was almost sure I heard him speak . . . but, of course, as soon as I came in—I remembered. . . . But some one must have called me.

FREDERIK. No.

PETER *stands looking at them, perplexed; not being able to comprehend as yet that he is not seen.*

CATHERINE. Isn't it curious . . . to hear your name and turn and . . . [*Unconsciously, she looks in* PETER'S *face.*] no one there?

REV. MR. BATHOLOMMEY. [*Kindly.*] Nerves . . . imagination.

FREDERIK. You need a complete change. [*Crossing to the door.*] For heaven's sake, let's have more light or we shall all be hearing voices.

PETER. Strange. . . . Nobody seems to see me. . . . It's—it's extraordinary! Katie! . . . Katie! . . . [*His eyes have followed* CATHERINE *who is now at the door.*

CATHERINE. [*Pausing.*] Perhaps it was the book I was reading that made me think I heard . . . The Doctor lent it to me.

FREDERIK. [*Pooh-poohing.*] Oh!

CATHERINE. [*Half to herself.*] If he *does* know, if he *can* see, he'll be comforted by the thought that I'm going to do everything he wanted. [*She passes out of the room.*

PETER. [*Showing that he does not want her to carry out his wishes.*] No, no, don't . . . Frederik, I want to speak to you.

[FREDERIK, *not glancing in* PETER'S *direction, lights a cigarette.*

MRS. BATHOLOMMEY. Well, Frederik, I hope the old gentleman can see his mistake *now.*

PETER. I can see several mistakes. [REV. MR. BATHOLOMMEY *rises and goes towards the door, pausing in front of* PETER *to take out his watch.*] . . . Mr. Batholommey, I'm glad to see you in my house . . . I'm very sorry that you can't see *me.* I wasn't pleased with my funeral sermon; it was very gloomy—very. I never was so depressed in my life.

MRS. BATHOLOMMEY. [*To* FREDERIK.] Do you know what I should like to say to your uncle?

PETER. I know.

REV. MR. BATHOLOMMEY. I hope at least you'll care for the parish poor as your uncle did—and keep on with *some* of his charities.

PETER. [*Putting his hand on* REV. MR. BATHOLOMMEY'S *shoulder.*] That's all attended to. I arranged all that with Frederik. He must look after my charities.

FREDERIK. I might as well tell you now—you needn't look to me. It's Uncle Peter's fault if your charities are cut off.

REV. MR. BATHOLOMMEY. [*Half-doubtingly.*] It doesn't seem possible that he made no arrangements to continue his good works. [FREDERIK *remains stolid.* REV. MR. BATHOLOMMEY *puts back his watch after glancing at it.*] Just thirty minutes to make a call. [*Goes into the hall to put on his overshoes, coat, &c., leaving* PETER'S *hand extended in the air.*

COLONEL LAWTON. [*Rising.*] I must be toddling. [*Pauses.*] It's queer, Frederik, how things turn out in this world. [*He stands, thinking matters over—cigar in mouth, his hand on his chin.*

PETER. [*Slipping his hand through* COLONEL LAWTON'S *arm. They seem to look each other in the eye.*] You were perfectly right about it, Thomas, I *should* have made a will . . . I—suppose it *is* a little too late, isn't it? . . . It would be—er—unusual to do it now, wouldn't it?

COLONEL LAWTON, *who has heard nothing—seen nothing—moves away as though* PETER *had never held his arm, and goes up into the hall for his cape and overshoes.*

COLONEL LAWTON. [*Noticing an old gold-headed walking-stick in the hall.*] Oh, er—what are you going to do with all the old man's family relics, Frederik?

FREDERIK. The junk, you mean? I shall lay it on some scrap-heap, I suppose. It's not worth a penny.

COLONEL LAWTON. I'm not so sure of that. They say there's a lot of money paid for this sort of trash.

FREDERIK. Is that so? Not a bad idea to have a dealer in to look it over.

PETER *stands listening, a faint smile on his face.*

MRS. BATHOLOMMEY. If I could have the old clock—cheap, Frederik, I'd take it off your hands.

FREDERIK. I'll find out how much it's worth. I shall have everything appraised. [*Sets his watch by the clock.* MRS. BATHOLOMMEY *gives him a look and joins her husband at the door.*

COLONEL LAWTON. Good-night. [*Exit, closing the door.*

MRS. BATHOLOMMEY. [*As* REV. MR. BATHOLOMMEY *goes out—calling after him.*] Henry, Catherine wants you to come back for supper. [MRS. BATHOLOMMEY *leaves the room too disgusted for words.* FREDERIK *goes into the office.*

PETER. [*Now alone.*] We live and learn . . . and oh! what I have learned since I came back. . . . [*He goes to his own particular peg in the vestibule and hangs up his hat. He glances at the wedding presents. Presently he sees the flowers which* CATHERINE *has placed on the desk. With a smile, he touches the flowers.* MARTA *enters with another lamp, which she places on a table. As* PETER'S *eyes rest on* MARTA, *he nods and smiles in recognition, waiting for a response.*] Well, Marta? . . . Don't you know your old master? . . . No? . . . No? . . . [*She winds the clock and leaves the room.*] I seem to be a stranger in my own house . . . yet the watch-dog knew me and wagged his tail as I came in. [*He stands trying to comprehend it all.*] Well! Well!

FREDERIK. [*Looking at his watch, re-enters from the office and goes to the 'phone, which presently rings.* FREDERIK *instantly lifts the receiver as though not wishing to attract attention. In a low voice.*] Yes. . . I was waiting for you. How are you, Mr. Hicks? [*Listens.*] I'm not anxious to sell—no. I prefer to carry out my dear old uncle's wishes. [PETER *eyes him—a faint smile on his lips.*] If I got my price? Well . . . of course in that case . . . I might be tempted. To-morrow? No, I can't see you to-morrow. I'm going to be married to-morrow, and leave at once for New York. Thank you. [*Listens.*] To-night? Very well, but I don't want it known. I'll sell, but it must be for more than the price my uncle refused. Make it ten thousand more and it's done. [*Listens.*] You'll come to-night? . . . Yes, yes . . . [*Listens at the 'phone.*] The dear old man told you his plans never failed, eh? God rest his soul! [*Laughing indulgently.*] Ha! Ha! Ha!

PETER. Ha! Ha! Ha!

FREDERIK. [*Echoing* HICKS' *words.*] What would he say if he knew? What could he say? Everything must change.

A far-away rumble of thunder is heard—the lightning flickers at the window and a flash is seen on the telephone which tinkles and responds as though from the electric shock. Exclaiming "Ugh," FREDERIK *drops the receiver—which hangs down.*

PETER. [*The storm passes as he speaks into the receiver without touching the telephone.*] Good-evening, my friend. We shall soon meet—face to face. You won't be able to carry this matter through. . . . [*Looking into space as though he could see the future.*] You're not well and you're going out to supper to-night; . . . you will eat something that will cause you to pass over. . . . I shall see you to-morrow. . . . A happy crossing!

FREDERIK. [*Picks up the receiver.*] Hello? . . . You don't feel well, you say? [*Then echoing the purport of* HICKS' *answer.*] I see . . . . Your lawyer can attend to everything to-night without you. Very well. It's entirely a question of money, Mr. Hicks. Send your lawyer to the Grimm Manor Hotel. I'll arrange at once for a room. Good-bye. [*Hangs up the receiver.*] That's off my mind. [*He lights a fresh cigarette—his face expressing the satisfaction he feels in the prospect of a perfectly idle future.* PETER *looks at him as though to say: "And that's the boy whom I loved and trusted!"* FREDERIK *gets his hat, throws his coat over his arm, and hastens out.*

PETER. [*Turns and faces the door leading into the next room, as though he could feel the presence of some one waiting there.*] Yes . . . I am still in the house. Come in . . . come in . . . [*He repeats the signal of the first act.*] Ou—oo. [*The door opens slowly—and* CATHERINE *enters as though at* PETER'S *call. She looks about her, not understanding. He holds out his arms to her.* CATHERINE *walks slowly towards him. He takes her in his arms, but she does not respond. She does not know that she is being held.*] There! There! . . . Don't worry. . . . It's all right. . . . We'll arrange things very differently. I've come back to change all my plans. [*She moves away a step—just out of his embrace. He tries to call her back.*] Katie! . . . Can't I make my presence known to *you?* Katie! Can't my love for you outlive *me?* Isn't it here in the home? . . . Don't cry. [*She moves about the room in thought. As* PETER *watches her—she pauses near his desk.*

CATHERINE. [*Suddenly.*] Crying doesn't help matters.

PETER. She hears me. She doesn't know it, but she hears me. She's cheering up. [*She inhales the flowers—a half smile on her lips.*] That's right, you haven't smiled before since I died.

[*Suddenly giving way to the realization of her loss,* CATHERINE *sighs.*

PETER. [*Correcting himself.*] I—I mean—since I learned that there was a happier place than the world I left. . . . I'm a trifle confused. I've not had time to adjust myself to these new conditions. [CATHERINE *smiles sadly—goes up to the window, and, leaning against the pane, looks out into the night.* PETER *continues comfortingly.*] The dead have never really died, you know. We couldn't die if we tried. We're all about you. . . . Look at the gardens: they've died, haven't they? But there they are all the better for it. Death is the greatest thing in the world. It's really a—Ha!—delightful experience. What is it, after all? A nap from which we waken rested, refreshened . . . a sleep from which we spring up like children tumbling out of bed—ready to frolic through another world. I was an old man a few days ago; now I'm a boy. I feel much younger than you—much younger. [*A conflict is going on in* CATHERINE'S *mind. She walks to the chair by the fireplace and sits—her back to the audience. He approaches her and lays a tender hand on her shoulder.*] I know what you're thinking. . . . Katie, I want you to break that very foolish promise I asked you to make. You're almost tempted to. Break it! Break it at once; then— [*Glancing smilingly towards the door through which he came—as though he wished to leave—like a child longing to go back to play.*] then I could—take the journey back in peace. . . . I can't go until you do—and I . . . I long to go. . . Isn't my message any clearer to you? [*Reading her mind.*] You have a feeling . . . an impression of what I'm saying; but the words . . . the words are not clear . . . Mm . . . let me see. . . If you can't understand me—there's the Doctor, he'll know how to get the message—he'll find the way. . . .Then I can hurry back . . . home. . .

CATHERINE. [*Helplessly—changing her position like a tired child.*] Oh, I'm so alone.

PETER. [*Cheerily.*] Not alone at all—not at all. I shall drop in very often . . . and then, there's your mother. [*Suddenly remembering.*] Oh, yes, I had almost forgotten. I have a message for you, Katie. . . . [*He seats himself in a chair which is almost in front of her.*] I've met your mother. [*She sits in a reverie.*

PETER *continues with the air of a returned traveller relating his experiences.*] She heard that I had crossed over and there she was—waiting for me. You're thinking of it, aren't you? Wondering if we met. . . . Yes, that was the first interesting experience. She knew me at once. "You were Peter Grimm," she said, "before you knew better"—that's what *they* call leaving *this* world—"to *know better*." You call it "dying." [*Confidentially.*] She's been here often, it seems, watching over you. I told her how much I loved you and said that you had a happy home. I spoke of your future—of my plans for you and Frederik. "Peter Grimm," she said, "you've over-looked the most important thing in the world—love. You haven't given her *her right* to the choice of her lover—*her right!*" Then it came over me that I'd made a terrible mistake . . . and at that minute, you called to me. [*Impressively.*] In the darkness surrounding all I had left behind, there came a light . . . a glimmer where you stood . . . a clear call in the night. . . . It seemed as though I had not been away one second . . . but in that second, you had suffered. . . . Now I am back to show you the way. . . . I am here to put my hand on your dear head and give you your mother's blessing; to say she will be with you in spirit until she holds you in her arms—you and your loved husband— [CATHERINE *turns in her chair and looks towards the door of the room in which* JAMES *is working.* PETER *catches the thought.*] —yes, James, it's you . . . And the message ended in this kiss. [*Prints a kiss on her cheek.*] Can't you *think* I'm with you, dear child? Can't you *think* I'm trying to help you? Can't you even hope? Oh, come, at least hope! Anybody can hope.

CATHERINE *rises with an entire change of manner—takes a bright red blossom from the vase on* PETER'S *desk—then deliberately walks to the door of the room in which* JAMES *is working.* PETER *follows her action hopefully. She does not tap on the door, however, but turns and sits at the piano—in thought—not facing the piano. She puts* PETER'S *flowers against her face. Then, laying the flowers on the piano, sings softly three or four bars of the song she sang in the first act—and stops abruptly.*

CATHERINE. [*To herself.*] That I should sit here singing—at a time like this!

PETER. Sing! Sing! Why not? Lift up your voice like a bird! Your old uncle doesn't sleep out there in the dust. That's only the dream. He's here—here—alive. All his age gone and youth glowing in his heart. If I could only tell you what lies before you —before us all! If people even *suspected* what the next life really is, they wouldn't waste time here—I can tell you *that.* They'd do dreadful things to get away from this existence—make for the nearest pond or— [*Pausing abruptly.*] Ah, here comes someone who'll know all about it! [*The* DOCTOR *comes from* WILLIAM'S *room.* PETER *greets him in a cordial but casual way, as though he had parted from him only an hour before.*] Well, Andrew, I apologize. [*Bowing obsequiously.*] You were right. I apologize.

CATHERINE. How is he, Doctor?

DR. MACPHERSON. William is better. Dropped off to sleep again. Can't quite understand him.

PETER. I apologize. I said that if I could come back, I would; and here I am—apologizing. Andrew! Andrew! [*Trying to attract* DR. MACPHERSON'S *attention.*] I have a message, but I can't get it across. This is your chance. I want *you* to take it. I don't wish Catherine to marry Frederik.

DR. MACPHERSON. He's somewhat feverish yet.

PETER. Can't *you* understand one word?

DR. MACPHERSON. It's a puzzling case. . . .

PETER. What? Mine?

DR. MACPHERSON. [*Getting a pad from his pocket—writing out a prescription with his fountain pen.*] I'll leave this prescription at the druggist's—

PETER. I'm quite shut out. . . . They've closed the door and turned the key on me.

DR. MACPHERSON. [*Suddenly noticing that* CATHERINE *seems more cheerful.*] What's happened? I left you in tears and here you are—all smiles.

CATHERINE. Yes, I—I am happier—for some reason. . . For the last few minutes I—I've had such a strange feeling.

DR. MCPHERSON. That's odd: so have I! Been as restless as a hungry mouse. Something seemed to draw me down here—can't explain it.

PETER. I'm beginning to be felt in this house.

DR. MACPHERSON. Catherine, I have the firm conviction that, in a very short time, I shall hear from Peter. [*Sitting at the table.*

PETER. I hope so. It's high time now.

DR. MACPHERSON. What I want is some positive proof; some absolute test; some—er— [*Thinks.*

CATHERINE *has seated herself at the table.—Unconsciously they both occupy the same seats as in the first act.*

PETER. The trouble is with other people, not with us. You want us to give all sorts of proofs; and here we are just back for a little while—very poorly put together on the chance that you'll see us at all.

DR. MACPHERSON. Poor old Peter—bless his heart! [*His elbow on the table as though he had been thinking over the matter.* CATHERINE *sits quietly listening.*] If he kept that compact with me, and came back,—do you know what I'd ask him first? If our work goes on.

PETER. Well, now, that's a regular sticker. It's bothered me considerably since I crossed over.

CATHERINE. What do you mean, Doctor?

DR. MACPHERSON. The question *every man wants the answer to:* what's to become of me—*me—my work?* Am I going to be a bone setter in the next life and he a tulip man? . . . I wonder.

PETER. Andrew, I've asked everybody—Tom, Dick and Harry. One spirit told me that sometimes our work *does* go on; but he was an awful liar—you know we don't drop our earth habits at once. He said that a genius is simply a fellow who's been there before in some other world and knows his business. Now then: [*Confidentially preparing to open an argument—sitting in his old seat at the table, as in the first act.*] it stands to reason, Andrew, doesn't it? What chance has the beginner compared with a fellow who knew his business before he was born?

DR. MACPHERSON. [*Unconsciously grasping the thought.*] I believe it is possible to have more than one chance at our work.

PETER. There . . . you caught that. . . . Why can't you take my message to Catherine?

DR. MACPHERSON. [*Rising to get his shawl—gruffly.*] Thought over what I told you concerning this marriage? Not too late to back out.

PETER. He's beginning to take the message.

CATHERINE. Everything's arranged: I shall be married as Uncle Peter wished. I sha'n't change my mind.

DR. MACPHERSON. H'm! [*Picks up his shawl.*

PETER. [*Trying to detain the* DOCTOR*—tugging at his shawl without seeming to pull it.*] Don't give up! Don't give up! A girl can always change her mind—while there's life. Don't give up! [*The* DOCTOR *turns, facing* PETER, *looking directly at him as he* *puts his hand in his coat pocket.*] You heard that, eh? . . . Didn't you? Yes? Did it cross over? . . . What? . . . It did? . . . You're looking me in the face, Andrew; can you see me? [*The* DOCTOR *takes a pencil out of his pocket, writes a prescription, throws his shawl over his shoulder—turning his back towards* PETER *and facing* CATHERINE.] Tc! Tc! Tc!

DR. MACPHERSON. Good-night.

CATHERINE. Good-night. [CATHERINE *goes quietly to the fire-place, kneeling down, mends the fire, and remains there sitting on an ottoman.*

PETER. [*Calling after the* DOCTOR.] If I could only make some sign—to start you thinking; but I can't depend upon *you*, I see that. . . . [*Then changing—as though he had an idea.*] Ah, yes! There *is* another way. Now to work. [*With renewed activity, he taps in the direction of the office door, although he himself stands three feet away from it. The door opens promptly and* JAMES *appears on the threshold—pen in hand—as though something had made him rise suddenly from his desk.* CATHERINE, *still seated, does not see* JAMES, *who stands looking at her—remembering that she is to be married on the following day.* PETER *tempts* JAMES.] Yes, she *is* pretty, James . . . young and lovely. . . . Look! . . . There are kisses tangled in her hair where it curls . . . . hundreds of them. . . . Are you going to let her go? Her lips are red with the red of youth. Every smile is an invocation to life. Who could resist her smiles? Can you, James? No, you will not let her go. And her hands, James. . . . Look! Hands made to clasp and cling to yours. Imagine her little feet trudging happily about *your* home. . . . Look at her shoulders . . . shaped for a resting-place for a little head. . . . Youwere right, James, we should ask nothing of our girls but to marry the men they love and be happy wives and happy mothers of happy children. You feel what I am saying. . . . You couldn't live without her, could you? No? Very well, then— [*Changing abruptly.*] Now, it's your turn.

JAMES *pauses a moment. There is silence. Then he comes forward a step and* CATHERINE, *hearing him, turns and rises.*

JAMES. [*Coldly—respectfully.*] Miss Grimm . . .

CATHERINE. James . . .

JAMES. I felt that you were here and wished to speak to me. I—I don't know why . . .

PETER. Good for James.

CATHERINE. [*Shaking hands with him.*] I'm very glad to see you again, James. [*When* PETER *sees that he has brought the two young people together, he stands in the background. The lovers are in the shadow, but* PETER'S *figure is marked and clear.*] Why did you go away?

JAMES. Oh—er—

CATHERINE. And without saying a word.

JAMES. Your uncle sent me away. I told him the truth again.

CATHERINE. Oh . . .

JAMES. I am going in a few hours.

CATHERINE. Where are you going? What do you intend to do?

JAMES. [*Half-heartedly.*] Father and I are going to try our luck together. We're going to start with a small fruit farm. It will give me a chance to experiment. . . .

CATHERINE. It will seem very strange when I come back home . . . Uncle gone . . . and you, James. [*Her voice trembling.*

JAMES. I hope you'll be happy, Catherine.

CATHERINE. James, Uncle died smiling at me—thinking of me . . . and just before he went, he gave me his mother's wedding ring and asked me to marry Frederik. I shall never forget how happy he was when I promised. That was all he wanted. His last smile was for me . . . and there he sat—still smiling after he was gone . . . the smile of a man leaving the world perfectly satisfied—at peace. It's like a hand on my heart—hurting it—when I question anything he wanted. I couldn't meet him in the hereafter if I didn't do everything he wished; I couldn't say my prayers at night; I couldn't speak his name in them. . . . He trusted me; depended upon me; did everything for me; so I must do this for him. . . . I wanted you to know this, James, because . . .

JAMES. Why haven't you told Frederik the truth?

CATHERINE. I have.

JAMES. That you don't love him? [CATHERINE *doesn't answer, but* JAMES *knows.*] . . . And he's willing to take you like that?—a little girl like you—in *that* way. . . . God! He's rotten all the way through. He's even worse than I thought. Katie, I didn't mean to say a word of this to-day—not a word; but a moment since—something made me change my mind—I don't know what! . . . [PETER *smiles.*] I felt that I *must* talk to you. You looked so young, so helpless, such a child. You've never had to think for yourself—you don't know what you're doing. You *couldn't* live under it, Catherine. You're making the greatest mistake possible, if you marry where you don't love. Why should you carry out your uncle's plans? You're going to be wretched for life to please a dead man who doesn't know it; or, if he does know it, regrets it bitterly.

PETER. I agree with you now, James.

CATHERINE. You musn't say that, James.

JAMES. But I will say it—I will speak my mind. I don't care how fond you were of your uncle or how much he did for you—it wasn't right to ask this of you. It wasn't fair. The whole thing is the mistake of a *very* obstinate old man.

CATHERINE. James!

JAMES. I loved him, too; but he *was* an obstinate old man. Sometimes I think it was the Dutch blood in his veins.

PETER. A very frank, outspoken fellow. I like to hear him talk—now.

JAMES. Do you know why I was sent away? Why I quarrelled with your uncle? I said that I loved you . . . he asked me. . . . I didn't tell him because I had any hopes—I hadn't. . . . I haven't now. . . . [*Struck.*] But in spite of what I'm saying . . . I don't know what makes me think that I . . . I could take you in my arms and you would let me . . . but I do think it.

CATHERINE. [*Retreats, backing towards* PETER.] No! . . . Don't touch me, James—you mustn't! Don't! . . . Don't!

PETER *pushes her into* JAMES' *arms, without touching her. She exclaims* "Oh, James!" *and fairly runs towards* JAMES *as though violently propelled. In reality, she thinks that she is yielding to an impulse. As she reaches him, she exclaims* "No," *and turns back, but* JAMES, *with outstretched arms, catches her.*

JAMES. You love me. [*Draws her to him.*

CATHERINE. Don't make me say that, James.

JAMES. I *will* make you say it! You *do* love me.

CATHERINE. No matter if I do, that won't alter matters.

JAMES. What? What?

CATHERINE. No, no, don't say any more. . . . I won't hear it. [*She stands free of* JAMES—*then turns and walks to the stairs.*] Good-bye, Jim.

JAMES. Do you mean it? Are you really going to sacrifice yourself because of— Am I really losing you? . . . Catherine! Catherine!

CATHERINE. [*In tears—beseechingly.*] Please don't. . . Please don't. . . .

FREDERIK *enters. Until the entrance of* FREDERIK, PETER *has had hope in his face, but now he begins to feel apprehensive.*

FREDERIK. [*Throwing his hat and coat on a chair.*] I have some work to do—more of my uncle's unopened mail; then I'll join you, Hartman. We must—er—make haste.

JAMES *looks at* CATHERINE, *then at* FREDERIK. CATHERINE *gives him an imploring glance—urging him not to speak.* FREDERIK *has gone to* PETER'S *desk.*

JAMES. I'll come back later. [*Goes towards the hall.*

FREDERIK. Catherine, have you asked James to be present at the ceremony to-morrow?

CATHERINE. No.

FREDERIK. James, will you—

JAMES. I shall be leaving early in the morning.

FREDERIK. Too bad! [*Exit* JAMES.

FREDERIK *lights the desk candles, takes the mail out of the drawer—opens two letters—tears them up after barely glancing at them—then sees* CATHERINE *still standing at the foot of the stairs—her back to him. He lays the cigar on the desk, crosses, and, taking her in his arms, kisses her.*

CATHERINE. [*With a revulsion of feeling.*] No! No! No! [*She covers her face with her hands—trying to control herself.*] Please! . . . Not now. . . .

FREDERIK. Why not *now?* [*Suspiciously.*] Has Hartman been talking to you? What has he been saying to you? [CATHERINE *starts slowly up the stairs.*] Wait a moment, please. . . . [*As she retreats a step up the stairs, he follows her.*] Do you really imagine you—you care for that fellow?

CATHERINE. Don't—please.

FREDERIK. I'm sorry to insist. Of course, I knew there was a sort of school-girl attachment on your part; . . . that you'd known each other since childhood. I don't take it at all seriously. In three months, you'll forget him. I must insist, however, that you do *not* speak to him again to-night. After to-morrow—after we are married—I'm quite sure that you will not forget you are my wife, Catherine—my wife.

CATHERINE. I sha'n't forget. [*She escapes into her room.* FREDERIK *goes to his desk.*

PETER. [*Confronting* FREDERIK.] Now, sir, I have something to say to you, Frederik Grimm, my beloved nephew! I had to die to find you out; but I know you! [FREDERIK *is reading a letter.*] You sit there opening a dead man's mail—with the heart of a stone—thinking: "He's gone! he's gone!—so I'll break every promise!" But there is something you have forgotten—something that always finds us out: the law of reward and punishment. Even now it is overtaking you. Your hour has struck. [FREDERIK *takes up another letter and begins to read it; then, as though disturbed by a passing thought, he puts it down. As though perplexed by the condition of his own mind, he ponders, his eyes resting unconsciously on* PETER.] Your hour has struck.

FREDERIK. [*To himself.*] What in the world is the matter with me to-night?

PETER. Read!

FREDERIK. [*Has opened a long, narrow, blue envelope containing a letter on blue paper and a small photograph. He stares at the letter, aghast.*] My God! Here's luck. . . . Here's luck! From that girl Annamarie to my uncle. Oh, if he had read it!

PETER. [*Standing in front of* FREDERIK *looks into space—as though reading the letter in the air.*] "Dear Mr. Grimm: I have not written because I can't do anything to help William, and I am ashamed."

FREDERIK. Wh! [*As though he had read the first part to himself, now reads aloud.*] "Don't be too hard upon me. . . . I have gone hungry trying to save a few pennies for him, but I never could; and now I see that I cannot hope to have him back. William is far better off with you. I—" [*Hesitates.*

PETER. [*Going back of the desk, standing behind* FREDERIK'S *chair.*] Go on. . . .

FREDERIK. "I wish that I might see him once again. Perhaps I could come and go in the night."

PETER. That's a terrible thing for a mother to write.

FREDERIK. [*Who has been looking down at the letter—suddenly feeling* PETER'S *presence.*] Who's that? Who's in this room? [*Looks over his shoulder—then glances about.*] I could have sworn somebody was looking over my shoulder . . . or had come in at the door . . . or . . . [*But seeing no one— he continues.*] "I met someone from home; . . . if there is any truth in the rumour of Catherine's marriage—it mustn't be, Mr. Grimm—it mustn't be . . . not to Frederik. For Frederik is my little boy's—" [FREDERIK *gives a furtive glance upstairs at the door of the child's room. Picks up the small picture which was in the envelope.*] Her picture . . . [*Turns it over—looks at the back—reads.*] "For my boy, from Annamarie." [FREDERIK, *conscious-stricken for the time being, bows his head.*

PETER. For the first time since I entered this house, you are yourself, Frederik Grimm. Once more a spark of manhood is alight in your soul. Courage! It's not too late to repent. Turn back, lad! Follow your impulse. Take the little boy in your arms. Go down on your knees and ask his mother's pardon. Turn over a fresh page, that I may leave this house in peace. . . .

FREDERIK. [*Looks about uneasily, then glances towards the door leading into the hall.*] Who is at the door? Curious . . . I thought I heard someone at . . .

PETER. I am at the door—I, Peter Grimm! Annamarie is at the door—the little girl who is ashamed to come home; the old mother in the kitchen breaking her heart for some word. William is at the door—your own flesh and blood—nameless; Katie, sobbing her heart out—you can hear her; all—we are all at the door—every soul in this house. We are all at the door of your conscience, Frederik. . . . Don't keep us waiting, my boy. It's very hard to kill the love I had for you. I long to love you again—to take you back to my heart—lies and all. [FREDERIK *rises—in deep thought.*] Yes! Call her! Tell her the truth. Give her back her promise. . . . Give her back her home. . . . Close the door on a peaceful, happy, silent room and go. Think—think of that moment when you give her back her freedom! Think of her joy, her gratitude, her affection. It's worth living for, lad. Speak! Make haste and call her, Fritz. [FREDERIK *takes several steps—then turns back to the desk. He tears the letter in two, muttering to himself,* "Damn the woman," *and sinks into his chair.*] Frederik Grimm, stand up before me! [FREDERIK *starts to rise, but changes his mind.*] Stand up! [FREDERIK *rises—not knowing why he has risen.* PETER *points an accusing finger at* FREDERIK.] Liar to the dead! Cheat, thief, hypocrite! You sha'n't have my little girl. You only want her for a week, a day, an hour. I refuse. I have come back to take her from you and you cannot put me to rest. . . . I have come back. . . . You cannot drive me from your thoughts—I am there. . . . [*Tapping his forehead, without touching it.*] I am looking over your shoulder . . . in at the window . . . under the door. . . . You are breathing me in the air. . . . I am looking at your heart. [*He brings his clenched fist down on the desk in answer to* FREDERIK'S *gesture; but, despite the seeming violence of the blow, he makes no sound.*] Hear me! You shall hear me! Hear me! [*Calling loudly.*] Hear me! Hear me! Hear me! Will nobody hear me? Is there no one in this house to hear me? No one? Has my journey been in vain? . . . [*For the first time fully realizing the situation.*] Oh, must we stand or fall by the mistakes we made here and the deed we did? Is there no second chance in this world?

FREDERIK. [*With a sneer on his lips as though trying to banish his thoughts.*] Psh!

MARTA *enters with a tray, containing a pot of coffee and a plate of small cakes.* PETER, *who has watched her with appealing eyes, like a dog craving attention, glances from her to the desk and from the desk back to* MARTA—*trying to tempt her to look at the torn letter.* FREDERIK, *deep in thought, does not notice her.* PETER *points to the desk as though to say, "Look!" After a pause, she picks up the picture and the letter—holding them in one hand to clear a spot for the tray which she is about to set on the desk.*

PETER. [*Speaking in a hushed voice.*] Marta, see what you have in your hand . . . that letter . . . there . . . read it. . . . Run to Catherine with it. Read it from the house-tops. . . . The letter . . . Look! There you have the story of Annamarie. . . . It is the one way to know the truth in this house—the only way. . . . There in your hand—the letter. . . . He will never speak. . . . The letter for Catherine.

MARTA *sets down the picture and the letter; but something prompts her to look at them; however, before she can carry out her impulse,* FREDERIK *starts up.*

FREDERIK. My God! How you startled me! [MARTA *sets down the tray.*] Oh! To be off and out of this old rat-trap. [*He wipes his forehead with his black-bordered handkerchief.*] I mean—our loss comes home to us so keenly here where we are accustomed to see him.

MARTA. A cup of coffee, sir?

FREDERIK. No, no, no.

MARTA. [*Pathetically.*] I thought you wished to keep to your uncle's customs. . . . He always took it at this time.

FREDERIK. [*Recovering.*] Yes, yes, of course.

MARTA. . . . No word? . . .

FREDERIK. [*Hesitates.*] What do you mean?

MARTA. No letter?

FREDERIK. Letter? . . . [*Covering the letter with his hand.*] From whom? . . .

MARTA. From . . . At a time like this, I thought . . . I felt . . . that Annamarie . . . that there should be some message. . . . Every day I expect to hear . . .

FREDERIK. No.

PETER *gestures to* MARTA—*pointing to the picture and letter, now covered by* FREDERIK'S *hand.*

MARTA. [*Hesitating.*] Are you certain?

FREDERIK. Quite certain. [*She curtsies and leaves the room.* FREDERIK, *as though relieved to see her go, jumps to his feet, and, tearing the letter in smaller pieces, lights them in the candle, dropping the burning pieces on a tray. As the flame dies out,* FREDERIK *brushes the blackened paper into the waste-basket.*] There's an end to *that!*

PETER *crouches near the basket—hovering over it, his hands clasped helplessly. After a pause, he raises his hand, until it points to a bedroom above. An echo of the circus music is very faintly heard; not with the blaring of brasses, but with the sounds of elfin horns, conveying the impression of a phantom circus band. The door of* WILLIAM'S *room opens, and he comes out as though to listen to the music. He wears a sleeping suit and is bare-footed. He has come down stairs before* FREDERIK *sees him.* FREDERIK *quickly puts aside the photograph, laying it on the desk, covering it with his hand.*

FREDERIK. [*Gruffly.*] Why aren't you in bed? If you're ill, that's the proper place for you.

WILLIAM. I came down to hear the circus music.

FREDERIK. Circus music?

WILLIAM. It woke me up.

FREDERIK. The circus left town days ago. You must have been dreaming.

WILLIAM. The band's playing now. Don't you hear it, sir? The procession's passing. [*He runs to the window and opens it. The music stops. A breeze sweeps through the room—bellies out the curtains and causes the lustres to jingle on the mantel. Surprised.*] No. It's almost dark. There's no procession . . . . no shining horses. . . . [*Turning sadly away from the window.*] I wonder what made me think the—I must have been dreaming. [*Rubbing his eyes.*

FREDERIK. [*Goes to the window, closes it. The child looks at him and, in retreating from him, unconsciously backs towards* PETER.] Are you feeling better?

WILLIAM. Yes, sir, I feel better—and hungry.

FREDERIK. Go back to bed.

WILLIAM. Yes, sir. [FREDERIK *sits.*

PETER. Where's your mother, William?

WILLIAM. Do you know where Annamarie is?

PETER. Ah!

FREDERIK. Why do you ask me? What should I know of her?

WILLIAM. Grandmother doesn't know; Miss Catherine doesn't know; nobody knows.

FREDERIK. I don't know, either. [*Tears up the picture—turning so that* WILLIAM *does not see what he is doing.* PETER, *who has been smiling at* WILLIAM, *motions him to come nearer.* WILLIAM, *feeling* PETER'S *presence, looks round the room.*

WILLIAM. Mr. Frederik, where's *old* Mr. Grimm?

FREDERIK. Dead.

WILLIAM. Are you sure he's dead? 'Cause— [*Puzzled—unable to explain himself, he hesitates.*

FREDERIK. [*Annoyed.*] You'd better go to bed.

WILLIAM. [*Pointing to a glass of water on a tray.*] Can I have a drink of water, please?

FREDERIK. Go to bed, sir, or you'll be punished. Water's not good for little boys with fever.

WILLIAM. [*Going towards the stairs.*] Wish I could find a cold brook and lie in it. [*Goes slowly up the stairs.* FREDERIK *would destroy the pieces of the picture; but* PETER *faces him as though forbidding him to touch it, and, for the first time,* FREDERIK *imagines he sees the apparition of his uncle.*

FREDERIK. [*In a very low voice—almost inaudibly.*] My God! I thought I saw . . . [*Receding a step and yet another step as the vision of* PETER *is still before him, he passes out of the room, wiping the beads of sweat from his forehead.* WILLIAM, *hearing the door close, comes down stairs and, running to the table at back, drinks a glass of water.*

WILLIAM. Um! That's good!

PETER. William! [WILLIAM *doesn't see* PETER *yet, but he feels his influence.*

WILLIAM. Wish it *had* been the circus music.

PETER. You shall hear it all again. [*Gestures towards the plate of cakes on the tray.*] Come, William, here's something very nice.

WILLIAM. [*Seeing the cakes.*] Um! Cakes! [*He steals to the tray, looking over his shoulder in fear of being caught.*

PETER. Don't be frightened. I'm here to protect you. Help yourself to the cakes. William, do you think you could deliver a message for me . . . a very important message? . . .

The circus music is heard. WILLIAM *sits at the tray and* PETER *seats himselj opposite as though he were the host doing the honours.* WILLIAM, *being unconsciously coaxed by* PETER, *is prevailed upon to choose the biggest cake. He takes a bite, looking towards* PETER.

WILLIAM. [*To himself.*] Ha! . . . Think I *am* dreaming. [*Rubbing his little stomach ecstatically.*] Hope I won't wake up and find there wasn't any cake.

PETER. Don't worry, you won't. [WILLIAM *has taken another piece of cake which he nibbles at—now holding a piece in each hand.*] Pretty substantial dream, eh? There's a fine, fat raisin. [WILLIAM *eats the raisin, then looks into the sugar-bowl.*] Don't hesitate, William. Sugar won't hurt you now. Nothing can hurt you any more. Fall to, William—help yourself. [WILLIAM *looks over his shoulder, fearing the return of* FREDERIK.] Oh, he won't come back in a hurry. Ha! Frederik *thought* he saw me, William; well, he didn't. He had a bad conscience—hallucination. [WILLIAM *nibbles a lump of sugar.*] Now, William, I have a message for you. Won't you try and take it for me, eh? [*But* WILLIAM *eats another lump of sugar.*] I see . . . I can't expect to get any assistance from a boy while his little stomach's calling. [WILLIAM *empties the cream jug and helps himself to cakes. Presently the music dies out.*] Now I'm going to tell you something. [*Impressively.*]

You're a very lucky boy, William; I congratulate you. Do you know why—of all this household—you are the only one to help me? . . . This is the secret: in a little time—it won't be long—you're going— [*As though he were imparting the most delightful information.*] —to know better! Think of *that!* Isn't the news splendid? [*But* WILLIAM *eats on.*] Think of what most of us have to endure before *we* know better! Why, William, you're going into the circus without paying for a ticket. You're laying down the burden before you climb the hill. And in your case, William, you are fortunate indeed; for there are some little soldiers in this world already handicapped when they begin the battle of life. . . . Their parents haven't fitted them for the struggle. . . . Like little moon moths,—they look in at the windows; they beat at the panes; they see the lights of happy firesides—the lights of home; but they never get in. . . . You are one of these wanderers, William. . . . And so, it is well for you that before your playing time is over—before your man's work begins,—you're going to know the great secret. Happy boy! No coarsening of your child's heart, until you stand before the world like Frederik; no sweat and toil such as dear old James is facing; no dimming of the eye and trembling of the hand such as the poor old Doctor shall know in time to come; no hot tears to blister your eyes, . . . tears such as Katie is shedding now; but, in all your youth, your faith—your innocence,—you'll fall asleep and oh! the awakening, William! . . . "It is well with the *child.*" [WILLIAM *lays down the cake and, clasping his hands, thinks.* PETER *answers his thoughts.*] What? No—don't think of it! Nonsense! You *don't* want to grow up to be a man. Grow up to fail? Or, still worse—to succeed—to be famous? To wear a heavy laurel wreath? A wreath to be held up by tired hands that ache for one hour's freedom. No, no, you're to escape all that, William; joy is on the way to meet you with sweets in its outstretched hands and laughter on its lips. [WILLIAM *takes the last swallow of a piece of cake, exclaims* "Hm!" *in a satisfied way, brushes the crumbs off his lap, and sits back in his chair.*] Have you had enough? Good! William, I want you to try to understand that you're to help me, will you? Will you tell Miss Catherine that—

WILLIAM. [*Without looking up, his hands folded in his lap.*] Take me back with you, Mr. Grimm?

PETER. Can you see me, William?

WILLIAM. No, sir; but I know.

PETER. Come here. [WILLIAM *doesn't move.*] Here . . . here . . . [WILLIAM *advances to the center of the room and pauses hesitatingly.*] Take my hand . . . [WILLIAM *approaches in the direction of the voice.* PETER *takes* WILLIAM'S *outstretched hand.*] Have you got it?

WILLIAM. No, sir. . . .

PETER. [*Putting his hand on* WILLIAM'S *head.*] Now? . . . Do you feel it?

WILLIAM. I feel something, yes, sir. [*Puts his hand on* PETER'S *hand, which is still on his head.*] But where's *your* hand? There's nothing there.

PETER. But you hear me?

WILLIAM. I can't really hear you. . . . It's a dream. [*Coaxingly.*] Oh, Mr. Grimm, take me back with you.

PETER. You're not quite ready to go with me yet, William— not until we can see each other face to face.

WILLIAM. Why did you come back, Mr. Grimm? Wasn't it nice where you were?

PETER. It was indeed. It was like— [*Whimsically.*] —new toys.

WILLIAM. [*To whom the idea appeals.*] As nice as that!

PETER. Nicer. But I had to come back with this message. I want you to help me to deliver it. [*Indicating the picture.*

WILLIAM. Where's the bosom of Abraham, Mr. Grimm?

PETER. Eh?

WILLIAM. The minister says you're asleep there.

PETER. Stuff and nonsense! I haven't been near the bosom of Abraham.

WILLIAM. Too bad you died before you went to the circus, Mr. Grimm. But it must be great to be in a place where you can look down and see the circus for nothing. Do you remember the clown that sang: "Uncle Rat has gone to town?"

PETER. Yes, indeed; but let us talk of something more important. Come here, William [*He starts towards the desk.*]; would you like to see someone whom all little boys love— love more than anybody else in the whole world? [PETER *is standing at the desk with his finger on the torn pieces of the picture.*

WILLIAM. Yes, the clown in the circus. . . . No . . . it it isn't a clown; . . . it's our mother. . . . Yes, I want to see my mother, Annamarie. [*Unconsciously* WILLIAM *comes to the desk and sees the torn picture—picks up a piece and looks at it. Very simply.*] Why . . . there she is! . . . That's her face.

PETER. Ah! You recognize her. Mother's face is there, William, but it's in little bits. We must put her together, William. We must show her to everybody in the house, so that everybody will say: "How in the world did she ever get here? To whom does this picture belong?" We must set them to thinking.

WILLIAM. Yes. Let us show her to everybody. [*He sits and joins the pieces under the guidance of* PETER.] Annamarie . . . Annamarie . . .

PETER. You remember many things, William . . . things that happened when you lived with Annamarie, don't you?

WILLIAM. I was very little. . . .

PETER. Still, you remember. . . .

WILLIAM. [*Evasively.*] I was afraid. . . .

PETER. You loved her.

WILLIAM. [*To picture.*] Oh, yes . . . yes, I loved you.

PETER. Now, through that miracle of love, you can remember many things tucked away in your childish brain,—things laid away in your mind like toys upon a shelf. Come, pick them up and dust them off and bring them out again. It will come back. When you lived with Annamarie . . . there was you . . . and Annamarie . . . and—

WILLIAM. —and the other one.

PETER. Ah! We're getting nearer! Who *was* the other one?

WILLIAM. [*Gives a quick glance towards the door—then as though speaking to the picture.*] I must put you together before *he* comes back. [*He fits the other pieces together—*PETER *trying to guide him. Presently* WILLIAM *hums as a child will when at play, singing the tune of "Uncle Rat."*] "Uncle Rat has gone to town."

PETER *and* WILLIAM. [*Singing together.*] "Ha! H'm!" [*At this instant,* PETER *is indicating another piece of the picture.*

WILLIAM. Her other foot. [*Then sings.*]

"Uncle Rat has gone to town,
To buy his niece a wedding gown."

[*Adjusting a piece of the picture.*] Her hand.

WILLIAM *and* PETER. [*Singing.*] "Ha! H'm!"

WILLIAM. Her other hand. [*Sings.*]

"What shall the wedding breakfast be?
Hard boiled eggs and—"

[*Speaking.*] Where's— [WILLIAM *pauses—looking for a piece of the picture.*

PETER. [*Finishing the verse.*] "A cup of tea." [*With a gesture as though knocking on the door of the adjoining room to attract* MRS. BATHOLOMMEY'S *attention.*

WILLIAM. [*Speaks.*] There's her hat.

WILLIAM *and* PETER. [*Singing.*] "Ha! H'm!"

WILLIAM. [*Stops singing and claps his hands with boyish delight—staring at the picture.*] Annamarie! Annamarie! You're not in bits any more—you're all put together.

By this time, PETER *is going up the stairs, and, as he stands in front of* CATHERINE'S *door, it opens.* PETER *passes in and* CATHERINE *comes out.*

CATHERINE. [*Astonished.*] Why, William! What are you doing here?

WILLIAM. Miss Catherine! Come down! Come down! I have something to show you.

CATHERINE. [*Not coming down.*] No, dear—come upstairs; there's a good boy. You mustn't play down there. Come to bed. [*Passes into* WILLIAM'S *room.*

MRS. BATHOLOMMEY. [*Who has entered, and sees* WILLIAM.] William!

WILLIAM. Look—look! [*Pointing to the picture.*] See what old Mr. Grimm brought back with him.

MRS. BATHOLOMMEY. [*Alarmed.*] What are you talking about, William? *Old* Mr. Grimm is dead.

WILLIAM. No, he isn't; . . . he's come back. . . . He has been in this room.

MRS. BATHOLOMMEY. Absurd!

WILLIAM. I was talking to him.

MRS. BATHOLOMMEY. You're feverish again. I must get the Doctor. [*Comes down to* WILLIAM.] And I thought you were feeling better! [*Seeing* CATHERINE, *who appears on the balcony as though wondering why* WILLIAM *doesn't come to bed.*] The child's mind is wandering. He imagines all sorts of things. I'll call the Doctor—

PETER. [*Who has re-entered.*] You needn't—he's coming now. Come in, Andrew. I'm giving you one more chance.

The DOCTOR *enters, wearing his skull-cap, and carrying his pipe in his hand. It is evident that he has come over in a hurry.*

MRS. BATHOLOMMEY. [*Surprised.*] I was just going for you. How fortunate that you came.

DR. MACPHERSON. I thought I'd have another peep at William.

By this time, CATHERINE *has seated herself on a chair, and takes* WILLIAM *on her lap. He puts his arms round her neck.*

MRS. BATHOLOMMEY. He's quite delirious.

DR. MACPHERSON. Doesn't look it. [*Putting his hand on* WILLIAM'S *cheek and forehead.*] Very slight fever. What makes you think he was delirious? [*Taking* WILLIAM'S *pulse.*

MRS. BATHOLOMMEY. [*Interrupting.*] He said that old Mr. Grimm was in this room—that he was talking to him.

DR. MACPHERSON. [*Interested.*] Yes? Really? Well, possibly he is. Nothing remarkable in *that,* is there?

PETER. Well, at last!

MRS. BATHOLOMMEY What? Oh, of course, you believe in—

DR. MACPHERSON. In fact, I had a compact with him to return if—

MRS. BATHOLOMMEY. A compact? Of all the preposterous—

DR. MACPHERSON. Not at all. Dozens of cases on record—as I can show you—where these compacts have actually been kept. [*Suddenly struck—looking at* WILLIAM.] I wonder if that boy's a sensitive. [*Hand on his chin.*] I wonder . . .

CATHERINE. [*Echoing the* DOCTOR'S *words.*] A sensitive?

MRS. BATHOLOMMEY. What's that?

DR. MACPHERSON. It's difficult to explain. I mean a human organism so constituted that it can be *informed* or *controlled* by those who—er—have— [*With a gesture.*] crossed over.

MRS. BATHOLOMMEY. I think I'll put the boy to bed, Doctor.

DR. MACPHERSON. Just a moment, Mistress Batholommey. I'm here to find out what ails William. William, what makes you think that Mr. Grimm is in this room?

MRS. BATHOLOMMEY. I wouldn't have the child encouraged in such ideas, Catherine. I—

DR. MACPHERSON. Sh! Please, please. [*Taking the boy on his knee.*] What makes you think Peter Grimm is in this room?

WILLIAM. [*Hesitating.*] . . . The things he said to me.

MRS. BATHOLOMMEY. Said to you?

CATHERINE. [*Wonderingly.*] William, . . . are you sure he . . .

DR. MACPHERSON. Said to *you*, eh? [WILLIAM *nods assent.*] *Old* Mr. Grimm? [WILLIAM *nods.*] Sure of that, William?

WILLIAM. Oh, yes, sir.

DR. MACPHERSON. Think before you speak, my boy; what did Mr. Grimm say to you?

WILLIAM. Lots of things . . .

MRS. BATHOLOMMEY. Really!

DR. MACPHERSON. [*Raises his hand for silence.*] How did he look, William?

WILLIAM. I didn't see him.

MRS. BATHOLOMMEY. Ha!

DR. MACPHERSON. You must have seen something.

WILLIAM. I thought once I saw his hat on the peg where it used to hang. [*Looks at the peg.*] No, it's gone.

MRS. BATHOLOMMEY. [*Remonstrating.*] Doctor!

DR. MACPHERSON. [*Thinking.*] I wonder if he really did—

CATHERINE. Do you think he could have seen Uncle Peter?

PETER. [*Pointing to the desk.*] William!

WILLIAM. Look! . . . [*Points to the picture.*] That's what I wanted to show you when you were upstairs.

CATHERINE. [*Seeing the picture.*] It's his mother—Annamarie.

MRS. BATHOLOMMEY. The Lord save us—his mother! I didn't know you'd heard from Annamarie.

CATHERINE. We haven't.

MRS. BATHOLOMMEY. Then how'd that picture get into the house?

PETER. Ah! I knew *she'd* begin! Now that she's wound up, we shall get at the truth.

MRS. BATHOLOMMEY. It's a new picture. She's much changed. How ever did it find its way here?

CATHERINE. I never saw it before. It's very strange. . . . We've all been waiting for news of her. Even her mother doesn't know where she is, or—could Marta have received this since I—

MRS. BATHOLOMMEY. I'll ask her. [*Exit into dining-room.*

CATHERINE. If not, who had the picture? . . . And why weren't we *all* told? . . . Who tore it up? Did you, William? [WILLIAM *shakes his head, meaning "No."*] Who has been at the desk? No one save Frederik . . . Frederik . . . and surely he— [*She pauses—perplexed.*

MRS. BATHOLOMMEY. [*Re-entering.*] No, Marta hasn't heard a word; and, only a few minutes ago, she asked Frederik if some message hadn't come, but he said "No, nothing." I didn't tell her of the picture.

CATHERINE. [*Looking at the picture.*] I wonder if there was any message with it.

MRS. BATHOLOMMEY. I remember the day that picture came . . . the day your uncle died. . . . It was in a long blue envelope—the size of the picture. . . . I took it from the postman myself because every one was distracted and rushing about. It dropped to the floor and as I picked it up I thought I knew the writing; but I couldn't remember whose it was. . . . It was directed to your uncle. . . . [*Looking from the desk to the waste-basket.*] There's the envelope [*Holding up a scrap of blue envelope.*] and paper; . . . some one has burned it.

CATHERINE. Annamarie wrote to my uncle . . .

DR. MACPHERSON. [*Not understanding.*] But what could Peter have to say to *me* concerning Annamarie? [*Making a resolution—rising.*] We're going to find out. You may draw the curtains, Catherine, if you please. [CATHERINE *draws the curtains. The* DOCTOR *turns the lights down and closes the door. A pause.*] Peter Grimm . . .

PETER. Yes, Andrew? . . .

DR. MACPHERSON. [*Not hearing.*] If you have come back . . . if you are in the room . . . and the boy speaks truly—give me some sign . . . some indication . . .

PETER. I can't give you a sign, Andrew. . . . I have spoken to the boy . . . the boy. . .

DR. MACPHERSON. If you cannot make your presence known to me—I know there are great difficulties—will you try and send your message by William? I presume you have one—

PETER. Yes, that's right.

DR. MACPHERSON. —or else you wouldn't have come back.

PETER. That's just the point I wanted to make, Andrew. You understand perfectly.

DR. MACPHERSON. [*As before.*] I am waiting. . . . We are all waiting. [*Noticing that a door is a trifle ajar.*] The door's open again. [MRS. BATHOLOMMEY, *without making a sound, closes it and sits as before.*

PETER. Sh! Listen! [*A pause.*

WILLIAM. [*In a peculiar manner—as though in a half dream—but not shutting his eyes. As though controlled by* PETER.] There was Annamarie and me and the other.

DR. MACPHERSON. [*Very low, as though afraid to interrupt* WILLIAM'S *train of thought.*] What other?

WILLIAM. The man . . . that came.

DR. MACPHERSON. What man?

WILLIAM. The man that made Annamarie cry.

CATHERINE. Who was he?

WILLIAM. I don't know . . .

PETER. Yes, you do. Don't tell lies, William.

DR. MACPHERSON. What man made Annamarie cry?

WILLIAM. I can't remember. . .

PETER. Yes, you can. . . . You're afraid. . . .

CATHERINE. [*In a low voice.*] So you do remember the time when you lived with Annamarie; . . . you always told me that you didn't . . . [*To* DR. MACPHERSON.] I must know more of this— [*Pauses abruptly.*] Think, William, who came to the house?

PETER. That's what *I* asked you, William.

WILLIAM. That's what *he* asked . . .

DR. MACPHERSON. Who?

WILLIAM. Mr. Grimm.

DR. MACPHERSON. When, William?

WILLIAM. Just now . . .

CATHERINE *and* MRS. BARTHOLOMMEY. [*Together.*] Just now!

DR. MACPHERSON. H'm. . . . You both ask the same question, eh? The man that came to see—

MRS. BATHOLOMMEY. [*Perplexed.*] It can't be possible that the child knows what he's talking about.

DR. MACPHERSON. [*Ignoring her.*] What did you tell Mr. Grimm when he asked you?

PETER. You'd better make haste, William. Frederik is coming back.

WILLIAM. [*Looking uneasily over his shoulder.*] I'm afraid.

CATHERINE. Why does he always look towards that door? You're not afraid now, William?

WILLIAM. [*Looking towards the door.*] N-no—but. . . Please, please don't let Mr. Frederik come back. 'Cause then I'll be afraid again.

DR. MACPHERSON. Ah!

PETER. William! William!

WILLIAM. [*Rising quickly.*] Yes, Mr. Grimm?

PETER. You must say that I am very unhappy.

WILLIAM. He says he is very unhappy.

DR. MACPHERSON. Why is he unhappy? . . . Ask him.

WILLIAM. Why are you unhappy, Mr. Grimm?

PETER. I am thinking of Catherine's future. . . .

WILLIAM. [*Not understanding the last word—puzzled.*] Eh?

PETER. To-morrow . . .

WILLIAM. [*After a slight pause.*] To-morrow . . .

PETER. Catherine's—

WILLIAM. [*Looks at* CATHERINE*—hesitating.*] Your— [*Stops.* CATHERINE *gives the* DOCTOR *a quick glance—she seems to divine the message.*

DR. MACPHERSON. [*Prompting.*] Her—

CATHERINE. What, William? What of to-morrow?

PETER. She must not marry Frederik.

WILLIAM. I mustn't say *that.*

DR. MACPHERSON. What?

WILLIAM. What he wanted me to say. [*Points towards* PETER. *All instinctively look towards the spot to which* WILLIAM *points, but they see no one.*

PETER. [*Speaking slowly to the boy.*] Catherine—must—not—marry Frederik Grimm.

DR. MACPHERSON. Speak, William. No one will hurt you.

WILLIAM. Oh, yes, *he* will. . . . [*Looking timidly towards the door* FREDERIK *passed through.*] I don't want to tell his name—'cause . . . 'cause . . .

DR. MACPHERSON. Why don't you tell the name, William?

PETER. Make haste, William, make haste.

WILLIAM. [*Trembling.*] I'm afraid . . . I'm afraid . . . he will make Annamarie cry; . . . he makes me cry . . .

CATHERINE. [*With suppressed excitement—half to herself.*] Why are you afraid of him? Was Frederik the man that came to see Annamarie?

MRS. BATHOLOMMEY. Catherine!

CATHERINE. [*On her knees before* WILLIAM.] Was he? Was it Frederik Grimm? Tell me, William.

MRS. BATHOLOMMEY. Surely you don't believe . . .

CATHERINE. [*In a low voice.*] I've thought of a great many things to-day . . . little things . . . little things I'd never noticed before. . . . I'm putting them together just as he put that picture together. . . . I must know the truth.

PETER. William, make haste. . . . Frederik is listening at the door.

WILLIAM. [*Frightened.*] I won't say any more. He's there . . . at the door. . . [*He looks over his shoulder and* CATHERINE *goes towards the door.*

DR. MACPHERSON. William, tell me.

PETER. William!

CATHERINE *opens the door suddenly.* FREDERIK *is standing, listening. He is taken unawares and for a few seconds he does not move—then he recovers.*

WILLIAM. Please don't let him scold me. I'm afraid of him. [*Going towards the stairs—looking at* FREDERIK.] I was afraid of him when I lived with Annamarie and he came to see us and made her cry.

DR. MACPHERSON. Are you sure you remember that? Weren't you too small?

WILLIAM. No, I *do* remember. . . . I always did remember; only for a little while I—I forgot. . . . I must go to bed. He told me to. [*Goes upstairs.*

PETER. [*Calling after* WILLIAM.] You're a good boy, William. [WILLIAM *goes to his room.*

CATHERINE. [*After a slight pause—simply.*] Frederik, you've heard from Annamarie. . . . [*Gestures towards the desk.* FREDERIK *sees the photograph and is silent.*] You've had a letter from her. You tried to destroy it. Why did you tell Marta that you'd had no message—no news? You went to see her, too. Why did you tell me that you'd never seen her since she went away? Why did you lie to me? Why do you hate that child?

FREDERIK. Are you going to believe what that boy—

CATHERINE. I'm going to find out. I'm going to find out where she is, before I marry you. That child may be right or wrong; but I'm going to know what his mother was to you. I want the truth.

DR. MACPHERSON. [*Who has been in thought—now looking up.*] We've heard the truth. We had that message from Peter Grimm himself.

CATHERINE. Yes, it *is* true. I believe Uncle Peter Grimm was in this room to-night.

FREDERIK. [*Not surprised—glancing towards the spot where* PETER *stood when he thought he saw him.*] Oh! You, too? Did you see him, too?

MRS. BATHOLOMMEY. [*Incredulously.*] Impossible!

CATHERINE. I don't care what anyone else may think—people have the right to think for themselves; but I believe he has been here—he *is* here. Uncle Peter, if you can hear me now, give me back my promise—or—or I'll take it back!

PETER. [*Gently—smilingly—relieved.*] I did give it back to you, my dear; but what a time I have had getting it across!

CURTAIN.

ACT III.

The third act takes place at twenty minutes to twelve on the same night.

The fire is out. The table on which PETER *took his coffee in the first act is now being used by the* DOCTOR *for* WILLIAM'S *medicines, two bottles, two glasses, two teaspoons, a clinical thermometer, &c.* WILLIAM, *who has been questioned by the* DOCTOR, *is now asleep upstairs.* PETER'S *hat hangs on the peg in the shadow. Although the hour is late, no one has thought of going to bed.* FREDERIK *is waiting at the hotel for the lawyer whom* HICKS *was to send to arrange for the sale of* PETER GRIMM'S *nurseries, but he has not arrived. The* DOCTOR, *full of his theories, is seated before the fire, writing the account of* PETER GRIMM'S *return, for the American Branch of the "London Society for Psychical Research." It is now a fine, clear night. The clouds are almost silvery and a hint of the moon is showing.*

DR. MACPHERSON. [*Reading what he has written.*] "To be forwarded to the 'London Society for Psychical Research': Dr. Hyslop: Dear Sir: This evening at the residence of Peter—" [*Pauses and inserts "the late" and continues to read after inserting the words.*] "—the late Peter Grimm—the well-known horticulturist of Grimm Manor, New York, certain phenomena were observed which would clearly indicate the return of Peter Grimm, ten days after his decease. While he was invisible to all, three people were present besides myself—one of these, a child of eight, who received the message. No spelling out by signals nor automatic writing was employed, but word of mouth." [*A rap sounds.*] Who will that be at this hour? . . . [*Looks at the clock.*] Nearly midnight. [*Opening the door.*] Yes?

A VOICE. [*Outside.*] Telegram for Frederik Grimm.

DR. MACPHERSON. Not in. I'll sign. [*He signs and, receiving the telegram, sets it against a candle-stick on the desk and resumes his seat. Reads:*] "I made a compact with Peter Grimm, while he was in the flesh, that whichever went first was to return and give the other some sign; and I propose to give positive proof—" [*He hesitates—thinks—then repeats.*] "positive proof that he kept this compact and that I assisted in the carrying out of his instructions."

MRS. BATHOLOMMEY. [*Enters—evidently highly wrought up by the events of the evening.*] Who was that? Who knocked?

DR. MACPHERSON. Telegram.

MRS. BATHOLOMMEY. I thought perhaps Frederik had come back. Don't you consider William much better?

DR. MACPHERSON. Mm . . .

MRS. BATHOLOMMEY. Dear, dear! The scene that took place to-night has completely upset me. [*The* DOCTOR *takes up his pen and reads to himself.*] Well, Doctor: [*She pushes forward a chair and sits at the other side of the table—facing him.*] the breaking off of the engagement is rather sudden, isn't it? We've been talking it over in the front parlour, Mr. Batholommey and I. James has finished his work and has just joined us. I suggest sending out a card—a neat card—saying that, owing to the bereavement in the family, the wedding has been indefinitely postponed. Of course, it isn't exactly true.

DR. MACPHERSON. Won't take place at all. [*Goes on reading.*

MRS. BATHOLOMMEY. Evidently not; but if the whole matter looks very strange to me—how is it going to look to other people; especially when we haven't any—any rational explanation—as yet? We must get out of it in some fashion.

DR. MACPHERSON. Whose business is it?

MRS. BATHOLOMMEY. Nobody's, of course. But Catherine's position is certainly unusual; and the strangest part of it all is—

she doesn't seem to feel her situation. She's sitting alone in the library, seemingly placid and happy. What I really wish to consult you about is this: shouldn't the card we're going to send out have a narrow black border? [*The* DOCTOR *is now writing.*] Doctor, you don't appear to be interested. You might at least answer my question.

DR. MACPHERSON. What chance have I had to answer? You've done all the talking.

MRS. BATHOLOMMEY. [*Rising—annoyed.*] Oh, of course, all these little matters sound trivial to you; but men like you couldn't look after the workings of the *next* world if other people didn't attend to *this*. Some one has to do it.

DR. MACPHERSON. I fully appreciate the fact, Mistress Batholommey, that other people are making it possible for me to be myself. I'll admit that; and now if I might have a few moments in peace to attend to something really important—

The REV. MR. BATHOLOMMEY *has entered with his hat in his hand.*

REV. MR. BATHOLOMMEY. Doctor, I've been thinking things over. I ran in for a moment to suggest that we suspend judgment until the information William has volunteered can be verified. I can scarcely believe that—

DR. MACPHERSON. Ump! [*Rises and goes to the telephone on the desk.*] Four-red.

REV. MR. BATHOLOMMEY. I regret that Frederik left the house without offering some explanation.

DR. MACPHERSON. [*At the 'phone.*] Marget, I'm at Peter's. I mean—I'm at the Grimms'. Send me my bag. I'll stay the night with William. Bye. [*Seats himself at the table.*

REV. MR. BATHOLOMMEY. Tell Frederik that, if he cares to consult me, I shall be at home in my study. Good-night, Doctor. Good-night, Rose.

DR. MACPHERSON. Hold on, Mr. Batholommey! [*The* REV. MR. BATHOLOMMEY *turns.*] I'm writing an account of all that's happened here to-night—

REV. MR. BATHOLOMMEY. [*Dubiously.*] Indeed!

DR. MACPHERSON. I shall verify every word of the evidence by William's mother for whom I am searching. [*The* REV. MR. BATHOLOMMEY *smiles faintly behind his hand.*] Then I shall send in my report, and not until then. What I wish to ask is this: would you have any objection to the name of Mrs. Batholommey being used as a witness?

REV. MR. BATHOLOMMEY. [*Looks perplexed.*] Well,—er—a—

MRS. BATHOLOMMEY. Oh, no, you don't! You may flout our beliefs; but wouldn't you like to bolster up your report with "the wife of a clergyman who was present!" It sounds so respectable and sane, doesn't it? No, sir! You cannot prop up your wild-eyed—

REV. MR. BATHOLOMMEY. Rose, my dear!

MRS. BATHOLOMMEY. [*Sweeping on.*] —theories against the good black of a minister's coat. *I* think myself that you have *probably* stumbled on the truth about William's mother.

REV. MR. BATHOLOMMEY. *Can* it be true? Oh, dreadful! Dreadful!

MRS. BATHOLOMMEY. But that child knew it all along. He's eight years old and he was with her until five—and five's the age of memory. Every incident of his mother's life has lingered in his little mind. Supposing you do find her and learn that it's all true: what do you prove? Simply that *William remembered.* and that's all there is to it.

REV. MR. BATHOLOMMEY. Let us hope that there's not a word of truth in it. Don't you think, Doctor—mind, I'm not opposing your ideas as a clergyman,—I'm just echoing what *everybody else* thinks—don't you believe these spiritualistic ideas, leading *away* from the Heaven *we* were taught to believe in, tend towards irresponsibility—er—eccentricity—and—often—er—insanity? Is it healthy—that's the idea—is it healthy?

DR. MACPHERSON. Well, Batholommey, religion has frequently led to the stake, and I never heard of the Spanish Inquisition being called *healthy* for anybody taking part in it. Still, religion flourishes. But your old-fashioned, unscientific, gilt, ginger-bread Heaven blew up ten years ago—went out. My Heaven's just coming in. It's new. Dr. Funk and a lot of the clergymen are in already. You'd better get used to it, Batholommey, and get in line and into the procession.

REV. MR. BATHOLOMMEY. You'll have to convince me first, Doctor—and that no man can do. I made up my mind at twenty-one, and my Heaven is just where it was then.

DOCTOR MACPHERSON. So I see. It hasn't improved a particle.

REV. MR. BATHOLOMMEY. [*Tolerantly.*] Well, well. Good-night. [MRS. BATHOLOMMEY *follows him in the hall.*

MRS. BATHOLOMMEY. Good-night, Henry; I'll be home to-morrow. You'll be glad to see me, dear, won't you?

REV. MR. BATHOLOMMEY. My church mouse! [*He pats her cheek, kisses her good-night and goes.*

MRS. BATHOLOMMEY. [*Who has gone to the door of her room—giving* DR. MACPHERSON *a parting shot.*] Write as much as you like, Doctor; words are but air. We didn't see Peter Grimm and you know and I know and everybody knows that *seeing* is believing.

DR. MACPHERSON. [*Looking up.*] Damn everybody! It's everybody's ignorance that has set the world back a thousand years. Where was I before you—Oh, yes. [*Reads as* MRS. BATHOLOMMEY *leaves the room.*] "I assisted in the carrying out of his instructions." [FREDERIK GRIMM *enters.*

FREDERIK. Anybody in this house come to their senses yet?

DR. MACPHERSON. I think so, my boy. I think several in this house have come to their senses. Catherine has, for one. I'm very glad to see you back, Frederik. I have a few questions to put to you.

FREDERIK. Why don't you have more light? It's half dark in this room. [*He picks up the lamp from the* DOCTOR'S *table and holds it so that he can look searchingly in the direction of the desk to see if* PETER'S *apparition is still there. His eye is suddenly riveted on the telegram resting against the candlestick on the desk.*] Is that telegram for me?

DR. MACPHERSON. Yes.

FREDERIK. Oh. . . . It may explain perhaps why I've been kept waiting at the hotel. . . . [*Tries to go to the desk but cannot muster up courage.*] I had an appointment to meet a man who wanted to buy the gardens. I may as well tell you, I'm thinking of selling out root and branch.

DR. MACPHERSON. [*Amazed.*] Selling out? Peter Grimm's gardens? So this is the end of Peter's great work?

FREDERIK. You'll think it strange, Doctor; but I—I simply can't make up my mind to go near that old desk of my uncle's. . . . I have a perfect terror of the thing! Would you mind handing me that telegram? [*The* DOCTOR *looks at him with scarcely veiled contempt, and hands him the telegram. After a glance at the contents,* FREDERIK *gives vent to a long-drawn breath.*] Billy Hicks—the man I was to sell to—is dead. . . . [*Tosses the telegram across the table towards* DR. MACPHERSON, *who does not take it. It lies on the table.*] I knew it this afternoon! I knew he would die . . . but I wouldn't let myself believe it. Someone told it to me . . . whispered it to me . . . . Doctor, as sure as you live—somebody else is doing my thinking for me in this house.

DR. MACPHERSON. [*Studying* FREDERIK.] What makes you say that?

FREDERIK. To-night—in this room, I thought I saw my uncle . . . [*Pointing towards the desk.*] there.

DR. MACPHERSON. Eh? . . .

FREDERIK. And just before I—I saw him—I—I had the . . . the strangest impulse to go to the foot of the stairs and call Kitty—give her the house—and run—run—get out of it.

DR. MACPHERSON. Oh, a good impulse, I see! Very unusual, I should say.

FREDERIK. I thought he gave me a terrible look—a terrible look.

DR. MACPHERSON. Your uncle?

FREDERIK. Yes. My God! I won't forget that look! And as I started out of the room—he blotted out. . . I mean—I *thought* I saw him blot out; . . . then I left the photograph on the desk and—

DR. MACPHERSON. That's how William came by it. [*Jots down a couple of notes.*] Did you ever have this impulse before—to give up Catherine—to let her have the cottage?

FREDERIK. Not much, I hadn't. Certainly not. I told you someone else was thinking for *me*. I don't want to give her up. It's folly! I've always been fond of her. But if she has turned against me, I'm not going to sit here and cry about it. I shall be up and off. [*Rising.*] But I'll tell you one thing: from this time, I propose to think for myself. I've taken a room at the hotel and a few things for the night. I've done with this house. I'd like to sell it along with the gardens, and let a stranger raze it to the ground; but—[*Thinks as he looks towards the desk.*] when I walk out of here to-night—it's hers—she can have it. . . . I wouldn't sleep here. . . . I give her the home because . . .

DR. MACPHERSON. Because you don't believe anything; but you want to be on the safe side in case he—[*Gesturing to desk.*] was there.

FREDERIK. [*Puzzled—awed—his voice almost dropping to a whisper.*] How do you account for it, Doctor?

DR. MACPHERSON. It might have been an hallucination or perhaps you did see him, though it could have been inflammation of conscience, Frederik: when did you last see Annamarie?

FREDERIK. [*Angrily.*] Haven't I told you already that I refuse to answer any questions as to my—

DR. MACPHERSON. I think it only fair to tell you that it won't make a particle of difference whether you answer me or not. I have someone on the track now—working from an old address; I've called in the detectives and I'll find her, you may be sure of that. As long as I'm going to know it, I may as well hear your side of it, too. When did you last see Annamarie?

FREDERIK. [*Sits—answers dully, mechanically, after a pause.*] About three years ago.

DR. MACPHERSON. Never since?

FREDERIK. No.

DR. MACPHERSON. What occurred the last time you saw her?

FREDERIK. [*Quietly, as before.*] What *always* occurs when a young man realizes that he has his life before him, must be respected—looked up to, settle down, think of his future and forget a silly girl?

DR. MACPHERSON. A scene took place, eh? Was William present?

FREDERIK. Yes. She held him in her arms.

DR. MACPHERSON. And then?

FREDERIK. I left the house.

DR. MACPHERSON. Then it's all true. [FREDERIK *is silent.*] What are you going to do for William?

FREDERIK. Nothing. I'm a rich man now—and if I recognize him—he'll be at me till the day he dies. His mother's gone to the dogs and under her influence, the boy—

DR. MACPHERSON. Be silent, you damned young scoundrel. Oh! What an act of charity if the good Lord took William, and I say it with all my heart. Out of all you have—not a crumb for—

FREDERIK. I want you to know I've sweat for that money, and I'm going to keep it!

DR. MACPHERSON. *You've* sweat for—

FREDERIK. [*Showing feeling.*]—Yes! How do you think I got the money? I went to jail for it—jail, jail. Every day I've been in this house has been spent in prison. I've been doing time. Do you think it didn't get on my nerves? I've gone to bed at nine o'clock and thought of what I was missing in New York. I've got up at cock-crow to be in time for grace at the breakfast table. I took charge of a class in Sabbath-school, and I handed out the infernal cornucopias at the church Christmas tree, while he played Santa Claus. What more can a fellow do to earn his money? Don't you call that sweating? No, sir; I've danced like a damned hand-organ monkey for the pennies he left me, and I had to grin and touch my hat and make believe I liked it. Now I'm going to spend every cent for my own personal pleasure.

DR. MACPHERSON. Will rich men never learn wisdom!

FREDERIK. [*Rising.*] No, they won't! But in every fourth generation there comes along a *wise* fellow—a spender who knows how to distribute the money others have hoarded: I'm the spender.

DR. MACPHERSON. Shame upon you and your like! Your breed should be exterminated.

FREDERIK. [*Taking a little packet of letters from the desk.*] Oh, no, we're quite as necessary as you are. And now—I shall answer no more questions. I'm done. Good-night, Doctor.

DR. MACPHERSON. Good-night and good-bye. [*With a look of disgust, he has gone to the table, held a medicine bottle to the light to look at the label and poured a spoonful into a wine-glass filled with water. As* FREDERIK *leaves the house, the* DOCTOR *taps on a door and calls.*] Catherine! [CATHERINE *enters, and shows by the glance she directs at the front door that she knows* FREDERIK *has been in the room and has just left the house.*] Burn up your wedding dress. We've made no mistake. I can tell you *that!* [*Goes up the stairs to* WILLIAM'S *room, taking the lamp with him.* JAMES *has entered, and, taking* CATHERINE'S *hand, holds it for a moment.*

JAMES. Good-night, Catherine. [*She turns and lays her hand on his shoulder.*

CATHERINE. I wonder, James, if *he* can see us now.

JAMES. That's the big mystery! . . . Who can tell? But any man who works with flowers and things that grow—knows there is no such thing as death—there's nothing but life—life and always life. I'll be back in the morning. . . . Won't you . . . . see me to the door?

CATHERINE. Yes . . . yes. . . . [*They go up together,* CATHERINE *carrying a candle into the dark vestibule. The moment they disappear, a lamp standing on the piano goes out as though the draught from the door or an unseen hand had extinguished it. It is now quite dark outside, and the moon is hidden for a moment. At the same time, a light, seemingly coming from nowhere, reveals* PETER GRIMM *standing in the room at the door—as though he had been there when the young people passed out. He is smiling and happy. The moon is not seen, but the light of it (as though it had come out from behind a cloud) now reveals the old windmill. From outside the door the voices of* JAMES *and* CATHERINE *are heard as they both say:*] Good-night.

JAMES. Catherine, . . . I won't go without it. . . .

PETER. [*Knowing that* JAMES *is demanding a kiss.*] Aha! [*Rubs his hands in satisfaction—then listens—and after a second pause exclaims, with an upraised finger, as though he were hearing the kiss.*] Ah! Now I can go. . . . [*He walks to the peg on which his hat hangs, and takes it down. His work is done.* CATHERINE *re-enters, darting into the hall in girlish confusion,*

JAMES' HAPPY VOICE. [*Outside.*] Good-night!

CATHERINE. [*Calling to him through the crack in the door.*] Good-night! [*She closes the door, turns the key and draws the heavy bolt—then leans against the door, candle-stick in hand—the wind has blown out the candle.*] Oh, I'm so happy! I'm *so* happy!

PETER. Then good-night to you, my darling: love cannot say good-bye. [*She goes to* PETER'S *chair, and, sitting, thinks it all over—her hands clasped in her lap—her face radiant with happiness.*] Here in your childhood's home I leave you. Here in the years to come, the way lies clear before you. [*His arm upraised.*] "*Lust in Rust*"—Pleasure and Peace go with you. [CATHERINE *looks towards the door—remembering* JAMES' *kiss—half smiling.*] [*Humorously.*] Y—es; I saw you. I heard . . . I know. . . . Here on some sunny, blossoming day when, as a wife, you look out upon my gardens—every flower and tree and shrub shall bloom enchanted to your eyes. . . . All that happens—happens again. And if, at first, a little knock of poverty taps at the door, and James finds the road hard and steep—what is money?—a thing,—a good thing to have,—but still a thing . . . and happiness will come without it. And when, as a mother, you shall see my plantings with new eyes, my

Catherine,—when you explain each leaf and bud to your little people—you will remember the time when *we* walked together through the leafy lanes and I taught you—even as you teach them—you little thing! . . . So, I shall linger in your heart. And some day, should your children wander far away and my gardens blossom for a stranger who may take my name from off the gates,—what *is* my name? Already it grows faint to my ears. [*Lightly.*] Yes, yes, yes, let others take my work. . . . Why should *we* care? All that happens, happens again. [*She rests her elbow on the chair, half hides her face in her hand.*] And never forget this: I shall be waiting for you—I shall know all your life. I shall adore your children and be their grandfather just as though I were here; I shall find it hard not to laugh at them when they are bad, and I shall worship them when they are good—and I don't want them too good. . . . Frederik was good. . . . I shall be everywhere about you . . . . in the stockings at Christmas, in a big, busy, teeming world of shadows just outside your threshold, or whispering in the still noises of the night. . . . And oh! as the years pass, [*Standing over her chair.*] you cannot imagine what pride I shall take in your comfortable middle life—the very *best* age, I think— when you two shall look out on your possessions arm in arm—and take your well-earned comfort and ease. How I shall love to see you look fondly at each other as you say: "Be happy, Jim—you've worked hard for this;" or James says: "Take your comfort, little mother, let them all wait upon *you*—*you* waited upon *them.* Lean back in your carriage—you've earned it!" And towards the end—[*Sitting on a chair by her side and looking into her face.*] after all the luxuries and vanities and possessions cease to be so important—people return to very simple things, dear. The evening of life comes bearing its own lamp. Then, perhaps, as a little old grandmother, a little old child whose bed-time is drawing near, I shall see you happy to sit out in the sunlight of another day; asking nothing more of life than the few hours to be spent with those you love, . . . telling your grandchildren, at your knees, how much brighter the flowers blossomed when *you* were young. Ha! Ha! Ha! All that happens, happens again. . . . And when, one glad day, glorified, radiant, young once more, the mother and I shall take you in our arms,—oh! what a reunion! [*Inspired.*] The flight of love—to love. . . . And now . . . [*He bends over her and caresses her hand.*]

good-night. [CATHERINE *rises and, going to the desk, buries her face in the bunch of flowers placed there in memory of* PETER.

CATHERINE. Dear Uncle Peter. . . .

MARTA *enters—pausing to hear if all is quiet in* WILLIAM'S *room.* CATHERINE, *lifting her face, sees* MARTA *and rapturously hugs her, to* MARTA'S *amazement—then goes up the stairs.*

PETER. [*Whose eyes never leave* CATHERINE.] *"Lust in Rust!"* Pleasure and Peace! Amen! [CATHERINE *passes into her room, the music dying away as her door closes.* MARTA, *still wondering, goes to the clock and winds it.*] Poor Marta! Every time she thinks of me, she winds my clock. We're not quite forgotten.

DR. MACPHERSON. [*Re-appears, carrying* WILLIAM, *now wrapped up in an old-fashioned Dutch patchwork quilt. The* DOCTOR *has a lamp in his free hand.*] So you want to go downstairs, eh? Very good! How do you feel, laddie?

WILLIAM. New all over.

DR. MACPHERSON. [*Placing the lamp on the little table right, and laying* WILLIAM *on the couch.*] Now I'll get you the glass of cold water. [*Goes into the dining-room, leaving the door open.*

PETER. [*Calling after the* DOCTOR.] Good-night, Andrew. I'm afraid the world will have to wait a little longer for the *big* guesser. Drop in often. I shall be glad to see you here.

WILLIAM. [*Quickly rising on the couch, looks towards the peg on which* PETER GRIMM'S *hat hung. Calling.*] Mr. Grimm! Where are you? I knew that you were down here. [*Seeing* PETER.] Oh, [*Raising himself to his knees on the sofa.*] I see you *now!*

PETER. Yes? [*There is an impressive pause and silence as they face each other.*

WILLIAM. Oh, you've got your hat; . . . it's off the peg. . . . You're going. Need you go right away—Mr. Grimm? Can't you wait a little while?

PETER. I'll wait for you, William.

WILLIAM. May I go with you? Thank you. I couldn't find the way without you.

PETER. Yes, you could. It's the surest way in this world. But I'll wait,—don't worry.

WILLIAM. I sha'n't. [*Coaxingly.*] Don't be in a hurry . . . I want—[*Lies down happily.*] to take a nap first. . . . I'm sleepy. [*He pulls the covering up and sleeps.*

PETER. I wish you the pleasantest dream a little boy can have in *this* world.

Instantly, as though the room were peopled with faint images of WILLIAM'S *dream, the phantom circus music is heard, with its elfin horns; and, through the music, voices call "Hai! Hai!" The sound of the cracking of a whip is heard, and the blare of a clown's ten-cent tin horn. The phantom voice of the* CLOWN *(very faint) calls:*

CLOWN'S VOICE. Billy Miller's big show and monster circus is in town this afternoon! Don't forget the date! Only one ring—no confusion. Circus day comes but once a year, little sir. Come early and see the wild animals and hear the lion roar-r-r! Mind, I shall expect *you!* Wonderful troupe of trained mice in the side-show.

During the above, the deeper voice of a "HAWKER"*—muffled and far off—cries:*

HAWKER'S VOICE. Peanuts, pop-corn, lemonade—ice cold lemo—lemo—lemonade! Circus day comes but once a year.

Breaking in through the music, and the voices of the CLOWN *and* HAWKER, *the gruff voice of a* "BARKER" *is heard calling.*

BARKER'S VOICE. Walk in and see the midgets and the giant! Only ten cents—one dime!

As these voices die away, the CLOWN, *whose voice indicates that he is now perched on the head of the couch, sings:*

CLOWN'S VOICE.

"Uncle Rat has gone to town,
Ha! H'm!
Uncle Rat has gone to town
To buy his niece"—

His voice ends abruptly—the music stops. Everything is over. There is silence. Then three clear knocks sound on the door.

PETER. Come in. . . . [*The door opens. No one is there—but a faint path of phosphorous light is seen.*] Oh, friends! Troops of you! [*As though he recognizes the unseen guests.*] I've been gone so long that you came for me, eh? I'm quite ready to go back. I'm just waiting for a happy little fellow who's going back with us. . . . We'll follow. Do you all go ahead—lead the way. [*He looks at* WILLIAM, *holds out his arms, and* WILLIAM *jumps up and runs into them.*] Well, William! You *know better* now. Come! [*Picking up* WILLIAM.] Happy, eh? [WILLIAM *nods, his face beaming.*

WILLIAM. Oh, yes!

PETER. Let's be off, then. [*As they turn towards the door.*

DR. MACPHERSON. [*Re-entering, goes to the couch with the water, and suddenly, setting down the glass, exclaims in a hushed voice:*] My God! He's dead! [*He half raises up a boy that appears to be* WILLIAM. *The light from the lamp on the table falls on the dead face of the child. Then the* DOCTOR *gently lays the boy down again on the couch, and sits pondering over the mystery of death.*

PETER. [*To the* DOCTOR.] Oh, no! There never was so fair a prospect for *life!*

WILLIAM. [*In* PETER'S *arms.*] I *am* happy!

Outside a hazy moonlight shimmers. A few stars twinkle in the far-away sky; and the low moon is seen back of the old windmill.

PETER. [*To* WILLIAM.] If the rest of them only knew what they're missing, eh?

WILLIAM. [*Begins to sing, joyously.*]

"Uncle Rat has gone to town."

PETER *dances up a few steps towards the door, singing with* WILLIAM.

PETER *and* WILLIAM.

"Ha! H'm!
Uncle Rat has gone to town
To buy his niece a wedding gown.
Ha! H'm!"

PETER. [*Gives one last fond look towards* CATHERINE'S *room. To* WILLIAM.] We're off! [*Putting the boy over his shoulder, they sing together, as they go up, the phantom circus music accompanying them.*]

"What shall the wedding breakfast be?
Ha! H'm!"

PETER. [*Alone.*]

"What shall the wedding breakfast be?
Hard boiled eggs and a cup of tea."

WILLIAM *and* PETER. "Ha! H'm!"

PETER GRIMM *has danced off with the child through the faint path of light. As he goes, the wind or an unseen hand closes the door after them. There is a moment's pause until their voices are no longer heard—then the curtain slowly descends. The air of the song is taken up by an unseen orchestra and continues as the audience passes out.*

CURTAIN.

THE AUTHORS AND THEIR PLAYS

RIP VAN WINKLE

The details are given specifically in the Introduction to the play, where the different dramatizations are discussed.

GEORGE HENRY BOKER

Born, Philadelphia, Pa., October 6, 1823. Died, Philadelphia, January 2, 1890. Author of the following plays, with their dates of first production, or when written: "Calaynos" (London: Sadler's Wells Theatre, May 10, 1849) (Philadelphia: Walnut Street Theatre, January 20, 1850); "Anne Boleyn" (1850); "The Betrothal" (Philadelphia: Walnut Street Theatre, September 25, 1850) (New York: Broadway Theatre, November 18, 1850); "All the World a Mask" (Philadelphia: Walnut Street Theatre, April 21, 1851); "The Podesta's Daughter" (1852); "The Widow's Marriage" (1852); "Leonor de Guzman" (Philadelphia: Walnut Street Theatre, October 3, 1853) (New York: Broadway Theatre, April 24, 1853); "Francesca da Rimini" (New York: Broadway Theatre, September 26, 1855); "The Bankrupt" (MS. 1853); "Königsmark" (1857, 1869); "Nydia" (1885); "Glaucus" (1886), based on Bulwer-Lytton.

OLIVER BELL BUNCE

The details are given specifically in the Introduction to "Love in '76".

STEELE MACKAYE

Born, Buffalo, New York, June 6, 1842. Died, Timpas, Colorado, on board train, February 25, 1894. Author of the following plays, with their dates of first production: "Monaldi" (New York: St. James Theatre, January 8, 1872), in collaboration with Francis Durivage; "Marriage," adapted from the French of Feuillet (New York: St. James Theatre, February 12, 1872); "A Radical Fool," written in London (1873-1874); "Arkwright's Wife," in collaboration with Tom Taylor (Leeds, England: Theatre Royal, July 7, 1873); "Silas Marner," a dramatization of George Eliot's novel, written in London (1873);

"Jealousy," with Charles Reade, written in London (1873-1874); "Rose Michel," based on a French play, in its turn based on Victor Hugo (New York: Union Square Theatre, November 23, 1875); "Queen and Woman," in collaboration with J. V. Pritchard (Brooklyn, N. Y.: Theatre, February 14, 1876); "Twins," in collaboration with A. C. Wheeler (New York: Wallack's Theatre, April 12, 1876); "Won at Last" (New York: Wallack's Theatre, December 10, 1877); "Through the Dark" (New York: Fifth Avenue Theatre, March 10, 1879); "An Iron Will" (Providence, R. I., Low's Opera House, October 27, 1879); "Hazel Kirke" (New York: Madison Square Theatre, February 4, 1880); "A Fool's Errand," dramatization from a novel by Judge Tourgee (Philadelphia: Arch Street Theatre, October 26, 1881); "Dakolar," based on Georges Ohnet's "Le Maître de Forges" (New York: Lyceum Theatre, April 6, 1885); "In Spite of All," founded on Sardou (New York: Lyceum Theatre, September 15, 1885); "Rienzi," based on Bulwer-Lytton's novel (Washington: Albaugh's Opera House, December 13, 1886; New York production, Niblo's Garden, May 2, 1887); "The Drama of Civilization," a pageant (New York: Madison Square Garden, November 27, 1887); "Anarchy" (Buffalo, N. Y.: Academy of Music, May 30, 1887); "Paul Kauvar; or, Anarchy" (New York: Standard Theatre, December 24, 1887); "A Noble Rogue" (Chicago: Opera House, July 3, 1888); "An Arrant Knave" (Chicago: Opera House, September 30, 1889); "Colonel Tom" (Boston: Tremont Theatre, January 20, 1890); "Money Mad" (New York: Standard Theatre, April 7, 1890); "Cousin Larry," written in 1891; "The World Finder," a spectatorio (Chicago; Spectatorium, 1893, World's Fair).

BRONSON HOWARD

Born, Detroit, Michigan, October 7, 1842. Died, Avon-by-the-Sea, New Jersey, August 4, 1908. Author of the following plays, with their dates of first production: "Fantine" (Detroit, Mich., 1864); "Saratoga" (New York: Fifth Avenue Theatre, December 21, 1870); "Diamonds" (New York: Fifth Avenue Theatre, September 26, 1872); "Moorcroft; or, The Double Wedding" (New York: Fifth Avenue Theatre, October 17, 1874); "Lilian's Last Love" (Chicago: Hooley's Theatre, September 4, 1877); "Hurricanes" (Chicago: Hooley's Theatre, May 27,

1878); "Old Love Letters" (New York: Park Theatre, August 31, 1878); "The Banker's Daughter," being a revision of "Lilian's Last Love" (New York: Union Square Theatre, September 30, 1878); "Wives," being an adaptation from Molière (New York: Daly's Theatre, October 18, 1879); "Fun in the Green-room" (New York: Booth's Theatre, April 10, 1882); "The Young Mrs. Winthrop" (New York: Madison Square Theatre, October 9, 1882); "One of Our Girls" (New York: Lyceum Theatre, November 10, 1885); "Met by Chance" (New York: Lyceum Theatre, January 11, 1887); "The Henrietta" (New York: Union Square Theatre, September 26, 1887); "Baron Rudolph," first named "Rudolph von Hallenstein" (New York: Fourteenth Street Theatre, October 25, 1887); "Shenandoah" (New York: Star Theatre, September 9, 1889); "Aristocracy" (New York: Palmer's Theatre, November 14, 1892); "Peter Stuyvesant," in collaboration with Brander Matthews (New York: Wallack's Theatre, October 2, 1899). Plays that have never been acted are: "Knave & Queen," in collaboration with Sir Charles Young, and "Kate," issued, 1906, in book form by Harper & Brothers.

AUGUSTUS THOMAS

Born, St. Louis, Mo., January 8, 1859. Author of the following plays, with their dates of first production: "Editha's Burglar," with Mrs. F. H. Burnett (St. Louis: Pope's Theatre, July 1, 1884); "The Burglar" (Boston: Park Theatre, June, 1888); "A Man of the World" (New York: Madison Square Theatre, October 30, 1889); "Afterthoughts" (New York: Madison Square Theatre, November 24, 1890); "Reckless Temple" (New York: Standard Theatre, October 27, 1890); "Alabama" (New York: Madison Square Theatre, April 1, 1891); "Colonel Carter of Cartersville," from the novel by F. Hopkinson Smith (New York: Palmer's Theatre, March 22, 1892); "Holly-Tree Inn" (New York: Union Square Theatre, April 11, 1892); "In Mizzoura" (Chicago: Hooley's Theatre, August, 1893); "New Blood" (New York: Palmer's Theatre, September 19, 1894; previously in Chicago); "The Man Upstairs" (New York: Hoyt's Theatre, April 9, 1895); "The Capitol" (New York: Standard Theatre, September 9, 1895); "That Overcoat" (1898); "The Hoosier Doctor" (New York: Fourteenth Street Theatre, April 18, 1898); "The Meddler" (New York:

Wallack's Theatre, September 1, 1898); "Arizona" (Chicago: Grand Opera House, June 12, 1899); "Oliver Goldsmith" (New York: Fifth Avenue Theatre, March 19, 1900); "On the Quiet" (New York: Hoyt's Theatre, February 11, 1901); "Colorado" (New York: Palmer's Theatre, January 12, 1902); "Soldiers of Fortune," from the novel by Richard Harding Davis (New York: Savoy Theatre, March 17, 1902); "The Earl of Pawtucket" (New York: Madison Square Theatre, February 5, 1903); "The Other Girl" (New York: Criterion Theatre, December 23, 1903); "Mrs. Leffingwell's Boots" (New York: Savoy Theatre, January 11, 1905); "The Education of Mr. Pipp," from pictures by Charles Dana Gibson, (New York: Liberty Theatre, February 20, 1905); "Delancey" (New York: Empire Theatre, September 4, 1905); "The Embassy Ball" (New York: Daly's Theatre, March 5, 1906); "The Ranger" (New York: Wallack's Theatre, September 2, 1907); "The Witching Hour" (New York: Hackett's Theatre, November 18, 1907); "The Harvest Moon" (New York: Garrick Theatre, October 18, 1909); "The Member from Ozark" (Detroit, Mich., Opera House, 1910); "As a Man Thinks" (New York: 39th Street Theatre, March 13, 1911); "The Model" (New York: Harris Theatre, August 31, 1912); "Mere Man" (New York: Harris Theatre, November 25, 1912); "Indian Summer" (New York: Criterion Theatre, October 27, 1913); "Rio Grande" (New York: Empire Theatre, April 4, 1916); "The Copperhead" (Hartford, Conn., January 22, 1918); "Palmy Days" (New York: The Playhouse, October 27, 1919); "Under the Bough," previously called "The Blue Devil" and "Speak of the Devil" (Boston: Colonial Theatre, May 31, 1920). Other plays credited to Mr. Thomas are: "A Leaf from the Woods," one act (St. Louis: Pope's Theatre, 1883); "A New Year's Call," one act (St. Louis: Pope's Theatre, 1883); "A Night's Frolic" (New York: Herald Square Theatre, 1888); "A Proper Impropriety," one act (New York: Union Square Theatre, 1889); "Alone" (St. Louis: Pickwick Theatre, 1881); "Chimmie Fadden," from the book of E. W. Townsend (New York: Palmer's Theatre, 1881); "Combustion" (St. Louis: Pope's Theatre, 1883); "For Money" (New York: Star Theatre, 1890); "Love Will Find the Way," written for amateurs; "The Big Rise" (St. Louis: Pope's Theatre, 1881); "The Dress Suit," written for amateurs only; "The Jucklins" (on the road, 1896); "The Music Box," written for amateurs only.

CLYDE FITCH

Born, Elmira, New York, May 2, 1865. Died at Chalôns-sur-Marne, September 4, 1909. Author of the following plays, with their dates of first production: "Beau Brummell" (New York: Madison Square Theatre, May 17, 1890); "Frédéric Lemaître" (New York: Daly's Theatre, December 1, 1890); "Betty's Finish" (Boston Museum, December 29, 1890); "Pamela's Prodigy" (London: Royal Court Theatre, October 21, 1891); "A Modern Match" (New York: Union Square Theatre, March 14, 1892. Later played by the Kendals as "Marriage"); "The Masked Ball," from the French of Bisson (New York: Palmer's Theatre, October 3, 1892); "The Harvest," afterwards used in "The Moth and the Flame" (Theatre of Arts and Letters, New York: Fifth Avenue Theatre, January 26, 1893); "April Weather" (Chicago: Opera House, May 29, 1893); "A Shattered Idol," from the French of Balzac, "Old Goriot" (St. Paul, Minn.: Globe Theatre, July 31, 1893); "The Social Swim," adapted from the French of Sardou (New York: Harlem Opera House, September 22, 1893); "An American Duchess," from the French of Lavadan (New York: Lyceum Theatre, November 20, 1893); "Mrs. Grundy, Jun.," from the French, (1894); "Gossip," from the French of Claretie, in collaboration with Leo Ditrichstein (New York: Palmer's Theatre, March 11, 1895); "His Grace de Grammont" (Brooklyn: Park Theatre, September 11, 1895); "Mistress Betty" (New York: Garrick Theatre, October 15, 1895); "Bohemia," from the French (New York: Empire Theatre, March 9, 1896); "The Liar," from the French of Bisson (New York: Hoyt's Theatre, September 2, 1896); "A Superfluous Husband," adapted from the German, with Leo Ditrichstein (New York: Miner's Fifth Avenue Theatre, January 4, 1897); "The Moth and the Flame" (New York: Lyceum Theatre, April 11, 1898); "The Head of the Family," adapted from the German, with Leo Ditrichstein (New York: Knickerbocker Theatre, December 6, 1898); "Nathan Hale" (New York: Knickerbocker Theatre, January 2, 1899, having been given in Chicago the previous January); "Barbara Frietchie" (New York: Criterion Theatre, October 24, 1899); "The Cowboy and the Lady" (New York: Knickerbocker Theatre, December 25, 1899); "Sapho," from the French of Daudet (New York: Wallack's Theatre, February

16, 1900); "The Climbers" (New York: Bijou Theatre, January 21, 1901); "Lovers' Lane" (New York: Manhattan Theatre, February 6, 1901); "Captain Jinks of the Horse Marines" (New York: Garrick Theatre, February 4, 1901); "The Last of the Dandies" (London, October 24, 1901); "The Way of the World" (New York: Hammerstein's Victoria, November 4, 1901); "The Girl and the Judge" (New York: Lyceum Theatre, December 4, 1901); "The Stubbornness of Geraldine" (New York: Garrick Theatre, November 3, 1902); "The Girl with the Green Eyes" (New York: Savoy Theatre, December 25, 1902); "The Bird in the Cage" (New York: Bijou Theatre, January 12, 1903); "Her Own Way" (New York: Garrick Theatre, September 28, 1903); "Algy" (Chicago: Garrick Theatre, October 4, 1903); "Major André" (New York: Savoy Theatre, November 11, 1903); "Glad of It" (New York: Savoy Theatre, December 28, 1903); "The Frisky Mrs. Johnson" (New York: Garrick Theatre, May 16, 1904); "The Coronet of a Duchess" (New York: Garrick Theatre, September 21, 1904); "Granny" (New York: Lyceum Theatre, October 24, 1904); "Cousin Billy," adapted from the French (New York: Criterion Theatre, January 2, 1905); "The Woman in the Case" (New York: Herald Square Theatre, January 30, 1905); "Her Great Match" (New York: Criterion Theatre, September 4, 1905); "Wolfville," a dramatization of a novel by Alfred Henry Lewis, the play in collaboration with Willis Steell, (Philadelphia, October 20, 1905); "The Toast of the Town," a re-writing of "Mistress Betty" (New York: Daly's Theatre, November 27, 1905); "Toddles," from the French (New York: Garrick Theatre, March 16, 1906); "The House of Mirth," a dramatization of Mrs. Edith Wharton's novel (New York: Savoy Theatre, October 22, 1906); "The Girl Who Has Everything" (New York: Liberty Theatre, December 4, 1906); "The Truth" (New York: Criterion Theatre, January 7, 1907; London: Comedy Theatre, April 6, 1907); "The Straight Road" (New York: Astor Theatre, January 7, 1907); "Her Sister," in collaboration with Cosmo Gordon-Lennox (New York: Hudson Theatre, December 24, 1907); "Toddles" (New York: Garrick Theatre, March 16, 1908); "Girls" (New York: Daly's Theatre, March 23, 1908); "The Blue Mouse," adapted from the German (New York: Lyric Theatre, November 30, 1908); "The Bachelor" (New

York: Maxine Elliott Theatre, March 15, 1909); "A Happy Marriage" (New York: Garrick Theatre, April 12, 1909); "The City" (New York: Lyric Theatre, December 22, 1909).

LANGDON MITCHELL

Born, Philadelphia, February 17, 1862. The details are given specifically in the Introduction to the play.

EUGENE WALTER

Born, Cleveland, Ohio, November 27, 1874. Author of the following plays, with their dates of production: "Sergeant James" (Boston Theatre, 1901; later called "Boots and Saddles," 1909); "The Undertow" (New York: Harlem Opera House, April 22, 1907); "Paid in Full" (New York: Astor Theatre, February 25, 1908); "The Wolf" (New York: Bijou Theatre, April 18, 1908); "The Easiest Way" (New York: Belasco Theatre, January 19, 1908); "Just a Wife" (New York: Belasco Theatre, January 31, 1909); "The Trail of the Lonesome Pine," being a dramatization of John Fox's novel (New York: New Amsterdam Theatre, January 29, 1912); "Fine Feathers" (New York: Astor Theatre, January 7, 1913); "The Knife" (New York: Bijou Theatre, April 12, 1917); "The Heritage," called also "The Assassin" (New York: The Playhouse, January 14, 1917); "Nancy Lee" (New York: Hudson Theatre, April 19, 1918); "The Challenge" (Season of 1919-1920).

DAVID BELASCO.

Born, San Francisco, Cal., July 25, 1853. A complete chronology of Mr. Belasco's plays is to be found in the Winter biography. Here are only listed those plays written after his arrival in New York. The list does not include the plays presented by him merely in the capacity as manager. "May Blossom" (New York: Madison Square Theatre, April 12, 1884); "Valerie," from Sardou (New York: Wallack's Theatre, February 15, 1886); "Baron Rudolph," with Bronson Howard (New York: Fourteenth Street Theatre, October 24, 1887); "The Wife," with Henry DeMille (New York: Lyceum Theatre, November 1, 1887); "Lord Chumley," with Henry DeMille (New York: Lyceum Theatre, August 21, 1888); "The Charity

Ball," with Henry DeMille (New York: Lyceum Theatre, November 19, 1889); "Men and Women," with Henry DeMille (New York: Proctor's 23rd Street Theatre, October 21, 1890); "Miss Helyett," from the French (New York: Star Theatre, November 3, 1891); "The Girl I Left Behind Me," with Franklyn Fyles (New York: Empire Theatre, January 25, 1893); "The Younger Son," from the German (New York: Empire Theatre, October 24, 1893); "The Heart of Maryland" (New York: Herald Square Theatre, October 22, 1895); "Zaza," from the French of Berton and Simon (New York: Garrick Theatre, January 8, 1899); "Naughty Anthony" (New York: Herald Square Theatre, January 8, 1900); "Madame Butterfly," from the novel by John Luther Long (New York: Herald Square Theatre, March 5, 1900); "Du Barry" (New York: Criterion Theatre, December 25, 1901); "The Darling of the Gods" (New York: Belasco Theatre, now the Republic, December 3, 1902); "Sweet Kitty Bellairs," from a novel by the Edgertons (New York: Belasco Theatre, now the Republic, December 8, 1903); "Adrea," with John Luther Long (Belasco Theatre, New York, now the Republic, January 11, 1905); "The Girl of the Golden West" (New York: Belasco Theatre, now the Republic, November 14, 1905); "The Rose of the Rancho," with Richard Walton Tully (New York: Belasco Theatre, now the Republic, November 27, 1906); "A Grand Army Man," in collaboration (New York: Stuyvesant Theatre, now the Belasco, October 16, 1907); "The Lily," from the French of Wolff and Leroux (New York: Stuyvesant Theatre, now the Belasco, December 23, 1909); "The Return of Peter Grimm" (New York: Belasco Theatre, January 2, 1911); "The Secret," from the French of Henry Bernstein (New York: Belasco Theatre, December 23, 1913); "Van Der Decken" (Wilmington, Del.: The Playhouse, December 12, 1915.) This list represents only a small part of Mr. Belasco's activities.